World Economic and Financial Surveys

WORLD ECONOMIC OUTLOOK
April 2012

Growth Resuming, Dangers Remain

International Monetary Fund

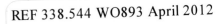

Cover and Design: Luisa Menjivar and Jorge Salazar
Composition: Maryland Composition

Cataloging-in-Publication Data

World economic outlook (International Monetary Fund)
World economic outlook : a survey by the staff of the International Monetary Fund. — Washington, DC : International Monetary Fund, 1980–
v. ; 28 cm. — (1981–1984: Occasional paper / International Monetary Fund, 0251-6365). — (1986– : World economic and financial surveys, 0256-6877)

Semiannual. Some issues also have thematic titles.
Has occasional updates, 1984–

1. Economic development — Periodicals. 2. Economic forecasting — Periodicals. 3. Economic policy — Periodicals. 4. International economic relations — Periodicals. I. International Monetary Fund. II. Series: Occasional paper (International Monetary Fund). III. Series: World economic and financial surveys.

HC10.80

ISBN 978-1-61635-246-2

Publication orders may be placed online, by fax, or through the mail:
International Monetary Fund, Publication Services
P.O. Box 92780, Washington, DC 20090, U.S.A.
Tel.: (202) 623-7430 Fax: (202) 623-7201
E-mail: publications@imf.org
www.imfbookstore.org
www.elibrary.imf.org

CONTENTS

Tables

Online Tables

Figures

ASSUMPTIONS AND CONVENTIONS

A number of assumptions have been adopted for the projections presented in the *World Economic Outlook.* It has been assumed that real effective exchange rates remained constant at their average levels during February 13–March 12, 2012, except for the currencies participating in the European exchange rate mechanism II (ERM II), which are assumed to have remained constant in nominal terms relative to the euro; that established policies of national authorities will be maintained (for specific assumptions about fiscal and monetary policies for selected economies, see Box A1); that the average price of oil will be $114.71 a barrel in 2012 and $110.00 a barrel in 2013 and will remain unchanged in real terms over the medium term; that the six-month London interbank offered rate (LIBOR) on U.S. dollar deposits will average 0.7 percent in 2012 and 0.8 percent in 2013; that the three-month euro deposit rate will average 0.8 percent in 2012 and 2013; and that the six-month Japanese yen deposit rate will yield on average 0.6 percent in 2012 and 0.1 percent in 2013. These are, of course, working hypotheses rather than forecasts, and the uncertainties surrounding them add to the margin of error that would in any event be involved in the projections. The estimates and projections are based on statistical information available through early April 2012.

The following conventions are used throughout the *World Economic Outlook:*

. . . to indicate that data are not available or not applicable;

– between years or months (for example, 2011–12 or January–June) to indicate the years or months covered, including the beginning and ending years or months;

/ between years or months (for example, 2011/12) to indicate a fiscal or financial year.

"Billion" means a thousand million; "trillion" means a thousand billion.

"Basis points" refer to hundredths of 1 percentage point (for example, 25 basis points are equivalent to ¼ of 1 percentage point).

As in the September 2011 *World Economic Outlook,* fiscal and external debt data for Libya are excluded for 2011 and later due to the uncertain political situation.

Data for the Syrian Arab Republic are excluded for 2011 and later due to the uncertain political situation.

As in the September 2011 *World Economic Outlook,* Sudan's data for 2011 exclude South Sudan after July 9. Projections for 2012 and onward pertain to the current Sudan.

If no source is listed on tables and figures, data are drawn from the World Economic Outlook (WEO) database.

When countries are not listed alphabetically, they are ordered on the basis of economic size.

Minor discrepancies between sums of constituent figures and totals shown reflect rounding.

As used in this report, the terms "country" and "economy" do not in all cases refer to a territorial entity that is a state as understood by international law and practice. As used here, the term also covers some territorial entities that are not states but for which statistical data are maintained on a separate and independent basis.

Composite data are provided for various groups of countries organized according to economic characteristics or region. Unless otherwise noted, country group composites represent calculations based on 90 percent or more of the weighted group data.

The boundaries, colors, denominations, and any other information shown on the maps do not imply, on the part of the International Monetary Fund, any judgment on the legal status of any territory or any endorsement or acceptance of such boundaries.

FURTHER INFORMATION AND DATA

This version of the *World Economic Outlook* is available in full through the IMF eLibrary (www.elibrary.imf.org) and the IMF website (www.imf.org). Accompanying the publication on the IMF website is a larger compilation of data from the WEO database than is included in the report itself, including files containing the series most frequently requested by readers. These files may be downloaded for use in a variety of software packages.

The data appearing in the *World Economic Outlook* are compiled by the IMF staff at the time of the WEO exercises. The historical data and projections are based on the information gathered by the IMF country desk officers in the context of their missions to IMF member countries and through their ongoing analysis of the evolving situation in each country. Historical data are updated on a continual basis as more information becomes available, and structural breaks in data are often adjusted to produce smooth series with the use of splicing and other techniques. IMF staff estimates continue to serve as proxies for historical series when complete information is unavailable. As a result, WEO data can differ from other sources with official data, including the IMF's *International Financial Statistics.*

The WEO data and metadata provided are "as is" and "as available," and every effort is made to ensure, but not guarantee, their timeliness, accuracy, and completeness. When errors are discovered, there is a concerted effort to correct them as appropriate and feasible. Corrections and revisions made after publication are incorporated into the electronic editions available from the IMF eLibrary (www.elibrary.imf.org) and on the IMF website (www.imf.org). All substantive changes are listed in detail in the online tables of contents.

For details on the terms and conditions for usage of the WEO database, please refer to the IMF Copyright and Usage website, www.imf.org/external/terms.htm.

Inquiries about the content of the *World Economic Outlook* and the WEO database should be sent by mail, fax, or online forum (telephone inquiries cannot be accepted):

World Economic Studies Division
Research Department
International Monetary Fund
700 19th Street, N.W.
Washington, DC 20431, U.S.A.
Fax: (202) 623-6343
Online Forum: www.imf.org/weoforum

PREFACE

The analysis and projections contained in the *World Economic Outlook* are integral elements of the IMF's surveillance of economic developments and policies in its member countries, of developments in international financial markets, and of the global economic system. The survey of prospects and policies is the product of a comprehensive interdepartmental review of world economic developments, which draws primarily on information the IMF staff gathers through its consultations with member countries. These consultations are carried out in particular by the IMF's area departments—namely, the African Department, Asia and Pacific Department, European Department, Middle East and Central Asia Department, and Western Hemisphere Department—together with the Strategy, Policy, and Review Department; the Monetary and Capital Markets Department; and the Fiscal Affairs Department.

The analysis in this report was coordinated in the Research Department under the general direction of Olivier Blanchard, Economic Counsellor and Director of Research. The project was directed by Jörg Decressin, Deputy Director, Research Department, and by Thomas Helbling, Division Chief, Research Department, with assistance from Petya Koeva Brooks, Mr. Helbling's predecessor as division chief.

The primary contributors to this report are Abdul Abiad, John Bluedorn, Rupa Duttagupta, Deniz Igan, Florence Jaumotte, Joong Shik Kang, Daniel Leigh, Andrea Pescatori, Shaun Roache, John Simon, Steven Snudden, Marco E. Terrones, and Petia Topalova. Other contributors include Bas Bakker, Julia Bersch, Phakawa Jeasakul, Edda Rós Karlsdóttir, Yuko Kinoshita, M. Ayhan Kose, Prakash Loungani, Frańek Rozwadowski, and Susan Yang. Gavin Asdorian, Shan Chen, Angela Espiritu, Nadezhda Lepeshko, Murad Omoev, Ezgi O. Ozturk, Katherine Pan, David Reichsfeld, Jair Rodriguez, Marina Rousset, Min Kyu Song, and Bennet Voorhees provided research assistance. Christopher Carroll, Kevin Clinton, Jose De Gregorio, and Lutz Killian provided comments and suggestions. Tingyun Chen, Mahnaz Hemmati, Toh Kuan, Rajesh Nilawar, Emory Oakes, and Steve Zhang provided technical support. Skeeter Mathurin and Claire Bea were responsible for word processing. Linda Griffin Kean of the External Relations Department edited the manuscript and coordinated the production of the publication, with assistance from Lucy Scott Morales. External consultants Amrita Dasgupta, Anastasia Francis, Aleksandr Gerasimov, Wendy Mak, Shamiso Mapondera, Nhu Nguyen, and Pavel Pimenov provided additional technical support.

The analysis has benefited from comments and suggestions by staff from other IMF departments, as well as by Executive Directors following their discussion of the report on March 30, 2012. However, both projections and policy considerations are those of the IMF staff and should not be attributed to Executive Directors or to their national authorities.

FOREWORD

Soon after the September 2011 *World Economic Outlook* went to press, the euro area went through another acute crisis.

Market worries about fiscal sustainability in Italy and Spain led to a sharp increase in sovereign yields. With the value of some of the banks' assets now in doubt, questions arose as to whether those banks would be able to convince investors to roll over their loans. Worried about funding, banks froze credit. Confidence decreased, and activity slumped.

Strong policy responses turned things around. Elections in Spain and the appointment of a new prime minister in Italy gave some reassurance to investors. The adoption of a fiscal compact showed the commitment of EU members to dealing with their deficits and debt. Most important, the provision of liquidity by the European Central Bank (ECB) removed short-term bank rollover risk, which in turn decreased pressure on sovereign bonds.

With the passing of the crisis, and some good news about the U.S. economy, some optimism has returned. It should remain tempered. Even absent another European crisis, most advanced economies still face major brakes on growth. And the risk of another crisis is still very much present and could well affect both advanced and emerging economies.

Let me first focus on the baseline. One must wonder why, with nominal interest rates expected to remain close to zero for some time, demand is not stronger in advanced economies. The reason is that they face, in varying combinations, two main brakes on growth: fiscal consolidation and bank deleveraging. Both reflect needed adjustments, but both decrease growth in the short term.

Fiscal consolidation is in effect in most advanced economies. With an average decrease in the cyclically adjusted primary deficit slightly under 1 percentage point of GDP this year, and a multiplier of 1, fiscal consolidation will be subtracting roughly 1 percentage point from advanced economy growth this year.

Bank deleveraging is affecting primarily Europe. While such deleveraging does not necessarily imply lower credit to the private sector, the evidence suggests that it is contributing to a tighter credit supply. Our best estimates are that it may subtract another 1 percentage point from euro area growth this year.

These effects are reflected in our forecasts. We forecast that growth will remain weak, especially in Europe, and unemployment will remain high for some time.

Emerging economies are not immune to these developments. Low advanced economy growth has meant lower export growth. And financial uncertainty, together with sharp shifts in risk appetite, has led to volatile capital flows. For the most part, however, emerging economies have enough policy room to maintain solid growth. As is typically the case, such a statement masks heterogeneity across countries. Some countries need to watch overheating, while others still have a negative output gap and can use policy to sustain growth. Overall, while we have revised our forecast down somewhat from September, we still project sustained growth in emerging economies.

Turning to risks, geopolitical tension affecting the oil market is surely a risk. The main one, however, remains another acute crisis in Europe. The building of the firewalls, when it is completed, will represent major progress. If and when needed, funds can be mobilized to help some countries survive the effects of adverse shifts in investor sentiment and give them more time to implement fiscal consolidation and reforms. By themselves, however, firewalls cannot solve the difficult fiscal, competitiveness, and growth issues some of these countries face. Bad news on the macroeconomic or political front still carries the risk of triggering the type of dynamics we saw last fall.

Turning to policy, many of the policy debates revolve around how best to balance the adverse short-term effects of fiscal consolidation and bank deleveraging versus their favorable long-term effects.

In the case of fiscal policy, the issue is complicated by the pressure from markets for immediate fiscal consolidation. It is further complicated by the fact that markets appear somewhat schizophrenic—they ask for fiscal consolidation but react badly when consolidation leads to lower growth. The right strategy remains the same as before. While some immediate adjustment is needed for credibility, the search should be for credible long-term commitments—through a combination of decisions that decrease trend spending and put in place fiscal institutions and rules that automatically reduce spending and deficits over time. Insufficient progress has been made along these lines, especially in the United States and in Japan. In the absence of greater progress, the current degree of short-term fiscal consolidation appears roughly appropriate.

In the case of bank deleveraging, the challenge is twofold. As with fiscal policy, the first challenge is to determine the right speed of overall deleveraging. The second is to make sure that deleveraging does not lead to a credit crunch, either at home or abroad. Partial public recapitalization of banks does not appear to be on the agenda anymore, but perhaps it should be. To the extent that it would increase credit and activity, it could easily pay for itself—more so than most other fiscal measures.

Turning to policies aimed at reducing risks, the focus is clearly on Europe. Measures should be taken to decrease the links between sovereigns and banks, from the creation of euro level deposit insurance and bank resolution to the introduction of limited forms of Eurobonds, such as the creation of a common euro bill market. These measures are urgently needed and can make a difference were another crisis to take place soon.

Taking one step back, perhaps the highest priority, but also the most difficult to achieve, is to durably increase growth in advanced economies, and especially in Europe. Low growth not only makes for a subdued baseline forecast, but also for a harder fiscal adjustment and higher risks along the way. For the moment, the focus should be on measures that increase demand. Looking forward, however, the focus should also be on measures that increase potential growth. The Holy Grail would be measures that do both. There are probably few of those. More realistically, the search must be for reforms that help in the long term but do not depress demand in the short term. Identifying these reforms, and addressing their potentially adverse short-term effects, should be very high on the policy agenda.

Olivier Blanchard
Economic Counsellor

EXECUTIVE SUMMARY

After suffering a major setback during 2011, global prospects are gradually strengthening again, but downside risks remain elevated. Improved activity in the United States during the second half of 2011 and better policies in the euro area in response to its deepening economic crisis have reduced the threat of a sharp global slowdown. Accordingly, weak recovery will likely resume in the major advanced economies, and activity is expected to remain relatively solid in most emerging and developing economies. However, the recent improvements are very fragile. Policymakers need to continue to implement the fundamental changes required to achieve healthy growth over the medium term. With large output gaps in advanced economies, they must also calibrate policies with a view to supporting still-weak growth over the near term.

Global growth is projected to drop from about 4 percent in 2011 to about 3½ percent in 2012 because of weak activity during the second half of 2011 and the first half of 2012. The January 2012 *WEO Update* had already marked down the projections of the September 2011 *World Economic Outlook,* mainly on account of the damage done by deteriorating sovereign and banking sector developments in the euro area. For most economies, including the euro area, growth is now expected to be modestly stronger than predicted in the January 2012 *WEO Update.* As discussed in Chapter 1, the reacceleration of activity during the course of 2012 is expected to return global growth to about 4 percent in 2013. The euro area is still projected to go into a mild recession in 2012 as a result of the sovereign debt crisis and a general loss of confidence, the effects of bank deleveraging on the real economy, and the impact of fiscal consolidation in response to market pressures. Because of the problems in Europe, activity will continue to disappoint for the advanced economies as a group, expanding by only about 1½ percent in 2012 and by 2 percent in 2013. Job creation in these economies will likely remain sluggish, and the unemployed will need further income support and help with skills development, retraining, and job searching. Real GDP growth in the emerging and developing economies is projected to slow from 6¼ percent in 2011 to 5¾ percent in 2012 but then to reaccelerate to 6 percent in 2013, helped by easier macroeconomic policies and strengthening foreign demand. The spillovers from the euro area crisis, discussed in Chapter 2, will severely affect the rest of Europe; other economies will likely experience further financial volatility but no major impact on activity unless the euro area crisis intensifies once again.

Policy has played an important role in lowering systemic risk, but there can be no pause. The European Central Bank's three-year longer-term refinancing operations (LTROs), a stronger European firewall, ambitious fiscal adjustment programs, and the launch of major product and labor market reforms helped stabilize conditions in the euro area, relieving pressure on banks and sovereigns, but concerns linger. Furthermore, the recent extension of U.S. payroll tax relief and unemployment benefits has forestalled abrupt fiscal tightening that would have harmed the U.S. economy. More generally, many advanced economies have made good progress in designing and implementing strong medium-term fiscal consolidation programs. At the same time, emerging and developing economies continue to benefit from past policy improvements. With no further action, however, problems could easily flare up again in the euro area and fiscal policy could tighten very abruptly in the United States in 2013.

Accordingly, downside risks continue to loom large, a recurrent feature in recent issues of the *World Economic Outlook.* Unfortunately, some risks identified previously have come to pass, and the projections here are only modestly more favorable than those identified in a previous downside scenario.[1] The most immediate concern is still that

[1]See the downside scenario in the January 2011 *WEO Update.*

further escalation of the euro area crisis will trigger a much more generalized flight from risk. This scenario, discussed in depth in this issue, suggests that global and euro area output could decline, respectively, by 2 percent and 3½ percent over a two-year horizon relative to WEO projections. Alternatively, geopolitical uncertainty could trigger a sharp increase in oil prices: an increase in these prices by about 50 percent would lower global output by 1¼ percent. The effects on output could be much larger if the tensions were accompanied by significant financial volatility and losses in confidence. Furthermore, excessively tight macroeconomic policies could push another of the major economies into sustained deflation or a prolonged period of very weak activity. Additionally, latent risks include disruption in global bond and currency markets as a result of high budget deficits and debt in Japan and the United States and rapidly slowing activity in some emerging economies. However, growth could also be better than projected if policies improve further, financial conditions continue to ease, and geopolitical tensions recede.

Policies must be strengthened to solidify the weak recovery and contain the many downside risks. In the short term, this will require more efforts to address the euro area crisis, a temperate approach to fiscal restraint in response to weaker activity, a continuation of very accommodative monetary policies, and ample liquidity to the financial sector.

- In the euro area, the recent decision to combine the European Stability Mechanism (ESM) and the European Financial Stability Facility (EFSF) is welcome and, along with other recent European efforts, will strengthen the European crisis mechanism and support the IMF's efforts to bolster the global firewall. Sufficient fiscal consolidation is taking place but should be structured to avoid an excessive decline in demand in the near term. Given prospects for very low domestic inflation, there is room for further monetary easing; unconventional support (notably LTROs and purchases of government bonds) should continue to ensure orderly conditions in funding markets and thereby facilitate the pass-through of monetary policy to the real economy. In addition, banks must be recapitalized—this may require direct support from a more flexible EFSF/ESM.
- In the United States and Japan, sufficient fiscal adjustment is planned over the near term but there is still an urgent need for strong, sustainable fiscal consolidation paths over the medium term. Also, given very low domestic inflation pressure, further monetary easing may be needed in Japan to ensure that it achieves its inflation objective over the medium term. More easing would also be needed in the United States if activity threatens to disappoint.
- More generally, given the weak growth prospects in the major economies, those with room for fiscal policy maneuvering, in terms of the strength of their fiscal accounts and credibility with markets, can reconsider the pace of consolidation. Others should let automatic stabilizers operate freely for as long as they can readily finance higher deficits.

Looking further ahead, the challenge is to improve the weak medium-term growth outlook for the major advanced economies. The most important priorities remain fundamental reform of the financial sector; more progress with fiscal consolidation, including ambitious reform of entitlement programs; and structural reforms to boost potential output. In addition to implementing new consensus regulations (such as Basel III) at the national level, financial sector reform must address many weaknesses brought to light by the financial crisis, including the problems related to institutions considered too big or too complex to fail, the shadow banking system, and cross-border collaboration between bank supervisors. Reforms to aging-related spending are crucial because they can greatly reduce future spending without significantly harming demand today. Such measures can demonstrate policymakers' ability to act decisively and thereby help rebuild market confidence in the sustainability of public finances. This, in turn, can create more room for fiscal and monetary policy to support financial repair and demand without raising the specter of inflationary government deficit financing. Structural reforms must be deployed on many fronts—for example, in the euro area, to improve economies' capacity to adjust to competitiveness shocks, and in Japan, to boost labor force participation.

Policies directed at real estate markets can accelerate the improvement of household balance sheets and thus support otherwise anemic consumption. Countries that have adopted such policies, such as Iceland, have seen major benefits, as discussed in Chapter 3. In the United States, the administration has tried various programs but, given their limited success, is now proposing a more forceful approach. Elsewhere, the authorities have left it to banks and households to sort out the problems. In general, fears about moral hazard—by letting individuals who made excessively risky or speculative housing investments off the hook—have stood in the way of progress. These issues are similar to those that are making it so difficult to address the euro area crisis, although in Europe the moral hazard argument is being applied to countries rather than individuals. But in both cases, the use of targeted interventions to support demand can be more effective than much more costly macroeconomic programs. And the moral hazard dimension can be addressed in part through better regulation and supervision.

Emerging and developing economies continue to reap the benefits of strong macroeconomic and structural policies, but domestic vulnerabilities have been gradually building. Many of these economies have had an unusually good run over the past decade, supported by rapid credit growth or high commodity prices. To the extent that credit growth is a manifestation of financial deepening, this has been positive for growth. But in most economies, credit cannot continue to expand at its present pace without raising serious concerns about the quality of bank lending. Another consideration is that commodity prices are unlikely to grow at the elevated pace witnessed over the past decade, notwithstanding short-term spikes related to geopolitical tensions. This means that fiscal and other policies may well have to adapt to lower potential output growth, an issue discussed in Chapter 4.

The key near-term challenge for emerging and developing economies is how to appropriately calibrate macroeconomic policies to address the significant downside risks from advanced economies while keeping in check overheating pressures from strong activity, high credit growth, volatile capital flows, still-elevated commodity prices, and renewed risks to inflation and fiscal positions from energy prices. The appropriate response will vary. For economies that have largely normalized macroeconomic policies, the near-term focus should be on responding to lower external demand from advanced economies. At the same time, these economies must be prepared to cope with adverse spillovers and volatile capital flows. Other economies should continue to rebuild macroeconomic policy room and strengthen prudential policies and frameworks. Monetary policymakers need to be vigilant that oil price hikes do not translate into broader inflation pressure, and fiscal policy must contain damage to public sector balance sheets by targeting subsidies only to the most vulnerable households.

The latest developments suggest that global current account imbalances are no longer expected to widen again, following their sharp reduction during the Great Recession. This is largely because the excessive consumption growth that characterized economies that ran large external deficits prior to the crisis has been wrung out and has not been offset by stronger consumption in surplus economies. Accordingly, the global economy has experienced a loss of demand and growth in all regions relative to the boom years just before the crisis. Rebalancing activity in key surplus economies toward higher consumption, supported by more market-determined exchange rates, would help strengthen their prospects as well as those of the rest of the world.

Austerity alone cannot treat the economic malaise in the major advanced economies. Policies must also ease the adjustments and better target the fundamental problems—weak households in the United States and weak sovereigns in the euro area—by drawing on resources from stronger peers. Policymakers must guard against overplaying the risks related to unconventional monetary support and thereby limiting central banks' room for policy maneuvering. While unconventional policies cannot substitute for fundamental reform, they can limit the risk of another major economy falling into a debt-deflation trap, which could seriously hurt prospects for better policies and higher global growth.

CHAPTER 1

GLOBAL PROSPECTS AND POLICIES

Recent Developments

After suffering a major setback during 2011, global prospects are gradually strengthening again, but downside risks remain elevated. Through the third quarter, growth was broadly in line with the estimates in the September 2011 *World Economic Outlook* (WEO). Real GDP in many emerging and developing economies was somewhat weaker than expected, but growth surprised on the upside in the advanced economies. However, activity took a sharp turn for the worse during the fourth quarter, mainly in the euro area (Figure 1.1, panels 1 and 2).

- The future of the Economic and Monetary Union (EMU) became clouded by uncertainty, as the sovereign debt crisis caused sharp increases in key government bond rates (Figure 1.2, panels 2 and 3). Plummeting confidence and escalating financial stress were major factors in the 1.3 percent (annualized) contraction of the euro area economy. Real GDP also contracted in Japan, reflecting supply disruptions related to floods in Thailand and weaker global demand. In the United States, by contrast, activity accelerated, as consumption and inventory investment strengthened. Credit and the labor market also began to show signs of life.
- Activity softened in emerging and developing economies, with factors unrelated to the euro area crisis also playing an important role, but remained relatively strong (Figure 1.1, panel 3). In emerging Asia and in Latin America, trade and production slowed noticeably, owing partly to cyclical factors, including recent policy tightening. In the Middle East and North Africa (MENA), activity remained subdued amid social unrest and geopolitical uncertainty. In sub-Saharan Africa (SSA), growth has continued largely unabated, helped by favorable commodity prices. In emerging Europe, weak growth in the euro area had a larger impact than elsewhere. However, concerns about a potentially sharp slowdown in Turkey and a weakened policy framework in Hungary also detracted from activity.

Although the recovery was always expected to be weak and vulnerable because of the legacy of the financial crisis, other factors have played important roles. In the euro area, these include EMU design flaws; in the United States, an acrimonious debate on fiscal consolidation, which undermined confidence within financial markets; and elsewhere, natural disasters as well as high oil prices because of supply-side disruptions. Thus, past and present WEO projections for only modest growth have their origins in various developments and regions (Figure 1.1, panel 4). Some of these developments are now unwinding, which will support a reacceleration of activity.

High-frequency indicators point to somewhat stronger growth. Manufacturing purchasing managers' index indicators for advanced and emerging market economies have edged up in the most recent quarter (Figure 1.3, panel 1). The disruptive effects on supply chains caused by the Thai floods appear to be receding, leading to stronger industrial production and trade in various Asian economies. In addition, reconstruction is continuing to boost output in Japan. Global financial conditions have improved: data have come in stronger than expected by markets, and fears of an imminent banking or sovereign crisis in the euro area have diminished. Recent improvements in the ability of major economies on the periphery to roll over sovereign debt, narrower sovereign and interbank spreads relative to December highs, and a partial reopening of bank funding markets have helped reduce these fears, but concerns linger (Figure 1.2, panels 2 and 3). More generally, market volatility has declined and flows to emerging market economies have rebounded (Figure 1.4, panels 1 and 2). Appreciating currencies have prompted renewed exchange rate intervention (for example, in Brazil and Colombia).

Policy has played an important role in recent improvements, but various fundamental problems remain unresolved. The European Central

Table 1.1. Overview of the *World Economic Outlook* Projections

(Percent change unless noted otherwise)

	Year over Year						Q4 over Q4		
			Projections		Difference from January 2012 WEO Projections		Estimates	Projections	
	2010	2011	2012	2013	2012	2013	2011	2012	2013
World Output[1]	**5.3**	**3.9**	**3.5**	**4.1**	**0.2**	**0.1**	**3.2**	**3.7**	**4.1**
Advanced Economies	**3.2**	**1.6**	**1.4**	**2.0**	**0.2**	**0.1**	**1.2**	**1.6**	**2.2**
United States	3.0	1.7	2.1	2.4	0.3	0.2	1.6	2.0	2.6
Euro Area	1.9	1.4	–0.3	0.9	0.2	0.1	0.7	–0.2	1.4
Germany	3.6	3.1	0.6	1.5	0.3	0.0	2.0	0.9	1.6
France	1.4	1.7	0.5	1.0	0.3	0.0	1.3	0.5	1.4
Italy	1.8	0.4	–1.9	–0.3	0.2	0.3	–0.4	–2.0	0.7
Spain	–0.1	0.7	–1.8	0.1	–0.2	0.4	0.3	–2.5	1.3
Japan	4.4	–0.7	2.0	1.7	0.4	0.1	–0.6	2.0	1.8
United Kingdom	2.1	0.7	0.8	2.0	0.2	0.0	0.5	1.5	2.3
Canada	3.2	2.5	2.1	2.2	0.3	0.2	2.2	2.0	2.3
Other Advanced Economies[2]	5.8	3.2	2.6	3.5	0.0	0.1	2.5	3.6	2.9
Newly Industrialized Asian Economies	8.5	4.0	3.4	4.2	0.1	0.1	3.1	4.8	3.1
Emerging and Developing Economies[3]	**7.5**	**6.2**	**5.7**	**6.0**	**0.2**	**0.1**	**5.8**	**6.3**	**6.4**
Central and Eastern Europe	4.5	5.3	1.9	2.9	0.8	0.5	3.8	1.6	3.6
Commonwealth of Independent States	4.8	4.9	4.2	4.1	0.5	0.3	3.7	3.8	4.0
Russia	4.3	4.3	4.0	3.9	0.7	0.4	3.7	3.9	4.1
Excluding Russia	6.0	6.2	4.6	4.6	0.2	–0.1	. . .	. . .	. . .
Developing Asia	9.7	7.8	7.3	7.9	0.0	0.1	7.2	8.1	7.7
China	10.4	9.2	8.2	8.8	0.1	0.0	8.9	8.4	8.4
India	10.6	7.2	6.9	7.3	–0.1	0.0	6.1	6.9	7.2
ASEAN-5[4]	7.0	4.5	5.4	6.2	0.2	0.6	2.5	8.5	5.5
Latin America and the Caribbean	6.2	4.5	3.7	4.1	0.2	0.1	3.6	3.9	4.8
Brazil	7.5	2.7	3.0	4.1	0.1	0.1	1.4	4.7	3.4
Mexico	5.5	4.0	3.6	3.7	0.1	0.2	3.7	3.6	3.8
Middle East and North Africa (MENA)	4.9	3.5	4.2	3.7	0.6	–0.2	. . .	. . .	. . .
Sub-Saharan Africa	5.3	5.1	5.4	5.3	–0.1	0.0	. . .	. . .	. . .
South Africa	2.9	3.1	2.7	3.4	0.1	0.0	2.6	3.0	3.7
Memorandum									
European Union	2.0	1.6	0.0	1.3	0.1	0.1	0.9	0.2	1.7
World Growth Based on Market Exchange Rates	4.2	2.8	2.7	3.3	0.3	0.1	2.3	2.7	3.4
World Trade Volume (goods and services)	**12.9**	**5.8**	**4.0**	**5.6**	**0.2**	**0.2**	**. . .**	**. . .**	**. . .**
Imports									
Advanced Economies	11.5	4.3	1.8	4.1	–0.2	0.2	. . .	. . .	. . .
Emerging and Developing Economies	15.3	8.8	8.4	8.1	1.3	0.4	. . .	. . .	. . .
Exports									
Advanced Economies	12.2	5.3	2.3	4.7	–0.1	0.0	. . .	. . .	. . .
Emerging and Developing Economies	14.7	6.7	6.6	7.2	0.5	0.2	. . .	. . .	. . .
Commodity Prices (U.S. dollars)									
Oil[5]	27.9	31.6	10.3	–4.1	15.2	–0.5	20.8	10.8	–6.2
Nonfuel (average based on world commodity export weights)	26.3	17.8	–10.3	–2.1	3.7	–0.4	–6.4	0.1	–2.4
Consumer Prices									
Advanced Economies	1.5	2.7	1.9	1.7	0.3	0.4	2.8	1.7	1.6
Emerging and Developing Economies[3]	6.1	7.1	6.2	5.6	0.0	0.1	6.5	5.5	4.5
London Interbank Offered Rate (percent)[6]									
On U.S. Dollar Deposits	0.5	0.5	0.7	0.8	–0.2	–0.1	. . .	. . .	. . .
On Euro Deposits	0.8	1.4	0.8	0.8	–0.3	–0.4	. . .	. . .	. . .
On Japanese Yen Deposits	0.4	0.3	0.6	0.1	0.0	–0.1	. . .	. . .	. . .

Note: Real effective exchange rates are assumed to remain constant at the levels prevailing during February 13–March 12, 2012. When economies are not listed alphabetically, they are ordered on the basis of economic size. The aggregated quarterly data are seasonally adjusted.

[1]The quarterly estimates and projections account for 90 percent of the world purchasing-power-parity weights.

[2]Excludes the G7 (Canada, France, Germany, Italy, Japan, United Kingdom, United States) and Euro Area countries.

[3]The quarterly estimates and projections account for approximately 80 percent of the emerging and developing economies.

[4]Indonesia, Malaysia, Philippines, Thailand, and Vietnam.

[5]Simple average of prices of U.K. Brent, Dubai, and West Texas Intermediate crude oil. The average price of oil in U.S. dollars a barrel was $104.01 in 2011; the assumed price based on futures markets is $114.71 in 2012 and $110.00 in 2013.

[6]Six-month rate for the United States and Japan. Three-month rate for the euro area.

Bank's (ECB's) three-year longer-term refinancing operations (LTROs) have forestalled an imminent liquidity squeeze that could have led to a banking crisis. Together with the recent commitment to increase the euro area firewall as well as fiscal and structural reforms (notably in Italy and Spain), this lowered sovereign risk premiums, notwithstanding some widening again lately. The recent extension of payroll tax relief and unemployment benefits has averted excessive fiscal tightening that would have harmed the U.S. economy. Nonetheless, markets are still very concerned about prospects in the euro area's weaker economies. Moreover, the challenges posed by risk sharing and governance in the euro area and by medium-term fiscal consolidation in the United States and Japan demand further action.

What Went Wrong in the Euro Area?

The euro area crisis is the product of the interaction among several underlying forces. As in other advanced economies, these forces include mispriced risk, macroeconomic policy misbehavior over many years, and weak prudential policies and frameworks. These interacted with EMU-specific flaws, accelerating the buildup of excessive public and private sector imbalances in several euro area economies, which were exposed in the aftermath of the Great Recession. The resulting crisis has had drastic consequences.

While the overall public and external debt levels of the euro area are lower than those of the United States and Japan, the crisis has exposed flaws in EMU governance. The Stability and Growth Pact was devised to bring about fiscal discipline but failed to forestall bad fiscal policies. Markets became increasingly integrated, with enormous cross-border bank lending, but supervision and regulation remained at a national level. The ECB was explicitly *not* allowed to be a lender of last resort, yet markets operated under the assumption that the authorities—governments and central banks—would be ready with a safety net if things went wrong. The perception that economies or banking systems were too big or too complex to fail underlay the idea that their liabilities had implicit guarantees. Under these circumstances, market forces did not function properly: sovereign and credit risks

Figure 1.1. Global Indicators

Indicators of global trade and production retreated during the second half of 2011. The forecast is for a reacceleration of activity starting in the second quarter of 2012. Disappointments relative to past projections are related to developments in the United States and Japan in 2011 and in Europe, notably the euro area, in 2012.

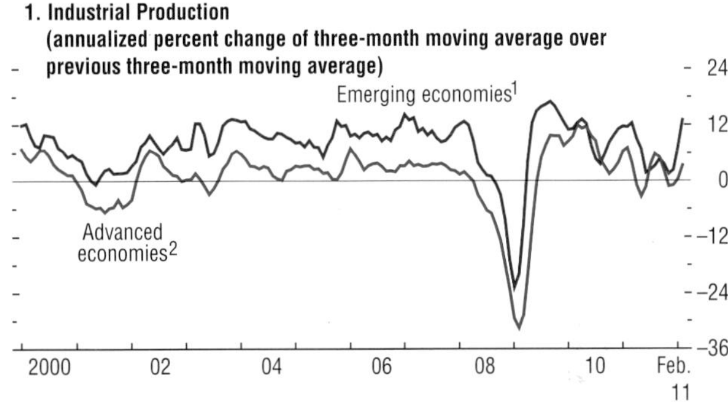

Real GDP Growth
(annualized quarterly percent change)

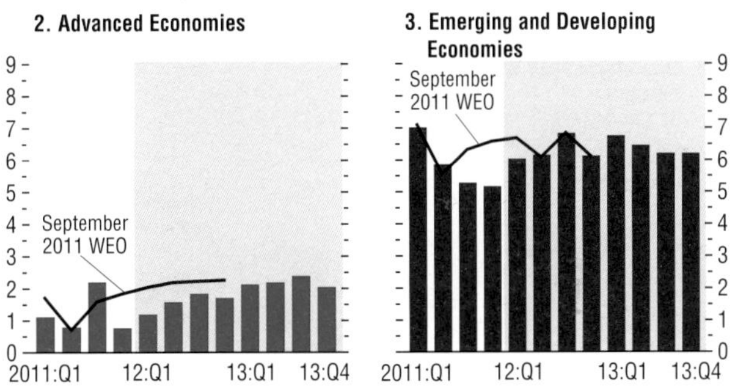

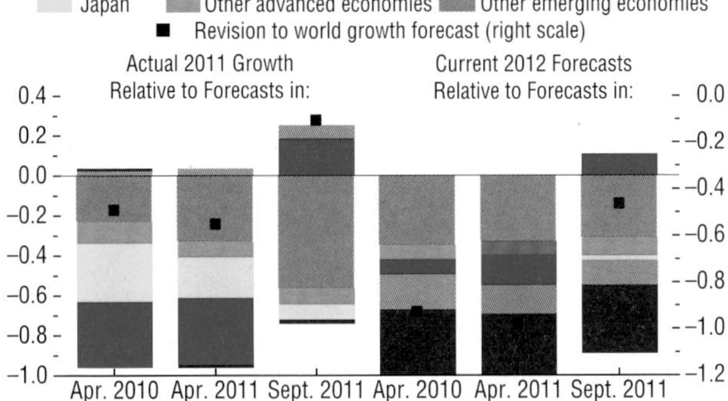

Source: IMF staff estimates.

[1]Argentina, Brazil, Bulgaria, Chile, China, Colombia, Hungary, India, Indonesia, Latvia, Lithuania, Malaysia, Mexico, Pakistan, Peru, Philippines, Poland, Romania, Russia, South Africa, Thailand, Turkey, Ukraine, and Venezuela.

[2]Australia, Canada, Czech Republic, Denmark, euro area, Hong Kong SAR, Israel, Japan, Korea, New Zealand, Norway, Singapore, Sweden, Switzerland, Taiwan Province of China, United Kingdom, and United States.

Figure 1.2. Recent Financial Market Developments

Financial conditions worsened appreciably in the fall of 2011 but have since improved. Economic data have surprised on the upside, most notably in the United States, and policy actions have brought down sovereign and bank risk premiums in the euro area.

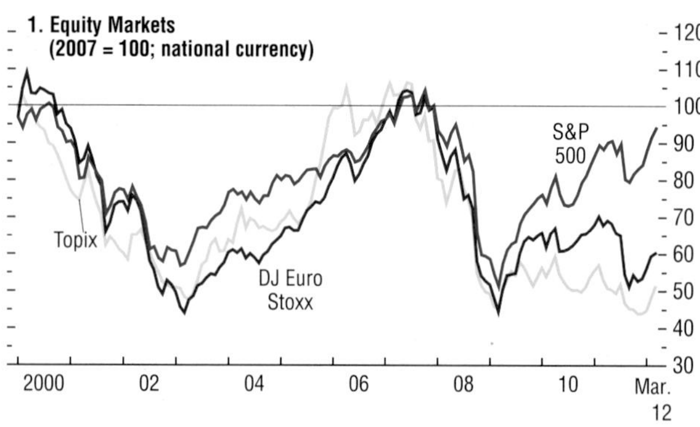

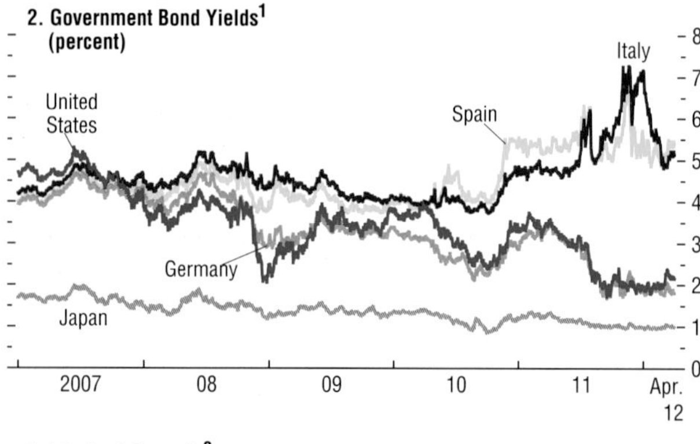

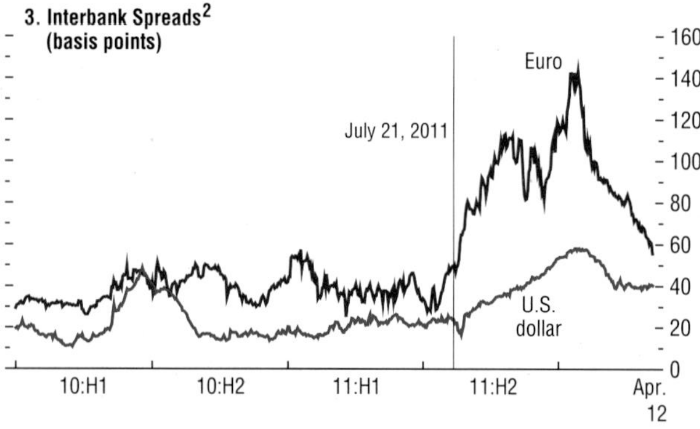

Sources: Bank of America/Merrill Lynch; Bloomberg Financial Markets; Citigroup; and IMF staff calculations.

[1] Ten-year government bonds.

[2] Three-month London interbank offered rate minus three-month government bill rate.

were underestimated and mispriced, resulting in large cross-country divergences in fiscal and external current account balances.

Since the crisis hit, the euro area has had to develop new mechanisms of support to heavily indebted members while implementing severe fiscal restraint. Concerns about bailing out investors and burdening public budgets prompted euro area members to entertain sovereign debt restructuring for Greece. The Greek crisis then escalated over the summer as negotiations continued concerning private sector involvement, raising concern in markets that other sovereigns could consider debt restructuring as a partial alternative to strong fiscal restraint and support from their euro area peers. Markets reassessed the riskiness of Italian bonds in particular: corporate, bank, and government securities were marked down. Following European Banking Authority (EBA) stress tests, the euro area initially had neither a clear road map nor visibly available resources to recapitalize banks found to be in need of more capital.

Policy efforts to fix the problems are ongoing. Since September, progress has accelerated. Steps include the recent decision to combine the European Stability Mechanism (ESM) and the European Financial Stability Facility (EFSF), the introduction of three-year LTROs by the ECB, the publication of bank recapitalization plans by the EBA, the December summit decision to advance the implementation of the ESM treaty to mid-2012 and to improve fiscal governance and policy coordination, and national measures to strengthen fiscal balances and introduce structural reforms, including in Spain and Italy. The risk of a crisis has also been reduced as a result of the progress achieved in Greece, although the problems there and in other economies on the euro area periphery will likely persist for a long time.

Prospects

The outlook for the global economy is slowly improving again but is still very fragile. Real GDP growth should pick up gradually during 2012–13 from the trough reached during the first quarter of 2012 (Table 1.1; Figure 1.1, panels 2 and 3). Improved financial conditions, accommodative monetary policies, a similar pace of fiscal tightening as in 2011, and special factors (reconstruction in Japan and Thailand) will drive the reacceleration. However, the recovery will remain vulnerable to several major downside risks. Regarding risks from Europe, the WEO projections assume that policymakers will prevent a Greek-style downward spiral from taking hold of another economy on the euro area periphery. However, it is assumed that additional support will be forthcoming only in the event of reintensified market turmoil. Thus, sovereign spreads and euro area banking system stress are expected to remain volatile and come down only gradually.

Tighter Financial Conditions, Mainly in the Euro Area

Financial conditions are projected to ease but stay tighter than those assumed in the September 2011 *World Economic Outlook*. The April 2012 *Global Financial Stability Report* underscores the continued high risks to financial stability relative to six months ago, despite policy steps to contain the euro area debt and banking crisis. In the euro area, sovereigns and banks face significant refinancing requirements for 2012, estimated at 23 percent of GDP. Deleveraging pressures are also likely to stay elevated, as banks undergo $2.6 trillion in balance sheet reduction over the next two years. Although these pressures are likely to affect mainly economies in the euro area periphery and in emerging Europe, they will be a drag on growth in core economies that could worsen if funding conditions deteriorate.

The ECB's LTROs have averted a liquidity-driven crisis by replacing private funding with official financing, but fundamental weaknesses remain. The recent EBA assessment of banks' capital plans suggests that, in aggregate, capital measures will adequately address the shortfalls, which will limit the negative impact on lending to the real economy. The LTROs also have helped boost demand for sovereign paper (including by banks), contributing to lower risk spreads. Lower spreads have supported a recovery of equity prices and mitigated pressures for rapid deleveraging by banks. In addition, the LTROs may have been interpreted by markets as signaling greater ECB resolve to do what it takes to stabilize financial conditions.

Nonetheless, stress in sovereign funding markets remains and will likely recede only slowly from pres-

Figure 1.3 Current and Forward-Looking Growth Indicators[1]

Leading indicators suggest that activity is bottoming out. Global output may be boosted by inventory rebuilding and investment as supply-side disruptions from the earthquake and tsunami in Japan and the floods in Thailand continue to unwind. Oil prices are projected to rise much less than in 2011, which will give some support to consumption growth.

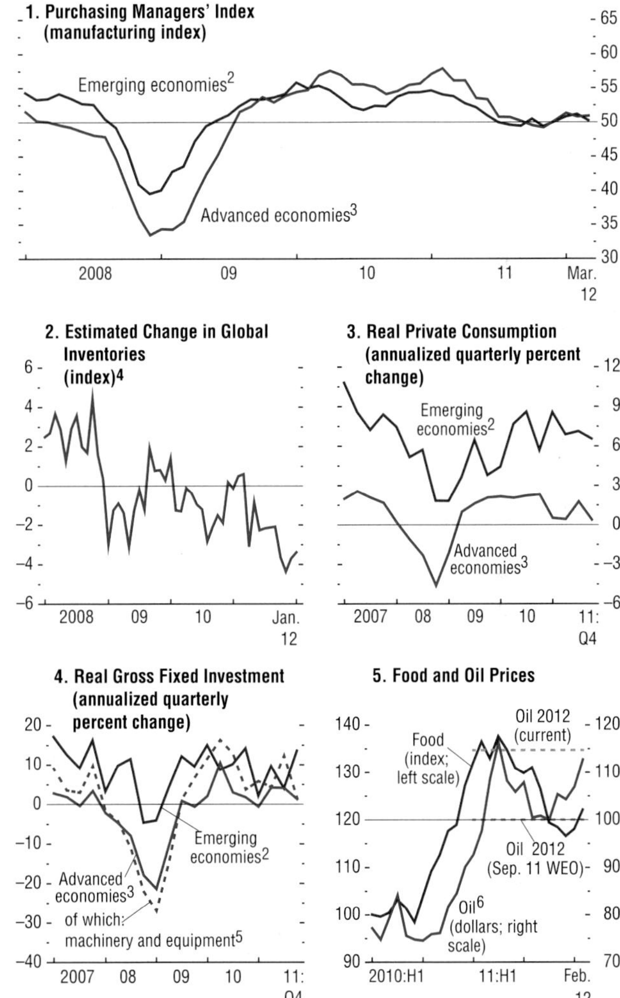

Sources: Haver Analytics; and IMF staff calculations.

[1]Not all economies are included in the regional aggregations. For some economies, monthly data are interpolated from quarterly series.

[2]Argentina, Brazil, Bulgaria, Chile, China, Colombia, Hungary, India, Indonesia, Latvia, Lithuania, Malaysia, Mexico, Peru, Philippines, Poland, Romania, Russia, South Africa, Thailand, Turkey, Ukraine, and Venezuela.

[3]Australia, Canada, Czech Republic, Denmark, euro area, Hong Kong SAR, Israel, Japan, Korea, New Zealand, Norway, Singapore, Sweden, Switzerland, Taiwan Province of China, United Kingdom, and United States.

[4]Based on deviations from an estimated (cointegral) relationship between global industrial production and retail sales.

[5]Purchasing-power-parity-weighted averages of metal products and machinery for the euro area, plants and equipment for Japan, plants and machinery for the United Kingdom, and equipment and software for the United States.

[6]U.S. dollars a barrel: simple average of spot prices of U.K. Brent, Dubai Fateh, and West Texas Intermediate crude oil.

Figure 1.4. Emerging Market Conditions

Financial conditions in emerging markets began to tighten during the fall of 2011. Amid a general flight from risk, interest rate spreads rose. Funding conditions worsened for banks, contributing to a tightening of lending standards, and capital inflows diminished. However, these flows are now returning with new vigor, and risk spreads have come down again.

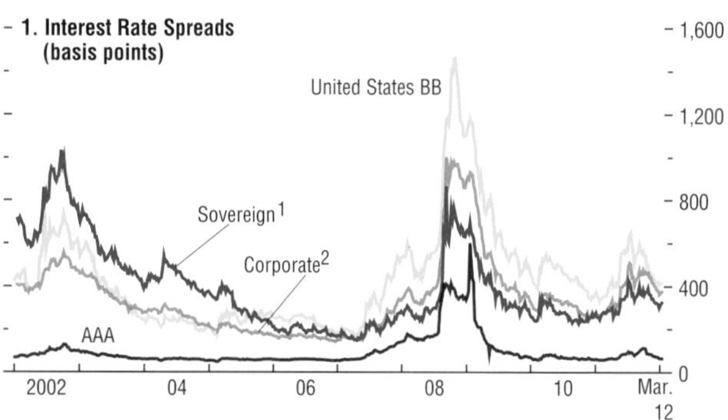

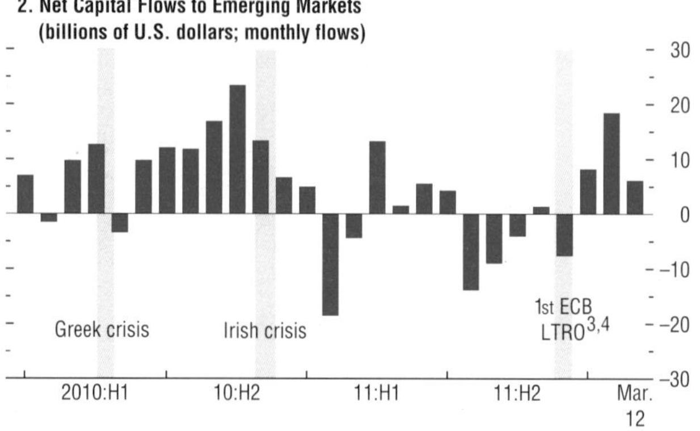

Emerging Market Bank Lending Conditions (diffusion index; neutral = 50)

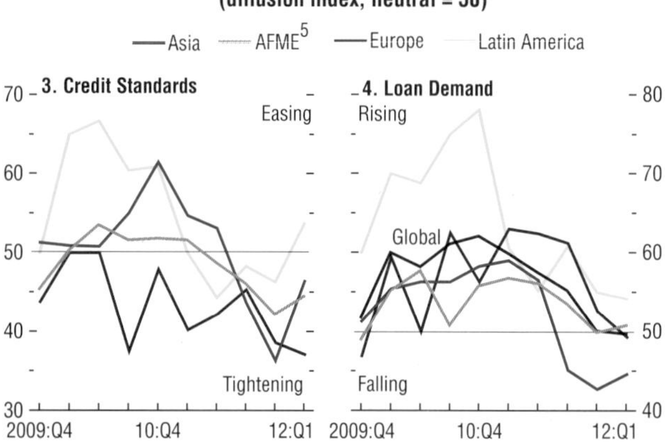

Sources: Bloomberg Financial Markets; Capital Data; EPFR Global; Haver Analytics; IIF Emerging Markets Bank Lending Survey; and IMF staff calculations.
[1]JPMorgan EMBI Global Index spread.
[2]JPMorgan CEMBI Broad Index spread.
[3]ECB = European Central Bank.
[4]LTRO = Longer-term refinancing operations.
[5]AFME = Africa and Middle East.

ent levels, as governments gradually regain the trust of investors through successful consolidation and structural reform. Together with weaker activity, this stress will continue to affect corporate funding markets. In the meantime, the risk of a renewed flare-up will continue to weigh on financial conditions.

Under these circumstances, bank lending in the crisis-hit economies of the euro area, which has already dropped sharply, is likely to stay very low (Figure 1.5, panel 1) as banks seek to strengthen their balance sheets with a view to staving off public intervention or resolution and to regain access to market funding.[1] In the core economies, financial conditions will likely remain much less tight than in the economies on the periphery. Nonetheless, even if subject to a considerable amount of uncertainty, it appears from the April 2012 *Global Financial Stability Report* calculations for a "current policies" scenario that balance sheet deleveraging could result in an appreciable drop in lending for the euro area as a whole, with the bulk of the reduction falling on economies on the periphery.

Outside Europe, spillovers from the euro area are likely to have limited effects on economic activity for as long as the euro area crisis is contained, as is assumed in the projections. The key channels are lower confidence, less trade, and greater financial tension (Figure 1.6). These are discussed in more depth in Chapter 2 and in the Spillover Feature in Chapter 2.

- The bond markets of Germany, Japan, Switzerland, the United Kingdom, and the United States have experienced safe haven inflows, which has lowered long-term government bond rates (see Figure 1.2, panel 2). This has offset the effects of rising risk aversion on the cost of corporate funding in some of these markets. In Japan and Switzerland, the inflows have led to significant exchange rate volatility, prompting official intervention.
- Contagion from the turbulence in the euro area caused a significant drop in capital inflows to many emerging market economies, resulting in higher interest spreads and lower asset prices. However, the recent easing of strains has already

[1]However, reduced lending is expected to contribute only modestly to raising core Tier 1 capital ratios to the 9 percent level recommended by the EBA, according to banks' plans (see also the April 2012 *Global Financial Stability Report*).

caused a sharp reversal in flows (see Figure 1.4, panel 2). The real effects of the outflows were small in most regions, not least because they helped bring down overvalued currencies and lower pressure on overheating sectors. Capital flows are likely to stay volatile, complicating policymaking. As noted in the April 2012 *Global Financial Stability Report*, with many emerging market economies at a later stage in the credit cycle, there is now less room to ease credit policies if capital flows deteriorate.

Spillovers from bank deleveraging are being felt more strongly, mainly in Europe (Figure 1.6, panel 2). Central and eastern European (CEE) and various Commonwealth of Independent States (CIS) economies are most vulnerable and already saw appreciable deleveraging during the third quarter of 2011; this likely continued at a more rapid pace during the fourth quarter. However, some of the larger economies are continuing to see significant portfolio inflows. In other emerging market economies, exposure to European bank deleveraging either is more limited or local institutions have the capacity to step in—albeit at higher cost. However, if disruptions in the euro area worsen, access to funding is very likely to tighten everywhere.

Domestic developments generally point to modest financial tightening elsewhere in the world, except in the United States. U.S. bank lending behavior and recent surveys suggest gradually easing conditions, but from very tight levels. Lending by midsize and small banks may be constrained for some time by market funding issues and weak real-estate-related portfolios. In many emerging markets, lending surveys suggest tightening conditions as a result of more difficult access to local and international funding (Figure 1.4, panels 3 and 4). Bank loan growth has slowed in China and India amid concerns about deteriorating loan quality. Continued elevated or accelerated loan growth is, to varying degrees, raising concern in Argentina, Brazil, Colombia, Indonesia, and Turkey.

Modestly Easing Global Monetary Conditions

Monetary policy is generally expected to maintain an easy stance (Figure 1.7, panel 1). Many central

Figure 1.5. Credit Market Conditions

Lending conditions tightened noticeably in the euro area recently, and credit growth slumped in late 2011. Developments were more positive in the United States and Japan. Looking ahead, conditions can be expected to ease somewhat. While the central bank balance sheet has expanded noticeably in the United States and the euro area, it has not done so in Japan. Broad money growth has remained very subdued in the euro area and Japan but has picked up in the United States, consistent with improving activity.

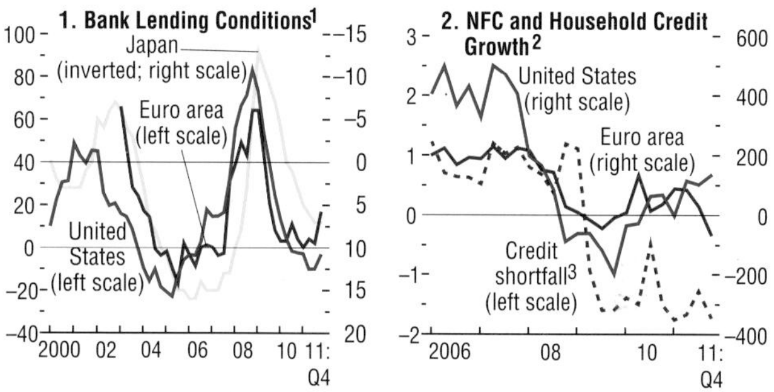

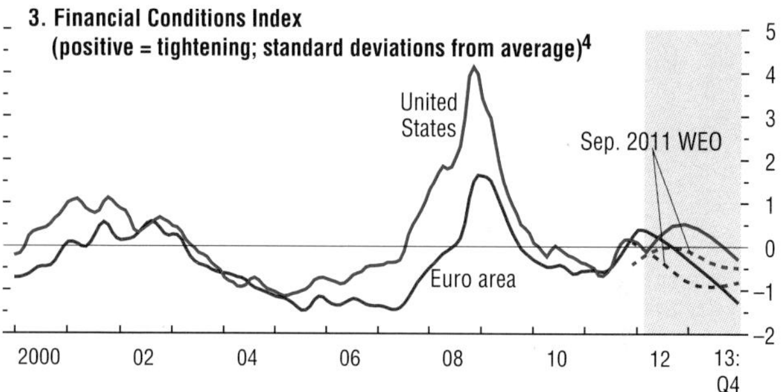

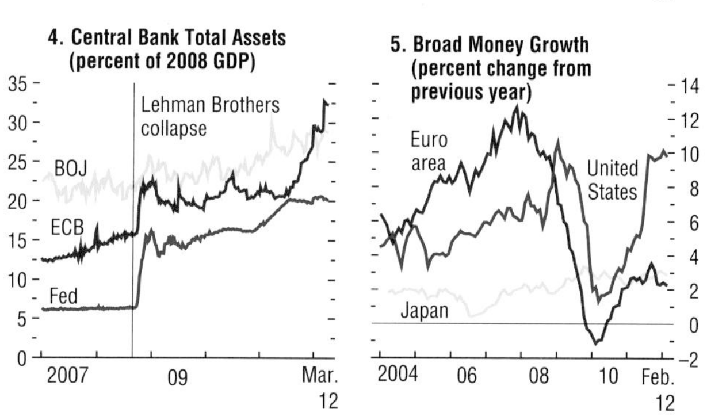

Sources: Bank of Japan (BOJ); Bloomberg Financial Markets; European Central Bank (ECB); Federal Reserve (Fed); Haver Analytics; and IMF staff estimates.

[1] Percent of respondents describing lending standards as tightening "considerably" or "somewhat" minus those indicating standards as easing "considerably" or "somewhat" over the previous three months. Survey of changes to credit standards for loans or lines of credit to firms for the euro area; average of surveys on changes in credit standards for commercial/industrial and commercial real estate lending for the United States; diffusion index of "accommodative" minus "severe," Tankan survey of lending attitude of financial institutions for Japan.

[2] NFC: nonfinancial corporation. Level change in amounts outstanding in billions of local currency units.

[3] Credit shortfall is the residual from a regression of real private sector credit growth on real GDP growth for the euro area.

[4] Historical data are monthly, and forecasts are quarterly.

Figure 1.6. Euro Area Spillovers[1]

Spillovers from the euro area to activity elsewhere are likely to be limited, except elsewhere within Europe, where there are strong trade and banking linkages.

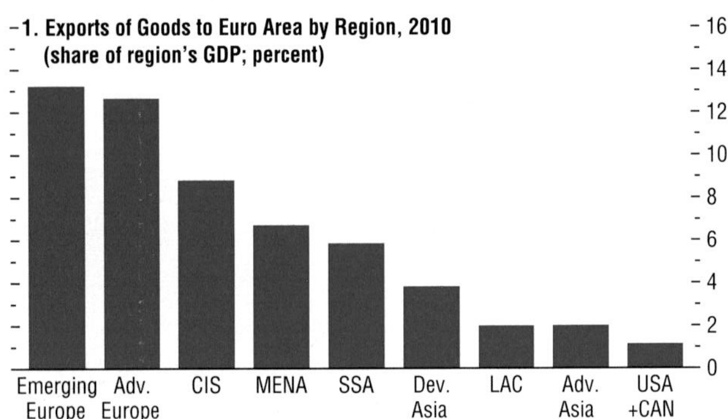

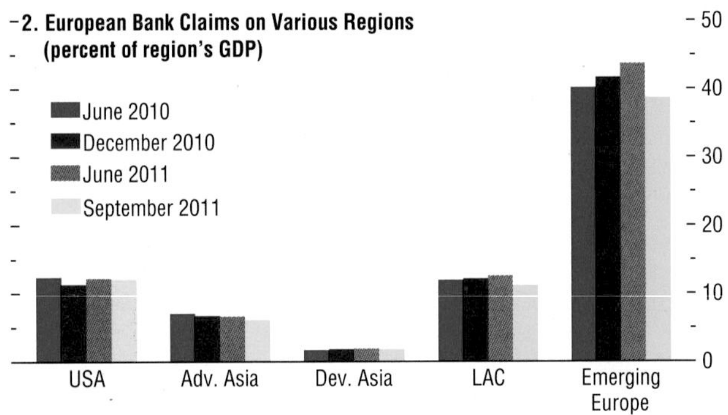

Sources: Bank for International Settlements; IMF, *Direction of Trade Statistics;* and IMF staff calculations.

[1]Adv. Asia: advanced Asia; Adv. Europe: advanced Europe excluding euro area countries; CAN: Canada; CIS: Commonwealth of Independent States; Dev. Asia: developing Asia; LAC: Latin America and the Caribbean; MENA: Middle East and North Africa; SSA: sub-Saharan Africa; USA: United States.

banks have already responded to slowing activity by cutting policy rates (Australia, Brazil, euro area, Indonesia, Israel, Philippines, Romania, Thailand, Turkey). Recently, the Bank of Japan and Bank of England expanded their unconventional policy interventions, and the Federal Reserve signaled its conditional intention to maintain exceptionally low interest rates at least through late 2014; this may have helped lower interest rates further into the future and weakened the U.S. dollar.

- Rates are expected to stay close to the zero lower bound in the United States and Japan for at least the next two years. For the euro area, markets are pricing in modest easing; policy rates in other advanced economies are expected to stay on hold or decline modestly.
- Across emerging market economies, rates are generally expected to be stable or decline somewhat. In economies where macroprudential measures have successfully dampened overheating real estate markets, the authorities may lighten some of these measures.

Continued Tightening of Fiscal Policy

Fiscal policy at the global level will tighten in 2012 by slightly less than in 2011, mainly because of reconstruction efforts in Japan and substantially less tightening in emerging market economies. The tightening will be concentrated in the advanced economies (Figure 1.7, panels 2 and 3).

- In the euro area, the fiscal withdrawal in 2012 is projected to amount to about 1½ percent of GDP, up from about 1 percent of GDP in 2011. In the United States, the projected tightening for 2012 is about 1¼ percent of GDP, up from less than ¾ percent of GDP in 2011. In Japan, earthquake-related reconstruction spending (equivalent to ¾ percent of GDP) will contribute to raising the structural deficit by about ½ percent of GDP. In 2013, the pace of tightening is expected to drop off in the euro area but pick up in the United States and Japan.
- In emerging and developing economies, the pace of fiscal tightening is projected to drop from about 1¼ percent of GDP in 2011 to less than ¼ percent of GDP in 2012, primarily as a result

of less ambitious fiscal restraint in some major emerging market economies (for example, China, India, Russia).

Gross-debt-to-GDP ratios will rise further in many advanced economies, with a particularly steep increase in the G7 economies, to about 130 percent by 2017. Without more action than currently planned, debt ratios are expected to reach 256 percent in Japan, 124 percent in Italy, close to 113 percent in the United States, and 91 percent in the euro area over the forecast horizon. In the G7 economies of the euro area, these ratios would be reached in 2013, after which they would fall, whereas in Japan and the United States the debt ratios are projected to rise through the forecast horizon, which extends to 2017. In a striking contrast, many emerging and developing economies will see a decline in debt-to-GDP ratios, with the overall ratio for the group dropping to below 30 percent by 2017. The April 2012 *Fiscal Monitor* provides more detail at the country level and discusses the role of growth and interest rate assumptions in driving the debt dynamics.

Volatile or Falling Commodity Prices

Oil prices rose sharply during 2010 and early 2011 to about $115 a barrel, then eased to about $100 a barrel, and now are back up to about $115 a barrel (Figure 1.3, panel 5). Production recovered in Libya but fell in various other Organization of Petroleum Exporting Countries (OPEC) producers, and non-OPEC output remained relatively weak. In addition, geopolitical risks—notably those centered on the Islamic Republic of Iran—have boosted oil prices. Projections for 2012–13 assume that oil prices recede to about $110 a barrel in 2013, in line with prices in futures markets, but in the current environment low stocks and limited spare capacity present important upside risks.

Other commodity prices have recently been given a temporary boost by better-than-expected macroeconomic results, but they continue to run much lower than in 2011. WEO projections assume a decline in the nonfuel commodity price index of 10.3 percent in 2012 and 2.7 percent in 2013 (see Table 1.1). An important factor here is improved prospects for the food supply during 2012. Stocks

Figure 1.7. Monetary and Fiscal Policies

Policy rates are expected to stay on hold for a prolonged period in advanced economies. Fiscal policy is projected to continue tightening in 2012 but at broadly the same pace as in 2011: more in advanced economies but much less in emerging and developing economies. Public debt is projected to reach a very high level in advanced economies in 2017 but to stay low in emerging and developing economies.

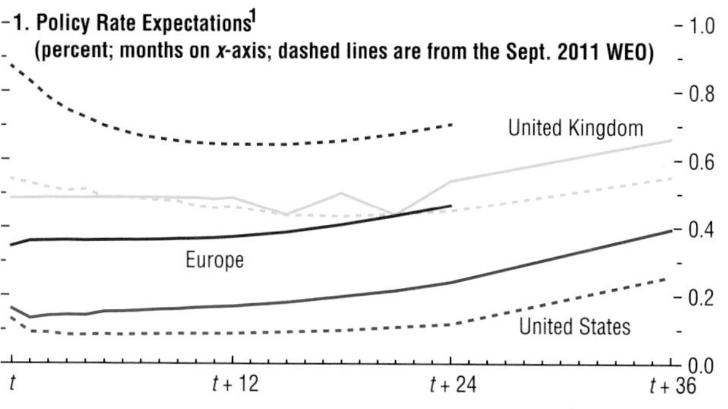

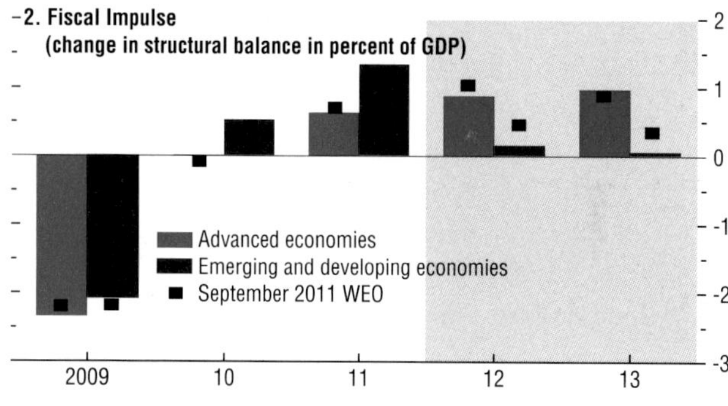

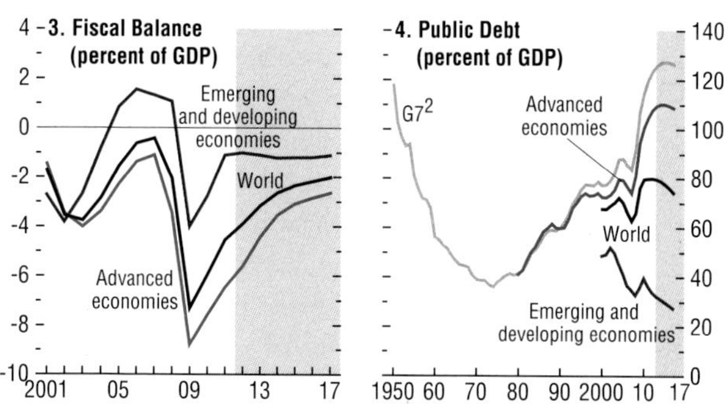

Sources: Bloomberg Financial Markets; and IMF staff estimates.

[1] Expectations are based on the federal funds rate for the United States, the sterling overnight interbank average rate for the United Kingdom, and the euro interbank offered forward rates for Europe; updated April 3, 2012.

[2] G7 comprises Canada, France, Germany, Italy, Japan, United Kingdom, and United States.

are still low, which poses risks, but a return to more normal levels appears to be under way. This is good news for many vulnerable households.

Forecast for 2012–13

Real GDP growth is forecast to slow to about 3½ percent in 2012, from about 4 percent in 2011, and to return to 4 percent in 2013 (see Table 1.1). In the advanced economies, growth is projected at about 1½ percent in 2012 and 2 percent in 2013. Because of weak confidence, fiscal consolidation, and still-tight financial conditions in a number of economies, euro area GDP is forecast to contract in 2012 by about ¼ percent, after expanding by about 1½ percent in 2011. Helped by improving financial conditions and less fiscal tightening, growth should rebound to about 1 percent in 2013—nonetheless, the output gap would stay above 2 percent of potential GDP, up from about 1½ percent in 2011. U.S. real GDP growth is projected to strengthen somewhat relative to 2011, at about 2 to 2½ percent during 2012–13, implying only modest change in the 5 percent of GDP output gap. In Japan, real GDP growth is projected at about 2 percent in 2012, recovering from the output losses in 2011 related to the earthquake and Thai floods. Labor market conditions are likely to remain very difficult in many advanced economies. A further concern is that much of the increase in GDP since the trough has flowed to profits (Box 1.1), and it is likely to be some time before conditions favor sustained real wage increases. Accordingly, governments must provide adequate assistance to the unemployed in the form of income support, skill building and professional training, and job search resources.

Expansion in the emerging and developing economies is projected to remain at about 5½ to 6 percent through 2013. Modest negative spillovers from the euro area are expected to be largely offset by monetary easing and reduced fiscal policy tightening—except in various CEE and CIS economies. In emerging Asia, recovery from the Thai floods and more demand from Japan will help propel output. In Latin America, financial conditions and commodity prices remain favorable; the recent policy tightening will weigh on activity for some time, but prospects should improve later in 2012. In the MENA region, the near-term outlook is challenging. Oil importers' growth is not expected to pick up given heightened domestic uncertainty and difficult external conditions, and the outlook for oil exporters is also muted, reflecting flat oil and gas production. (The increase in growth projected for 2012 reflects the rebound of activity in Libya.) In SSA economies, activity should remain relatively strong, helped by growing production of both crude oil and minerals. The labor market challenges in emerging and developing economies vary widely. Unemployment rates are very high in various CEE and CIS economies that have been hit by the crisis as well as in the MENA region, where job creation has been subdued but many young people are entering the labor force. By contrast, unemployment rates are relatively low in many emerging Asian and Latin American economies, thanks to strong growth in recent years.

Consumption dynamics are forecast to improve modestly in 2012 relative to 2011. Continued deleveraging by households and governments means that household consumption will not accelerate much in the major advanced economies (Figure 1.3, panel 3). This stands in sharp contrast to the consumption dynamics in the emerging and developing economies, which have been a hallmark of the recovery thus far (Box 1.2). In the United States, consumption is expected to withstand the fiscal tightening, thanks to improvements in the labor market and fewer energy and food price hikes. The saving rate is projected to be broadly stable, at about 4 to 4½ percent. Low real estate prices are depressing net worth, which encourages saving, even as debt-to-income ratios have fallen back to 2004 levels (Figure 1.8, panel 1). In the euro area, prospects for consumption are generally weak because of fallen confidence, employment, and incomes and high debt in various economies on the periphery. Germany and a few other countries may break the pattern. In many emerging and developing economies, consumption is expected to stay robust, consistent with strong labor markets.

Greater uncertainty, accelerated deleveraging by banks in the euro area, and credit tightening in selected emerging market economies suggest that the growth of fixed investment is likely to slow (Figure 1.3, panel 4). Investment (including inventories) may be boosted temporarily by a need to expand capacity as production makes up the losses related to natural disasters (Figure 1.3, panel 2). But high uncertainty and tighter financial conditions will push in the opposite direction in the euro area and the CEE and CIS economies. In various emerging market economies, notably China, real estate markets are cooling down, which implies slowing investment in construction.

Despite appreciable slack in the major advanced economies, other economies will operate close to or above full capacity, and thus inflation dynamics will vary (Figure 1.9).

- Commodity price hikes have held up headline inflation in major advanced economies. At the same time, core inflation and wage gains have remained low. In the United States and the euro area, unit labor costs have receded or stagnated, respectively, over the past few years. As labor markets improve only very gradually, headline inflation in the United States is projected to fall to about 2 percent in 2013 (Figure 1.9, panel 1). The projection for the euro area is about 1½ percent for 2013. Prices in Japan are projected to move broadly sideways.
- Inflation prospects are more diverse across emerging market economies (Figure 1.9, panels 3 and 4). As discussed in Chapter 2, the recent easing of inflation is partly a result of lower commodity prices. In emerging Europe the picture is mixed, but pressures are expected to ease during 2012. In emerging Asia, headline inflation is slowing and expected to continue on this path. However, inflation is projected to stay elevated in parts of the region, notably in India, and to accelerate in Indonesia. In Latin America, many of the major economies are operating close to full capacity and inflation is forecast to decline only modestly. In the CIS, MENA, and parts of SSA, inflation pressure is expected to stay quite elevated, reflecting accommodative macroeconomic policies and supply-side disruptions.

Medium-Term Prospects and Global Imbalances

Medium-term prospects remain very challenging for advanced economies but much better for emerging and developing economies. A key question is whether the forecasts for emerging Asia and Latin America are too optimistic, considering the downward revisions to the

Figure 1.8. Balance Sheets and Saving Rates

(Percent unless noted otherwise)

Balance sheets have improved in the United States but household net worth remains low, weighing on consumption. Saving rates are projected to move broadly sideways. In the euro area, balance sheets have strengthened to a lesser extent, and house prices may need to correct further.

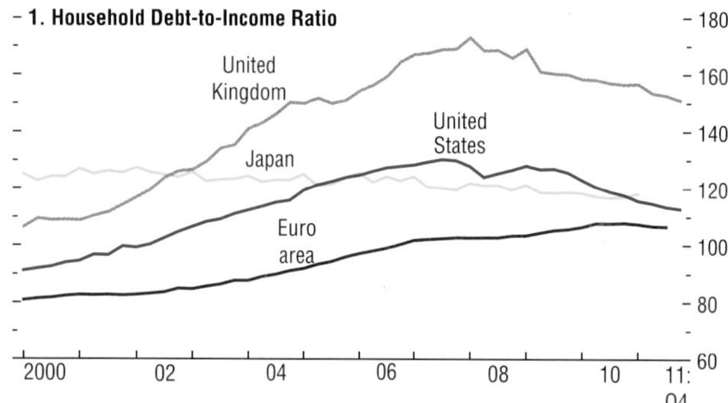

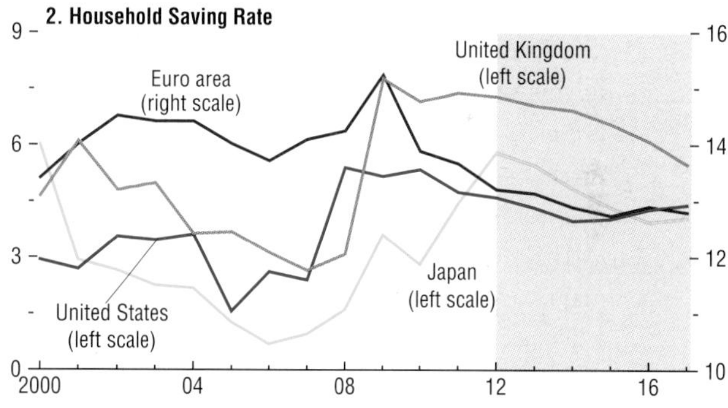

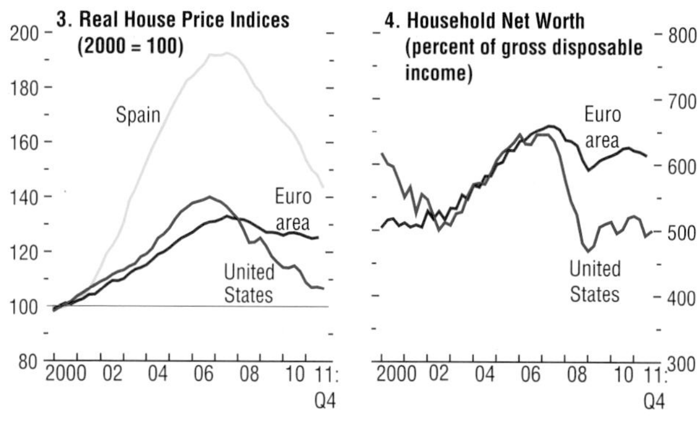

Sources: Haver Analytics; Organization for Economic Cooperation and Development; and IMF staff estimates.

Figure 1.9. Global Inflation

(Twelve-month change in the consumer price index unless noted otherwise)

Inflation pressure is easing. In the major advanced economies, domestic inflation pressure, as measured by the GDP deflator, is low. In emerging market economies, pressure varies widely but is generally projected to recede modestly.

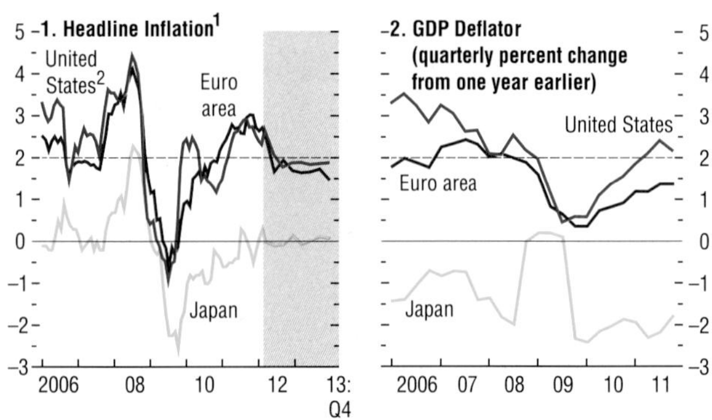

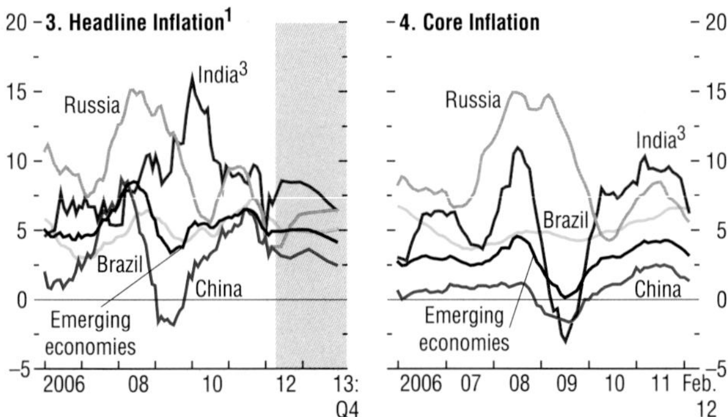

Sources: Haver Analytics; and IMF staff estimates.
[1]Historical data are monthly, and forecasts are quarterly.
[2]Personal consumption expenditure deflator.
[3]Consumer price index for industrial workers for headline inflation; wholesale price index excluding food and energy for core inflation.

potential output of advanced economies (Figure 1.10, panel 1) and modest but persistent disappointments over the past couple of years (see Figure 1.1, panel 4). Previous issues of the *World Economic Outlook* have cited high credit growth rates (Figure 1.10, panels 2 and 3), booming real-estate-related activity, and strong commodity prices as drivers of growth. Evidence suggests that episodes of high credit and GDP growth are typically followed by episodes of much lower growth. This also holds following episodes with booming commodity prices, which is discussed further in Chapter 4. Policymakers therefore should not assume that strong recent performance that largely reflects these same factors is a good guide to future performance.

The latest WEO projections suggest that global imbalances are no longer expected to widen, reflecting mainly the contribution of lower surpluses from Japan and the oil exporters and of lower deficits from the United States and elsewhere (Figure 1.11, panel 3). Because the sharp drop in consumption relative to precrisis projections in the United States and other deficit economies has not been offset by higher domestic demand growth in surplus economies, including China, the result has been a major drop in global demand relative to precrisis projections. This outcome reflects excesses in the deficit economies that had to unwind and policy shortcomings in surplus economies.

The implications of the new current account projections are still under study as a new methodology for assessing the multilateral consistency of the real effective exchange rate is being developed. The main change among the major currencies since publication of the September 2011 *World Economic Outlook* is a 6 to 7 percent increase in the real effective exchange rates of the U.S. dollar and the renminbi and a large downward revision to the medium-term forecast for China's current account surplus. However, its surplus is still expected to rise from present levels as cyclical factors unwind (Box 1.3) and to reach a relatively high share in global GDP. Thus the contribution of emerging Asia to current account balances in not forecast to narrow (see Figure 1.11, panel 3). In addition, the decline in China's external imbalance has been accompanied by growing tension from internal imbalances—high levels of investment and low consumption—which remain to be addressed. This calls for additional structural reforms and exchange rate adjustment to shift incentives away from investment, particularly in the tradables sector, and toward higher household income and greater consumption.

Many emerging market economies continue to build up international reserves or other foreign assets (Figure 1.11, panel 2). In some instances, this behavior is understandable; in others, reserves have reached very high levels, and the continued accumulation reflects a desire to maintain a competitive exchange rate.

Risks

Recent policy actions have helped bring down risks, as borne out by various market risk metrics, but the global economy remains unusually vulnerable. The two most immediate risks are renewed escalation of the euro area crisis and heightened geopolitical uncertainty, which could trigger a sharp increase in the price of oil. Other risks include growing disinflation pressure, especially in parts of the euro area and—over the medium term—disruptions to global bond markets from accident-prone political economies and high budget deficits and debt in the United States and Japan and unwinding credit booms in some emerging market economies. There are also upside risks: growth might turn out stronger than projected if there is more rapid recovery in the United States and the euro area, thanks to a stronger policy response to the euro area crisis and improved confidence, and if the geopolitical tensions recede and the risk premium in oil prices dissipates. Greater confidence and waning supply-side disruptions could also foster a more forceful rebound in global durables consumption and investment, helped by generally healthy corporate balance sheets and less costly capital.

The standard fan chart suggests that risks have receded relative to the September 2011 *World Economic Outlook* (Figure 1.12, panel 1). The width of the forecast's 90 percent confidence band is now somewhat narrower than in September. This narrowing reflects a smaller dispersion in analysts' forecasts for the term spread, oil prices, and the VIX—the Chicago Board Options Exchange Market Volatility Index (Figure 1.12, panel 3). In the September 2011 *World Economic Outlook*, quantitative indicators implied that the risk of a serious global slowdown—that is, global growth falling below 2 percent in 2012—was about 10 percent. According to the IMF

Figure 1.10. Emerging Market Economies[1]

Many emerging market economies in Asia and Latin America are growing above precrisis trends and are projected to continue to do so, unlike many advanced economies. However, WEO projections still see some slack. Credit growth in these economies is also still high. Usually, periods of high real GDP and credit growth are followed by periods of lower real GDP growth.

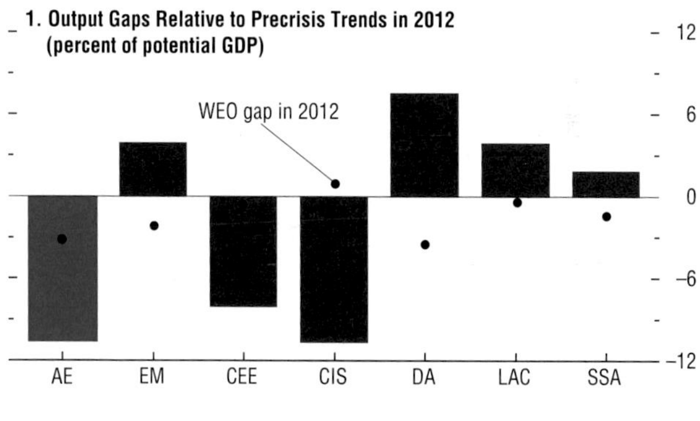

Real Credit Growth
(year-over-year percent change)

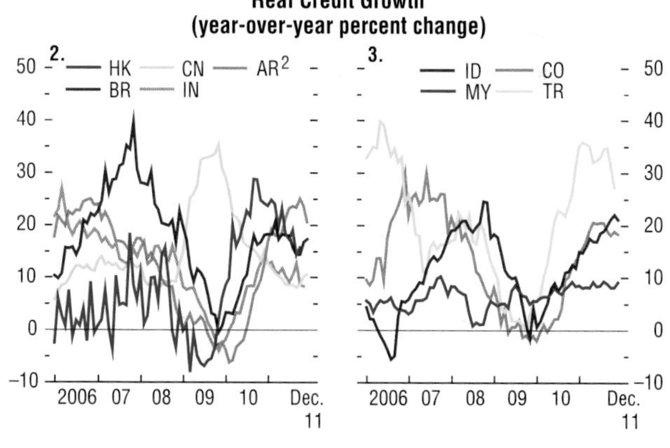

Sources: IMF, *International Financial Statistics;* and IMF staff calculations.

[1]AR: Argentina; AE: advanced economies; BR: Brazil; CEE: central and eastern Europe; CIS: Commonwealth of Independent States; CN: China; CO: Colombia; DA: developing Asia; EM: emerging economies; HK: Hong Kong SAR; ID: Indonesia; IN: India; LAC: Latin America and the Caribbean; MY: Malaysia; SSA: sub-Saharan Africa; TR: Turkey. Credit refers to bank credit to the private sector.

[2]Nominal credit is deflated using the IMF staff's estimate of average provincial inflation.

staff's methodology, the probability has declined to about 1 percent for 2012. There are four risk indicators underlying the fan chart (Figure 1.12, panel 2):

- *Term spread:* Judging by *Consensus Forecasts* for interest rates, risks to growth are to the upside for 2012.
- *S&P 500:* Options prices suggest that risks to growth are to the upside for 2012.
- *Inflation:* For 2012, there is an upside risk for global inflation, which, based on the fan chart, means a downside risk for global growth.[2]
- *Oil market:* Risks through 2013 remain to the upside for oil prices and thus to the downside for global growth.

The fan chart provides a market perspective on risks, whereas the Global Projection Model (GPM) uses the IMF staff's model-based analysis and projections for GDP and inflation. GPM estimates suggest that there is still substantial risk of a new (or prolonged) recession in several advanced economies. The probability of negative output growth in 2012 is about 55 percent for the euro area, 15 percent for the United States, 14 percent for Japan, and 3 percent for Latin America (Figure 1.13, panel 1). New shocks or policy mistakes could push one of the major advanced economies into prolonged deflation.

Over the medium term, the threat of a debt-deflation spiral continues to loom in several economies, especially in the euro area, where the GDP deflator growth has been about 1 percent only for three years already. The GPM inflation forecasts suggest that in the final quarter of 2013, the probability of a fall in consumer prices is above 25 percent for the euro area and above 35 percent in Japan (Figure 1.13, panel 2). By contrast, the corresponding probability for the United States is less than 10 percent. As gauged by a composite indicator, the risks of sustained deflation at the global level have retreated since 2008 (Figure 1.13, panel 3).[3] Nevertheless, deflation pressure is

Figure 1.11. Global Imbalances[1]

Recently, the U.S. dollar, yen, and renminbi have appreciated in real effective terms, while most other currencies have depreciated. Major emerging market economies, with the exception of China, have continued to build up international reserves. Global imbalances are no longer projected to widen. The latest revision to medium-term current account projections mainly reflects a lower surplus in China.

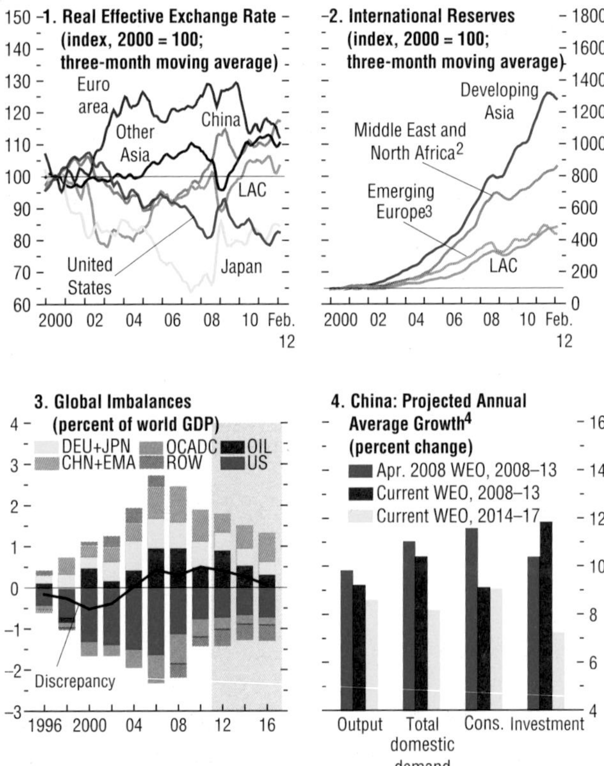

Sources: IMF, *International Financial Statistics;* and IMF staff estimates.

[1]CHN+EMA: China, Hong Kong SAR, Indonesia, Korea, Malaysia, Philippines, Singapore, Taiwan Province of China, and Thailand; DEU+JPN: Germany and Japan; LAC: Latin America and the Caribbean; OCADC: Bulgaria, Croatia, Czech Republic, Estonia, Greece, Hungary, Ireland, Latvia, Lithuania, Poland, Portugal, Romania, Slovak Republic, Slovenia, Spain, Turkey, and United Kingdom; OIL: oil exporters; ROW: rest of the world; US: United States.

[2]Bahrain, Djibouti, Egypt, Islamic Republic of Iran, Jordan, Kuwait, Lebanon, Libya, Oman, Qatar, Saudi Arabia, Sudan, Syrian Arab Republic, United Arab Emirates, and Republic of Yemen.

[3]Bulgaria, Croatia, Hungary, Latvia, Lithuania, Poland, Romania, and Turkey.

[4]Variables in real terms. Cons. is total consumption.

[2]Based on past experience, the fan chart methodology assumes that causation goes from inflation to growth rather than vice versa. A risk of lower inflation then means that monetary policy could ease more than expected, which would generate higher growth. For further discussion, see Elekdag and Kannan (2009). At present, however, in the major advanced economies there is much less room than usual for cutting interest rates.

[3]For details on the construction of this indicator, see Decressin and Laxton (2009).

prominent in various economies on the periphery of the euro area (Greece, Ireland, Spain).

Increased Bank and Sovereign Stress in the Euro Area

In the near term, a key downside risk is reintensification of adverse feedback loops between bank asset quality and sovereign risk in the euro area. Figure 1.14 presents this downside scenario, which assumes that banks tighten lending standards and constrain credit growth to rebuild capital buffers, consistent with the April 2012 *Global Financial Stability Report* "weak policies" scenario. Given the resulting weaker growth outlook, concerns over fiscal sustainability intensify and sovereign spreads rise. In addition, increased market concern means that several euro area sovereigns are forced into more front-loaded fiscal consolidation, which further depresses near-term demand and growth. This in turn leads to further deterioration of bank asset quality—owing to higher losses on sovereign debt holdings—and an increase in nonperforming loans to the private sector, prompting further tightening in credit standards, and so on. In the simulation, private investment declines by almost 15 percent (relative to WEO projections). Euro area output falls by 3½ percent relative to the WEO forecast, and domestic inflation would fall close to zero. Assuming that credit contractions in other regions follow those contained in the *Global Financial Stability Report* weak policies scenario, and taking into consideration spillovers via international trade, global output would be lower than the WEO projections by about 2 percent. The repercussions of this scenario for the various regions are discussed in Chapter 2.

Adverse Oil Supply Shock

The impact on oil prices of a potential or actual disruption in oil supplies involving the Islamic Republic of Iran—the world's third largest exporter of crude oil—would be large if not offset by supply increases elsewhere. A halt of Iran's exports to Organization for Economic Cooperation and Development (OECD) economies (if not offset) would likely trigger an initial oil price increase of about 20 to 30 percent, with other producers or

Figure 1.12. Risks to the Global Outlook

Risks around the WEO projections have diminished, consistent with market indicators, but they remain large and tilted to the downside. The various indicators do not point in a consistent direction. Inflation and oil price indicators suggest downside risks to growth. The term spread and S&P 500 options prices, however, point to upside risks.

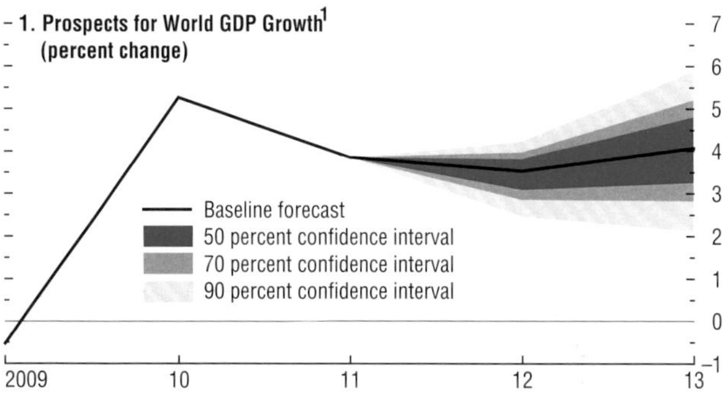

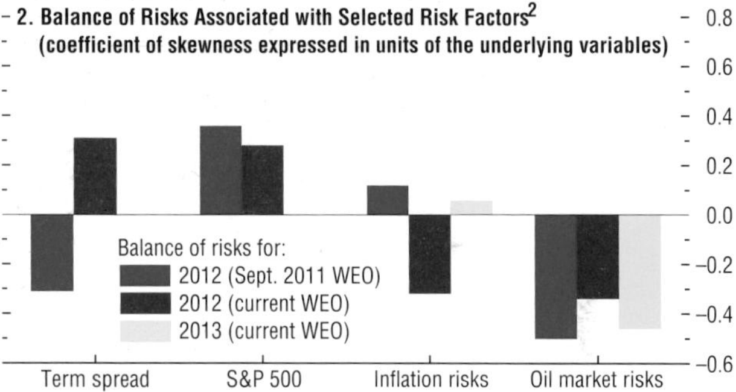

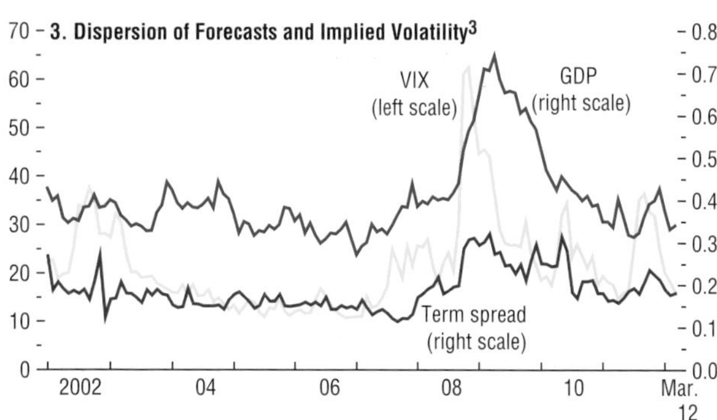

Sources: Bloomberg Financial Markets; Chicago Board Options Exchange; Consensus Economics; and IMF staff estimates.

[1]The fan chart shows the uncertainty around the WEO central forecast with 50, 70, and 90 percent confidence intervals. As shown, the 70 percent confidence interval includes the 50 percent interval, and the 90 percent confidence interval includes the 50 and 70 percent intervals. See Appendix 1.2 in the April 2009 *World Economic Outlook* for details.

[2]The values for inflation risks and oil market risks are entered with the opposite sign, since they represent downside risks to growth.

[3]GDP measures the dispersion of GDP forecasts for the G7 economies (Canada, France, Germany, Italy, Japan, United Kingdom, United States), Brazil, China, India, and Mexico. VIX: Chicago Board Options Exchange Market Volatility Index. Term spread measures the dispersion of term spreads implicit in interest rate forecasts for Germany, Japan, United Kingdom, and United States.

Figure 1.13. Recession and Deflation Risks

Risks for a prolonged recession and for sustained deflation are elevated in the euro area, notably in economies on the periphery. While the risk of a recession is low in Japan, the risk of deflation continues to be a problem. In other areas, the risks are significantly lower.

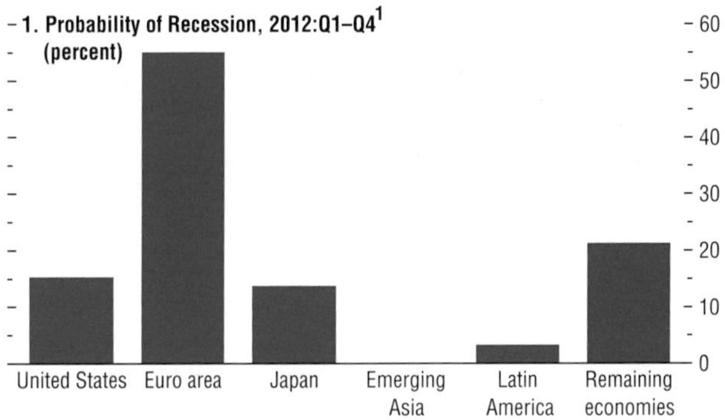

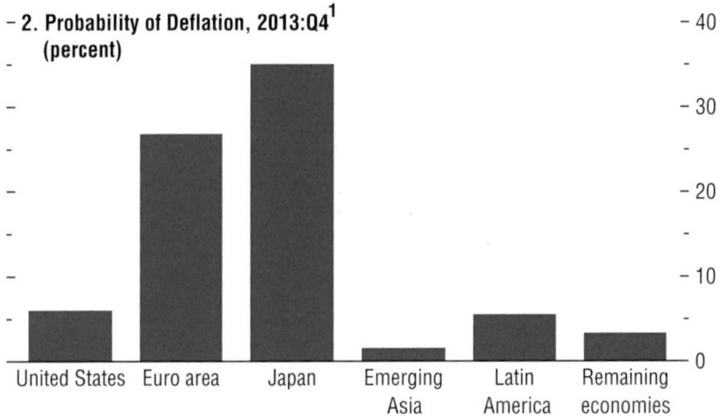

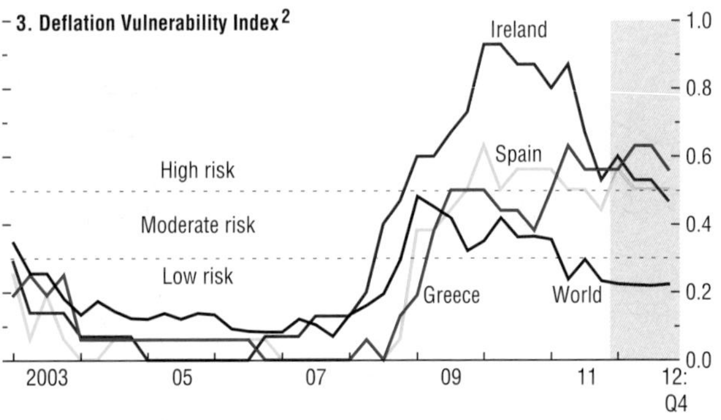

Source: IMF staff estimates.
[1]Emerging Asia: China, Hong Kong SAR, India, Indonesia, Korea, Malaysia, Philippines, Singapore, Taiwan Province of China, and Thailand; Latin America: Brazil, Chile, Colombia, Mexico, and Peru; remaining economies: Argentina, Australia, Bulgaria, Canada, Czech Republic, Denmark, Estonia, Israel, New Zealand, Norway, Russia, South Africa, Sweden, Switzerland, Turkey, United Kingdom, and Venezuela.
[2]For details on the construction of this indicator, see Kumar (2003) and Decressin and Laxton (2009). The indicator is expanded to include house prices.

emergency stock releases likely providing some offset over time—a part of this is likely priced in already. Further uncertainty about oil supply disruptions could trigger a much larger price spike. Figure 1.15 presents a downside scenario in which a negative supply shock raises the real price of oil by slightly more than 50 percent on average over the first two years. This reduces the already sluggish growth of real household income and raises production costs, eroding profitability. These factors undermine the recovery in private consumption and investment growth for economies in all regions, except for net oil exporters. At the global level, output is reduced by about 1¼ percent. The short-term impact could be significantly larger if the adverse oil shock damages confidence or spills over to financial markets, effects that are not included in this scenario.

Reevaluation of Potential Output Growth in Emerging Market Economies

Another downside risk stems from a fundamental reevaluation of sustainable growth in emerging market economies. This could be precipitated by banks and authorities tightening lending standards, given concerns about the quality of loan portfolios as they reevaluate the viability of some investment projects financed during recent rapid credit expansion. Figure 1.16 presents a downside scenario in which credit growth in emerging Asia is lower by 3 percent each year over five years relative to the path implicit in WEO projections. The scenario also assumes that the long-term level of potential GDP in emerging Asia is lower by roughly 10 percent because previous investment was based on an overly optimistic view of external demand growth. In this scenario, lower demand from Asia causes a fall in commodity prices, which has an adverse impact on commodity exporters. Expectations for potential growth are downgraded for these economies, the level of output is reduced by about 5 percent, and credit growth slows proportionately. In advanced economies, there is also a mild slowdown in credit growth, and the monetary policy response to the adverse external shock is assumed to be constrained by the zero interest rate bound. Nevertheless, the deleterious effects on the real economy are smaller than in emerging market economies but noticeable, with output levels declining by 3 percent in Japan, 2¼ percent in the euro area, and 1¼ percent in the United States.

Improving Euro Area Prospects and Easing Tensions in Global Credit and Oil Markets

This scenario assumes a variety of improvements. Policies in the euro area are stronger than projected, consistent with the April 2012 *Global Financial Stability Report* "complete policies" scenario, fostering a larger-than-expected easing in banking and sovereign stress (Figure 1.17). The average euro area sovereign risk premium is assumed to decline by 50 basis points and, relative to the baseline, credit to the private sector expands. Outside the euro area, credit conditions also ease, most notably in the United States, where lending to small and medium-size firms is assumed to pick up much more quickly than in the WEO baseline scenario. Geopolitical tensions are assumed to ease, with the price of oil assumed to be roughly 10 percent below that in the baseline. Under this scenario, in 2013, global GDP is roughly 1½ percent higher, led by an improvement of about 2¼ percent in the euro area, roughly 1½ percent in the United Sates, close to 1½ percent in emerging Asia, and ¾ percent in Japan. The improvement in Latin America is more modest, reflecting the drag from lower oil prices on oil exporters in the region.

Tail Risks

Several tail risks are hard to quantify but merit attention:

- The potential consequences of a disorderly default and exit by a euro area member are unpredictable and thus not possible to map into a specific scenario. If such an event occurs, it is possible that other euro area economies perceived to have similar risk characteristics would come under severe pressure as well, with a full-blown panic in financial markets and depositor flight from several

Figure 1.14. WEO Downside Scenario for Increased Bank and Sovereign Stress in the Euro Area

(Percent or percentage point deviation from WEO baseline)

This scenario uses a six-region version of the Global Economy Model (GEM) to estimate the global impact of heightened adverse feedback between banking and sovereign stress in the euro area. The scenario assumes that banks tighten lending standards and constrain credit growth to rebuild capital buffers, consistent with the April 2012 *Global Financial Stability Report* (GFSR) "weak policies" scenario. The resulting weaker growth outlook amplifies concern over fiscal sustainability, and sovereign spreads rise temporarily by roughly 100 basis points. Given increased market concern, several euro area sovereigns are forced into more front-loaded fiscal consolidation, averaging to an additional 1 percentage point of GDP in 2012 and 2013, which further depresses near-term demand and growth. Also, credit in other regions of the world is assumed to contract as it does in the GFSR weak policies scenario. Monetary policy in many advanced economies is constrained by the zero lower bound on nominal interest rates, amplifying the negative impact on activity of these adverse conditions. The global macroeconomic implications are presented below.

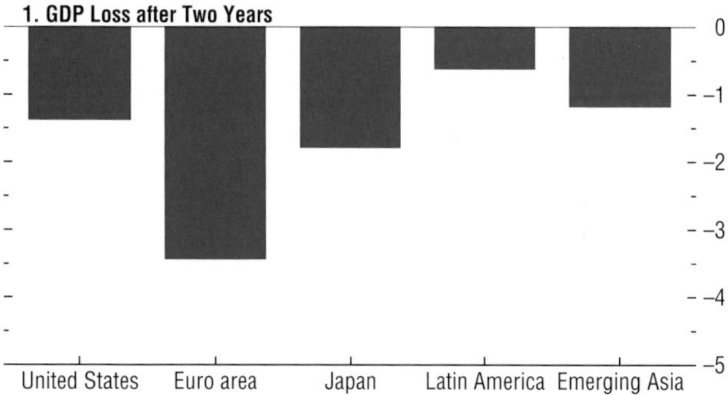

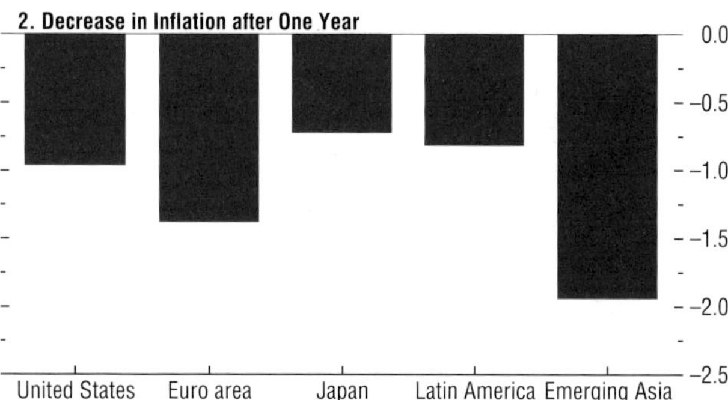

Source: GEM simulations.

Figure 1.15. WEO Downside Scenario for a Disruption in the Global Oil Supply[1]

(Percent or percentage point deviation from WEO baseline)

This scenario uses a six-region version of the Global Economy Model (GEM) to estimate the global impact of a disruption in global oil supply. The impact on oil prices of intensified concern about an Iran-related oil supply shock (or an actual disruption) would be large if not offset by supply increases elsewhere, given limited inventory and spare capacity buffers, as well as the still-tight physical market conditions expected throughout 2012. Here a negative supply shock raises the real price of oil to average a little over 50 percent above the WEO baseline during the first two years, after which it settles about 40 percent above the baseline. This reduces the already sluggish growth of real household incomes and raises production costs, eroding profitability. These factors undermine the recovery in private consumption and investment growth in all regions except those that are net oil exporters. The macroeconomic impact is presented below. The short-term impact could be significantly larger than suggested if the adverse oil shock damages confidence or spills over to financial markets, effects that are not included in this scenario.

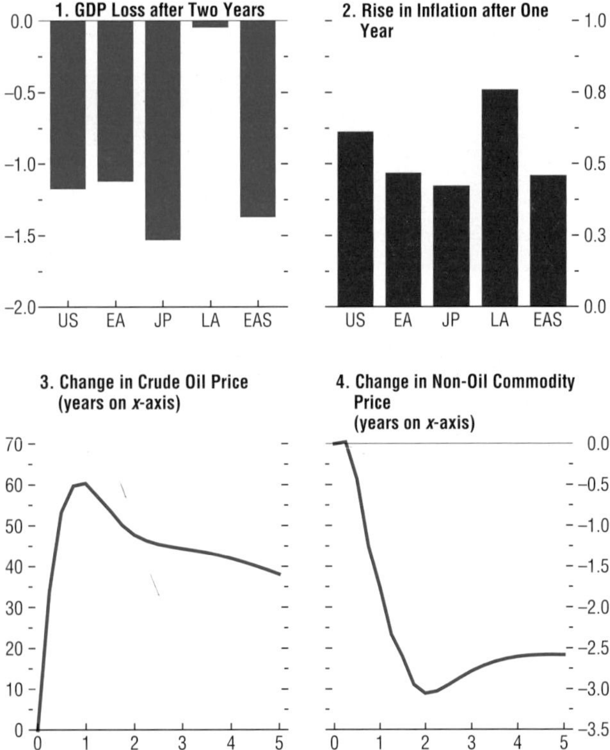

Source: GEM simulations.
[1]US: United States; EA: euro area; JP: Japan; LA: Latin America; EAS: emerging Asia.

banking systems. Under these circumstances, a breakup of the euro area could not be ruled out. The financial and real spillovers to other regions, especially emerging Europe, would likely be very large. This could cause major political shocks that could aggravate economic stress to levels well above those after the Lehman collapse.

- In the current environment of limited policy room, there is also the possibility that several adverse shocks could interact to produce a major slump reminiscent of the 1930s. For instance, intensified concern about an oil supply shock related to the Islamic Republic of Iran could cause a spike in oil prices that depresses output in the euro area, amplifying adverse feedback loops between the household, sovereign, and banking sectors. In the meantime, the oil price shock could also trigger a reassessment of the sustainability of credit booms and potential growth in emerging Asia, leading to hard landings in these economies. This could, in turn, prompt a collapse in non-oil commodity prices that would hurt many emerging and developing economies, especially in Latin America and Africa. More generally, a concurrent rise in global risk aversion could lead to a sudden reversal of capital flows to emerging and developing economies.
- Sovereign debt markets in Japan and the United States have remained calm and have even benefited from safe haven flows. However, continued failure to adopt and implement strong medium-term consolidation plans could erode the safe haven status of these economies, a risk that is particularly pertinent for Japan. This could severely destabilize global bond markets, with potentially large effects on global output.

Policy Challenges

The main concern is that the global economy will continue to be susceptible to major downside risks that weigh on consumer and investor confidence and that the recovery will remain anemic in the major advanced economies, with large output gaps persisting for some time. These challenges call for more policy action, especially in advanced economies: implementing agreed medium-term fiscal consolidation plans without overdoing adjustment; maintaining a very accommodative monetary policy stance and providing ample liquidity to help repair household and financial sector balance sheets; and resolving the euro area crisis without delay. More rapid progress could greatly lower the risk of self-perpetuating pessimism and bad equilibriums. With respect to emerging and developing economies, policies must be geared toward ensuring a soft landing in economies that have seen sustained, very strong credit growth.

Policies in Advanced Economies

The major advanced economies are still reeling from the shocks that triggered the Great Recession. Overcoming these shocks requires a continuation of exceptionally low monetary policy rates and unconventional support, limited fiscal consolidation in the short term where possible, and major fiscal adjustment in the medium and long term. Further efforts are also needed to strengthen and reform financial sectors. In the euro area, governance reforms and structural policies to improve competitiveness can, over time, counter the negative impact on output from balance sheet deleveraging. The most immediate challenge, however, is to contain the spillovers from the crisis in the periphery.

Structural and institutional reforms are essential to repair the damage done by the crisis and lower the chance of future crises. These reforms must address a broad range of issues: pensions and health care systems, labor and product markets, housing sectors, and, perhaps most important, financial sectors. The specific requirements vary across economies and are discussed in depth in the following sections.

Progressing toward more sustainable public finances

Given still-large output gaps in many advanced economies, the best course for fiscal policy is to adopt measures that do the least short-term harm to demand and preclude unsustainable long-term paths. Economies that are not under market pressure and where tax rates are not high could usefully undertake balanced-budget fiscal expansion (including around present consolidation paths) and major measures to

Figure 1.16. WEO Downside Scenario for a Reevaluation of Potential Output Growth in Emerging Market Economies

(Percent or percentage point deviation from WEO baseline)

This scenario uses a six-region version of the Global Economy Model (GEM) to estimate the global impact of a reevaluation of potential output growth in emerging market economies that also leads to slower credit growth. Here credit growth in emerging Asia is lower by 3 percent each year over five years relative to the path implicit in WEO projections. The scenario also assumes that the level of potential GDP in emerging Asia is lower in the long term by roughly 10 percent, since investment was previously based on overly optimistic expectations of growth in external demand. In this scenario, lower demand from emerging Asia causes a fall in commodity prices, which has an adverse impact on emerging markets, particularly Latin America. Expectations about potential growth are downgraded for these economies, and the level of potential output is reduced by about 5 percent in the long term, with a proportionate slowing in credit growth. In advanced economies, there is also a mild slowing in credit growth, and the monetary policy response to the external shock is assumed to be constrained, as policy rates are at the zero lower bound. The macroeconomic implications of this scenario are presented below.

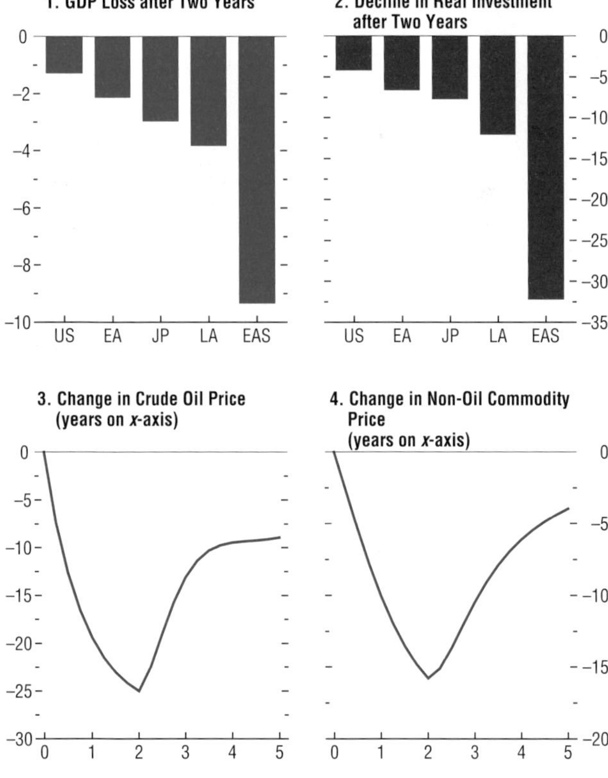

Source: GEM simulations.

[1] US: United States; EA: euro area; JP: Japan; LA: Latin America; EAS: emerging Asia.

Figure 1.17. WEO Upside Scenario[1]

(Percent or percentage point deviation from WEO baseline)

This scenario uses a six-region version of the Global Economy Model (GEM) to estimate the global impact of a larger-than-expected easing in banking and sovereign stress in the euro area, an improvement in private market credit conditions in other regions, and lower global oil prices. The average euro area sovereign risk premium is assumed to decline by 50 basis points and, relative to the baseline, credit expansion to the private sector is consistent with the April 2012 *Global Financial Stability Report*'s "complete policies" scenario. Outside the euro area, credit conditions also ease, most notably in the United States. The price of oil is assumed to be roughly 10 percent below the price in the WEO baseline. The macroeconomic implications of this scenario are presented below.

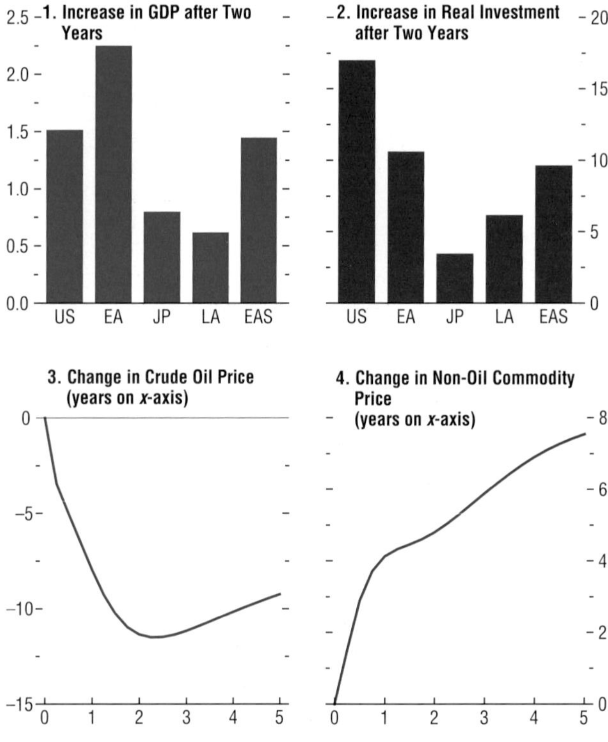

Source: GEM simulations.
[1] US: United States; EA: euro area; JP: Japan; LA: Latin America; EAS: emerging Asia.

build credibility and cut entitlement spending in the future.

- Given concerns about fiscal room, a balanced-budget fiscal expansion could support activity and employment while keeping fiscal consolidation plans on track. For example, temporary tax hikes matched by increases in government purchases—for much-needed infrastructure—could lead to an almost equal rise in output.[4] Government spending targeted to distressed households that spend all their disposable income will yield a similar increase in output. Alternatively, low-multiplier spending could be cut while high-multiplier spending is increased. By supporting activity, such balanced-budget fiscal expansion could also support the targeted reduction in government-debt-to-GDP ratios.
- The April 2012 *Fiscal Monitor* underscores the benefits of strengthening fiscal institutions, adopting and committing to respect sound fiscal rules, and reforming entitlement programs (for example, linking retirement age to life expectancy and improving incentives in the health care sector). Reforms of entitlement programs appear to be the most promising path because they demonstrate policymakers' ability to act. Depending on their design, such reforms can reduce off-balance-sheet public liabilities with only limited short-term negative impact on output. In this regard, several advanced economies are aggressively tackling pension and health care reform, which offers by far the largest potential benefits.[5] Progress with respect to improving fiscal rules and governance has been better, but markets continue to question the enforceability of those rules and have lingering concerns about broader governance issues.

Realistic medium-term plans for fiscal adjustment are necessary to maintain or rebuild credibility and help anchor expectations. Many advanced economies have already adopted such plans. Given the weak

[4]Simulations of policy models developed at six institutions—the Federal Reserve, ECB, European Commission, OECD, Bank of Canada, and IMF—are consistent with this result. See Coenen and others (2012). Note that balanced-budget fiscal policy changes are a double-edged sword. On the downside, matched temporary decreases in taxes and expenditures will lead to decreases in output.

[5]See Statistical Table 9 in the September 2011 *Fiscal Monitor*.

growth prospects in the major economies, those with room for fiscal policy maneuvering, in terms of strength of their fiscal accounts and credibility with markets, can reconsider the pace of consolidation. Others should let automatic stabilizers operate freely for as long as they can readily finance higher deficits and should consider measures that achieve balanced-budget fiscal expansion. In the meantime, the United States and Japan should urgently adopt credible medium-term fiscal adjustment plans. From the near-term perspective, under current U.S. laws many tax provisions begin to expire in 2013, just when deep automatic spending cuts kick in. If this were to materialize, it would significantly undermine the economic recovery. To minimize attendant uncertainties, policymakers should agree as soon as possible on their fiscal plans for next year as well as for the medium term. Given the relatively low revenue ratio, policymakers should adopt spending cuts as well as tax increases over the medium term. Japan intends to cut the primary deficit in half by 2015 and achieve a primary surplus by 2020, and the authorities have proposed a set of measures to achieve the first milestone, including doubling the consumption tax to 10 percent by 2015. Nonetheless, more needs to be done to put debt on a downward path. Possible measures and their pros and cons are discussed in the April 2012 *Fiscal Monitor* and in several earlier issues.

Strengthening financial sectors

There are major challenges confronting prudential authorities, as discussed in the April 2012 *Global Financial Stability Report*. In many large economies, financial sectors became bloated and overleveraged during the decade before the financial crisis. Over time, shrinkage and deleveraging are necessary steps to improving system stability: financial excesses were both a major source of shocks and a major factor in undermining the system's capacity to absorb shocks of any origin.

The challenge for policymakers now, most immediately in Europe, is to prevent disorderly and destructive deleveraging of the banking system and to promote an adequate flow of credit to the private sector. This involves finding the right balance between addressing and alleviating short-term pressures and sustained adjustment over the medium term. Just as fiscal adjustment that is too rapid can become self-defeating, so can drastic balance sheet deleveraging. The dilemma in Europe is that even though the scale of bank recapitalization, restructuring, or resolution has been inadequate, rapid tightening of bank credit is the opposite of what the economy needs. Supervisors must ensure that deleveraging is achieved in a way that limits harm to the economy. For example, if banks shed legacy assets or sell noncore businesses to strong institutions, it will not reduce credit to the economy as much as if they curtail new loan originations or reduce credit lines and loan portfolios. The specific policy implications for euro area authorities are discussed below.

Policymakers elsewhere should stand ready to backstop liquidity in their banking systems. The effects of deleveraging in the euro area are not projected to have a major impact outside Europe. However, if the euro area downside scenario materializes, financial spillovers could be much larger. Policymakers should consider offering liquidity backstops—for example, through swap lines with the Federal Reserve to alleviate dollar shortages, regional pooling arrangements or IMF support, drawing down the large stock of foreign reserves (in some economies), and enhanced deposit guarantees. Thinly capitalized banks should be directed to increase their capital buffers. Policymakers should also remain alert to the need for a continuing supply of credit to credit-rationed agents (small and medium-size firms, households) and the maintenance of trade financing, possibly stepping in through temporary government programs.

Better prudential policies and frameworks remain essential for rebuilding the global financial system. Much progress has been made in strengthening the prudential frameworks for banks, even in the face of the continued problems posed by institutions too big or too complex to fail. Nonetheless, many challenges remain, including implementing consensus regulations (such as Basel III) at the national level, improving regulation and supervision of shadow banking, ensuring that banks are not too reliant on fickle wholesale funding, and bringing transparency to large derivatives markets. Furthermore, day-to-day cross-border collaboration between supervisory authorities must be stepped up. The uneven or limited progress in these domains is of growing concern.

Maintaining an accommodative monetary policy

In past financial crises, interest rate cuts and currency devaluations helped pull economies out of recession. Neither of these options has much scope in the largest advanced economies, except in the euro area.

- The ECB has some room to further lower the policy rate, given that inflation is projected to fall appreciably below the ECB's "close to but below" 2 percent inflation target over the medium term and that risks of second-round effects from high oil prices or tax and administrative price hikes appear small—WEO projections see headline consumer price index inflation falling to about 1½ percent by 2013, below the ECB's target.[6] Low levels of domestic inflation can hinder much-needed improvement in debtors' balance sheets and stand in the way of much-needed adjustments in competitiveness. The ECB's unconventional policies need to continue to ensure orderly conditions in funding markets and thereby facilitate the pass-through of monetary policy to the real economy.
- Policy rates in Japan, the United Kingdom, and the United States are already close to or at the lower bound. Should downside risks to the growth outlook threaten to materialize, their central banks could step up their unconventional policies, preferably in a way that eases credit conditions for small and medium-size firms and households. Given very low domestic inflation pressure in Japan, further monetary easing may in any case be needed to ensure achievement of the inflation objective over the medium term.

Policymakers could also consider other actions targeted to credit-constrained agents. As discussed in Chapter 3, fiscal programs to restructure mortgages can offer efficient ways to relieve indebted households. In the United States, for example, programs have reached far fewer households than initially envisaged, but additional measures have now been adopted. Borrowing costs could be directly lowered for small and medium-size firms through temporary subsidies and programs by public development banks.

Central banks' balance sheets, and the scope for losses in their financial accounts, have expanded appreciably as they have stepped up purchases of securities and broadened collateral standards (Figure 1.5, panel 4). However, the size of these balance sheet expansions tells very little about the risk of inflation. Because of increased uncertainty, banks and other economic agents are holding much more liquidity than before the crisis. As economic conditions improve and the supply of credit accelerates, central banks can absorb this liquidity—for example, by allowing refinancing operations to lapse, selling securities they bought earlier, or issuing their own paper. Problems arise when the public sector faces political or practical limits on the longer-term capacity to cut deficits. Chronically high inflation would result only if such an impasse were highly likely. To guard against this, central banks must maintain the independence to pursue a low inflation target, and government budgets must be sustainable over time, in terms of political feasibility as well as the projected size of the deficit.[7] The more effectively fiscal policy addresses this intertemporal challenge, the more leeway monetary policy has to act in a supportive manner.

Dealing with the euro area crisis

The near-term focus must be on crisis management so as to prevent the downside risks discussed earlier from materializing. Supplying sufficient liquidity will help forestall abnormal funding costs for sovereigns and banks and help avoid contagion. To that end, the euro area requires a credible firewall that is large, robust, and flexible enough to stem contagion and facilitate the adjustment process in the highly indebted countries. The recent decision to combine the ESM and the EFSF is thus welcome and, along with other recent European efforts, will strengthen the European crisis mechanism and support the IMF's efforts to bolster the global firewall. The crisis facilities (EFSF/ESM) should also have the flexibility to take

[6] An average inflation rate of 1½ percent will have very different manifestations in the core and in the periphery of the euro area.

[7] Central banks' capital and revaluation reserves are not a major consideration. Accounting losses do not matter as long as central banks are independent and fiscal policies are considered sustainable.

direct stakes in banks and assist in the restructuring of financial institutions where necessary. This will help stem the negative feedback loop between banking and sovereign risks in the euro area.

It is also critical to break the adverse feedback loops between subpar growth, deteriorating fiscal positions, increasing bank recapitalization needs, and deleveraging, which raise the risk of a prolonged period of deflation. The ECB should implement additional monetary easing to ensure that inflation develops in line with its target over the medium term and guard against deflation risks, thereby also facilitating much-needed adjustments in competitiveness.[8] Moreover, country banking authorities should work together with host supervisors to monitor and limit deleveraging of their banks at home and abroad. Bank supervisors must do whatever possible to avoid excessively fast deleveraging that curtails lending to the real economy. To that end, more capital must be injected into euro area banks. This may require the use of public funds for recapitalization—including from the EFSF/ESM.

The key challenge is to chart a way back to sustained growth. Structural reform gaps vary across countries, but there is a widespread need for efforts to lower barriers to entry in product and services markets and to allow labor markets to deliver higher employment. Economies with weak external positions face the prospect of having to achieve very low inflation or deflation—"internal devaluations"—to help restore competitiveness because the channel of currency depreciation is unavailable to them as members of a currency union. Internal devaluations, however, would add to the problem of debt overhang in the short to medium term..

Over the medium term, many difficult decisions will be required to remedy EMU design flaws that contributed to the crisis.

- A strong mechanism that delivers responsible fiscal policies is urgently needed. In this regard, the recently agreed "fiscal compact" marks important progress in improving fiscal credibility with little detriment to fiscal flexibility—which is important given the period of weak growth ahead. However, enforcement will be key, and this might mean that EU institutions will need to be actively involved in national budgetary plans, as envisaged by current proposals (the "two pack"). The fiscal compact will also need to be complemented by greater fiscal risk sharing to ensure that economic dislocation in one country does not develop into a costly fiscal and financial crisis for the entire region.
- There is also need for a mechanism to share private sector risks that is grounded in a more integrated euro area financial system.[9] This could be achieved by moving toward a model of common supervision and resolution, including a shared backstop and common deposit insurance—with joint responsibility for supervision comes joint responsibility for financial support. The current absence of such a common system distorts monetary policy and competition in the financial system: healthy banks in economies on the periphery can now obtain market funding only at much greater cost than their peers in the core economies—if they can obtain it at all—because of the weakness of their sovereigns. The ECB's LTROs are helping correct this but can do so only temporarily.
- There must be better adjustment to real as well as fiscal and financial imbalances. Accelerating the completion of the single market for goods and services and reforms to labor markets could help boost growth and adjustment. Various economies in the euro area periphery are in the process of implementing major reforms, especially to labor markets. The importance of progress in these domains for a well-functioning monetary union cannot be overemphasized.

Policies in Emerging and Developing Economies

Emerging and developing economies need to avoid overstimulating activity to make up for less demand from advanced economies. Overheating pressures from strong activity, high credit growth, and still-elevated commodity prices remain in a variety of economies (Figure 1.18). Among the overheating indicators, it is mainly those related to

[8]Broad indicators of domestic (GDP) inflation have been running close to 1 percent since 2009. Under such conditions, internal rebalancing is very challenging to achieve.

[9]The financial sector, including ownership of diversified financial assets, accounts for a great deal of risk sharing in the United States (see Asdrubali, Sorensen, and Yosha, 1996).

Figure 1.18. Overheating Indicators for the G20 Economies[1]

Various indicators suggest that overheating pressure has diminished in emerging market economies. However, this reflects mostly a reduction in capital flows and financial market developments, which are now turning around and could lead to renewed overheating.

2012 estimates above the 1997–2006 average by:

● Less than 0.5 standard deviation ● Greater than or equal to 0.5 but less than 1.5 standard deviations ● Greater than or equal to 1.5 standard deviations

	Domestic					External				Financial					
	Output relative to trend[2]	Output gap	Unem-ployment	Inflation[3]	Summary	Terms of trade	Capital inflows	Current account	Summary	Credit growth[4]	House prices[4]	Equity prices[4]	Summary	Fiscal balance[5]	Real interest rate[6]
Advanced Economies															
Japan	●	●	●	●	●	●	●	●	● ↗	●	●	●	●	↘	↘
Canada	●	●	●	●	●	●	●	●	● ↘	●	●	●	●	↗	↘
France	●	●	●	●	●	●	●	●	●	●	●	●	●	↗	↘
Germany	●	●	●	●	●	●	●	●	●	●	●	●	●	—	↘
Italy	●	●	●	●	●	●	●	●	● ↘	●	●	●	●	↗	↘
United Kingdom	●	●	●	●	● ↘	●	●	●	●	●	●	●	●	↗	↘
Australia	●	●	●	●	● ↘	●	●	●	● ↘	●	●	●	●	↗	—
Korea	●	●	●	●	● ↘	●	●	●	●	●	●	●	●	—	—
United States	●	●	●	●	●	●	●	●	●	●	●	●	●	↗	↘
Emerging Market Economies															
Brazil	●	●	●	●	●	●	●	●	● ↘	●	●	●	● ↘	↗	↗
Argentina[7]	●	●	●	●	●	●	●	●	● ↘	●		●	● ↘	—	↘
Turkey	●	●	●	●	●	●	●	●	● ↗	●		●	● ↘	↘	—
India	●	●		●	●	●	●	●	● ↘	●	●	●	●	—	—
China	●	●	●	●	● ↘	●	●	●	● ↗	●	●	●	●	—	↗
South Africa	●	●	●	●	● ↗	●	●	●	●	●	●	●	●	↗	—
Saudi Arabia	●			●	●	●		●	●	●		●	●		↘
Indonesia	●	●	●	●	●	●	●	●	●	●	●	●	● ↘	↗	—
Russia	●	●	●	●	● ↘	●	●	●	● ↘	●	●	●	●	↘	—
Mexico	●	●	●	●	●	●	●	●	●	●	●	●	●		—

Sources: Australia Bureau of Statistics; Bank for International Settlements; CEIC China Database; Global Property Guide; Haver Analytics; IMF, *Balance of Payments Statistics;* IMF, *International Financial Statistics;* Organization for Economic Cooperation and Development; and IMF staff estimates.

[1]For each indicator, except as noted below, economies are assigned colors based on projected 2012 values relative to their precrisis (1997–2006) average. Each indicator is scored as red = 2, yellow = 1, and blue = 0; summary scores are calculated as the sum of selected component scores divided by the maximum possible sum of those scores. Summary colors are assigned red if the summary score is greater than or equal to 0.66, yellow if greater than or equal to 0.33 but less than 0.66, and blue if less than 0.33. Arrows up (down) indicate hotter (colder) conditions compared with the September 2011 WEO predicted values for 2011.

[2]Output more than 2.5 percent above the precrisis trend is indicated by red. Output less than 2.5 percent below the trend is indicated by blue.

[3]For the following inflation-targeting economies, the target inflation rate was used instead of the 1997–2006 average in the calculation of the inflation indicator: Australia, Brazil, Canada, Indonesia, Korea, Mexico, South Africa, Turkey, United Kingdom. For the non-inflation-targeting economies, red was assigned if inflation is approximately 10 percent or higher, yellow if inflation is approximately 5 to 9 percent, and blue if inflation is less than 5 percent.

[4]The indicators for credit growth, house price growth, and share price growth refer to the latest 2012 values relative to the 1997–2006 average of output growth.

[5]Arrows in the fiscal balance column represent the forecast change in the structural balance as a percent of GDP over the period 2011–12. An improvement of more than 0.5 percent of GDP is indicated by an up arrow; a deterioration of more than 0.5 percent of GDP is indicated by a down arrow.

[6]Real policy interest rates below zero are identified by a down arrow; real interest rates above 3 percent are identified by an up arrow. Real policy interest rates are deflated by two-year-ahead inflation projections.

[7]Calculations are based on Argentina's official GDP data. The IMF has called on Argentina to adopt remedial measures to address the quality of the official GDP data. The IMF staff is also using alternative measures of GDP growth for macroeconomic surveillance, including data produced by private analysts, which have shown significantly lower real GDP growth than the official data since 2008. Nominal variables are deflated using the IMF staff's estimate of average provincial inflation.

external developments that augur some reprieve, but this could change quickly because capital flows are returning. Appropriate policy responses will vary. For economies that have largely normalized macroeconomic policies, the near-term focus should be on responding to moderating domestic demand and slowing external demand from advanced economies. At the same time, these economies must be prepared to cope with adverse spillovers from advanced economies and with volatile capital flows. Other economies should avoid further stimulus and instead continue to rebuild fiscal room, remove monetary accommodation, and strengthen prudential policies and frameworks.

IMF staff models point to a need for only limited, if any, monetary tightening. However, requirements vary across G20 economies. To differing degrees, more tightening may be needed in Argentina, India, Indonesia, Russia, and Turkey (Figure 1.19, panels 1 and 2). Economies with diminishing inflation pressure can afford to hold steady (China, Mexico), although China has to manage lending to overheating sectors (such as real estate). Where inflation expectations have moved above target, room for policy maneuvering is now more limited (Brazil). Inflation pressure is still strong in a number of MENA and SSA economies, and they may have to further tighten monetary and credit conditions. If downside risks to external demand materialize, monetary policy should generally be the first line of response. Regarding the risks posed by higher oil prices, central banks must take heed that these do not translate into broader inflation pressure—fortunately, lower prices for food, which typically accounts for a much larger share of household spending, are helping contain these risks.

Fiscal policy in emerging and developing economies should respond to the different conditions and risks they face but, in general, should continue to rebuild policy room (Figure 1.19, panel 3). Against this backdrop, the modest fiscal tightening that is in the works appears appropriate (see Figure 1.7, panel 2). A number of economies in emerging Asia have room to make policy more supportive of economic activity (a notable exception is India), given favorable debt dynamics. Among G20 economies, more tightening than currently projected

Figure 1.19. Policy Requirements in Emerging Market Economies

Most emerging market economies should, in principle, not cut interest rates, despite some easing of inflation pressure. These economies are operating with limited (if any) slack, still-high credit growth, and lower real interest rates than before the crisis. However, given downside risks, those with relatively high interest rates can pause or even cut policy rates a little. In the meantime, many emerging market economies must continue to rebuild room for fiscal policy maneuvering.

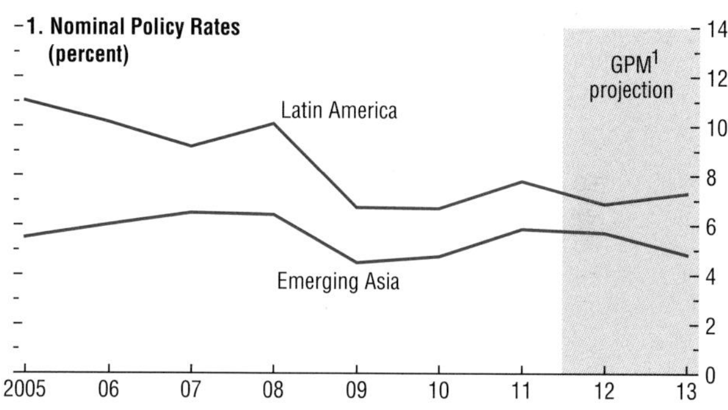

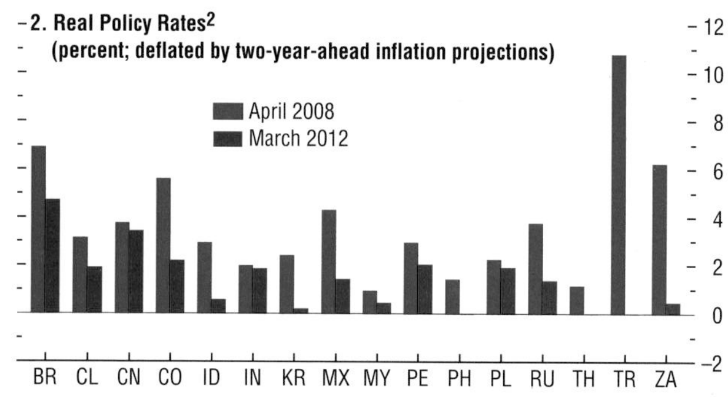

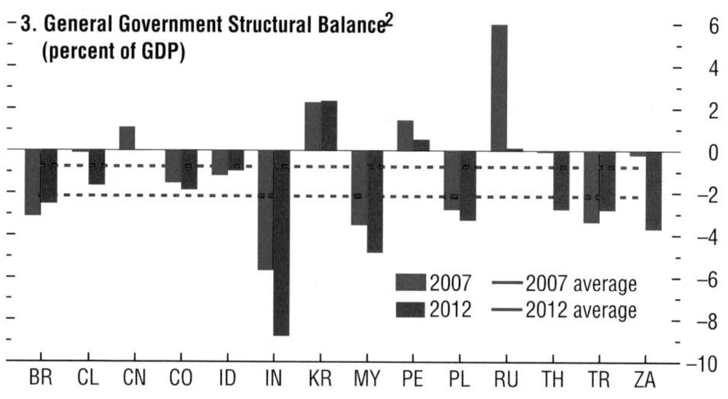

Source: IMF staff estimates.
[1]GPM = Global Projection Model.
[2]BR: Brazil; CL: Chile; CN: China; CO: Colombia; ID: Indonesia; IN: India; KR: Korea; MX: Mexico; MY: Malaysia; PE: Peru; PH: Philippines; PL: Poland; RU: Russia; TH: Thailand; TR: Turkey; ZA: South Africa.

appears necessary in Argentina, India, Russia, and Turkey. In other economies, higher deficits than before the crisis mean that further stimulus should be avoided, while automatic stabilizers should be allowed to operate freely. Emerging and developing economies that are highly dependent on commodity revenues and external inflows must also cautiously assess the risks of a large and protracted deceleration in such funding. In general, if external downside risks to growth materialize, automatic stabilizers should be allowed to operate, as long as financing is available and sustainability concerns permit. In economies with low deficit and debt levels, there may also be room to use discretionary fiscal stimulus. In China, fiscal policy should be the first line of defense against weakening external demand and should foster more consumption—the credit overhang from the 2008–09 stimulus is still working its way through the system, and a renewed lending boom could jeopardize bank loan portfolios. Risks to fiscal balances from energy subsidies should be contained by narrowly targeting subsidies to the most vulnerable households. The specific requirements are discussed in more detail in the April 2012 *Fiscal Monitor*.

It is important to further improve prudential policies and frameworks to address financial fragility. In recent years, many emerging and developing economies expanded rapidly, supported by ample credit growth and buoyant asset prices. To some extent, the credit booms were due to financial deepening, which is positive for growth. However, in most cases, they raise serious concerns about the eventual quality of banks' loan portfolios. In this setting, stronger prudential policies and frameworks are essential to address growing financial stability risks.

In a highly uncertain global environment, managing volatile capital inflows could be another policy challenge for many emerging market economies. Some economies have already started using macroprudential measures designed to manage capital inflows, such as taxes on certain inflows, minimum holding periods, and currency-specific requirements. For example, Brazil and India rolled back the level of such taxes and restrictions as capital flows slackened. Brazil has recently changed tack again as inflows have resumed. Other macroeconomic tools for responding to restive capital flows remain as options: allowing the exchange rate to respond, adjusting international foreign reserve levels, and calibrating monetary and fiscal policies. Better prudential policies and frameworks could also play an important role in ameliorating the impact of volatile capital flows on financial stability.

Special Feature: Commodity Market Review

Global commodity markets lost some of their luster in 2011. Commodity prices, while still high in real terms, declined during much of 2011 (Figure 1.SF.1, panel 1), except for the price of crude oil, which became increasingly driven by geopolitical supply risks toward the end of the year. Commodity prices rebounded in the first quarter of 2012, but generally remain below their levels at the end of 2010. A number of developments have led to doubts about whether commodity prices have broad further upside potential, as reflected, for example, in recent downgrades of commodity assets to underweight from the customary overweight rating of the past few years.

The leading factor behind the commodity price declines in 2011 was higher-than-usual uncertainty about near-term global economic prospects. Second, growth in emerging and developing economies slowed more than expected, and the slowdown in the Chinese real estate market has renewed concerns about a hard landing there. Third, the broad-based boom in commodity markets started about a decade ago (with some differences across commodities), and there are doubts about its continued sustainability, given that high prices have begun to elicit supply responses, especially for some major grains and base metals.

Crude oil prices have diverged from broader commodity price trends in recent months. They did not fall along with other commodity prices when global growth expectations for 2012 were downgraded in the second half of 2011. As of mid-March 2012, oil prices had risen above previous peak values reached in April 2011 immediately after the Libyan supply disruptions. Increased geopolitical risks explain much recent oil price divergence, but other supply setbacks over the past year also illustrate how difficult and fragile continued growth in global oil production remains.

The Commodity Market Review analyzes the factors underlying recent developments and discusses

Figure 1.SF.1. Commodity Prices and the Global Economy

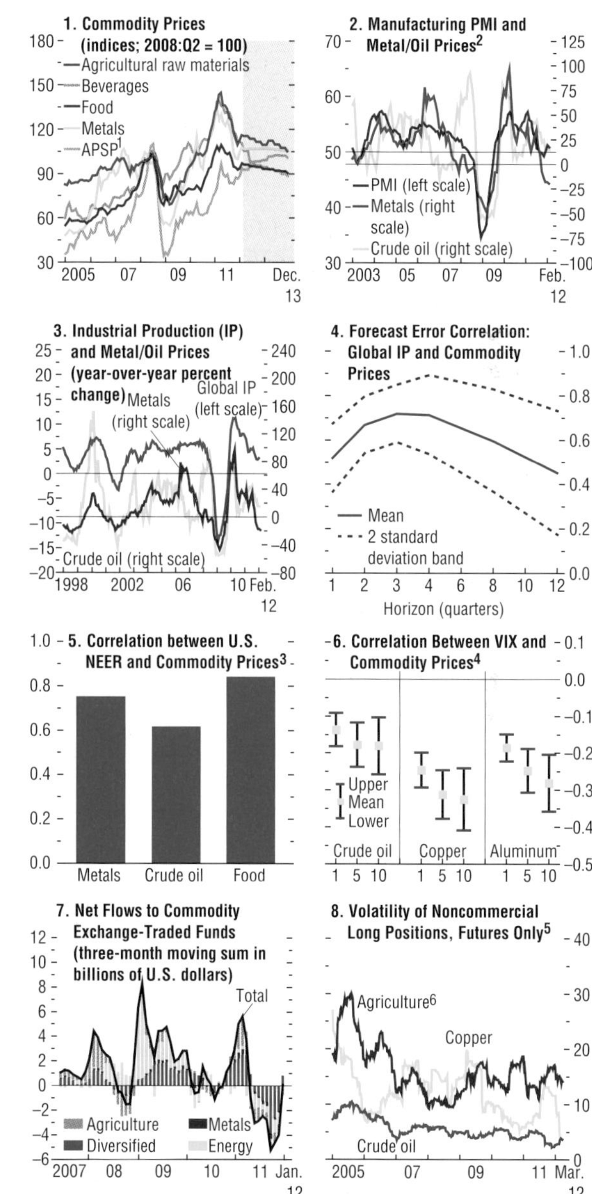

Sources: IMF, Primary Commodity Price System; and IMF staff calculations.
[1]Average petroleum spot price (APSP) is a simple average of Brent, Dubai Fateh, and West Texas Intermediate spot prices.
[2]Global manufacturing Purchasing Manager's Index (PMI): values above 50 indicate expansion. Commodity prices are in year-over-year percent change.
[3]Correlation between rolling two-year standard deviations of monthly changes in the U.S. nominal effective exchange rate (NEER) and commodity prices.
[4]Chart shows forecast error correlation derived with bivariate vector autoregressions with daily data; upper and lower denote 2 standard deviation band; days on *x*-axis.
[5]Rolling 26-week standard deviations of weekly changes in positions.
[6]Sum of corn, wheat, and soybeans.

The authors are Thomas Helbling, Joong Shik Kang, and Shaun Roache, with support from Marina Rousset.

Table 1.SF.1. Share of Commodity Price Variance Associated with Static Common Factors[1]
(Based on optimal number of common factors)

	Including Great Recession (2008:Q3–2009:Q1)			Excluding Great Recession (2008:Q3–2009:Q1)		
	Full Sample	Mid-Size Sample	Short Sample	Full Sample	Mid-Size Sample	Short Sample
	1979:Q1–2011:Q2	1995:Q1–2011:Q2	2003:Q1–2011:Q2	1979:Q1–2011:Q2	1995:Q1–2011:Q2	2003:Q1–2011:Q2
Agricultural Raw Materials						
Average	0.42	0.48	0.60	0.37	0.40	0.51
Food and Beverages						
Average	0.43	0.43	0.52	0.41	0.38	0.58
Base Metals						
Average	0.54	0.51	0.64	0.60	0.40	0.51
Energy						
Crude Oil, Dated Brent	0.95	0.87	0.86	0.95	0.85	0.56
Crude Oil, West Texas Intermediate	0.91	0.86	0.85	0.89	0.80	0.53
Natural Gas, U.S.	0.25	0.31	0.37	0.18	0.17	0.19
Average	0.67	0.68	0.72	0.62	0.58	0.47
Average, All Commodities	0.49	0.50	0.59	0.44	0.43	0.54

Sources: IMF Primary Commodity Price System; and IMF staff calculations.

[1]Based on logarithmic first differences of commodity prices in constant U.S. dollars.

their implications for the near-term commodity market outlook.

Commodity Prices and the Global Economy

Global economic factors, such as industrial activity, are common influences on all commodity prices. They affect prices through the same channels, including the demand for commodities and the cost of carrying inventories. There is robust empirical evidence that just a few common factors, typically one or two, explain a large share of price fluctuations (as measured by the variance of price changes) across all major commodity groups (Table 1.SF.1).[10]

The aggregate common factor in commodity prices is closely related to fluctuations in global industrial production—a proxy measure for global economic activity. This close relationship is reflected in the synchronization of commodity price cycles with cycles in global economic activity (Figure 1.SF.1, panel 2). Indeed, turning points in commodity prices tend to overlap with turning points in global economic activity.[11] Global industrial production also has predictive content for commodity prices in the sample and, in some cases, even outside the sample (for example, Alquist, Kilian, and Vigfusson, 2011, for crude oil—Figure 1.SF.1, panel 3). Conversely, forecast errors in global industrial production and the common factor in commodity prices are strongly and positively correlated (Figure 1.SF.1, panel 4).

Against this backdrop, the recent commodity price declines in response to the increasingly widespread downgrading of projections for global growth in 2011 and 2012 reflect standard patterns. Conversely, when leading indicators in the first quarter, notably manufacturing purchasing managers' indices, suggested an uptick in near-term activity, cyclical commodity prices rebounded, especially for base metals and crude oil.

Other global economic and financial developments also weighed on commodity prices in 2011. In particular, when the euro area crisis began to escalate in late summer, the U.S. dollar appreciated against most other currencies thanks to safe haven flows, while general financial market volatility

[10]Table1.SF.1 is based on an approximate factor model approach applied to a panel including the prices of 36 commodities. The common factors were estimated using principal components, a consistent estimate even in the presence of some serial and cross-sectional correlation as well as heteroscedasticity in the idiosyncratic errors in individual prices (see, for example, Bai and Ng, 2002). The number of static factors was determined using information criteria (Bai and Ng, 2002). The static factors embody an underlying structure driven by an even smaller number of dynamic factors (Bai and Ng, 2007). For the panel of 36 commodity prices, the optimal number of static factors is on the order of three to four, depending on the sample period; the optimal number of dynamic factors is one to two.

[11]See Box 5.2 in the April 2008 *World Economic Outlook*.

increased. Commodity prices in U.S. dollars, the unit of account for most international commodity market transactions, tend to be negatively correlated with shocks to the external value of the U.S. dollar, given the shifts in purchasing power and costs outside the dollar area implied by U.S. currency movements (Figure 1.SF.1, panel 5).

Unexpected changes in financial market volatility also tend to be negatively associated with global commodity prices. Shocks to the VIX, a widely used proxy for financial market volatility, usually are negatively correlated with commodity prices (Figure 1.SF.1, panel 6). The negative correlation can be explained in part by increased uncertainty about near-term economic prospects when the VIX increases.[12] Increased uncertainty also feeds into financial conditions, which tighten in response. The related increases in risk premiums in turn affect commodity markets. In commodity derivative markets, noncommercial investors seek higher risk premiums on their derivative positions, which raises hedging costs.[13] This rise, together with higher risk premiums on commodity-related credit, raises the carry costs of inventories. With higher uncertainty about future activity and lower incentives for inventory holdings, spot prices tend to fall.

Because commodity derivatives are in effect high-beta assets based on near-term global economic prospects, the increase in uncertainty has also had an effect on investor sentiment. In addition, the continued strong correlation between commodity prices and global equity prices, both driven by uncertainty, has made commodity assets less attractive for diversification purposes. Investors withdrew funds from commodity funds through much of 2011 (Figure 1.SF.1, panel 7). Overall, cumulative withdrawals during 2011 exceeded those during the 2008–09 global financial crisis. The increased volatility of noncommercial futures positions in late 2011 is another reflection of what appears to be greater reluctance to take risks in commodity derivative markets (Figure 1.SF.1, panel 8).

In the constrained global growth environment expected for 2012–13, commodity prices are projected to remain broadly unchanged. Cyclical commodity prices may pick up, if global growth is stronger than currently expected. This pickup would likely remain moderate, however, because growth in 2012 is not likely to recover above the rates expected before renewed escalation of uncertainty in 2011. Similarly, the expected reduction in potential growth in China and other emerging market economies, even if moderate, would dampen cyclical upward pressure.

Growth Slowdown and the Inventory Cycle in China

China's growth has moderated since mid-2011, and there is so far little sign of a sharp correction in the potentially overheated real estate sector and most related activities, despite widespread concerns about a hard landing (Figure 1.SF.2, panel 1). At the same time, commodity imports and apparent consumption of more cyclical commodities—especially base metals but also crude oil—have increased at a robust pace, in part due to continued solid domestic investment growth (Figure 1.SF.2, panels 2 and 3).

Another concern is commodity inventory levels in China. In retrospect, it appears that inventory demand accounted for much of the sharp increase in China's commodity demand in 2009 and early 2010. Identifying China's position on the inventory cycle is more difficult than for other large economies because of the key role of state-owned reserve management agencies, notably the State Reserve Bureau. Official holdings of commodities are quite usual in a number of areas, notably for strategic purposes (for example, crude oil) and in agriculture (for food security and as a result of government intervention in agricultural markets). In China, however, there is also important public sector involvement in other areas. For example, recent estimates put China's total copper inventory (excluding what is held in exchange-bonded warehouses) at about 1.78 million tons, or 9 percent of total annual production for 2011. (More conservative estimates put it at about 1 million tons). At the same time, China's agencies disclose very little information about the size of their stocks. For crude oil and products, for example, the authorities do not provide data on inventory levels, which complicates the assessment of global oil market developments. An assessment of China's

[12]See, among others, Bloom (2009).

[13]See, for example, Etula (2009) and Acharya, Lochstoer, and Ramadorai (2010).

Figure 1.SF.2. China: Recent Commodity Market Developments

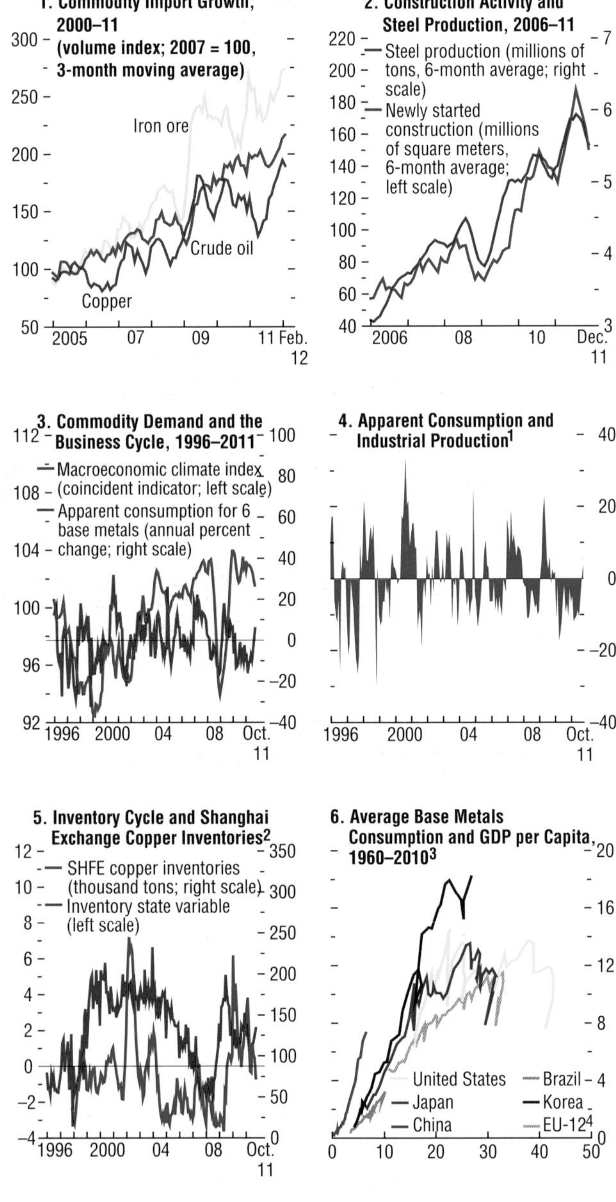

Sources: CEIC; Haver Analytics; World Bureau of Metal Statistics; IMF, *World Economic Outlook;* and IMF staff calculations.

[1]Difference between annual growth rate of apparent consumption and industrial production, in percentage points.

[2]State variable calculated using the Kalman filter and a four-variable latent factor model; SHFE = Shanghai Futures Exchange.

[3]Aggregate of aluminum, copper, lead, nickel, tin, and zinc. Real GDP per capita in thousands of purchasing-power-parity-adjusted U.S. dollars on the *x*-axis; metal consumption per capita in kilograms on the *y*-axis.

[4]Aggregate for Austria, Belgium, Denmark, Finland, France, Germany, Italy, Netherlands, Norway, Sweden, Switzerland, and United Kingdom.

inventory cycle must therefore rely on circumstantial evidence. Given that cyclical commodities such as base metals are used as inputs in the production process, one indicator might be the gap between indicators of economic activity (such as imports) and indicators of demand for these commodities (such as "apparent consumption," defined as domestic production, plus imports, minus exports). If activity picks up when apparent consumption declines, this might indicate that inventories are falling (and vice versa). If China's inventory holders target a "normal" level of stock over the cycle, this would also provide some clues to the prospects for inventory demand, with high inventory accumulation suggesting weaker future demand (Figure 1.SF.2, panel 4).

A dynamic factor model that tries to uncover movement in China's unobservable base metals inventory cycle provides an alternative perspective. This approach considers the comovement of a number of indicators that should be useful in identifying changes in base metals demand. The results shown here are from a four-variable model, which includes China's macroeconomic coincident indicator (including industrial production, employment, and other activity variables), apparent consumption and imports for six base metals, and inventories of copper held in Shanghai futures exchange bonded warehouses.[14] This final indicator is narrower than the others, reflecting in part data availability. It is assumed that these variables are a function of two unobserved (latent) variables that are interpreted to be the business cycle and the inventory cycle. In particular, the business cycle is assumed to affect all four of these variables, while the inventory cycle affects only the base-metals-specific demand and inventory indicators. In China, fluctuations in key sectors are also likely to contribute significantly—and separately from the broader

[14]The model is specified in a state-space framework. The four signal equations included the seasonally adjusted monthly log change in the China macroeconomic indicator, China's apparent consumption and imports for a number of base metals, and Shanghai exchange inventories of copper. Each observable variable is estimated as a function of one or both latent variables (a business cycle and a commodity inventory cycle), both of which follow stationary AR(1) processes. The shocks to the latent variables are assumed to be orthogonal, and the estimated latent variables are recovered using the Kalman filter. The model is estimated using maximum likelihood and monthly data over a sample period from January 1995 through October 2011.

business cycle—to changes in base metals demand, particularly those related to the construction and real estate sectors. These effects are not explicitly identified in this model due to a lack of data.[15]

The base metals inventory cycle generated by this model shows a pattern similar to the gap between apparent consumption and industrial production, but there are noticeable differences in publicly available exchange inventories (Figure 1.SF.2, panel 5). In particular, the variable for the inventory state has a longer duration cycle, and its turning points have, in the past, preceded those for exchange stockpiles. In the run-up to the global financial crisis, as commodity prices surged, China appeared to run down its inventories significantly. Following the rapid buildup in stocks before China's fiscal stimulus in 2009, there was steady destocking until the middle of 2011, after which inventories began to rise again. This analysis suggests that base metals inventories are now broadly close to "normal" levels. China's demand in the near term may therefore rely much more on real economic activity than on large swings in desired inventory holdings.

China's impact on global commodity markets in the near term will depend on its ability to engineer a soft landing for growth in 2012 and the evolution of its inventory cycle. Current *World Economic Outlook* projections anticipate annual growth of 8.2 percent in 2012, which is consistent with continued robust, albeit less buoyant, Chinese demand across a broad range of commodities. These projections assume that China does not unexpectedly enter another period of destocking. In fact, the recent increase in canceled warrants relative to total stocks in London Metal Exchange warehouses, which is a leading indicator of declining metal inventory buffers in the near term, reflects expectations of robust growth in the demand for base metals—consistent with waning concern about a hard landing in China and incoming data suggesting stronger-than-expected activity in the United States (Figure 1.SF.3, panel 1).[16]

The prospect for China's commodity demand over the medium term depends on the pace and composition of its economic growth. Investment growth has remained rapid in the aftermath of China's 2009–10 macroeconomic stimulus, in part due to cyclical factors. Structural factors also help explain the persistently large share of investment in China's economy—including an artificially low cost of capital—that lies behind its highly commodity-intense economic growth. China's government has committed to rebalancing demand away from investment and exports and toward consumption, which may gradually moderate the growth of demand for many commodities. But, compared with the experience of other economies, China's per capita commodity demand will continue to increase as incomes rise, given current income levels (Figure 1.SF.2, panel 6). Against this backdrop, the main risk to global commodity demand will remain closely related to China's growth prospects. In contrast, risks of a transition to less commodity-intensive growth do not seem imminent. More generally, industrialization, urbanization, and income convergence in emerging and developing economies will remain important sources of commodity demand growth.

Commodity Price Divergence and Supply Developments

Common factors play an important role in commodity price fluctuations, as noted above. Nevertheless, there can also be substantial divergence in price changes across commodities because of specific factors. One measure of price divergence, the 75–25 interquartile range of price changes—defined as the difference between the 75th and 25th percentiles of the cross section of price changes of all 51 commodities included in the IMF's commodity price index—shows that divergence narrowed to below the 30-year average during the second half of 2011 (Figure 1.SF.3, panel 2). This narrowing followed an unusually large widening that started during the fuel and food crisis of 2007–08. The divergence between price changes in crude oil and other commodities, however, widened noticeably during the second half of 2011. The price divergence between base metals

[15]Lack of data on activity in specific sectors at a monthly frequency (and a relatively long history) precludes this type of analysis. In practical terms, sectoral effects would be identified in this model by including a range of observable activity variables (for example, construction activity or new building starts) in the measurement equations that, together with commodity demand, are determined in part by unobservable sectoral cycles.

[16]Metal on warrant represents inventories stored at the warehouse; canceled warrants represent metal earmarked for delivery. Investors cancel their warrants because they want to take it out of the warehouse.

Figure 1.SF.3. Commodity Supply and Inventory Developments I

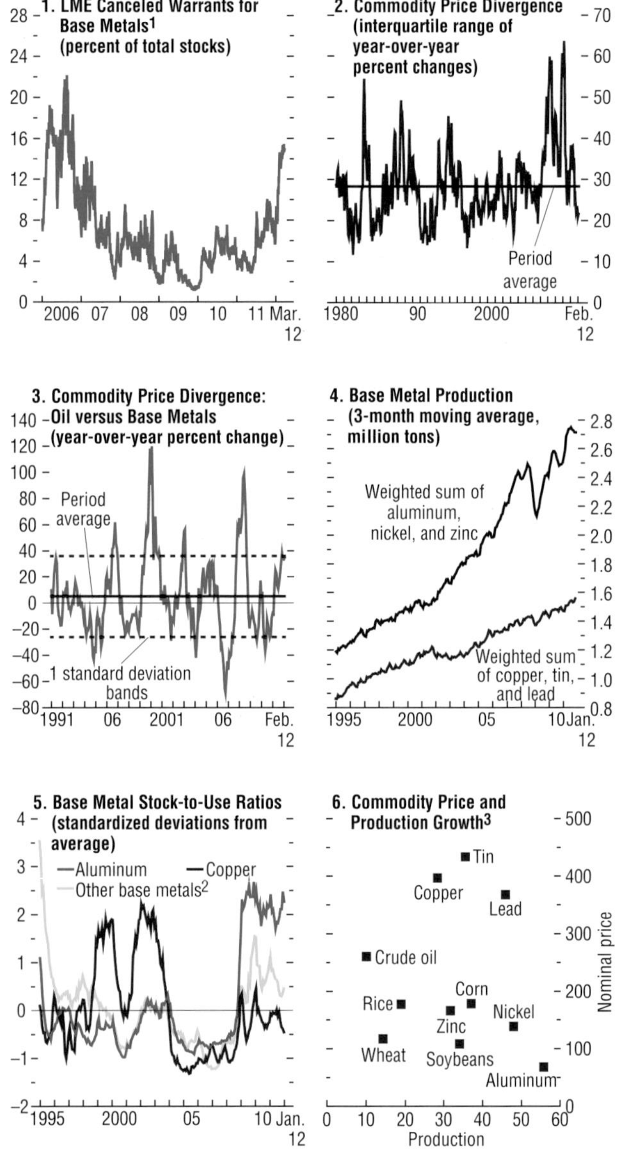

Sources: Bloomberg; IMF, Primary Commodity Price System; International Energy Agency; United States Department of Agriculture; World Bureau of Metal Statistics; and IMF staff estimates.

[1]Average across aluminum, copper, lead, nickel, tin, and zinc. LME = London Metal Exchange.

[2]Weighted average of lead, nickel, tin, and zinc.

[3]Cumulative percent change from 2003 to 2011.

and crude oil—cyclical commodities—is particularly noteworthy (Figure 1.SF.3, panel 3).

Broad-based narrowing in commodity price divergence is consistent with a situation in which commodity-specific factors have become relatively less important compared with common factors. In the short to medium term, commodity-specific factors typically are supply-related events or developments.[17] Indeed, in global food markets, favorable harvest outcomes during the past crop year and expectations of better harvests this crop year led to unwinding within a year—as is usually the case—of the adverse supply shock that hit global grain markets in 2010. In contrast, oil prices have remained high, mirroring tight physical market conditions, largely from supply shocks through much of 2011 and because of geopolitical risks.

Differences in supply and inventory responses also correspond to price divergence over the medium term. Between 2003 and 2011, the cumulative price increases for aluminum and nickel were smaller than for other base metals, reflecting increased inventory buffers supported by stronger production responses to high prices (Figure 1.SF.3, panels 4 and 5). In contrast, copper and tin prices took off, consistent with smaller inventory buffers and more constrained production growth (Figure 1.SF.3, panel 6; Figure 1.SF.4, panel 1).

Global Oil Supply and Geopolitical Risks

Global oil demand in 2011 was lower than projected at the end of 2010, consistent with weaker-than-expected global activity. Nevertheless, the flow-supply shortfall that characterized market conditions in early 2011—a legacy of the spike in oil demand in the second half of 2010—persisted through much of the year, mainly because of supply disruptions in major oil-producing economies (especially Libya) and longer-than-expected maintenance and other outages

[17]Commodity-specific factors include both demand and supply factors. The main commodity-specific factors on the supply side are supply outcomes, notably harvests, and the level of inventory buffers. The latter are important because the effective supply during a period is given by the sum of production and changes in inventories. Technological innovations can be important both on the demand side—changes in the scope for substitution with other commodity inputs or the efficiency of use (for example, of fuels)—or on the supply side (for example, new extraction technologies).

in producers that are not members of OPEC, the Organization of Petroleum Exporting Countries (Table 1.SF.2; Figure 1.SF.4, panel 2). Additional production in other OPEC members, especially Saudi Arabia, and weakening demand finally led to balanced demand and supply in the late fall. At that time, however, industry oil stocks of Organization for Economic Cooperation and Development (OECD) economies and OPEC spare capacity had fallen below their five-year averages—which are frequently used industry benchmarks (Figure 1.SF.4, panel 3). At the same time, geopolitical risks started increasing again, raising precautionary demand for inventories. These developments took place in an overall context of persistent oil scarcity, with oil production remaining below trend.[18]

Geopolitical oil supply risks were a prominent feature throughout 2011. They first increased in early 2011 with the unrest in the Middle East and North Africa. While Libya-related risks subsided toward the end of the year (by February 2012, Libyan oil production had recovered to about four-fifths of the pre-unrest level), risks have increased elsewhere, including in the Islamic Republic of Iran, the Syrian Arab Republic, the Republic of Yemen, Sudan and South Sudan, and Iraq. Since the International Atomic Energy Agency released its report on Iran's nuclear program in November 2011, Iran-related risks are the biggest concern. As a result of the recent EU oil import embargo, other countries' tighter sanctions, and Iran's partial oil export embargo, the potential Iranian oil supply shock is morphing into an actual shock because lower Iranian oil production and exports seem inevitable during 2012 and beyond. The extent and speed of the decline, however, are difficult to predict: outcomes will depend on economic and strategic considerations of a small number of players, including major emerging net importers.

The larger the reduction in the Iranian oil supply, the greater the risk of global oil market tightening. For example, a reduction in oil exports equal to total exports to OECD economies would amount to about 1½ million barrels a day, equivalent to a shock of about 2.4 times the standard deviation of regular fluctuations in global production (Table 1.SF.3).[19] The global oil supply

[18]See Chapter 3 of the April 2011 *World Economic Outlook*.

[19]From a historical perspective, disruption of this magnitude would constitute an above-average disruption, both in terms of total barrels and as a percent of global production.

Figure 1.SF.4. Commodity Supply and Inventory Developments II

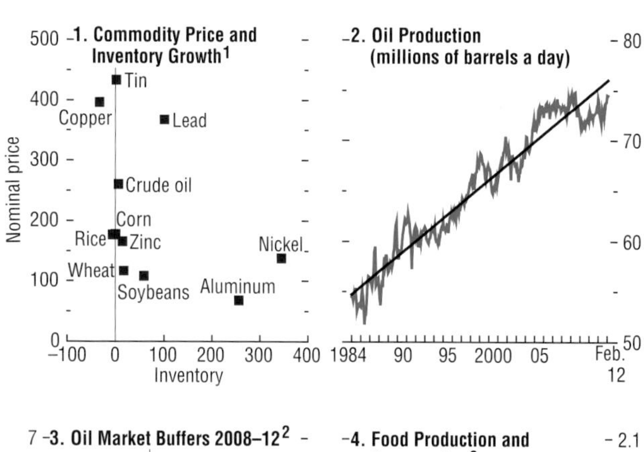

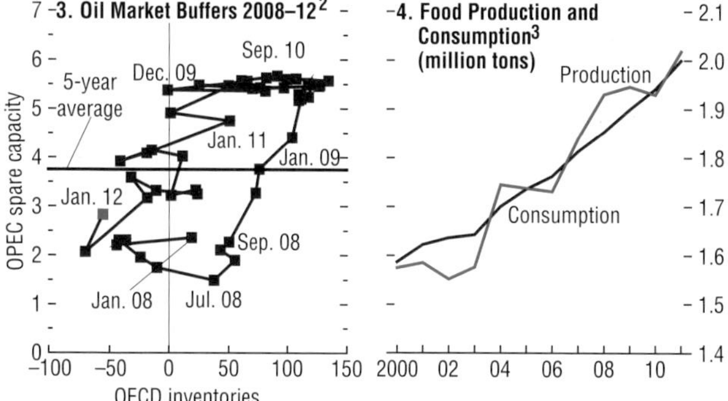

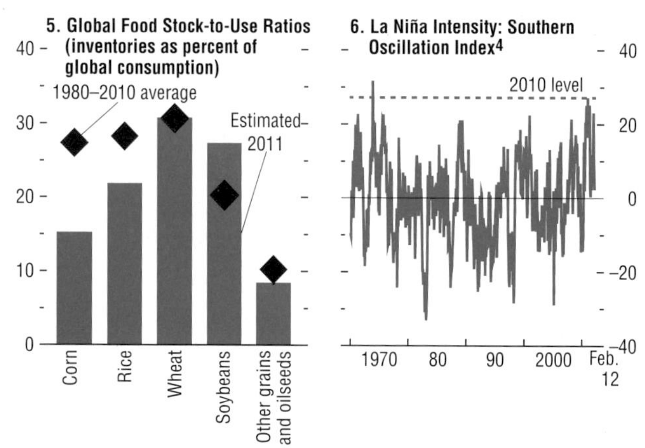

Sources: IMF, Primary Commodity Price System; International Energy Agency; U.S. National Oceanic and Atmospheric Administration; U.S. Department of Agriculture; World Bureau of Metal Statistics; and IMF staff calculations.

[1]Cumulative percent change from 2003 to 2011.

[2]Organization for Economic Cooperation and Development (OECD) stocks, deviations from five-year average (million barrels) on *x*-axis; Organization of Petroleum Exporting Countries (OPEC) effective spare capacity (million barrels a day) on *y*-axis (excluding Iraq, Nigeria, and Venezuela for the entire time period, and Libya since November 2011).

[3]Sum of corn, wheat, and milled rice. Crop year on *x*-axis; 2001 denotes 2000–01 crop year.

[4]Large positive values often indicate La Niña episodes.

Table 1.SF.2. Global Oil Demand and Production by Region
(Millions of barrels a day)

						Year-over-Year Percent Change							
	2009	2010	2011 Proj.	2010: H2	2011: H1	2004–06 Avg.	2007	2008	2009	2010	2011 Proj.	2010: H2	2011: H1
Demand													
Advanced Economies	45.7	45.1	44.7	44.9	45.2	–0.1	–3.5	–3.9	1.5	–1.3	–0.8	–0.6	–2.0
Of Which:													
United States	19.5	19.2	19.1	19.3	19.1	–0.1	–5.9	–3.7	2.2	–1.5	–0.5	–0.1	–2.9
Euro Area	10.6	10.3	10.0	10.2	10.3	–0.4	–0.4	–5.6	–0.2	–2.9	–2.4	–2.0	–3.7
Japan	4.5	4.5	4.5	4.4	4.6	–1.8	–4.9	–8.2	1.3	0.8	0.9	–1.3	2.7
Newly Industrialized Asian Economies	4.8	4.7	4.8	4.7	4.8	2.7	–2.7	3.3	3.9	–1.2	0.7	–1.9	–0.6
Emerging and Developing Economies	42.6	44.0	45.2	43.5	44.5	3.9	2.9	2.1	5.1	3.2	2.7	3.7	2.6
Of Which:													
Commonwealth of Independent States	4.5	4.7	4.8	4.5	4.8	2.3	2.3	–1.2	6.8	5.1	1.9	4.1	6.0
Developing Asia	24.8	25.8	26.7	26.0	25.7	3.5	1.5	4.6	5.9	4.1	3.3	5.1	3.1
China	9.1	9.5	9.9	9.5	9.5	5.4	2.2	4.1	12.5	4.9	3.9	7.8	2.2
India	3.3	3.5	3.6	3.5	3.4	4.9	4.0	4.7	2.4	4.2	3.3	3.5	5.0
Middle East and North Africa	9.3	9.4	9.7	9.2	9.6	5.2	5.0	3.6	3.2	1.1	2.8	1.3	1.0
Western Hemisphere	5.9	6.1	6.3	6.0	6.2	4.4	4.9	0.0	5.3	3.0	2.6	3.4	2.7
World	88.3	89.1	89.9	88.4	89.7	1.6	–0.7	–1.2	3.2	0.8	0.9	1.5	0.2
Production													
OPEC (current composition)[1,2]	34.8	35.8	36.2	35.5	36.1	1.7	3.3	–5.7	2.2	2.7	1.3	2.9	2.6
Of Which:													
Saudi Arabia	9.8	10.7	. . .	10.4	11.1	–0.2	4.9	–9.5	3.1	9.9	. . .	8.3	11.5
Nigeria	2.5	2.6	. . .	2.6	2.6	–1.9	–7.6	–0.4	15.7	3.9	. . .	8.7	–0.3
Venezuela	2.7	2.7	. . .	2.8	2.7	1.8	0.8	–3.6	–4.6	–0.3	. . .	1.8	–2.4
Iraq	2.4	2.7	. . .	2.7	2.8	2.0	14.3	2.5	–2.2	13.3	. . .	13.7	12.9
Non-OPEC[2]	52.6	52.7	53.6	52.5	52.9	0.4	–0.2	1.8	2.1	0.2	. . .	0.3	0.1
Of Which:													
North America	14.1	14.5	15.0	14.3	14.8	–1.2	–3.6	2.1	3.5	3.1	. . .	2.3	3.8
North Sea	3.8	3.4	3.4	3.5	3.3	–7.0	–4.7	–5.3	–8.6	–9.8	. . .	–10.7	–8.8
Russia	10.5	10.6	10.7	10.5	10.6	2.5	–0.7	2.0	2.4	1.2	. . .	1.2	1.3
Other Former Soviet Union[3]	3.1	3.0	3.1	3.1	3.0	9.9	3.1	8.7	1.3	–1.7	. . .	–0.3	–2.9
Other Non-OPEC	21.2	21.1	21.5	21.1	21.2	1.4	3.0	2.0	3.4	–0.2	. . .	0.8	–1.1
World	87.4	88.5	89.9	88.0	89.0	0.9	1.2	–1.4	2.2	1.2	. . .	1.3	1.1
Net Demand[4]	**0.9**	**0.6**	**. . .**	**0.5**	**0.7**	**0.5**	**–0.2**	**0.0**	**1.0**	**0.7**	**. . .**	**0.5**	**0.8**

Sources: International Energy Agency, *Oil Market Report*, August 2011; and IMF staff calculations.

[1]OPEC = Organization of Petroleum Exporting Countries. Includes Angola (subject to quotas since January 2007) and Ecuador, which rejoined OPEC in November 2007 after suspending its membership from December 1992 to October 2007.

[2]Totals refer to a total of crude oil, condensates, natural gas liquids, and oil from nonconventional sources.

[3]Other Former Soviet Union includes Azerbaijan, Belarus, Georgia, Kazakhstan, Kyrgyz Republic, Tajikistan, Turkmenistan, Ukraine, and Uzbekistan.

[4]Difference between demand and production. In the percent change columns, the figures are percent of world demand.

disruption is likely to be smaller because other producers will make up part of the difference, as Saudi Arabia and other OPEC producers did in the case of the Libyan disruption. Saudi Arabia has indeed signaled its intention to raise production further in case of another large-scale supply disruption. Nevertheless, event study and time series analyses suggest that such offsets rarely compensate for the total difference and that significant local oil supply disruptions are associated with declines in global oil supply, at least temporarily.

Iran-related geopolitical oil supply risks extend beyond the reduction in oil production and exports that appears to be in the making already and is priced in by markets. Iran's location at the Strait of Hormuz, the choke point for shipment of about 40 percent of global oil exports (25 percent of global production), and its geographic proximity to other major oil producers means that there is a risk of a large-scale, possibly unprecedented, oil supply disruption in the event of military conflict or attempts to close the

Table 1.SF.3. Mean and Standard Deviations of Oil Production
(Based on monthly changes in production)

	1984–2011			2001–11			2006–11		
		Standard Deviation			Standard Deviation			Standard Deviation	
Producer	Mean	Percent	mbd[1]	Mean	Percent	mbd[1]	Mean	Percent	mbd[1]
World	0.1	1.2	0.9	0.1	0.9	0.6	0.0	0.8	0.6
Non-OPEC[2]	0.0	0.9	0.4	0.0	0.8	0.3	0.0	0.9	0.4
OPEC	0.2	3.0	0.9	0.1	1.7	0.5	–0.1	1.5	0.5
Islamic Republic of Iran	0.2	6.5	0.2	0.0	3.5	0.1	–0.2	2.4	0.1
Memorandum									
Iranian exports to OECD[3]									
Ratio to Standard Deviation, World Production[4]						2.36			2.47
Ratio to Standard Deviation, Non-OPEC Production[4]						4.30			3.96
Ratio to Standard Deviation, Iranian Production[4]						11.46			17.24

Source: U.S. Energy Information Administration; International Energy Agency; and IMF staff calculations.
[1]The standard deviation in terms of percent change applied to latest production data available (November 2011); mbd = millions of barrels a day.
[2]OPEC = Organization of Petroleum Exporting Countries.
[3]Crude oil exports as of September 2011; OECD = Organization for Economic Cooperation and Development.
[4]Ratio of crude oil exports to standard deviation of monthly production levels.

strait.[20] Given the low responsiveness of global oil demand to price changes in the short term, such oil supply disruption would require a very large price response to maintain global supply-demand balance.

Geopolitical risk is unlikely to subside soon; this risk has increased precautionary demand for oil inventories. Activity-related oil demand growth is also likely to strengthen as the recovery in global activity advances. With supply outside OPEC expected to increase only modestly in the near term, prospects are for oil market conditions to ease only gradually. Oil futures prices suggest that spot prices are expected to ease gradually but remain above the average 2011 level through 2012–13. Given below-average spare capacity and inventory buffers, upside risks to oil prices remain a prominent concern in this environment, notwithstanding downside risks to global economic growth and oil demand.

Supply Rebound in Global Food Markets

With more favorable harvest outcomes in the past crop year, global food inventories started to be rebuilt in 2011 (Figure 1.SF.4, panel 4).[21] As a result, and against expectations of further harvest improvements this crop year, food prices declined during the second half of 2011, broadly in tandem with cyclical commodity prices. Nevertheless, global demand continues to grow at a robust pace, and vulnerability to adverse weather events and other adverse supply shocks remains a concern (Figure 1.SF.4, panel 5). Global food inventories remain significantly below the average level over the past four decades in terms of stock-to-use ratios, especially for corn and rice. The legacy of the decline in global food inventories during the years before the 2007–08 global food crisis is therefore still present.

The weather pattern known as La Niña represents the most prominent risk to the food supply. Following the strongest La Niña in three decades in 2010, the return of the weather pattern this year has been unexpectedly powerful (Figure 1.SF.4, panel 6). The effects of La Niña on crop yields have historically been ambiguous, but the strength of this current cycle increases the prospect of drought in South America and excessive rain in Asia. Soybeans are the crop most at risk, largely because of their concentrated production in Argentina and Brazil, but also because they have taken the place on the supply side of hitherto higher-priced corn. La Niña also has the potential to reduce rice yields in Asia, but a very large increase in harvested area there should ensure positive supply growth, which will prevent a decline in inventory buffers.

[20]The Strait of Hormuz is also an important choke point for shipments of liquefied natural gas (LNG)—some 20 percent of the global LNG supply according to some estimates.

[21]In the *World Agricultural Supply and Demand Estimates* of the U.S. Department of Agriculture, crop years vary by crop, but they run broadly from the second half of one year to the first half of the next.

Box 1.1. The Labor Share in Europe and the United States during and after the Great Recession

Inequality has been of concern lately because of its linkages to the sustainability of growth (Berg and Ostry, 2011) and its impact on social cohesion. Changes in the labor share (the share of labor compensation in GDP) are a commonly used measure of inequality.[1] There has been an overall downward trend in the labor share in many advanced economies since the early 1980s for which various explanations have been advanced. These include the college premium (the premium on wages of those with a bachelor's degree), the superstar effect (the disproportionate compensation of the top 1 percent of the income distribution), and the "hollowing out" of the middle class as a result of skill-biased technological change or the offshoring of medium-skill jobs (Rajan, 2010; Atkinson, Piketty, and Saez, 2011; Acemoglu and Autor, 2011). This box, however, focuses more narrowly on the cyclical behavior of the labor share, especially during the Great Recession and the subsequent recovery. Did workers shoulder a larger share of the adjustment during the Great Recession? Have they been left out during the recovery? Is the behavior of the labor share different from that during previous recovery episodes?

The Theory

Economic theory makes no clear association between fluctuations in aggregate income and the labor share. In many models, the labor share is constant throughout the business cycle. In others, it is positively correlated with the gap between output and potential, but not necessarily with the level of output itself. Finally, when there is labor hoarding during a recession, the labor share is expected to behave countercyclically. However, a number of empirical studies present evidence that the labor share is typically countercyclical—rising during recessions and falling during recoveries.

Figure 1.1.1. Evolution of the Labor Share during the Great Recession and Recovery

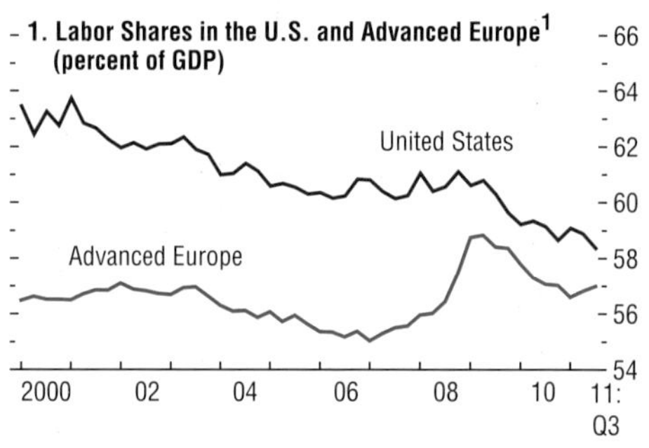

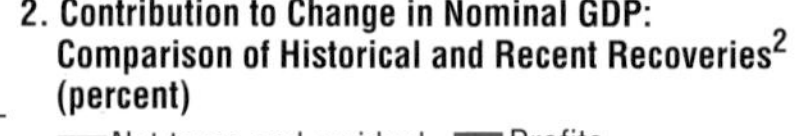

2. Contribution to Change in Nominal GDP:
Comparison of Historical and Recent Recoveries²
(percent)

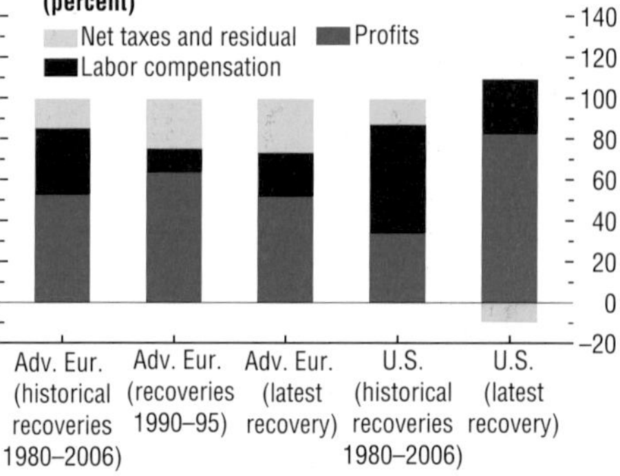

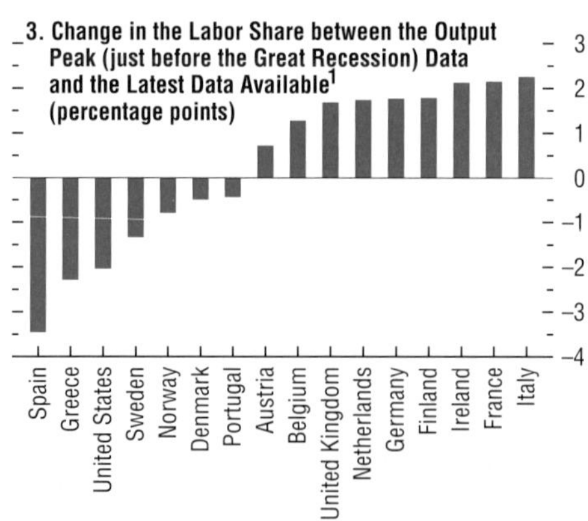

Sources: Eurostat; Organization for Economic Cooperation and Development; U.S. Bureau of Labor Statistics; and IMF staff calculations.

[1]The labor share is defined as the ratio of labor compensation to GDP.

[2]The peaks and troughs in output are determined using the Harding and Pagan (2002) version of the Bry and Boschan algorithm. Recovery is defined as four quarters following the trough.

The main author of this box is Florence Jaumotte, with support from Jair Rodriguez.

[1]While the size of the labor share is commonly associated with inequality, this link is not straightforward. Under some circumstances, a decline in the labor share could imply no change in income inequality, for instance if more workers are compensated by way of stock options.

Box 1.1. *(continued)*

This Time Around

Labor share data point to countercyclical behavior, with an increase in the labor share of national income during the Great Recession and a decline (or stabilization) during the recovery (Figure 1.1.1).[2] During the recession, profits were the component that contributed most often to the decline in income. In most economies, labor compensation actually increased, except in Greece, Ireland, Spain, and the United States. The labor share increased only very modestly during the recession in the United States and Spain.[3] During the recovery, although all components of GDP increased, profits rebounded quite strongly in most economies, leading to a decline in the labor share. Labor compensation increased again in all countries, with the exception of Portugal and Spain.

In advanced Europe, the behavior of the labor share during the most recent recovery seems broadly similar to what took place during other recoveries between 1980 and 2006: profits increased quite strongly relative to labor income.[4]

In contrast, the recent recovery in the United States appears unusual from a historical perspective. The rebound in profits relative to labor income is much stronger this time around (although during all recoveries the labor share tends to fall). In fact, the most recent U.S. recovery looks very much like a typical European recovery. One possibility is that workers' fear of long-term unemployment has led to more subdued wages relative to labor productivity growth during the recent recovery. But it will take further research to determine the actual causes.

In many European economies, workers are not worse off after the Great Recession in terms of their share of national income. The labor share is still higher today than just before the Great Recession in many economies. Yet, in the United States and in a few European economies (especially Greece and Spain), the labor share remains well below the precrisis peak. Only time will tell the extent to which the latest labor share losses will add to the general trend decline.

[2]National accounts data provide information on the compensation of employees, but do not break down the labor income of other categories of workers (self-employed, employers, family workers), which is included in the category "gross operating surplus and mixed income." The assumption to calculate the labor share is that workers in these other categories command the same compensation per worker as employees.

[3]Net taxes declined in most economies and contributed substantially to lower GDP in a number of them (Italy, Norway, Portugal).

[4]Two definitions of recovery are used: (1) four quarters following the trough (shown in Figure 1.1.1); and (2) the period between the trough and the quarter during which output returns to its precrisis peak (available on request). The findings are broadly similar for both definitions. An alternative definition of recovery not used here is the period between the trough and the quarter during which output returns to trend.

Box 1.2. The Global Recovery: Where Do We Stand?

The recovery from the Great Recession has been unusually uneven: very weak in many advanced economies but surprisingly strong in many emerging and developing economies. The trajectory of the ongoing recovery in advanced economies has so far displayed some disturbing similarities with the sluggish recovery following the much shallower 1991 global recession. More recently, the recovery in advanced economies has weakened, raising concern about the pace and durability of the global recovery. This box explores three major questions to put the ongoing recovery in historical perspective. How different is the current global recovery from past recoveries? How do developments in advanced and emerging economies compare with those during earlier episodes? And where do we stand in the recovery process? To address these questions, this box briefly examines the main features of global recoveries during the past 50 years and the experiences of advanced and emerging market economies during these episodes.

A global recovery is defined as a period (usually the first three years) of increasing economic activity following a global recession. This box focuses on the recoveries that followed the global recessions of 1975, 1982, 1991, and 2009, which involved declines in world real GDP per capita.[5] The 2009 episode stands out as the most severe and synchronized global recession during the postwar period. This raises the question of whether the recovery from the Great Recession differs much from past recoveries. To analyze the dynamics of the global recovery, the behavior of a set of macroeconomic and financial variables during the current recovery is compared with that of the previous three episodes.

How Similar? How Different?

The ongoing global recovery has several similarities with previous ones but also exhibits some important differences. At the global level, real GDP, trade, credit, and house and equity prices have not displayed an unusual pattern during the current recovery (Figure 1.2.1). In fact, GDP, consumption, and investment have rebounded more strongly than after most past global recessions. However, the declines were much deeper in 2009, and an unprecedented degree of macroeconomic policy expansion has helped drive the current recovery (Figure 1.2.2).[6] Despite the strong rebound in global economic activity, the level of unemployment has remained much higher than during previous episodes. These aggregate observations mask, however, important differences between the recoveries experienced by advanced economies and emerging market economies.

One distinguishing feature of the current recovery is its uneven nature. As documented in Box 1.1 of the October 2010 *World Economic Outlook*, emerging market economies have performed better than in past episodes. In fact, they account for the lion's share of world growth since 2009, driven largely by buoyant domestic demand, vibrant asset markets, strong capital inflows, and expansionary policies.[7] The strong performance of emerging markets reflects in part some structural improvements such as better-regulated financial systems and stronger macroeconomic frameworks that allowed them to pursue more credible and effective countercyclical policies. Notable exceptions are the emerging European economies, which suffered a financial shock qualitatively similar to the shock in many advanced economies.

In contrast, the current recovery in advanced economies has been extremely weak, reflecting in

The authors of this box are M. Ayhan Kose, Prakash Loungani, and Marco E. Terrones. Ezgi O. Ozturk and M. Angela Espiritu provided research assistance.

[5]These global recessions are identified by applying at the global level the two standard methods of dating peaks and troughs in individual country business cycles—statistical procedures and discretionary methods such as the one used by the National Bureau of Economic Research for the United States. Both methods yield the same turning points in global activity (Kose, Loungani, and Terrones, 2009). A per capita measure of global GDP is considered to account for the heterogeneity in population growth rates across countries—in particular, emerging and developing economies tend to have faster GDP growth than advanced economies, but they also have higher population growth.

[6]For a discussion of the scope of expansionary macroeconomic policies following the recent global recession, see Dao and Loungani (2010).

[7]Kose, Otrok, and Prasad (forthcoming) present a detailed account of many differences in cyclical performance between advanced and emerging market economies in recent years.

Box 1.2. *(continued)*

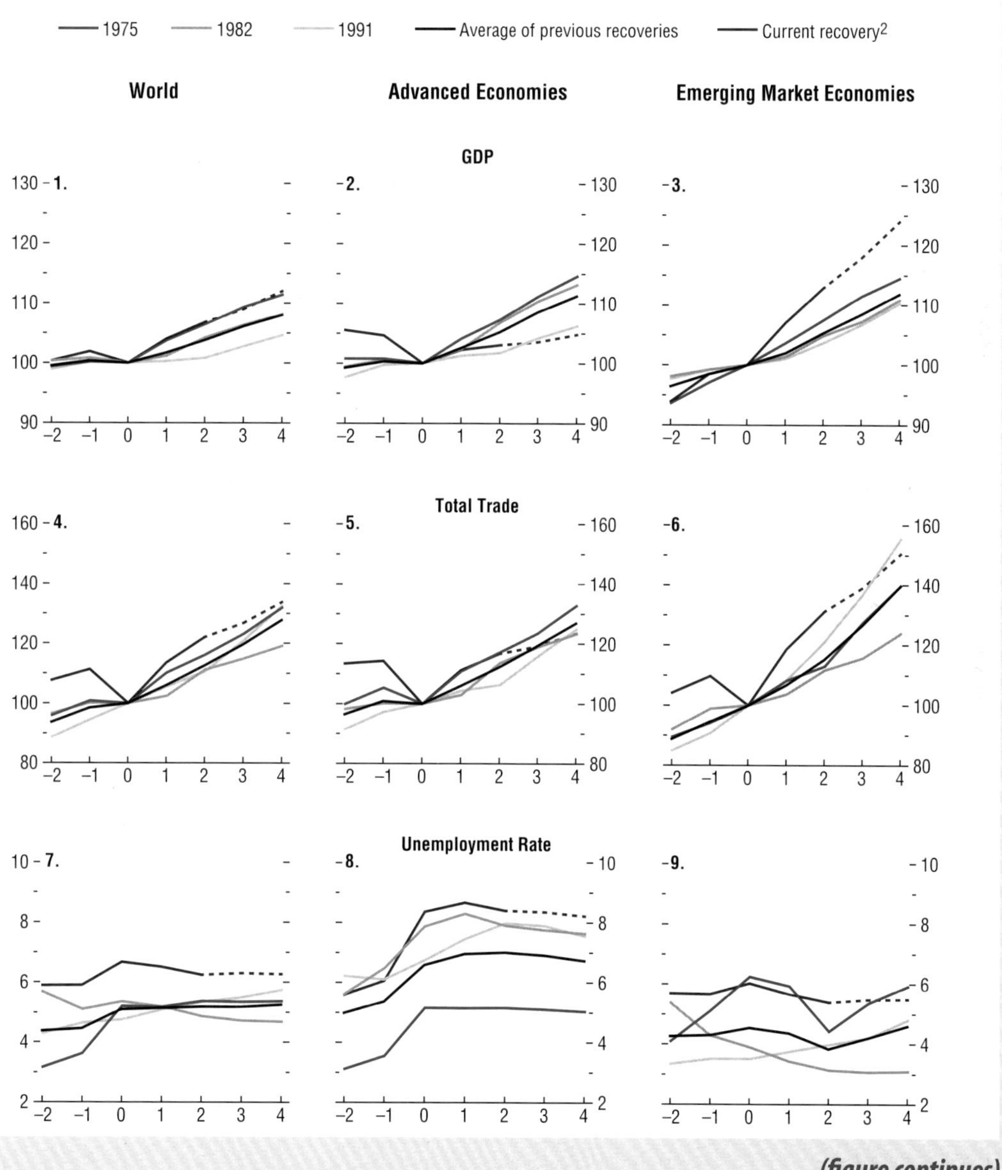

(figure continues)

Box 1.2. *(continued)*

Figure 1.2.1. Dynamics of Global Recoveries: Selected Variables[1] *(concluded)*

(Years on x-axis; t = 0 in the year of the trough; indexed to 100 at the trough; in real terms unless noted otherwise)

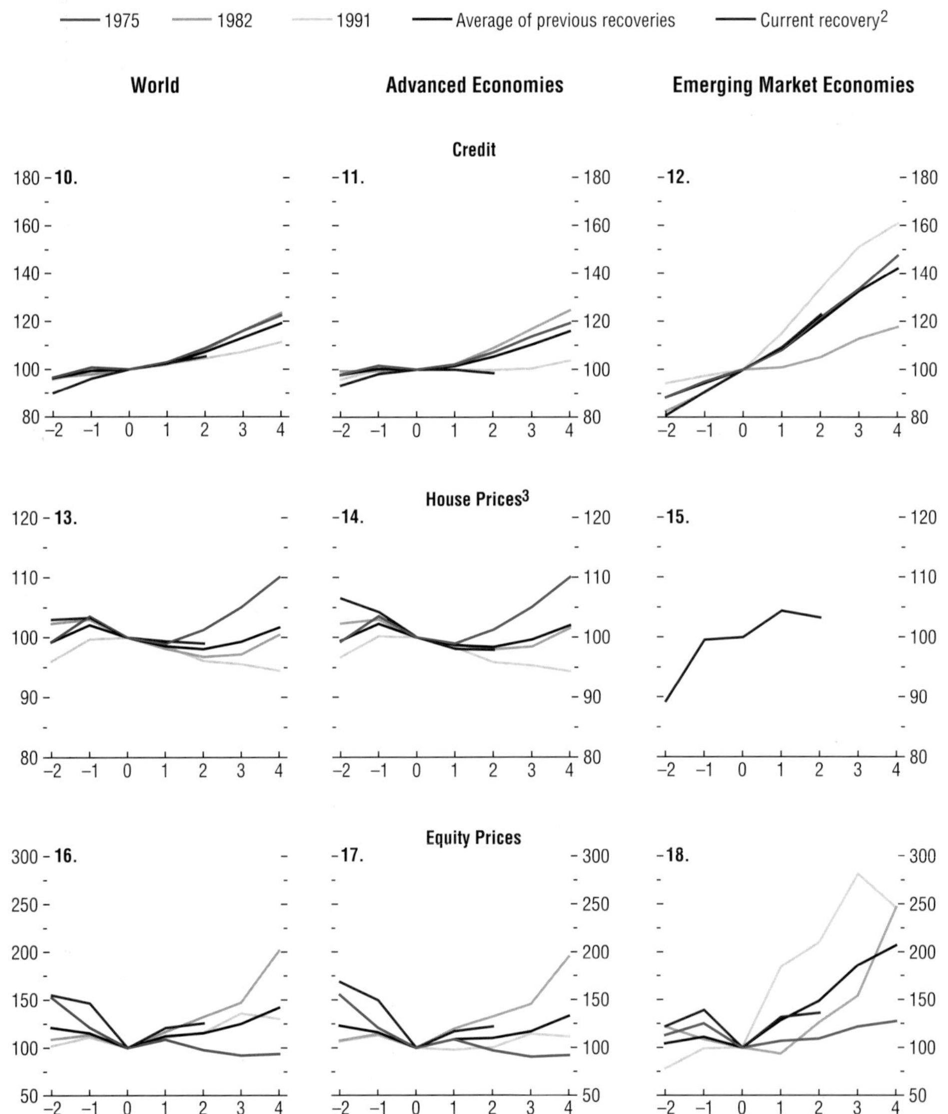

Source: IMF staff estimates.

[1]Aggregates for GDP are purchasing-power-parity-weighted per capita real GDP indices. Aggregates for total trade are trade-weighted real trade indices. Aggregates for unemployment rate are labor-force-weighted unemployment rates in percent. Aggregates for real credit, real house prices, and real equity prices are market-weighted by GDP in U.S. dollars.

[2]Dashed lines denote WEO forecasts, where available.

[3]House price series for the previous global recoveries are not available for emerging market economies.

Box 1.2. *(continued)*

part the legacy of the global financial crisis, particularly the ongoing need for balance sheet repair in the household and financial sectors.[8] Specifically, the 2012 forecast of economic activity, if realized, would mean that the current recovery is the weakest for advanced economies during the postwar era. In a number of advanced economies, output has not yet rebounded to the levels observed before the recession, unemployment remains well above historical norms, and cumulative growth in consumption and investment has been much smaller.

Another distinct feature of the current recovery is a sharp and sustained contraction in investment in structures in advanced economies. The severity of the contraction can be traced to deterioration in the credit and housing markets. Still, developments in these market segments have thus far not been significantly worse than after the 1991 recession.

Interestingly, equity markets have performed better on average than after previous recessions. One explanation is that many nonfinancial corporations now operate on a global level and have benefited from the overall improvement in global activity, particularly in emerging markets—which, as noted, have recovered better than after previous worldwide recessions.

Advanced Economies: Reliving the Early 1990s?

Despite the fact that the Great Recession was markedly more severe than the 1991 global recession, the underlying causes of these two episodes and the evolution of activity during the succeeding recoveries are remarkably similar for the advanced economies.

- These two recoveries were preceded by recessions associated with a bust in credit and housing markets in key advanced economies.[9] In particular, the 1991 recession was associated with disrup-

Figure 1.2.2. Growth during Global Recessions and Recoveries: Selected Variables

(Annual percent change; in real terms)

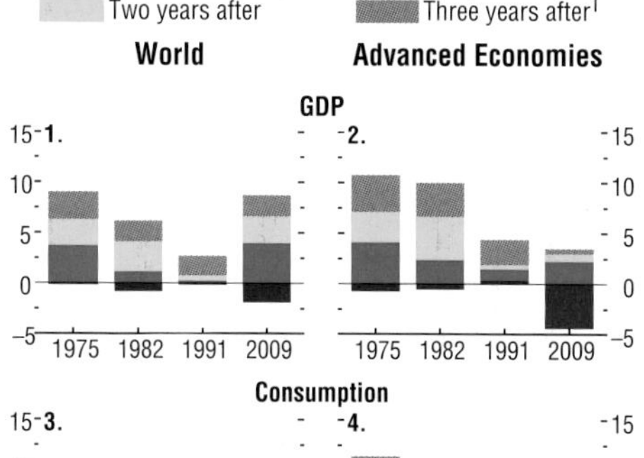

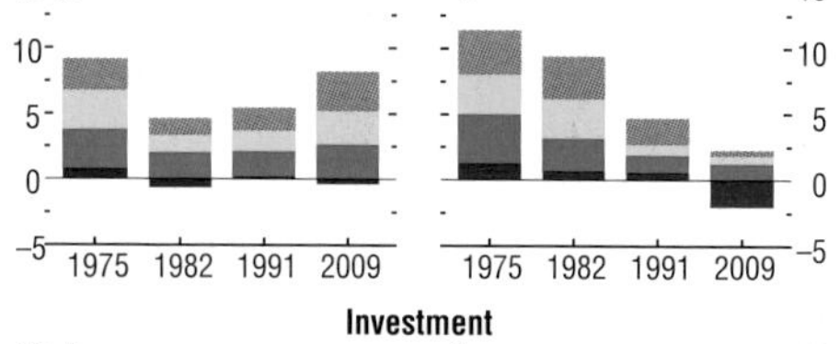

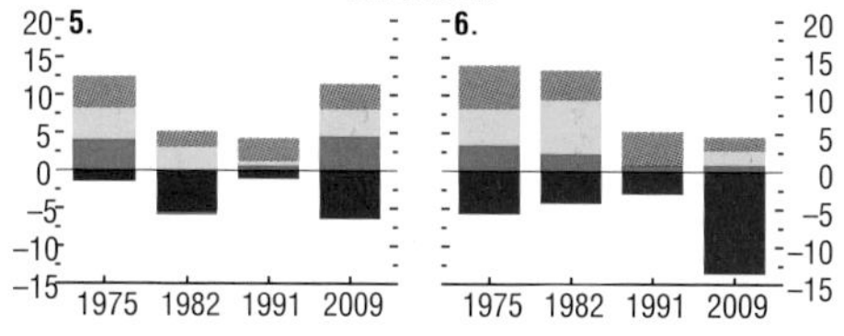

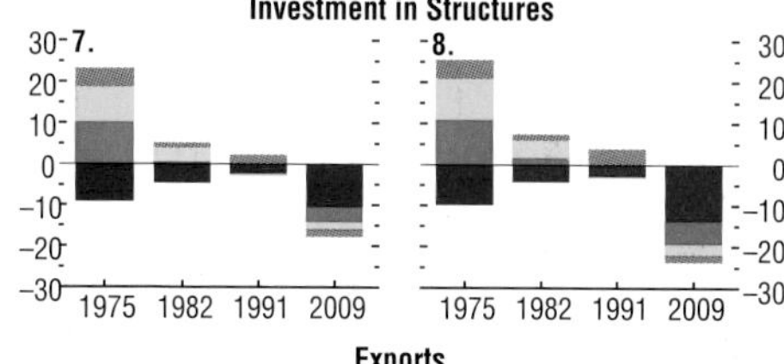

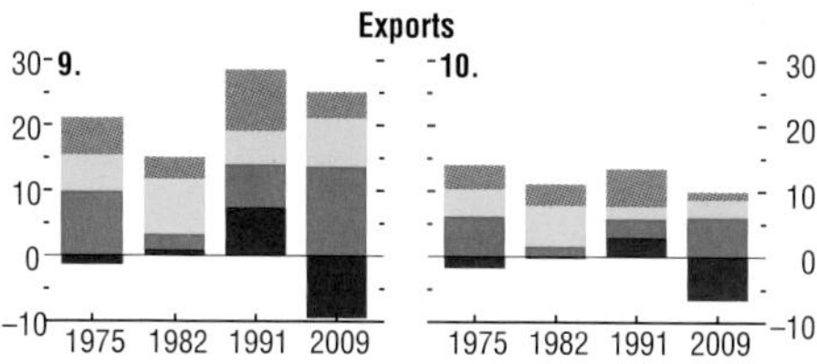

Source: IMF staff estimates.

Note: Each bar represents the percent change in the respective variable in the years of the global recessions and recoveries. Growth rates of all variables, except exports, are per capita and weighted for purchasing power parity. Investment in structures includes both residential investment and other buildings and structures. Export growth is weighted by the U.S. dollar value of total trade as a share of the group's total trade.

[1] Figures for 2012 (global recession year 2009) are forecasts.

[8] In many ways, this outcome was expected. For example, Claessens, Kose, and Terrones (forthcoming) present evidence suggesting that recoveries following turmoil in financial markets tend to be weaker. They also find that recoveries associated with rapid growth in credit and house prices are often stronger.

[9] Before both the 2008–09 global financial crisis and the ERM crisis, advanced economies experienced highly synchronized credit booms (Mendoza and Terrones, forthcoming).

Box 1.2. *(continued)*

tions in credit and asset markets in the United States and Japan. Similarly, the Great Recession involved severe problems in credit and housing markets in the United States and a number of other advanced economies, including Ireland, Spain, and the United Kingdom.

- Both recoveries were slowed down in part by challenges in Europe. The earlier recovery episode was shaped by downturns in many European economies during the European Exchange Rate Mechanism (ERM) crisis of 1992–93. Interest rates had to be raised during that period to defend the exchange rate arrangement, and several advanced European economies were forced to reduce their large fiscal deficits. This suppressed economic activity and further depressed credit and housing markets in the region. Currently, high sovereign risk premiums are inflicting similar or even worse damage on fiscal balances and growth. In both cases, lack of a timely, credible, and coordinated policy strategy heightened the financial turmoil.
- The trajectories of the two recoveries were quite similar because advanced economies experienced meager growth in both cases. In part, this is a result of the disappointing growth in domestic consumption and investment driven by the legacy of the financial crisis—balance sheet repair, weak credit expansion, and lingering problems in housing markets—and loss of competitiveness in some economies. Both episodes are also marked by persistently high unemployment.[10] However, considering the deep fall in output in 2009, the rise in unemployment has been more limited. This is particularly true in Europe and may well reflect policies involving more job-friendly wage setting and greater labor hoarding in some of these economies.

Conclusions

Although the strong rebound in world output during this global recovery is comparable with previous episodes, the divergence of advanced and emerging market economies' fortunes sets the current recovery apart. Emerging market economies have rebounded strongly and have been the engine of world growth during this recovery. The robust performance of these economies can be explained in part by their strong macroeconomic frameworks and structural reforms.

In contrast, for advanced economies, the current recovery is predicted to be the weakest of the postwar era. The trajectory of the ongoing recovery in advanced economies has so far paralleled the recovery following the 1991 recession to a surprising degree. Both of these recoveries were hampered by housing and financial market problems in these economies. These problems are likely to continue sapping the strength of the recovery unless policymakers adopt stronger policies to address them.

[10]Loungani (2012) discusses evidence for the theory that the drop in output through aggregate demand channels explains much of the increase in unemployment in advanced economies. For the United States, labor market slack could be better reflected in the persistent drop in the employment-to-population ratio.

Box 1.3. Where Is China's External Surplus Headed?

China's current account surplus has declined from a precrisis peak of 10.1 percent of GDP in 2007 to 2.8 percent of GDP in 2011—a reversal that was sharper and more persistent than expected. It has long been challenging to forecast China's current account, given the economy's rapid structural change, the uncertainties surrounding prospects for the terms of trade, the *World Economic Outlook* forecast assumption of a constant real exchange rate, and the volatility of the global economy in recent years. This box examines the links between the recent decline in China's current account surplus, shifts in domestic spending, changes in global prices and trade patterns, and domestic costs and external competitiveness. It also considers the implications and outlook for China's external surplus over the medium term.

The primary cause of the decline in the current account surplus is a compression of the trade surplus, although the income balance contributed as well (Figure 1.3.1). This took place in the context of cyclically weak demand from China's main trading partners, which was 6½ percentage points lower for 2008–11 than forecast in early 2008. Demand was especially weak in the United States and the euro area, which account for about 40 percent of China's exports.

At the same time, investment became increasingly important in supporting growth (Figure 1.3.2). Investment was initially boosted by stimulus measures, which raised public spending on infrastructure in response to the rapidly deteriorating global economic conditions during the Great Recession. However, as public stimulus waned after mid-2009, there was a significant pick-up in private capital formation, first in housing construction and, more recently, for renewed expansion of manufacturing capacity, often in relatively higher-end industries. This investment proved to be significantly more import-intensive than domestic consumption, which put downward pressure on the trade balance.

Another factor in the reversal of the current account surplus has been ongoing secular deterioration in China's terms of trade.[1] As noted, the run-up in investment spending was more import-intensive, particularly for commodities and minerals, for which global supply is relatively inelastic and prices have been rising. At the same time, exports became increasingly tilted toward machinery and equipment, for which global supply is relatively elastic, competition is significant, and relative prices have been falling. In fact, because of its economic size, China is no longer a price taker in global markets, so its strong investment has added to downward pressure on the prices of its export goods. As a consequence, aside from a temporary rebound in 2009, China's terms of trade have declined by 10½ percentage points more than forecast in early 2008.

Figure 1.3.1. China's Current Account and Components, 1971–2011
(Percent of GDP)

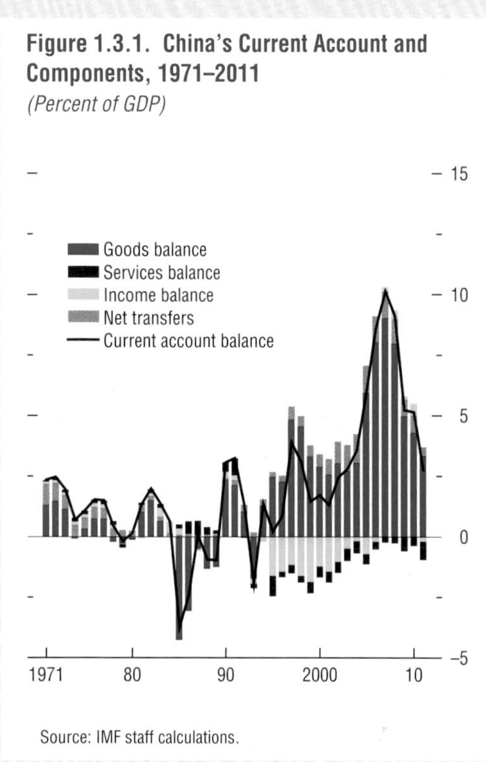

Source: IMF staff calculations.

The main authors of this box are Ashvin Ahuja, Nigel Chalk, Malhar Nabar, and Papa N'Diaye. The box draws on Ahuja and others (forthcoming).

[1]From a historical perspective, the secular terms-of-trade deterioration is not surprising. Other economies in the region—notably Japan and the newly industrialized Asian economies—also suffered similar, lasting terms-of-trade declines as they gained significant export market share and moved along their development path.

Box 1.3. *(continued)*

Figure 1.3.2. China's Fixed Asset Investment, 2004–11
(Percent unless noted otherwise)

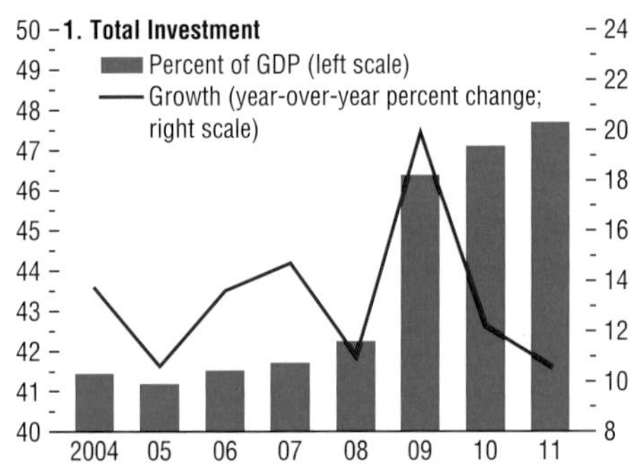

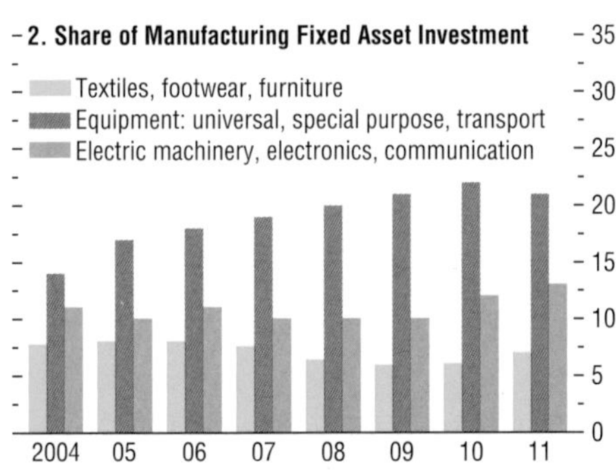

Source: IMF staff calculations.

Figure 1.3.3. Profitability of China's Manufacturing Sector, 2003–11

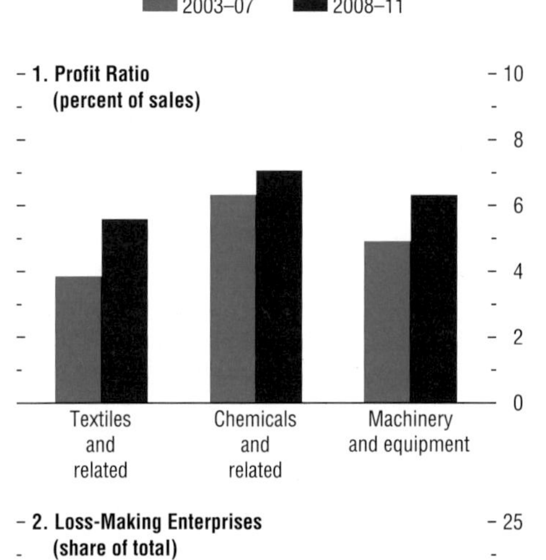

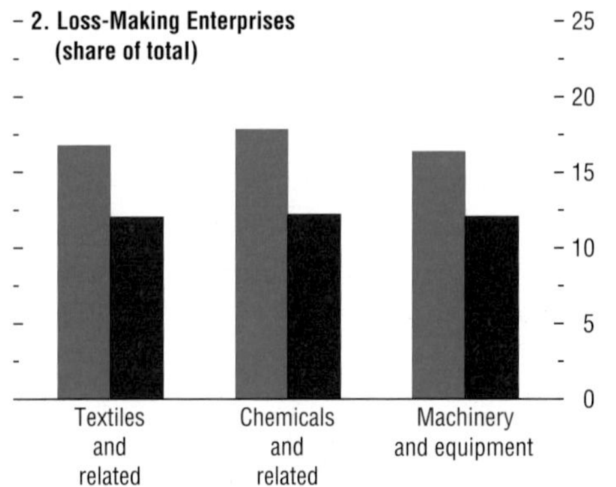

Source: IMF staff calculations.

Rising domestic costs are also cited as a reason for the decline in China's trade surplus. There is significant anecdotal evidence of rising costs, and official data suggest that nominal wages have been rising at about 15 percent a year. At the same time, the renminbi has been appreciating in real, trade-weighted terms (14¾ percent between April 2008 and the end of 2011). However, there is not yet strong evidence suggesting that these rising costs are making a large impact on competitiveness. Indeed, profit margins have been rising, and there has been a decline in the share of loss-making enterprises across a range of industries (Figure 1.3.3.). Several developments have contained the impact of rising domestic costs and facilitated productivity improvements, including relocation of industries away from the coastal provinces to lower-cost inland areas, economies of scale associated with a growing domestic market, and the continuing low cost of key inputs (land, water, energy, capital).

How much has each of these factors contributed to the observed decline in China's current account surplus? There is no easy answer to this question because all factors are interrelated and influenced by other developments. Their individual contributions are therefore difficult to identify precisely. Nevertheless, illustrative IMF staff calculations using simplifying assumptions can shed some light on this question. The calculations compare actual developments against a counterfactual scenario for

Box 1.3. *(continued)*

Table 1.3.1. Estimated Contributions to Decline in China's Current Account Surplus, 2007–11[1]
(Percent of GDP)

	Estimated Trade Elasticities[2]	Reduced-Form Current Account Equation
Actual 2007	10.1	10.1
Actual 2011[3]	2.8	2.8
Change, 2007–11	–7.3	–7.3
Contributing Factors		
Terms of Trade	–1.6	–3.6
Foreign Demand	–1.1	–1.4
Investment	–1.8	–2.6
Real Effective Exchange Rate	–2.1	–1.3
Others	–0.8	1.5

Source: IMF staff calculations.
[1]See Ahuja and others (forthcoming).
[2]Elasticities based on estimated calculations for exports and imports of goods and services.
[3]Preliminary.

the four key variables and are based on two different approaches to obtain the relevant elasticities.[2] The counterfactual scenario assumes that growth in China's trading partners remains at potential during 2007–11, that the real exchange rate stays constant, and that China's terms of trade and investment-to-GDP ratio remain at their 2007 levels. The calculations suggest that the terms-of-trade decline caused between one-fifth and two-fifths of the decline in the current account surplus over the past four years (Table 1.3.1). The acceleration in investment accounted for one-quarter to one-third of the decline, while the appreciation of the currency contributed between one-fifth and one-third. Below-potential growth in partner countries had a slightly smaller effect. Overall, the conclusion is that growing domestic investment, worsening terms of trade, weakening external demand, and a rising real effective exchange rate (REER) explain a large share of the postcrisis decline in the current account surplus. That said, these calculations are based on a partial equilibrium approach and therefore must be interpreted with some caution, in particular because they do not account for feedback effects between the various factors (such as linkages between high investment in China and rising global commodity prices).

[2]Again see Ahuja and others (forthcoming).

Figure 1.3.4. China's Current Account Balance as a Share of World GDP, 2006–17
(Percent of world nominal GDP)

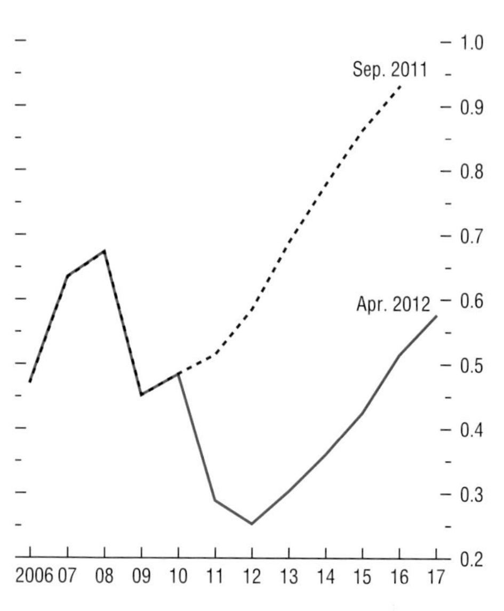

Source: IMF staff estimates.

The forecast in this issue of the *World Economic Outlook* projects another rise in China's current account surplus—but at most to about 4 to 4½ percent of GDP by 2017, a much smaller external imbalance than in previous forecasts. However, China will still account for a rising share of the overall global current account surplus as its economy grows (Figure 1.3.4). These projections assume that many of the recent shifts underpinning the current account reversal will persist. In particular, the terms of trade are assumed to deteriorate steadily (by ½ percent a year) and the investment ratio to remain close to current levels while the rebalancing toward consumption gradually gains traction. China also is assumed to gain global market share at the same average pace as over the past decade. The projections are also based on the

Box 1.3. *(concluded)*

Figure 1.3.5. Change in China's Global Market Share, 2001–10
(Change from previous year; percentage points)

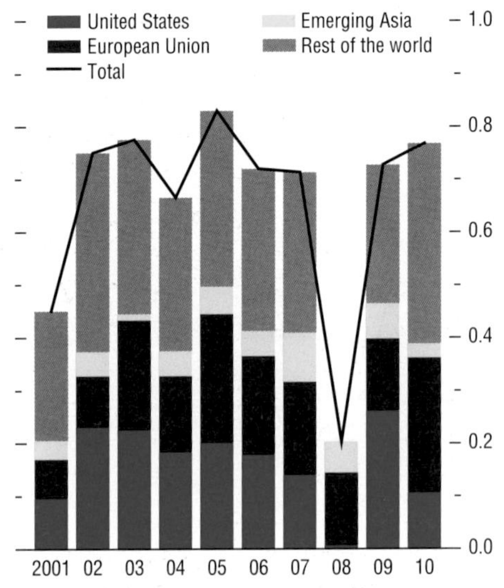

Source: IMF staff calculations.
Note: The 27 EU member countries are listed in Table C of the Statistical Appendix.

usual WEO assumption that the REER will remain at the level prevailing when the current WEO forecasts were prepared. Under these conditions, net exports will likely improve in real terms as global demand recovers, but the current account surplus is not expected to rise to anywhere near the levels recorded before the Great Recession.

The downside risks to the current account projections are considerable. They are tied in part to the global outlook but also to uncertainty about the pace of structural change in China's economy. The rapid growth of China's export market share during the past decade was the result of a variety of factors that have largely run their course, including the beneficial impact of World Trade Organization accession, strong growth in manufacturing productivity, large-scale relocation of global production facilities to China, and low production costs (Figure 1.3.5). Continued export growth will involve a shifting product mix toward higher-end manufacturing, a process that will face headwinds from the slow recovery in global demand. In addition, existing markets will become saturated, there will be fewer opportunities for productivity gains from technology transfer, and fewer overseas production facilities will relocate to China.

In conclusion, the decline in China's external surplus has been sizable and has contributed to a changing constellation of global imbalances. However, this adjustment has largely been the result of very high levels of investment. Available official data on consumption and saving, which cover the period until the end of 2010, do not yet indicate that domestic consumption is rising as a share of GDP or that national saving is falling. The policy thrust of the 12th Five-Year Plan, however, is focused on raising household income, boosting consumption, and facilitating expansion of the service sector. If these ongoing structural reforms are implemented, China has the potential for domestic consumption, rather than investment, to drive future declines in its current account surplus. This would ultimately be a more lasting transformation that would increase the welfare of the Chinese people and contribute significantly to strong, sustained, and balanced global growth.

References

Acemoglu, Daron, and David Autor, 2011, "Skills, Tasks and Technologies: Implications for Employment and Earnings," in *Handbook of Labor Economics,* Vol. 4, ed. by Orley Ashenfelter and David E. Card (Amsterdam: Elsevier).

Acharya, Viral, Lars Lochstoer, and Tarun Ramadorai, 2010, "Limits to Arbitrage and Hedging: Evidence from Commodity Markets" (unpublished; New York: New York University).

Ahuja, Ashvin, Rudolf Bems, Nigel Andrew Chalk, Malhar Nabar, Papa M'B. P. N'Diaye, and Nathaniel John Porter, forthcoming, "An End to Global Imbalances? A View from China," IMF Working Paper (Washington: International Monetary Fund).

Alquist, Ron, Lutz Kilian, and Robert Vigfusson, 2011, "Forecasting the Price of Oil," Working Paper No. 2011-15 (Ottawa: Bank of Canada).

Asdrubali, Pierfederico, Bent Sorensen, and Oved Yosha, 1996, "Channels of Interstate Risk Sharing: United States 1963–90," *Quarterly Journal of Economics*, Vol. 111, pp. 1081–110.

Atkinson, Tony, Thomas Piketty, and Emmanuel Saez, 2011, "Top Incomes in the Long Run of History," *Journal of Economic Literature*, Vol. 49, No. 1, pp. 3–71.

Bai, Jushan, and Serena Ng, 2002, "Determining the Number of Factors in Approximate Factor Models," *Econometrica*, Vol. 70, No. 1, pp. 191–221.

———, 2007, "Determining the Number of Primitive Shocks in Factor Models," *Journal of Business and Economics Statistics*, Vol. 25, pp. 52–60.

Berg, Andrew, and Jonathan Ostry, 2011, "Inequality and Unsustainable Growth: Two Sides of the Same Coin?" IMF Staff Discussion Note No. 11/08 (Washington: International Monetary Fund).

Bloom, Nicholas, 2009, "The Impact of Uncertainty Shocks," *Econometrica*, Vol. 77, No. 3, pp. 623–85.

Claessens, Stijn, M. Ayhan Kose, and Marco E. Terrones, forthcoming, "How do Business and Financial Cycles Interact?" *Journal of International Economics*.

Coenen, Günter, Christopher J. Erceg, Charles Freedman, Davide Ferceri, Michael Kumhof, René Lalonde, Douglas Laxton, Jesper Lindé, Annabelle Mourougane, Dirk Muir, Susanna Mursula, Carlos de Resende, John Roberts, Werner Roeger, Stephen Snudden, Mathias Trabandt, and Jan in 't Veld, 2012, "Effects of Fiscal Stimulus in Structural Models," *American Economic Journal*, Vol. 4, No. 1, pp. 22–68.

Dao, Mai, and Prakash Loungani, 2010, "The Human Cost of Recessions: Assessing It, Reducing It," IMF Staff Position Note No. 10/17 (Washington: International Monetary Fund).

Decressin, Jörg, and Douglas Laxton, 2009, "Gauging Risks for Deflation," IMF Staff Position Note No. 09/01 (Washington: International Monetary Fund).

Elekdag, Selim, and Prakash Kannan, 2009, "Incorporating Market Information into the Construction of the Fan Chart," IMF Working Paper No. 09/178 (Washington: International Monetary Fund).

Etula, Erkko, 2009, "Broker-Dealer Risk Appetite and Commodity Returns," Staff Report No. 406 (New York: Federal Reserve Bank).

Harding, Don, and Adrian Pagan, 2002, "Dissecting the Cycle: A Methodological Investigation, *Journal of Monetary Economics,* Vol. 49, No. 2, pp. 365–81.

Kose, M. Ayhan, Prakash Loungani, and Marco E. Terrones, 2009, "Out of the Ballpark," *Finance & Development,* Vol. 46, No. 2, pp. 25–28.

Kose, M. Ayhan, Christopher Otrok, and Eswar Prasad, forthcoming, "Global Business Cycles: Convergence or Decoupling?" *International Economic Review.*

Kumar, Manmohan S., 2003, *Deflation: Determinants, Risks, and Policy Options,* IMF Occasional Paper No. 221 (Washington: International Monetary Fund).

Lee, Jaewoo, Gian Maria Milesi-Ferretti, Jonathan Ostry, Alessandro Prati, and Luca Antonio Ricci, 2008, *Exchange Rate Assessments: CGER Methodologies,* IMF Occasional Paper No. 261 (Washington: International Monetary Fund).

Loungani, Prakash, 2012, "Unemployment through the Prism of the Great Recession," *IMF Research Bulletin* (March).

Mendoza, Enrique, and Marco E. Terrones, forthcoming, "An Anatomy of Credit Booms and Their Demise," ed. by Carmen Reinhart and Miguel Fuentes, *Capital Mobility and Monetary Policy.*

Rajan, Raghuram G., 2010, *Fault Lines: How Hidden Fractures Still Threaten the World Economy* (Princeton, New Jersey: Princeton University Press).

CHAPTER 2

COUNTRY AND REGIONAL PERSPECTIVES

The world economy has changed dramatically since September 2011. European growth has slowed sharply, and many economies in the region are now in or close to recession. In the Middle East and North Africa (MENA), unrest has spread, further depressing the outlook for the region even as some economies rebuild after earlier conflicts. In other regions, however, developments have been more positive. The United States has seen a spate of encouraging economic news, with growth increasing and unemployment falling. Asia has weathered the global slowdown well and looks headed for a soft landing. Latin America has shown resilience to the swings in risk aversion flowing from European developments over recent months. Finally, sub-Saharan Africa (SSA) has been surprisingly resilient to the European slowdown, reflecting an ongoing redirection of its economic linkages toward Asia.

While growth prospects in much of the world have been marked down since the September 2011 *World Economic Outlook*, they are expected to improve in the latter half of 2012 as a result of the combined policy measures taken across developed and emerging market economies. These developments are reflected in Figure 2.1, which shows revisions to the 2012 growth forecasts relative to the September 2011 *World Economic Outlook*. Revisions to the outlook have generally been negative, but to varying degrees. And the revisions partly reflect spillovers from the deterioration of prospects in Europe—the scatterplot shows that economies with the strongest trade ties to Europe have generally seen the largest downgrades. We return to this theme of spillovers throughout the chapter. To set the scene for the discussion of spillovers, Figure 2.2 shows the average effects of the euro area crisis scenario discussed in Chapter 1 on each of the regions considered in this chapter. This scenario models the likely effects of an intensification of the euro area crisis—a sharp drop in risk appetite, asset and commodity prices, and global demand. While Europe is obviously the region most strongly affected, the pattern of spillovers is varied, with the strength of trade

Figure 2.1. Revisions to 2012 WEO Growth Projections and Trade Linkages with Europe[1]

Revisions to the outlook have generally been downward, but to varying degrees. And the revisions partly reflect spillovers from the deterioration of prospects in Europe—economies that have the strongest trade ties with Europe have generally seen the largest downgrades.

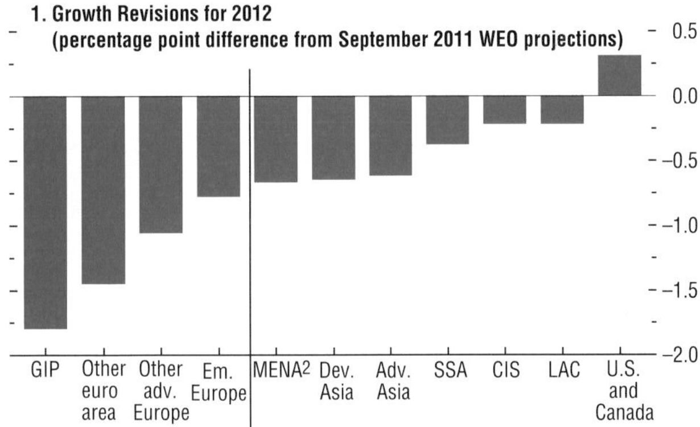

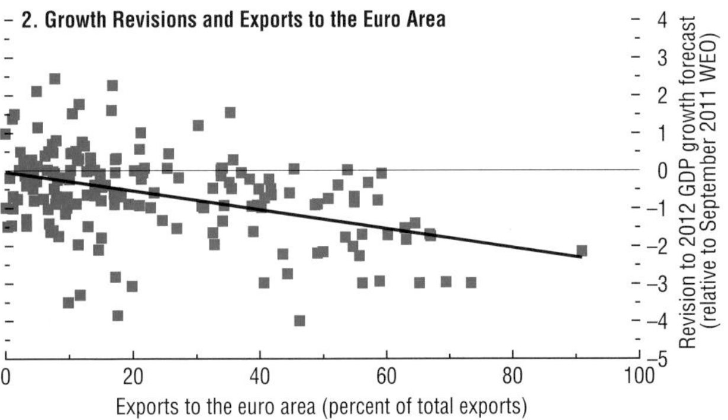

Sources: IMF, *Direction of Trade Statistics;* and IMF staff estimates.
[1]Adv. Asia: advanced Asia; CIS: Commonwealth of Independent States; Dev. Asia: developing Asia; Em. Europe: emerging Europe; GIP: Greece, Ireland, Portugal; LAC: Latin America and the Caribbean; MENA: Middle East and North Africa; Other adv. Europe: Czech Republic, Denmark, Iceland, Norway, Sweden, Switzerland, United Kingdom; Other euro area: Austria, Belgium, Cyprus, Estonia, Finland, France, Germany, Italy, Luxembourg, Malta, Netherlands, Slovak Republic, Slovenia, Spain; SSA: sub-Saharan Africa.
[2]Excludes Libya and Syrian Arab Republic. Excludes South Sudan after July 9, 2011.

Figure 2.2. The Effects of an Intensified Euro Area Crisis on Various Regions
(Peak deviation of output from WEO baseline)

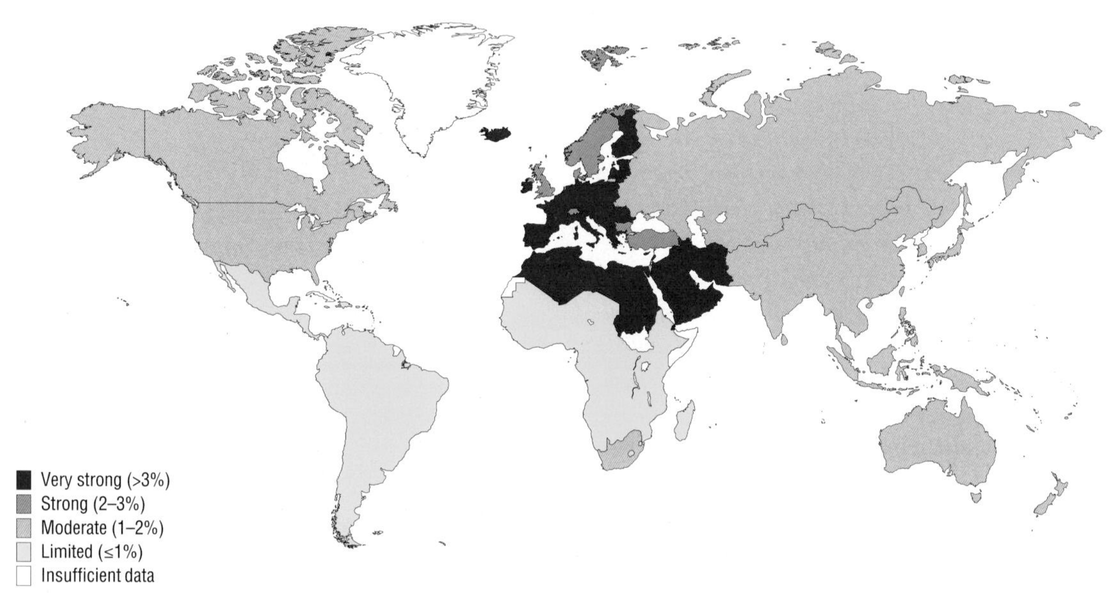

Source: IMF staff estimates.
Note: Peak deviation of output from the WEO baseline under the first downside scenario described in Chapter 1 (increased bank and sovereign stress in the euro area). Simulations were conducted using the IMF's Global Economic Model, which is a six-region model (supplemented with satellite models) that does not explicitly model individual countries (except the United States and Japan).

ties, financial market linkages, and euro area bank exposures all playing a role. These individual channels, and their regional expression, are discussed in more detail in the sections below.

The chapter begins with a detailed discussion of the outlook for Europe, including intraregional spillovers from the periphery to the core of the euro area and from the euro area to the rest of Europe. The remaining sections discuss the outlook for the United States and Canada, Asia, Latin America and the Caribbean (LAC), the Commonwealth of Independent States (CIS), the Middle East and North Africa, and sub-Saharan Africa.

Europe: Crisis, Recession, and Contagion

In the last quarter of 2011, renewed fears that the euro area crisis would escalate and spread led to another bout of uncertainty and widening risk spreads that contributed to an unexpectedly sharp slowing in the euro area, with spillovers to the rest of Europe and beyond. The European Central Bank (ECB) alleviated funding pressure in the banking sector through longer-term refinancing operations (LTROs). These measures, in combination with steps toward strengthening the fiscal compact, structural reforms, and fiscal consolidation, succeeded in stabilizing market sentiment and lowering uncertainty. The recent decision to enhance the European firewall reinforces these policy efforts. The baseline outlook is for a gradual return to recovery through 2012–13. The possibility that the crisis will escalate again remains a major downside risk to growth and financial sector stability until the underlying issues are resolved.

Real activity in Europe slowed by more than expected during the fourth quarter of 2011, with output contracting in many economies. As a result, downward revisions to 2012 growth relative to the September 2011 *World Economic Outlook* are generally larger for Europe than for other regions (Figures 2.1 and 2.3).

The unexpectedly strong slowdown was importantly driven by a spike in perceived risks about growth prospects, competitiveness, and sovereign solvency in crisis-hit periphery countries and Italy. The banking sector has played a key role in transmitting this shock throughout the region.

Figure 2.3. Europe: Revisions to 2012 GDP Growth Forecasts
(Change in percentage points from September 2011 WEO projections)

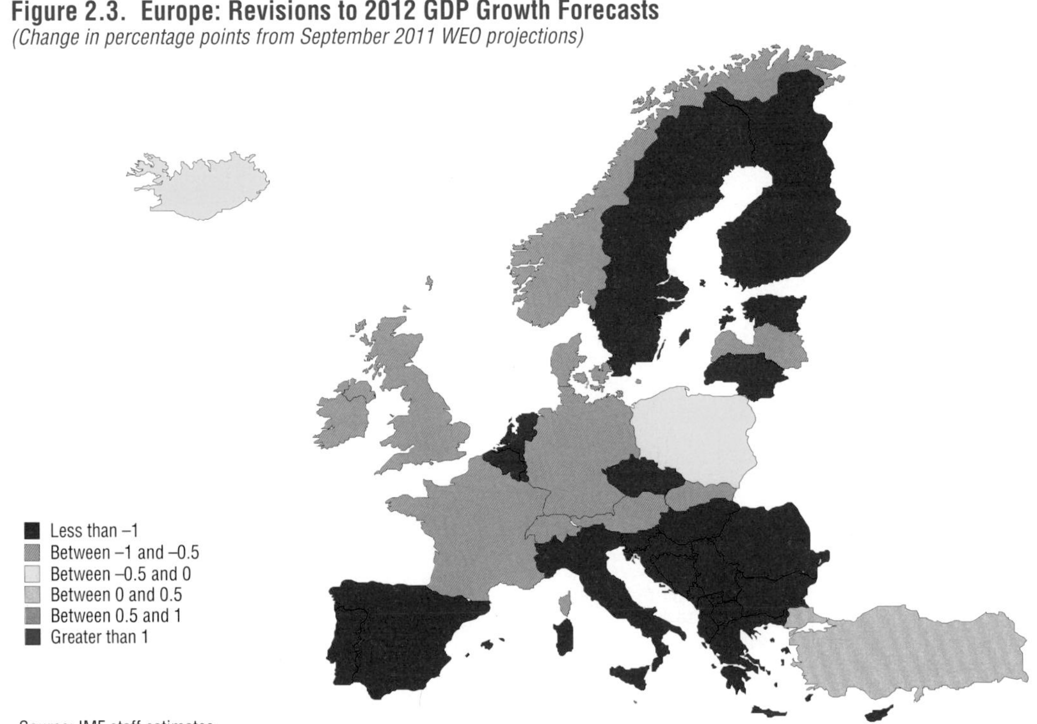

Source: IMF staff estimates.

Because of banks' holdings of government bonds, the elevation of perceived sovereign risks triggered renewed funding pressures and increased yields and risk premiums. As a result, balance sheet deleveraging accelerated during the second half of 2011, as detailed in the Spillover Feature later in this chapter. This process amounted, in effect, to a bank credit supply shock that contributed to slower growth or outright declines in credit to the private sector. The link between euro area bank deleveraging and credit growth had an important cross-border dimension, notably in eastern Europe (Box 2.1).

The extent to which these broad trends slowed growth in individual European economies reflects both their exposure to crisis conditions and underlying shocks and their initial conditions, especially with respect to fiscal positions and financial sector fragility. Among euro area members, growth divergences are wider than during the 2003–08 expansion (Figure 2.4). Greece, Ireland, and Portugal remain at the heart of the crisis. Its intensification during the fall most strongly affected Italy and, to a lesser extent, Spain, where economic activity contracted markedly in the fourth quarter. In other European economies, inside and outside the euro area, activity weakened, dipping into or stopping just short of mild recession territory.

The situation stabilized since early January, with improving financial market sentiment and encouraging signals for activity. In bond markets, sovereign yield spreads against German bunds retreated from their recent highs, except for the economies in crisis. This improvement reflects the success of the ECB's three-year LTROs in mid-December in reducing liquidity-related solvency risks for euro area banks, reforms and new consolidation measures, and upside surprises to activity in other regions, notably the United States.

Near-term prospects and risks for Europe depend importantly on the course of events in the euro area. The *World Economic Outlook* (WEO) baseline projections assume that policymakers succeed in containing the sovereign crisis through continued crisis management and further advancing measures toward its resolution. Volatility and sovereign

Figure 2.4. Europe: Back in Recession[1]

Europe tipped back into recession, resulting from renewed escalation of perceived euro area crisis risks in late 2011. The aggregate masks growth divergences in the region, with sharp recessions forecast for the euro area crisis economies. Strong regional trade and financial linkages imply a weaker outlook for the rest of Europe as well. Credit conditions are weak and may tighten further. Inflation is expected to retreat throughout the region, as domestic demand remains weak.

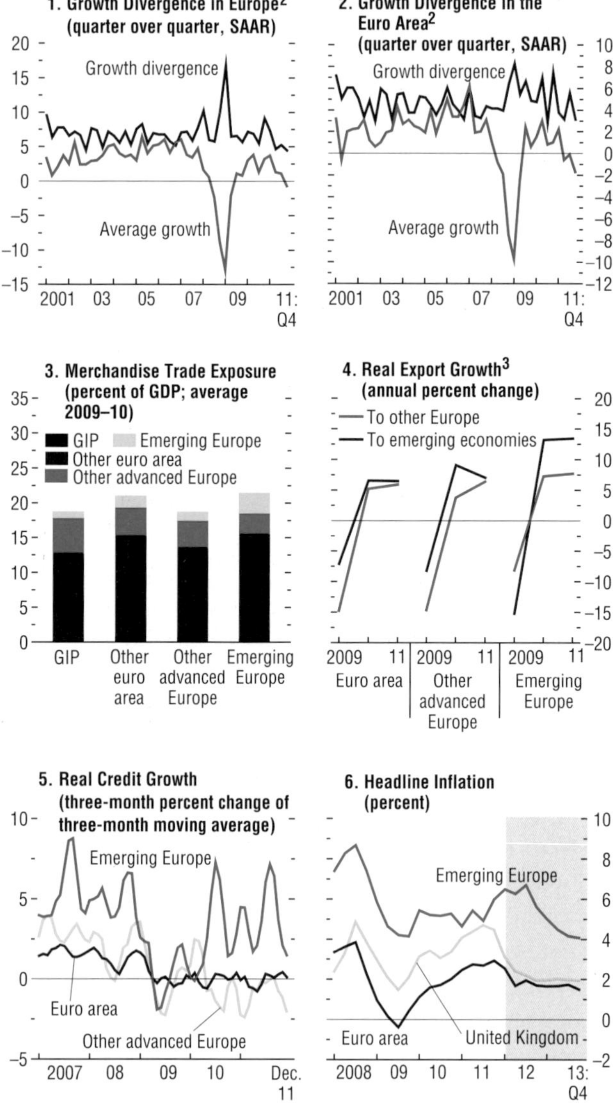

Sources: IMF, *Direction of Trade Statistics;* IMF, *International Financial Statistics* (IFS); and IMF staff estimates.

[1]GIP: Greece, Ireland, Portugal. Other advanced Europe: Czech Republic, Denmark, Iceland, Norway, Sweden, Switzerland, United Kingdom. Emerging Europe: Albania, Bosnia and Herzegovina, Bulgaria, Croatia, Hungary, Kosovo, Latvia, Lithuania, former Yugoslav Republic of Macedonia, Montenegro, Poland, Romania, Serbia, Turkey.

[2]Growth divergence is 85th percentile growth minus 15th percentile growth. SAAR: seasonally adjusted annual rate.

[3]Nominal trade values are deflated using world export price deflators from the IFS database. The country composition of "other Europe" differs for each export group and consists of all European economies not in that export group. Export growth for 2011 is calculated as year-over-year growth from November 2010 through November 2011.

yields are expected to normalize further after recent improvements, although greater fiscal consolidation will weigh on growth in some cases.

In this baseline, economic growth in Europe is expected to strengthen during the course of 2012. Annual growth will be ¼ percent in 2012, markedly weaker than in 2011 (2 percent), largely because of the negative carryover from the second half of 2011. The divergence in growth performance among European economies is expected to narrow in the baseline, although prospects still vary considerably for 2012–13 (Table 2.1).

- In the euro area, real GDP is projected to contract at an annual rate of ½ percent in the first half of 2012 and to start recovering thereafter. The recession is expected to be shallow and short-lived in many economies—confidence and financial conditions have already improved, and external demand from other regions will likely strengthen. In contrast, in Greece and Portugal, where adjustment under joint EU/IMF programs continues, and in Italy and Spain, where yield spreads remain elevated despite stepped-up fiscal efforts, the recessions will be deeper and recovery is expected to start only in 2013.
- Growth in other advanced economies in Europe is projected to rebound during 2012, largely on improving global demand and strengthening prospects in the euro area core. Many of these economies avoided large precrisis imbalances, and balance sheet pressure on households and governments has been weaker. This has helped cushion the spillovers from the euro area crisis. In contrast, growth in the United Kingdom, where the financial sector was hit hard by the global crisis, will be weak in early 2012, before recovering there as well.
- Near-term growth prospects in emerging Europe will be closely tied to developments in the euro area core. Under the baseline, much of the spillover from the euro area slowdown in late 2011 will already have been absorbed, and trade growth and manufacturing activity are expected to pick up, both in the euro area and globally, through 2012. However, tighter funding as a result of deleveraging by euro area parent banks is likely to weigh on credit growth.

Inflation in many economies moderated during the second half of 2011 and is expected to remain

Table 2.1. Selected European Economies: Real GDP, Consumer Prices, Current Account Balance, and Unemployment

(Annual percent change unless noted otherwise)

	Real GDP			Consumer Prices[1]			Current Account Balance[2]			Unemployment[3]		
		Projections			Projections			Projections			Projections	
	2011	2012	2013	2011	2012	2013	2011	2012	2013	2011	2012	2013
Europe	**2.0**	**0.2**	**1.4**	**3.2**	**2.7**	**2.2**	**0.5**	**0.6**	**0.8**	...	...	...
Advanced Europe	**1.4**	**–0.1**	**1.1**	**2.8**	**2.1**	**1.7**	**1.1**	**1.3**	**1.5**	**9.4**	**10.0**	**9.9**
Euro Area[4,5]	1.4	–0.3	0.9	2.7	2.0	1.6	–0.3	0.7	1.0	10.1	10.9	10.8
Germany	3.1	0.6	1.5	2.5	1.9	1.8	5.7	5.2	4.9	6.0	5.6	5.5
France	1.7	0.5	1.0	2.3	2.0	1.6	–2.2	–1.9	–1.5	9.7	9.9	10.1
Italy	0.4	–1.9	–0.3	2.9	2.5	1.8	–3.2	–2.2	–1.5	8.4	9.5	9.7
Spain	0.7	–1.8	0.1	3.1	1.9	1.6	–3.7	–2.1	–1.7	21.6	24.2	23.9
Netherlands	1.3	–0.5	0.8	2.5	1.8	1.8	7.5	8.2	7.8	4.5	5.5	5.5
Belgium	1.9	0.0	0.8	3.5	2.4	1.9	–0.1	–0.3	0.4	7.2	8.0	8.3
Austria	3.1	0.9	1.8	3.6	2.2	1.9	1.2	1.4	1.4	4.2	4.4	4.3
Greece	–6.9	–4.7	0.0	3.1	–0.5	–0.3	–9.7	–7.4	–6.6	17.3	19.4	19.4
Portugal	–1.5	–3.3	0.3	3.6	3.2	1.4	–6.4	–4.2	–3.5	12.7	14.4	14.0
Finland	2.9	0.6	1.8	3.3	2.9	2.1	–0.7	–1.0	–0.3	7.8	7.7	7.8
Ireland	0.7	0.5	2.0	1.1	1.7	1.2	0.1	1.0	1.7	14.4	14.5	13.8
Slovak Republic	3.3	2.4	3.1	4.1	3.8	2.3	0.1	–0.4	–0.4	13.4	13.8	13.6
Slovenia	–0.2	–1.0	1.4	1.8	2.2	1.8	–1.1	0.0	–0.3	8.1	8.7	8.9
Luxembourg	1.0	–0.2	1.9	3.4	2.3	1.6	6.9	5.7	5.6	6.0	6.0	6.0
Estonia	7.6	2.0	3.6	5.1	3.9	2.6	3.2	0.9	–0.3	12.5	11.3	10.0
Cyprus	0.5	–1.2	0.8	3.5	2.8	2.2	–8.5	–6.2	–6.3	7.8	9.5	9.6
Malta	2.1	1.2	2.0	2.4	2.0	1.9	–3.2	–3.0	–2.9	6.4	6.6	6.5
United Kingdom[5]	0.7	0.8	2.0	4.5	2.4	2.0	–1.9	–1.7	–1.1	8.0	8.3	8.2
Sweden	4.0	0.9	2.3	1.4	2.5	2.0	6.7	3.0	2.9	7.5	7.5	7.7
Switzerland	1.9	0.8	1.7	0.2	–0.5	0.5	14.0	12.1	11.6	3.1	3.4	3.6
Czech Republic	1.7	0.1	2.1	1.9	3.5	1.9	–2.9	–2.1	–1.9	6.7	7.0	7.4
Norway	1.7	1.8	2.0	1.3	1.5	2.0	14.6	14.8	13.7	3.3	3.6	3.5
Denmark	1.0	0.5	1.2	2.8	2.6	2.2	6.2	4.8	4.5	6.1	5.8	5.5
Iceland	3.1	2.4	2.6	4.0	4.8	3.5	–6.5	–2.8	–1.5	7.4	6.3	6.0
Emerging Europe[6]	**5.3**	**1.9**	**2.9**	**5.3**	**6.2**	**4.5**	**–6.0**	**–5.6**	**–5.5**	...	...	...
Turkey	8.5	2.3	3.2	6.5	10.6	7.1	–9.9	–8.8	–8.2	9.9	10.3	10.5
Poland	4.3	2.6	3.2	4.3	3.8	2.7	–4.3	–4.5	–4.3	9.6	9.4	9.1
Romania	2.5	1.5	3.0	5.8	2.9	3.1	–4.2	–4.2	–4.7	7.2	7.2	7.1
Hungary	1.7	0.0	1.8	3.9	5.2	3.5	1.6	3.3	1.2	11.0	11.5	11.0
Bulgaria	1.7	0.8	1.5	3.4	2.1	2.3	1.9	2.1	1.6	12.5	12.5	12.0
Serbia	1.8	0.5	3.0	11.2	4.1	4.3	–9.1	–8.6	–7.9	23.7	23.9	23.6
Croatia	0.0	–0.5	1.0	2.3	2.2	2.4	0.9	0.4	–0.2	13.2	13.5	12.7
Lithuania	5.9	2.0	2.7	4.1	3.1	2.5	–1.7	–2.0	–2.3	15.5	14.5	13.0
Latvia	5.5	2.0	2.5	4.2	2.6	2.2	–1.2	–1.9	–2.5	15.6	15.5	14.6

[1]Movements in consumer prices are shown as annual averages. December–December changes can be found in Tables A6 and A7 in the Statistical Appendix.

[2]Percent of GDP.

[3]Percent. National definitions of unemployment may differ.

[4]Current account position corrected for reporting discrepancies in intra-area transactions.

[5]Based on Eurostat's harmonized index of consumer prices.

[6]Also includes Albania, Bosnia and Herzegovina, Kosovo, former Yugoslav Republic of Macedonia, and Montenegro.

well contained, given the slowdown in activity and declines in commodity prices. Where inflation either increased or remained above target, the causes were primarily one-time factors such as increases in energy prices and indirect taxes.

The balance of risks to Europe's near-term growth prospects remains to the downside. Despite the progress in strengthening crisis management in recent months, a renewed escalation of the euro crisis remains a possibility as long as the underlying issues are not resolved. Because most economies in the region are in close orbit, the pull from tight trade and financial linkages means that the possible escalation of the euro area crisis remains the most important downside risk.

Figure 2.5. Trade and Financial Linkages with the Euro Area[1]

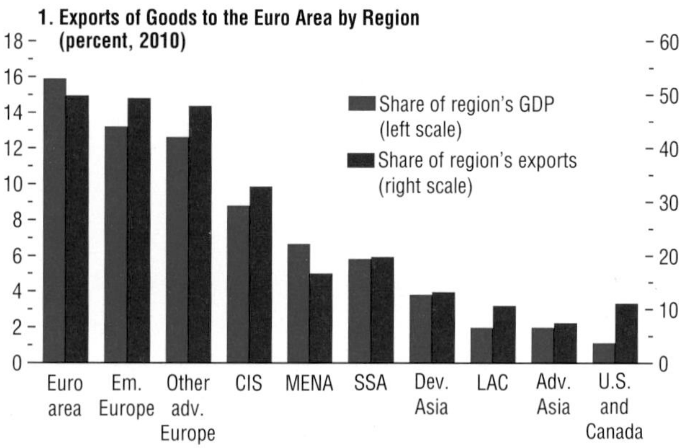

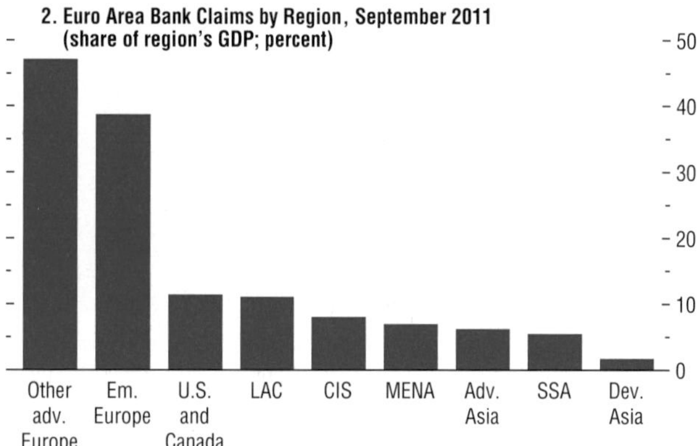

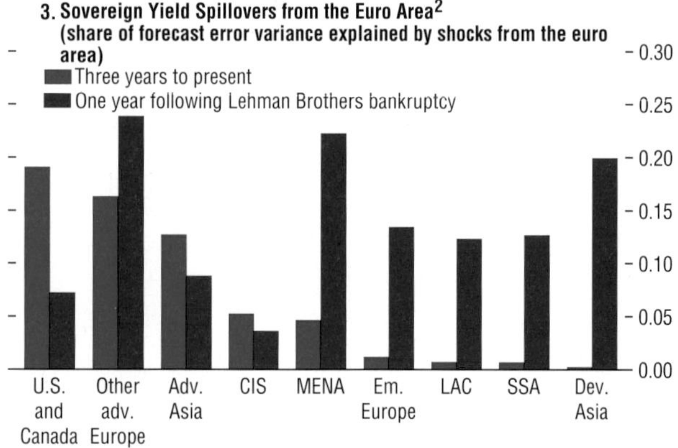

Sources: Bank for International Settlements; IMF, *Direction of Trade Statistics;* and IMF staff calculations.

[1]Adv. Asia: advanced Asia; CIS: Commonwealth of Independent States; Dev. Asia: developing Asia; Em. Europe: emerging Europe; LAC: Latin America and the Caribbean; MENA: Middle East and North Africa; Other adv. Europe: Czech Republic, Denmark, Iceland, Norway, Sweden, Switzerland, United Kingdom; SSA: sub-Saharan Africa.

[2]Spillover indices using the Diebold and Yilmaz (2012) methodology, applied to daily changes in long-term sovereign yields for various regions.

Spillovers from the Euro Area to Other Regions

If the euro area crisis escalates, adverse feedback loops between rising funding pressure in the banking system, increasing fiscal vulnerability, and slowing aggregate demand could start anew. The model simulations underlying the euro area downside scenario described in Chapter 1 and presented in Figure 2.2 illustrate how an escalation of the crisis could play out. First, financial market comovement could increase to much higher levels, such as those seen during 2008–09, with rising yields and risk premiums. Second, the spike in uncertainty and global risk aversion could lead to deterioration in confidence, immediately dampening domestic demand. In addition, international trade (particularly in durables) would decline by more than overall output, which could negatively affect export-oriented economies. Third, oil and other commodity prices would likely decline, affecting commodity-exporting regions.

The impact of the spillovers also depends on exposure. For many countries, the strongest links to Europe are through trade. Panel 1 of Figure 2.5 shows the relative importance of exports to the euro area for each region. Trade linkages are strongest within Europe (both within the euro area and with advanced and emerging European economies outside the euro area). Outside the continent, trade linkages are strongest with the CIS, followed by the MENA and SSA regions; they are relatively small for Asia, Latin America, and the United States.

Exposures through financial linkages have been more limited, except through the role of euro area banks and their central and eastern European subsidiaries (Figure 2.5, panel 2; Spillover Feature; Chapter 1 of the April 2012 *Global Financial Stability Report*). Panel 3 of Figure 2.5 shows that financial market spillovers from Europe have been relatively small—accounting for less than one-fifth of the variation in other regions' financial market movements—and these spillovers are in general smaller than from U.S. financial markets. Nevertheless, during periods of intense financial stress, such as after the bankruptcy of Lehman Brothers in 2008, financial spillovers could strengthen.

Policy Challenges

The overarching policy priority in Europe is to prevent further escalation of the sovereign debt and growth crisis in the euro area while working toward resolution of the underlying causes. This requires policy adjustment in a number of areas at both the country and the euro area levels. Most economies in the region need a policy mix that supports the recovery while addressing fiscal sustainability challenges and financial sector vulnerabilities.

Appropriate fiscal consolidation is an obvious priority. Euro area economies in crisis and countries with weaker fiscal positions (Italy, Slovenia) need to implement recently agreed plans to tighten the fiscal stance. Spain's new deficit target aims for a large consolidation, which is broadly appropriate, although it could have accommodated more fully the impact of the weak growth outlook. Many other euro area economies, however, should allow automatic stabilizers to operate freely to prevent still-weak activity and downside risks from dampening market confidence about growth prospects. Those with room for fiscal policy maneuvering, in terms of the strength of their fiscal accounts and their credibility with markets, should consider slowing the pace of fiscal consolidation and focusing on measures aimed at enhancing medium-term debt sustainability (Germany). In advanced economies outside the euro area, market pressure has generally remained benign and sovereign funding costs are low, so automatic stabilizers should not be constrained. In addition, some advanced economies in Europe have appropriately allowed the pace of structural fiscal adjustment to slow. Further slowing could be considered if economic conditions deteriorate. In emerging Europe, the need for fiscal consolidation varies widely; economies that have faced increased market pressure and rising yields in recent months must continue with steady consolidation (Hungary).

Given the broad need for fiscal adjustment, much of the burden of supporting growth falls on monetary policy. The policy stance should generally remain accommodative, given downside risks to growth and little danger of inflation pressure in the near term. The ECB should lower its policy rate while continuing to use unconventional policies to address banks' funding and liquidity problems. Central banks in many other advanced economies in Europe have little or no scope for easing through conventional means and must support the recovery using unconventional policies. In the United Kingdom, with inflation expected to fall below the 2 percent target amid weaker growth and commodity prices, the Bank of England can further ease its monetary policy stance. In emerging Europe, inflation pressure is set to decline rapidly in many countries, giving central banks new room for easing.

Structural reforms to boost growth are also needed urgently given that the sovereign risks at the heart of the current crisis are partly related to growth prospects—or lack thereof. Product and labor market reforms can boost productivity, and they are paramount in economies with competitiveness problems and internal or external imbalances. When implemented, they can support market confidence and the sustainability of fiscal positions.

Forestalling further escalation of the crisis also requires intervention along two dimensions at the euro area level. First, crisis management facilities need to be strong. In this respect, the recent decision to combine the European Stability Mechanism (ESM) with the European Financial Stability (EFSF) is welcome and, along with other recent European efforts, will strengthen the European crisis mechanism and support the IMF's efforts to bolster the global firewall. To limit damaging deleveraging, banks need to raise capital levels, in some cases through direct government support. There is a need for a pan-euro-area facility with the capacity to take direct stakes in banks, including in countries with little fiscal room to do so themselves.

Second, as underscored in Chapter 1, over the medium term policymakers must urgently address the Economic and Monetary Union design flaws that contributed to the crisis. This is essential to the permanent restoration of market confidence. Strong mechanisms are needed to enforce responsible fiscal policies. To make the inevitable loss of national policy discretion palatable, there needs to be more fiscal risk sharing across countries, including, for example, through an expanded ESM. Other priorities are further progress in integrating financial sectors in the euro area, including through cross-border supervision, as well as resolution mechanisms and deposit insurance with a common backstop.

The United States and Canada: Regaining Some Traction

The U.S. economy has gained some traction (Figure 2.6), with growth improving through 2011 and signs of expansion in the job market. Risks to the outlook are more balanced but still tend to the downside given fiscal uncertainty, weakness in the housing market, and potential spillovers from Europe. Bold policy measures in the housing market could help accelerate the recovery. And recent changes to the communications strategy of the Federal Reserve may enhance the expansionary effect of current monetary policy settings. However, the difficulty of reaching agreement on extending temporary policy measures—such as the Bush tax cuts—and the current inability to agree on a medium-term fiscal consolidation strategy could undermine market confidence and outcomes. In Canada, the recovery is well advanced, and the economy is well positioned with room for policymakers to respond flexibly to changes in the economic outlook, including by allowing full operation of automatic fiscal stabilizers and resorting to stimulus should the recovery threaten to falter.

Growth in the United States was determined primarily by domestic factors in 2011, with the economy pulling itself up by its bootstraps—again. After a weak start, U.S. economic activity gained strength through the year, with the quarterly growth rate rising each quarter (Figure 2.7, panel 1). Inflation has been subdued recently, but higher oil prices may push up inflation in the near term. And while some job growth is evident, wage growth has been negative in real terms for the past two years and remains weak (Figure 2.7, panel 3).

Figure 2.6. United States and Canada: Revisions to 2012 GDP Growth Forecasts
(Change in percentage points from September 2011 WEO projections)

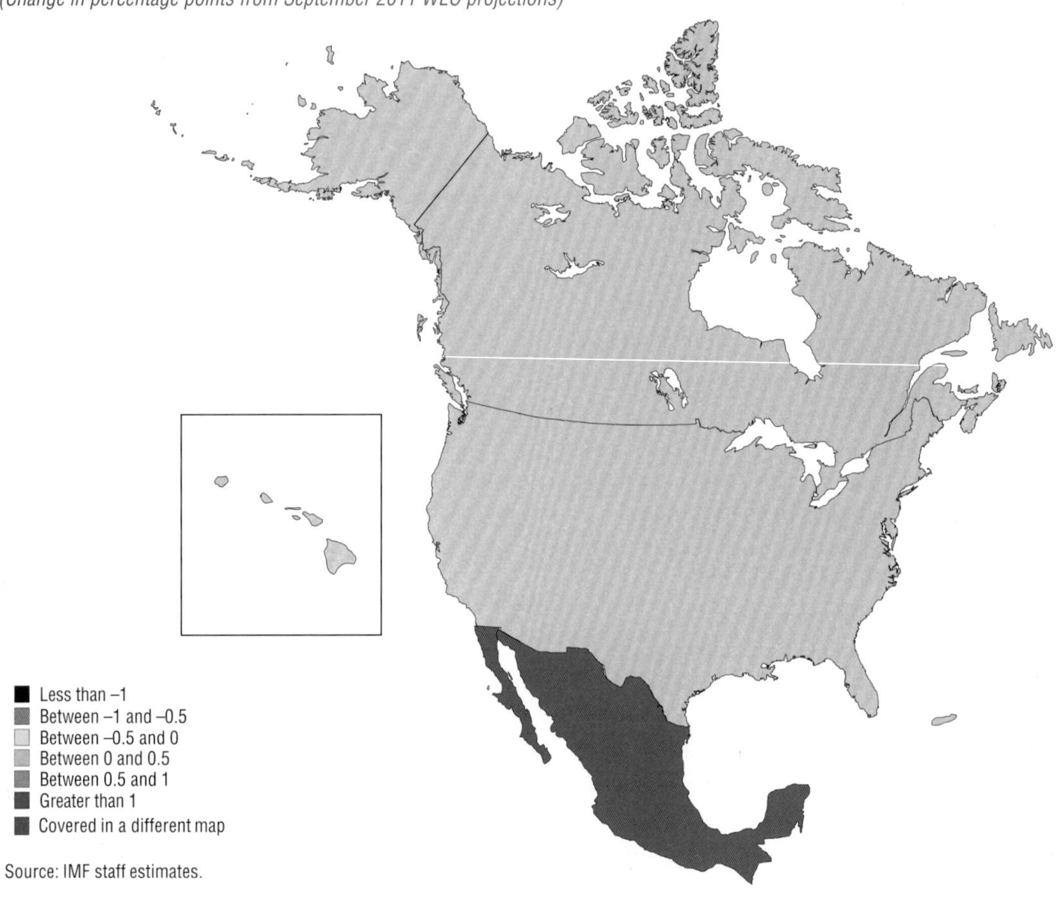

Source: IMF staff estimates.

U.S. economic growth is projected at 2 percent in 2012 and 2½ percent in 2013 (Table 2.2), reflecting ongoing weakness in house prices, pressures to deleverage, and a weak labor market. Although recent labor market outcomes have been promising, with unemployment falling to 8¼ percent in March, the outlook is for only modest increases in employment during 2012 and 2013. The persistent output gap will keep inflation in check, with headline inflation receding from 3 percent in 2011 to about 2 percent in 2012 and 2013. External factors have a relatively limited effect on the baseline outlook.

In Canada, in contrast, the determinants of growth are both external and internal—externally, world commodity prices and demand from the United States will influence growth; internally, the planned fiscal tightening and high household debt are constraints. Growth is forecast to moderate from 2½ percent in 2011 to 2 percent in 2012, reflecting retreating commodity prices, ongoing fiscal withdrawal, and slow recovery in the United States. As a result, inflation is projected to fall to the midpoint of the target band by 2013.

Downside risks to the outlook are significant. Financial market spillovers from the euro area to the United States and Canada are relatively strong, reflecting U.S. prominence as a financial center and safe haven (see Figure 2.5, panel 3). While the recent bout of concern over European sovereigns caused a flight to safety, the positive effects of this on government bond yields were offset by higher volatility and other negative effects on bank funding costs, corporate bonds, and equities. A flare-up in the euro area from increased sovereign and bank stress could easily undermine confidence in the U.S. corporate sector and thereby squeeze investment and demand, undermining growth. Modeling (see Figure 2.2) suggests that under such a scenario U.S. output could fall by 1½ percent relative to the baseline, about 40 percent of the size of the decline in Europe. A particularly strong contributor to the magnitude of this spillover is the zero lower bound on monetary policy interest rates.

Despite the importance of Europe for the external outlook, there are other, more pressing domestic sources of risk. Under current U.S. laws many tax provisions, including the tax cuts enacted under President

Figure 2.7. United States: Pulling Itself up by Its Bootstraps

Growth in the United States surprised with the quarterly pace increasing through the year. This was reflected in stronger labor market outcomes, although wage growth is still weak. The United States is facing significant policy challenges related to housing market weakness, the zero lower interest rate bound of monetary policy, and increasing government debt. Recent innovations to the Federal Reserve's communications strategy may help with the zero lower bound, but much more needs to be done on multiple fronts.

Sources: Board of Governors of the Federal Reserve; Congressional Budget Office (CBO); Haver Analytics; and IMF staff estimates.

[1]Each dot denotes the value of an individual Federal Open Market Committee (FOMC) participant's judgment of the appropriate level of the target federal funds rate at the end of the specified time period, as recorded during the January 24–25, 2012, FOMC meeting.

Table 2.2. Selected Advanced Economies: Real GDP, Consumer Prices, Current Account Balance, and Unemployment
(Annual percent change unless noted otherwise)

	Real GDP			Consumer Prices[1]			Current Account Balance[2]			Unemployment[3]		
		Projections			Projections			Projections			Projections	
	2011	2012	2013	2011	2012	2013	2011	2012	2013	2011	2012	2013
Advanced Economies	**1.6**	**1.4**	**2.0**	**2.7**	**1.9**	**1.7**	**–0.2**	**–0.4**	**–0.2**	**7.9**	**7.9**	**7.8**
United States	1.7	2.1	2.4	3.1	2.1	1.9	–3.1	–3.3	–3.1	9.0	8.2	7.9
Euro Area[4,5]	1.4	–0.3	0.9	2.7	2.0	1.6	–0.3	0.7	1.0	10.1	10.9	10.8
Japan	–0.7	2.0	1.7	–0.3	0.0	0.0	2.0	2.2	2.7	4.5	4.5	4.4
United Kingdom[4]	0.7	0.8	2.0	4.5	2.4	2.0	–1.9	–1.7	–1.1	8.0	8.3	8.2
Canada	2.5	2.1	2.2	2.9	2.2	2.0	–2.8	–2.7	–2.7	7.5	7.4	7.3
Other Advanced Economies[6]	3.2	2.6	3.5	3.0	2.5	2.5	4.9	3.4	3.1	4.5	4.5	4.5
Memorandum												
Newly Industrialized Asian Economies	4.0	3.4	4.2	3.6	2.9	2.7	6.5	5.9	5.7	3.6	3.5	3.5

[1]Movements in consumer prices are shown as annual averages. December–December changes can be found in Table A6 in the Statistical Appendix.

[2]Percent of GDP.

[3]Percent. National definitions of unemployment may differ.

[4]Based on Eurostat's harmonized index of consumer prices.

[5]Current account position corrected for reporting discrepancies in intra-area transactions.

[6]Excludes the G7 economies (Canada, France, Germany, Italy, Japan, United Kingdom, United States) and euro area countries.

George W. Bush, begin to expire in 2013, just as deep automatic spending cuts kick in. Such a massive adjustment could significantly undermine the economic recovery. The repeated difficulty of extending temporary policy measures implies that these provisions may expire nonetheless. Furthermore, given the lengthy election season and ongoing gridlock in the U.S. Congress, there is little chance of meaningful medium-term debt reduction before 2013. Should growth disappoint, the lack of a fiscal consolidation strategy may increase the U.S. risk premium, which could have spillover effects for other major economies. Another downside risk, given ongoing problems in resolving household debt burdens and clearing the market overhang of foreclosed homes, is that the recovery in house prices will be more protracted than assumed under the baseline. On the other hand, if the job market continues to positively surprise and, thereby, provide more widespread support to consumption, growth could become more resilient and ultimately strengthen.

In Canada, the housing market is an area of potential vulnerability, with high house prices and rising household indebtedness. Strong spillovers to Canada from the United States mean it is also exposed to the risks discussed above.

Given the outlook and the ongoing problems in Europe, the first priority for U.S. authorities is to agree on and commit to a credible fiscal policy agenda that places public debt on a sustainable track over the medium term. But reflecting lessons being learned in Europe, the U.S. authorities must make efforts to support near-term recovery. The recent agreement to extend payroll tax relief and unemployment benefits is welcome, but more effort is required toward medium-term consolidation. The Congressional Budget Office estimates that current policies will lead to a rise in federal debt held by the public to about 90 percent of GDP by 2020—an uncomfortably high burden (Figure 2.7, panel 6). Conversely, if all temporary tax reductions and stimulus measures were allowed to expire—a path that would significantly undermine the recovery and economic growth—debt would fall to just under 65 percent of GDP.

Another important policy priority is for support the housing market. A recent white paper on housing released by the Federal Reserve Board (BGFRS, 2012) and Chapter 3 of this issue of the *World Economic Outlook* highlight multiple ways that growth is constrained by the overhang of foreclosed homes and the prevalence of households with negative equity. Recent improvements to the Home Affordable Modification Program are welcome, but will likely struggle to be effective without strong participation from government-sponsored enterprises Fannie Mae and Freddie Mac. The adoption of the administration's proposals on mortgage refinancing would also be a step in the right direction, and both Chapter 3 and the Federal Reserve Board white paper discuss a number of additional possibilities. Regardless of the approach, however, bold policy action that supports the housing market could lead to a significant boost in consumption and overall growth and is strongly recommended.

The recent change in the way the Federal Reserve communicates its decisions and policy assumptions has the potential to bolster its support for the economy. Specifically, it has announced an inflation target of 2 percent over the medium term within its dual mandate and has started publishing policy rate forecasts with a view to influencing long-term interest rates and better anchoring inflation expectations (see Figure 2.7).[1] It should also stand ready to implement unconventional support if activity threatens to disappoint, so long as inflation expectations remain subdued.

Canada is in a sounder fiscal and financial position than the United States. Ongoing fiscal tightening should continue, although there is policy room to slow the pace if downside risks to growth materialize.

Asia: Growth Is Moderating

Much weaker external demand has dimmed the outlook for Asia (Figure 2.8). But resilient domestic demand in China, limited financial spillovers, room for policy easing, and the capacity of Asian banks to step in as European banks deleverage suggest that the soft landing under way is likely to continue.

[1]Explicit forecasts are more transparent, given the parsing that took place in the past over the distinctions in meaning between, for example, "for some time," "for an extended period," and "at least through mid-2013."

Figure 2.8. Asia: Revisions to 2012 GDP Growth Forecasts
(Change in percentage points from September 2011 WEO projections)

Less than –1
Between –1 and –0.5
Between –0.5 and 0
Between 0 and 0.5
Between 0.5 and 1
Greater than 1
Insufficient data

Source: IMF staff estimates.

Figure 2.9. Asia: Growth Is Moderating[1]

Slowing exports, particularly to Europe, are dampening Asia's growth prospects. But Chinese demand provides a buffer to the region's commodity exporters, and domestic demand remains strong in some parts of developing Asia. Market turmoil in late 2011 was greater for countries with closer links to euro area banks. Inflation has moderated in many economies, but there is less fiscal room now than in 2007.

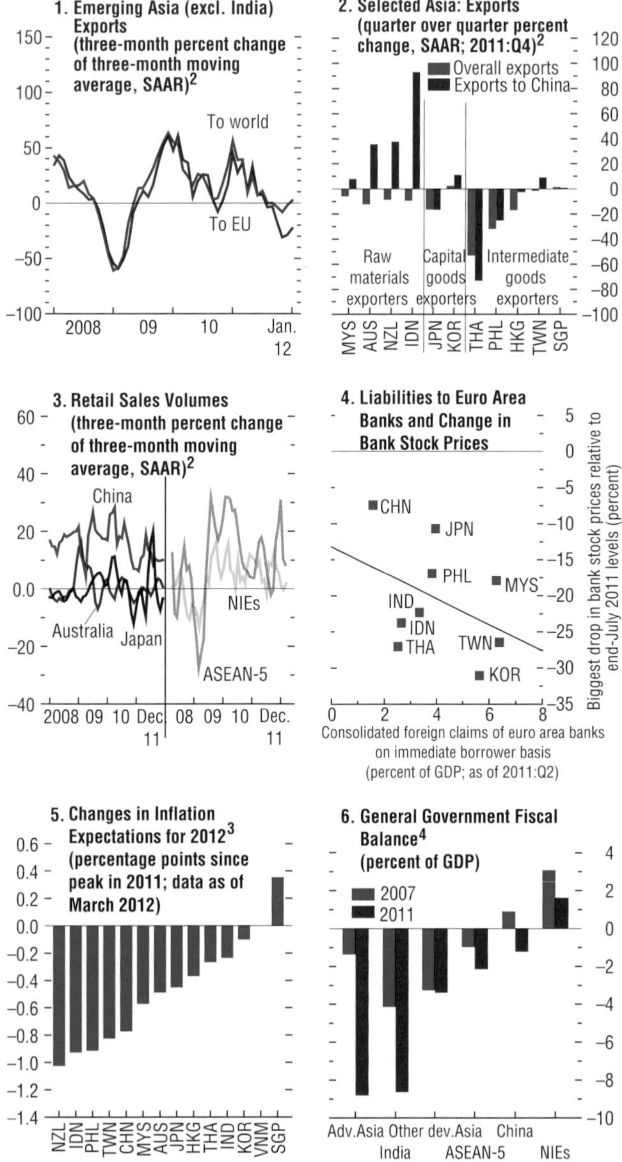

Sources: Bank for International Settlements; CEIC; Consensus Economics; IMF, *Direction of Trade Statistics;* and IMF staff calculations.

[1]Advanced Asia (Adv. Asia): Australia (AUS), Japan (JPN), New Zealand (NZL); ASEAN-5: Indonesia (IDN), Malaysia (MYS), Philippines (PHL), Thailand (THA), Vietnam (VNM); CHN: China; IND: India; Newly Industrialized Asian Economies (NIEs): Hong Kong SAR (HKG), Korea (KOR), Singapore (SGP), Taiwan Province of China (TWN).

[2]SAAR: seasonally adjusted annual rate.

[3]For India, the change in expectations refers to the average annual wholesale price inflation for fiscal year ending in March 2013.

[4]Other developing Asia (Other dev. Asia): Afghanistan, Bangladesh, Bhutan, Brunei Darussalam, Cambodia, Fiji, Kiribati, Lao PDR, Maldives, Myanmar, Nepal, Pakistan, Papua New Guinea, Samoa, Solomon Islands, Sri Lanka, Timor-Leste, Vanuatu.

Activity across Asia slowed during the last quarter of 2011, reflecting both external and domestic developments. The effect of spillovers from Europe can be seen in the weakness of Asia's exports to that region (Figure 2.9, panel 1). In some economies, such as India, domestic factors also contributed to the slowdown, as a deterioration in business sentiment weakened investment and policy tightening raised borrowing costs. The historic floods that hit Thailand significantly curtailed that country's growth in the last quarter of the year, shaving 2 percentage points off annual growth in 2011, and led to negative spillovers on other economies (for example, Japan). In some other Asian economies, however, robust domestic demand helped offset the drag on growth of slowing exports. Investment and private consumption remained strong in China, buoyed by solid corporate profits and rising household income (Figure 2.9, panel 2). Moreover, the rebound from the supply-chain disruptions caused by the March 2011 Japanese earthquake and tsunami was stronger than anticipated.

While financial turmoil in the euro area spilled over to Asian markets late last year, the effects were limited. Portfolio flows turned sharply negative in late 2011, equity prices fell sharply, sovereign and bank credit default swap (CDS) spreads increased, and regional currencies depreciated. Overall, however, market movements in late 2011 were smaller than the gyrations observed during 2008–09. The movements had limited economic impact and were partially reversed in early 2012.

In emerging Asia, adverse market developments were correlated with countries' reliance on euro area banks (Figure 2.9, panel 4). As described in more detail in this chapter's Spillover Feature, euro area banks have already begun reducing their cross-border lending. Asian banks are generally in good financial health, and many large Asian banks have sufficient capacity to step up lending further.[2] But euro area banks handle a substantial share of trade credit in the region and often specialize in complex project financing, for which it could be difficult to find quick substitutes.

[2]See Chapter 3 of the April 2012 *Regional Economic Outlook: Asia and Pacific*.

Table 2.3. Selected Asian Economies: Real GDP, Consumer Prices, Current Account Balance, and Unemployment
(Annual percent change unless noted otherwise)

	Real GDP			Consumer Prices[1]			Current Account Balance[2]			Unemployment[3]		
		Projections			Projections			Projections			Projections	
	2011	2012	2013	2011	2012	2013	2011	2012	2013	2011	2012	2013
Asia	**5.9**	**6.0**	**6.5**	**5.0**	**3.9**	**3.6**	**2.0**	**1.4**	**1.7**	...	...	...
Advanced Asia	**1.3**	**2.6**	**2.8**	**1.6**	**1.4**	**1.4**	**2.2**	**1.8**	**2.0**	**4.3**	**4.3**	**4.2**
Japan	–0.7	2.0	1.7	–0.3	0.0	0.0	2.0	2.2	2.7	4.5	4.5	4.4
Australia	2.0	3.0	3.5	3.4	2.7	3.0	–2.2	–4.6	–5.1	5.1	5.2	5.2
New Zealand	1.4	2.3	3.2	4.0	2.1	2.4	–4.1	–5.4	–6.3	6.5	6.0	5.4
Newly Industrialized Asian Economies	**4.0**	**3.4**	**4.2**	**3.6**	**2.9**	**2.7**	**6.5**	**5.9**	**5.7**	**3.6**	**3.5**	**3.5**
Korea	3.6	3.5	4.0	4.0	3.4	3.2	2.4	1.9	1.5	3.4	3.3	3.3
Taiwan Province of China	4.0	3.6	4.7	1.4	1.3	1.8	8.8	8.0	8.4	4.4	4.4	4.3
Hong Kong SAR	5.0	2.6	4.2	5.3	3.8	3.0	4.1	3.2	3.5	3.4	3.5	3.5
Singapore	4.9	2.7	3.9	5.2	3.5	2.3	21.9	21.8	21.3	2.0	2.1	2.1
Developing Asia	**7.8**	**7.3**	**7.9**	**6.5**	**5.0**	**4.6**	**1.8**	**1.2**	**1.4**	...	...	...
China	9.2	8.2	8.8	5.4	3.3	3.0	2.8	2.3	2.6	4.0	4.0	4.0
India	7.2	6.9	7.3	8.6	8.2	7.3	–2.8	–3.2	–2.9	...	...	...
ASEAN-5	**4.5**	**5.4**	**6.2**	**5.9**	**5.4**	**4.7**	**2.8**	**1.7**	**1.4**	...	...	...
Indonesia	6.5	6.1	6.6	5.4	6.2	6.0	0.2	–0.4	–0.9	6.6	6.4	6.3
Thailand	0.1	5.5	7.5	3.8	3.9	3.3	3.4	1.0	1.4	0.7	0.7	0.7
Malaysia	5.1	4.4	4.7	3.2	2.7	2.5	11.5	10.8	10.4	3.2	3.1	3.0
Philippines	3.7	4.2	4.7	4.8	3.4	4.1	2.7	0.9	1.0	7.0	7.0	7.0
Vietnam	5.9	5.6	6.3	18.7	12.6	6.8	–0.5	–1.6	–1.4	4.5	4.5	4.5
Other Developing Asia[4]	**4.6**	**5.0**	**5.0**	**10.6**	**9.7**	**9.2**	**–0.7**	**–2.0**	**–2.0**	...	...	...
Memorandum												
Emerging Asia[5]	7.3	6.8	7.4	6.1	4.7	4.3	2.5	1.9	2.0	...	...	...

[1]Movements in consumer prices are shown as annual averages. December–December changes can be found in Tables A6 and A7 in the Statistical Appendix.

[2]Percent of GDP.

[3]Percent. National definitions of unemployment may differ.

[4]Other Developing Asia comprises Islamic Republic of Afghanistan, Bangladesh, Bhutan, Brunei Darussalam, Cambodia, Republic of Fiji, Kiribati, Lao People's Democratic Republic, Maldives, Myanmar, Nepal, Pakistan, Papua New Guinea, Samoa, Solomon Islands, Sri Lanka, Timor-Leste, Tonga, Tuvalu, and Vanuatu.

[5]Emerging Asia comprises all economies in Developing Asia and the Newly Industrialized Asian Economies.

Although the external environment is challenging, a soft landing is projected under the baseline forecast, given robust domestic demand, favorable financial conditions, and room for policy easing. Growth in the region is projected at 6 percent in 2012 before gradually recovering to 6½ percent in 2013 (Table 2.3).

- In China, even with the drag from external demand, growth is projected to be above 8 percent in 2012 and 2013 because consumption and investment are expected to remain robust.
- In India, while part of the expected slowdown to 7 percent in 2012 is a cyclical response to higher interest rates and lower external demand, policy uncertainty and supply bottlenecks are playing a role and will need to be tackled in the near term to ensure that potential growth does not decline.
- With a timely boost from reconstruction spending, Japan is projected to grow at 2 percent in 2012. The crisis in Europe and problems regarding energy supply are likely to dampen Japanese economic activity and exports. Growth is expected to remain subdued at 1¾ percent in 2013, reflecting the weak global environment and a decline in reconstruction spending.
- In Korea, a rebound in construction is expected to offset a muted outlook for private consumption and investment due to increased global uncertainty.
- Exports from the ASEAN-5[3] were hit particularly hard, but strong domestic demand helped offset the external slowdown, especially in Indonesia. In

[3]The Association of Southeast Asian Nations (ASEAN) has 10 members; the ASEAN-5 are Indonesia, Malaysia, the Philippines, Thailand, and Vietnam.

Thailand, a rebound following last year's flooding is expected in the first half of 2012, supported by monetary easing and a large fiscal package in response to the floods.

As the pace of economic activity in the region has slowed and capital flows have diminished, inflation pressure has waned and credit growth has slowed. Inflation in the region is expected to recede from 5 percent last year to just under 4 percent in 2012 and to 3½ percent in 2013.

There are significant downside risks to the outlook. In particular, an escalation of the euro area crisis—the downside scenario described in Chapter 1 and illustrated in Figure 2.2—could lower emerging Asia's output by 1¼ percent relative to the baseline, and Japan's output by 1¾ percent. For Asia's open economies, trade would be the most important channel of transmission. For Japan, the simulation results suggest that the spillover effects of decreased external demand are magnified by the constraint on monetary policy of the zero nominal interest rate floor.

A sharp rise in global risk aversion and uncertainty would also produce significant spillovers, not only through its effect on financial market conditions (Figure 2.5, panel 3), but also because of its dampening effect on trade in durables. As shown in panel 2 of Figure 2.5, the region's exposure to euro area banks is smaller than that of other regions. Nevertheless, banking systems in the region that have the greatest reliance on foreign wholesale funding (the newly industrialized Asian economies—NIEs—Australia, New Zealand) remain vulnerable to deleveraging in the global financial system.

An additional external risk is that tensions in the Middle East will cause another oil price spike. Among the internal risks is balance sheet vulnerability from slowing real estate and export sectors in China. These appear manageable on their own, but a large external shock could bring these risks to the fore, precipitating a decline in investment and activity in China that would also have implications for its trading partners.

Policy in the region needs to be set with an eye toward these risks. For economies with relatively low levels of public debt (ASEAN-5, China, NIEs), the pace of fiscal consolidation could be slowed if downside risks materialize. Many Asian economies could also advance their plans to boost social safety nets and increase investment in infrastructure if another round of fiscal stimulus is warranted—these policies have long-term positive effects on economic rebalancing and income inequality that are beneficial even in good times. However, fiscal consolidation remains a priority in India and Japan, to anchor confidence and rebuild room to meet future challenges.

Although monetary tightening has been appropriately paused in many Asian economies, and cautiously reversed in some, room for further easing is constrained in economies where underlying inflation pressures remain (India, Indonesia, Korea) and in those that are still working through previous credit expansion (China). In Japan, by contrast, further monetary easing can help strengthen growth prospects, and asset purchases under existing programs may need to be expanded to accelerate an exit from deflation.

If euro area bank deleveraging escalates, policymakers will need to ensure that the supply of credit is maintained for those vulnerable to credit rationing, such as small and medium-size firms. Programs developed precisely for this purpose during the 2008–09 crisis could be reactivated as needed. Dollar-funding pressures, which became evident during the previous crisis (notably in Korea, Malaysia, and Taiwan Province of China), remain a vulnerability. Should global liquidity dry up as a result of an intensified euro area crisis, policymakers should stand ready to backstop liquidity in the region.

The fragility of the external outlook highlights the need for the region to rebalance growth by strengthening domestic sources of demand over the coming years. In China, a continuation of recent currency appreciation and progress in implementing the policies identified in the 12th Five-Year Plan would ensure that the recent decline in the external surplus is sustained (see Box 1.3). Elsewhere in emerging Asia, including in many ASEAN economies and India, strengthening domestic demand will require improving the conditions for private investment, including by addressing infrastructure bottlenecks and enhancing governance and public service delivery.

Latin America and the Caribbean: On a Glide Path to Steady Growth

The swings in risk aversion in global markets over the past six months have had significant effects on the region. Initially a rise in risk aversion took some pressure off a number of economies in the region that were threatening to overheat. But, after this pause, capital flows are returning and exchange rates are once again under pressure. Earlier policy tightening, however, is beginning to bear fruit. This combination of policy gains and recent resilience in the face of global sentiment swings means that the outlook is promising (Figure 2.10). Nevertheless, inflation remains above the midpoint of the target band in many economies and credit growth is still elevated. At the same time, there is continued potential for downdrafts from Europe. While risks are broadly balanced, these tensions are complicating the tasks of policymakers.

The LAC region grew strongly during 2011. External factors had a significant influence on these developments. High commodity prices supported activity in many of the region's commodity exporters despite a general slowdown in global growth and capital flows, which helped contain overheating pressures. Internally, the tightening of fiscal, monetary, and prudential policies also helped moderate the pace of expansion (Figure 2.11). In Central America and the Caribbean, while economic activity is still subdued, strong real linkages with the United States

Figure 2.10. Latin America and the Caribbean: Revisions to 2012 GDP Growth Forecasts
(Change in percentage points from September 2011 WEO projections)

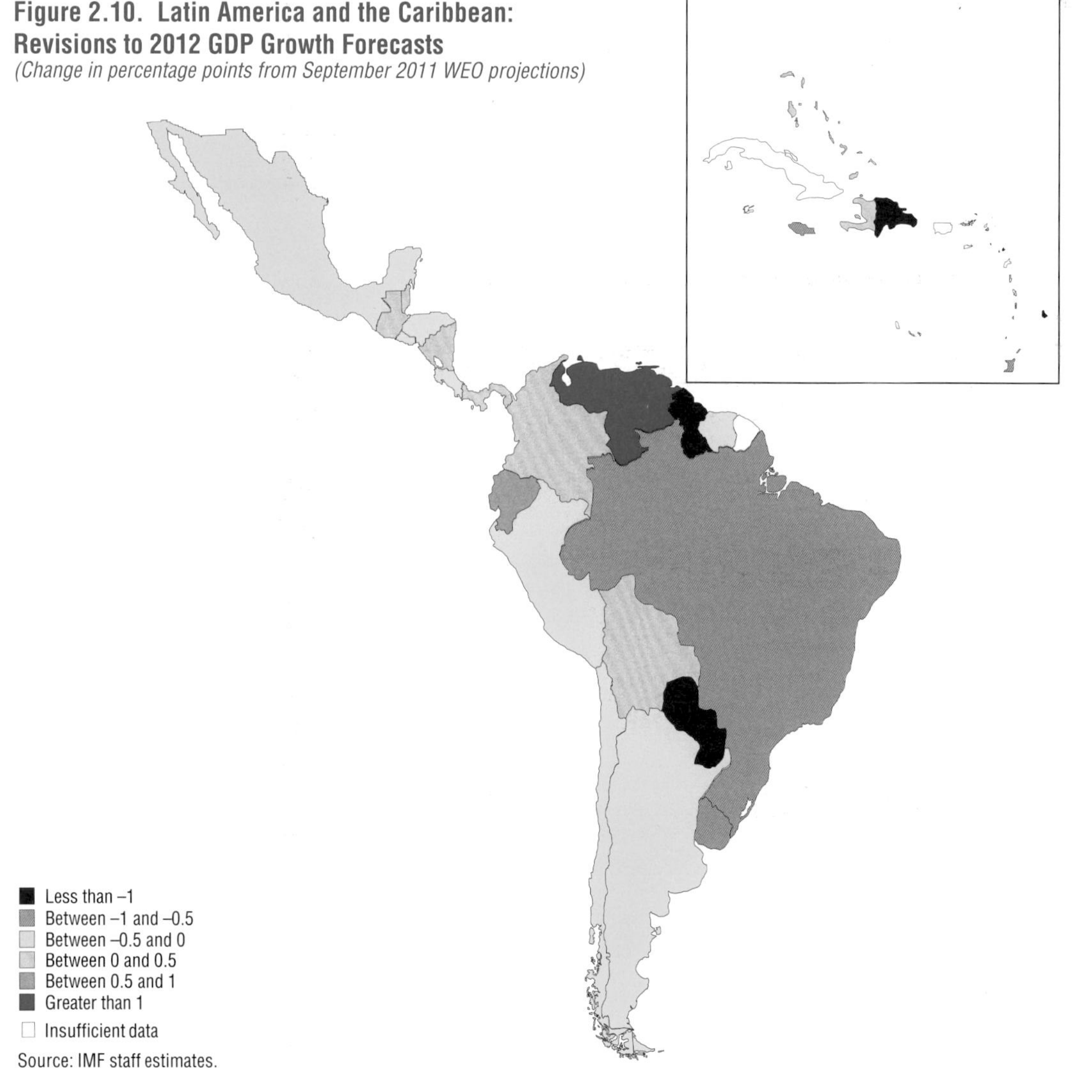

Source: IMF staff estimates.

Figure 2.11. Latin America: Watch Out for Downdrafts[1]

Swings in risk aversion over the past six months led at first to a moderation of capital flows and exchange rates but, more recently, to a renewal of capital flows and pressure on exchange rates. Policy tightening began to bear fruit, leading to stabilization of real credit growth—albeit at high levels. Nonetheless, inflation is still above the midpoint of the target in many countries. Policymakers need to remain vigilant to possible downdrafts from Europe and updrafts from capital flows.

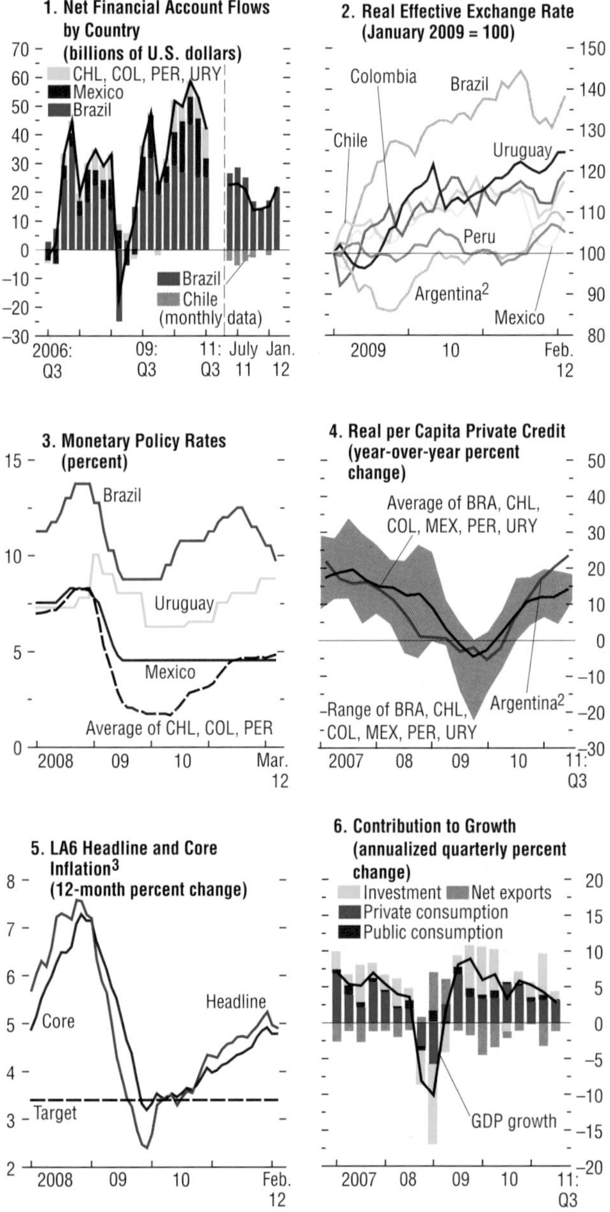

Sources: Haver Analytics; IMF, *International Financial Statistics;* and IMF staff calculations.
[1]BRA: Brazil; CHL: Chile; COL: Colombia; MEX: Mexico; PER: Peru; URY: Uruguay.
[2]Nominal variables for Argentina are deflated using IMF staff estimates of average provincial inflation.
[3]LA6: Brazil, Chile, Colombia, Mexico, Peru, and Uruguay.

offer some upside prospects as the United States slowly recovers.

Spillovers to the region through trade, financial, and banking channels were active during recent months but with only limited effects on activity. As implied above, trade spillovers are predominantly commodity related and, as such, linked to Asian growth. Financial spillovers have been more closely related to European developments—a rise in risk aversion stemming from concerns about developments in Europe led to a temporary reduction in capital flows to the region. There was not, however, a reversal of flows and, as such, this development has been a net positive for the region. Nevertheless, the region has had difficulty absorbing hot money in the past and this remains an ongoing source of vulnerability. Spillovers to the region from Europe, however, are channeled most directly through the region's exposure to the operations of European banks. There is a relatively large European bank presence in the region, particularly of Spanish banks (see Figure 2.5, panel 2). The sale by Santander of shares in its local subsidiaries in late 2011 caused a temporary fall in regional bank stock indices, which points to the possibility that weakness in the European parent banks could cause problems for regional financial markets and for the supply of credit. However, the regional operations of these banks are predominantly conducted by subsidiaries and funded by local deposits, so it is likely that future financial spillovers will be small.

Growth in the LAC region is projected to moderate to 3¾ percent in 2012, before returning to about 4 percent in 2013 (Table 2.4). Among the commodity exporters, strong domestic demand growth moderated, as tighter macroeconomic policies began to bear fruit and the external environment weakened. This is most apparent in Brazil, where growth for 2011 was 2¾ percent and monetary policy has already been loosened. In combination, these forces mean that overheating risks have receded (see Figure 1.18). However, elevated credit and import growth suggests that overheating risks are not completely under control and could reemerge if capital flows return to previous levels. In Mexico, growth was strong in 2011 and, as in the United States, surprised to the upside. Growth is forecast at between 3½ and 3¾ percent

Table 2.4. Selected Western Hemisphere Economies: Real GDP, Consumer Prices, Current Account Balance, and Unemployment
(Annual percent change unless noted otherwise)

	Real GDP			Consumer Prices[1]			Current Account Balance[2]			Unemployment[3]		
		Projections			Projections			Projections			Projections	
	2011	2012	2013	2011	2012	2013	2011	2012	2013	2011	2012	2013
North America	**2.0**	**2.2**	**2.5**	**3.1**	**2.3**	**2.0**	**–3.0**	**–3.1**	**–2.9**	...	...	...
United States	1.7	2.1	2.4	3.1	2.1	1.9	–3.1	–3.3	–3.1	9.0	8.2	7.9
Canada	2.5	2.1	2.2	2.9	2.2	2.0	–2.8	–2.7	–2.7	7.5	7.4	7.3
Mexico	4.0	3.6	3.7	3.4	3.9	3.0	–0.8	–0.8	–0.9	5.2	4.8	4.6
South America[4]	**4.8**	**3.8**	**4.3**	**7.8**	**7.4**	**7.0**	**–1.0**	**–1.9**	**–2.0**	...	...	...
Brazil	2.7	3.0	4.1	6.6	5.2	5.0	–2.1	–3.2	–3.2	6.0	6.0	6.5
Argentina[5]	8.9	4.2	4.0	9.8	9.9	9.9	–0.5	–0.7	–1.1	7.2	6.7	6.3
Colombia	5.9	4.7	4.4	3.4	3.5	3.1	–2.8	–2.7	–2.4	10.8	11.0	10.5
Venezuela	4.2	4.7	3.2	26.1	31.6	28.8	8.6	7.4	5.6	8.1	8.0	8.1
Peru	6.9	5.5	6.0	3.4	3.3	2.6	–1.3	–2.0	–1.9	7.5	7.5	7.5
Chile	5.9	4.3	4.5	3.3	3.8	3.0	–1.3	–2.4	–2.4	7.1	6.6	6.9
Ecuador	7.8	4.5	3.9	4.5	5.7	4.8	–0.3	0.5	0.6	6.0	5.8	6.2
Uruguay	5.7	3.5	4.0	8.1	7.4	6.6	–2.2	–3.6	–3.2	6.1	6.0	6.0
Bolivia	5.1	5.0	5.0	9.9	4.9	4.5	2.2	1.6	1.1	...	...	...
Paraguay	3.8	–1.5	8.5	6.6	5.0	5.0	–1.2	–3.5	–1.4	5.6	5.8	5.5
Central America[6]	**4.7**	**4.0**	**4.0**	**5.6**	**5.3**	**5.2**	**–6.9**	**–6.9**	**–6.7**	...	...	...
Caribbean[7]	**2.8**	**3.5**	**3.6**	**7.2**	**5.5**	**5.2**	**–3.5**	**–3.6**	**–3.7**	...	...	...
Memorandum												
Latin America and the Caribbean[8]	4.5	3.7	4.1	6.6	6.4	5.9	–1.2	–1.8	–2.0	...	...	...
Eastern Caribbean Currency Union[9]	–0.2	1.5	2.2	3.4	3.5	2.4	–19.9	–21.4	–20.5	...	...	...

[1]Movements in consumer prices are shown as annual averages. December–December changes can be found in Tables A6 and A7 in the Statistical Appendix.

[2]Percent of GDP.

[3]Percent. National definitions of unemployment may differ.

[4]Also includes also Guyana and Suriname.

[5]Figures are based on Argentina's official GDP and consumer price index (CPI-GBA) data. The IMF has called on Argentina to adopt remedial measures to address the quality of the official GDP and CPI-GBA data. The IMF staff is also using alternative measures of GDP growth and inflation for macroeconomic surveillance, including data produced by private analysts, which have shown significantly lower real GDP growth than the official data since 2008, and data produced by provincial statistical offices and private analysts, which have shown considerably higher inflation figures than the official data since 2007.

[6]Central America comprises Belize, Costa Rica, El Salvador, Guatemala, Honduras, Nicaragua, and Panama.

[7]The Caribbean comprises Antigua and Barbuda, The Bahamas, Barbados, Dominica, Dominican Republic, Grenada, Haiti, Jamaica, St. Kitts and Nevis, St. Lucia, St. Vincent and the Grenadines, and Trinidad and Tobago.

[8]Latin America and the Caribbean comprises Mexico and economies from the Caribbean, Central America, and South America.

[9]Eastern Caribbean Currency Union comprises Antigua and Barbuda, Dominica, Grenada, St. Kitts and Nevis, St. Lucia, and St. Vincent and the Grenadines as well as Anguilla and Montserrat, which are not IMF members.

for 2012 and 2013, a slight slowdown but still above potential. In Central America, growth is expected to be about 4 percent and in the Caribbean, about 3½ percent. High public debt and weak tourism and remittance flows continue to constrain the outlook for the Caribbean. The outlook for Central America, like that for Mexico, is closely tied to developments in the United States.

Spillovers to the region, both real and financial, from renewed crisis in Europe are likely to be limited. It is estimated that a reemergence of crisis in Europe, one of the downside scenarios described in Chapter 1 and presented in Figure 2.2, could lower regional output by about ¾ percent relative to the baseline. This is toward the lower end of estimated effects, reflecting the relatively low level of trade with Europe (which accounts for only about 10 percent of the region's goods exports) and limited financial spillovers (see Figure 2.5). As discussed above, despite the relatively large presence of European banks in the region, spillovers through European banking operations are expected to be moderate. Conversely, the region, and particularly the Southern Cone, is very dependent on commodity prices. In this respect, it could be affected if a crisis in Europe spills over into a more general slowdown, particularly if it affects China and emerging Asia. Counterbalancing this external vulnerability is the sway of the Brazilian economy, which is driven predominantly by internal factors.

Against this backdrop, policies must be alert to domestic overheating and must build on a strong foundation of prudential measures developed during the most recent periods of robust capital flows. While external pressures abated briefly, they are returning—it would be premature to relax policy settings while inflation is still above the midpoint of target bands and risks tend to the upside. These concerns are particularly acute in Venezuela, where policy has not tightened noticeably and inflation continues at high levels. Similarly, in Argentina, although it is not affected by international credit flows in the same way, high credit growth and high inflation are worrisome. Recent swings in capital flows provide a strong argument for regional governments to continue strengthening their prudential frameworks to ensure that they are prepared for any future booms or busts in these flows. In Mexico, given firmly anchored inflation expectations and continuing softness in the United States, monetary policy can remain accommodative as long as inflation pressure and expectations remain at bay.

Fiscal consolidation should continue (especially where it is needed to maintain debt sustainability), but social and infrastructure spending should be protected too. Fiscal policy in commodity exporters should focus on saving any windfall revenue gains while commodity prices are still strong, to build room for supportive action in case downside risks to the outlook begin to materialize (see Chapter 4). In Central America, policies should shift toward rebuilding the policy buffers used during the crisis and adopting structural reforms aimed at boosting medium-term growth. Greater resolve is required in reducing debt overhang in the Caribbean while addressing weak competitiveness.

Figure 2.12. Commonwealth of Independent States: Revisions to 2012 GDP Growth Forecasts
(Change in percentage points from September 2011 WEO projections)

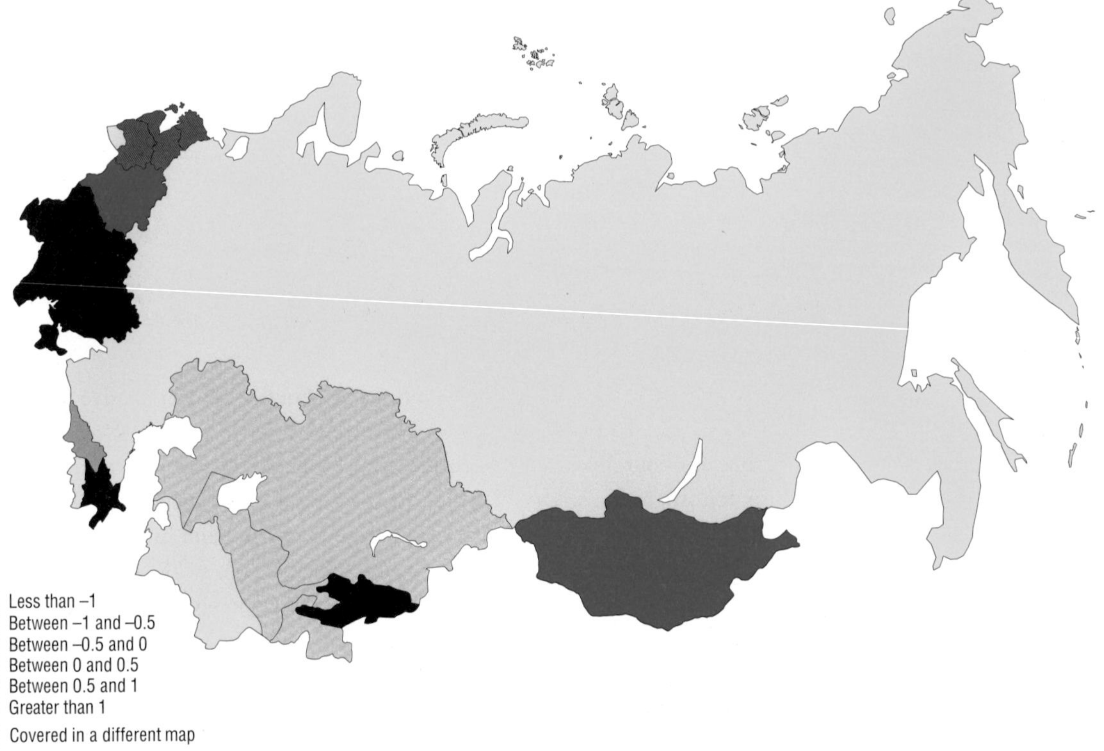

Less than –1
Between –1 and –0.5
Between –0.5 and 0
Between 0 and 0.5
Between 0.5 and 1
Greater than 1
Covered in a different map

Source: IMF staff estimates.
Note: Includes Georgia and Mongolia.

Commonwealth of Independent States: Commodity Prices Are the Main Spillover Channel

Weaker exports to Europe along with policy tightening in some economies will moderate growth in the CIS this year (Figure 2.12), even though commodity prices are expected to remain high. If the euro area crisis intensifies, the fall in global demand together with the associated decline in commodity prices will be a significant constraint on the region's growth.

The CIS continued to grow strongly during the second half of 2011, supported by still-strong oil and commodity prices, a rebound in agricultural output in a number of economies (Armenia, Belarus, Kazakhstan, Russia) following the drought in 2010, and strong domestic demand (Figure 2.13).

The region, however, has been affected by spillovers from the euro area. The rise in global financial turmoil in late 2011 and the resulting flight to safety contributed to significant capital outflows from Russia, a rise in CDS spreads (particularly for Ukraine), and depreciation of a number of regional currencies, including the Russian ruble. The onset of recession in the euro area is reflected in weaker exports and a slowdown in industrial production in the region's larger economies.

Reflecting the much weaker external outlook, growth in the CIS is expected to slow to 4¼ percent in 2012, from 5 percent in 2011 (Table 2.5). This slowdown is expected to occur even with oil prices remaining relatively high.

- Growth in Russia will benefit from high oil prices. Current projections of 4 percent growth this year are only slightly below the forecasts in the September 2011 *World Economic Outlook*. Growth in 2013 has also been revised down to just below 4 percent because oil prices are expected to weaken somewhat.
- In the region's other energy-exporting economies, growth is also projected to moderate slightly, to 5¾ percent in 2012 and 5½ percent in 2013. Despite weaker external conditions, growth in these economies will be supported by strong terms of trade, as well as investment in oil and mining (Kazakhstan) and infrastructure (Kazakhstan, Uzbekistan). Following a sharp fall in oil output

Figure 2.13. Commonwealth of Independent States: Buoyed by Commodity Prices, Buffeted by Euro Area Headwinds[1]

Weaker external demand, especially from Europe, has been a drag on growth in the CIS. The region has benefited from still-high commodity prices, but an escalation of the euro area crisis would cause a big terms-of-trade shock for the region. Inflation has eased, but fiscal room has not yet been rebuilt to precrisis levels.

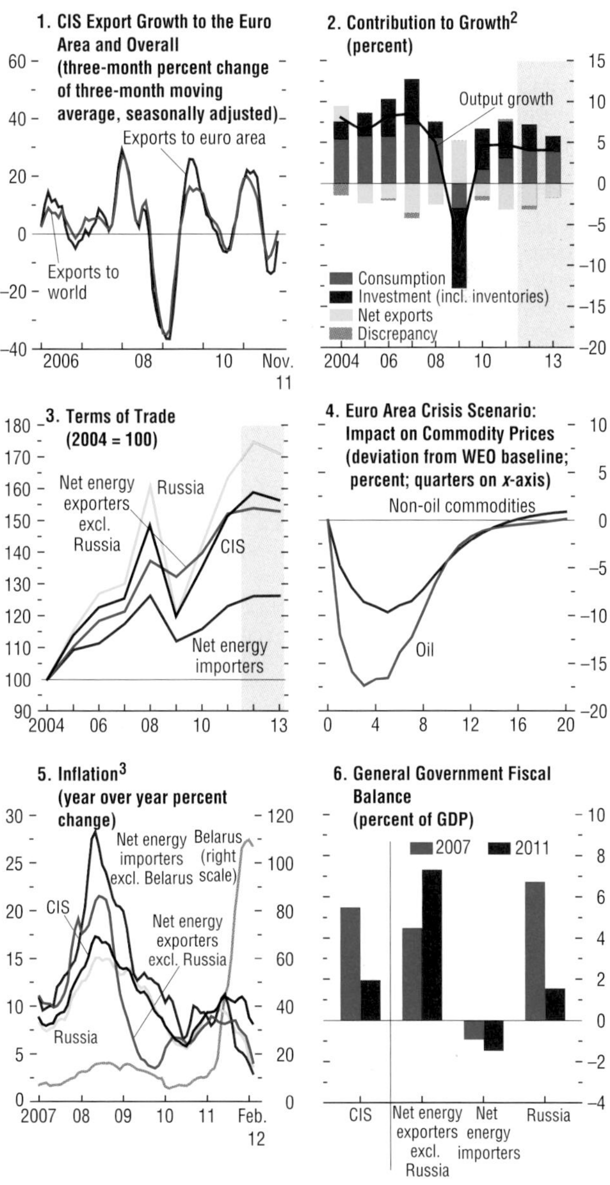

Sources: Haver Analytics; IMF, *Direction of Trade Statistics*; and IMF staff estimates.

[1]Net energy exporters: Azerbaijan, Kazakhstan, Russia, Turkmenistan, Uzbekistan. Net energy importers: Armenia, Belarus, Georgia, Kyrgyz Republic, Moldova, Mongolia, Tajikistan, Ukraine.

[2]Azerbaijan, Georgia, Tajikistan, Turkmenistan, and Uzbekistan are excluded due to data limitations.

[3]Due to data limitations, Turkmenistan and Uzbekistan are excluded from the group of net energy exporters excluding Russia; Kyrgyz Republic, Mongolia, and Tajikistan are excluded from the group of net energy importers excluding Belarus.

Table 2.5. Commonwealth of Independent States: Real GDP, Consumer Prices, Current Account Balance, and Unemployment
(Annual percent change unless noted otherwise)

	Real GDP			Consumer Prices[1]			Current Account Balance[2]			Unemployment[3]		
		Projections			Projections			Projections			Projections	
	2011	2012	2013	2011	2012	2013	2011	2012	2013	2011	2012	2013
Commonwealth of Independent States (CIS)[4]	**4.9**	**4.2**	**4.1**	**10.1**	**7.1**	**7.7**	**4.6**	**4.0**	**1.7**	. . .	. . .	. . .
Net Energy Exporters	**4.7**	**4.3**	**4.2**	**8.5**	**5.1**	**6.6**	**6.2**	**5.4**	**2.6**	. . .	. . .	. . .
Russia	4.3	4.0	3.9	8.4	4.8	6.4	5.5	4.8	1.9	6.5	6.0	6.0
Kazakhstan	7.5	5.9	6.0	8.3	5.5	7.0	7.6	6.6	5.6	5.4	5.4	5.3
Uzbekistan	8.3	7.0	6.5	12.8	12.7	10.9	5.8	2.8	3.0	0.2	0.2	0.2
Azerbaijan	0.1	3.1	1.9	7.9	5.6	6.1	26.3	21.8	16.4	6.0	6.0	6.0
Turkmenistan	14.7	7.0	6.7	5.8	6.2	7.0	1.8	2.1	1.3	. . .	. . .	. . .
Net Energy Importers	**5.7**	**3.7**	**3.9**	**18.2**	**17.4**	**13.3**	**–8.0**	**–7.1**	**–5.8**	. . .	. . .	. . .
Ukraine	5.2	3.0	3.5	8.0	4.5	6.7	–5.6	–5.9	–5.2	8.2	8.2	7.9
Belarus	5.3	3.0	3.3	53.2	66.0	35.8	–10.4	–6.2	–6.5	0.6	0.6	0.6
Georgia	7.0	6.0	5.5	8.5	1.7	5.5	–12.7	–10.3	–9.3	14.9	14.1	13.5
Armenia	4.4	3.8	4.0	7.7	4.0	4.2	–12.3	–11.0	–9.5	19.0	19.0	18.5
Tajikistan	7.4	6.0	6.0	12.4	7.9	8.4	–2.3	–3.6	–5.0	. . .	. . .	. . .
Mongolia	17.3	17.2	11.8	9.5	13.6	12.5	–30.4	–24.4	–1.8	3.0	3.0	3.0
Kyrgyz Republic	5.7	5.0	5.5	16.6	4.1	8.1	–3.1	–4.8	–4.2	7.9	7.7	7.6
Moldova	6.4	3.5	4.5	7.6	5.5	5.0	–10.6	–9.7	–9.9	6.7	6.6	6.4
Memorandum												
Low-Income CIS Economies[5]	7.3	6.1	5.9	11.7	8.7	8.7	–1.7	–2.6	–2.2	. . .	. . .	. . .
Net Energy Exporters Excluding Russia	6.8	5.7	5.4	8.9	7.1	7.7	10.6	8.8	7.1	. . .	. . .	. . .

[1]Movements in consumer prices are shown as annual averages. December–December changes can be found in Table A7 in the Statistical Appendix.
[2]Percent of GDP.
[3]Percent. National definitions of unemployment may differ.
[4]Georgia and Mongolia, which are not members of the Commonwealth of Independent States, are included in this group for reasons of geography and similarities in economic structure.
[5]Low-income CIS economies comprise Armenia, Georgia, Kyrgyz Republic, Moldova, Tajikistan, and Uzbekistan.

in 2011, Azerbaijan's hydrocarbon output is expected to remain broadly stable this year, and continued strong growth in the nonhydrocarbon sector is expected to help the economy expand by 3 percent in 2012.

- In the energy-importing economies of the CIS, both external and domestic factors are contributing to the slowdown in growth this year. Waning export demand and tighter monetary and financial conditions will contribute to a slowdown in Ukraine's growth from 5¼ percent last year to 3 percent this year. Growth in Belarus is also expected to slow to 3 percent this year from 5¼ percent in 2011, as a result of last year's currency crisis and the monetary and fiscal tightening that was required to bring inflation down from triple digits.

After rising in mid-2011 due to high food and fuel prices (as well as to excess demand pressures in a number of economies), headline inflation began to moderate in many CIS economies in the second half of last year and early this year. Contributing to the decline are good harvests that reduced food price inflation, a moderation in economic activity, and monetary tightening in a number of economies. As a result, inflation is projected to moderate this year in almost all economies in the region, with depreciation-driven inflation in Belarus a notable exception.

The most important risk to the region is the possible escalation of the crisis in the euro area. Direct spillovers will come through trade linkages—the euro area accounts for about a third of the region's exports, the most for any region outside Europe (Figure 2.5, panel 1). Even CIS economies with less direct trade exposure to the euro area will be affected via Russia, which is the largest trade partner (and a source of remittances and foreign direct investment) for many economies in the region. An indirect but potentially more important channel is the effect a euro area crisis and global downturn would have on commodity prices.

In the euro area crisis scenario described in Chapter 1, oil and commodity prices would be lower by 17 and 10 percent, respectively, relative to the baseline, resulting in a significant terms-of-trade shock for the region (Figure 2.13, panel 4). And as was demonstrated late last year, increased capital outflows would put pressure on the region's currencies and exacerbate funding pressure for economies with large external financing needs, such as Ukraine. While the region's financial linkages with euro area banks are relatively limited (see Figure 2.5, panel 2), distress in a systemically important euro area bank could cause an abrupt withdrawal of funding and raise the likelihood of banking sector distress in Russia.[4] An upside risk for CIS energy exporters is a further rise in oil prices as a result of renewed tensions in the Middle East.

Fortifying the region against such risks calls for rebuilding policy room in most CIS economies, notably through fiscal consolidation. Fiscal balances are much lower than they were before the 2008–09 crisis. In Russia, the non-oil deficit has more than tripled since the crisis, and the oil reserve fund has been drawn down; in Ukraine, public finances remain vulnerable to pressures from higher wage, pension, and capital spending; and in Belarus, tight wage policy in the budget sector will be crucial to the reduction of inflation expectations.

The moderation of inflation in the region gives policymakers some room for monetary maneuvering. Nevertheless, monetary policy should continue to focus on reducing inflation under the baseline scenario, because inflation remains high in a number of economies (Belarus, Russia, Uzbekistan). Should downside risks materialize, monetary and fiscal authorities should stand ready to adjust their policies. Greater exchange rate flexibility, which was a welcome development in Russia last year but is still lacking in other economies in the region, would also help these economies adjust to adverse shocks.

[4]See IMF (2011).

Middle East and North Africa: Growth Stalled, Outlook Uncertain

In addition to significant internal challenges in several economies in the region and geopolitical risks associated with the Islamic Republic of Iran, there are large potential spillovers to the region from Europe. Internal challenges, exemplified by ongoing social unrest, have spurred an increase in social transfers. Key policy priorities will be preserving or rebuilding macroeconomic stability in the face of the ongoing unrest while evolving toward a model for inclusive growth that does not depend so heavily on government transfers. External challenges come from two main sources—oil prices and trade linkages with Europe. For oil exporters, a renewal of crisis in Europe could depress oil prices and undermine the recent increases in government spending on social support. In North Africa, trade, remittance, and tourism links with Europe are historically important and currently depressed.

Growth in the MENA region was below trend in 2011, primarily because of country-specific factors.[5] Among oil exporters, strong oil prices contributed to growth of 4 percent in 2011, which was held down by lower outcomes in the Islamic Republic of Iran related to a poor harvest and the effect of the subsidy reform. Among oil importers, growth was 2 percent even after the exclusion of data from the Syrian Arab Republic. This low growth is a direct reflection of the effects of social unrest. Other than through their effects on oil prices, global factors and European developments have had a relatively minor effect on the region to date—revisions primarily reflect regional developments (Figure 2.14).

Regional spillovers from the social unrest have been large, particularly on tourism and capital flows, which have declined throughout the region (Figure 2.15). Given the size of economy-specific shocks and their strong regional spillovers, it is difficult to isolate a Europe-specific effect, except the weakening of remittances. Even so, the potential spillovers from a reemergence of crisis in Europe, as modeled in the first downside scenario of Chapter 1 and illustrated

[5]The Syrian Arab Republic has been excluded from the data and projections due to the uncertain political situation. Growth in Libya, which is included, is strongly affected by the civil war and projected bounce back in 2012.

Figure 2.14. Middle East and North Africa: Revisions to 2012 GDP Growth Forecasts
(Change in percentage points from September 2011 WEO projections)

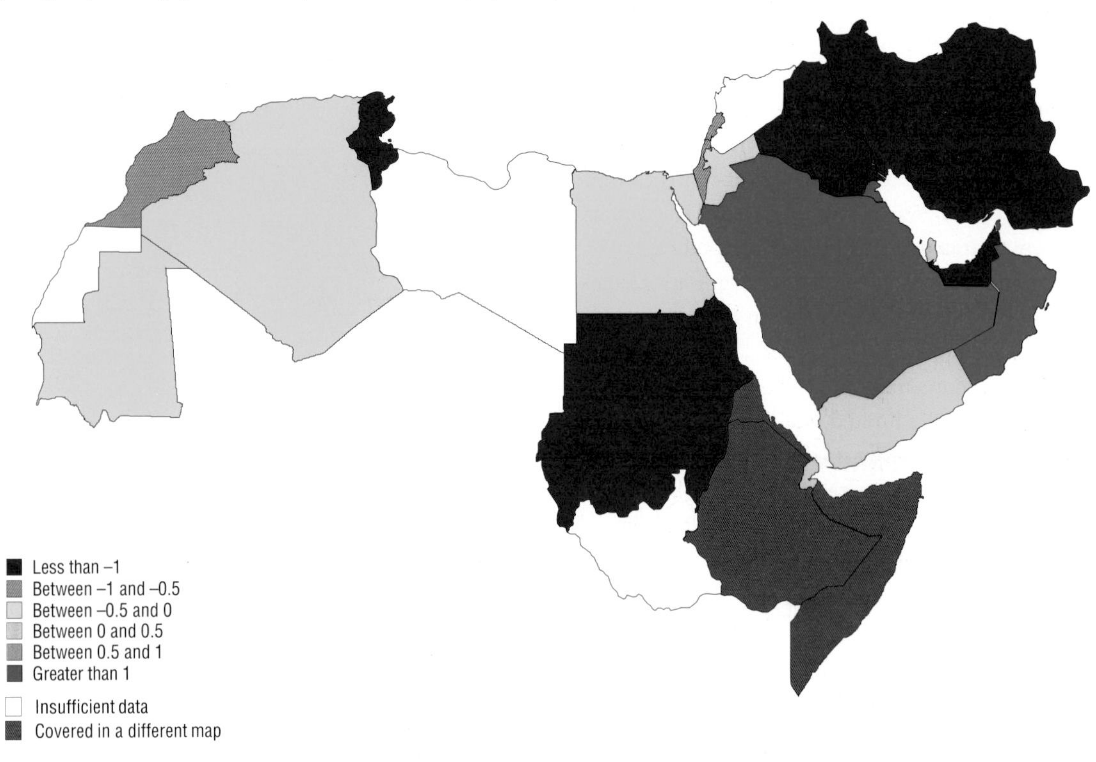

Source: IMF staff estimates.

in Figure 2.2, could lower regional output by about 3¼ percent relative to the baseline—the largest spillover effect for any region outside Europe. Of this, most is attributable to weaker oil prices. The remaining effect reflects strong spillovers from weaker trading partner demand on the region—predominantly through effects on foreign financing flows, trade, tourism, and remittances. These links are best seen in the pattern of trade for the region (see Figure 2.5, panel 1). Goods exports to Europe account for approximately 20 percent of exports, or 7 percent of GDP—higher than for Asia, Canada, Latin America, the SSA region, or the United States. Figure 2.5 also shows that, although current financial linkages appear weak, spillovers to the MENA region were among the strongest in the year immediately following the collapse of Lehman Brothers in 2008.

These strong spillovers from Europe shape the risks to the outlook, but the baseline is predominantly determined by regional factors. The baseline forecast is for growth of 4¼ percent in 2012 and 3¾ percent in 2013 (Table 2.6). Among oil importers, strong oil prices, anemic tourism associated with social unrest in the region, and lower trade and remittance flows reflecting ongoing problems in Europe are the major constraints. Among oil exporters, negative developments in the Islamic Republic of Iran are projected to be offset by increased oil production in Iraq and Saudi Arabia and a bounce back in Libya. Given the relatively subdued growth outlook and receding non-oil commodity prices, inflation in the region is projected to fall slightly over the forecast horizon from 9½ percent in 2011 to 8¾ percent in 2013.

As mentioned above, external risks revolve around developments in Europe. Internal risks are dominated by political developments. Domestic instability caused a significant decline in tourism for the region, which has yet to recover to earlier levels (Figure 2.15, panel 2). A more intense recession in

Europe could further undermine the already shaky tourism sector with follow-on effects to the rest of the economy. For oil exporters, risks revolve around the price of oil—which, on the downside, is predominantly tied to the possibility of an intensified crisis in Europe that spills over into slower growth in the rest of the world. Government expenditures have risen to such a degree that a relatively modest fall in the price of oil can lead to budget deficits. Conversely, despite being already elevated because of regional political uncertainty, oil prices could rise further on the back of intensified concerns about an Iran-related oil supply shock, unrest in the region, or an actual disruption in oil supplies. Such effects could be dramatic given limited inventory and spare capacity buffers, as well as the still-tight physical market conditions expected throughout 2012.

Given these risks and outlook, the region faces serious policy challenges. The primary challenge is to secure economic and social stability, but there is also a short-term need to place public finances on a sustainable footing. For oil exporters, governments need to seize the opportunity presented by high oil prices to move toward sustainable and more diversified economies. In addition, the social disruption highlights the need for an inclusive medium-term growth agenda that establishes strong institutions to stimulate private sector activity, opens up greater access to economic opportunities, and addresses chronically high unemployment, particularly among the young.

A key medium-term fiscal policy objective is the reorientation of fiscal policies toward poverty reduction and the promotion of productive investment. However, increased spending on fuel and food subsidies (with the Islamic Republic of Iran an important exception), along with pressures to raise civil service wages and pensions, is straining public finances (particularly for oil-importing economies), which will not be sustainable over the medium term. Increased targeting of subsidies, and fuel subsidy reforms in particular, will help ease the strain.[6]

[6]See Annex 3.2 of the April 2011 *Regional Economic Outlook: Middle East and Central Asia,* and Coady and others (2010) for discussion of these issues.

Figure 2.15. Middle East and North Africa: A Sea of Troubles[1]

The uncertain political environment in many economies in the region is undermining growth prospects. The legacy of social unrest and of weakness in Europe can be seen in weak tourism and remittance numbers and capital outflows. An increase in social transfer expenditures means that, for oil exporters, government budgets are increasingly dependent on continued high oil prices.

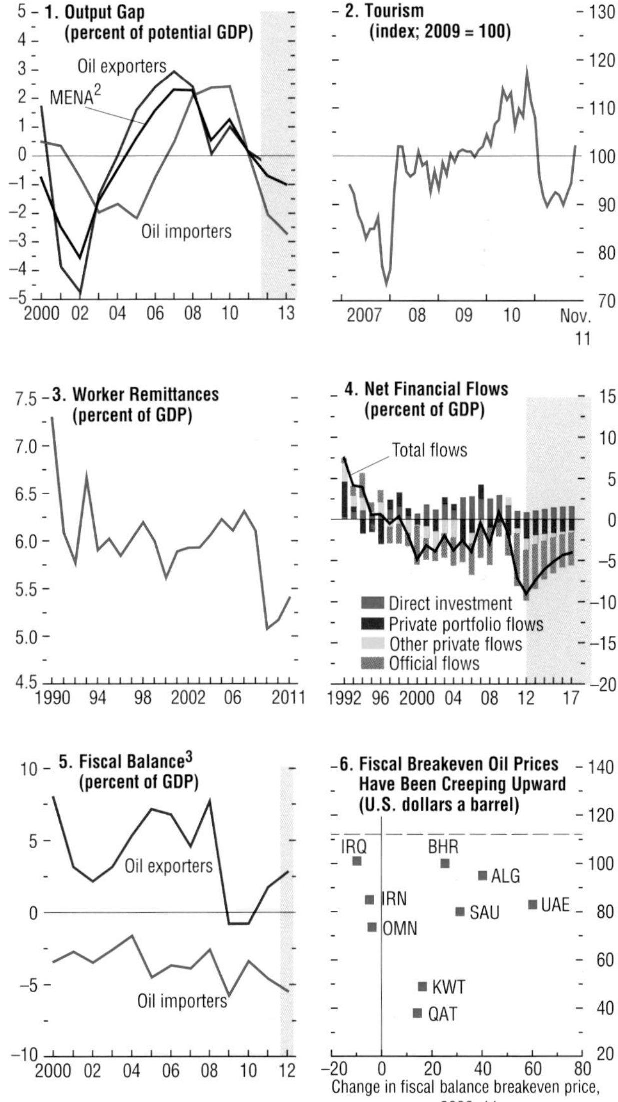

Sources: Haver Analytics; national authorities; and IMF staff estimates.

[1]Oil exporters: Algeria (ALG), Bahrain (BHR), Islamic Republic of Iran (IRN), Iraq (IRQ), Kuwait (KWT), Libya, Oman (OMN), Qatar (QAT), Saudi Arabia (SAU), Sudan, United Arab Emirates (UAE), Republic of Yemen. Oil importers: Djibouti, Egypt, Jordan, Lebanon, Mauritania, Morocco, Syrian Arab Republic, Tunisia. Data exclude Syrian Arab Republic for 2011 onward and South Sudan after July 9, 2011.

[2]MENA: Middle East and North Africa.

[3]Data exclude Libya.

Table 2.6. Selected Middle East and North African Economies: Real GDP, Consumer Prices, Current Account Balance, and Unemployment

(Annual percent change unless noted otherwise)

	Real GDP			Consumer Prices[1]			Current Account Balance[2]			Unemployment[3]		
		Projections			Projections			Projections			Projections	
	2011	2012	2013	2011	2012	2013	2011	2012	2013	2011	2012	2013
Middle East and North Africa	**3.5**	**4.2**	**3.7**	**9.6**	**9.5**	**8.7**	**13.2**	**14.5**	**12.7**	. . .	. . .	. . .
Oil Exporters[4]	**4.0**	**4.8**	**3.7**	**10.3**	**10.3**	**8.8**	**16.9**	**18.2**	**16.0**	. . .	. . .	. . .
Islamic Republic of Iran	2.0	0.4	1.3	21.3	21.8	18.2	10.7	6.6	5.1	15.1	16.7	18.1
Saudi Arabia	6.8	6.0	4.1	5.0	4.8	4.4	24.4	27.9	22.7	. . .	. . .	. . .
Algeria	2.5	3.1	3.4	4.5	5.5	4.5	10.3	10.0	7.9	10.0	9.7	9.3
United Arab Emirates	4.9	2.3	2.8	0.9	1.5	1.7	9.2	10.3	10.4	. . .	. . .	. . .
Qatar	18.8	6.0	4.6	2.0	4.0	4.0	28.4	31.5	29.0	. . .	. . .	. . .
Kuwait	8.2	6.6	1.8	4.7	3.5	4.0	41.8	46.2	41.9	2.1	2.1	2.1
Iraq	9.9	11.1	13.5	6.0	7.0	6.0	7.9	9.1	10.8	. . .	. . .	. . .
Sudan[5]	–3.9	–7.3	–1.5	18.1	23.2	26.0	2.1	–4.6	–4.0	12.0	10.8	9.6
Oil Importers[6]	**2.0**	**2.2**	**3.6**	**7.5**	**6.9**	**8.4**	**–5.3**	**–5.3**	**–4.9**	. . .	. . .	. . .
Egypt	1.8	1.5	3.3	11.1	9.5	12.1	–2.0	–2.6	–2.1	10.4	11.5	11.3
Morocco	4.3	3.7	4.3	0.9	2.0	2.5	–7.4	–5.9	–6.0	9.0	8.9	8.8
Tunisia	–0.8	2.2	3.5	3.5	5.0	4.0	–7.4	–7.1	–7.1	18.9	17.0	16.0
Lebanon	1.5	3.0	4.0	5.0	4.0	3.3	–14.4	–14.2	–13.4	. . .	. . .	. . .
Jordan	2.5	2.8	3.0	4.4	4.9	5.6	–9.5	–8.3	–6.8	12.9	12.9	12.9
Memorandum												
Israel	4.7	2.7	3.8	3.4	2.0	2.0	0.1	–0.9	0.0	5.6	6.0	5.8
Maghreb[7]	–1.7	11.0	5.9	3.9	4.0	3.0	2.7	5.3	6.2	. . .	. . .	. . .
Mashreq[8]	1.8	1.8	3.4	10.0	8.6	10.8	–4.3	–4.7	–4.1	. . .	. . .	. . .

[1]Movements in consumer prices are shown as annual averages. December–December changes can be found in Tables A6 and A7 in the Statistical Appendix.

[2]Percent of GDP.

[3]Percent. National definitions of unemployment may differ.

[4]Also includes Bahrain, Libya, Oman, and Republic of Yemen.

[5]Data for 2011 exclude South Sudan after July 9. Data for 2012 onward pertain to the current Sudan.

[6]Also includes Djibouti and Mauritania. Excludes Syrian Arab Republic for 2011 onward.

[7]The Maghreb comprises Algeria, Libya, Mauritania, Morocco, and Tunisia.

[8]The Mashreq comprises Egypt, Jordan, Lebanon, and Syrian Arab Republic. Excludes Syrian Arab Republic for 2011 onward.

Sub-Saharan Africa: Resilience Should Not Breed Complacency

Sub-Saharan Africa has recorded another year of strong growth and was one of the regions least affected by recent financial turmoil and deterioration in the global outlook (Figure 2.16). Rebuilding policy buffers remains a priority in most economies, but sluggish growth in South Africa may require some policy support. Containing the surge in inflation is a policy priority in east Africa.

The SSA region turned in another solid performance in 2011, expanding by about 5 percent. This occurred despite a slowdown in South Africa (due in part to the slowdown in the euro area), adverse supply shocks from drought in both eastern and western Africa, and civil conflict in Côte d'Ivoire.

The region's resilience reflects a number of factors, including its relative insulation from financial spillovers emanating from the euro area. The region's limited financial linkages with Europe (see Figure 2.5, panels 2 and 3) helped protect it from the turmoil in late 2011, with South Africa a notable exception—there it led to rand depreciation and stock price volatility. Furthermore, the diversification of exports toward fast-growing emerging markets has reduced the region's trade exposure to Europe.[7] Exports to the euro area now account for only one-fifth of the region's exports, down from two-fifths in the early 1990s (Figure 2.5, panel 1; Figure 2.17, panel 4). High commodity prices also benefited the region's commodity exporters and

[7]See Chapter 3 of the October 2011 *Regional Economic Outlook: Sub-Saharan Africa.*

Figure 2.16. Sub-Saharan Africa: Revisions to 2012 GDP Growth Forecasts
(Change in percentage points from September 2011 WEO projections)

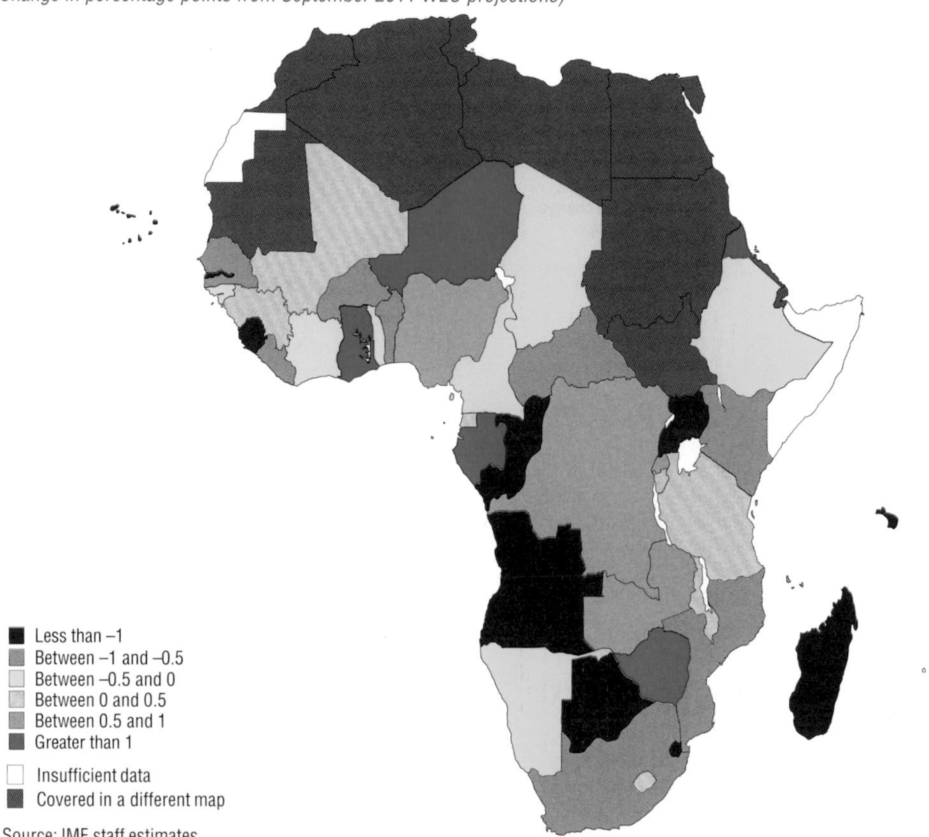

Source: IMF staff estimates.

boosted investment in natural resource extraction. And policy stances remain relatively accommodative in many economies in the region.

Reflecting this resilience, the downward revision to the SSA outlook was small (Figure 2.1, panel 1; Figure 2.17, panel 1). SSA growth is expected to pick up somewhat in 2012 to 5½ percent, from 5 percent in 2011 (Table 2.7), helped by the coming onstream of new mineral and oil production and the reversal of the adverse supply shocks experienced in 2011. That said, several economies will experience a significant slowdown:

- The region's middle-income economies, which are growing the least rapidly, saw large downward revisions to their growth, reflecting their stronger trade and financial ties with slowing Europe. South Africa is projected to expand by only 2¾ percent this year, 1 percentage point less than projected in the September 2011 *World Economic Outlook*. This reflects deterioration in the external environment, weaker terms of trade, and a general loss of business confidence. Growth is also expected to slow in Botswana to 3¼ percent this year due in large part to weaker global demand for diamonds. After the one-time boost from the start of oil production last year, Ghana's growth is set to moderate to a still-robust 8¾ percent this year.
- Growth in the oil-exporting economies is expected to accelerate to 7¼ percent in 2012 from 6¼ percent last year, largely because new oil fields coming onstream in Angola are expected to boost GDP growth there to 9¾ percent this year. In Nigeria, non-oil GDP growth is projected to ease somewhat this year, reflecting tighter fiscal and monetary policies, although with some rebound in oil output, overall GDP growth should remain about 7 percent.
- Among the low-income economies, a rebound in agricultural output and in hydroelectricity generation following last year's drought is expected to support

Figure 2.17. Sub-Saharan Africa: Continued Resilience[1]

Sub-Saharan Africa has seen only small downward revisions to its growth projections. Exports to Europe have slowed, especially for middle-income economies, but strong terms of trade and increased diversification toward fast-growing emerging markets have helped support the region. Inflation pressure and reduced fiscal room give policymakers less ability to maneuver if downside risks materialize.

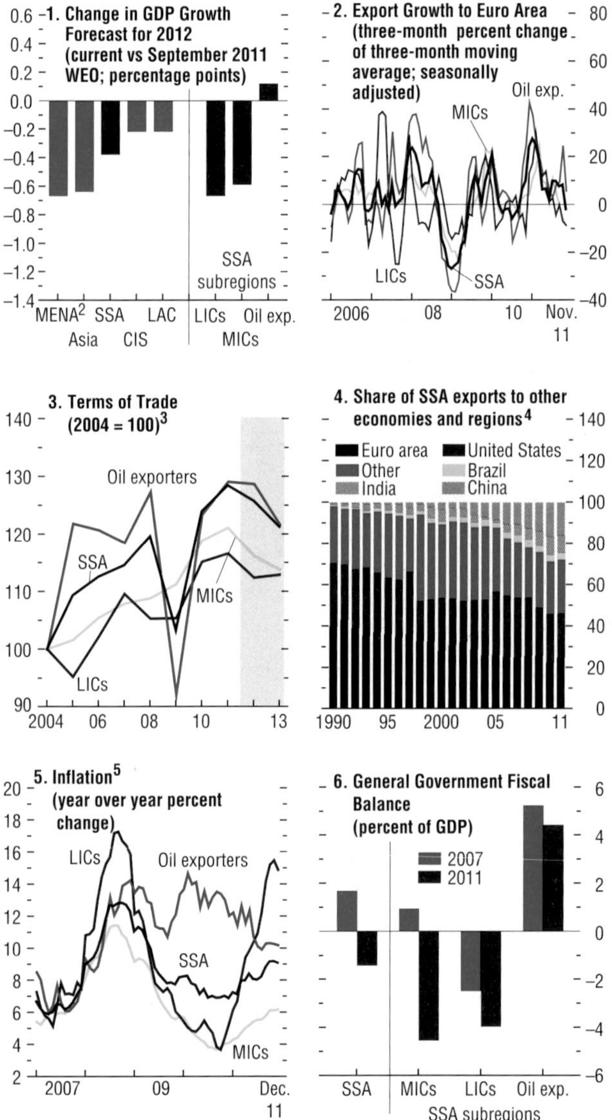

Sources: Haver Analytics; IMF, *Direction of Trade Statistics;* and IMF staff estimates.

[1]CIS: Commonwealth of Independent States; LAC: Latin America and the Caribbean; LIC: low-income country (SSA); MENA: Middle East and North Africa; MIC: middle-income country (SSA); Oil exp.: oil exporters; SSA: sub-Saharan Africa.

[2]Excludes Libya and Syrian Arab Republic. Excludes South Sudan after July 9, 2011.

[3]Excludes Liberia and Zimbabwe due to data limitations.

[4]The value for 2011 is based on the data from January to November.

[5]Due to data limitations, the following are excluded: Chad, Republic of Congo, and Equatorial Guinea from oil exporters; Zambia from MICs; Benin, Central African Republic, Comoros, Democratic Republic of Congo, Eritrea, Ethiopia, Guinea, Liberia, Malawi, São Tomé and Príncipe, Sierra Leone, and Zimbabwe from LICs.

growth in Kenya, which is projected to grow by 5¼ percent in 2012 and by 5¾ percent in 2013. But power shortages and macroeconomic tightening to stem inflation pressure are expected to temper growth in Uganda and, to a lesser extent, Tanzania.

The SSA region is relatively less exposed to the global slowdown, but it is not immune to spillovers. In the euro area crisis scenario described in Chapter 1 and presented in Figure 2.2, SSA output would be reduced by 1 percent relative to the baseline. The euro area crisis would negatively affect the region through its effect on exports, remittances, official aid, and private capital flows. It would also result in a sharp drop in oil and non-oil commodity prices relative to the baseline forecasts, by 17 and 10 percent, respectively. As a result, commodity exporters and middle-income economies that are more integrated into global markets would be the most affected by an escalation of the euro area crisis.

South Africa may also transmit global shocks to the rest of the region. It is more exposed to weaknesses in the world economy—particularly to Europe, which remains a major market for its high-value-added exports. Adverse shocks affecting South Africa can quickly spread to neighboring economies, through their effect on migrant workers' incomes, trade, regional investment, and finance.

For now, policymakers should focus on rebuilding policy buffers. Many economies in the region have already begun to reduce fiscal deficits and tighten monetary policy, particularly where inflation spiked last year. Indeed, inflation pressure has already begun to abate in much of the region, mostly on account of lower food prices. Budgetary discipline will also help generate the room needed to refocus spending on priority areas such as infrastructure, health, and education. If downside risks materialize, economies without significant financing constraints should be prepared to loosen policy levers. The challenge is different in South Africa, which is struggling with subpar growth and very high unemployment. Support for activity remains an important policy objective, and in the event of a protracted slowdown, further monetary easing could be a potential source of stimulus as long as inflation expectations and the core inflation rate remain well contained.

Table 2.7. Selected Sub-Saharan African Economies: Real GDP, Consumer Prices, Current Account Balance, and Unemployment

(Annual percent change unless noted otherwise)

	Real GDP			Consumer Prices[1]			Current Account Balance[2]			Unemployment[3]		
		Projections			Projections			Projections			Projections	
	2011	2012	2013	2011	2012	2013	2011	2012	2013	2011	2012	2013
Sub-Saharan Africa	**5.1**	**5.4**	**5.3**	**8.2**	**9.6**	**7.5**	**–1.8**	**–2.0**	**–2.6**	...	...	...
Oil Exporters	**6.2**	**7.3**	**6.2**	**10.2**	**10.2**	**8.7**	**5.6**	**6.9**	**4.9**	...	...	...
Nigeria	7.2	7.1	6.6	10.8	11.2	9.7	6.2	7.3	5.3	23.9	...	...
Angola	3.4	9.7	6.8	13.5	11.1	8.3	8.1	9.7	6.2	...	...	...
Equatorial Guinea	7.1	4.0	6.8	7.3	7.0	7.0	–9.7	–9.0	–6.6	...	...	...
Gabon	5.8	5.6	2.3	1.3	2.3	2.6	12.0	11.7	7.5	...	...	...
Chad	1.6	6.9	0.1	1.9	5.5	3.0	–17.7	–10.0	3.3	...	...	...
Republic of Congo	4.5	3.1	5.4	1.9	2.7	2.9	6.2	4.3	3.8	...	...	...
Middle-Income[4]	**3.9**	**3.8**	**4.2**	**5.4**	**5.8**	**5.4**	**–3.8**	**–4.9**	**–5.2**	...	...	...
South Africa	3.1	2.7	3.4	5.0	5.7	5.3	–3.3	–4.8	–5.5	24.5	23.8	23.6
Ghana	13.6	8.8	7.4	8.7	9.6	8.9	–10.0	–6.9	–6.0	...	...	...
Cameroon	4.1	4.1	4.5	2.9	3.0	3.0	–3.5	–4.8	–3.3	...	...	...
Côte d'Ivoire	–4.7	8.1	6.2	4.9	2.0	2.5	6.7	–2.8	–3.0	...	...	...
Botswana	4.6	3.3	4.6	8.5	7.8	6.7	–6.8	–4.1	–1.4	...	...	...
Senegal	2.6	3.8	4.5	3.4	3.0	2.2	–8.3	–10.0	–10.7	...	...	...
Low-Income[5]	**5.8**	**5.9**	**5.9**	**10.6**	**15.5**	**9.6**	**–9.7**	**–11.1**	**–9.9**	...	...	...
Ethiopia	7.5	5.0	5.5	18.1	33.9	23.1	–0.2	–8.4	–7.6	...	...	...
Kenya	5.0	5.2	5.7	14.0	10.6	5.2	–11.8	–9.6	–8.4	...	...	...
Tanzania	6.7	6.4	6.7	7.0	17.4	9.5	–9.7	–12.3	–11.2	...	...	...
Uganda	6.7	4.2	5.4	6.5	23.4	7.6	–11.1	–12.5	–10.7	...	...	...
Democratic Republic of Congo	6.9	6.5	6.7	15.5	12.7	9.4	–8.7	–7.8	–6.5	...	...	...
Mozambique	7.1	6.7	7.2	10.4	7.2	5.6	–13.0	–12.7	–12.4	...	...	...

[1]Movements in consumer prices are shown as annual averages. December–December changes can be found in Table A7 in the Statistical Appendix.

[2]Percent of GDP.

[3]Percent. National definitions of unemployment may differ.

[4]Also includes Cape Verde, Lesotho, Mauritius, Namibia, Seychelles, Swaziland, and Zambia.

[5]Also includes Benin, Burkina Faso, Burundi, Central African Republic, Comoros, Eritrea, The Gambia, Guinea, Guinea-Bissau, Liberia, Madagascar, Malawi, Mali, Niger, Rwanda, São Tomé and Príncipe, Sierra Leone, Togo, and Zimbabwe.

Spillover Feature: Cross-Border Spillovers from Euro Area Bank Deleveraging

Euro area banks have been reducing assets, which has raised concern about the possibility of a credit crunch and the effects on real GDP growth and financial stability, not only in the euro area but also in other regions of the world. This Spillover Feature analyzes the potential spillovers of euro area bank deleveraging on other economies.

Concerns about global spillovers from euro area bank deleveraging stem from the major role these banks play in all sectors of global lending. This includes interbank funding, nonbank private credit (including trade finance), and, to a more moderate extent, public sector lending. The recent three-year longer-term refinancing operations (LTROs) of the European Central Bank (ECB) have likely been a key element in smoothing deleveraging pressure on euro area banks, but, as explained in the April 2012 *Global Financial Stability Report,* fundamental deleveraging dynamics are likely to persist. The most exposed regions are emerging Europe and a region designated "other advanced Europe."[8] The decline in total banks' foreign claims in the third quarter of 2011 has been relatively modest so far compared with the period following the collapse of Lehman Brothers in 2008. But the effects on several emerging markets and on the region designated "other advanced Asia" (Australia, Hong Kong SAR, Korea, New Zealand, Singapore, Taiwan Province of China) were sizable, and risk aversion, which has been declining from recent highs since early 2012, is not expected to return to precrisis levels soon, given continued downside risks to global growth. Simulations of euro area bank deleveraging suggest that it could have a moderate impact on growth in some regions. Although current WEO baseline projections already incorporate some deleveraging, even moderate additional growth effects from greater-than-expected deleveraging would be worrisome in the context of the current fragile global recovery and ongoing fiscal consolidation.[9] While there could be some offset from other sources of funding, the risk of stronger financial tensions and effects on economic activity remain, especially if deleveraging by European banks triggers a broad and sharp increase in risk aversion.

Deleveraging Pressures on Euro Area Banks and Spillover Channels

Several factors have put pressure on euro area banks to reduce their assets. First, market funding has become costly and scarce, reflecting adverse feedback loops between the sovereign crisis and bank balance sheets and a general lack of confidence between counterparties in the financial system. Although ECB operations are helping ease funding pressures, fundamental deleveraging dynamics appear to be at work. Markets are challenging a bank business model that relies heavily on wholesale funding to increase leverage. Second, some banks remain undercapitalized, and the decline in banks' equity prices has made it difficult and costly to raise private capital. Finally, in response to these developments, the European authorities asked banks in fall 2011 to raise core Tier 1 capital ratios to 9 percent and build an exceptional capital buffer for sovereign debt exposures by June 30, 2012, with a view to restoring stability and confidence and maintaining lending to the real economy. However, the banks' deleveraging plans submitted to the European Banking Authority suggest that in aggregate, the shortfalls are expected to be supported by capital measures, which would limit the negative impact on lending to the real economy.

Bank deleveraging can have undesirable consequences for economic activity and financial stability. A reduction in bank credit leads to tighter financing conditions and lower economic growth. Regarding real activity, this is because banks play a spe-

The main author is Florence Jaumotte, with support from Min Kyu Song and David Reichsfeld. Model simulations used in this focus were prepared by Keiko Honjo and Stephen Snudden.

[8]For this analysis, Israel is included in this region, along with Czech Republic, Denmark, Iceland, Norway, Sweden, Switzerland, and the United Kingdom.

[9]The growth effects of deleveraging mentioned in this Spillover Feature (and in the April 2012 *Global Financial Stability Report*) are not relative to the WEO baseline, which since September 2011 already incorporates some deleveraging.

cial role in the intermediation between savers and borrowers (Adrian, Colla, and Shin, 2012). When a bank reduces assets and liabilities, investors who previously lent to banks can channel funds to the real economy through other means (for example, through purchases of corporate bonds). But investors typically demand higher yields because they are less able to solve asymmetric information problems, are more risk averse, and do not use leverage as banks do to provide cheaper credit.[10] As for financial stability, a reduction in bank funding to other financial institutions can generate funding distress. Fire sales of assets can spread across banks, potentially leading to a vicious circle of selling and price declines. Large divestiture by foreign affiliates can substantially weaken financial institutions' equity prices, as was the case recently in Latin America. Finally, sales of sovereign bonds could intensify the funding distress of sovereigns, with adverse feedback effects for banks and the real economy.

Euro area bank deleveraging could affect other regions of the world, especially if banks initially concentrate their deleveraging on foreign locations, as suggested by market intelligence (see the April 2012 *Global Financial Stability Report*).[11] The first direct channel of cross-border spillover is the withdrawal of claims of euro area banks on foreign countries. But second-round effects could follow if foreign banks'—especially internationally active U.K. and U.S. banks'—loss of euro area funding forces them to deleverage as well. Depending on the extent of funding withdrawal, deleveraging could undermine global confidence, with broader effects. With a rise in global risk aversion, emerging markets would likely suffer generalized capital outflows, whereas economies with an international reserve currency or deep domestic financial markets (Japan, United States) could face capital inflows from safe haven effects, accompanied by currency appreciation. In this case, the relevant measure of exposure is not just euro area claims on an economy, but total foreign claims. Finally, foreign countries' exports could suffer if the domestic deleveraging of euro area banks lowers growth in the euro area.[12]

Pattern of Exposure and Vulnerability

The major role played by euro area banks in global lending is good reason to be concerned about deleveraging by these entities and the effects elsewhere. Based on Bank for International Settlements (BIS) data, euro area banks are major players in global foreign claims of banks in general and in each sector of lending, with shares between 25 and 40 percent (even after excluding lending to other euro area countries—Figure 2.SF.1). Moreover, a substantial share of euro area banks' foreign claims have maturities of less than one year, which makes them easy to unwind. Trade credit might be particularly vulnerable: maturities for this kind of credit are typically short, and euro area banks are major players in this market in all regions.[13]

The regions most exposed to foreign claims from euro area banks are other advanced Europe and emerging Europe (Figure 2.SF.2).[14,15] Financial centers across the world are also very exposed. Japan and developing Asia are the least exposed regions. Emerging Europe and other advanced Europe

[10]Moreover, small and medium-size firms are heavily dependent on bank credit and have little access to bond or equity financing.

[11]There may be several reasons for this. First, these assets may not be part of their core activity. Second, the risk of negative feedback to a bank's performance because of a reduction in its profits and an increase in nonperforming loans as a result of deteriorating economic conditions abroad is smaller. Finally, the recent European Banking Authority guidelines encourage maintaining the flow of credit to EU economies. Some banking groups may, however, prefer not to deleverage in strategic emerging markets that are highly profitable.

[12]The distress in euro area banks will also affect other regions through those regions' claims on the euro area; however, this channel is beyond the topic of deleveraging.

[13]Bank-intermediated trade finance is about 35 to 40 percent of total trade finance. Another niche market that could be affected is project finance.

[14]The regions considered in the analysis are as follows: North America comprises Canada and the United States; other advanced Europe comprises Czech Republic, Denmark, Iceland, Israel, Norway, Sweden, Switzerland, United Kingdom; other Advanced Asia comprises Australia, Hong Kong SAR, Korea, New Zealand, Singapore, Taiwan Province of China. Emerging Europe, the Commonwealth of Independent States (CIS), Developing Asia, Latin America and the Caribbean (LAC), the Middle East and North Africa (MENA), and sub-Saharan Africa (SSA) are defined according to the classification in the Statistical Appendix. Financial centers are included in the aggregates for their respective regions because they are often hubs of regional financing and may thus have spillover effects on the rest of the region.

[15]This is the case in all sectors (private, public, banks). North America and other advanced Asia are also relatively exposed in the banking sector, as is LAC in the public sector.

Figure 2.SF.1. Euro Area Bank Participation in Global Lending, September 2011

The major role played by euro area banks in global lending and the short-term nature of a substantial share of their foreign claims are good reasons to be concerned about their deleveraging.

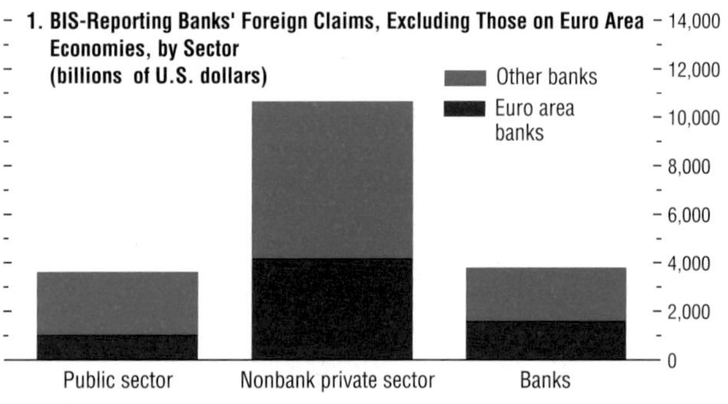

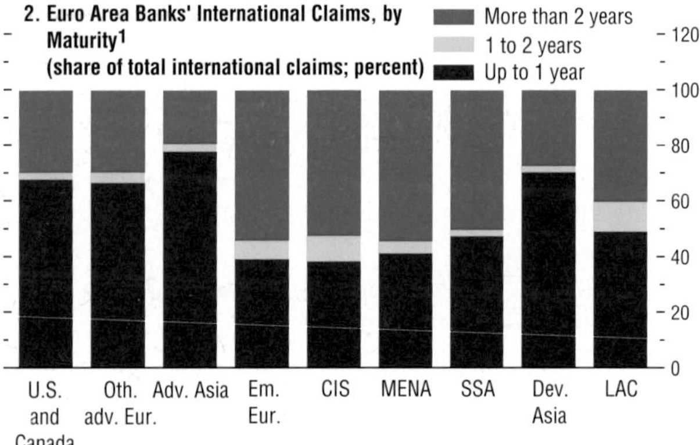

Sources: Bank for International Settlements (BIS); and IMF staff calculations.
[1]Advanced Asia (Adv. Asia): Australia, Hong Kong SAR, Japan, Korea, New Zealand, Singapore, Taiwan Province of China; CIS: Commonwealth of Independent States; Dev. Asia: developing Asia; Em. Eur.: emerging Europe; LAC: Latin America and the Caribbean; MENA: Middle East and North Africa; Other advanced Europe (Oth. adv. Eur.): Czech Republic, Denmark, Iceland, Israel, Norway, Sweden, Switzerland, United Kingdom; SSA: sub-Saharan Africa.

remain the most exposed regions, even considering that a portion of the foreign claims is funded by local deposits in affiliates and hence is less likely to be withdrawn (Cerutti, Claessens, and McGuire, 2011) or taking into account differences in financial deepening across regions.[16] Regions that are directly exposed to banks from euro area countries that have been under market pressure, such as Greece, Ireland, Italy, Portugal, Spain, and Belgium, as opposed to the rest of the euro area, might be more vulnerable. For most regions, the bulk of exposures are to banks from the core of the euro area. But banks in the economies under market pressure have significant claims in other parts of advanced Europe (Ireland), emerging Europe, and Latin America (Spain).

Were global risk aversion to rise significantly, broader vulnerability would play a crucial role in determining the extent to which countries are affected. When total foreign exposure to banks—not just to euro area banks—is taken into account, the potential for broader vulnerability is much higher, especially in other advanced Europe, but also in advanced Asia and North America. When broader indicators are considered, emerging Europe and the CIS appear especially vulnerable (Figure 2.SF.3). Despite sharp declines in current account deficits, these economies have large external financing needs and low reserve coverage of short-term debt and the current account deficit. A significant share of public debt is financed externally, and fiscal financing requirements are large in a number of these economies. Finally, they have a high share of foreign-currency-denominated loans, which could imply large negative balance sheet effects on the private sector in the event of exchange rate pressure and could expose banks to indirect foreign currency risk. The MENA region also exhibits some vulnerability, with high public domestic rollover needs in some economies, which could be problematic if domestic sources of public financing, such as banks, are affected by the euro area crisis. Although external rollover needs are

[16]The adjusted measure proposed by Cerutti, Claessens, and McGuire (2011) has two partially offsetting corrections. On the one hand, subtracting foreign claims funded by local deposits reduces the size of the exposure. On the other hand, the measure adds off-balance-sheet commitments (such as unused credit lines and trade credit guarantees) to capture the maximum exposure.

also very large, most economies in the region hold ample international reserves.

More generally, risk is higher because policy room is much more limited than during the post-Lehman deleveraging, when massive injections of liquidity and recapitalization programs were made possible by ample fiscal room and greater scope for central bank intervention.

How Much Deleveraging So Far?

According to consolidated BIS data, which capture banks' cross-border deleveraging, euro area banks reduced their (adjusted) foreign claims by 3 percent during the third quarter of 2011 (the most recent data point available). Overall, global bank foreign claims declined only ½ percent thanks to some offsets by banks from North America and Japan (Figure 2.SF.4).[17] The overall retrenchment so far is small in comparison with the 2008 crisis, when global foreign claims fell by about 20 percent (although that retrenchment took place over several quarters). But since June 2011 the reduction in foreign claims has affected more regions outside the euro area, especially emerging Europe, LAC, SSA, and advanced Asia.[18] In addition to fewer euro area bank claims, several emerging markets have suffered outflows of funding from non-euro-area banks, while advanced economies have seen inflows of such funding, which may signal a rise in global risk aversion.[19] Total foreign bank claims were lower by 2 percentage points of GDP in emerging Europe and by 0.6 percentage point of GDP in Latin America and the Caribbean and advanced Asia.[20] In addition, euro

[17]Based on BIS consolidated foreign claims at ultimate risk, adjusted for the exchange rate and breaks in series (Cerutti, 2012).

[18]While the discussion focuses on broad regions, the impact of deleveraging has been heterogeneous in some regions. Country-specific factors have been, and will continue to be, crucial.

[19]More recent data on fund flows to emerging markets, however, suggest that global risk aversion has declined again.

[20]Claims on the nonbank private sector have fallen the most. However, because the data are consolidated by banking group, they may reflect a fall in loans to affiliates that were used for lending to the nonbank sector. Claims on (nonaffiliated) banks have so far fallen mostly in Europe, but not much in other regions. Claims on the public sector have fallen significantly in emerging Europe and Latin America.

Figure 2.SF.2. Regional Exposure to Banks' Foreign Claims[1]

The regions most exposed to foreign claims from euro area banks are other advanced Europe and emerging Europe. This is true even if affiliates' claims funded with local deposits (which are less likely to be withdrawn) are ignored or if differences in financial deepening across regions are taken into account. Total foreign exposures show a much higher potential for broader vulnerability, especially in other advanced Europe, advanced Asia, and North America.

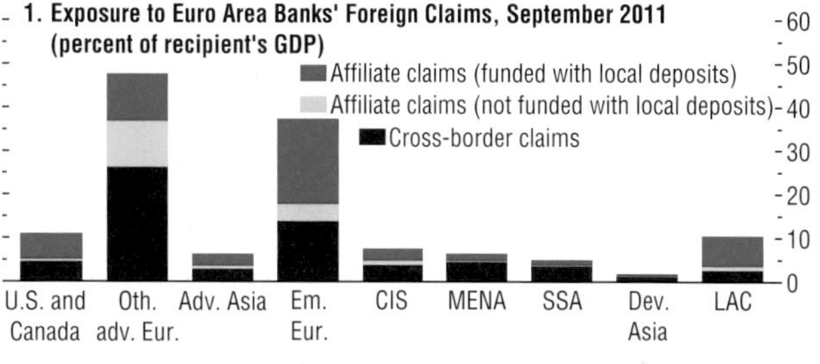

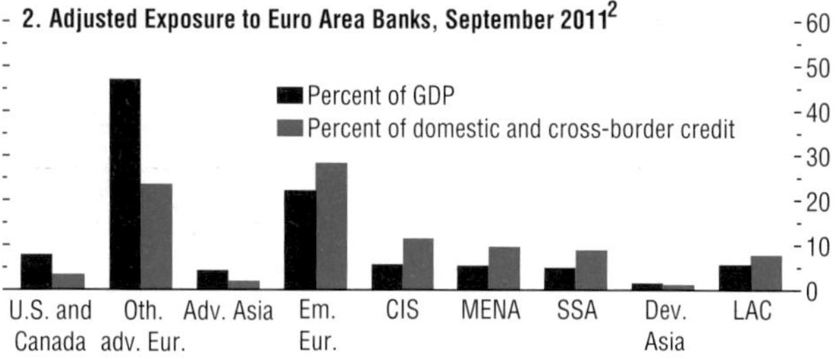

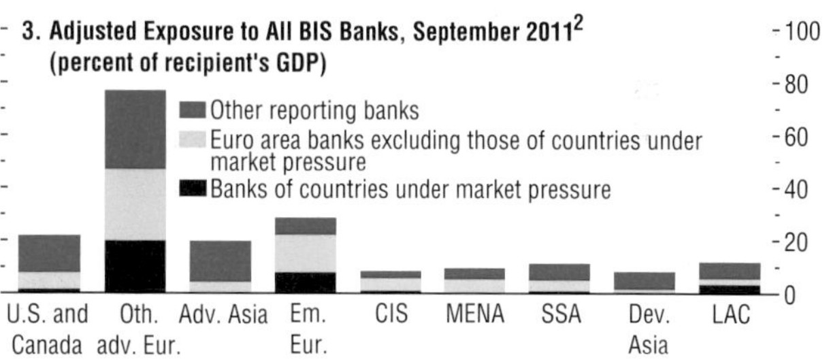

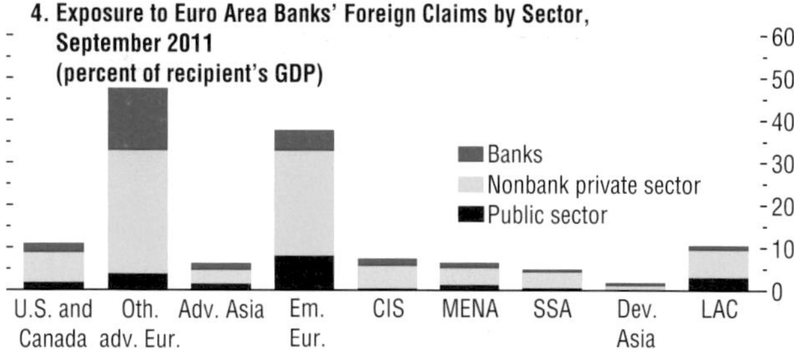

Sources: Bank for International Settlements (BIS); Cerutti, Claessens, and McGuire (2011); and IMF staff estimates.

[1]Advanced Asia (Adv. Asia): Australia, Hong Kong SAR, Japan, Korea, New Zealand, Singapore, Taiwan Province of China; CIS: Commonwealth of Independent States; Dev. Asia: developing Asia; Em. Eur.: emerging Europe; LAC: Latin America and the Caribbean; MENA: Middle East and North Africa; Other advanced Europe (Oth. adv. Eur.): Czech Republic, Denmark, Iceland, Israel, Norway, Sweden, Switzerland, United Kingdom; SSA: sub-Saharan Africa.

[2]Adjusted borrowers' exposure to BIS-reporting banks is defined as the sum of cross-border claims, off-balance-sheet credit commitments, and affiliate claims not funded through local deposits. See Cerutti, Claessens, and McGuire (2011). Countries under market pressure: Belgium, Greece, Ireland, Italy, Portugal, Spain.

area banks tightened lending standards strongly during the third and fourth quarters of 2011, reflecting difficult access to market funding as well as weaker economic activity. And expectations are for further tightening in early 2012.

General lending conditions in the various regions (including domestic banks' deleveraging) deteriorated significantly in emerging markets during the third and fourth quarters of 2011. The strongest declines were in emerging Europe, Africa, and the Middle East. Data on growth of real credit to the private sector do not yet show a significant change in trend, but there is a lag in recording these data.[21] The deterioration in international market funding conditions was a major reason for the tightening, and a majority of respondents in all regions attributed the tightening at least in part to financial strains in the euro area.[22] Some tightening was also observed in the major advanced economies (Japan, United Kingdom, United States). U.S. dollar funding pressures had been building since the summer, but when six major central banks decided in November to lower the interest rate on dollar swap lines and extend the swap facilities until February 1, 2013, it provided some relief. In the wake of events in the euro area, credit default swap (CDS) spreads of banks around the world also rose in fall 2011, though they have eased somewhat recently.

There were also indications of pressure in trade finance, though it appears manageable so far. Trade finance surveys indicate deterioration in supply conditions as a result of financial constraints (less credit or liquidity available at counterparty banks and less credit from international financial institutions), reflecting at least in part euro area bank deleveraging.[23] But so far the impact has been more on pricing than on volume because other banks have stepped in to fill the gap.[24]

Figure 2.SF.3. Regional Vulnerabilities

Emerging Europe and the Commonwealth of Independent States (CIS) also have broader external vulnerabilities, which could make them more vulnerable should global risk aversion rise significantly.

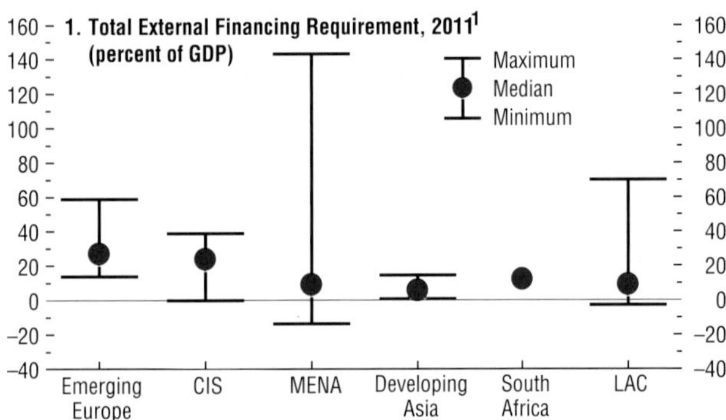

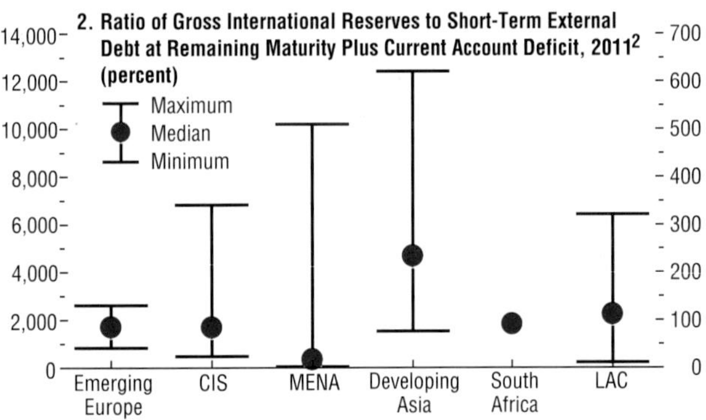

Source: IMF staff calculations.
[1]CIS: Commonwealth of Independent States. MENA: Middle East and North Africa. LAC: Latin America and the Caribbean.
[2]MENA on left scale; others on right scale.

[21]Credit growth remains high in most emerging markets (with the exception of the MENA and SSA regions) and weak or negative in most advanced regions (with the exception of other advanced Asia).

[22]Institute of International Finance Survey of Emerging Markets Bank Lending Conditions.

[23]Institute of International Finance Survey of Emerging Markets Bank Lending Conditions and ICC-IMF Market Snapshot, January 2012.

[24]There is also more concern about long-term trade and project financing, for which the syndication market has shut down. It is

Finally, issuances in bond and equity markets—an alternative to bank credit—had been weakening across the board, but the most recent data on fund flows to emerging markets show strong inflows of late, signaling that global risk aversion may have decreased (see Chapter 1).

How Much Impact on Growth?

The impact of bank credit reduction on growth depends on several factors: (1) the extent to which other sources of funding can replace bank credit, (2) the evolution of the demand for credit, and (3) various regions' policy room to react to funding tightening. As for substitution of bank credit with other funding, although a full offset is unlikely (see above), other sources of funding could substantially close the gap. In many countries, domestic financial systems appear on average well capitalized and may have the potential to fill gaps.[25] In general, countries with strong domestic growth may be in a better position to substitute funding thanks to healthy banking and corporate sectors. Bond and equity markets could substitute for bank loans in advanced economies, but in emerging markets, these are still small relative to the size of the economy. The offsetting potential will depend greatly on global risk aversion. If euro area bank deleveraging were to cause a substantial rise in global risk aversion, a broader retrenchment of all sources of funding is likely.

The growth impact of bank deleveraging also depends on credit demand. For instance, if overly indebted households or firms are trying to repair their balance sheets, bank deleveraging will not be as binding and may not add to deterioration in growth beyond what is reflected in falling credit demand. Weakening credit demand in some of the

hard for new entrants to step in owing to the complex nature of the contracts.

[25]Banks appear well capitalized on average in most regions, with regulatory Tier 1 capital to risk-weighted assets well above 9 percent, a high return to equity (except in the United States and the United Kingdom), and low numbers of nonperforming loans (except in emerging Europe and some CIS economies). This does not preclude risks of financial instability, however. As we have learned from the crisis, a handful of financial institutions can bring down the whole financial system, even if the financial system is sound and healthy on average.

Figure 2.SF.4. Evolution of Banks' Adjusted Foreign Claims over Time[1]

Since June 2011, there has been a retrenchment of global foreign claims affecting several emerging markets but also advanced Asia. In addition to reductions in euro area bank claims, several emerging markets have suffered outflows of funding from non-euro-area banks, while advanced economies have seen inflows of non-euro-area funding.

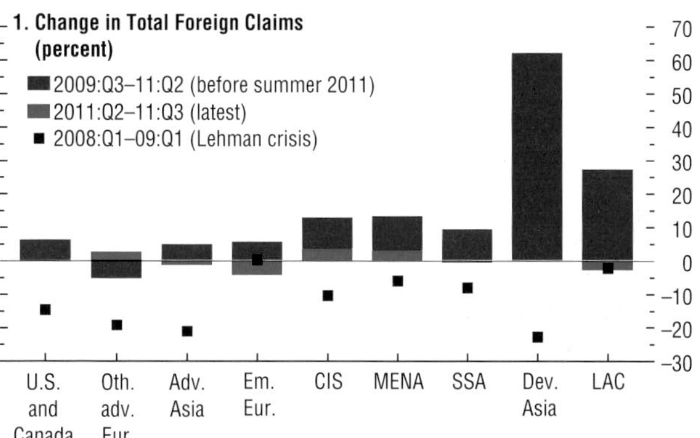

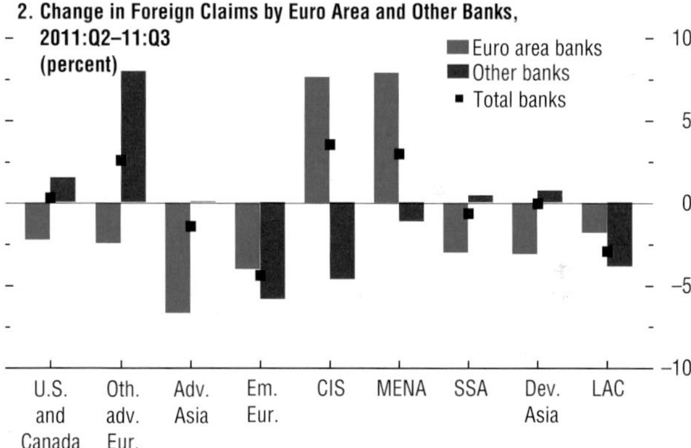

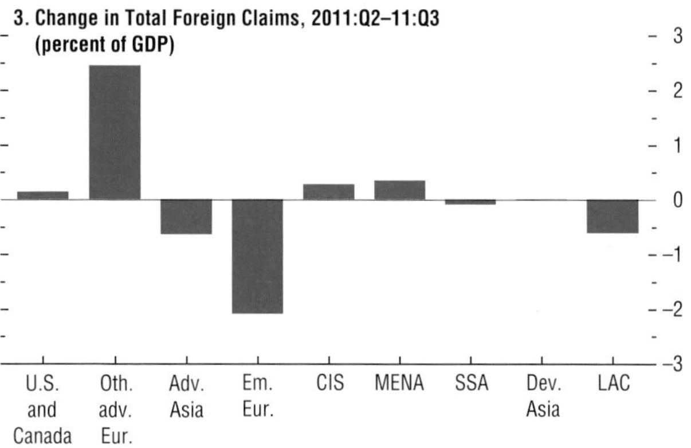

Sources: Bank for International Settlements (BIS); and IMF staff estimates.
[1]Based on BIS consolidated foreign claims at ultimate risk basis, adjusted for the exchange rate and breaks in series (Cerutti, 2012). Advanced Asia (Adv. Asia): Australia, Hong Kong SAR, Japan, Korea, New Zealand, Singapore, Taiwan Province of China; CIS: Commonwealth of Independent States; Dev. Asia: developing Asia; Em. Eur.: emerging Europe; LAC: Latin America and the Caribbean; MENA: Middle East and North Africa; Other advanced Europe (Oth. adv. Eur.): Czech Republic, Denmark, Iceland, Israel, Norway, Sweden, Switzerland, United Kingdom; SSA: sub-Saharan Africa.

most exposed regions, such as emerging Europe and some advanced economies (euro area, Japan, United Kingdom, United States) may thus mitigate harm to growth caused by a reduction in credit. In other emerging markets, especially Asia and Latin America, credit demand is holding up well, but strong economic growth may generate additional sources of financing that can substitute for bank lending.

Finally, in countries where there is enough policy room, policymakers may be able to offset some of the impact of deleveraging by relaxing fiscal or monetary policy. Compared with 2007, the fiscal position of most regions, measured by the fiscal balance and public debt, has deteriorated substantially, especially in advanced economies. Debt levels and deficits remain more moderate in emerging markets on average, but some economies (for example, in emerging Europe and the CIS) lack fiscal room and may actually have to tighten fiscal policy in case of a renewed downturn due to fiscal financing pressures. Advanced economies (euro area, Japan, United Kingdom, United States) already have very low interest rates and are close to or have hit the zero-bound constraint to easing monetary policy. Room for monetary easing could also be constrained in some emerging market economies facing inflation pressure (India, Indonesia, Korea) or still working through the previous credit expansion is still being worked through (China). However, in these economies less credit would help reduce overheating pressures.

Simulations of Deleveraging Effects

To illustrate the potential impact of bank deleveraging on growth in the various regions of the world, we use the baseline European bank deleveraging scenario explained in the *Global Financial Stability Report*. This scenario features (1) funding pressures partly offset by the ECB's two LTROs; (2) a 9 percent core Tier 1 ratio by June 2012; (3) announced deleveraging plans; (4) progress toward the net stable funding ratio imposed by Basel III; and (5) a home bias—that is, banks deleverage first outside the European Union, next in the European Union but not in the home country, and finally in the home country. In this scenario, more than 50 percent of the reduction in the amount of credit by euro area banks takes place outside the euro area, and outside the euro area the largest declines in percent of GDP are in the group that includes emerging Europe, the CIS, and other developing economies (specifically, the MENA and SSA regions) (Figure 2.SF.5). These amounts of deleveraging are relative to a scenario without deleveraging. Some deleveraging was likely already planned by banks before September 2011, consistent with the IMF staff's sluggish growth projections; some was likely triggered by developments since September.

The impact of deleveraging is simulated using the IMF's Global Economy Model, a quarterly, multiregion dynamic stochastic general equilibrium model. In this simulation, the reduction in regional bank credit calculated in the *Global Financial Stability Report* scenario is calibrated through an increase in the region's corporate spread.[26] It should be noted that there are some limitations to the model simulations, which suggests that the estimates probably represent upper bounds of the likely effects on economic growth of the change in credit supply: (1) The model does not incorporate offsets from other sources of funding, including domestic banks. (2) The simulations cannot distinguish credit supply from credit demand; hence, they may be overestimating the impact of the change in credit supply in some regions. (3) The response of monetary policy in the euro area, Japan, and the United States is constrained by the zero bound on nominal interest rates and does not take into account the possibility of further quantitative easing under a downside scenario. The largest effect of deleveraging is in the euro area, with growth reductions of 0.9 and 0.6 percentage point, respectively, in 2012 and 2013. Outside the euro area, the United States, Japan, emerging Asia, and Latin America are only slightly affected, largely through

[26]The model is calibrated to reflect existing estimates, suggesting that a 1 percent reduction in credit reduces growth by about 0.35 percentage point. Estimates are for the euro area, emerging Europe, and the United States, but a similar coefficient is used for all the regions. An important assumption behind the simulations is that the response of monetary policy to the slowdown in the euro area, Japan, and the United States is constrained by the zero bound on nominal interest rates. The zero-bound constraint on nominal interest rates is particularly damaging for growth in the United States (relative to Japan or the euro area) because of high price flexibility: the decline in prices from lower activity pushes real interest rates higher, further dampening activity.

lower exports as a result of reduced euro area growth. Growth in other economies (which includes emerging Europe, CIS, and the MENA and SSA regions) is more affected, especially in 2012 (by about 0.8 percentage point). The model does not provide separate estimates for emerging Europe, but regression estimates suggest that the growth effect of deleveraging could also be 0.7 percentage point.[27] Thus, overall, the growth impact of euro area bank deleveraging would be relatively moderate, except in Europe.

Policy Implications

Policymakers are taking action to mitigate the expected impact of deleveraging by euro area banks and should be prepared to do more if needed, both in the euro area and in the rest of the world. For the euro area, continued provision by the ECB of ample liquidity at short and longer maturities is the key to smooth deleveraging. Given the currently very unfavorable market conditions for raising private capital, increased public funding to inject capital into banks would reduce the risk of a credit crunch. Making the European Financial Stability Facility more attractive and effective for bank recapitalization and ensuring that it is adequately funded would be especially helpful for economies subject to market pressures, but could also give other economies a leg up (reflecting highly linked financial systems and real economies in the euro area). If the 9 percent core Tier 1 capital ratio appears to be triggering swift deleveraging, it may be necessary to give banks more flexibility to reconstitute their capital buffers.

Policymakers in the rest of the world should be prepared to mitigate the impact of euro area bank deleveraging on growth through fiscal and monetary easing—provided there is enough policy room. Policymakers should also be ready to backstop liquidity in their banking systems should the need arise. Options range from swap lines with the Federal Reserve to alleviate dollar shortages for countries that currently do not have them to regional pooling arrangements, drawing down the

[27]The estimated regressions are from Chapter 4 of the October 2011 *Regional Economic Outlook: Europe.*

Figure 2.SF.5. Potential Impact of European Bank Deleveraging on Growth[1]

The impact of deleveraging on growth absent any significant rise in global risk aversion is very moderate, except in the euro area countries under market pressure and in the group of other economies (which includes CIS, emerging Europe, MENA, and SSA). Some of this deleveraging was already planned and ongoing before the fall of 2011. These are upper-bound estimates. Indeed, the model does not account for the fact that other sources of funding, including domestic banks in some non-euro-area countries, are providing some offset; it does not distinguish credit supply from credit demand; and advanced economies could engage in further unconventional monetary easing if growth weakens.

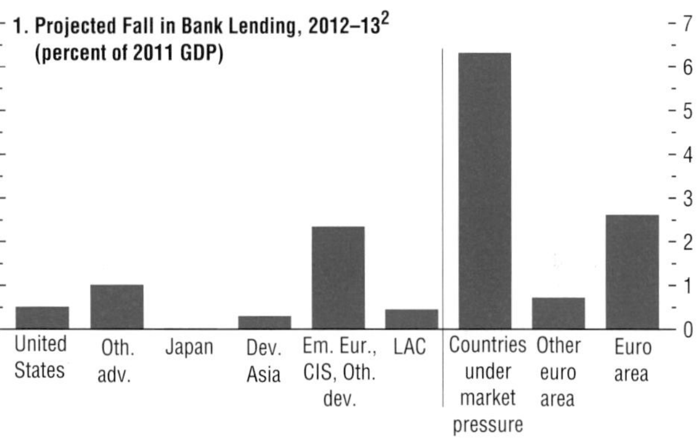

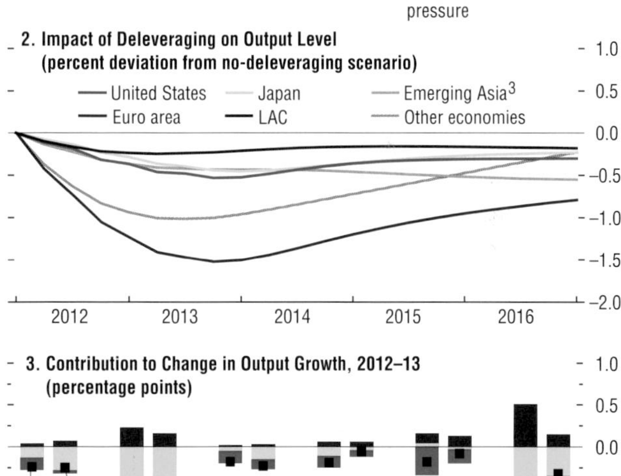

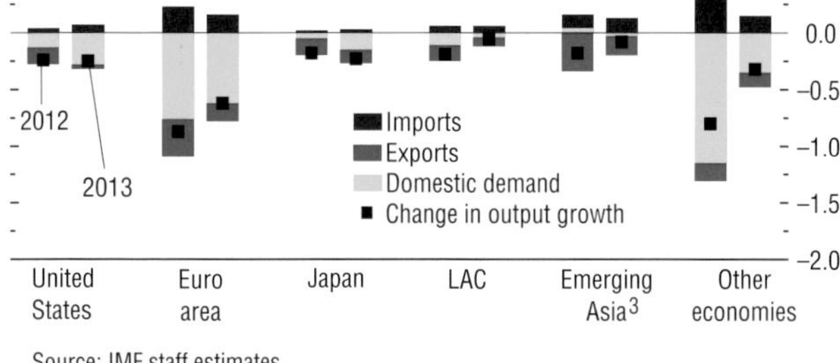

Source: IMF staff estimates.

[1]Based on the *GFSR* baseline scenario of European bank deleveraging.

[2]The projected fall in bank lending supply is from the 58 EU banks in the *GFSR* bank deleveraging exercise (baseline scenario). For the euro area, and for four of the economies included in the other advanced group (Czech Republic, Denmark, Sweden, United Kingdom), it also includes the projected fall in bank lending supply from other domestic banks in the economy. CIS: Commonwealth of Independent States; Countries under market pressure: Greece, Ireland, Italy, Portugal, Spain; Dev. Asia: developing Asia; Em. Eur.: emerging Europe; LAC: Latin America and the Caribbean; Other advanced (Oth. adv.): Australia, Canada, Czech Republic, Denmark, Hong Kong SAR, Iceland, Israel, Korea, New Zealand, Norway, Singapore, Sweden, Switzerland, Taiwan Province of China, United Kingdom; Other developing (Oth. dev.): Middle East and North Africa and sub-Saharan Africa; Other euro area: Austria, Belgium, Cyprus, Estonia, Finland, France, Germany, Luxembourg, Malta, Netherlands, Slovak Republic, Slovenia.

[3]Emerging Asia: developing Asia and Hong Kong SAR, Korea, Singapore, and Taiwan Province of China.

large stock of foreign reserves (in some economies), and enhanced deposit guarantees. Thinly capitalized banks should be directed to increase their capital buffers. Finally, policymakers should ensure that the supply of credit is maintained for credit-rationed agents (small and medium-size firms, households) and for trade financing, possibly stepping in through government programs if needed, without creating distortions in the allocation of credit.

Box 2.1. East-West Linkages and Spillovers in Europe

Regional economic and financial integration between western and eastern Europe has advanced rapidly since the fall of the Iron Curtain.[1] As a result, regional spillovers have also increased. They were prominent during the 2008–09 crisis and again in fall 2011, when the euro area crisis escalated. This box reviews recent developments in integration and analyzes spillovers between western and eastern Europe.

Regional economic and financial integration between western and eastern Europe has increased in many areas. Two prominent features are banking sector integration and the buildup of production chains within the context of greater general trade integration.

- The financial sector in eastern Europe has become closely integrated with the banking sector in western Europe through both ownership and financing. Much of the banking system in the region is now owned by banks in western Europe, particularly parent banks headquartered in Austria, France, and Italy. During the precrisis boom years, parent banks increased both financing to their subsidiaries and direct cross-border lending to nonbanks. As a result, banks reporting to the Bank for International Settlements (BIS), most of which are headquartered in western Europe, now have a significant market share in eastern Europe. Their assets account for more than half of total assets in the banking system in a number of economies (Figure 2.1.1).
- Trade integration has grown rapidly. For western Europe, eastern Europe is the most dynamic export market, with exports increasing from slightly less than 1 percent of GDP in 1995 to about 3¼ percent in 2010. They are now higher than those to Asia or the Western Hemisphere. Conversely, western Europe is eastern Europe's largest export market, with exports to that destination accounting for about 15 percent of the region's GDP.

The authors of this box are Bas B. Bakker, Phakawa Jeasakul, and Yuko Kinoshita.

[1]In this box "eastern Europe" refers to countries in central, eastern, and southeastern Europe (CESEE); "western Europe" refers to the euro area, Denmark, Iceland, Norway, Sweden, Switzerland, and the United Kingdom.

Figure 2.1.1. Eastern Europe: Financial Linkages with Western Europe[1]

1. Funding from BIS-Reporting Banks, 2011:Q3 (exposure relative to GDP; percent)

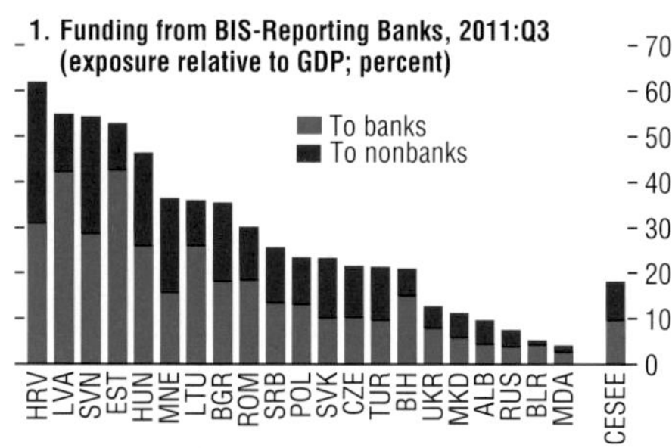

2. Consolidated Claims of BIS-Reporting Banks by Country of Bank Ownership, 2011:Q3[2] (relative to banking system's total assets; percent)

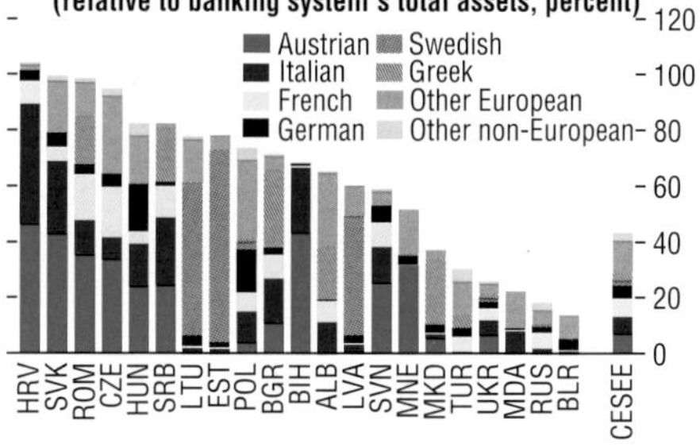

Sources: Bank for International Settlements (BIS) Locational and Consolidated Banking Statistics (Tables 6A, 6B, 9B); and IMF staff calculations.

[1]ALB: Albania; BGR: Bulgaria; BLR: Belarus; BIH: Bosnia and Herzegovina; CESEE: Central, eastern, and southeastern Europe; CZE: Czech Republic; EST: Estonia; HRV: Croatia; HUN: Hungary; LTU: Lithuania; LVA: Latvia; MDA: Moldova; MKD: former Yugoslav Republic of Macedonia; MNE: Montenegro; POL: Poland; ROM: Romania; RUS: Russia; SRB: Serbia; SVK: Slovak Republic; SVN: Slovenia; TUR: Turkey; UKR: Ukraine.

[2]The bottom figure is constructed using BIS consolidated banking statistics, which show the stock of gross assets owned by BIS-reporting banks in each CESEE country. These assets may be funded domestically (for example, through domestic deposits), through parent banks, or through the international wholesale market. Although in many CESEE countries financial integration with western Europe is also visible through the high volume of funding from parent banks, in some other countries (for example, Czech Republic, Slovak Republic) domestic banking systems are mostly domestically financed even though they are owned mostly by western European banking groups.

- Cross-border production chains have multiplied, especially in the automobile sector. German firms in particular have relocated some of their production to the region. Within these produc-

Box 2.1. *(continued)*

tion chains, eastern European economies have specialized in final assembly, while core components are produced in western Europe. The stock of foreign direct investment in the region is about 42 percent of GDP on average, most of it owned by firms in western Europe.

Within these broad trends, the degree of integration varies across countries. Central Europe and the Baltics are the most intertwined with western Europe. Southeastern Europe is less integrated. It has fewer cross-border production chains and less trade with western Europe.

Growth, Trade, and Financial Spillovers

Given the tight linkages, it has long been recognized that shocks originating in western Europe can affect eastern Europe's economies. But reverse spillovers can also be important. Germany's export growth during the precrisis years was boosted by strong demand from eastern Europe, while the sharp contraction in eastern Europe in 2009 exacerbated the German downturn.[2] In financial markets, increases in credit default swap (CDS) spreads of Austrian parent banks in early 2009 partly reflected their exposure to the crisis in some eastern European countries.

A variety of empirical models confirms that growth and trade spillovers are quantitatively important, with a shock in western Europe affecting eastern Europe as much as one for one.[3] In particular, a vector autoregression model, which implicitly involves spillovers through many channels of transmission, suggests even larger spillover effects. A shock to growth in western Europe has a one-for-one effect on growth in eastern Europe. In contrast, a growth shock in eastern Europe has no significant effect on growth in western Europe. However, the effects of a shock emanating from central Europe on growth in western Europe are statistically significant, with spillover magnitudes of about one-third.

Models also confirm that financial spillovers matter, with funding from western European parent banks strongly affecting credit and domestic demand growth in eastern Europe. The financing provided by western European banks added 1½ percentage points to eastern Europe's annual GDP growth during 2003–08, when annual average growth was 6½ percent. Financial and trade spillovers also interact because shocks to financial flows from western Europe to eastern Europe are soon felt in trade flows. An estimated 57 cents of each euro of bank financing from western Europe ended up being spent on imports from that region.

Spillovers from the Euro Area Crisis

Until early fall 2011, there had been little impact of the euro area crisis on eastern Europe. While CDS spreads in the euro area periphery rose steadily, those in eastern Europe remained flat or declined, as the region recovered from the deep recession of 2008–09.

The picture changed when the euro area crisis intensified late last year. East-West banking linkages proved to be an important channel of transmission. CDS spreads widened for large western European banks, reflecting their significant funding pressure. These, in turn, triggered sizable balance sheet deleveraging, including of assets in eastern Europe. BIS locational statistics show that western European banks' exposure to the region declined by almost 5 percent in the third quarter of 2011, the biggest quarterly decline since the 2008–09 crisis. Financial market spillovers also mattered. Sovereign CDS spreads in the region increased—the magnitude of the increases varied with underlying vulnerability, with those on Hungarian bonds particularly large—and currencies came under pressure.

Reflecting these spillovers, and notwithstanding improved euro area sentiment, growth in eastern Europe is expected to slow sharply this year, and downside risks are significant. This outlook highlights how greater economic and financial integration and the potential for greater cross-border spillovers have raised new policy challenges

[2]During 2003–08, German exports to central, eastern, and southeastern Europe grew by 16 percent annually in real terms, raising total export growth 6½ percent to 8¼ percent; in 2009, they dropped by 26 percent, which worsened the contraction of Germany's exports from 12¼ to 16¼ percent.

[3]The models are described in Chapter 4 of the October 2011 *Regional Economic Outlook: Europe.*

Box 2.1. ***(continued)***

for eastern European economies. A key concern is that funding from foreign parent banks could be constrained for some time. Measures to support bank financing from domestic sources, including the domestic deposit base, could help to enable appropriate business and consumer credit expansion. Adequate liquidity and solvency of the domestic banking sector will play an important role in supporting depositors' confidence, as will policies geared toward lowering macroeconomic imbalances and vulnerability. Compared with 2008, some areas of vulnerability are lower. High current account deficits are no longer an issue in most economies. But in other areas vulnerability is still high—external debt in many economies is still large, and foreign currency balance sheet exposure remains a problem. In addition, a number of new weaknesses have emerged—including a high number of nonperforming loans and large fiscal deficits—which have only been partially addressed.

References

Adrian, Tobias, Paolo Colla, and Hyun Song Shin, 2012, "Which Financial Frictions? Parsing the Evidence from the Financial Crisis of 2007–09," paper presented at the Annual Meeting of the American Economic Association, Chicago, January.

Board of Governors of the Federal Reserve System (BGFRS), 2012, "The U.S. Housing Market: Current Conditions and Policy Considerations" (Washington).

Cerutti, Eugenio, 2012, "Foreign Bank Default Exposures and Rollover Risks: Measurement, Evolution, and Determinants," (unpublished; Washington: International Monetary Fund).

———, Stijn Claessens, and Patrick McGuire, 2011, "Systemic Risks in Global Banking: What Available Data Can Tell Us and What More Data Are Needed," IMF Working Paper 11/222 (Washington: International Monetary Fund).

Coady, David, Robert Gillingham, Rolando Ossowski, John Piotrowski, Shamsuddin Tareq, and Justin Tyson, 2010, "Petroleum Product Subsidies: Costly, Inequitable, and Rising," IMF Staff Position Note No. 10/05 (Washington: International Monetary Fund).

Diebold, Francis X., and Kamil Yilmaz, 2012, "Better to Give than to Receive: Predictive Directional Measurement of Volatility Spillovers," *International Journal of Forecasting*, Vol. 28, pp. 57–66.

International Monetary Fund (IMF), 2008, *International Financial Statistics*, IMF Statistics Department (Washington).

———, 2011, *Euro Area Policies: Spillover Report for the 2011 Article IV Consultation and Selected Issues,* IMF Country Report No. 11/185 (Washington).

CHAPTER 3

DEALING WITH HOUSEHOLD DEBT

Does household debt amplify downturns and weaken recoveries? Based on an analysis of advanced economies over the past three decades, we find that housing busts and recessions preceded by larger run-ups in household debt tend to be more severe and protracted. These patterns are consistent with the predictions of recent theoretical models. Based on case studies, we find that government policies can help prevent prolonged contractions in economic activity by addressing the problem of excessive household debt. In particular, bold household debt restructuring programs such as those implemented in the United States in the 1930s and in Iceland today can significantly reduce debt repayment burdens and the number of household defaults and foreclosures. Such policies can therefore help avert self-reinforcing cycles of household defaults, further house price declines, and additional contractions in output.

Household debt soared in the years leading up to the Great Recession. In advanced economies, during the five years preceding 2007, the ratio of household debt to income rose by an average of 39 percentage points, to 138 percent. In Denmark, Iceland, Ireland, the Netherlands, and Norway, debt peaked at more than 200 percent of household income. A surge in household debt to historic highs also occurred in emerging economies such as Estonia, Hungary, Latvia, and Lithuania. The concurrent boom in both house prices and the stock market meant that household debt relative to assets held broadly stable, which masked households' growing exposure to a sharp fall in asset prices (Figure 3.1).

When house prices declined, ushering in the global financial crisis, many households saw their wealth shrink relative to their debt, and, with less income and more unemployment, found it harder to meet mortgage payments. By the end of 2011, real house prices had fallen from their peak by about 41 percent in Ireland, 29 percent in Iceland, 23 percent in Spain and the United States, and 21 percent in Denmark. Household defaults, underwater mortgages (where the loan balance exceeds the house value), foreclosures, and fire sales are now endemic to a number of economies. Household deleveraging by paying off debts or defaulting on them has begun in some countries. It has been most pronounced in the United States, where about two-thirds of the debt reduction reflects defaults (McKinsey, 2012).

What does this imply for economic performance? Some studies suggest that many economies' total gross debt levels are excessive and need to decline.[1] For example, two influential reports by McKinsey (2010, 2012) emphasize that to "clear the way" for economic growth, advanced economies need to reverse the recent surge in total gross debt. Yet others suggest that the recent rise in debt is not necessarily a reason for concern. For example, Fatás (2012) argues that the McKinsey reports' focus on gross debt is "very misleading," since what matters for countries is net wealth and not gross debt.[2] A high level of private sector debt as a share of the economy is also often interpreted as a sign of financial development, which in turn is beneficial for long-term growth (see, for example, Rajan and Zingales, 1998). Similarly, Krugman (2011) notes that because gross debt is "(mostly) money we owe to ourselves," it is not immediately obvious why it should matter. However, Krugman also cautions that gross debt can become a problem. Overall, there is no accepted wisdom about whether and how gross debt may restrain economic activity.

The main authors of this chapter are Daniel Leigh (team leader), Deniz Igan, John Simon, and Petia Topalova, with contributions from Edda Rós Karlsdóttir and Franek Rozwadowski and support from Shan Chen and Angela Espiritu. Christopher Carroll was the external consultant.

[1]Sovereign debt rose sharply in advanced economies as a result of the crisis, and overall gross debt has reached levels not seen in half a century.

[2]To illustrate this point, Fatás (2012) refers to Japan, where the gross-debt-to-GDP ratio is exceptionally high but where, reflecting years of current account surpluses, the economy is a net *creditor* to the rest of the world. Similarly, the elevated Japanese gross government debt stock corresponds to large private sector assets.

Figure 3.1. Household Debt, House Prices, and Nonperforming Mortgage Loans, 2002–10

Household debt and house prices soared in the years leading up to the Great Recession. When house prices declined, ushering in the global financial crisis, household nonperforming mortgage loans rose sharply in a number of economies.

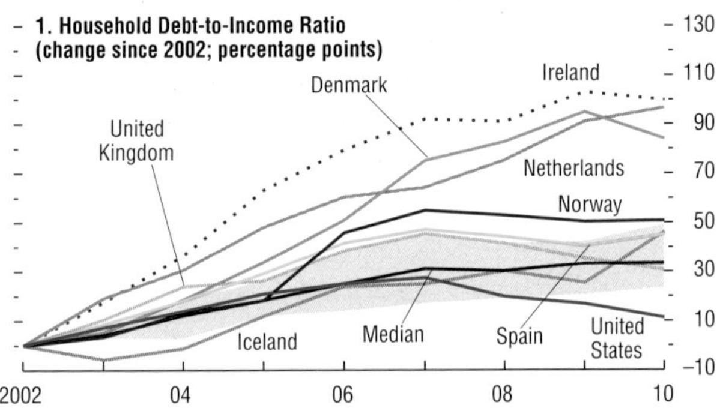

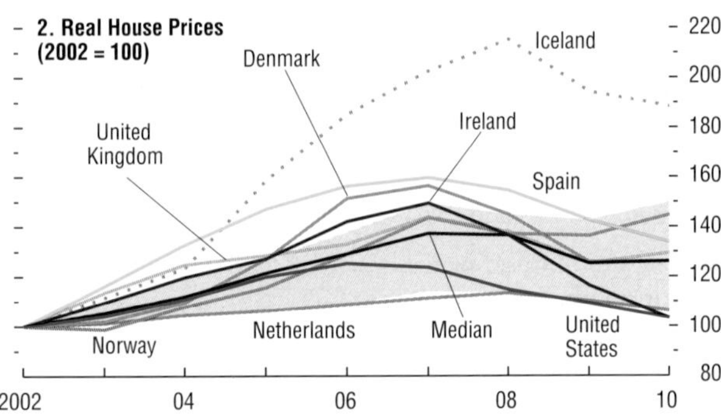

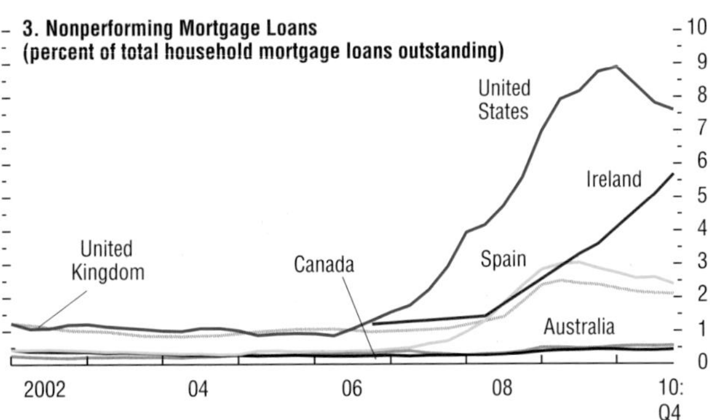

Sources: Eurostat; Haver Analytics; Federal Reserve Bank of New York; Reserve Bank of Australia; Bank of Spain; U.K. Council of Mortgage Lenders; Central Bank of Ireland; Chapter 3 of the April 2011 *Global Financial Stability Report*; and IMF staff calculations.

Note: The shaded areas in panels 1 and 2 denote the interquartile range of the change in the household debt-to-income ratio since 2002 and the real house price index, respectively. Nonperforming loans are loans more than 90 days in arrears.

This chapter contributes to the debate over gross debt by focusing on the household sector. Previous studies have focused more on deleveraging by other sectors.[3] In particular, we address the following questions:

- What is the relationship between household debt and the depth of economic downturns? Are busts that are preceded by larger run-ups in gross household debt typically more severe?
- Why might gross household debt be a problem? What are the theoretical mechanisms by which gross household debt and deleveraging may restrain economic activity?[4]
- What can governments do to support growth when household debt becomes a problem? In particular, what policies have been effective in reducing the extent of household debt overhang and in averting unnecessary household defaults, foreclosures, and fire sales? How effective have recent initiatives been?[5]

To address these questions, we first conduct a statistical analysis of the relationship between household debt and the depth of economic downturns. Our purpose is to provide prima facie evidence rather than to establish causality. We focus on housing busts, given the important role of the housing market in triggering the Great Recession, but also consider recessions more generally. We then review the theoretical reasons why household debt might constrain economic activity. Finally, we use selected case studies to investigate which government policies have been effective in dealing with excessive house-

[3]For example, see Chapter 3 of the October 2010 *World Economic Outlook,* which assesses the implications of sovereign deleveraging (fiscal consolidation). Since deleveraging by various sectors—household, bank, corporate, and sovereign—will have different implications for economic activity, each is worth studying in its own right.

[4]A related question is what level of household debt is optimal, but such an assessment is beyond the scope of this chapter.

[5]We do not investigate which policies can help prevent the excessive buildup of household debt before the bust, an issue that is addressed in other studies. These two sets of policies are not mutually exclusive. For example, policies that prevent an excessive buildup in household debt during a boom can alleviate the consequences of a bust. See Crowe and others (2011), Chapter 3 of the September 2011 *Global Financial Stability Report,* and Dell'Ariccia and others (forthcoming) for policies designed to avert real estate price booms and restrain rapid growth in private sector debt.

hold debt. The episodes considered are the United States in the 1930s and today, Hungary and Iceland today, Colombia in 1999, and the Scandinavian countries in the early 1990s. In each case, there was a housing bust preceded by or coinciding with a substantial increase in household debt, but the policy responses were very different.

These are the chapter's main findings:

- Housing busts preceded by larger run-ups in gross household debt are associated with significantly larger contractions in economic activity. The declines in household consumption and real GDP are substantially larger, unemployment rises more, and the reduction in economic activity persists for at least five years. A similar pattern holds for recessions more generally: recessions preceded by larger increases in household debt are more severe.
- The larger declines in economic activity are not simply a reflection of the larger drops in house prices and the associated destruction of household wealth. It seems to be the *combination* of house price declines and prebust leverage that explains the severity of the contraction. In particular, household consumption falls by more than four times the amount that can be explained by the fall in house prices in high-debt economies. Nor is the larger contraction simply driven by financial crises. The relationship between household debt and the contraction in consumption also holds for economies that did not experience a banking crisis around the time of the housing bust.
- Macroeconomic policies are a crucial element of forestalling excessive contractions in economic activity during episodes of household deleveraging. For example, monetary easing in economies in which mortgages typically have variable interest rates, as in the Scandinavian countries, can quickly reduce mortgage payments and avert household defaults. Similarly, fiscal transfers to households through social safety nets can boost households' incomes and improve their ability to service debt, as in the Scandinavian countries. Such automatic transfers can further help prevent self-reinforcing cycles of rising defaults, declining house prices, and lower aggregate demand. Macroeconomic stimulus, however, has its limits. The zero lower bound on nominal interest rates can prevent sufficient rate cuts, and high government debt may constrain the scope for deficit-financed transfers.
- Government policies targeted at reducing the level of household debt relative to household assets and debt service relative to household repayment capacity can—at a limited fiscal cost—substantially mitigate the negative effects of household deleveraging on economic activity. In particular, bold and well-designed household debt restructuring programs, such as those implemented in the United States in the 1930s and in Iceland today, can significantly reduce the number of household defaults and foreclosures. In so doing, these programs help prevent self-reinforcing cycles of declining house prices and lower aggregate demand.

The first section of this chapter conducts a statistical analysis to shed light on the relationship between the rise in household debt during a boom and the severity of the subsequent bust. It also reviews the theoretical literature to identify the channels through which shifts in household gross debt can have a negative effect on economic activity. The second section provides case studies of government policies aimed at mitigating the negative effects of household debt during housing busts. The last section discusses the implications of our findings for economies facing household deleveraging.

How Household Debt Can Constrain Economic Activity

This section sheds light on the role of gross household debt in amplifying slumps by analyzing the experience of advanced economies over the past three decades. We also review the theoretical reasons gross household debt can deepen and prolong economic contractions.

Stylized Facts: Household Debt and Housing Busts

Are housing busts more severe when they are preceded by large increases in gross household debt? To answer this question, we provide some stylized facts about what happens when a housing bust occurs in two groups of economies. The first has a

Figure 3.2. The Great Recession: Consumption Loss versus Precrisis Rise in Household Debt
(Percent)

The Great Recession was particularly severe in economies that experienced a larger run-up in household debt prior to the crisis.

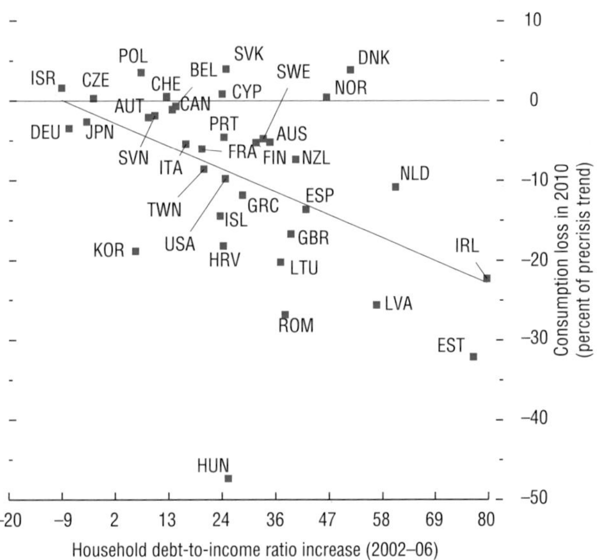

Sources: Eurostat; Haver Analytics; and IMF staff calculations.
Note: The consumption loss in 2010 is the gap between the (log) level of real household consumption in 2010 and the projection of where real household consumption would have been that year based on the precrisis trend. The precrisis trend is defined as the extrapolation of the (log) level of real household consumption based on a linear trend estimated from 1996 to 2004. AUS: Australia; AUT: Austria; BEL: Belgium; CAN: Canada; CHE: Switzerland; CYP: Cyprus; CZE: Czech Republic; DEU: Germany; DNK: Denmark; ESP: Spain; EST: Estonia; FIN: Finland; FRA: France; GBR: United Kingdom; GRC: Greece; HRV: Croatia; HUN: Hungary; IRL: Ireland; ISL: Iceland; ISR: Israel; ITA: Italy; JPN: Japan; KOR: Korea; LTU: Lithuania; LVA: Latvia; NLD: Netherlands; NOR: Norway; NZL: New Zealand; POL: Poland; PRT: Portugal; ROM: Romania; SVK: Slovak Republic; SVN: Slovenia; SWE: Sweden; TWN: Taiwan Province of China; USA: United States.

housing boom but no increase in household debt. The other has a housing boom and a large increase in household debt. We focus on housing busts, given how prevalent they were in advanced economies during the Great Recession.[6] But we also report results for recessions in general, whether or not they are associated with a housing bust. We start by summarizing how different economies fared during the Great Recession depending on the size of their household debt buildup. We then use a more refined statistical approach to consider the broader historical experience with housing busts and recessions and to distinguish the role of household debt from the roles of financial crises and house price declines.

The Great Recession

The Great Recession was particularly severe in economies that had a larger buildup in household debt prior to the crisis. As Figure 3.2 shows, the consumption loss in 2010 relative to the precrisis trend was greater for economies that had a larger rise in the gross household debt-to-income ratio during 2002–06.[7] The consumption loss in 2010 is the gap between the (log) level of real household consumption in 2010 and the projection of where real household consumption would have been that year based on the precrisis trend. The precrisis trend is, in turn, defined as the extrapolation of the (log) level of real household consumption based on a linear trend estimated from 1996 to 2004, following the methodology of Chapter 4 of the September 2009 *World Economic Outlook*. The estimation of the precrisis trend ends several years before the crisis so that it is not contaminated by the possibility of an unsustainable boom during the run-up to the crisis or a precrisis slowdown. The slope of the regression line is –0.26, implying that for each additional 10 percentage point rise in household debt prior to the crisis, the consumption loss was larger by 2.6

[6]Housing-related debt (mortgages) comprises about 70 percent of gross household debt in advanced economies. The remainder consists mainly of credit card debt and auto loans.

[7]See Appendix 3.1 for data sources. Glick and Lansing (2010) report a similar finding for a smaller cross-section of advanced economies.

percentage points, a substantial (and statistically significant) relationship.[8]

Historical experience

Is the Great Recession part of a broader historical pattern—specifically, are busts that are preceded by larger run-ups in gross household debt usually more severe? To answer this question, we use statistical techniques to relate the buildup in household debt during the boom to the nature of economic activity during the bust. Given the data available on gross household debt, we focus on a sample of 24 Organization for Economic Cooperation and Development (OECD) economies and Taiwan Province of China during 1980–2011. First, we identify housing busts based on the turning points (peaks) in nominal house prices compiled by Claessens, Kose, and Terrones (2010).[9] For our sample of 25 economies, this yields 99 housing busts. Next, we divide the housing busts into two groups: those that involved a large run-up in the household debt-to-income ratio during the three years leading up to the bust and those that did not.[10] We refer to the two groups as "high-debt" and "low-debt" busts, respectively. Other measures of leverage (such as debt-to-assets and debt-to-net-worth ratios) are not widely available for our multicountry sample. Finally, we regress measures of economic activity on the housing bust dummies for the two groups using a methodology similar to that of Cerra and Saxena (2008), among others. Given our focus on the household sector, we start by considering the behavior of household consumption and then report results for GDP and its components, unemployment, and house prices.

Specifically, we regress changes in the log of real household consumption on its lagged values (to capture the normal fluctuations of consumption) as well as on contemporaneous and lagged values of the housing bust dummies. Including lags allows household consumption to respond with a delay to housing busts.[11] To test whether the severity of housing busts differs between the two groups, we interact the housing bust dummy with a dummy variable that indicates whether the bust was in the high-debt group or the low-debt group. The specification also includes a full set of time fixed effects to account for common shocks, such as shifts in oil prices, and economy-specific fixed effects to account for differences in the economies' normal growth rates. The estimated responses are cumulated to recover the evolution of the level of household consumption following a housing bust. The figures that follow indicate the estimated response of consumption and 1 standard error band around the estimated response.

The regression results suggest that housing busts preceded by larger run-ups in household debt tend to be followed by more severe and longer-lasting declines in household consumption. Panel 1 of Figure 3.3 shows that the decline in real household consumption is 4.3 percent after five years for the high-debt group and only 0.4 percent for the low-debt group. The difference between the two samples is 3.9 percentage points and is statistically significant at the 1 percent level, as reported in Appendix 3.2. These results survive a variety of robustness tests, including different estimation approaches (such as generalized method of moments), alternative specifications (changing the lag length), and dropping outliers (as identified by Cook's distance). (See Appendix 3.2 on the robustness checks.)

[8]The sharper fall in consumption in high-debt growth economies does not simply reflect the occurrence of banking crises. The relationship between household debt accumulation and the depth of the Great Recession remains similar and statistically significant after excluding the 18 economies that experienced a banking crisis at some point during 2007–11, based on the banking crises identified by Laeven and Valencia (2010). The sharper contraction in consumption also does not reflect simply a bigger precrisis consumption boom. The finding of a strong inverse relationship between the precrisis debt run-up and the severity of the recession is similar and statistically significant when controlling for the precrisis boom in consumption.

[9]Claessens, Kose, and Terrones (2010) identify turning points in nominal house prices using the Harding and Pagan (2002) algorithm.

[10]For our baseline specification, we define a "large" increase in debt as an increase above the median of all busts, but, as the robustness analysis in Appendix 3.2 reports, the results do not depend on this precise threshold. The median is an increase of 6.7 percentage points of household income over the three years leading up to the bust, and there is a wide variation in the size of the increase. For example, the household debt-to-income ratio rose by 17 percentage points during the period leading up to the U.K. housing bust of 1989 and by 68 percentage points before the Irish housing bust of 2006.

[11]Appendix 3.2 provides further details on the estimation methodology.

Figure 3.3. Economic Activity during Housing Busts

Real household spending and GDP fall more during housing busts preceded by a larger run-up in household debt, and the unemployment rate rises more. There is a greater fall in domestic demand, which is partly offset by a rise in net exports.

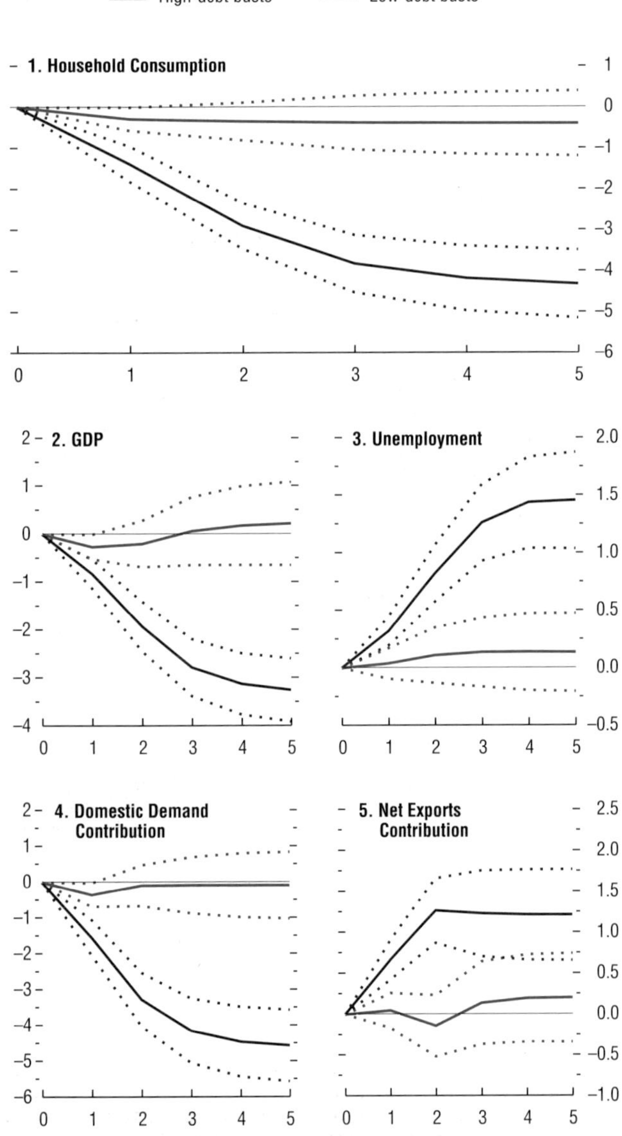

Source: IMF staff calculations.
Note: *X*-axis units are years, where $t = 0$ denotes the year of the housing bust. Dashed lines indicate 1 standard error bands. High- and low-debt busts are defined, respectively, as above and below the median increase in the household debt-to-income ratio during the three years preceding the bust. The unemployment rate and the contributions to GDP are in percentage points; all other variables are in percent.

Housing busts preceded by larger run-ups in household leverage result in more contraction of general economic activity. Figure 3.3 shows that real GDP typically falls more and unemployment rises more for the high-debt busts. Net exports typically make a more positive contribution to GDP—partially offsetting the fall in domestic demand—but this reflects a greater decline in imports rather than a boom in exports.[12]

A logical question is whether the larger decline in household spending simply reflects larger declines in house prices. Panel 1 of Figure 3.4 shows that real house prices do indeed fall significantly more after highly leveraged busts. The fall in real house prices is 10.8 percentage points larger in the high-debt busts than in the low-debt busts, and the difference between the two samples is significant at the 1 percent level. However, this larger fall in house prices cannot plausibly explain the greater decline in household consumption. Real consumption declines by more than 3.9 percentage points more in the high-debt busts, implying an elasticity of about 0.4, well above the range of housing wealth consumption elasticities in the literature (0.05–0.1). Based on this literature, the fall in house prices therefore explains at most one-quarter of the decline in household consumption. To further establish that the decline in consumption reflects more than just house price declines, we repeat the analysis while replacing the housing bust dummy variable with the decrease in house prices (in percent). The results suggest that for the same fall in real house prices (1 percent), real household consumption falls by about twice as much during high-debt busts as during low-debt busts. Therefore, it seems to be the *combination* of house price declines and the prebust leverage that explains the severity of the contraction of household consumption.

Moreover, household deleveraging tends to be more pronounced following busts preceded by a larger run-up in household debt. In particular, the household debt-to-income ratio declines by 5.4 per-

[12]Estimation results for investment also show a larger fall for the high-debt busts. Estimation results for residential investment (for which data are less widely available) also show a larger fall for the high-debt busts, but the responses are not precisely estimated due to the smaller sample size.

centage points following a high-debt housing bust (Figure 3.5). The decline is statistically significant. In contrast, there is no decline in the debt-to-income ratio following low-debt housing busts. Instead, there is a small and statistically insignificant increase. This finding suggests that part of the stronger contraction in economic activity following high-debt housing busts reflects a more intense household deleveraging process.

It is important to establish whether the results are driven by financial crises. The contractionary effects of such crises have already been investigated by previous studies (Cerra and Saxena, 2008; Chapter 4 of the September 2009 *World Economic Outlook*; and Reinhart and Rogoff, 2009, among others). We find that the results are not driven by the global financial crisis—similar results apply when the sample ends in 2006, as reported in Appendix 3.2. Moreover, we find similar results when we repeat the analysis but focus only on housing busts that were not preceded or followed by a systemic banking crisis, as identified by Laeven and Valencia (2010), within a two-year window on either side of the housing bust. For this limited set of housing busts, those preceded by a larger accumulation of household debt are followed by deeper and more prolonged downturns (Figure 3.6). So the results are not simply a reflection of banking crises.

Finally, it is worth investigating whether high household debt also exacerbates the effects of other adverse shocks. We therefore repeat the analysis but replace the housing bust dummies with recession dummies. We construct the recession dummies based on the list of recession dates provided by Howard, Martin, and Wilson (2011). Figure 3.6 also shows that recessions preceded by a larger run-up in household debt do indeed tend to be more severe and protracted.

Overall, this analysis suggests that when households accumulate more debt during a boom, the subsequent bust features a more severe contraction in economic activity. These findings for OECD economies are consistent with those of Mian, Rao, and Sufi (2011) for the United States. These authors use detailed U.S. county-level data for the Great Recession to identify the causal effect of household debt. They conclude that the greater decline in

Figure 3.4. Housing Wealth and Household Consumption

House prices fall more during housing busts preceded by a larger run-up in debt, but this alone cannot explain the sharper decline in consumption in the wake of such busts. The larger fall in house prices explains about a quarter of the greater decline in consumption based on a standard elasticity of consumption with respect to housing wealth. Also, a 1 percent decline in real house prices is typically associated with a larger decline in real household consumption when it is preceded by a larger run-up in household debt.

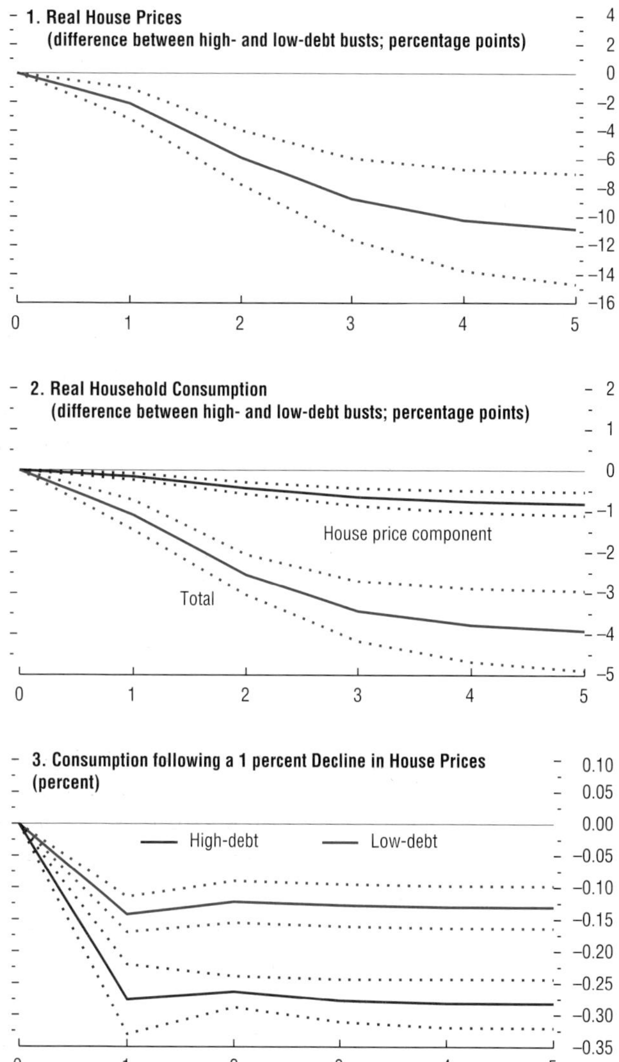

Source: IMF staff calculations.

Note: *X*-axis units are years, where $t = 0$ denotes the year of the housing bust. Dashed lines indicate 1 standard error bands. House price component is defined as the fall in real house prices multiplied by a benchmark elasticity of consumption relative to real housing wealth, based on existing studies (0.075). High- and low-debt are defined, respectively, as above and below the median increase in the household debt-to-income ratio during the three years preceding the fall in house prices.

Figure 3.5. Household Debt during Housing Busts
(Percentage points)

The reduction in household debt (deleveraging) is more pronounced during housing busts preceded by a larger buildup in indebtedness.

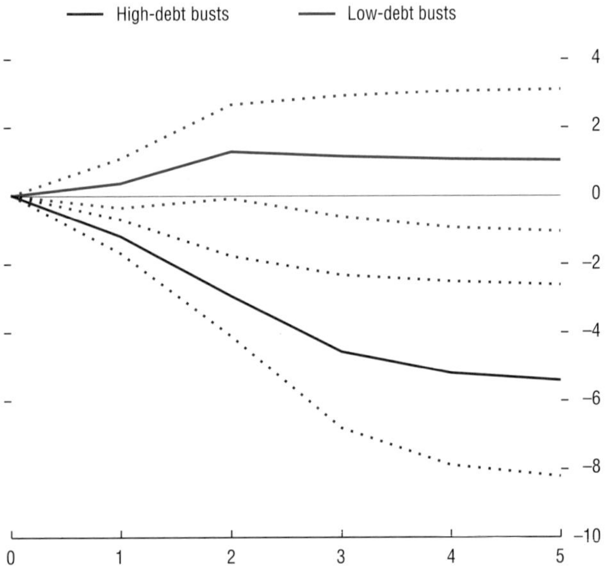

Source: IMF staff calculations.
Note: *X*-axis units are years, where $t = 0$ denotes the year of the housing bust. Dashed lines indicate 1 standard error bands. High- and low-debt busts are defined, respectively, as above and below the median increase in the household debt-to-income ratio during the three years preceding the bust.

consumption after 2007 in U.S. counties that accumulated more debt during 2002–06 is too large to be explained by the larger fall in house prices in those counties.[13] This is consistent with the cross-country evidence in Figure 3.4. They also find evidence of more rapid household deleveraging in high-debt U.S. counties, which underscores the role of deleveraging and is consistent with the cross-country evidence in Figure 3.5. In related work, Mian and Sufi (2011) show that a higher level of household debt in 2007 is associated with sharper declines in spending on consumer durables, residential investment, and employment (Figure 3.7). Based on their findings, they conclude that the decline in aggregate demand driven by household balance sheet weakness explains the majority of the job losses in the United States during the Great Recession (Mian and Sufi, 2012).

The findings are also broadly consistent with the more general finding in the literature that recessions preceded by economy-wide credit booms—which may or may not coincide with household credit booms—tend to be deeper and more protracted than other recessions (see, for example, Claessens, Kose, and Terrones, 2010; and Jordà, Schularick, and Taylor, 2011). This conclusion is also consistent with evidence that consumption volatility is positively correlated with household debt (Isaksen and others, 2011).

Why Does Household Debt Matter?

We have found evidence that downturns are more severe when they are preceded by larger increases in household debt. This subsection discusses how the pattern fits with the predictions of theoretical models. A natural starting point is to consider a closed economy with no government debt. In such an economy, net private debt must be zero, because one person's debt is another's asset. Some people may accumulate debt, but this would simply

[13]In particular, by comparing house price declines with consumption declines in counties with high and low levels of household debt, they obtain an *implicit* elasticity of consumption relative to house prices of 0.3 to 0.7, which is well above the range of estimates in the literature. This suggests that only 14 to 30 percent of the greater decline in consumption in high-debt counties is due to the larger falls in house prices in those counties.

represent "money we owe to ourselves" (Krugman, 2011) with no obvious macroeconomic implications. Nevertheless, even when changes in gross household debt imply little change in economy-wide net debt, they can influence macroeconomic performance by amplifying the effects of shocks. In particular, a number of theoretical models predict that build-ups in household debt drive deep and prolonged downturns.[14]

We now discuss the main channels through which household debt can amplify downturns and weaken recoveries. We also highlight the policy implications. In particular, we explain the circumstances under which government intervention can improve on a purely market-driven outcome.

Differences between borrowers and lenders

The accumulation of household debt amplifies slumps in a number of recent models that differentiate between borrowers and lenders and feature liquidity constraints. A key feature of these models is the idea that the distribution of debt within an economy matters (Eggertsson and Krugman, 2010; Guerrieri and Lorenzoni, 2011; Hall, 2011).[15] As Tobin (1980) argues, "the population is not distributed between debtors and creditors randomly. Debtors have borrowed for good reasons, most of which indicate a high marginal propensity to spend from wealth or from current income or from any other liquid resources they can command."[16] Indeed, household debt increased more at the lower ends

[14]In an open economy, gross household debt can have additional effects. In particular, a reduction in household debt could signal a transfer of resources from domestic to foreign households, implying even larger macroeconomic effects than in a closed economy.

[15]In an earlier theoretical sketch, King (1994) discusses how differences in the marginal propensity to consume between borrowing and lending households can generate an aggregate downturn when household leverage is high.

[16]Differences in the propensity to consume can arise for a number of reasons. Life-cycle motives have been emphasized as a source of differences in saving behavior across cohorts (see Modigliani, 1986, among others). Others have focused on the role of time preferences, introducing a class of relatively impatient agents (see Iacoviello, 2005; and Eggertsson and Krugman, 2010). Dynan, Skinner, and Zeldes (2004) find a strong positive relationship between personal saving rates and lifetime income, suggesting that the rich consume a smaller proportion of their income than the poor.

Figure 3.6. Household Consumption
(Percent)

The finding that consumption falls more during housing busts preceded by a larger run-up in household debt is not driven by banking crises. It holds for a subset of housing busts not associated with a systemic banking crisis within a two-year window. In addition, recessions are generally deeper if they are preceded by a larger run-up in household debt.

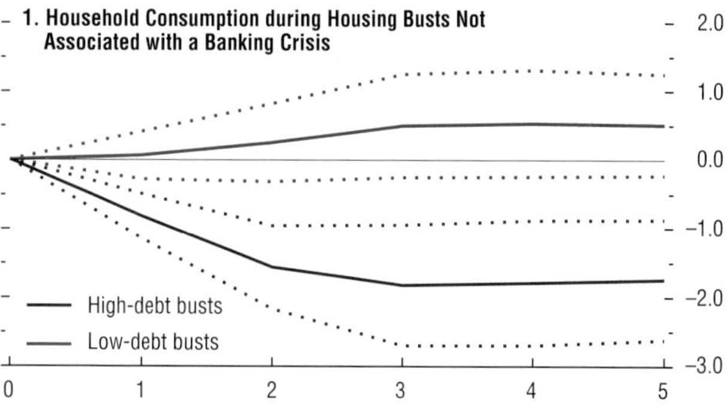

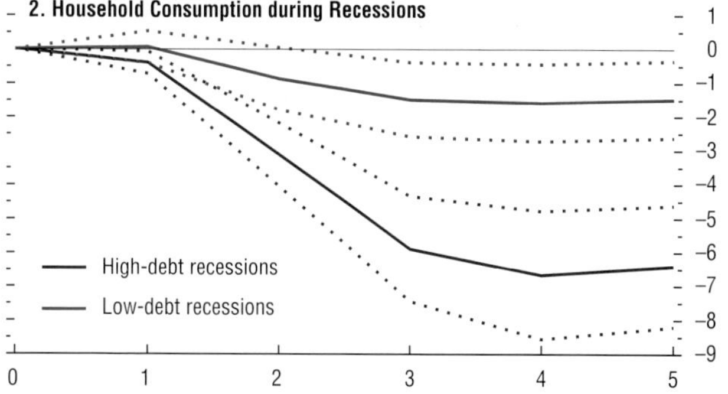

Source: IMF staff calculations.

Note: In panel 1, *x*-axis units are years, where $t = 0$ denotes the year of the housing bust. Housing busts associated with a systemic banking crisis within two years of the bust are not considered in the analysis. Systemic banking crisis indicators are from the updated Laeven and Valencia (2010) database. Dashed lines indicate 1 standard error bands. High- and low-debt busts are defined, respectively, as above and below the median increase in the household debt-to-income ratio during the three years preceding the housing bust. In panel 2, *x*-axis units are years, where $t = 0$ denotes the year of the recession. Dashed lines indicate 1 standard error bands. High- and low-debt recessions are defined, respectively, as above and below the median increase in the household debt-to-income ratio during the three years preceding the recession.

Figure 3.7. Economic Activity during the Great Recession in the United States
(Index; 2005:Q4 = 100)

Mian and Sufi (2011) find that in U.S. counties where households accumulated more debt before the Great Recession there was deeper and more prolonged contraction in household consumption, investment, and employment.

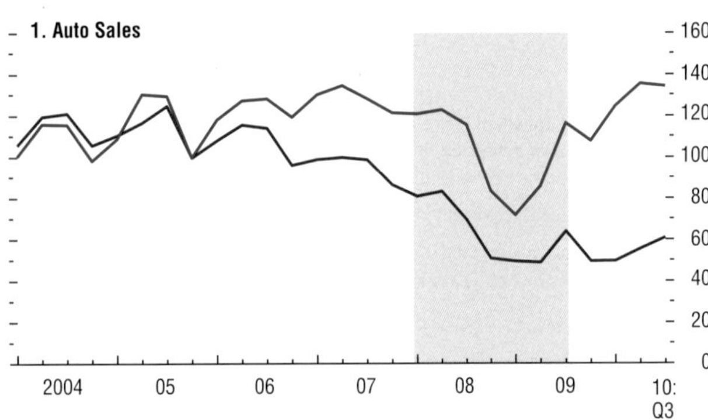

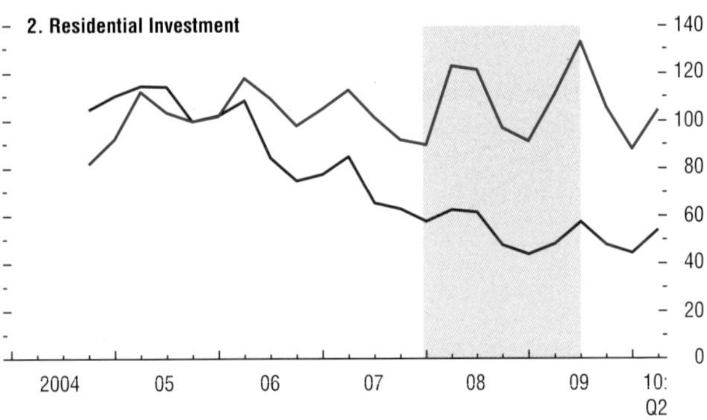

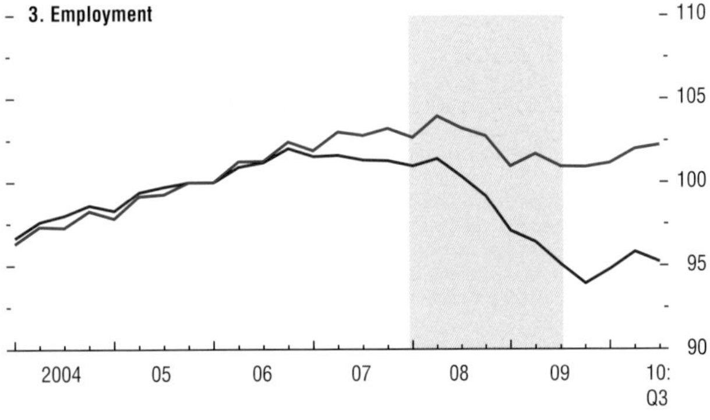

Source: Mian and Sufi (2011).
Note: Shaded area indicates U.S. recession based on National Bureau of Economic Research dates.

of the income and wealth distribution during the 2000s in the United States (Kumhof and Rancière, 2010).

A shock to the borrowing capacity of debtors with a high marginal propensity to consume that forces them to reduce their debt could then lead to a decline in aggregate activity. Deleveraging could stem from a realization that house prices were overvalued (as in Buiter, 2010; and Eggertsson and Krugman, 2010), a tightening in credit standards (Guerrieri and Lorenzoni, 2011), a sharp revision in income expectations, or an increase in economic uncertainty (Fisher, 1933; Minsky, 1986). Here, a sufficiently large fall in the interest rate could induce creditor households to spend more, thus offsetting the decline in spending by the debtors. But, as these models show, the presence of the zero lower bound on nominal interest rates or other price rigidities can prevent these creditor households from picking up the slack. This feature is particularly relevant today because policy rates are near zero in many advanced economies.

Consumption may be further depressed following shocks in the presence of uncertainty, given the need for precautionary saving (Guerrieri and Lorenzoni, 2011; Carroll, Slacalek, and Sommer, 2011). The cut in household consumption would then be particularly abrupt, "undershooting" its long-term level (as it appears to have done in the United States today; see Glick and Lansing, 2009). Such a sharp contraction in aggregate consumption would provide a rationale for temporarily pursuing expansionary macroeconomic policies, including fiscal stimulus targeted at financially constrained households (Eggertsson and Krugman, 2010; Carroll, Slacalek, and Sommer, 2011), and household debt restructuring (Rogoff, 2011).

Negative price effects from fire sales

A further negative effect on economic activity of high household debt in the presence of a shock, postulated by numerous models, comes from the forced sale of durable goods (Shleifer and Vishny, 1992; Mayer, 1995; Krishnamurthy, 2010; Lorenzoni, 2008). For example, a rise in unemployment reduces households' ability to service their debt, implying a rise in household defaults, foreclosures, and creditors selling foreclosed properties at distressed, or fire-sale, prices. Estimates suggest that a single foreclosure lowers the price of a neighboring property by about 1 percent, but that the effects can be much larger when there is a wave of foreclosures, with estimates of price declines reaching almost 30 percent (Campbell, Giglio, and Pathak, 2011). The associated negative price effects in turn reduce economic activity through a number of self-reinforcing contractionary spirals. These include negative wealth effects, a reduction in collateral value, a negative impact on bank balance sheets, and a credit crunch. As Shleifer and Vishny (2010) explain, fire sales undermine the ability of financial institutions and firms to lend and borrow by reducing their net worth, and this reduction in credit supply can reduce productivity-enhancing investment. Such externalities—banks and households ignoring the social cost of defaults and fire sales—may justify policy intervention aimed at stopping household defaults, foreclosures, and fire sales.

The case of the United States today illustrates the risk of house prices "undershooting" their equilibrium values during a housing bust on the back of fire sales. The IMF staff notes that "distress sales are the main driving force behind the recent declines in house prices—in fact, excluding distress sales, house prices had stopped falling" and that "there is a risk of house price undershooting" (IMF, 2011b, p. 20). And Figure 3.8 suggests that U.S. house prices may have fallen below the levels consistent with some fundamentals.[17]

Inefficiencies and deadweight losses from debt overhang and foreclosures

A further problem is that household debt overhang can give rise to various inefficiencies. In the case of firms, debt overhang is a situation in which existing debt is so great that it constrains the ability to raise funds to finance profitable investment projects (Myers, 1977). Similarly, homeowners with debt overhang may invest little in their property. They may, for example, forgo investments that improve the net present value of their homes, such

[17]Slok (2012) and *The Economist* (2011) report that U.S. house prices are undervalued.

Figure 3.8. Estimated House Price Misalignment in the United States
(Percent)

U.S. house prices are now at or below the levels implied by regression-based estimates and some historical valuation ratios.

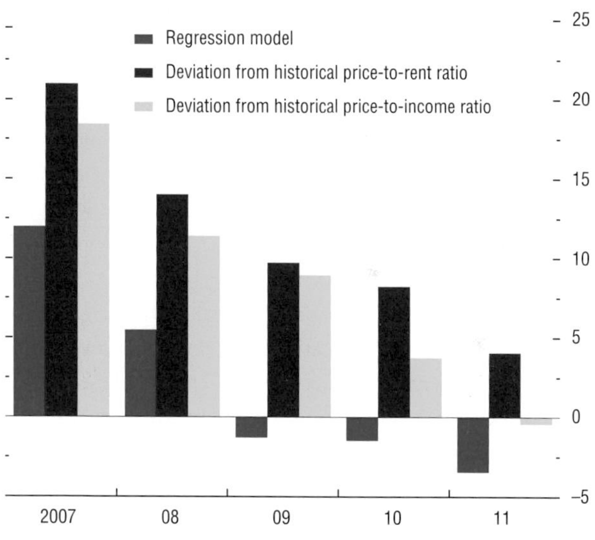

Sources: Federal Housing Administration; Organization for Economic Cooperation and Development; IMF, *International Financial Statistics*; and IMF staff calculations.
Note: The regression model measure indicates the implied house price misalignment when house price changes are modeled as a function of changes in personal disposable income, working-age population, credit and equity prices, interest rate levels, and construction costs. See Chapter 1 of the October 2009 *World Economic Outlook*, Box 1.4, and Igan and Loungani (forthcoming) for further details. The price-to-rent ratio and price-to-income ratio depict the percent deviation of these ratios from their historical averages, calculated over 1970–2000.

as home improvements and maintenance expenditures. This effect could be large. Based on detailed household-level U.S. data, Melzer (2010) finds that homeowners with debt overhang (negative equity) spend 30 percent less on home improvements and maintenance than homeowners without debt overhang, other things equal. While privately renegotiating the debt contract between the borrower and the lender could alleviate such debt overhang problems, renegotiation is often costly and difficult to achieve outside bankruptcy because of free-rider problems or contract complications (Foote and others, 2010).

Foreclosures and bankruptcy can be an inefficient way of resolving households' inability to service their mortgage debt, giving rise to significant "deadweight losses" (BGFRS, 2012). These deadweight losses stem from the neglect and deterioration of properties that sit vacant for months and their negative effect on neighborhoods' social cohesion and crime (Immergluck and Smith, 2005, 2006). Deadweight losses are also due to the delays associated with the resolution of a large number of bankruptcies through the court system.

Overall, debt overhang and the deadweight losses of foreclosures can further depress the recovery of housing prices and economic activity. These problems make a case for government involvement to lower the cost of restructuring debt, facilitate the writing down of household debt, and help prevent foreclosures (Philippon, 2009).

Dealing with Household Debt: Case Studies

Having established that household debt can amplify slumps and weaken recoveries, we now investigate how governments have responded during episodes of household deleveraging. We start by reviewing four broad policy approaches that can, in principle, allow government intervention to improve on a purely market-driven outcome. These approaches are not mutually exclusive and can be complementary. Each has benefits and limitations. The approach a government decides to use is likely to reflect institutional and political features of the economy, the available policy room, and the size of the household debt problem.

- *Temporary macroeconomic policy stimulus:* As discussed above, household deleveraging following a balance sheet shock can imply an abrupt contraction in household consumption to well below the long-term level (overshooting). The costs of the associated contraction in economic activity can be mitigated by an offsetting temporary macroeconomic policy stimulus. In an economy with credit-constrained households, this provides a rationale for temporarily pursuing an expansionary fiscal policy, including through government spending targeted at financially constrained households (Eggertsson and Krugman, 2010; Carroll, Slacalek, and Sommer, 2011).[18] For example, simulations of policy models developed at six policy institutions suggest that, in the current environment, a temporary (two-year) transfer of 1 percent of GDP to financially constrained households would raise GDP by 1.3 percent and 1.1 percent in the United States and the European Union, respectively (Coenen and others, 2012).[19] Financing the temporary transfer by a lump-sum tax on all households rather than by issuing government debt would imply a "balanced-budget" boost to GDP of 0.8 and 0.9 percent, respectively. Monetary stimulus can also provide relief to indebted households by easing the debt service burden, especially in countries where mortgages have variable rates, such as Spain and the United Kingdom. In the United States, the macroeconomic policy response since the start of the Great Recession has been forceful, going much beyond that of several other countries. It included efforts by the Federal Reserve to lower long-term interest rates, particularly in the key mortgage-backed-

[18]The presence of financially constrained households with a high marginal propensity to consume out of disposable income increases the effectiveness of fiscal policy changes—it renders the economy non-Ricardian—in a wide range of models (see Coenen and others, 2012, for a discussion). The presence of the zero lower bound on interest rates further amplifies the multipliers associated with temporary fiscal policy changes (Woodford, 2010).

[19]The six policy institutions are the U.S. Federal Reserve Board, the European Central Bank, the European Commission, the OECD, the Bank of Canada, and the IMF. The simulations assume that policy interest rates are constrained by the zero lower bound—a key feature of major advanced economies today—and that the central bank does not tighten monetary policy in response to the fiscal expansion. See Coenen and others (2012) for further details.

security segment relevant for the housing market. Macroeconomic stimulus, however, has its limits. High government debt may constrain the available fiscal room for a deficit-financed transfer, and the zero lower bound on nominal interest rates can prevent real interest rates from adjusting enough to allow creditor households to pick up the economic slack caused by lower consumption by borrowers.

- *Automatic support to households through the social safety net:* A social safety net can automatically provide targeted transfers to households with distressed balance sheets and a high marginal propensity to consume, without the need for additional policy deliberation. For example, unemployment insurance can support people's ability to service their debt after becoming unemployed, thus reducing the risk of household deleveraging through default and the associated negative externalities.[20] However, as in the case of discretionary fiscal stimulus, allowing automatic stabilizers to operate fully requires fiscal room.[21]
- *Assistance to the financial sector:* When the problem of household sector debt is so severe that arrears and defaults threaten to disrupt the operation of the banking sector, government intervention may be warranted. Household defaults can undermine the ability of financial institutions and firms to lend and borrow by reducing their net worth, and this reduction in credit supply can reduce productive investment (Shleifer and Vishny, 2010). A number of policies can prevent such a tightening in credit availability, including recapitalizations and government purchases of distressed assets.[22] Such support mitigates the effects of household balance sheet distress on the financial sector. The U.S. Troubled Asset Relief Program established in 2008 was based, in part, on such considerations. Similarly, in Ireland, the National Asset Management Agency was created in 2009 to take over distressed loans from the banking sector. Moreover, assistance to the financial sector can enable banks to engage in voluntary debt restructuring with households. However, strong capital buffers may be insufficient to encourage banks to restructure household debt on a large scale, as is evident in the United States today. In addition, this approach does not prevent unnecessary household defaults, defined as those that occur as a result of temporary liquidity problems. Moreover, financial support to lenders facing widespread defaults by their debtors must be designed carefully to avoid moral hazard—indirectly encouraging risky lending practices in the future.
- *Support for household debt restructuring:* Finally, the government may choose to tackle the problem of household debt directly by setting up frameworks for voluntary out-of-court household debt restructuring—including write-downs—or by initiating government-sponsored debt restructuring programs. Such programs can help restore the ability of borrowers to service their debt, thus preventing the contractionary effects of unnecessary foreclosures and excessive asset price declines. To the extent that the programs involve a transfer to financially constrained households from less financially constrained agents, they can also boost GDP in a way comparable to the balanced-budget fiscal transfer discussed above. Such programs can also have a limited fiscal cost. For example, as we see later on, they may involve the government buying distressed mortgages from banks, restructuring them to make them more affordable, and later reselling them, with the revenue offsetting the initial cost. They also sometimes focus on facilitating case-by-case restructuring by improving the institutional and legal framework for debt renegotiation between the lender and the borrower, which implies no fiscal cost. However, the success of these programs depends on a combination of careful

[20]The generosity and duration of the associated welfare payments differ by country. In Sweden, for example, workers are eligible for unemployment insurance for up to 450 days, although at declining replacement rates after 200 days. By contrast, in the United States, unemployment insurance is normally limited to 26 weeks, and extended benefits are provided during periods of high unemployment. The maximum duration of unemployment insurance was extended to 99 weeks (693 days) in February 2009, and this extension was renewed in February 2012.

[21]Furthermore, to provide targeted support in a timely manner, the safety net needs to be in place before household debt becomes problematic.

[22]See Honohan and Laeven (2005) for a discussion of the various policies used for the resolution of financial crises.

design and implementation.[23] In particular, such programs must address the risk of moral hazard when debtors are offered the opportunity to avoid complying with their loan's original terms.

It is worth recognizing that any government intervention will introduce distortions and lead to some redistribution of resources within the economy and over time. The question is whether the benefits of intervention exceed the costs. Moreover, if intervention has a budgetary impact, the extent of intervention should be constrained by the degree of available fiscal room. The various approaches discussed above differ in the extent of redistribution involved and the associated winners and losers. For example, the presence and generosity of a social safety net reflect a society's preferences regarding redistribution and inequality. Government support for the banking sector and household debt restructuring programs may involve clearer winners than, say, monetary policy stimulus or an income tax cut. The social friction that such redistribution may cause could limit its political feasibility. Mian, Sufi, and Trebbi (2012) discuss the political tug-of-war between creditors and debtors and find that political systems tend to become more polarized in the wake of financial crises. They also argue that collective action problems—struggling mortgage holders may be less well politically organized than banks—can hamper efforts to implement household debt restructuring. Moreover, all policies that respond to the consequences of excessive household debt need to be carefully designed to minimize the potential for moral hazard and excessive risk taking by both borrowers and lenders in the future.

To examine in practice how such policies can mitigate the problems associated with household debt, we investigate the effectiveness of government action during several episodes of household deleveraging. We focus on policies that support household debt restructuring directly because of the large amount of existing literature on the other policy approaches. For example, there is a large literature on the determinants and effects of fiscal and monetary policy. There are also a number of studies on the international experience with financial sector policies.

The episodes we consider are the United States in the 1930s and today, Hungary and Iceland today, Colombia in 1999, and three Scandinavian countries (Finland, Norway, Sweden) in the 1990s. In each of these cases, there was a housing bust preceded by or coinciding with a substantial increase in household debt, but the policy response was different.[24] We start by summarizing the factors that led to the buildup in household debt and what triggered household deleveraging. We then discuss the government response, focusing on policies that directly address the negative effect of household debt on economic activity. Finally, we summarize the lessons to be learned from the case studies.[25]

Factors Underlying the Buildup in Household Debt

In each of these episodes, a loosening of credit constraints allowed households to increase their debt. This increase in credit availability was associated with financial innovation and liberalization and declining lending standards. A wave of household optimism about future income and wealth prospects also played a role and, together with the greater credit availability, helped stoke the housing and stock market booms.

The United States in the 1920s—the "roaring twenties"—illustrates the role of rising credit avail-

[23]Laeven and Laryea (2009) discuss in detail the principles that should guide government-sponsored household debt restructuring programs.

[24]We do not discuss the real estate bust in Japan in the 1990s because household leverage relative to both safe and liquid assets was low at the time and household deleveraging was not a key feature of the episode. As Nakagawa and Yasui (2009) explain: "The finances of Japanese households were not severely damaged by the mid-1990s bursting of the bubble. Banks, however, with their large accumulation of household deposits on the liability side of their balance sheets, were victims of their large holdings of defaulted corporate loans and the resulting capital deterioration during the bust; in response, banks tightened credit significantly during this period" (p. 82).

[25]Other economies today have also implemented measures to address household indebtedness directly. For example, in the United Kingdom, the Homeowners Mortgage Support Scheme aimed to ease homeowners' debt service temporarily with a government guarantee of deferred interest payments, the Mortgage Rescue Scheme attempted to protect the most vulnerable from foreclosure, while the expansion of the Support for Mortgage Interest provided more households with help in meeting their interest payments. Reforms currently being implemented in Ireland include modernizing the bankruptcy regime by making it less onerous and facilitating voluntary out-of-court arrangements between borrowers and lenders of both secured and unsecured debt. In Latvia, the authorities' efforts have focused on strengthening the framework for market-based debt resolution (see Erbenova, Liu, and Saxegaard, 2011).

ability and consumer optimism in driving household debt. Technological innovation brought new consumer products such as automobiles and radios into widespread use. Financial innovation made it easier for households to obtain credit to buy such consumer durables and to obtain mortgage loans. Installment plans for the purchase of major consumer durables became particularly widespread (Olney, 1999). General Motors led the way with the establishment of the General Motors Acceptance Corporation in 1919 to make loans for the purchase of its automobiles. By 1927, two-thirds of new cars and household appliances were purchased on installment. Consumer debt doubled from 4.5 percent of personal income in 1920 to 9 percent of personal income in 1929. Over the same period, mortgage debt rose from 11 percent of gross national product to 28 percent, partly on the back of new forms of lending such as high-leverage home mortgage loans and early forms of securitization (Snowden, 2010). Reflecting the economic expansion and optimism that house values would continue rising, asset prices boomed.[26] Real house prices rose by 19 percent from 1921 to 1925,[27] while the stock market rose by 265 percent from 1921 to 1929.

Rising credit availability due to financial liberalization and declining lending standards also helped drive up household debt in the more recent cases we consider. In the Scandinavian countries, extensive price and quantity restrictions on financial products ended during the 1980s. Colombia implemented a wave of capital account and financial liberalization in the early 1990s. This rapid deregulation substantially encouraged competition for customers, which, in combination with strong tax incentives to invest in housing and optimism regarding asset values, led to a household debt boom in these economies.[28] Similarly, following Iceland's privatization and liberalization of the banking system in 2003, household borrowing constraints were eased substantially.[29] It became possible, for the first time, to refinance mortgages and withdraw equity. Loan-to-value (LTV) ratios were raised as high as 90 percent by the state-owned Housing Financing Fund, and even further by the newly private banks as they competed for market share. In Hungary, pent-up demand combined with EU membership prospects triggered a credit boom as outstanding household debt grew from a mere 7 percent of GDP in 1999 to 33 percent in 2007. The first part of this credit boom episode was also characterized by a house price rally, driven by generous housing subsidies. In the United States in the 2000s, an expansion of credit supply to households that had previously been unable to obtain loans included increased recourse to private-label securitization and the emergence of so-called exotic mortgages, such as interest-only loans, negative amortization loans, and "NINJA" (no income, no job, no assets) loans.

Factors That Triggered Household Deleveraging

The collapse of the asset price boom, and the associated collapse in household wealth, triggered household deleveraging in all of the historical episodes we consider. The U.S. housing price boom of the 1920s ended in 1925, when house prices peaked. Foreclosure rates rose steadily thereafter (Figure 3.9), from 3 foreclosures per 1,000 mortgaged properties in 1926 to 13 per 1,000 by 1933. Another shock to household wealth came with the stock market crash of October 1929, which ushered in the Great Depression. A housing bust also occurred in the Scandinavian countries in the late 1980s and in Colombia in the mid-1990s. Similarly, the end of a house price boom and a collapse in stock prices severely dented household wealth in Iceland and the United States at the start of the Great Recession. In all these cases, household

[26]Regarding the reasons for this optimism, Harriss (1951) explains that "In the twenties, as in every period of favorable economic conditions, mortgage debt was entered into by individuals with confidence that the burden could be supported without undue difficulty … over long periods the value of land and improvements had often risen enough to support the widely held belief that the borrower's equity would grow through the years, even though it was small to begin with" (p. 7).

[27]In certain areas, such as Manhattan and Florida, the increase was much higher (30 to 40 percent).

[28]In Finland the ratio of household debt to disposable income rose from 50 percent in 1980 to 90 percent in 1989; in Sweden it rose from 95 percent to 130 percent. In Colombia bank credit to the private sector rose from 32 percent of GDP in 1991 to 40 percent in 1997.

[29]Financial markets in Iceland were highly regulated until the 1980s. Liberalization began in the 1980s and accelerated during the 1990s, not least because of obligations and opportunities created by the decision to join the European Economic Area in 1994. Iceland's three new large banks were progressively privatized between the late 1990s and 2003, amid widespread accusations of political favoritism (see OECD, 2009).

Figure 3.9. Foreclosures and Household Debt during the Great Depression in the United States

After the peak in house prices in 1925, foreclosure rates rose steadily for the following eight years. While widespread defaults lowered the stock of outstanding nominal debt starting in 1930, the collapse in household income meant that the debt-to-income ratio continued to rise until 1933.

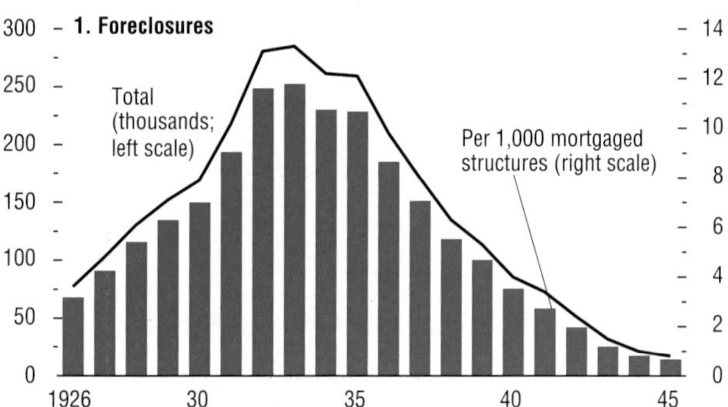

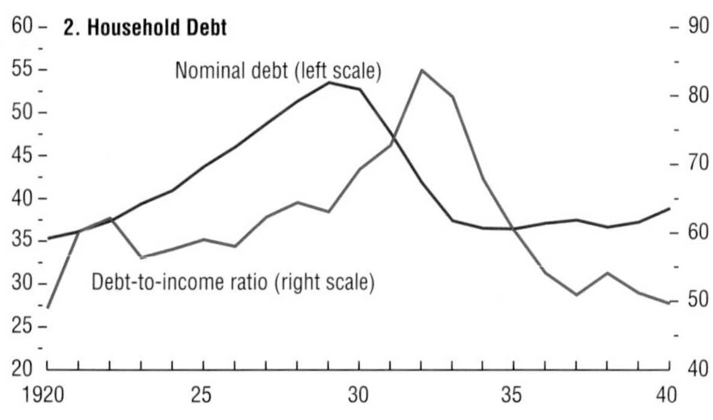

Source: IMF staff calculations.
Note: The debt-to-income ratio is in percentage points; nominal household debt is in billions of dollars.

deleveraging started soon after the collapse in asset prices. In addition, a tightening of available credit associated with banking crises triggered household deleveraging during all these episodes. The distress in household balance sheets due to the collapse of their wealth spread quickly to financial intermediaries' balance sheets, resulting in tighter lending standards and forcing further household deleveraging.

The experience of Iceland in 2008 provides a particularly grim illustration of how a collapse in asset prices and economic prospects, combined with a massive banking crisis, leads to household overindebtedness and a need for deleveraging. Iceland's three largest banks fell within one week in October 2008. Household balance sheets then came under severe stress from a number of factors (Figure 3.10). First, the collapse in confidence triggered sharp asset price declines, which unwound previous net wealth gains. At the same time, the massive inflation and large depreciation of the krona during 2008–09 triggered a sharp rise in household debt since practically all loans were indexed to the consumer price index (CPI) or the exchange rate. CPI-indexed mortgages with LTV ratios above 70 percent were driven underwater by a combination of 26 percent inflation and an 11 percent drop in house prices. Likewise, with the krona depreciating by 77 percent, exchange-rate-indexed mortgages with LTV ratios above 40 percent went underwater. Inflation and depreciation also swelled debt service payments, just as disposable income stagnated. The combination of debt overhang and debt servicing problems was devastating. By the end of 2008, 20 percent of homeowners with mortgages had negative equity in their homes (this peaked at 38 percent in 2010), while nearly a quarter had debt service payments above 40 percent of their disposable income.

The Policy Response

Having summarized the factors that drove up household debt and triggered household deleveraging, we turn to the policies that governments pursued to mitigate the negative effects on economic activity. For each episode, we start with an overview of the policies implemented and of the political context in which they were introduced. We then consider how effective the policies were in addressing the negative effects of household debt on economic activity. In particular, we investigate whether the policies helped prevent foreclosures (by restructuring a large share of mortgages), provide transfers to credit-constrained households with a high marginal propensity to consume, and reduce debt overhang. At the same time, the small number of episodes considered and the lack of counterfactual experiences complicate quantifying the effect of these policies on macroeconomic aggregates, such as real GDP.

The discussion starts with two cases that illustrate broadly successful approaches to dealing with household debt—the United States during the Great Depression and Iceland since the Great Recession. We then contrast these cases with less successful episodes—Colombia in the 1990s and Hungary and the United States since the Great Recession. Finally, we consider the case of the Scandinavian countries during the 1990s, when, despite a large increase in household debt, the authorities did not adopt discretionary household debt restructuring policies.

The United States during the Great Depression

This episode exemplifies a bold and broadly successful government-supported household debt restructuring program designed to prevent foreclosures, the U.S. Home Owners' Loan Corporation (HOLC). HOLC was established in 1933 because a series of earlier initiatives designed to stop the rising number of foreclosures had achieved little (see Figure 3.9), and social pressure for large-scale intervention was high.[30] As Harriss (1951) explains, "The tremendous social costs imposed by these conditions of deep depression are vividly and movingly revealed in the files of the Home Owners' Loan Corporation. Demands for direct action by the government were insistent and nearly unanimous" (p. 9). In April 1933, a newly elected President Franklin Roosevelt urged Congress to pass legislation that would

[30]The earlier policies included a number of state initiatives to impose moratoriums on foreclosures and the Federal Home Loan Bank (FHLB) Act of 1932, designed to increase bank lending by providing funding for liquidity-constrained banks. The FHLB Act accepted only 3 out of 41,000 applications within its first two years.

Figure 3.10. Household Balance Sheets during the Great Recession in Iceland

The financial position of Iceland's households came under severe stress in 2008. The collapse in asset prices unwound previous net wealth gains, while widespread indexation coupled with higher inflation and exchange rate depreciation led to a rise in nominal household debt. The share of mortgage holders with negative equity in their homes rose steadily, reaching close to 40 percent by 2010.

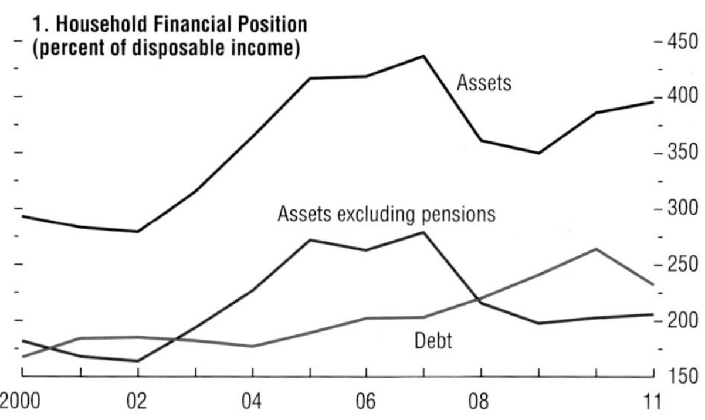

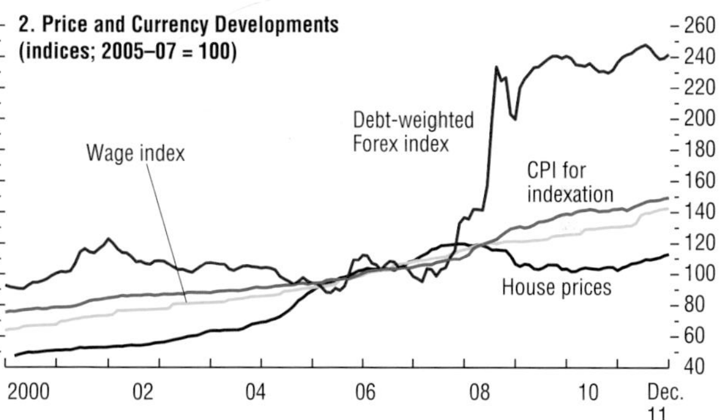

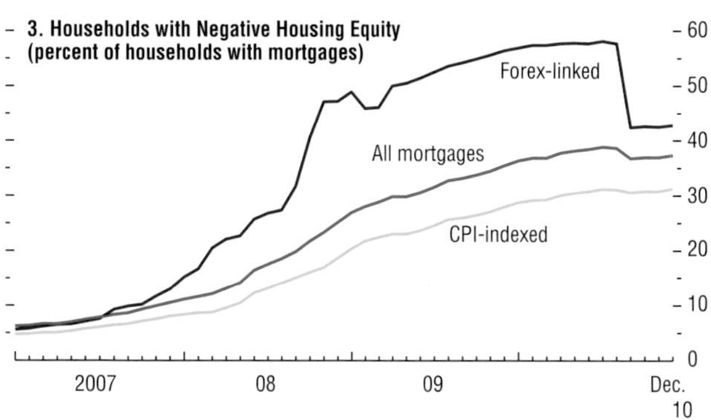

Sources: Central Bank of Iceland; Statistics Iceland; and IMF staff estimates.
Note: In panel 1, pension assets are corrected for an estimated tax of 25 percent. CPI = consumer price index; Forex = foreign exchange.

prevent foreclosures, and HOLC was established that summer.[31]

To prevent mortgage foreclosures, HOLC bought distressed mortgages from banks in exchange for bonds with federal guarantees on interest and principal. It then restructured these mortgages to make them more affordable to borrowers and developed methods of working with borrowers who became delinquent or unemployed, including job searches (Box 3.1 provides further details on the program). HOLC bought about 1 million distressed mortgages that were at risk of foreclosure, or about one in five of all mortgages. Of these million mortgages, about 200,000 ended up foreclosing when the borrowers defaulted on their renegotiated mortgages. The HOLC program helped protect the remaining 800,000 mortgages from foreclosure, corresponding to 16 percent of all mortgages (Table 3.1).[32] HOLC mortgage purchases amounted to $4.75 billion (8.4 percent of 1933 GDP), and the mortgages were sold over time, yielding a nominal profit by the time of the HOLC program's liquidation in 1951. The HOLC program's success in preventing foreclosures at a limited fiscal cost may explain why academics and public figures called for a HOLC-style approach during the recent recession.

A key feature of HOLC was the effective transfer of funds to credit-constrained households with distressed balance sheets and a high marginal propensity to consume, which mitigated the negative effects on aggregate demand discussed above. The objective, emphasized by President Roosevelt in a message to Congress, was to relieve "the small home owner … of the burden of excessive interest and principal payments incurred during the period of higher values and higher earning power" (Harriss, 1951, p. 9). Accordingly, HOLC extended mortgage terms from a typical length of 5 to 10 years, often at variable rates, to fixed-rate 15-year terms, which were sometimes extended to 20 years (Green and Wachter, 2005). By making mortgage payments more affordable, it effectively transferred funds to households with distressed mortgages that had a higher marginal propensity to consume and away from lenders with (presumably) a lower marginal propensity to consume.[33] In a number of cases, HOLC also wrote off part of the principal to ensure that no loans exceeded 80 percent of the appraised value of the house, thus mitigating the negative effects of debt overhang discussed above.

Iceland during the Great Recession

The case of Iceland illustrates how a multipronged approach can provide debt relief to a large share of households and stem the rise in defaults. Iceland's bold policy response was motivated by the sheer scale of its household debt problem (see Figure 3.10) and intense social pressure for government intervention. In some of the largest protests ever seen in Iceland, thousands of people took to the streets demanding debt write-downs. Over a two-year period, the government provided a framework for dealing with household debt in the context of an IMF-supported program.

The approach to resolving the household debt problem had several elements. At the outset, stopgap measures offered near-term relief in order to ensure that families did not lose their homes owing to temporary problems and to prevent a spike in foreclosures leading to a housing market meltdown. The measures included a moratorium on foreclosures, a temporary suspension of debt service for exchange-rate- and CPI-indexed loans, and rescheduling (payment smoothing) of these loans. About half the households with eligible loans took advantage of payment smoothing, which reduced current debt service payments by 15 to 20 percent and 30 to 40 percent for CPI-indexed and foreign-exchange-indexed loans, respectively.

At a later stage, households were given the option of restructuring their loans out of court by negotiating with their lenders directly or with the help of a (newly created) Office of the Debtor's Ombudsman

[31]Household debt had been falling in nominal terms since 1929 on the back of defaults but continued to rise as a share of households' shrinking incomes until 1933 (see Figure 3.9).

[32]Fishback and others (2010) and Courtemanche and Snowden (2011) offer evidence that this action provided relief to the housing market by supporting home values and home ownership.

[33]HOLC also changed adjustable-rate, interest-only mortgages to fixed-rate, fully amortizing mortgages. This reduced uncertainty about future debt service obligations and implied less need for precautionary saving and helped homeowners avoid a large lump-sum payment at the loan's maturity.

acting on their behalf. The negotiations are on a case-by-case basis but use templates developed through dialogue between the government and the financial institutions. The templates provide for substantial write-downs designed to align secured debt with the supporting collateral, and debt service with the ability to repay. The case-by-case negotiations safeguard property rights and reduce moral hazard, but they take time. As of January 2012, only 35 percent of the case-by-case applications for debt restructuring had been processed. To speed things up, a debt forgiveness plan was introduced, which writes down deeply underwater mortgages to 110 percent of the household's pledgeable assets. In addition, a large share of mortgage holders receives a sizable interest rate subsidy over a two-year period, financed through temporary levies on the financial sector. Box 3.2 provides a detailed description of the household debt restructuring framework.[34]

Iceland's financial institutions had both the incentive and the financial capacity to participate. After the spectacular collapse of the country's banking system, the three large new banks that were assembled from the wreckage acquired their loan portfolios at fair value that took into account the need for write-downs. This gave them the financial room to bear the costs of write-downs, and they frequently took the initiative. Much of the cost of debt restructuring was borne indirectly by foreign creditors, who took significant losses when the banks collapsed. Aligning households' incentives to participate was more complicated. The combination of indexation, inflation, and falling housing prices meant that the longer households waited, the larger the write-down. The unconditional moratorium on foreclosures and the suspension of debt service also reduced the incentive to resolve debt problems, and frequent revisions of the debt restructuring framework created an expectation of ever more generous offers. It was only when a comprehensive framework was put in place with a clear expiration date that debt write-downs finally took off. As of January 2012, 15 to 20 percent of all mortgages have either been—or are in the process of being—written down (see Table 3.1).

[34]For a full discussion of household debt restructuring in Iceland, see Karlsdóttir, Kristinsson, and Rozwadowski (forthcoming).

Overall, while the jury is still out on Iceland's approach to household debt, the policy response seems to address the main channels through which household debt can exert a drag on the economy. A spike in foreclosures was averted by the temporary moratorium and the concerted effort to find durable solutions to the household debt problem. By enabling households to reduce their debt and debt service, the debt restructuring framework transfers resources to agents with a relatively high marginal propensity to consume. The financial-sector-financed interest subsidy is playing a similar role. Finally, the write-down of a substantial portion of excess household debt (that is, in excess of household assets) mitigates the problems associated with debt overhang. The extent to which the Icelandic approach is able to achieve the ultimate goal of putting households back on their feet, while minimizing moral hazard, remains to be seen.

Colombia during the 1990s

This episode illustrates how household debt resolution measures that put the burden on a fragile banking sector can lead to a credit crunch. Following the sudden stop in capital inflows in 1997 triggered by the Asian and Russian crises, and the associated rise in interest rates, household defaults increased sharply and mortgage lenders suffered substantial losses (Fogafin, 2009).With their mortgage obligations increasing significantly while house prices collapsed and unemployment rose, many borrowers took their case to the courts (Forero, 2004). In response, the authorities conducted a bank restructuring program in 1999, and the constitutional court passed a series of rulings that aimed to lower households' mortgage debt burden and prevent foreclosures. In particular, the court ruled that mortgages were no longer full-recourse loans—households now had the option of walking away from their mortgage debt. The court also declared the capitalization of interest on delinquent loans unconstitutional.

These reforms represented a substantial transfer of funds to households with distressed balance sheets—those likely to have a high marginal propensity to consume—but imposed heavy losses on the fragile financial sector. The reforms also encouraged strategic

Table 3.1. Government-Supported Out-of-Court Debt Restructuring Programs in Selected Case-Study Countries

Program	Beneficiaries	Debt Modifications	Incentives and Burden Sharing	Take-up (in percent of mortgages, unless specified otherwise)
		United States 1929		
Home Owners' Loan Corporation	Households already in default (or at-risk mortgages held by financial institutions in distress)	Repayment burdens further reduced by extending loan terms and lowering interest rates. Principal reductions to a maximum loan-to-value (LTV) ratio of 80 percent	Moral hazard avoided because program was limited to those already in default. Participation was voluntary, but lenders were offered payouts above the amount they could recover in foreclosure. Eligibility criteria ensured that the borrower could service the new loan and limited the potential losses to be borne by taxpayers. Burden of principal reductions was shared between lenders and the government. Government bore risk on restructured mortgages.	Total households: 25 million Households with a mortgage: 5 million Eligible mortgages: 50 percent Applications: 38 percent Approved applications: 20 percent Foreclosures avoided: 800,000 Total authorization: $4.8 billion (8.5 percent of gross national product—GNP) Total restructurings: $3.1 billion (5.5 percent of GNP)
		Iceland 2008		
Payment Smoothing	Households with consumer price index (CPI)-linked and foreign exchange (FX)-linked mortgages and car loans	Debt service is reduced through rescheduling and maturity extension.	CPI-linked mortgages: Statutory requirement FX-linked loans: Agreement between government and lenders	Total households: 130,000 Households with a mortgage: 85,000 *Indicators of distress (excluding impact of measures):*[1] Households with negative equity (2010): 40 percent Households with debt service exceeding 40 percent of disposable income (2010): 30 percent Mortgages in default (2010): 15 percent *Take-up:* CPI- and FX-payment smoothing: 50 percent Approved and in-process restructurings: Sector Agreement: 1.6 percent DO: 3.9 percent Mortgage Write-down for Deeply Underwater Households: 14.9 percent
Sector Agreement (bank-administered voluntary restructuring)	Households with multiple creditors and debt service difficulties but able to service a mortgage amounting to at least 70 percent of the value of the house	Debt service is scaled down to capacity to pay. Debt is reduced to 100 percent of collateral value if households remain current on reduced payments for three years.	Government fostered agreement among largest lenders. Participation is voluntary. If agreement is not reached, debtors may apply to the Debtor's Ombudsman (DO) or the courts. The burden of restructuring the loans falls on the lenders.	
DO-Administered Voluntary Restructuring	Similar to Sector Agreement, but reaches less wealthy households. Aimed at households seeking advice and support in dealing with creditors.	Similar to Sector Agreement, but allows deeper temporary reduction in debt service. Procedures are more tailored and complex than under Sector Agreement.	Statutory framework that leads to court-administered restructuring in the event that negotiations are unsuccessful. The burden of restructuring the loans falls on the lenders.	

Program	Beneficiaries	Debt Modifications	Incentives and Burden Sharing	Take-up (in percent of mortgages, unless specified otherwise)
		Iceland 2008		
Mortgage Write-down for Deeply Underwater Households	Households with LTV ratio above 110 percent as of December 2010	Principal was reduced to 110 percent of the value of the debtor's pledgeable assets.	Agreement between mortgage lenders and government. Participation was voluntary, but lenders signed on because the written-down value exceeded the recovery likely through bankruptcy. Moral hazard was avoided because the program was limited to those with an LTV ratio above 110 percent in December 2010. The burden of restructuring the loans falls on the lenders.	
		United States 2009		
Home Affordable Modification Program (HAMP)[2]	Households in default	Focused on reducing repayment burdens through (1) interest rate reductions, (2) term extensions, (3) forbearance, and, since October 2010, principal reduction for loans outside the government-sponsored enterprises (Fannie Mae, Freddie Mac).	Participation is voluntary (except for receivers of Troubled Asset Relief Program funds). Principal write-down not often used, increasing the likelihood that the modified loan will redefault. Restructuring is initiated by servicers (not lenders), who have little incentive to participate. Securitization and junior-claim holders create conflict of interest.	Total number of households: 114 million Households with a mortgage: 51 million Households with negative equity: 23 percent Targeted reach: 6-8 percent Trial modifications: 4 percent Permanent modifications: 1.9 percent Total committed: $29.9 billion (0.2 percent of GDP)[3] Total amount used: $2.3 billion[3]
		Hungary 2011		
September 2011	Borrowers in good standing with FX-denominated mortgages	Principal write-down through the ability to prepay mortgages at a preferential exchange rate	Mandated by statute Burden of write-down borne by lenders alone Prepayment requirement limits ability of borrowers to participate.	Number of households: 4 million Households with a mortgage: 800,000 Mortgages in arrears: 90,000 Technically eligible: 90 percent Practically eligible: 25 percent Preliminary take-up: 15 percent
		Colombia 1999		
1999	Mortgage holders	Banks forced to retake underwater property and treat loan as fully repaid Repayment burden lowered through interest rate reduction	Participation mandated by court ruling Moral hazard and loss of confidence led to credit crunch.	Number of households: ±10 million Households with a mortgage: ±700,000 Mortgages in arrears: 126,000 (peak in 2002) Repossessed homes: 43,000 (1999–2003) Eligible borrowers: ±100 percent

[1]Near-universal indexation caused the indicators of distress to peak in 2010, two years after the crash.

[2]HAMP is the flagship debt restructuring program. As discussed in the text, there are other initiatives under the Making Home Affordable (MHA) program. The description of the program and cited numbers are as of the end of 2011.

[3]Source is Daily TARP Update for December 30, 2011 (Washington: U.S. Treasury). This reflects the amount obligated to all MHA initiatives. The total amount obligated for all housing programs under the Troubled Asset Relief Program is $45.6 billion.

default by households that would otherwise have repaid their loans, which further exacerbated lenders' losses.[35] Moreover, the court rulings weakened confidence regarding respect for private contracts and creditor rights. A severe and persistent credit crunch followed, and mortgage credit picked up only in 2005.

Hungary during the Great Recession

This episode illustrates how a compulsory program that is poorly targeted and puts the burden of debt restructuring on a fragile banking sector can jeopardize the stability of the financial system without achieving the desired economic objectives.

Hungarian households' indebtedness in foreign currency is among the highest in eastern Europe, although total household debt peaked at a relatively modest level, 40 percent of GDP, and is concentrated in roughly 800,000 households (or 20 percent of the total).[36] With the sharp depreciation of the Hungarian forint after the start of the global financial crisis, concerns that the rising debt service was undermining private consumption compelled the authorities to help foreign-currency-indebted households.[37] After a series of failed efforts to provide relief (such as a temporary moratorium on foreclosures and a voluntary workout initiative), the government introduced a compulsory debt restructuring program in September 2011, without prior consultation with stakeholders. During a fixed window (roughly five months), banks were forced to allow customers to repay their mortgages at a preferential exchange rate, roughly 30 percent below market rates. All losses from the implied debt reduction would be borne by the banks alone.

The compulsory debt restructuring program appears to have achieved high participation based on preliminary estimates—about 15 percent of all mortgages (see Table 3.1). However, it has three core limitations. First, it is poorly targeted as far as reaching constrained households with a high marginal propensity to consume. Only well-off households can repay outstanding mortgage balances with a one-time forint payment, implying limited redistribution toward consumers with a high marginal propensity to consume. Second, the compulsory program places the full burden of the losses on the banks, some of which are ill prepared to absorb such losses. Consequently, further bank deleveraging and a deepening of the credit crunch may result, with associated exchange rate pressure.[38] And finally, the implicit retroactive revision of private contracts without consulting the banking sector hurts the overall investment climate.

The United States since the Great Recession

This episode, which is ongoing, illustrates how difficult it is to achieve comprehensive household debt restructuring in the face of a complex mortgage market and political constraints. The key programs have reached far fewer households than initially envisaged in the three years since their inception. These shortfalls led the authorities to adopt additional measures in February 2012 to alleviate the pressure on household balance sheets.

Since the start of the Great Recession, a number of U.S. policymakers have advocated a bold household debt restructuring program modeled on the HOLC of the Great Depression.[39] However, support for such large-scale government intervention in the housing market has, so far, been limited.[40] Instead,

[35]In order to compensate lenders for losses incurred by the court ruling, the national deposit insurance company established a line of credit with favorable rates for lenders in 2000.

[36]By the time the crisis arrived in 2008, 100 percent of all new lending and 50 percent of household loans outstanding were in Swiss francs and collateralized by housing.

[37]As IMF (2011a) explains, debt service for holders of foreign-currency-denominated loans increased by more than 50 percent.

[38]Realizing the potential adverse impact of the legislation on the banking sector, the authorities adopted additional measures in December 2011 to spread the burden (see IMF, 2011a).

[39]Specific proposals for household debt policies along the lines of HOLC include those of Blinder (2008) and Hubbard and Mayer (2008). Blinder (2008) proposed a HOLC-style program to refinance 1 to 2 million distressed mortgages for owner-occupied residences by borrowing and lending about $300 billion. Hubbard and Mayer (2008) proposed lowering repayment amounts and preventing foreclosures and estimated that this would stimulate consumption by approximately $120 billion a year, or 0.8 percent of GDP a year. Approximately half of this effect was estimated to come through the wealth effect—higher house prices due to fewer foreclosures—and half through the transfer of resources to constrained households ("HOLC effect"). See Hubbard and Mayer (2008) and Hubbard (2011). Analysis accompanying IMF (2011b, Chapter II) suggests that, for each 1 million foreclosures avoided, U.S. GDP would rise by 0.3 to 0.4 percentage point.

[40]The case of "cramdowns" illustrates how political constraints affected the policy response. As IMF (2011b) explains, the

the authorities implemented a number of more modest policies.[41] Here, we focus on the Home Affordable Modification Program (HAMP), the flagship mortgage debt restructuring initiative targeted at households in default or at risk of default. Announced in February 2009, HAMP's goal was to stabilize the housing market and help struggling homeowners get relief by making mortgages more affordable through the modification of first-lien loans. The program was amended in October 2010 to allow principal write-downs under the Principal Reduction Alternative (PRA) and further enhanced in 2012, as discussed below. HAMP is part of the Making Home Affordable (MHA) initiative, which helps struggling homeowners get mortgage relief through a variety of programs that aid in modification, refinancing, deferred payment, and foreclosure alternatives. Other options under the MHA initiative include the Home Affordable Refinance Program (HARP), which also aims at reducing monthly mortgage payments. However, households already in default are excluded from HARP, and the impact on preventing foreclosures is likely to be more limited.[42]

HAMP had significant ambitions but has thus far achieved far fewer modifications than envisaged. Millions of households remain at risk of losing their homes. The stock of properties in foreclosure at the end of 2011 stood at about 2.4 million—a nearly fivefold increase over the precrisis level—and the so-called shadow inventory of distressed mortgages suggests that this number could rise significantly (Figure

authorities viewed allowing mortgages to be modified in courts (cramdowns) as a useful way to encourage voluntary modifications at no fiscal cost, but noted that a proposal for such a policy had failed to garner sufficient political support in 2009. Mian, Sufi, and Trebbi (2012) argue that creditors' greater ability to organize politically and influence government policy may be the reason they were better able to protect their interests during the recent financial crisis: "Debtors, on the other hand, were numerous and diffused, therefore suffering from typical collective action problems" (p. 20).

[41]Early attempts to fix the household debt problem were the Federal Housing Administration (FHA) Secure program, the Hope Now Alliance, the Federal Deposit Insurance Corporation's Mod in a Box, and Hope for Homeowners.

[42]The MHA initiative also includes the FHA's Short Refinance Program for borrowers with negative equity, Home Affordable Unemployment Program, Home Affordable Foreclosure Alternatives Program, Second Lien Modification Program, and Housing Finance Agency Innovation Fund for the Hardest Hit Housing Markets.

Figure 3.11. The U.S. Housing Market, 2000–11

There were about 2.4 million properties in foreclosure in the United States at the end of 2011, a nearly fivefold increase over the precrisis level, and the "shadow inventory" of distressed mortgages suggests that this number could rise further.

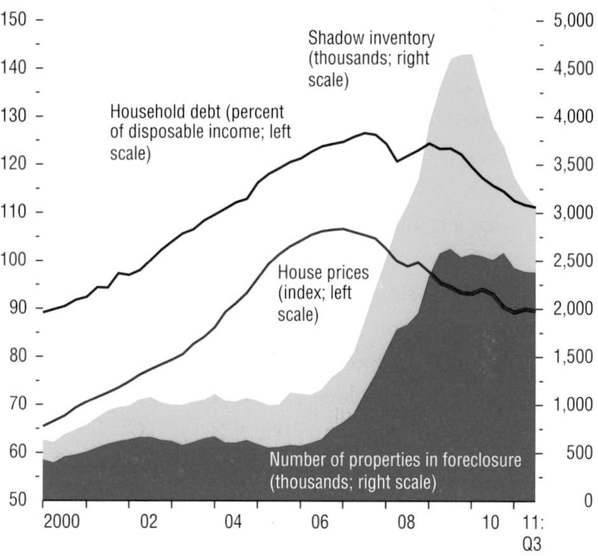

Sources: Office of the Comptroller of the Currency; Office of Thrift Supervision; U.S. Treasury; Federal Reserve; Haver Analytics; and IMF staff calculations.

Note: Shadow inventory indicates properties likely to go into foreclosure based on a number of assumptions. It includes a portion of all loans delinquent 90 days or more (based on observed performance of such loans); a share of modifications in place (based on redefault performance of modified mortgages); and a portion of negative equity mortgages (based on observed default rates). Data on modifications and negative equity are not available prior to 2008:Q2.

3.11). Meanwhile, the number of permanently modified mortgages amounts to 951,000, or 1.9 percent of all mortgages (see Table 3.1).[43] By contrast, some 20 percent of mortgages were modified by the Depression-era HOLC program, and HAMP's targeted reach was 3 to 4 million homeowners (MHA, 2010).[44] By the same token, the amount disbursed under MHA as of December 2011 was only $2.3 billion, well below the allocation of $30 billion (0.2 percent of GDP).

Issues with HAMP's design help explain this disappointing performance. The specific issues are as follows:

- Limited incentives for the parties to participate in the program and tight eligibility criteria for borrowers have resulted in low take-up. The initial legislation made creditor cooperation completely voluntary, thereby enabling many creditors to opt out of the program. Loan servicers have little incentive to initiate a costly renegotiation process given that they are already compensated for some (legal) costs when delinquent loans enter foreclosure.[45] The high probability of redefault may lead lenders and investors to prefer forbearance and foreclosure to modification (Adelino, Gerardi, and Willen, 2009). Securitization presents additional coordination and legal problems. In addition, conflicts of interest may arise, for example, when second-lien holders forestall debt restructuring (IMF, 2011b). Several factors also hamper borrower participation. For instance, many of the expenses related to the outstanding loan, such as late fees and accrued interest, get folded into the new, modified loan. Finally, many distressed borrowers are effectively locked out of the program due to tight eligibility requirements. The unemployed are ineligible to apply for HAMP (they are eligible for a different initiative under MHA that is designed for the unemployed), and households that suffered large income losses often fail to meet the postmodification debt-to-income requirements, especially without principal reduction. Overall, therefore, the program transfers only limited funds to distressed homeowners.
- HAMP has not reduced monthly mortgage payments enough to restore affordability in many cases. HAMP includes strict step-by-step instructions for modifying a loan, with the primary methods being interest rate reductions, term extensions, and forbearance. Certain exceptions to this step-by-step process are allowed. Non-GSE loans with an LTV above 115 percent may also be eligible for principal reductions under PRA.[46] As of the end of 2011, 11 percent of HAMP permanent modifications included a principal write-down.[47] The nonparticipation by GSEs, which hold about 60 percent of all outstanding mortgages, helps explain this low take-up. Importantly, the modifications focus on bringing a narrow definition of the mortgage repayment burden down to 31 percent of monthly gross income rather than the total repayment burden (including other installment loans and second mortgages). As a result, most borrowers remain seriously constrained even after the modifications, with after-modification total debt repayment burdens averaging 60 percent of monthly gross income and the after-modification LTV sometimes actually increasing (MHA, 2012). This helps explain the high redefault rate on the modified loans, which currently averages 27

[43]As MHA (2012) explains, as of January 2012, 1.79 million trials had been started, but only 951,000 of these trials succeeded in becoming "permanent." (The trial period allows the loan servicer to test the borrower's ability to make the modified loan payment before finalizing the loan modification.) Note that some 200,000 of these modifications were subsequently canceled, leaving 769,000 *active* permanent modifications.

[44]In a report on the implementation of the HAMP program, the Office of the Special Inspector General for the Troubled Asset Relief Program (SIGTARP) clarified that "Treasury has stated that its 3 to 4 million homeowner goal is not tied to how many homeowners actually receive sustainable relief and avoid foreclosure, but rather that 3 to 4 million homeowners will receive offers for a trial modification" (SIGTARP, 2010). The report criticizes measuring trial modification offers—rather than foreclosures avoided through permanent modifications—as "simply not particularly meaningful."

[45]As Kiff and Klyuev (2009) explain, a servicer's primary duty is to collect mortgage payments from borrowers and pass them to the mortgage holders (trusts, in the case of securitized loans). Servicers also manage the escrow accounts they hold on behalf of borrowers to pay property taxes and insurance, and they employ various loss-mitigation techniques should the borrower default. Servicers are paid a fee for this work.

[46]The GSEs—government-sponsored enterprises—include the Federal National Mortgage Association (Fannie Mae) and the Federal Home Loan Mortgage Corporation (Freddie Mac).

[47]As MHA (2012) explains, 47,000 permanent modifications received principal write-downs (p. 4), which is equivalent to 11 percent of the 432,000 permanent modifications between October 2010 and December 2011.

percent after 18 months and as high as 41 percent in cases where the monthly payment reduction was less than or equal to 20 percent (MHA, 2012).

In response to these shortcomings, the authorities adopted additional measures to alleviate the pressure on household balance sheets. In February 2012, the authorities announced an expansion of HAMP, including broader eligibility and a tripling of the incentives for lenders to offer principal reductions. In addition, the program was extended by one year. However, participation of the GSEs in the program remains subject to approval by the Federal Housing Finance Agency. Principal reductions are likely to reduce foreclosure rates and, if implemented on a large scale, would support house prices substantially—helping to eliminate the overall uncertainty weighing on the housing market via the shadow inventory.[48]

Scandinavia during the 1990s

The Scandinavian countries illustrate how institutional features, such as a large social safety net, may influence governments' adoption of discretionary household debt restructuring policies. In contrast to the cases discussed above, these episodes featured few government initiatives directly targeted at household debt. After housing prices peaked in the late 1980s and the subsequent onset of banking crises in these economies, the primary discretionary policy responses of the Scandinavian governments consisted of support for the financial system.

These economies did not initiate any household debt restructuring measures, but their large existing social safety nets supported household incomes and their ability to service their debt. The large safety nets are a result of a tradition of providing many public services, mainly as a way to promote equality in these economies.[49] For example, unemployment benefits as a percentage of previous wages averaged 65 percent in Finland, Norway, and Sweden in 1991, well above the 47 percent average in other OECD economies (OECD, 1995, p. 61). In Sweden, the wage replacement ratio was 83 percent. This government-provided insurance, along with other social safety net benefits, substantially mitigated the impact of job loss on households with distressed balance sheets and supported their ability to pay their mortgages. At the same time, the automatic transfer programs combined with the recession implied a substantial rise in government debt. The government debt-to-GDP ratio rose from an average of 31 percent in 1990 to 64 percent in 1994 (Figure 3.12).[50] In response, the authorities implemented cuts to social welfare payments in the mid- to late 1990s as part of a multiyear fiscal consolidation (Devries and others, 2011).

In addition, the variable mortgage rates prevalent in these economies allowed lower interest rates to pass through quickly to lower mortgage payments. The decline in short-term interest rates after the Scandinavian countries abandoned the exchange rate peg to the European Currency Unit in November 1992 was substantial. For example, the abandonment of the exchange rate peg allowed a cumulative 4 percentage point reduction in short-term interest rates in Sweden (IMF, 1993). By contrast, households in economies where mortgage rates tend to be fixed over multiyear terms often need to apply for a new mortgage (refinance) in order to reap the benefit of lower prevailing rates, a process that can be hampered by lower house values and negative equity.

Lessons from the Case Studies

Our investigation of the initiatives implemented by governments to address the problem of household debt during episodes of household deleveraging leads to the following policy lessons:

[48]Other measures include a pilot sale of foreclosed properties for conversion to rental housing. Transitioning properties into rentals should help reduce the negative impact of foreclosures on house prices. The authorities also called on Congress to broaden access to refinancing under HARP for both GSE-backed and non-GSE mortgages; these measures would support the recovery of the housing market. In particular, they would allow non-GSE loans to be refinanced through a streamlined program operated by the FHA.

[49]For example, IMF (1991) explains that in Norway, "the Government has traditionally sought to provide many basic services in the areas of health and education publicly, mainly as a way to promote equity but also for reasons of social policy. In addition, efforts to redistribute incomes and reduce regional differences have led to an extensive transfer system." (p. 19)

[50]The rise in government debt was also a result of financial support to the banking sector and discretionary fiscal stimulus aimed at reducing unemployment.

Figure 3.12. Government Debt in the Scandinavian Countries, 1988–95
(Percent of GDP)

Finland, Norway, and Sweden experienced a sharp increase in government debt following the housing bust and banking crisis of the early 1990s.

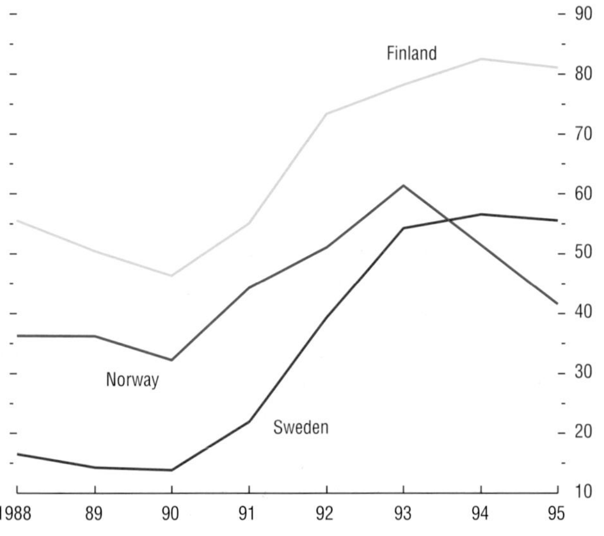

Source: IMF staff calculations.

- Bold household debt restructuring programs, such as those implemented in the United States in the 1930s and in Iceland today, can significantly reduce the number of household defaults and foreclosures and substantially reduce debt repayment burdens. In so doing, these programs help prevent self-reinforcing cycles of declining house prices and lower aggregate demand. The Icelandic experience also highlights the importance of a comprehensive framework, with clear communication to the public and an explicit time frame. It was only after such a framework was put in place that the process of household debt restructuring took off.
- Ensuring a strong banking sector is crucial during the period of household deleveraging. In Iceland, the fact that the new banks had acquired their loan portfolios at fair value meant that far-reaching household debt restructuring could proceed without affecting bank capital. This also gave banks incentives to initiate negotiations with borrowers. In contrast, in the case of Colombia in the 1990s and in Hungary today, an insufficiently capitalized banking sector could not absorb the losses associated with (mandatory) household debt restructuring. This resulted in a disruption of credit supply.
- Existing institutional features may influence whether or not governments implement discretionary policy initiatives to tackle the problems associated with household debt. In the Scandinavian countries, despite a significant buildup in household debt before the housing bust of the late 1980s, the authorities introduced few new policies targeted at household debt. We argue that this lack of a policy response may reflect the existence of substantial automatic fiscal stabilizers through the social safety net, in addition to variable mortgage interest rates that quickly transmitted monetary policy stimulus to homeowners.
- An important element in the design of targeted policies is sufficient incentives for borrowers and lenders to participate. For example, debt restructuring initiatives need to offer creditors and debtors a viable alternative to default and foreclosure. The case of the United States during the Great Depression demonstrates how specific provisions

can be implemented to ensure that the lenders willingly accept the government-supported modifications. In contrast, the case of the United States since the Great Recession, where loan modifications may open the door to potential litigation by investors, illustrates how poorly designed household debt restructuring efforts can result in low participation.

- Government support for household debt restructuring programs involves clear winners and losers. The friction caused by such redistribution may be one reason such policies have rarely been used in the past, except when the magnitude of the problem was substantial and the ensuing social and political pressures considerable.

Summary and Implications for the Outlook

Housing busts preceded by larger run-ups in gross household debt are associated with deeper slumps, weaker recoveries, and more pronounced household deleveraging. The decline in economic activity is too large to be simply a reflection of a greater fall in house prices. And it is not driven by the occurrence of banking crises alone. Rather, it is the combination of the house price decline and the prebust leverage that seems to explain the severity of the contraction. These stylized facts are consistent with the predictions of recent theoretical models in which household debt and deleveraging drive deep and prolonged slumps.

Macroeconomic policies are a crucial element of efforts to avert excessive contractions in economic activity during episodes of household deleveraging. For example, fiscal transfers to unemployed households through the social safety net can boost their incomes and improve their ability to service debt, as in the case of the Scandinavian economies in the 1990s. Monetary easing in economies in which mortgages typically have variable interest rates can quickly reduce mortgage payments and prevent household defaults. Support to the financial sector can address the risk that household balance sheet distress will affect banks' willingness to supply credit. Macroeconomic stimulus, however, has its limits. The zero lower bound on nominal interest rates can prevent sufficient rate cuts, and high government debt may constrain the scope for deficit-financed transfers.

Targeted household debt restructuring policies can deliver significant benefits. Such policies can, at a relatively low fiscal cost, substantially mitigate the negative impact of household deleveraging on economic activity. In particular, bold household debt restructuring programs such as those implemented in the United States in the 1930s and in Iceland today can reduce the number of household defaults and foreclosures and alleviate debt repayment burdens. In so doing, these programs help prevent self-reinforcing cycles of declining house prices and lower aggregate demand. Such policies are particularly relevant for economies with limited scope for expansionary macroeconomic policies and in which the financial sector has already received government support.

However, the success of such programs depends on careful design. Overly restrictive eligibility criteria or poorly structured incentives can lead to programs having a fraction of their intended effect. Conversely, overly broad programs can have serious side effects and undermine the health of the financial sector.

Appendix 3.1. Data Construction and Sources

Data on household balance sheets were collected from a variety of sources. The main source is the Organization for Economic Cooperation and Development (OECD) Financial Accounts Database. The data set contains detailed information on households' financial assets and liabilities for 33 economies, spanning the period 1950–2010, though the series for most of the economies begin in the 1990s. We focus on the household sector's total financial liabilities. For several economies, the series on total financial liabilities were extended back using data from national sources (Finland, Italy, Korea, New Zealand, Norway, Sweden, United Kingdom, United States). Household financial liabilities series for Australia, Belgium, France, Germany, Greece, the Netherlands, and Portugal going back to 1980 were obtained from Cecchetti, Mohanty, and Zampolli (2011). More recent data on household balance sheets for several non-OECD countries (Bulgaria, Latvia, Lithuania, Romania) were obtained from Eurostat. Data for the United States before 1950 come from the U.S. Bureau of Economic Analysis and from *Historical Statistics of the United States;*

for Iceland, data on household liabilities are from national sources.

The remainder of the series used in the chapter draw mostly on the IMF World Economic Outlook (WEO), World Bank World Development Indicators, OECD.Stat, and Haver Analytics databases. In particular, household disposable income, housing prices, and unemployment rates are taken from OECD.Stat and spliced with Haver Analytics data to extend coverage. House price information for Colombia and Hungary are from the *Global Property Guide;* for Iceland, the housing price index is from national sources. Macroeconomic variables, such as real and nominal GDP, private consumption, investment, and so on are from the WEO database.

Housing bust indicators are obtained from Claessens, Kose, and Terrones (2010), who use the Harding and Pagan (2002) algorithm to determine turning points in the (log) level of nominal house prices. Recession indicators are from Howard, Martin, and Wilson (2011), who define a recession as two consecutive quarters of negative growth. Because our empirical analysis relies on annual data, we assign the recession or housing bust, respectively, to the year of the first quarter of the recession or house price peak. Financial crisis indicators are from Laeven and Valencia (2010).

Appendix 3.2. Statistical Methodology and Robustness Checks

This appendix provides further details on the statistical methods used in the first section of the chapter and the robustness of the associated regression results.

Model Specification and Estimation

The baseline specification is a cross-section and time-fixed-effects panel data model estimated for 24 Organization for Economic Cooperation and Development economies and Taiwan Province of China during 1980–2011:

$$\Delta Y_{it} = \mu_i + \lambda_t + \sum_{j=0}^{2} \beta_j \Delta Y_{i,t-j} + \sum_{s=0}^{2} \beta_s Bust_{i,t-s} + \sum_{s=0}^{2} \gamma_s \{Bust_{i,t-s} \times HiDebt_{i,t-s-1}\} + \sum_{s=0}^{2} \theta_s HiDebt_{i,t-s-1} + v_{i,t}, \qquad (3.1)$$

where ΔY_{it} denotes the change in the variable of interest. We start with the (log) of real household consumption and then examine the components of GDP, unemployment, household debt, and house prices. The term *Bust* denotes a housing bust dummy that takes the value of 1 at the start of a housing bust; *HiDebt* is a dummy variable that takes the value of 1 if the rise in the household debt-to-income ratio in the three years before the bust was "high." In our baseline specification, we define the rise as high if it was above the median for all housing busts across all economies. We conduct a number of robustness checks on this definition of "high," finding similar results (see below). We include country and time fixed effects to allow for global shocks and country-specific trends. We cumulate the estimates of equation (3.1) to obtain estimates of the response of the *level* of the variable of interest (Y) along with the standard error (clustered by economy) using the delta method.

Robustness Checks

As Table 3.2 shows, the finding that housing busts preceded by a large buildup in household debt tend to be more severe holds up to a number of robustness checks. For each robustness check, we focus on the severity of the housing bust for the high- and low-debt groups in terms of the decline in real household consumption five years after the bust.[51] The robustness tests include the following:

- *Definition of "high-debt" group:* Our baseline places a housing bust in the high-debt group if it was preceded by an above-median rise in the household debt-to-income ratio during the three years leading up to the bust. The results do not depend on whether the rise is defined in absolute terms (percentage point increase in the ratio) or in relative terms (proportionate increase in percent). The results are also similar if we define "high debt" as being in the top quartile and "low debt"

[51]Similar results are obtained at horizons of less than five years, but these are not reported, given space constraints.

Table 3.2. Real Consumption following Housing Busts: Robustness

	High Debt	Low Debt	Difference
Baseline	−4.315***	−0.396	−3.918***
	(0.829)	(0.791)	(0.970)
Alternative Samples			
Excluding the Great Recession	−4.098***	−0.425	−3.673***
	(0.987)	(1.068)	(1.294)
Excluding Financial Crises	−1.757**	0.504	−2.261**
	(0.876)	(0.735)	(1.095)
Excluding Outliers	−2.978***	−0.133	−2.845***
	(0.755)	(0.726)	(0.946)
Alternative Statistical Models			
Generalized Method of Moments	−4.142***	−0.277	−3.865***
	(0.996)	(1.015)	(1.301)
Four Lags of Dependent Variable	−2.121**	0.984	−3.105**
	(1.071)	(1.273)	(1.310)
Alternative Definitions of High versus Low Debt			
Above versus Below Median (percent increase in debt)	−3.675***	−0.543	−3.132***
	(0.779)	(0.841)	(0.917)
Top versus Bottom Quartile (percentage point increase in debt)	−5.690***	−0.948	−4.742**
	(1.601)	(1.236)	(2.332)

Source: IMF staff calculations.

Note: The table presents the estimated cumulative response of real consumer spending following housing busts at year $t = 5$ for episodes with a low and high buildup in household debt in the three years prior to the housing bust. Robust standard errors, corrected for clustering at the economy level, are shown in parentheses. ***, **, and * indicate significance at the 1, 5, and 10 percent level, respectively.

as being in the bottom quartile of the increase in the debt-to-income ratio.

- *Time sample:* The results are not driven by the Great Recession. Ending the sample in 2006 produces similar results.
- *Outliers and specification:* The results regarding the more severe contraction in economic activity are robust to the exclusion of outliers using Cook's distance. (This involves excluding outlier data points with large residuals or high influence.) The results are also similar if we use a dynamic specification with four lags instead of the two lags in the baseline specification.
- *Alternative estimation procedure:* The results are also similar if we undertake the estimation using the Arellano-Bond (1991) estimator. This procedure addresses the possibility of bias because country fixed effects are correlated with the lagged dependent variables in the autoregressive equation.

Box 3.1. The U.S. Home Owners' Loan Corporation (HOLC)

HOLC, a program that involved government purchases of distressed loans, was established June 13, 1933. The explicit goals of HOLC, set forth in its authorizing statute, were as follows: "To provide emergency relief with respect to home mortgage indebtedness, to refinance home mortgages, to extend relief to the owners of homes occupied by them and who are unable to amortize their debt elsewhere, to amend the Federal Home Loan Bank Act, to increase the market for obligations of the United States, and for other purposes."

The program provided for (1) the exchange of HOLC bonds (with a federal guarantee at first of interest only but later, beginning in spring 1934, of both interest and principal) for home mortgages in default and, in a few cases, for (2) cash loans for payment of taxes and mortgage refinancing. HOLC loans were restricted to mortgages in default (or mortgages held by financial institutions in distress) and secured by nonfarm properties with dwelling space for not more than four families and appraised by HOLC officials at not more than $20,000 ($321,791 in 2008 dollars). No loans could exceed 80 percent of the HOLC appraisal, nor could any loan exceed $14,000. Loans were to carry no more than 5 percent interest and were to be amortized by monthly payments during their maturity of 15 years, which was sometimes extended to 20 years (Green and Wachter, 2005).

How It Worked

Eligibility criteria for borrowers and properties were stringently applied. In total (between June 13, 1933, and June 27, 1935) HOLC received 1,886,491 applications requesting $6.2 billion in refinancing, equivalent to roughly 35 percent of outstanding nonfarm mortgage loans, or 11 percent of gross national product, which exceeded its total authorization of $4.75 billion. Approximately 40 percent of those eligible for the program applied, and 46 percent of these applications were rejected or withdrawn. "Inadequate security" and "lack of distress" were the most cited reasons for rejection of an application. Some of the applications were withdrawn as a result of voluntary bilateral agreements between the applicant and the lender, at the encouragement of HOLC. Nevertheless, HOLC bought and restructured about 1 million distressed mortgages that were at risk of foreclosure, or about one in five of all mortgages.

The success crucially depended on the lenders' willingness to accept HOLC bonds in exchange for their outstanding mortgages. Lenders were reluctant to participate because of the initial limitation of the government guarantee to interest only, with no commitment on principal, and the belief that HOLC would lose money. The relatively low 4 percent interest rate—roughly one-third below the customary rate on mortgages, some financial institutions' legal restrictions on investment policies, and the lack of confidence in the government's credit were also reasons not to accept the exchange.

Yet the government guarantee of interest was much better than the promise of a distressed homeowner: an almost certain return of 4 percent was more attractive than an accruing but uncollectible 6 percent and came without collection and servicing costs or the expense of potential foreclosure. In addition, the appraisal standards might permit the receipt of more in bonds than could be obtained from sale at foreclosure. Finally, the bonds were exempt from state and local property taxes, and the income was exempt from state and federal normal income tax. To further improve the terms for the exchange, the legal restrictions on investment policies were lifted, the New York Real Estate Securities Exchange announced that the bonds would be admitted for trading, the Treasury authorized use of the bonds as collateral for deposits of public money, the Reconstruction Finance Corporation (RFC) agreed to accept the bonds as collateral at up to 80 percent of face value, and the Comptroller of the Currency reversed an earlier stand to permit receivers of national banks to accept the new bonds. In early 1934, the government guarantee was extended to the bond principal, undoubtedly enhancing their acceptability, and HOLC announced new 18-year bonds, callable in 10 years and bearing a 3 percent coupon.

Appraisal values were critical in providing incentives for participation in the refinancing program as well as ensuring adequate reach and burden sharing.

The author of this box is Deniz Igan.

Box 3.1. *(continued)*

The lower the valuation placed on properties, the less the risk for HOLC, but the fewer the number of homeowners who could benefit and the greater the sacrifice required from the former lenders. Appraisals were based on three equally weighted factors: "the market value at the time of appraisal; the cost of a similar lot at the time of the appraisal, plus the reproduction cost of the building, less depreciation; and the value of the premises as arrived at by capitalizing the monthly reasonable rental value of the premises over a period of the past ten years." The result often exceeded the current market value given the circumstances in the housing market.

A couple of complications arose in the case of mortgages held by recently failed banks and in the case of second mortgages and other junior claims. A wholesale operation was established to handle the cases involving recently failed banks: the RFC would make a loan to a bank in difficulty and accept mortgages as collateral, and then HOLC would process these mortgages and turn its bonds or cash over to the bank, which in turn repaid the RFC. About 13 percent of all HOLC-refinanced mortgages fell into this category. The policy for dealing with junior claim holders was to limit the total obligations on a property to 100 percent of its appraisal to ensure that borrowers could reasonably be expected to carry out their obligations. The junior lien had to be secured by a bond and mortgage, requiring foreclosure as a means of liquidation. (HOLC consent was required before the second-lien holder could foreclose.)

HOLC got off to a rough start: it underestimated the size of the task and was poorly organized. Its status as an independent organization gave it more freedom in terms of budgeting and administration, but the lack of precedent and the urgency of the situation posed challenges. Yet, within a few years, HOLC had gained a reputation for proper execution and efficient provision of much-needed relief.

Box 3.2. Household Debt Restructuring in Iceland

In the aftermath of Iceland's devastating financial crisis in 2008, the authorities sought to shield households from near-term distress, set them on a path to financial viability, and prevent a wave of foreclosures. Their policy initiatives fall into two broad categories: postponing or rescheduling debt service and reducing the stock of debt. The task was complicated by a Supreme Court finding, midway through the process, that most exchange-rate-linked obligations are illegal under a 2001 law. This stalled the debt reduction programs described below but also led to debt reduction equivalent to 10 percent of GDP, some of which would otherwise have been provided via those programs.[1] Much of the cost of debt restructuring was borne indirectly by foreign creditors, who took significant losses when the banks collapsed.

Postponing or Rescheduling Debt Service

The immediate goal was to shield households from a ballooning in debt service stemming from the near universal indexation of debt to the consumer price index (CPI) or the exchange rate, both of which had risen sharply. A first step was to suspend debt service, temporarily, on all exchange-rate-linked loans and some local-currency mortgages. Soon thereafter, the authorities introduced payment smoothing: a mechanism for rescheduling by rebasing debt service on an index that had risen much less than the CPI or the exchange rate. Payment smoothing provided up-front debt service relief of 15 to 20 percent for CPI-indexed loans and 30 to 40 percent for exchange-rate-indexed loans. The relief came at the cost of larger future payments and possible extensions of maturity. To encourage households to participate, payment smoothing was made the default option for CPI-indexed loans, and a three-year limit was placed on maturity extensions (with any remaining balances written off). About 50 percent of mortgages benefited from payment smoothing. A temporary moratorium on foreclosures of residential properties complemented these measures.

Debt Reduction

Several principles shaped Iceland's approach to debt reduction. First, the financial burden was to fall on the financial sector, which had financial buffers, rather than on the public sector, whose debt was already high. Second, the needs of distressed households were to be weighed against preserving creditors' rights. And finally, speed was an important consideration.

The approach rests on four pillars, each of which has been modified over time in light of experience. Three provide for case-by-case solutions administered, respectively, by the courts, the financial sector, and the newly created Office of the Debtor's Ombudsman (DO). The fourth is an agreement that allows fast-track write-downs for deeply underwater mortgages.

- *Court-administered solutions:* The authorities amended the Law on Bankruptcy in order to make it easier and cheaper for households to file for consolidation of unsecured debt and to shorten the discharge period in the event of bankruptcy. They also enacted the Law on Mitigation of Residential Mortgage Payments, aimed at households with moderately priced homes. This law allows lenders to write down mortgages to 110 percent of collateral value (later reduced to 100 percent) and convert the written-down portion to an unsecured claim. This framework is cumbersome, but its basic elements—reduced payments during a specified period, a subsequent reduction of the lien, and possible cancellation of unsecured debt—were the model and legal basis for the out-of-court initiatives that followed. It also serves as a backstop in case out-of-court negotiations break down.
- *Sector agreement:* The authorities supported a sectorwide agreement on a bank-administered framework for fast-track out-of-court debt mitigation. This agreement addresses many of the problems associated with court-administered

The authors of this box are Edda Rós Karlsdóttir and Franek Rozwadowski.

[1]The illegal loans were recalculated as if they had been made in domestic currency on the best terms available at the time of the original loan. A February 2012 Supreme Court decision modified this treatment, but its effect is still unclear and is not reflected in this discussion.

Box 3.2. *(continued)*

restructuring. It integrates the handling of secured and unsecured debt and sets out guidelines for third-party guarantees and collateral.

Under this framework, households seeking relief first liquidate nonessential assets and use any excess cash to reduce debt. Outstanding underwater mortgages (or auto loans) are then divided up into a secured loan, equal to 100 percent of the value of the collateral, and a provisionally unsecured loan. The general rule is that the household must service the secured loan in full and use its remaining "capacity to repay" to make partial pro rata payments on all unsecured loans.[2] But there are also provisions for a three-year suspension of up to 30 percent of the mortgage. If the household remains current on all these payments for three years, the outstanding balances of all unsecured loans are canceled.

- *The Debtor's Ombudsman:* A third case-by-case framework was set up by legislation under a DO and its supporting legal framework. The DO provides households with legal and financial advice and appoints a supervisor to represent them in negotiations. The legislation seeks to reduce delays by introducing time limits for processing applications; it also incentivizes lenders by introducing a formal procedure for lodging claims, making court-administered restructuring the fallback (and threat) should negotiations fail. DO-administered debt restructuring has the same basic features as restructuring under the sector agreement, but it allows for more tailoring to individual circumstances, brings in a wider set of borrowers and creditors, and may provide for a smaller write-down of unsecured claims.
- *Fast-track write-downs:* The final pillar, erected in December 2010, was a government-fostered agreement by lenders on relatively simple rules for writing down deeply underwater mortgages to 110 percent of pledgeable assets. This agreement removed households' incentive to hold back in the hope of a better deal later on by specifying the dates on which the mortgage and the property would be valued and by specifying the date on which the offer would expire. The fast-track write-downs have reduced more debt and reached more households than all the other programs. As of January 31, 2012, close to 15 percent of households with mortgages have benefited from the fast-track write-downs, compared with fewer than 6 percent who have used or are using the sector agreement and the DO. That said, the case-by-case approaches may be reaching a larger number of households with high debt service ratios since only about a quarter of the households benefiting from the fast-track write-downs were in this category (Ólafsson and Vignisdóttir, 2012).

Outcomes and Lessons

While the jury is still out on Iceland's approach to household debt, a number of conclusions can already be drawn. First, measures with simple eligibility criteria, such as write-downs of deeply underwater mortgages, can provide quick relief with rough-hewn targeting. Second, case-by-case out-of-court frameworks can help bail out households with complex problems faster than the courts. However, these frameworks are also slow: only 35 percent of the applications received had been processed by the end of January 2012. In part this is because key concepts (such as "capacity to repay") were not defined precisely. But it is also because the legislation and the sector agreement leave more to be decided on the basis of individual circumstances than is consistent with the fast-track objective. Finally, in the same vein, the more complex structure of the DO approach contributes to long processing periods.

There appears to be a trade-off between speedy resolution and fine-tuning debt relief in order to protect property rights and reduce moral hazard. One way to minimize this trade-off is through the use of parallel frameworks—general measures for severe cases in which write-downs appear inevitable and case-by-case measures for more complex cases. Indeed the authorities' decision to complement case-by-case frameworks with fast-track measures for deeply underwater mortgages is a step in the right direction.

[2]Capacity to pay is defined as the difference between disposable income and the "normal" cost of living.

References

Adelino, Manuel, Kristopher Gerardi, and Paul Willen, 2009, "Why Don't Lenders Renegotiate More Home Mortgages? Redefaults, Self-Cures, and Securitization," NBER Working Paper No. 15159 (Cambridge, Massachusetts: National Bureau of Economic Research).

Arellano, Manuel, and Stephen Bond, 1991, "Some Tests of Specification for Panel Data: Monte Carlo Evidence and an Application to Employment Equations," *Review of Economic Studies*, Vol. 58, pp. 277–97.

Blinder, Alan S., 2008, "From the New Deal, a Way Out of a Mess," *The New York Times*, February 24.

Board of Governors of the Federal Reserve System (BGFRS), 2012, "The U.S. Housing Market: Current Conditions and Policy Considerations," staff white paper (Washington, January).

Buiter, Willem H., 2010, "Housing Wealth Isn't Wealth," *Economics—The Open-Access, Open-Assessment E-Journal*, Vol. 4, No. 22, pp. 1–29.

Campbell, John, Stefano Giglio, and Parag Pathak, 2011, "Forced Sales and House Prices," *American Economic Review*, Vol. 101, No. 5, pp. 2108–31.

Carroll, Christopher, Jiri Slacalek, and Martin Sommer, 2011, "Dissecting Saving Dynamics: Measuring Credit, Wealth and Precautionary Effects" (unpublished; Baltimore: Johns Hopkins University Press).

Cecchetti, Stephen G., M. S. Mohanty, and Fabrizio Zampolli, 2011, "The Real Effects of Debt," BIS Working Paper No. 352 (Basel: Bank for International Settlements).

Cerra, Valerie, and Sweta Saxena, 2008, "Growth Dynamics: The Myth of Economic Recovery," *American Economic Review*, Vol. 98, No. 1, pp. 439–57.

Claessens, Stijn, Ayhan Kose, and Marco Terrones, 2010, "Financial Cycles: What? How? When?" in *NBER International Seminar on Macroeconomics,* ed. by Richard Clarida and Francesco Giavazzi (Chicago: University of Chicago Press), pp. 303–43.

Coenen, Günter, Christopher J. Erceg, Charles Freedman, Davide Furceri, Michael Kumhof, René Lalonde, Douglas Laxton, Jesper Lindé, Annabelle Mourougane, Dirk Muir, Susanna Mursula, Carlos de Resende, John Roberts, Werner Roeger, Stephen Snudden, Mathias Trabandt, and Jan in't Veld, 2012, "Effects of Fiscal Stimulus in Structural Models," *American Economic Journal: Macroeconomics*, Vol. 4, No. 1, pp. 22–68.

Courtemanche, Charles, and Kenneth Snowden, 2011, "Repairing a Mortgage Crisis: HOLC Lending and Its Impact on Local Housing Markets," *Journal of Economic History*, Vol. 71, No. 2, pp. 307–37.

Crowe, Christopher W., Giovanni Dell'Ariccia, Deniz Igan, and Pau Rabanal, 2011, "Policies for Macrofinancial Stability: Options to Deal with Real Estate Booms," IMF Staff Discussion Note No. 11/02 (Washington: International Monetary Fund).

Dell'Ariccia, Giovanni, Deniz Igan, Luc Laeven, and Hui Tong, forthcoming, "Policies for Macrofinancial Stability: Options to Deal with Credit Booms," IMF Staff Discussion Note (Washington: International Monetary Fund).

Devries, Pete, Jaime Guajardo, Daniel Leigh, and Andrea Pescatori, 2011, "A New Action-Based Dataset of Fiscal Consolidation in OECD Countries," IMF Working Paper No. 11/128 (Washington: International Monetary Fund).

Dynan, Karen, Jonathan Skinner, and Stephen P. Zeldes, 2004, "Do the Rich Save More?" *Journal of Political Economy*, Vol. 112, No. 2, pp. 397–444.

The Economist, 2011, "The Bursting of the Global Housing Bubble Is Only Halfway Through," Nov. 26. www.economist.com/node/21540231.

Eggertsson, Gauti B., and Paul Krugman, 2010, "Debt, Deleveraging, and the Liquidity Trap: A Fisher-Minsky-Koo Approach" (unpublished; Princeton, New Jersey: Princeton University).

Erbenova, Michaela, Yan Liu, and Magnus Saxegaard, 2011, "Corporate and Household Debt Distress in Latvia: Strengthening the Incentives for a Market-Based Approach to Debt Resolution," IMF Working Paper No. 11/85 (Washington: International Monetary Fund).

Fatás, Antonio, 2012, "No Need to Deleverage Gross Debt." http://fatasmihov.blogspot.com/2012/01/no-need-to-deleverage-gross-debt.html.

Fishback, Price V., Alfonso Flores-Lagunes, William Horrace, Shawn Kantor, and Jaret Treber, 2010, "The Influence of the Home Owners' Loan Corporation on Housing Markets During the 1930s," *Review of Financial Studies*, Vol. 24, No. 6, pp. 1782–813.

Fisher, Irving, 1933, "The Debt-Deflation Theory of Great Depressions," *Econometrica*, Vol. 1, No. 4, pp. 337–47.

Fondo de Garantías de Instituciones Financieras (Fogafin), ed., 2009, *Crisis Financiera Colombiana en los Años Noventa: Origen, Resolución y Lecciones Institucionales*, Universidad Externado de Colombia (Bogotá).

Foote, Christopher, Kristopher Gerardi, Lorenz Goette, and Paul Willen, 2010, "Reducing Foreclosures: No Easy Answers," *NBER Macroeconomics Annual 2009*, Vol. 24, pp. 89–138.

Forero, Efrain, 2004, "Evolution of the Mortgage System in Colombia: From the UPAC to the UVR1 System," paper presented at the XLI Conferencia Interamericana para la Vivienda, Panama City, August 11–13, 2003.

Glick, Reuven, and Kevin J. Lansing, 2009, "U.S. Household Deleveraging and Future Consumption Growth," *FRBSF Economic Letter*, May 15.

———, 2010, "Global Household Leverage, House Prices, and Consumption," *FRBSF Economic Letter*, January 11.

Green, Richard K., and Susan M. Wachter, 2005, "The American Mortgage in Historical and International Context," *Journal of Economic Perspectives*, Vol. 19, No. 4, pp. 93–114.

Guerrieri, Veronica, and Guido Lorenzoni, 2011, "Credit Crises, Precautionary Savings and the Liquidity Trap" (unpublished; Chicago: University of Chicago Press).

Hall, Robert E., 2011, "The Long Slump," *American Economic Review*, Vol. 101 (April), pp. 431–69.

Harding, Don, and Adrian Pagan, 2002, "Dissecting the Cycle: A Methodological Investigation," *Journal of Monetary Economics*, Vol. 49, No. 2, pp. 365–81.

Harriss, C. Lowell, 1951, "Background of Home Owners' Loan Corporation Legislation," in *History and Policies of the Home Owners' Loan Corporation* (Cambridge, Massachusetts: National Bureau of Economic Research).

Honohan, Patrick, and Luc Laeven, eds., 2005, *Systemic Financial Crises: Containment and Resolution* (Cambridge, United Kingdom: Cambridge University Press).

Howard, Greg, Robert Martin, and Beth Ann Wilson, 2011, "Are Recoveries from Banking and Financial Crises Really So Different?" Board of Governors of the Federal Reserve System International Finance Discussion Paper No. 1037 (Washington, November).

Hubbard, Glenn, 2011, "Q&A for Hubbard-Mayer Mortgage Refinancing Proposal." www.glennhubbard.net/papers/369-qaa-for-hubbard-mayer-mortgage-refinancing-proposal.html.

———, and Chris Mayer, 2008, "First, Let's Stabilize Home Prices," *The Wall Street Journal*, October 2. http://online.wsj.com/article/SB122291076983796813.html.

Iacoviello, Matteo, 2005, "House Prices, Borrowing Constraints, and Monetary Policy in the Business Cycle," *American Economic Review*, Vol. 95, No. 3, pp. 739–64.

Igan, Deniz, and Prakash Loungani, forthcoming, "Global Housing Cycles," IMF Working Paper (Washington: International Monetary Fund).

Immergluck, Dan, and Geoff Smith, 2005, "There Goes the Neighborhood: The Effect of Single-Family Mortgage Foreclosures on Property Values" (unpublished; Chicago: Woodstock Institute).

———, 2006, "The Impact of Single Family Mortgage Foreclosures on Neighborhood Crime," *Housing Studies*, Vol. 21, No. 6, pp. 851–66.

International Monetary Fund (IMF), 1991, *Recent Economic Developments,* Norway (Washington).

———, 1993, *Recent Economic Developments,* Sweden (Washington).

———, 2011a, *Hungary: Staff Report for the 2010 Article IV Consultation and Proposal for Post-Program Monitoring.* (Washington).

———, 2011b, *United States: Staff Report for the 2011 Article IV Consultation, Country Report No. 11/201* (Washington).

Isaksen, Jacob, Paul Lassenius Kramp, Louise Funch Sørensen, and Søren Vester Sørensen, 2011, "Household Balance Sheets and Debt—An International Country Study," Danmarks Nationalbank, *Monetary Review,* 4th Quarter 2011.

Jordà, Òscar, Moritz H.P. Schularick, and Alan M. Taylor, 2011, "When Credit Bites Back: Leverage, Business Cycles, and Crises," NBER Working Paper No. 17621 (Cambridge, Massachusetts: National Bureau of Economic Research).

Karlsdóttir, Edda Rós, Yngvi Örn Kristinsson, and Franek Rozwadowski, forthcoming, "Responses to Household Financial Distress in Iceland," IMF Working Paper (Washington: International Monetary Fund).

Kiff, John, and Vladimir Klyuev, 2009, "Foreclosure Mitigation Efforts in the United States: Approaches and Challenges," IMF Staff Position Note No. 09/02 (Washington: International Monetary Fund).

King, Mervyn, 1994, "Debt Deflation: Theory and Evidence," *European Economic Review*, Vol. 38, No. 3–4, pp. 419–45.

Krishnamurthy, Arvind, 2010, "Amplification Mechanisms in Liquidity Crises," *American Economic Journal: Macroeconomics*, Vol. 2, No. 3, pp. 1–30.

Krugman, Paul, 2011, "Debt Is (Mostly) Money We Owe to Ourselves." http://krugman.blogs.nytimes.com/2011/12/28/debt-is-mostly-money-we-owe-to-ourselves.

Kumhof, Michael, and Romain Rancière, 2010, "Leveraging Inequality," *Finance & Development*, Vol. 47, No. 4, pp. 28–31.

Laeven, Luc, and Thomas Laryea, 2009, "Principles of Household Debt Restructuring," IMF Staff Position Note No. 09/15 (Washington: International Monetary Fund).

Laeven, Luc, and Fabian Valencia, 2010, "Resolution of Banking Crises: The Good, the Bad, and the Ugly," IMF Working Paper 10/146 (Washington: International Monetary Fund).

Lorenzoni, Guido, 2008, "Inefficient Credit Booms," *Review of Economic Studies*, Vol. 75, No. 3, pp. 809–33.

Making Home Affordable Program (MHA), 2010, "Refinements to Existing Administration Programs Designed to Help Unemployed, Underwater Borrowers While Helping Administration Meet Its Goals" (Washington: Department of the Treasury, Department of Housing and Urban Development, and White House). www.makinghomeaffordable.gov/about-mha/latest-news/Pages/pr_03262010.aspx.

———, 2012, "January 2012 Making Home Affordable Report and Servicer Assessments for Fourth Quarter 2011" (Washington: Department of the Treasury, Department of Housing and Urban Development, and White House). www.treasury.gov/initiatives/financial-stability/results/MHA-Reports/Pages/default.aspx.

Mayer, Christopher J., 1995, "A Model of Negotiated Sales Applied to Real Estate Auctions," *Journal of Urban Economics*, Vol. 38, No. 1, pp. 1–22.

McKinsey Global Institute (McKinsey), 2010, *Debt and Deleveraging: The Global Credit Bubble and Its Economic Consequences* (Seoul, San Francisco, London, and Washington).

———, 2012, *Debt and Deleveraging: Uneven Progress on the Path to Growth* (Seoul, San Francisco, London, and Washington).

Melzer, Brian, 2010, "Debt Overhang: Reduced Investment by Homeowners with Negative Equity," Kellogg School of Management Working Paper (Chicago).

Mian, Atif, Kamalesh Rao, and Amir Sufi, 2011, "Household Balance Sheets, Consumption, and the Economic Slump," University of Chicago Booth School of Business Working Paper (Chicago).

Mian, Atif, and Amir Sufi, 2011, "Consumers and the Economy, Part II: Household Debt and the Weak U.S. Recovery," *FRBSF Economic Letter*, January 18.

———, 2012, "What Explains High Unemployment? The Aggregate Demand Channel," NBER Working Paper No. 17830 (Cambridge, Massachusetts: National Bureau of Economic Research).

Mian, Atif, Amir Sufi, and Francesco Trebbi, 2010, "The Political Economy of the U.S. Mortgage Default Crisis," *American Economic Review*, Vol. 95, pp. 587–611.

———, 2012, "Resolving Debt Overhang: Political Constraints in the Aftermath of Financial Crises," NBER Working Paper No. 17831 (Cambridge, Massachusetts: National Bureau of Economic Research).

Minsky, Hyman, 1986, *Stabilizing an Unstable Economy* (New Haven, Connecticut: Yale University Press).

Modigliani, Franco, 1986, "Life Cycle, Individual Thrift, and the Wealth of Nations," *American Economic Review*, Vol. 76, No. 3, pp. 297–313.

Myers, Stewart C., 1977, "Determinants of Corporate Borrowing," *Journal of Financial Economics*, Vol. 5, No. 2, pp. 147–75.

Nakagawa, Shinobu, and Yosuke Yasui, 2009, "A Note on Japanese Household Debt: International Comparison and Implications for Financial Stability," BIS Paper No. 46 (Basel: Bank for International Settlements).

Ólafsson, Tjörvi, and Karen Á. Vignisdóttir, 2012, "Households' Position in the Financial Crisis in Iceland," Central Bank of Iceland Working Paper (Reykjavik).

Olney, Martha L., 1999, "Avoiding Default: The Role of Credit in the Consumption Collapse of 1930," *The Quarterly Journal of Economics*, Vol. 114, No. 1, pp. 319–35.

Organization for Economic Cooperation and Development (OECD), 1995, *Economic Survey*, Sweden (Paris).

———, 2009, *Economic Survey*, Iceland (Paris).

Philippon, Thomas, 2009, "The Macroeconomics of Debt Overhang," paper presented at the 10th Jacques Polak Annual Research Conference, November 5–6.

Rajan, Raghuram, and Luigi Zingales, 1998, "Financial Dependence and Growth," *American Economic Review*, Vol. 88 (June), pp. 559–86.

Reinhart, Carmen M., and Kenneth Rogoff, 2009, *This Time Is Different: Eight Centuries of Financial Folly* (Princeton, New Jersey: Princeton University Press).

Rogoff, Kenneth, 2011, "Understanding the Second Great Contraction: An Interview with Kenneth Rogoff," *McKinsey Quarterly* (October). www.mckinseyquarterly.com/Understanding_the_Second_Great_Contraction_An_interview_with_Kenneth_Rogoff_2871.

Shleifer, Andrei, and Robert W. Vishny, 1992, "Liquidation Values and Debt Capacity: A Market Equilibrium Approach," *Journal of Finance*, Vol. 47, No. 4, pp. 1343–66.

———, 2010, "Fire Sales in Finance and Macroeconomics," NBER Working Paper No. 16642 (Cambridge, Massachusetts: National Bureau of Economic Research).

Slok, Torsten, 2012, "Global Home Prices—Several Countries Still Overvalued," presentation, Deutsche Bank Securities (New York).

Snowden, Kenneth, Jr., 2010, "The Anatomy of a Residential Mortgage Crisis: A Look Back to the 1930s," in *The Panic of 2008: Causes, Consequences and Proposals for Reform,* ed. by Lawrence Mitchell and Arthur Wilmarth (Northampton, Massachusetts: Edward Elgar).

Special Inspector General for the Troubled Asset Relief Program (SIGTARP), 2010, "Factors Affecting Implementation of the Home Affordable Modification Program," SIGTARP-10-005 (Washington, March 25).

Tobin, James, 1980, *Asset Accumulation and Economic Activity: Reflections on Contemporary Macroeconomic Theory* (Oxford: Basil Blackwell).

U.S. Office of the Comptroller of the Currency (OCC), 2011, *Mortgage Metrics Report*, Third Quarter (Washington).

Woodford, Michael, 2010, "Simple Analytics of the Government Expenditure Multiplier," NBER Working Paper No. 15714 (Cambridge, Massachusetts: National Bureau of Economic Research).

CHAPTER 4 COMMODITY PRICE SWINGS AND COMMODITY EXPORTERS

How do commodity price swings affect commodity exporters, and how should their policies respond? These questions have become relevant again with the confluence of a weak global economy and the sustained buoyancy of commodity markets following the slump of the 1980s and 1990s. This chapter reexamines the macroeconomic performance of commodity exporters during commodity price cycles. It highlights how performance moves with the price cycle. The economic effects on commodity exporters are strong when commodity prices are driven by the global economy. Countercyclical fiscal policies—which build buffers during commodity price upswings that can be used during downswings—can help insulate small commodity exporters that are exposed to economic volatility induced by commodity price fluctuations. However, when price increases endure permanently, higher public investment and lower labor and capital taxes can boost private sector productivity and welfare. Against the backdrop of near-record commodity prices, coupled with unusual uncertainty in the global outlook, the priority for commodity exporters is to upgrade their policy frameworks and institutions in addition to building fiscal buffers. However, if high price levels persist, a cautious approach—which maintains fiscal buffers while gradually incorporating new information to allow a smooth adjustment to potentially permanently higher prices—is a sensible way forward.

Commodity prices have risen dramatically over the past decade, interrupted only briefly by the global financial crisis. By the end of 2011, average prices for energy and base metals in real terms were three times as high as just a decade ago, approaching or surpassing their record levels over the past four decades (Figure 4.1). Food and raw material prices also rose markedly, although they remain well below the highs reached in the 1970s. Many analysts attribute elevated commodity prices to the sustained

Figure 4.1. World Commodity Prices, 1970–2011
(In real terms)

There has been a broad-based rise in commodity prices during the past decade.

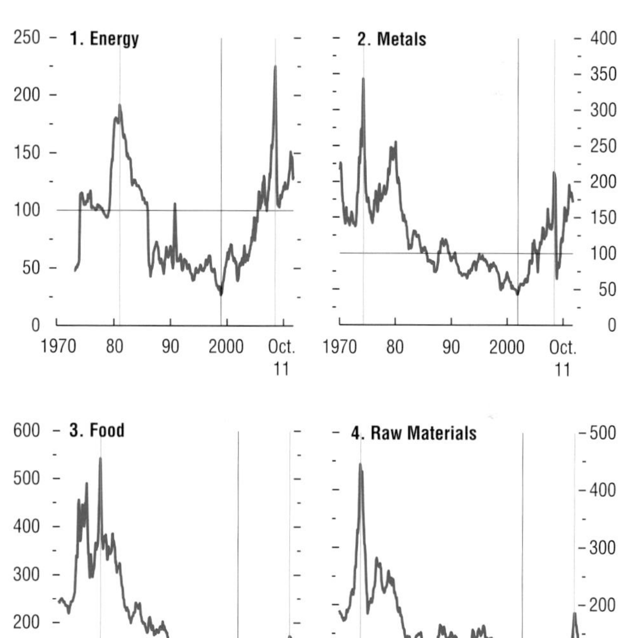

Source: IMF staff calculations.
Note: The real price index for a commodity group is the trade-weighted average of the global U.S. dollar prices of the commodities in the group deflated by the U.S. consumer price index and normalized to be 100 in 2005. The blue vertical lines indicate long cycle peaks, and the red vertical lines indicate long cycle troughs. The exact dates of these turning points are as follows (where M = month). Energy: 1981:M1, 1998:M12, 2008:M7. Metals: 1974:M4, 2001:M12, 2008:M6. Food: 1977:M4, 2001:M11, 2011:M2. Raw materials: 1973:M9, 2002:M1, 2011:M2. See Appendix 4.1 for a full description of the underlying data.

The main authors of this chapter are John Bluedorn, Rupa Duttagupta (team leader), Andrea Pescatori, and Stephen Snudden, with support from Murad Omoev, Katherine Pan, and Marina Rousset. Julia Bersch and Susan Yang also contributed.

growth in emerging market economies over the past decade.[1]

Looking ahead, given the weak global activity and heightened downside risks to the near-term outlook, commodity exporters may be in for a downturn (see Chapter 1). If downside risks to global economic growth materialize, there could be even greater challenges facing commodity exporters, most of which are emerging and developing economies (Figure 4.2). Conversely, if geopolitical risks to the supply of oil materialize, oil prices could rise temporarily, but the ensuing slowdown in global growth could lead to a decline in the prices of other commodities. This chapter addresses these concerns by asking the following questions:

- How is the economic performance of commodity exporters influenced by commodity price cycles? How do standard indicators such as real GDP growth, credit growth, and external and fiscal balance behave over the course of such cycles?
- What are the effects on exporters of commodity price fluctuations driven by unexpected changes in global activity?
- How should small, open commodity exporters shield their economies from commodity price swings? What is the role of fiscal policy? How should fiscal and monetary policy interact? How do the preexisting public debt level and other structural characteristics, such as the share of commodity exports in the economy, affect policy choices?

This chapter contributes to the policy debate in several ways. First, it sheds light on how exporters of different commodities—energy, metals, food, and agricultural raw materials—may have different sensitivities to commodity price cycles. It also recognizes that not all commodity price changes are alike in terms of their potential effects and identifies the economic effects of commodity market shocks driven by global activity.[2] Finally, using the IMF's workhorse Global Integrated Monetary and Fiscal model (GIMF), it assesses the optimal fiscal policy response to globally driven commodity price changes for small, open commodity exporters. This model-based analysis complements a related literature on the role of fiscal policy in commodity-exporting economies by distinguishing between the effects of global commodity price shocks that are demand driven from those that are supply driven. The analysis also highlights how the appropriate fiscal policy response depends on other prevailing policies and structural characteristics of the commodity exporter, as well as the implications of these domestically oriented policies for global economic stability.[3]

It is important to stress that macroeconomic stabilization in the face of commodity price volatility is only one of many policy priorities for commodity-exporting emerging market and developing economies. Others include resource exhaustibility, intergenerational equity, and Dutch disease challenges associated with resource discoveries. The relative priority of addressing various policy challenges depends on country-specific conditions, including the structure of the commodity endowment, institutional capacity, and the level of development.[4] Although we also consider the effects of permanent commodity price changes, a full-fledged analysis of optimal policies, given the whole gamut of cyclical and longer-term objectives of commodity exporters, is beyond the scope of this chapter.

The main conclusions of this analysis are as follows:

- Macroeconomic performance in commodity exporters tends to move with commodity price cycles. Economic activity and external and fiscal balances deteriorate (improve) during commodity price downswings (upswings), whether the latter entail long periods of falling (rising) commodity prices or shorter commodity price swings that last for only a few years. This behavior is generally

[1]See Heap (2005) and previous *World Economic Outlook* chapters (Chapter 5 in the September 2006 issue, Chapter 5 in April 2008, and Chapter 3 in October 2008).

[2]To do this we use a variant of the identification strategy in Kilian (2009); Kilian, Rebucci, and Spatafora (2009); and Kilian and Murphy (2010) for estimating the effect of global demand and commodity production shocks on crude oil, copper, coffee, and cotton prices.

[3]See IMF (2009) and Baunsgaard and others (forthcoming) for a discussion of the role of commodity exporters' fiscal institutions in addressing macroeconomic stabilization against commodity price shocks.

[4]See Baunsgaard and others (forthcoming), Medas and Zakharova (2009), Deaton (1999), Collier and Goderis (2007), and Eyzaguirre and others (2011) for a discussion of some of these issues.

Figure 4.2. Share of Net Commodity Exports in Total Exports and GDP
(Percent)

Net commodity exports comprise a sizable share of total goods exports and GDP in many emerging market and developing economies.

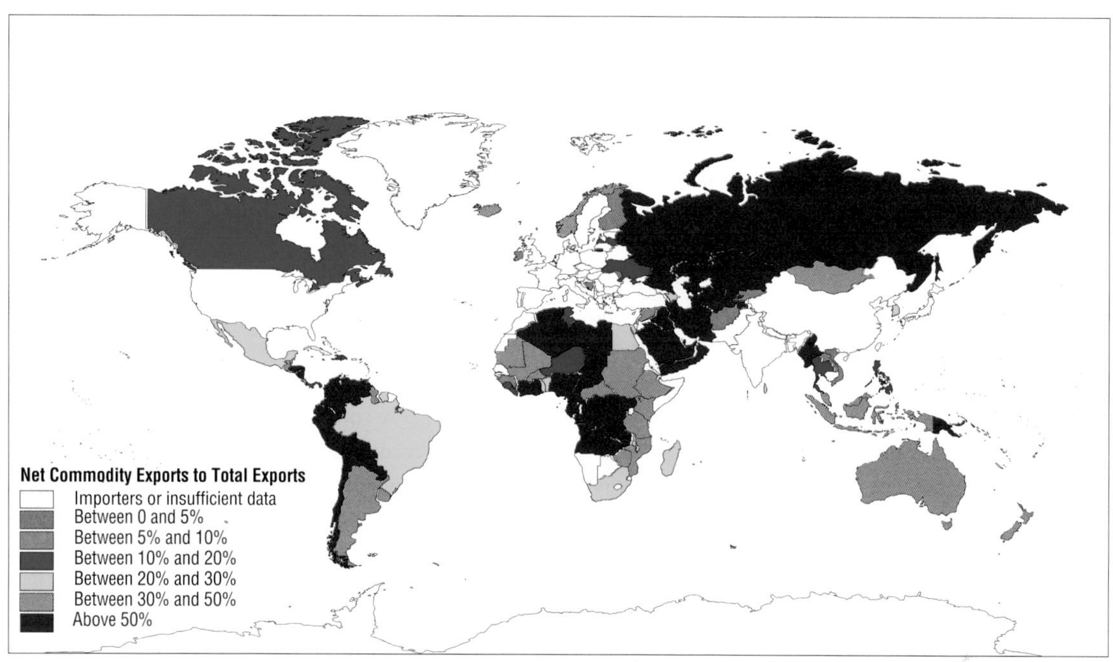

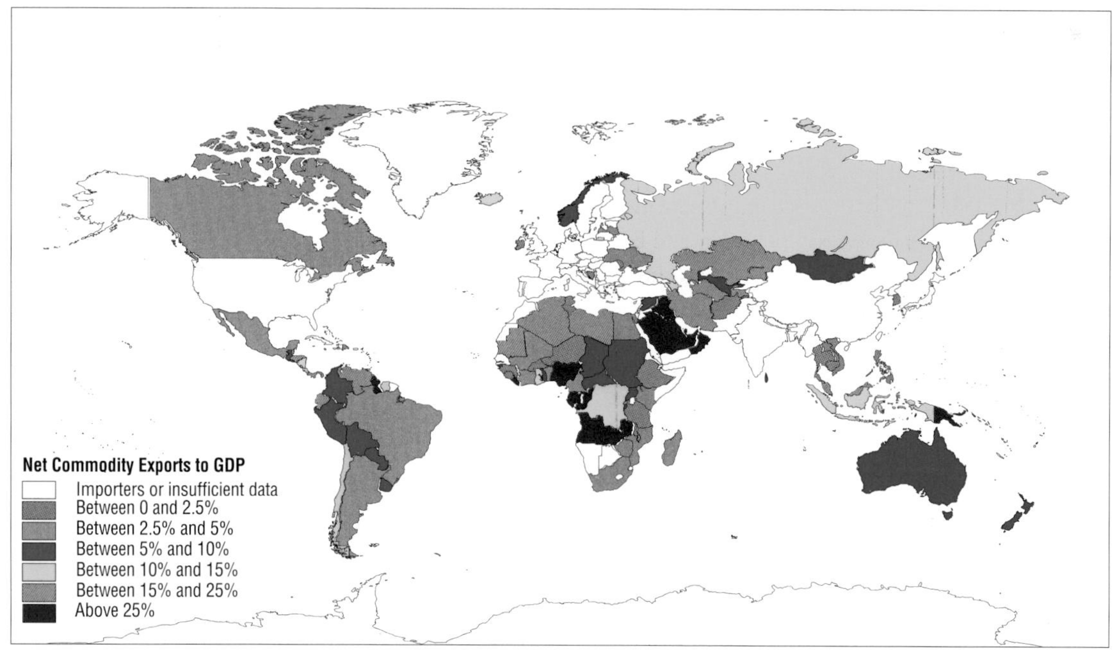

Source: IMF staff calculations.
Note: These maps show the economy averages using the available yearly data for 1962–2010. See Appendix 4.1 for a full description of the underlying data.

more prominent for energy and metal exporters than for exporters of food and raw materials, possibly because energy and metal prices are more sensitive to the global business cycle and because they generally account for a higher share in total exports and GDP.

- The source of the commodity price change matters in terms of its economic effects on commodity exporters. In particular, commodity prices underpinned by unexpected changes in global activity (demand) have a significant effect on exporters' real activity and external and fiscal balances, while those driven by unexpected changes to global commodity production (supply) are not always significant. This effect is generally stronger for oil exporters than for exporters of other commodities.
- The optimal fiscal policy response to commodity price fluctuations for small commodity exporters is a countercyclical policy stance: save commodity-related revenue increases during upswings and use these buffers during downswings. Such a fiscal stance dampens the macroeconomic volatility arising from commodity price fluctuations.
- The effectiveness of a countercyclical policy stance, however, also depends on the degree of monetary policy autonomy—fiscal policy is more effective under an inflation-targeting regime with a flexible exchange rate because monetary policy helps reduce inflation volatility. It also depends on the level of public net debt—at high levels of debt, debt reduction should become a priority to help reduce the sovereign risk premium and build credibility. Furthermore, for some commodity market shocks and under some circumstances, a less countercyclical policy response in major commodity exporters might be the preferred solution from the perspective of collective action.
- Under permanent commodity price changes, the pivotal issue becomes how best to adjust to the permanently higher or lower commodity-related fiscal revenue levels. For a permanent price increase, increases in public investment and reductions in taxes on labor and capital boost private sector productivity and welfare. However, distinguishing between temporary and permanent commodity price changes is not a trivial exercise. This underscores the need to enhance policy frameworks and fiscal buffers, while gradually incorporating new information about the persistence of commodity prices.

What messages do these findings provide for commodity exporters? The weak global economic outlook suggests that commodity prices are unlikely to increase at the pace of the past decade. In fact, under the baseline *World Economic Outlook* projections, commodity prices are forecast to decline somewhat during 2012–13 (see Chapter 1). Sizable downside risks to global growth also pose risks of further downward adjustment in commodity prices. In contrast, if oil prices were to rise sharply as a result of greater supply-side concerns, this could unexpectedly depress global demand and eventually lower the prices of all other commodities. If prices were to enter such a cyclical downswing, commodity exporters would likely suffer, given historical patterns. A number of commodity exporters are ready to handle such a downswing, having strengthened their policy frameworks over time or having already adopted operating principles to guide fiscal policy. Others should use the opportunity presented by strong prices to lower debt levels, strengthen institutions, and build fiscal room to support a timely countercyclical policy response in the event of a commodity price downswing.

What are the lessons for the longer term? Commodity prices may be experiencing a long upswing and prices may stay close to current historic highs.[5] Alternatively, they may retreat in response to increasing user efficiency and the unwinding of earlier supply constraints. Given the unusual uncertainty and the difficulty of projecting commodity market prospects in real time, the best approach is a cautious one that builds buffers to address cyclical volatilities and gradually incorporates new information to allow a smooth adjustment to potentially permanently higher commodity prices.[6]

The chapter is structured as follows. The first section presents stylized facts on domestic economic

[5]See the Commodity Market Review in Chapter 1, and Erten and Ocampo (2012).

[6]These conclusions are not without precedent. Frankel (2011) underscores the need for commodity exporters to avoid procyclical fiscal policy that exacerbates economic volatility. Baunsgaard and others (forthcoming) stress the importance of designing fiscal frameworks that gradually incorporate new information.

indicators during commodity price swings. The second discusses the economic effects of commodity market shocks. The third examines the optimal policy responses to commodity price changes. The final section summarizes and concludes.

Commodity Price Swings and Macroeconomic Performance

How does commodity exporters' economic performance relate to commodity prices?[7] This question is examined in two parts. First, we focus on performance during the two most prominent recent commodity price booms (periods of sustained increases in commodity prices)—the early 1970s and the 2000s—and the intervening period of slumping commodity prices during the 1980s and 1990s.[8] This exercise sheds light on how commodity exporters' performance relates to the level of commodity prices. Next, we study regular commodity price swings and cycles during the past 50 years. This sheds light on any comovements between exporters' economic conditions and commodity price cycles, regardless of the underlying trends in prices. These descriptive analyses uncover useful correlations between global commodity price cycles and domestic economic indicators, without implying any causal relation between the two. Differences are highlighted across four distinct commodity groups—energy, metals, food (and beverages), and agricultural raw materials. These groups differ across many dimensions—in terms of the basic structure of the underlying markets, the nature of the commodity (for example, renewable versus exhaustible resource bases), and their association with global activity (for example, metals and energy are more important for industrialization and infrastructure building, and as such their prices may be more strongly correlated with the global business cycle than the prices of food and agricultural raw materials). We also focus on one major commodity from each of the four groups—crude oil (energy), copper (metals), coffee (food), and cotton (raw materials)—so as to study whether the broad patterns observed for commodity groups also hold at the commodity-specific level.[9]

Economic Performance Leading into Commodity Price Booms and Slumps

Commodity exporters experienced stronger macroeconomic performance during the 1970s and 2000s, when commodity prices were high in real terms, compared with the 1980s and 1990s, when prices were weak (Table 4.1).[10] Real GDP growth for the median commodity exporter was 1½ to 3½ percentage points higher during the 1970s and 2 to 4 percentage points higher during the 2000s, compared with the interim period.[11] In addition, despite higher commodity prices, consumer price index (CPI) inflation was lower during both booms compared with the interim period, when many exporters experienced crises and struggled to achieve macroeconomic and financial stability.

Energy and metal exporters appear to have fared relatively better during the recent decade compared with the 1970s. They achieved strong gains in real GDP growth and sizable reductions in inflation during the past decade. The latter may represent a shift toward inflation targeting among emerging and developing economies in the 2000s, including among commodity exporters (Brazil, Chile, Colombia, South Africa, and Thailand, among others).[12] These economies also reduced their public debt levels considerably during the

[7]We define commodity exporters as those whose share of net exports of the commodity (or commodity group) in total goods exports is at least 10 percent. See Appendix 4.1 for details.

[8]We focus on three long stretches in commodity prices over the past 50 years (see Figure 4.1 and Radetzki, 2006): the run-up to the peak in the mid-1970s (energy prices peaked in the 1980s); the subsequent protracted slump until 2001 (energy prices troughed in 1998); and the rebound thereafter.

[9]These commodities are also notable as being relevant among the commodities within their groups for the largest number of commodity exporters in the sample (that is, the largest number of commodity exporters with at least a 10 percent share of net exports of these commodities in total goods exports).

[10]Throughout, we use real commodity prices for the study: the global U.S. dollar–denominated commodity prices are deflated by the U.S. CPI. See Appendix 4.1 for details.

[11]For each indicator, we take the cross-sample median value of the country averages.

[12]See Heenan, Peter, and Roger (2006) and Roger (2010) for cross-country evidence on the adoption of inflation targeting. Batini and Laxton (2005) find that emerging and developing economies that adopted inflation targeting made significant progress in anchoring inflation and inflation expectations.

Table 4.1. Average Economic Performance of Net Commodity Exporters, 1970–2010

	1970s Boom	1980–2000 Slump	2000s Boom	Average 1960–2010
		Real GDP Growth (percentage points)		
Net Energy Exporters	5.6	2.5	4.6	4.3
Net Metal Exporters	5.6	2.2	6.4	3.5
Net Food Exporters	5.1	2.9	4.5	4.0
Net Raw Material Exporters	5.0	3.3	5.3	4.3
		Differential in Real GDP Growth Relative to Emerging and Developing Noncommodity Exporters (percentage points)		
Net Energy Exporters	1.1	–0.8	–0.8	0.5
Net Metal Exporters	2.0	–1.8	0.5	–0.4
Net Food Exporters	0.6	–0.8	–0.6	0.2
Net Raw Material Exporters	1.4	–0.6	0.2	0.5
		Level of Public Debt to GDP (percent of GDP)		
Net Energy Exporters	31.3	63.9	24.1	44.4
Net Metal Exporters	36.2	52.7	27.3	52.4
Net Food Exporters	21.9	78.7	37.4	50.0
Net Raw Material Exporters	33.6	80.2	34.5	57.4
		Change in Public Debt to GDP (percentage points; increase = deterioration)		
Net Energy Exporters	0.7	1.1	–4.5	–0.4
Net Metal Exporters	1.5	1.2	–4.0	–0.4
Net Food Exporters	0.8	1.5	–3.9	0.4
Net Raw Material Exporters	0.1	1.7	–5.9	–0.3
		Average Inflation (percentage points)		
Net Energy Exporters	8.6	14.4	6.6	12.5
Net Metal Exporters	8.4	22.5	9.2	16.1
Net Food Exporters	6.4	13.2	7.3	10.7
Net Raw Material Exporters	4.6	12.4	6.8	10.1

Source: IMF staff calculations.

Note: Unless indicated otherwise, numbers represent the median value of the averages over the relevant period, except for the level of public debt to GDP, which is the median end-of-period value. Commodity exporters are those whose share of net exports of the particular commodity (or commodity group) in total goods exports is at least 10 percent; noncommodity exporters are those whose share is less than or equal to zero. See Figure 4.1 for the exact dates that mark the long cycles for each commodity group. Because the underlying data for the table are annual, the dates are rounded to the nearest year.

recent decade, relative to the 1970s boom.[13] Finally, only in the 2000s was there a marked improvement in average fiscal balances—proxied by the change in the public-debt-to-GDP ratio—for exporters in all commodity groups; there was none in the 1970s.

Macroeconomic policies in commodity exporters appear to have continued to improve during the 2000s. We examine the behavior of economic indicators in commodity exporters in three snapshots from the past decade—at the beginning of the boom, at mid-decade, and at the end of the decade (Table 4.2).[14] Inflation and public debt levels fell sharply through the 2000s, notwithstanding the Great Recession. In contrast, the overall and cyclically adjusted fiscal balance improved until mid-decade but deteriorated toward the end of the decade. The deterioration in fiscal positions in 2010 is likely related to fiscal action in response to the global crisis. Moreover, policies and economic conditions interacted such that despite the deterioration in fiscal balances, some debt reduction was accomplished by commodity exporters by the end of the decade.[15]

[13]We use the change in public debt to GDP as a proxy for fiscal position because the cyclically adjusted primary balance is not available for many countries over the period between 1960 and 2010. We also do not have data on noncommodity real GDP for all the commodity exporters in the sample, which could better gauge economic performance outside the commodity sector.

[14]Note that prices of energy and metal commodities peaked in 2008, while those of food and agricultural materials crested in 2010.

[15]Empirical analysis of the fiscal stance in commodity producers during commodity price cycles is relatively recent (compared

Table 4.2. Economic Performance of Net Commodity Exporters during the 2000s

	2001	2005	2010	Average 2001–10
		Public Debt to GDP (percent)		
Net Energy Exporters	59.8	38.7	20.7	41.1
Net Metal Exporters	52.7	41.1	36.4	47.6
Net Food Exporters	78.7	65.8	37.4	54.5
Net Raw Material Exporters	80.2	52.9	34.5	53.9
		Change in Public Debt to GDP (percentage points)		
Net Energy Exporters	–1.0	–6.7	–1.8	–4.2
Net Metal Exporters	–7.1	–7.6	–0.8	–3.0
Net Food Exporters	1.5	–5.4	–0.4	–3.4
Net Raw Material Exporters	–1.0	–6.5	–0.3	–4.8
		Overall Fiscal Balance (percent of GDP)		
Net Energy Exporters	–0.9	0.7	–1.3	–0.7
Net Metal Exporters	–1.8	0.8	–0.4	–0.9
Net Food Exporters	–3.4	–2.1	–2.1	–1.8
Net Raw Material Exporters	–2.6	–2.4	–2.3	–2.1
		Cyclically Adjusted Fiscal Balance (percent of potential GDP)		
Net Energy Exporters	2.5	0.3	–2.2	–0.9
Net Metal Exporters	0.8	–0.2	–3.1	–1.6
Net Food Exporters	–3.2	–2.6	–2.6	–3.2
Net Raw Material Exporters	–4.8	–1.6	–3.1	–2.6
		Inflation (percentage points)		
Net Energy Exporters	4.9	7.4	4.7	7.5
Net Metal Exporters	8.4	7.9	6.9	8.6
Net Food Exporters	5.7	7.2	4.8	7.7
Net Raw Material Exporters	5.1	6.9	5.3	7.0
		Change in Log Real Effective Exchange Rate (times 100)		
Net Energy Exporters	3.2	1.5	0.3	1.5
Net Metal Exporters	1.3	2.9	1.5	0.8
Net Food Exporters	1.6	2.2	–2.1	0.9
Net Raw Material Exporters	1.6	0.4	–2.8	1.0

Source: IMF staff calculations.

Note: Unless indicated otherwise, numbers represent the median value within the sample for the relevant year. Commodity exporters are those whose share of net exports of a particular commodity group in total goods exports is at least 10 percent.

Economic Performance during Shorter Commodity Price Swings

With some evidence of a positive correspondence between macroeconomic performance and commodity price booms and slumps, we now turn to the consequences of shorter-term commodity price cycles. To do this, we identify turning points in real prices within each commodity group from 1957 to October 2011.[16] This exercise yields more than 300 completed cycles for 46 commodities, with a median (average)

with studies that assess the procyclicality of fiscal policy with output cycles). See Chapter 3 in the September 2011 *Regional Economic Outlook—Western Hemisphere*; Medina (2010); and Kaminsky (2010) for procyclicality in Latin American commodity producers' fiscal policies, especially among lower- and middle-income economies. Céspedes and Velasco (2011), however, find that fiscal policies in commodity exporters (encompassing a wider group) have become less procyclical in the 2000s.

[16]Drawing on Cashin, McDermott, and Scott (2002), we use the Harding and Pagan (2002) methodology to identify peaks and troughs in the time path of real commodity prices. A candidate turning point is identified as a local maximum or minimum if the price in that month is either greater or less than the price in the two months before and the two months after. The sequence of resulting candidate turning points is then required to alternate between peaks and troughs. Furthermore, each phase defined by

upswing duration of 2 (2½) years and a median (average) downswing of 2½ (3) years. An average downswing entails a decline in real prices (from peak to trough) of 38 to 52 percent, with price changes sharper for energy and metal prices (see Appendix 4.2). The relationship between key economic indicators during commodity price upswings and downswings is summarized below.

With few exceptions, indicators of commodity exporters' domestic economic performance tend to move with commodity price cycles—improving during upswings and deteriorating during downswings. This pattern is observed for each of the four commodity groups. Moreover, the difference in economic performance across downswings and upswings tends to be amplified when cycles last longer and/or when they entail sharper price changes than average. Specifically:[17]

- *Real GDP* (Figure 4.3, panels 1 and 2): Across the four groups of commodity exporters, median real GDP growth is ½ to 1¼ percentage points lower during downswings than during upswings.
- *Credit growth* is 1 to 2 percentage points lower during typical downswings than during upswings for energy and metal exporters, while the difference is sharper for food exporters at 6 percentage points (Figure 4.3, panels 3 and 4).[18]
- *External balances* (Figure 4.3, panels 5 and 6): The current account balance deteriorates during downswings compared with upswings. The sharpest difference is for energy exporters, whose current account falls from a surplus of ¾ percent of GDP in an upswing to a deficit of 2¼ percent of GDP in a downswing. For all commodity exporters, the differences are larger when the underlying price phase lasts longer or price changes are sharper than during a typical phase. Thus, weaker terms of trade resulting from lower commodity export prices more than offset any positive demand effect from the lower price of the commodity.
- *Fiscal balances* (Figure 4.3, panels 9–12): The fiscal position is weaker in downswings compared with upswings. We present two measures of the fiscal position—change in the public-debt-to-GDP ratio and the overall fiscal balance.[19] These measures point to a deterioration in fiscal balance of ½ to 4 percentage points of GDP in downswings relative to upswings, with greater variation in energy and metal exporters.
- *Financial stability:* More commodity price downswings than upswings are associated with banking crises in commodity exporters (Table 4.3).
- *The real effective exchange rate (REER)* is generally stronger in the course of a commodity price upswing compared with a downswing (Figure 4.3, panels 7 and 8). The cumulative percentage change in the REER during an upswing (from trough to peak) is typically greater than during a downswing (from peak to trough). This variation is particularly remarkable for energy and metal exporters, whereas the pattern is not observed for food exporters.[20]

The pattern of cyclical synchronization in macroeconomic indicators and commodity prices becomes muddier for individual commodities within the commodity groups (Figure 4.4).

- *Activity:* Procyclical behavior in real GDP growth is more prominent for oil and copper exporters compared with coffee and cotton exporters. The stronger comovement of economic activity and commodity price cycles could reflect the greater

the turning points (upswing or downswing) is required to be at least 12 months in length. See Appendix 4.2 for details.

[17]The macroeconomic variables are studied for each phase (upswing or downswing) using three characteristics—cross-country median for the entire phase, median when the phase is in the top quartile in terms of duration (long swings), and median when the phase is in the top quartile in terms of amplitude (sharp swings). We also compared mean values (instead of median values) for the macroeconomic indicators across alternative commodity price swings. The pattern is the same, with slightly larger differences in variation between upswings and downswings.

[18]We do not have sufficient data on credit growth for raw materials exporters.

[19]The data coverage for the change in public debt is more comprehensive than for the overall fiscal balance.

[20]This is consistent with the empirical literature. For instance Chen, Rogoff, and Rossi (2010) find that commodity exporters' real exchange rates are higher during periods of increasing commodity prices. However, the average growth in the REER during a commodity price upswing is not always greater than its average growth in a downswing (not shown here), which is a bit puzzling. We offer two possible explanations. First, the REER (like the other variables analyzed) is affected not only by changes in commodity prices but also by underlying policies and other factors, none of which are identified or controlled for in this exercise. Second, there may be some overshooting of the REER in the beginning of an upswing, which unwinds somewhat during the rest of the phase, resulting in average growth of the REER that is not necessarily stronger in an upswing relative to a downswing.

Figure 4.3. Macroeconomic Performance of Commodity Exporters during Commodity Price Swings

Commodity exporters' economic performance moves in tandem with commodity price swings.

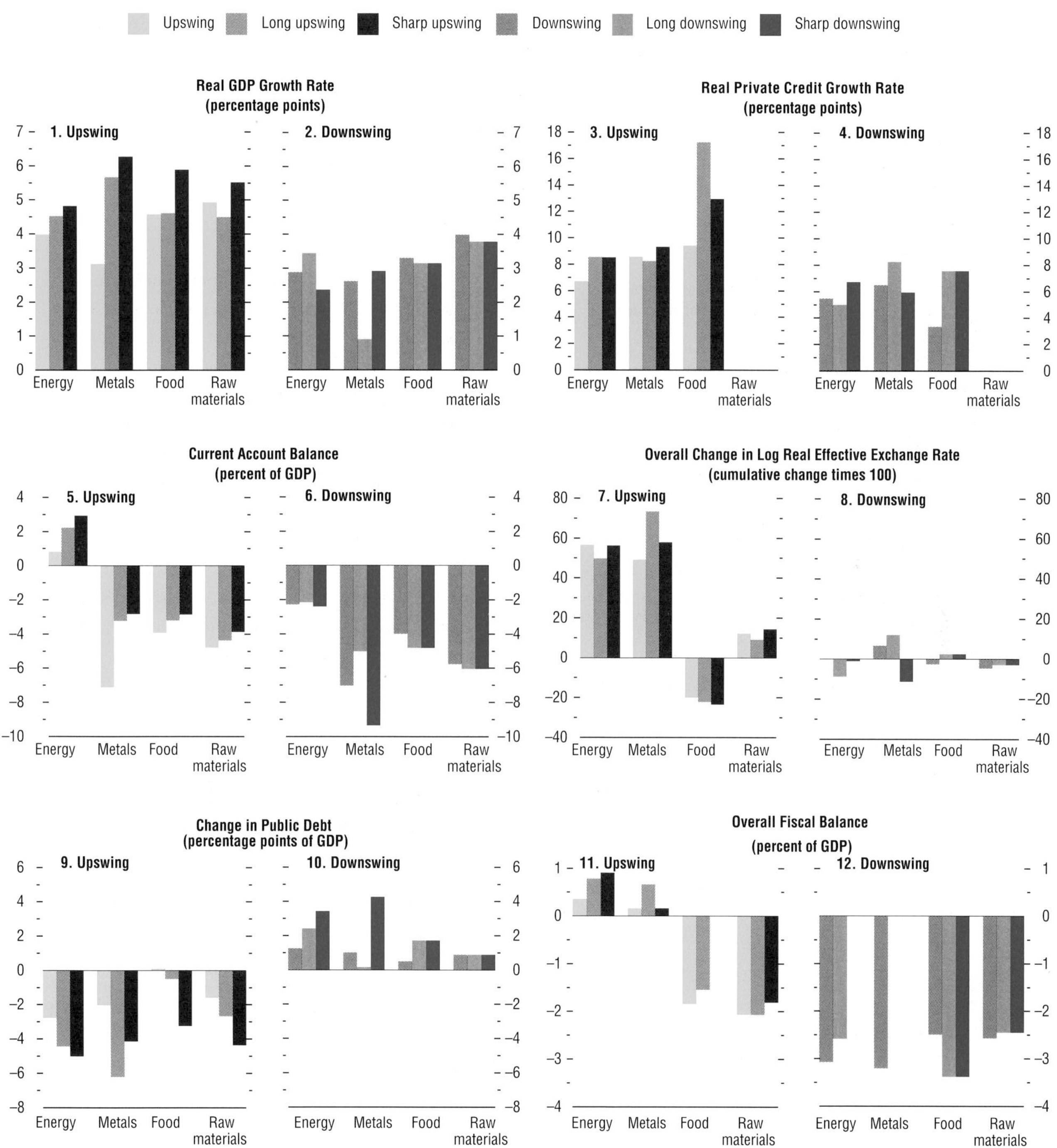

Source: IMF staff calculations.

Note: Each bar shows the median value of the economy-level averages within the relevant sample for each variable. Long swings are in the top quartile by duration, and sharp swings are in the top quartile by amplitude. Bars appear only if there are at least three years of data for at least three economies, and therefore bars are missing when these criteria are not met. See Appendix 4.1 for a full description of the underlying data.

Table 4.3. Relationship between Commodity Price Swings and Banking Crises in Commodity Exporters

(Number of observations)

	Net Energy Exporters		
	No Banking Crisis	Banking Crisis	Total
Upswing	409	67	476
Downswing	399	77	476
Total	808	144	952
	Net Metal Exporters		
	No Banking Crisis	Banking Crisis	Total
Upswing	262	25	287
Downswing	340	49	389
Total	602	74	676
	Net Food Exporters		
	No Banking Crisis	Banking Crisis	Total
Upswing	433	83	516
Downswing	825	168	993
Total	1,258	251	1,509
	Net Raw Material Exporters		
	No Banking Crisis	Banking Crisis	Total
Upswing	520	46	566
Downswing	492	105	597
Total	1,012	151	1,163

Source: IMF staff calculations.

Note: The table shows the cross tabulation of the indicated commodity price index phase with banking crises in the associated group of net commodity exporters. Observations are economy-years. The banking crisis indicator comes from Laeven and Valencia (2008, 2010). See Appendix 4.1 for a full description of the data.

importance of oil and copper in their exporters' economic activity—average net exports of oil to GDP are more than 20 percent and more than 10 percent for copper. For exporters of coffee and cotton, net exports to GDP average between 3 and 4 percent.

- *External balance:* The current account balance is procyclical in all commodity exporters, and the differences between upswings and downswings are amplified when the underlying cycle is longer or the price changes are sharper.
- *Fiscal balance:* The comovement of fiscal balances and commodity cycles is more prominent for exporters of crude oil and copper than for exporters of food and raw materials.

Commodity Price Cycles and Policy Regimes

Having established that domestic commodity exporters' economic conditions move with commodity price cycles, we next examine whether this comovement is dampened or accentuated under alternative policy regimes in commodity exporters. In particular, we focus on the nature of the exchange rate regime (pegged versus nonpegged) and the degree of capital account openness (relatively high versus low). As before, these basic correlations should not be misinterpreted as a causal link between structural characteristics and comovement of economic conditions and commodity price swings.

Exchange rate regime

The cyclical variability in macroeconomic indicators is slightly stronger with pegged exchange rate regimes relative to flexible regimes, especially for energy and metal exporters (Figure 4.5). Under pegged regimes, output growth falls more sharply during downswings for all except raw material exporters, while the current account balance differences are sharper for exporters of metals and energy. Conceptually, a fixed exchange rate can reduce economic volatility by limiting exchange rate fluctuations, but it is also unable to absorb external shocks, including changes in real commodity prices. We find weak evidence of the latter effect dominating for energy and metal exporters.[21]

Capital account openness

There is more comovement of macroeconomic indicators with commodity price cycles under greater capital account openness for energy and metal exporters but not for other commodity exporters (Figure 4.6). Overall, there may be offsetting forces at play. Economies with greater access to international capital markets should be better able to smooth output volatility when commodity prices fluctuate—for instance, by borrowing in international markets during downswings. Markets may, however, be procyclical for some—with capital flows increasing during commodity price upswings and declining during downswings.[22] The latter force appears to dominate for energy and

[21]See Rafiq (2011) for evidence from the Gulf Cooperation Council oil exporters, and Adler and Sosa (2011) for Latin American commodity exporters.

[22]Adler and Sosa (2011) find evidence of this procyclicality for Latin American commodity exporters.

Figure 4.4. Macroeconomic Performance of Exporters of Four Major Commodities during Commodity Price Swings

The comovement with commodity price cycles of domestic economic indicators is stronger for exporters of oil and copper than of coffee and cotton.

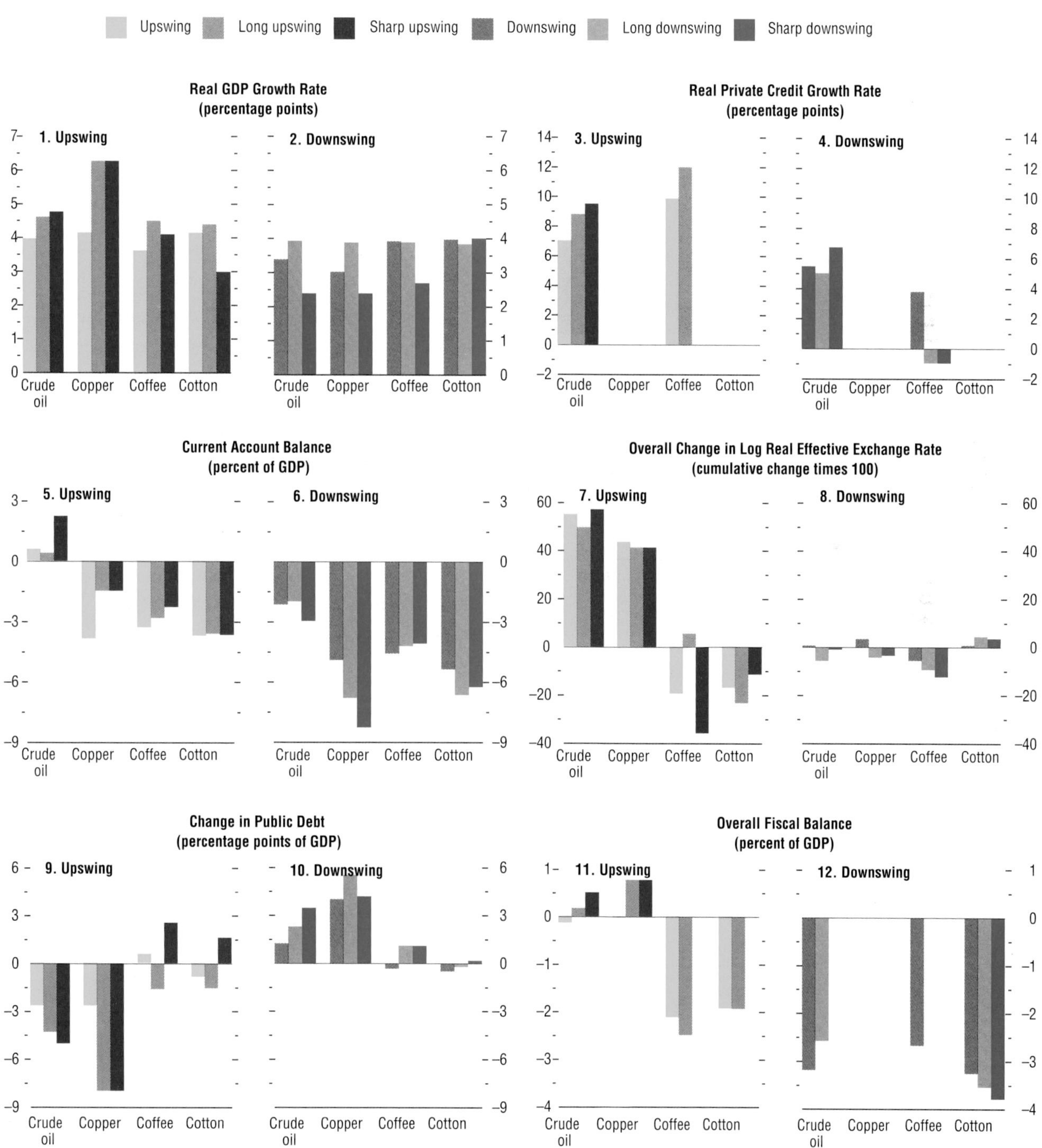

Source: IMF staff calculations.
Note: Each bar shows the median value of the economy-level averages within the relevant sample for each variable. Long swings are in the top quartile by duration, and sharp swings are in the top quartile by amplitude. Bars appear only if there are at least three years of data for at least three economies, and therefore bars are missing when these criteria are not met. See Appendix 4.1 for a full description of the underlying data.

Figure 4.5. The Exchange Rate Regime and Exporter Performance during Commodity Price Swings

The comovement of economic indicators with commodity price cycles is greater under pegged exchange rates for energy and metal exporters.

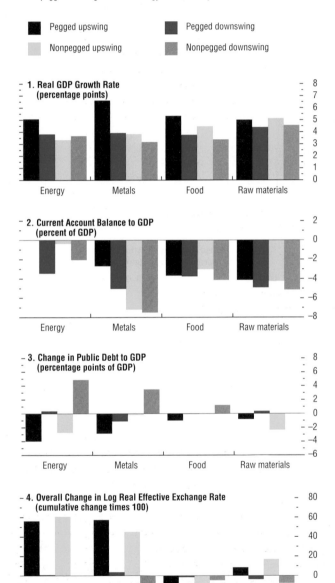

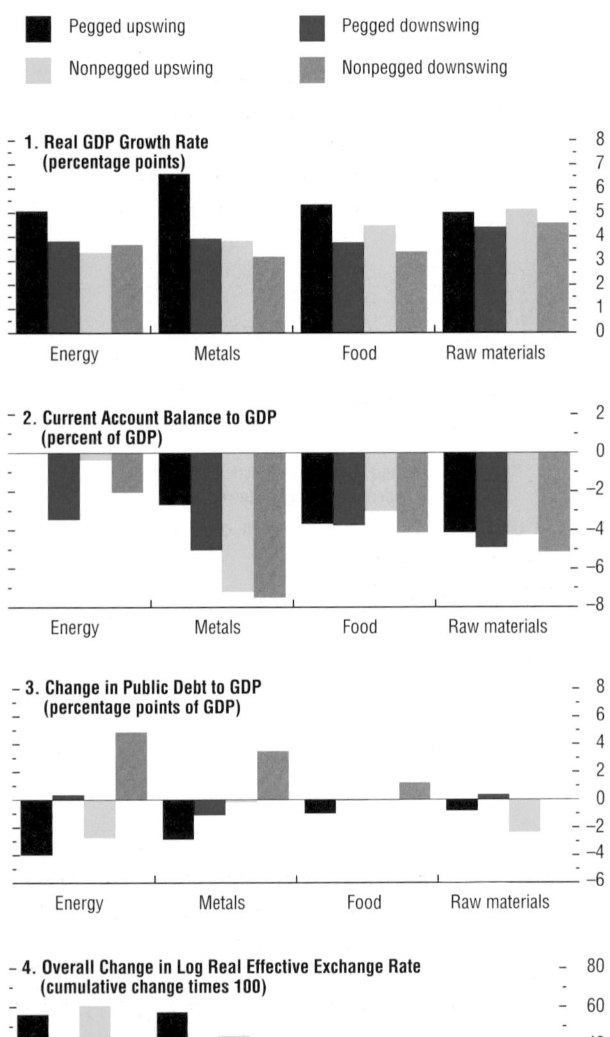

Source: IMF staff calculations.
Note: Each bar shows the median value of the economy-level averages within the relevant sample for each variable. Bars appear only if there are at least three years of data for at least three economies. Exchange rate regimes are from the "coarse" classification system in Ilzetzki, Reinhart, and Rogoff (2008), updated to 2010. See Appendix 4.1 for a full description of the underlying data.

metal exporters, but not for exporters of food and raw materials.

To sum up, the macroeconomic performance of commodity exporters is closely related to commodity price swings. This procyclical behavior with respect to commodity prices is accentuated when commodity price swings last a long time or involve sharp price changes. There are, however, considerable differences among commodity exporters. Energy and metal exporters are typically more synchronized with commodity price swings than exporters of food and raw materials, and their macroeconomic variation with commodity price swings tends to be more pronounced under fixed exchange rate regimes and greater capital account openness.

The generally sharper differences in macroeconomic performance between upswings and downswings for energy and metal exporters compared with food and agricultural commodities exporters may reflect in part steeper price changes for energy and metals compared with food and agricultural raw materials. But more generally, the above correlations do not control for policies that may dampen or accentuate the comovement between economic conditions and commodity price cycles. For instance, energy and metals generally carry larger royalties than other commodities, which, if spent during upswings, would reinforce the comovement of economic indicators with commodity price swings.

Commodity Market Drivers and Their Macroeconomic Effects

How does an unanticipated deterioration in the global economic outlook affect commodity prices and commodity exporters? To answer this question, this section first identifies how shocks to global economic activity affect commodity prices and then estimates the macroeconomic effects on commodity exporters.

Commodity Market Drivers

Using a structural vector autoregression (VAR) model of the global commodity markets for crude oil, copper, cotton, and coffee, we identify the contribution of global economic activity and commodity production shocks to commodity price fluctuations. The remaining (unaccounted for) fluctuations in the price reflect other factors that cannot be precisely identified but are likely a combination of commodity-specific demand factors and expectations about future global production and demand.[23]

Global demand shocks have a positive effect on the prices of all commodities except coffee (Table 4.4). A 1 standard deviation positive global demand shock (equal to a 0.6 percent rise in the monthly global industrial production index for oil and a 0.75 percent rise for copper) increases the real price in the impact year by 3.5 percent for oil and 2.4 percent for copper. For cotton, a 1 standard deviation rise in global demand, proxied by an increase in global real GDP of 0.8 percent, increases cotton prices by 0.7 percent. The positive effect of the global demand shock remains significant even after three years following the impact for crude oil and cotton prices.

In contrast, although global production shocks result in price movements in the opposite direction, the effect is not significant for any commodity except coffee. A 1 standard deviation positive production shock increases annual production by 7 percent for coffee and 4 percent for cotton in the same year. The average increases in monthly production for oil and copper are 0.5 and 1 percent, respectively. The negative price effect of this production increase is significant for coffee only,

[23]The VARs for oil and copper are estimated at monthly frequency, while those for coffee and cotton use annual data due to data limitations. See Appendix 4.3 for details on the baseline model and robustness checks. Examples of production shocks include unpredictable weather events, such as floods and droughts that adversely impact yields (for food and raw materials); production disruptions from unanticipated equipment breakdowns or work stoppages (for energy and metals); and unexpected technological breakthroughs that boost production. An example of a global activity shock includes a sudden fall in global activity due to an unanticipated hard landing in a systemically important country. Conversely, examples of commodity-specific shocks include a preference shift for coffee over tea (as happened over the past decade), gradual improvements in the intensity of commodity usage, and changes in expectations about future production and global activity. Thus, production or activity changes that are either wholly or partially anticipated would be in the unexplained component of the price, matched to the time at which the news about the forthcoming change is first received rather than at the time it actually occurs. An example of such an anticipated production shock might include the recent case of Libya, where political turmoil was expected to disrupt oil production and thereby the global oil supply, which pushed oil prices up in advance. Similarly, an anticipated increase in demand for commodities because of an ongoing real-estate-driven growth boom in China would push up commodity prices in advance.

Figure 4.6. Capital Account Openness and Exporter Performance during Commodity Price Swings

There is some evidence of greater comovement between economic indicators and commodity price cycles under greater capital account openness for energy and metal exporters.

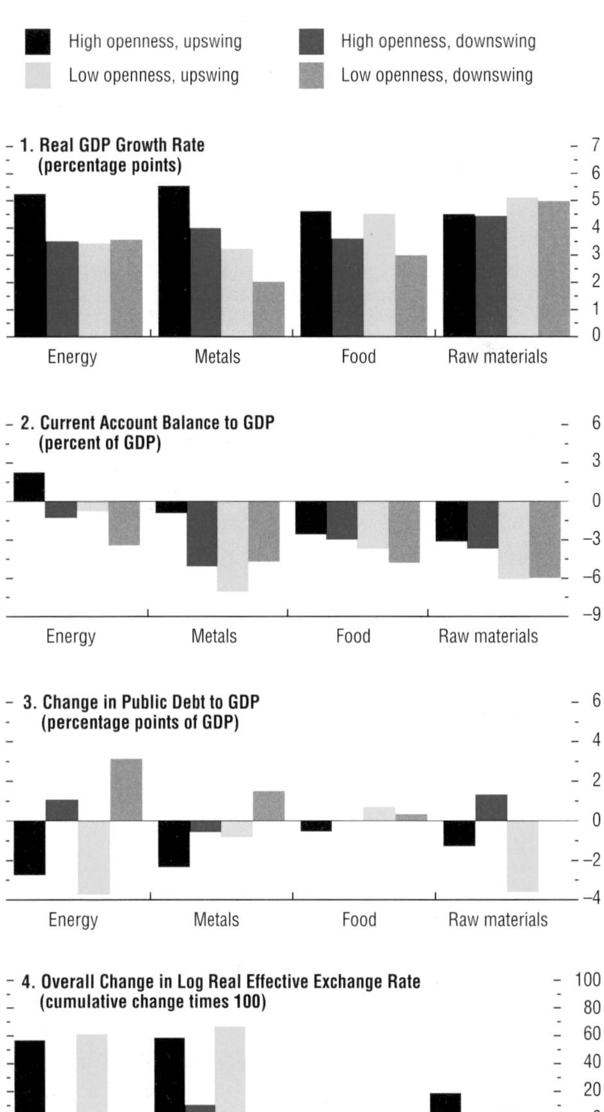

Source: IMF staff calculations.

Note: Each bar shows the median value of the economy-level averages within the relevant sample for each variable. Bars appear only if there are at least three years of data for at least three economies. An economy is classified as having high openness if its Chinn and Ito (2006, 2008) capital account openness measure is greater than or equal to the grand median of the sample. Otherwise, it is classified as having low openness. See Appendix 4.1 for a full description of the underlying data.

Table 4.4 Dynamic Effects of Global Commodity Market Shocks

		Commodity Production		Global Activity		Real Commodity Price	
Commodity	Shock	On Impact	At 3 Years	On Impact	At 3 Years	On Impact	At 3 Years
Oil	Production	0.488†	0.263	0.024	0.059	−1.098	1.975
	Global Activity	0.128†	−0.080	0.610†	0.215	3.526†	3.693†
Copper	Production	0.949†	0.696†	−0.031	−0.076	−0.873	−2.106
	Global Activity	0.305†	0.229	0.752†	0.475†	2.414†	0.693
Coffee	Production	6.933***	1.767	−0.144	−0.163	−1.050*	−1.481
		(0.731)	(1.175)	(0.156)	(0.321)	(0.557)	(1.252)
	Global Activity	. . .	2.393*	1.041***	1.162***	0.517	−1.466
		. . .	(1.263)	(0.110)	(0.328)	(0.544)	(1.319)
Cotton	Production	4.149***	0.095	0.370***	0.425	−0.038	−0.296
		(0.437)	(1.059)	(0.132)	(0.345)	(0.369)	(0.536)
	Global Activity	. . .	−3.005**	0.848***	1.320***	0.693*	1.410**
		. . .	(1.178)	(0.089)	(0.373)	(0.361)	(0.614)

Source: IMF staff calculations.

Note: Since the oil and copper commodity market models are at monthly frequency, the average effect over the corresponding year is shown for these commodities. A dagger is placed next to the statistic if at least 50 percent of the underlying statistics are individually significant at the 10 percent level. Standard errors are in parentheses underneath their corresponding estimate for the results from the annual frequency vector autoregression. *, **, and *** denote significance at the 10 percent, 5 percent, and 1 percent levels, respectively. The thought experiment is a 1 standard deviation rise in the commodity's global production shock or a 1 standard deviation rise in the global activity shock at the relevant frequency. No value is shown when the indicated shock is restricted to have no contemporaneous effect. See Appendix 4.3 for further details.

whose price falls by 1 percent on impact, and is not significant for the others. The result is contrary to the literature for oil, which argues that historical oil price shocks are largely underpinned by global supply.[24] This likely implies that historical supply disruptions in oil markets were mostly anticipated in advance. Conversely, weather-related supply shocks may be harder to predict than shocks to energy and metal supplies, resulting in more significant effects on prices of agricultural commodities, such as coffee.[25]

These findings demonstrate that not all commodity price effects are alike, and much depends on the source of the shock and the type of commodity. More important, changes in commodity prices driven by unexpected movements in global activity can be significant.

Domestic Macroeconomic Effects of Global Commodity Market Shocks

How do global-activity-driven commodity market shocks affect commodity exporters? We answer this question by estimating a dynamic panel model of the economic effects of alternative commodity market drivers for exporters of each commodity.[26] As described above, we are able to identify two types of underlying shocks that drive commodity price changes—shocks to global activity (demand) and shocks to global production of the commodity (supply). The following panel model is estimated by commodity for each set of exporters:[27]

$$Y_{i,t} = \alpha_i + \delta Y_{i,t-1} + \sum_{k=0}^{1} \sum_{j=0}^{2} (\beta_{k,j} u_{t-k,j} + \theta_k W_{i,t-k} + \varphi_{k,j} W_{i,t-k} u_{t-k,j}) + \eta_{i,t}, \quad (4.1)$$

where $Y_{i,t}$ is the macroeconomic variable of interest for economy i at time t. We focus on real GDP, current account balance as a ratio of GDP, and change in public debt to GDP. α_i is an economy-specific fixed effect, $u_{t,j}$ is the jth commodity market shock of interest at time t, $W_{i,t}$ is economy i's commodity exposure at time t, expressed as a lagged three-year moving average of net exports of the commodity to the economy's total GDP, and $\eta_{i,t}$ is a mean-zero error term. The interaction terms allow for the possibility

[24]See for instance Hamilton (2011). However, Kilian (2009) and Kilian and Murphy (2010) hold the opposite view.

[25]The fact that global demand does not significantly affect coffee prices may reflect their greater sensitivity to beverage-related preferences as well as low income elasticity (Bond, 1987).

[26]Commodity price movements can also have serious implications for commodity importers, many of which are low-income countries (LICs). While the chapter mainly focuses on exporters, Box. 4.1 provides a synopsis of the varying effects of food and fuel price increases on LICs.

[27]In the sample, each net commodity exporter's average share of net exports of the commodity to total goods exports over the entire sample period is at least 10 percent.

that the effects of commodity market variables vary with the economy's reliance on commodity exports.

The results confirm that global demand-driven commodity shocks have significant economic effects on commodity exporters (Figure 4.7; Table 4.5). This is not surprising, as global activity surprises may affect the demand for all goods. A diversified exporter of commodities will therefore face an increase in demand for all its exports. Specifically:

- A positive global activity shock improves economic conditions for all commodity exporters via real GDP growth or external balances or both. For oil, a typical global demand shock that increases the price of oil increases real GDP of net oil exporters by close to 0.4 percent in the impact year, while for coffee the increase is 0.6 percent (Table 4.5).[28] The real GDP effects for oil and coffee grow over the next three years, remaining positive and significant. For the remaining cases, the growth effects of demand shocks are not significant. However, there are significant improvements in the current account balance for all commodity exporters, and this effect remains significant even after three years for exporters of all commodities. Global demand shocks improve fiscal balances only for oil exporters, with the effect growing over a three-year horizon.
- In contrast, it is not surprising that a negative global production shock for the commodity, which increases its price, does not always have a significant economic effect. This is because a negative global production shock can be partially driven by a negative domestic production shock, or can result in a fall in global GDP, which could partly or fully offset the positive effect from the stronger terms of trade (as observed for copper and cotton).

How do the above economic effects of global activity versus global production manifest themselves over the entire phase of a commodity price upswing or downswing? To find out, we draw on the VAR model to separate the oil price upswings that are

[28]Note that a typical global demand (or production) shock for the case of oil and copper prices represents the annual average of the monthly structural shocks in the monthly VAR model. See Appendix 4.3 for details on using these results to obtain an estimate of the implied elasticities of real GDP with respect to price increases at an annual frequency.

Figure 4.7. Real Output Effects of Commodity Market Shocks
(Percent response)

Global demand-driven commodity price shocks can have significant economic effects on commodity exporters.

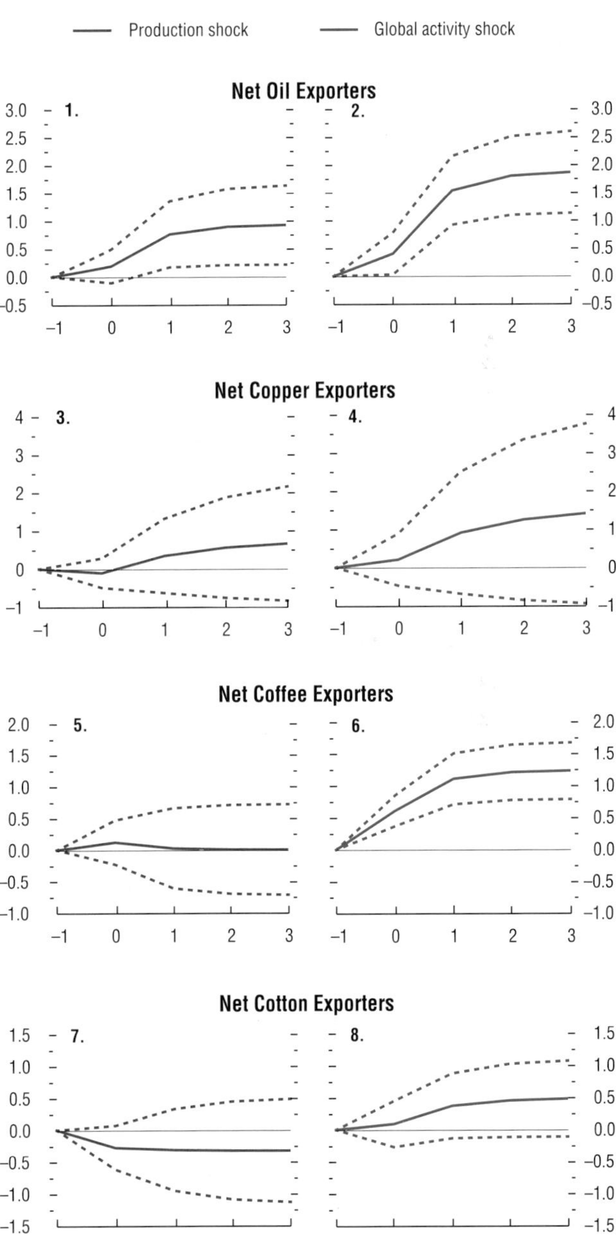

Source: IMF staff calculations.
Note: The *x*-axis shows the number of years elapsed, where time zero is the year that the shock occurs. The sample consists of net commodity exporters, where net exports of the commodity to total goods exports is at least 10 percent. Dashed lines denote 90 percent confidence bands. Shock magnitudes are a 1 standard deviation annual global production shock decline or annual global activity shock increase. See Appendix 4.3 for a description of the vector autoregression model used to estimate the underlying global activity and production shocks.

Table 4.5. Domestic Macroeconomic Effects of Global Commodity Market Shocks

		Real GDP		Current Account to GDP		Change in Public Debt to GDP	
Commodity	Shock	On Impact	At 3 Years	On Impact	At 3 Years	On Impact	At 3 Years
Oil	Production	0.191	0.923**	0.510	2.802	−1.990***	−4.316***
		(0.182)	(0.432)	(0.329)	(1.851)	(0.671)	(1.043)
	Global Activity	0.404*	1.862***	0.840***	5.458***	−1.333***	−3.269***
		(0.228)	(0.448)	(0.230)	(0.980)	(0.395)	(0.433)
Copper	Production	−0.104	0.658	0.098	−1.253**	0.984	−0.094
		(0.235)	(0.908)	(0.287)	(0.576)	(0.675)	(1.077)
	Global Activity	0.210	1.406	1.049**	2.486***	0.338	−0.851
		(0.412)	(1.428)	(0.549)	(0.952)	(0.752)	(1.191)
Coffee	Production	0.121	0.001	0.220	0.532	2.873*	0.860
		(0.212)	(0.437)	(0.237)	(0.560)	(1.657)	(1.090)
	Global Activity	0.603***	1.229***	0.364*	1.589*	4.579	6.128
		(0.146)	(0.270)	(0.217)	(0.915)	(4.192)	(5.895)
Cotton	Production	−0.275	−0.325	−0.399	−1.153	2.854	1.697
		(0.210)	(0.491)	(0.324)	(1.124)	(3.718)	(2.176)
	Global Activity	0.090	0.479	1.258*	4.110***	0.469	−0.435
		(0.218)	(0.359)	(0.648)	(1.588)	(2.074)	(1.464)

Source: IMF staff calculations.

Note: Standard errors are in parentheses underneath their corresponding estimate. *, **, and *** denote significance at the 10 percent, 5 percent, and 1 percent levels, respectively. The thought experiment is a 1 standard deviation annual global production shock decline of the commodity or a 1 standard deviation annual global activity shock rise. For oil and copper, the shocks are the average of the monthly shocks within a year, as taken from the model underlying Table 4.4, described in Appendix 4.3. The dynamic effects shown here are evaluated at the sample average value of the commodity exposure measure (net exports of the commodity of interest to GDP): for oil, this is 22.9 percent; for copper, 10.3 percent; for coffee, 4.2 percent; and for cotton, 3.2 percent.

driven predominantly by global demand from those that are driven primarily by changes in global production.[29] The results are summarized in Figure 4.8.

- The cyclical economic effect of oil price swings is somewhat larger when driven by global demand. The difference in real GDP growth between a typical upswing and a downswing is 1 percentage point for a demand-driven oil price cycle, compared with about 0.5 percent for all oil price cycles on average. The variation in the current account balance and the cumulative REER appreciation under a demand-driven oil price upswing relative to a downswing is similar to that observed in all oil price cycles on average.
- The fiscal position improves less during demand-driven oil price upswings relative to downswings. The fiscal balance proxied by the annual change in the public-debt-to-GDP ratio improves by about 2½ percentage points of GDP during a global demand-driven upswing (compared with an improvement of close to 4 percentage points of GDP for all oil price cycles on average). This may reflect a tendency for oil exporters to have a less countercyclical (or more procyclical) fiscal response to global demand shocks than to other shocks, which in turn could explain the greater domestic economic variation in response to demand-driven oil price cycles.

Distinguishing between the underlying sources of commodity price swings does matter, as these drivers have different price and macroeconomic effects for different commodity exporters. Overall, the economic effects of global activity shocks are significant for commodity exporters. These effects are strongest for crude oil, but also hold for other exporters. Oil exporters experience somewhat greater variation in real activity from global demand-driven oil price cycles than from other types of oil price cycles. These findings do not, however, shed light on how commodity exporters should respond to global commodity shocks to minimize their domestic economic effects. These questions are addressed in the next section.

Optimal Fiscal Policy Responses to Commodity Market Shocks

How should commodity exporters respond to commodity price fluctuations? The role of macroeconomic policies in lowering economic volatility may be more important for commodity exporters given the persistence and volatility of commodity price swings. As noted, a typical downswing in oil and metal prices

[29]Such a clear separation of demand-driven from production-driven price cycles is not possible for the other commodities. See Appendix 4.3 for details.

can last two to three years, can entail a real price decline from peak to trough of 40 to 50 percent, and can induce a setback in real GDP growth of ½ to 1 percentage point. In this regard, the role of fiscal policy may be crucial, given the direct effect of commodity prices on government coffers, and through the latter's actions, on the rest of the economy.[30]

This section focuses on the optimal fiscal policy response to commodity price fluctuations in a small, open commodity exporter and its interaction with monetary policy through the choice of exchange rate regime. Although the model is calibrated for oil, as discussed below, the qualitative results are equally applicable to other commodities. The section analyzes how the optimal fiscal policy choice is affected by the source of commodity price fluctuations, differences in underlying macroeconomic conditions, and structural characteristics of the commodity exporter. Recognizing some of the limitations of the model-based analysis, we also discuss possible trade-offs between optimal policies at the country versus the global level for the case of large commodity exporters, given the possibility for spillover of their policies. We also consider the optimal fiscal response to permanent commodity price changes. Finally, we consider how commodity exporters can best design their policies in light of prevailing uncertainty about the future direction of commodity prices.

The Setting

We use a two-region version of the Global Integrated Monetary and Fiscal model (GIMF) comprising a small, open oil exporter and the rest of the world, which is a *net* oil importer.[31] The small, open oil exporter takes the global oil price as given. It exports the bulk of its oil production, with net oil exports equivalent to 18 percent of its GDP and

[30]The empirical evidence, however, points to fiscal policies being procyclical, thereby exacerbating domestic volatility. For instance, Husain, Tazhibayeva, and Ter-Martirosyan (2008) find that fiscal policy reactions to oil price shocks raise real domestic volatility. As noted, Frankel (2011) argues that commodity exporters are too procyclical in their macroeconomic policies, while Céspedes and Velasco (2011) find that there may have been a decline in procyclical fiscal policies in commodity exporters in recent years.

[31]See Appendix 4.4 for details.

Figure 4.8. Oil Price Drivers, Cycles, and Performance in Net Oil Exporters

Global demand-driven oil price cycles lead to greater macroeconomic volatility.

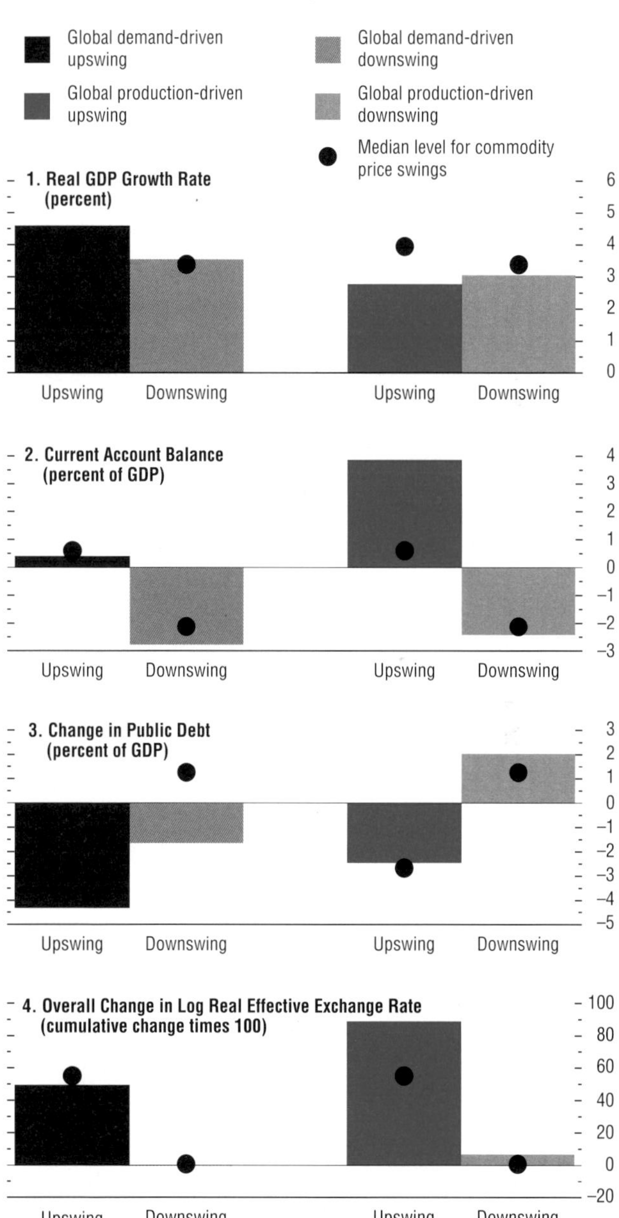

Source: IMF staff calculations.

Note: The black circles denote the sample median level during upswings and downswings, without taking into account their underlying driver. There are two production-driven oil price swings: a downswing (1996:M1–1998:M12) and an upswing (1999:M1–2000:M9). There are four demand-driven price swings: two downswings (1990:M10–1993:M12 and 2000:M10–2001:M12) and two upswings (1994:M1–1996:M10 and 2002:M1–2008:M7). See Appendix 4.1 for a full description of the underlying data. See Appendix 4.3 for a description of the vector autoregression model used to estimate the underlying global activity and production shocks.

representing 45 percent of its total exports.[32] This structure implies that a global demand-driven shock would affect the oil exporter not only through a change in the price of oil, but also through a change in the demand for other goods it exports (thereby allowing for Dutch-disease-type effects). The exporter is populated by households with overlapping generations as well as liquidity-constrained households, to more realistically capture the effects of fiscal policy. The government can borrow in international capital markets but faces a risk premium that is increasing with the level of its net external debt.[33] In the baseline, we also assume that (1) oil production is largely controlled by the government, which accrues most of the associated rent (through "commodity royalties"); (2) net public debt is relatively small, and the sensitivity of the sovereign risk premium to its changes is low; and (3) monetary policy follows an inflation-targeting regime, with a floating nominal exchange rate. These assumptions are relaxed in subsequent robustness analyses.

The fiscal policy stance is modeled through rules that target the government budget balance to minimize output and inflation volatility. Specifically, in each period the fiscal policy authority sets a fiscal instrument in response to deviations of non-oil tax receipts relative to their long-term level and deviations of commodity royalties from their long-term level. For example, if the global oil price and tax receipts temporarily rise unexpectedly, commodity royalties temporarily increase above their long-term levels and the fiscal authority may adjust the fiscal instrument in response. The specific instrument used is the labor tax rate, which is chosen for simplicity and does not constitute a policy recommendation. Also, policy conclusions do not depend on this choice. We consider three broad stances:

- *A balanced budget rule:* Under such a rule, the government budget is balanced in every period, so all exceptional commodity royalties and tax revenues are redistributed immediately to households through lower tax rates. This rule is procyclical by design but maintains fiscal balance and net debt at long-term targets.
- *A structural surplus rule:* Under this rule, exceptionally high commodity royalties and tax revenues are saved, while exceptionally low royalties and revenues result in dissavings (thereby avoiding increases in tax rates to offset the loss). This rule results in a one-for-one change in the overall fiscal balance and government debt in response to deviations of royalties and tax revenues from their long-term values. It is cyclically neutral, since it does not add to or subtract from aggregate demand.
- *A countercyclical rule:* Under this rule, the fiscal authority not only saves exceptionally high commodity royalties and tax revenues, but also increases taxes to dampen the stimulus to aggregate demand from higher oil revenue accruing to the private sector. In the case of exceptionally low royalties and tax revenues, taxes are lowered temporarily. This rule implies larger changes in budget surpluses and government debt in response to oil price changes. However, it acts countercyclically, increasing (reducing) the structural balance during periods of strong (weak) oil prices and/or economic activity.

In practice, fiscal policy behavior in a number of commodity exporters has been broadly influenced by rules of this kind. Chile and Norway have even adopted specific rules along the lines of those used in the model simulations. Chile follows a structural surplus rule, which allows for the presence of automatic stabilizers. Norway's rule targets a structural non-oil balance and also allows for the possibility of countercyclical responses over the business cycle.[34]

Response to Temporary Commodity Price Shocks

To compare the effects of the three fiscal policy stances, we analyze the results from simulations based on two oil-price-shock scenarios. In the first, the oil

[32]This is similar to the average shares for oil exporters in the sample (see Appendix 4.1).

[33]Net debt takes into account any positive foreign asset position (such as a sovereign wealth fund).

[34]Over the past two decades, there has been a marked increase in the adoption of rules-based fiscal policy, expressed through some concept of the fiscal balance or its components (revenue and/or expenditure) and/or the debt level. Fiscal rules are currently in use in some form in more than 65 countries. See IMF (2009).

price increases in response to unexpected increases in global activity. In the second, the increase is due to a negative shock to global oil production. In both scenarios, the shocks are calibrated to result in comparable oil price increases (close to 20 percent after one year). Also, the persistence of the oil price increases is about three years—within the distribution of the duration of oil price cycles in the empirical analysis.

We find that the effects of oil price increases on the domestic economy differ according to whether they are driven by external demand or external supply conditions, in line with the empirical results.

For the external supply-driven oil price increase, a temporary decline in oil supply in the rest of the world increases the real price of oil by 20 percent in the first year. The price gradually falls over the next two years (Figure 4.9). As the rest of the world's GDP declines so does real external demand for all goods exported by the small, open oil exporter. However, the fall in external demand is offset by an increase in the real value of the economy's oil exports, which improves its trade balance. Despite the increase in headline inflation resulting from higher oil prices, depressed global demand reduces the real price of final goods and in fact causes core inflation to fall. This is mitigated in part by slightly more stimulative monetary policy.

For the external demand-driven oil price increase, a temporary increase in liquidity in the rest of the world boosts global demand, driving up the real price of oil by about 20 percent in the first three years, after which global demand unwinds. Oil prices also experience a boom-bust cycle. Unlike a supply-driven oil price shock, the global demand boom drives up the demand and prices of *all* the small, open economy's exports.

For both shocks, a fiscal policy stance that aims at a balanced budget exacerbates macroeconomic volatility relative to the structural and countercyclical stances (Figures 4.9 and 4.10). Under a balanced budget rule, the excess tax revenues and oil royalties obtained during the boom are spent via a decline in labor taxes. Conversely, when the oil price increase unwinds, the fall in tax revenues and royalties is offset by an increase in labor taxes. In either direction, there is an increase in the output gap and in inflation volatility. With a structural surplus rule, the excess

Figure 4.9. Dynamic Effects of a Temporary Reduction in Oil Supply in the Rest of the World on a Small, Open Oil Exporter

A balanced budget fiscal policy in response to a global supply-driven oil price increase elevates domestic macroeconomic volatility in the oil exporter. A countercyclical fiscal response is the best way to reduce this volatility.

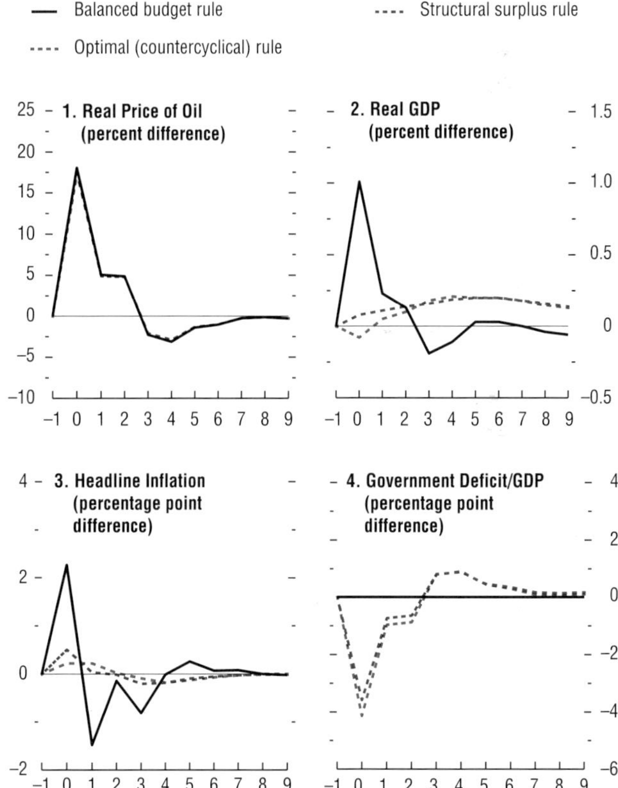

Source: IMF Global Integrated Monetary and Fiscal Model.
Note: The *x*-axis shows the number of years elapsed, where time zero is the year that the shock occurs. See Appendix 4.4 for a description of the model.

Figure 4.10. Dynamic Effects of a Temporary Increase in Liquidity in the Rest of the World on a Small, Open Oil Exporter

Domestic economic volatility induced by a global demand-driven oil price increase is even greater than that of a global supply-driven increase. In either case, a countercyclical fiscal policy dominates the balanced budget policy in terms of minimizing the volatility.

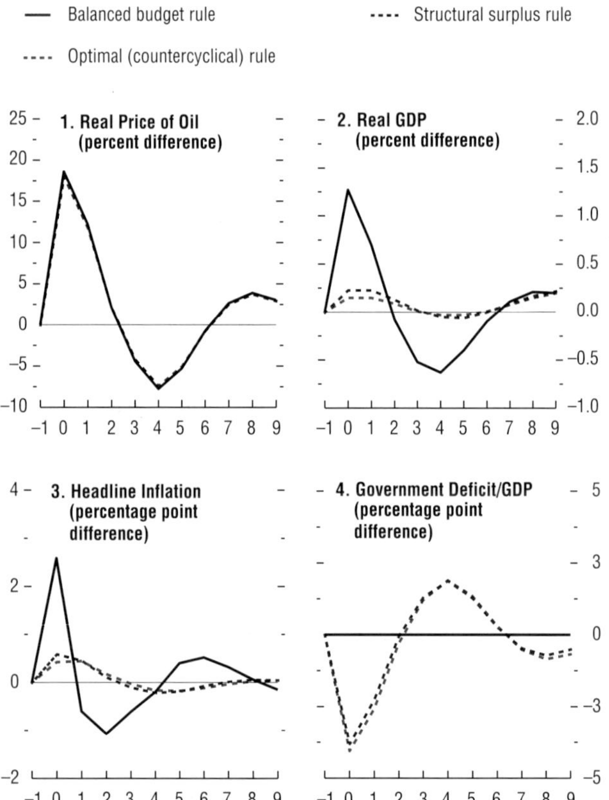

Source: IMF Global Integrated Monetary and Fiscal Model.
Note: The *x*-axis shows the number of years elapsed, where time zero is the year that the shock occurs. See Appendix 4.4 for a description of the model.

revenues and royalties during the price boom are saved, resulting in no change in labor taxes and a fall in the debt-to-GDP ratio. Conversely, these revenues are allowed to fall short of their potential levels when the boom unwinds. In either direction, the structural surplus rule helps dampen inflation and output volatility relative to a balanced budget rule.[35] Under a countercyclical rule, the labor tax rate rises with the boom, helping further dampen demand and inflation. Conversely, the labor tax rate is reduced when the boom unwinds, mitigating the fall in demand. Thus, a countercyclical rule reduces the output gap and inflation volatility more than a structural surplus rule under both types of cyclical commodity price shocks and constitutes the optimal fiscal response to them both. In the simulations, the size of countercyclical responses to the temporarily high royalties is quite small. This largely reflects the assumption that most of the oil royalties accrue to the government, which in turn implies that insulating the economy from changes in government oil revenues is broadly sufficient for macroeconomic stabilization.

Alternative Policy Frameworks and Structural Characteristics

The result that a countercyclical fiscal policy stance is optimal is generally robust to alternative assumptions about policy regimes and structural characteristics. Nevertheless, there are some nuances to consider (Figure 4.11).

Fixed exchange rate regime

Under a fixed exchange rate regime, the fiscal authority's countercyclical response to oil price shocks must be more aggressive. The main reason is that it lacks the support of the monetary authority, which, unlike under an inflation-targeting regime, is not complementary but procyclical in its response to commodity price shocks. For example, in the case of an unexpected oil price increase, the monetary policy stance is relaxed to offset the upward pressure on the nominal exchange rate. This feature is reminiscent of the empirical regularity that the comovement of the

[35]This is consistent with the findings of Kumhof and Laxton (2010), who find that a structural surplus rule can reduce macroeconomic volatility for a small copper exporter such as Chile.

domestic economy with the commodity price cycle is stronger with pegged exchange rates, as discussed earlier.[36]

Initial debt levels

The size of the countercyclical response might also reflect initial public net debt levels, depending on how strongly the sovereign risk premium reacts to changes in the level of net debt. In an alternative simulation with an initial net debt level of 100 percent of GDP (compared with the baseline of 30 percent), changes in the net debt level due to countercyclical policy responses can lead to a substantial change in the sovereign risk premium and hence domestic interest rates. In the case of an unexpected oil price drop, for example, a strong countercyclical response would result in a substantial increase in the risk premium due to higher public net debt, which would induce a sharp contraction in private domestic demand. This latter effect could be strong enough to fully offset the initial expansionary fiscal policy response.[37] Thus, at high levels of net debt, a higher priority is placed on reducing debt and building fiscal credibility prior to adopting a countercyclical fiscal response.

Different ownership structure in the oil sector

If there is a higher share of domestic private ownership in the oil sector, the saving behavior of households matters.[38] Assuming that a higher share of private sector oil royalties goes to households that can smooth their consumption by saving more (compared with the case of public sector ownership, when the government distributes revenues in a broadly similar way across households that smooth their consumption and those that do not), the ensuing output and inflation volatility is lower than in the baseline case. However, it is still optimal to have

[36]See also Broda (2004) or Rafiq (2011).

[37]See also Demirel (2010), who finds that optimal fiscal and monetary policies are procyclical (countercyclical) in the presence (absence) of the country spread. IMF (2009) finds that for a sample of Organization for Economic Cooperation and Development (OECD) countries, fiscal rules were more effective when public debt ratios were below a certain threshold.

[38]In this scenario, the private sector is assumed to own 90 percent of the oil production, compared with the baseline case, in which it owned only 10 percent.

Figure 4.11. Optimal Fiscal Policy Stance under Alternative Policy Frameworks and Structural Characteristics

This figure compares the optimal fiscal rule to the balanced budget rule for a temporary increase in global liquidity (similar to Figure 4.10). A countercyclical fiscal policy is consistently optimal for alternative macroeconomic conditions or different characteristics of commodity exporters. The exception is when the risk premium is highly sensitive to the level of sovereign debt, in which case the optimal fiscal response is closer to a structural surplus rule.

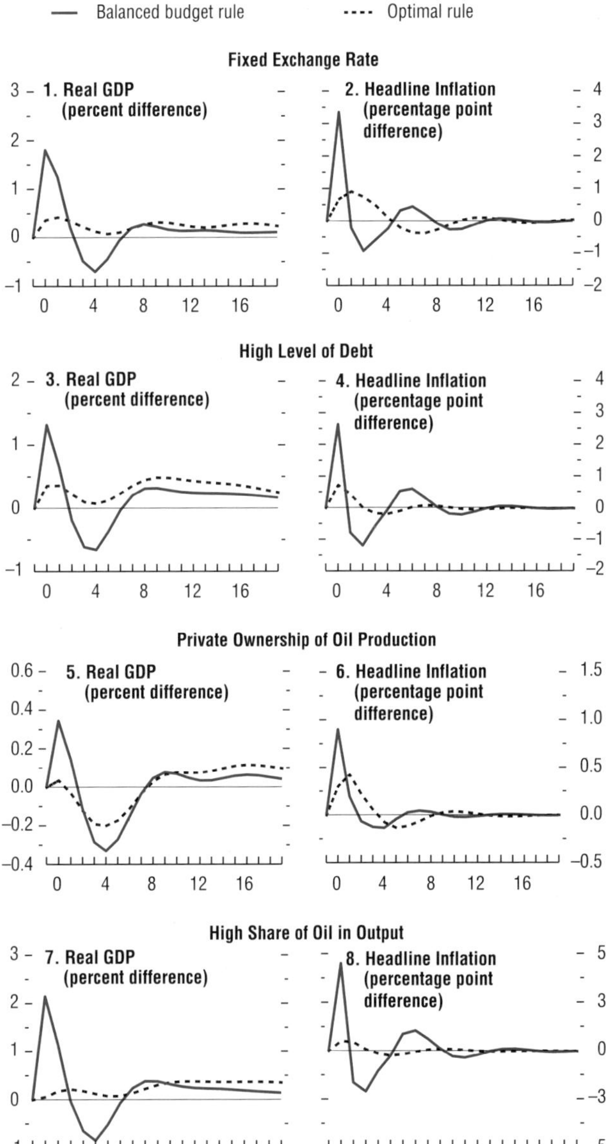

Source: IMF Global Integrated Monetary and Fiscal Model.
Note: The *x*-axis shows the number of years elapsed, where time zero is the year that the shock occurs. Panels 1 and 2 show the case when the exchange rate regime is fixed. Panels 3 and 4 show the case where net public debt is 100 percent of GDP. Panels 5 and 6 show the case where the share of private ownership in total oil production is 90 percent. Panels 7 and 8 show the case where the ratio of net oil exports to GDP is 36 percent.

a countercyclical fiscal response, which mitigates output and inflation volatility more than the other fiscal rules.

Higher share of oil in production

If the oil sector accounts for a larger share of output,[39] it is optimal to have a countercyclical fiscal response only to the changes in tax revenues, while saving the changes in oil royalties. Even though there are spillovers from the oil revenues into the non-oil sector, the non-oil sector contributes less to overall demand fluctuations relative to the baseline. Also, given the much larger share of the oil sector in the economy, a more countercyclical fiscal response to the increase in oil royalties can cause output to fall. Thus, saving the difference in government oil royalties may be enough for macroeconomic stabilization.

Subsidies for oil consumption

Many oil producers implicitly subsidize gasoline consumption and oil in domestic production. Such subsidies reduce the pass-through of changes in the price of oil into headline inflation. However, output fluctuations are similar to those considered in the baseline model because of changes in oil royalties and their effect on the non-oil economy. Thus, a countercyclical fiscal rule is still preferred to a structural rule for smoothing output volatility. A full analysis of the desirability of these subsidies should take into account the long-term viability of these subsidies, which is beyond the scope of this chapter.

Non-oil commodities

The results of the model are easily applicable to commodities other than oil. Although specific parameter values in the simulations have been chosen to replicate features of oil exporters, there is nothing about the structure of the model that makes it relevant only for oil.[40] For example, our results are broadly similar to those of Kumhof and Laxton (2010) for the case of copper in Chile. The main difference is that oil price shocks might have larger effects on headline inflation compared with copper and other industrial raw materials, since oil is more important in the consumption basket. In contrast, for food, the difference in headline inflation might be even more pronounced. Intuitively, the optimal size of the countercyclical fiscal response therefore increases with a higher share of the commodity in the consumption basket.

These findings underscore the importance of countercyclical fiscal policy in commodity exporters to ameliorate domestic volatility induced by temporary global commodity price shocks. A countercyclical fiscal stance is preferred under both fixed and flexible exchange rate regimes but needs to work harder under fixed rates when monetary policy becomes procyclical. Moreover, for a countercyclical policy to be effective and credible, public net debt levels should be low. When commodity production comprises a large share of an economy's value added, the size of the countercyclical fiscal response is closer to that of a structural surplus rule.

Where do commodity exporters stand vis-à-vis the policy lessons above? In general, they have been moving in the right direction by reducing their debt levels and strengthening their fiscal balances, especially over the past decade. However, economies vary greatly when it comes to macroeconomic and institutional readiness to implement fiscal policies aimed at macroeconomic stabilization. Some effectively now operate under a structural or countercyclical fiscal rule or fiscal responsibility laws (Botswana, Chile) and/or have moved toward further enhancement of their monetary policy frameworks by adopting inflation targeting (Indonesia, South Africa, and many Latin American economies). Some have achieved large debt reductions over the past decade (many OPEC members) or are in the process of

[39]In this scenario, the share of net oil exports in total GDP is 36 percent, as in some members of the Organization of Petroleum Exporting Countries (OPEC), compared with the baseline of 18 percent.

[40]When it comes to quantifying the optimal fiscal policy response to cyclical commodity price fluctuations, the structure of commodity exporters matters, of course, because of differences in demand and supply price elasticities across commodities, the heterogeneity of commodity prices across regions, and the level of production rents. In addition, economies that are more diversified across commodities are less inclined to experience domestic fluctuations from global supply shocks compared with broad-based global demand shocks. Moreover, structural characteristics such as high commodity intensity in total production and public ownership are more applicable to metal and oil production than to agricultural commodities.

formalizing fiscal institutions.[41] For those that have yet to initiate policy reforms, the current strength of commodity prices offers a good opportunity to build additional fiscal buffers and to ready fiscal and monetary institutions for any unexpected cyclical downturn in commodity prices.

Global Spillovers from Domestic Policies in Commodity Exporters

Could there be trade-offs between the optimal response to temporary commodity price shocks from the perspective of individual economies and the optimal response from the perspective of global economic stability? The analysis of optimal policies in this chapter was based on the assumption that commodity exporters are small and their policies do not affect economic activity in the rest of the world, including commodity markets. While this is a reasonable assumption for most commodity exporters and commodities, it may not be realistic for some large exporters. For instance, some oil exporters account for a substantial share of global absorption, wealth, and spare oil production capacity. When a commodity exporter is large, its policies can generate spillovers to other economies. Similarly, broadly identical policy responses by a group of relatively large commodity exporters may also generate important spillovers. This, in turn, raises the question of whether such spillovers could change the advice about optimal responses to commodity price changes.

A comprehensive analysis of optimal policies for large commodity exporters is beyond the scope of this chapter since it would need to consider not only the type of shock but also policies of other large economies, including commodity importers. Instead, this section touches on the possible conflicts between policies that are optimal for large oil exporters from a domestic perspective and policies that are optimal from a global perspective in the case of a temporary oil supply shock. The backdrop to this discussion is the current concern about increased geopolitical risks to the supply of oil as a source of downside risks to the global economy. Policy responses of large oil exporters are thus an important consideration in the global response to such shocks (see Chapter 1).

A temporary oil supply shock would have asymmetric effects on oil exporters for whom oil is a dominant source of exports compared with oil importers as well as other oil exporters. For exporters whose main export is oil, the terms-of-trade gains from the increase in oil prices in response to a supply shock would dominate any negative effect from a fall in external demand. The optimal domestic fiscal response to the windfall revenue gain in a small, open oil exporter (that does not experience the supply shock) would be a countercyclical one. Such a response by large exporters, however, would not be helpful in offsetting the negative direct effects of the shock on aggregate demand of oil importers. As a result, global output growth could slow or fall further than it would without such policies in oil exporters.[42] However, in normal times, the increased saving by large oil exporters could lower global real interest rates and boost interest-sensitive components of aggregate demand in importers.

Do such spillovers from large oil exporters' policies change the policy advice? Not necessarily. In many cases, the countercyclical fiscal response for oil exporters is still likely to be optimal. Importers can respond to the supply shock with countercyclical policies of their own. Nevertheless, there could be circumstances where other policy choices might be more relevant—for example, when the policy room in importers is limited or when the global economic downturn is so deep or protracted that the ensuing falloff in global demand can ultimately depress prices for all commodities, including oil. Under such circumstances, the countercyclical response may not be optimal in the first place for large exporters.

What are the policy options under these circumstances? The best option (from a global perspective) would be increased oil production by oil exporters

[41]See Céspedes and Velasco (2011), IMF (2009), De Gregorio and Labbé (2011), Ossowski and others (2008), and Roger (2010).

[42]This trade-off between domestic and global economic stability arises only when the effects of commodity market shocks are asymmetric across different economies. Therefore, there is no relevant trade-off when commodity prices are driven by global activity, which affects commodity exporters and the rest of the world in similar ways.

unaffected by the initial supply disruption, if they have spare capacity. This would offset the shock and stabilize global oil markets. If oil supply increases are not feasible, a less countercyclical policy response in large oil exporters combined with supportive economic policies in major importers (where possible) could also help alleviate the negative effect of the oil price increase on global output. How large could this effect be? If major oil exporters opted to spend all of their revenue windfalls from a 50 percent hike in the price of oil on imports, then real demand in the rest of the world could rise by up to ¾ percentage point, not a negligible amount.[43]

Fiscal Response to a Permanent Increase in the Price of Oil

Besides cyclical fluctuations, commodity prices also display long-term trends. While these trends are difficult to forecast, they nevertheless point to the possibility that some price shocks may have a permanent component. The main difference with respect to temporary price rises is the fact that a permanent oil price increase will have a permanent effect on potential royalties and possibly even on potential output. This naturally leads to the question of how a permanent windfall in oil royalties should be used most efficiently to maximize potential output and overall welfare.

A permanent oil price increase raises many policy issues, including those related to equity across generations, and an exhaustive analysis of these issues is beyond the scope of the chapter.[44] Nevertheless, using the GIMF, we can examine which fiscal instrument is most effective in maximizing output and welfare. By exploring a relatively wide array of fiscal instruments, we complement previous work on this topic, which has focused primarily on the desirability of investing savings in foreign assets (Davis and others, 2001; Barnett and Ossowski, 2003; Bems and de Carvalho Filho, 2011) or domestic government investment (Takizawa, Gardner, and Ueda, 2004; Berg and others, forthcoming). It should be emphasized that this analysis is conducted for an oil exporter, but as noted, the results also apply to other commodities.

The fiscal policy options in response to a permanent increase in oil royalties are increases in public investment (such as public infrastructure), increases in household transfers, reductions in distortionary tax rates (such as those on labor and capital income), and reductions in debt levels or increases in sovereign wealth invested abroad. The key features of this model are the assumption that higher investment and lower taxes boost labor demand and that higher transfers lower the supply of labor, which is in line with the empirical evidence.[45] To evaluate these options, we analyze their effects on the new long-term equilibrium in the model, compared with the long-term equilibrium before the shock. Because the speed of the transition to the new equilibrium differs depending on the fiscal policy options, the results also include the net present value of each option in terms of household utility (Table 4.6). It is important to bear in mind, however, that the results depend on the choice of underlying model parameters. The parameters used in this model closely follow those in the literature, but the results could vary according to economy-specific characteristics.

Increased public investment has the strongest effect on output (see also Takizawa, Gardner, and Ueda, 2004). However, it is important to stress that the simulations do not account for low-quality governance and production bottlenecks, which could substantially impede the efficient conversion of resources into public capital (see Box 4.2). In addition, the benefits of public investment accrue only slowly because it takes time to build up public

[43]These calculations present an upper bound on the positive effects from spending increases by large oil exporters that account for more than one-third of global oil production (such as a majority of the OPEC producers together). We assume that these oil exporters' fiscal revenues increase proportionately with the oil price increase and that they channel all the windfall fiscal revenues back to the rest of the world via increased import demand. See Beidas-Strom (2011) for a related analysis of global spillover effects of fiscal spending by Saudi Arabia.

[44]Among these questions are resource exhaustibility, Dutch disease effects, bequest objectives, and exporting economies' institutional and development needs. See Box 4.2 for a discussion of some of these issues.

[45]See Eissa and Hoynes (2004) and Keane (2010). Another implicit assumption is that the original equilibrium was not already at the optimal capital and output levels due to prevailing distortions in the economy, a reasonable assumption for most developing economies.

Table 4.6. Comparison of Policy Instruments for Permanent Increases in Oil Royalties

	Real GDP (percent)	Real Consumption (percent)	Current Account (percent of GDP)	Debt-to-GDP Ratio (percent of GDP)	NPV of Utility (percent)
Reduction in Labor Taxes	1.7	9.7	0.8	0.0	24.6
Reduction in Capital Taxes	12.2	11.9	–0.6	0.0	25.1
Increase in General Transfers	–0.6	6.5	0.2	0.0	21.8
Increase in Government Investment	53.7	31.6	0.3	0.0	19.0
Reduction in Net Debt from Low Initial Debt Position	4.1	12.6	5.5	–109.0	12.8
Reduction in Net Debt from High Initial Debt Position	15.4	21.5	7.6	–109.0	20.1

Source: IMF Global Integrated Monetary and Fiscal Model.

Note: The first four columns show the difference between the new long-term level and the old long-term level of each variable. The last column shows the net present value (NPV) of household utility evaluated over the transition to the new steady state.

capital. As a result, the net present value of the expected utility flow is lower than under some other options, although this result depends on how much policymakers discount the future. The more patient a country's policymakers and citizens, the more beneficial the public investment option becomes.[46] An increase in general transfers to households—even though it raises household income and, thus, private consumption—negatively affects labor supply, thus reducing the total hours worked and output in the long term.

However, there are trade-offs between maximizing output and maximizing welfare, with the ultimate choice of the instrument depending on country-specific preferences. For instance, an increase in general transfers to households raises the net present value of utility (from increases in consumption and leisure) by more than an increase in public investment, even though the former has less of an output effect. The public welfare benefits of using resource revenues to pay off debt are significant only when a country's initial debt level is high and debt reduction significantly lowers the sovereign risk premium. In this case, the main benefit is to lower sovereign risk, which means the government can borrow at lower interest rates to finance investment and service its debt (see, for example, Venables, 2010). Lower borrowing costs stimulate demand, while the lower cost of servicing the debt increases fiscal room. In contrast, paying off a low amount of debt and then accumulating assets (for example, via a sovereign wealth fund) yields a relatively small return—namely, investment income from safe international assets. This might be a good option in response to prudential and intergenerational equity demands, but in this model context, where there is no uncertainty, accumulating low-yielding foreign asset positions offers lower benefits in terms of both output and welfare.

The effects of various fiscal policy instruments are almost the same whether prices rise or fall. This would argue for a cut in general transfers to minimize the output effects under a permanent decline in oil prices, as the model assumes that increases in transfers reduce the labor supply. However, if optimizing the net present value of utility by meeting social needs were a concern, then cutting transfers would not be optimal. Another option, if the economy started at a relatively low net debt position, would be to reduce holdings of assets, with relatively small negative effects on both output and household welfare. Conversely, cutting public infrastructure investment would be the least desirable fiscal response if the objective were to minimize the output shortfall from permanently lower commodity prices.

Conclusions and Policy Lessons

This chapter presents evidence of commodity exporters' vulnerability to swings in commodity prices. Historically, exporters' macroeconomic performance has fluctuated with commodity price cycles—improving during upswings and deteriorating during downswings. The comovement of domestic economic conditions with commodity

[46]We assume a 5 percent discount factor.

price cycles is amplified when the underlying cycles are longer or deeper than usual. When the underlying drivers of commodity price changes are identified, we find that global demand-driven commodity market shocks have a positive and significant effect on exporters' activity and external balances. For oil exporters, domestic economic indicators tend to vary with global demand-driven oil price cycles.

What are the policy implications for commodity exporters? If all commodity price swings were temporary, the optimal fiscal policy response for a small commodity exporter would be a countercyclical one—save the windfall fiscal revenue and royalties during price upswings and spend them during downswings to ameliorate the macroeconomic volatility induced by commodity price cycles. These policies are desirable under both fixed and flexible exchange rate regimes but are more effective under a flexible exchange rate combined with inflation targeting, when monetary policy complements fiscal policy by reducing inflation volatility. When public debt levels are high, however, the priority should be on lowering debt and sovereign risk premium to build credibility prior to adopting countercyclical fiscal policies. For large commodity exporters whose policies generate spillovers for others, the optimal policy response may depend on the nature of the shock and the state of the global economy. Thus, when global demand is weak and policy room in the rest of the world is limited, there may be a case for a less countercyclical fiscal policy response.

Under a permanent increase in the commodity price, the key challenge is how best to use the permanently higher royalties to maximize welfare. Changes in public investment expenditures give the strongest output effect by raising private sector productivity (for instance, via improvements in education, health, and infrastructure) and subsequently by increasing private capital, labor and corporate incomes, and consumption. Conversely, if prices were to fall permanently, cutting general transfers could best limit the output shortfall, although the social welfare impact of such cuts must be taken into account.

What messages do these findings provide for commodity exporters? In the near term they face a weak global economy. If downside risks to the global outlook materialize, commodity prices could decline further. Over the longer term, commodity prices are even more unpredictable. They may stay at their current levels in real terms if rapid commodity-intensive growth continues in emerging and developing economies. On the other hand, prices may decline in response to increasing user efficiency and the unwinding of earlier supply constraints. In light of the unusually high uncertainty and the difficulty of forecasting prospects for commodity markets in real time, a cautious approach is the best option. This involves upgrading policy frameworks and institutions and building buffers to address cyclical volatility while gradually incorporating new information to smooth the adjustment to potentially permanently higher prices.

Appendix 4.1. Data Description

Real Commodity Prices

Monthly data on commodity prices come mainly from the IMF's Primary Commodity Price System. All prices are period averages and are representative of the global market price because they are determined by the largest exporter of a given commodity. The key exception is the monthly oil price, which is the U.S. Energy Information Administration (EIA) import price of crude oil to refiners between January 1974 and August 2011. The price is extended backward through 1973 with Barsky and Kilian's (2002) imputed series value. All prices are denominated in U.S. dollars and, in line with other work (such as Cashin, McDermott, and Scott, 2002), deflated by the U.S. consumer price index (CPI) to obtain a real commodity price (CPI is taken from the St. Louis Federal Reserve Economic Data database, series CPIAUCSL). These real prices are then normalized such that the average real price in 2005 is equal to 100. Annual data on real commodity prices are calculated by taking the mean of the data at a monthly frequency for the corresponding year.

Exports and Imports by Commodity

Annual data on imports and exports used in the chapter are taken from the UN-NBER bilateral country and commodity-level merchandise trade flows database, which covers the period 1962–2000 (Feenstra and others, 2005). These data are extended with the United Nations COMTRADE data from 2001–10, following the methodology described in Feenstra and others (2005) and using the Standard International Trade Classification (SITC) Version 2 to define trade in each commodity. These data are then aggregated to compute country-level total exports and imports and country-level exports and imports by commodity.

Commodity Price Indices

The four commodity group price indices (energy, metals, food and beverages, raw materials) are weighted averages of the real prices of the commodities within a group. The weight for each commodity is its once-lagged three-year moving average of total world exports of the commodity divided by total world exports of all commodities in the group.

Economy-Level Macroeconomic Variables

These data come largely from the World Economic Outlook (WEO) database: real output (series NGDP_R), nominal output in U.S. dollars (series NGDPD), the current account in current U.S. dollars (series BCA), the overall fiscal balance (GGXOFB), and the cyclically adjusted fiscal balance as a percent of potential GDP (series GGCB). The change in the public-debt-to-GDP ratio is taken from the Historical Public Debt database (Abbas and others, 2010). The real effective exchange rate is series EREER from the IMF's Information Notice System (INS) database, from 1980 to the present. We construct a comparable series for the years prior to 1980 by combining the INS weights with historical nominal, bilateral exchange rates. We take the growth rate of this constructed series and splice the original INS series using this growth rate as far back as possible. The underlying data for real private credit growth are the level of bank credit to the private sector in current local currency units, taken from line 22 of the IMF's International Financial Statistics (IFS) database. This private credit series is releveled whenever a level shift or break is observed in the series. These data are deflated using the economy's CPI to construct a real private credit level. The exchange rate regime indicator is taken from Ilzetzki, Reinhart, and Rogoff (2008). We collapse their coarse classification into a binary indicator, mapping their classes 1 and 2 to "fixed" and 3 and 4 to "flexible." To extend this indicator to the present, we take the 2008 value for the indicator by economy and assume that it is the same during 2009–11. The capital account openness indicator (high versus low) is calculated using Chinn and Ito's (2006, 2008) capital openness measure, KAOPEN. To extend this indicator to the present, we take the last value for the indicator by economy and carry it forward to the present. We then take the grand median of this measure and categorize an observation as high if it is above this grand median and low if it is below it. The banking crisis indicator comes from Laeven and Valencia (2008, 2010). It takes a value of 1 if the economy is deemed to be experiencing a systemic banking crisis and zero otherwise.

Commodity Production and Inventories

The four major commodities explored in this chapter are crude oil, copper, coffee, and cotton. Production data for these commodities came from various sources.

Monthly oil production data come from the EIA's *International Energy Statistics* for world petroleum production (thousands of barrels a day), from January 1974 to August 2011. These data are extended backward through 1973 with Barsky and Kilian's (2002) imputed value of the series. The monthly global inventory level for oil is proxied by total OECD inventories, taken from the EIA's *International Energy Statistics* for the total petroleum stock in the OECD, measured on an end-of-period basis in millions of barrels. For data prior to 1988, we follow the approach of Kilian and Murphy (2010) and splice the total OECD stock back to 1970 using the monthly growth rate of the U.S. stock (also taken from the EIA).

Monthly copper production data come from two sources. From January 1995 onward, world copper production comes from the World Bureau of Metal Statistics—WBMS (originally sourced from the U.S. Geological Survey). To recover a monthly measure of world copper production prior to 1995 requires two steps. First, we calculate the growth rate of monthly U.S. copper production—which goes back to 1955—from the Commodity Research Bureau (CRB). This growth rate series is then used to extend the WBMS U.S. series backward. Second, we add this resulting extended series to the "Outside of the U.S." production series from the CRB, starting in 1955 (originally sourced from the American Bureau of Metal Statistics). We then calculate the growth rate of the resulting world production series and use it to extend the WBMS world copper production series backward from 1995 to 1955. Monthly global copper inventories are the sum of copper inventory stocks recorded by the London Metal Exchange, COMEX (part of the New York Mercantile Exchange), and the Shanghai Metals Market. Data are in thousands of metric tons and were kindly shared with us by the Comisión Chilena del Cobre.

Yearly coffee and cotton production data are from the U.S. Department of Agriculture (USDA) Foreign Agricultural Service. We match the harvest year to the calendar year during which most of the production occurred. Inventories for these commodities are end-of-year amounts and are also from the USDA.

Global Activity

At the monthly frequency, global activity is measured as the change in the natural logarithm of a global industrial production index. This global industrial production index comes from the Netherlands Bureau for Economic Policy Analysis (CPB) for 1991 to the present. Prior to 1991, the growth rate of the advanced economies' industrial production index from the IFS was used to splice the CPB data backward. At the annual frequency, global activity is measured as the change in the natural logarithm of global real GDP, which is taken from the WEO database. In a robustness check for the vector autoregression at the monthly frequency, we used the global activity index of Kilian (2009). This is an index of detrended real shipping freight costs around the world.

Oil Price Forecast Error

The oil price forecasts used in Appendix 4.3 are the 12-month-ahead forecasts for the U.S. dollar price of West Texas Intermediate (WTI) crude oil, taken from the March/April survey of Consensus Economics. The forecast error is calculated as the difference between the log of this forecast and the actual log average spot price of WTI crude oil in March/April of the following year.

Global GDP Forecast Error

The global GDP growth forecast used in Appendix 4.3 is the weighted average of the GDP growth forecasts for the G7 economies plus Brazil, China, India, and Russia. The growth forecasts are the 12-month-ahead Consensus Economics forecasts from March/April. The weights are purchasing-power-parity GDP weights for 2011 from the WEO database. The forecast error is calculated as the difference between this forecast and the similarly weighted average of the actual growth rates of these economies.

Sample

The sample consists of emerging and developing economy commodity exporters with populations of at least 1 million, and each economy with a ratio of net commodity exports (for the relevant commodity group or commodity) to total goods exports that averages at least 10 percent over all available years (Table 4.7).

Table 4.7. Commodity Intensity in Exports

(Net exports of commodities over total goods exports times 100)

	International Financial Statistics Code	World Bank Code	All Commodities	Commodity Groups				Major Commodities			
				Energy	Metals	Food	Raw Materials	Oil	Copper	Coffee	Cotton
Islamic Republic of Afghanistan	512	AFG					23.5				
Algeria	612	DZA	60.5	68.4				53.7			
Angola	614	AGO	80.9	65.6		15.5		68.0		13.4	
Argentina	213	ARG	37.3			35.3					
Azerbaijan	912	AZE	27.8	38.1			13.5	45.2			13.0
Benin	638	BEN	27.7				32.5				31.3
Bolivia	218	BOL	61.4	22.0	26.1						
Brazil	223	BRA	29.0			29.4				14.4	
Burkina Faso	748	BFA	33.6				47.1				43.0
Burundi	618	BDI	70.7			64.4				63.2	
Cambodia	522	KHM					25.2				
Cameroon	622	CMR	78.8	22.8		33.5	19.4	33.0		13.7	
Central African Republic	626	CAF	43.8			15.8	28.5			15.9	12.9
Chad	628	TCD	83.0	13.9			70.0	68.2			68.5
Chile	228	CHL	51.2		48.5				48.9		
Colombia	233	COL	56.1	16.7		42.3		12.0		36.2	
Democratic Republic of Congo	636	COD	58.9	11.7	34.7			14.3	32.8		
Republic of Congo	634	COG	75.9	54.5			17.2	56.2			
Costa Rica	238	CRI	48.4			51.9				20.2	
Côte d'Ivoire	662	CIV	61.9			49.6	19.6			17.5	
Dominican Republic	243	DOM	19.8			17.9					
Ecuador	248	ECU	74.3	28.8		49.7		29.6			
Egypt	469	EGY	29.4	31.1			12.7	30.2			15.6
El Salvador	253	SLV	39.4			39.9				39.1	
Ethiopia	644	ETH	38.7			40.5				53.9	
Georgia	915	GEO			12.7						
Ghana	652	GHA	62.8			46.9					
Guatemala	258	GTM	44.6			41.2				29.2	
Haiti	263	HTI	12.9			14.7				17.8	
Honduras	268	HND	56.8			50.3				15.4	
India	534	IND				10.6					
Indonesia	536	IDN	49.1	32.1			10.6	24.3			
Islamic Republic of Iran	429	IRN	77.8	85.4				85.0			
Iraq	433	IRQ	61.1	89.8				93.5			
Kazakhstan	916	KAZ	69.0	44.1	19.0			42.8			
Kenya	664	KEN	30.2			39.8				23.6	
Kuwait	443	KWT	67.0	69.5				67.7			
Kyrgyz Republic	917	KGZ					12.0				
Lao People's Democratic Republic	544	LAO					32.6			13.8	
Latvia	941	LVA	15.4				13.2				
Liberia	668	LBR	19.4				14.5				
Libya	672	LBY	88.1	90.2				88.9			
Madagascar	674	MDG	26.7			29.1				20.4	
Malawi	676	MWI	23.2			25.0					
Malaysia	548	MYS	36.0				25.5				
Mali	678	MLI	43.4				57.5				55.0
Mauritania	682	MRT	49.8		26.0	22.5					
Mauritius	684	MUS	37.5			42.2					
Mexico	273	MEX	23.5	15.0				16.1			
Moldova	921	MDA			13.8						
Mongolia	948	MNG	34.0		16.3		12.7		15.8		
Mozambique	688	MOZ	40.3		15.9	13.6	10.2				
Myanmar	518	MMR	59.6			26.2	28.8				
Nicaragua	278	NIC	56.0			41.1	17.9			21.1	16.6
Niger	692	NER	19.0			10.7					

Table 4.7. Commodity Intensity in Exports *(continued)*

	International Financial Statistics Code	World Bank Code	All Commodities	Commodity Groups				Major Commodities			
				Energy	Metals	Food	Raw Materials	Oil	Copper	Coffee	Cotton
Nigeria	694	NGA	87.8	80.5				79.1			
Oman	449	OMN	85.1	89.3				86.4			
Panama	283	PAN	12.2			27.7					
Papua New Guinea	853	PNG	72.7		22.7	24.3	11.5	19.9	25.6	11.3	
Paraguay	288	PRY	58.5			40.1	22.8				13.3
Peru	293	PER	54.3		31.2	16.0			18.6		
Philippines	566	PHL	12.2			10.2					
Russia	922	RUS	55.5	34.8	12.1			28.7			
Rwanda	714	RWA	63.6			57.0				51.5	
Saudi Arabia	456	SAU	82.6	86.3				84.0			
Sierra Leone	724	SLE	11.4			12.5					
South Africa	199	ZAF	24.1		12.5						
Sri Lanka	524	LKA	26.3			24.4					
Sudan	732	SDN	47.9	14.3			33.8	39.0			32.3
Syrian Arab Republic	463	SYR	49.7	50.5			10.1	51.0			
Tajikistan	923	TJK	65.3		43.1		30.3				29.9
Tanzania	738	TZA	34.9			24.1	13.5			20.1	11.7
Thailand	578	THA	16.0			20.6					
Togo	742	TGO	27.1			18.9	10.3			11.1	
Tunisia	744	TUN	12.6	12.2				14.5			
Turkmenistan	925	TKM	68.8	48.2			23.9				23.3
Uganda	746	UGA	77.5			69.1	10.3			65.8	
Ukraine	926	UKR	15.4		34.9						
United Arab Emirates	466	ARE	65.5	67.7				69.9			
Uruguay	298	URY	35.6			26.3					
Uzbekistan	927	UZB	53.6	11.1			41.8				41.7
Venezuela	299	VEN	59.5	58.1				57.3			
Vietnam	582	VNM						16.1			
Republic of Yemen	474	YEM	67.0	80.4				79.4			
Zambia	754	ZMB	72.3		71.7				72.9		
Zimbabwe	698	ZWE	33.3		19.0						
Maximum			88.1	90.2	71.7	69.1	70.0	93.5	72.9	65.8	68.5
Mean			47.9	47.8	27.1	31.8	23.5	50.1	35.8	26.8	29.2
Median			49.4	46.2	22.7	28.4	19.5	51.0	29.2	20.2	26.6
Standard Deviation			21.8	28.0	15.9	15.5	14.4	26.6	21.7	17.2	17.6
Number of Economies			78	30	17	40	32	29	6	22	14

Source: IMF staff calculations.

Note: Entries are not shown if the share is less than 10 since this is the criterion used to define the sample. The table shows the averages of each share over the period 1962–2010 using all available data. For the commodity groups, the average share is calculated for each component and then these averages are added together. All Commodities includes gold and silver. See Appendix 4.1 for details on the source data.

Appendix 4.2. Statistical Properties of Commodity Price Cycles

We adopt the Harding and Pagan (2002) methodology used for dating business cycles to identify turning points (peaks and troughs) in the time path of real commodity prices.[47] A full cycle in real commodity prices comprises one upswing phase—the period from trough to peak—and one downswing phase—the period from peak to trough. Drawing on Cashin, McDermott, and Scott (2002), a candidate turning point is identified as a local maximum or minimum if the price in that month is either greater or less than the price in the two months before and the two months after. The set of resulting candidates is then required to alternate peaks and troughs. Furthermore, each phase defined by the turning points (either upswing or downswing) must be at least 12 months long, and thus a complete cycle must be at least 24 months.

This exercise gives us over 300 completed cycles for 46 commodities with an average duration of five years (Table 4.8). Among upswings and downswings, the average (median) duration of the former is about 2½ (2) years, and of the latter about 3 (2½) years (Figure 4.12). However, there are significant variations in the distribution within and across commodity groups. For instance, an average downswing in crude oil lasted 31 months compared with upswings of 33 months. Among nonfuel commodities, downswings typically lasted longer than upswings, especially for food and raw material prices. The latter could be affected by some persistent negative factors, related to weather, plant disease, and so forth, that do not generally affect the prices of energy and metals. With the exception of crude oil and a few metals' prices, the amplitude

[47]The business cycle literature has traditionally distinguished between classical cycles and growth cycles. In the former case, variables of interest are not pretreated or transformed before turning points are identified. In the latter case, variables are filtered prior to the dating analysis—for example, turning points are chosen to capture periods of above- or below-trend growth. Since we are agnostic about the presence of any trend in commodity prices, we focus on commodity prices in levels, distinguishing between periods of expansion and contraction. Even more important, this classical cycle approach avoids the need to choose between alternative filtering or detrending methods, which are known to introduce potentially spurious phase shifts, confounding the turning points algorithm.

Figure 4.12. Duration of Commodity Price Upswings and Downswings
(Months)

Downswings last somewhat longer than upswings for most commodity groups except energy.

Energy | Metals | Food | Raw materials

1. Trough-to-Peak Length (upswing)

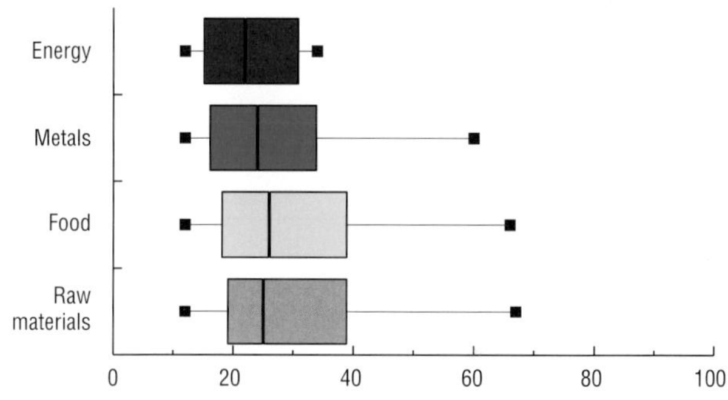

2. Peak-to-Trough Length (downswing)

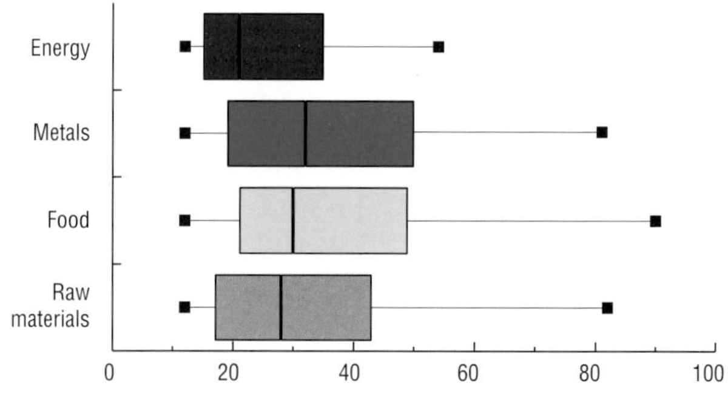

Source: IMF staff calculations.
Note: The vertical line inside each box is the median duration within the group; the left and right edges of each box show the top and bottom quartiles. The distance from the black squares (adjacent values) on either side of the box indicates the range of the distribution within that commodity group, excluding outliers. See Appendix 4.2 for a description of the algorithm used to identify peaks and troughs.

Figure 4.13. Amplitude of Commodity Price Upswings and Downswings
(Change in log real price)

With the exception of energy prices, the amplitude of commodity price downswings is generally greater than that of upswings.

1. Amplitude during Upswings

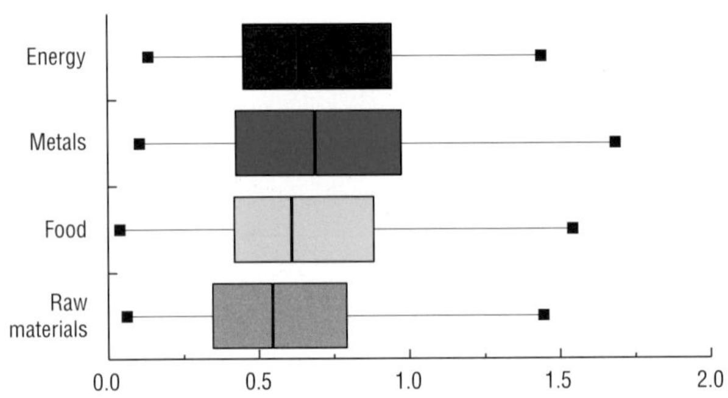

2. Amplitude during Downswings

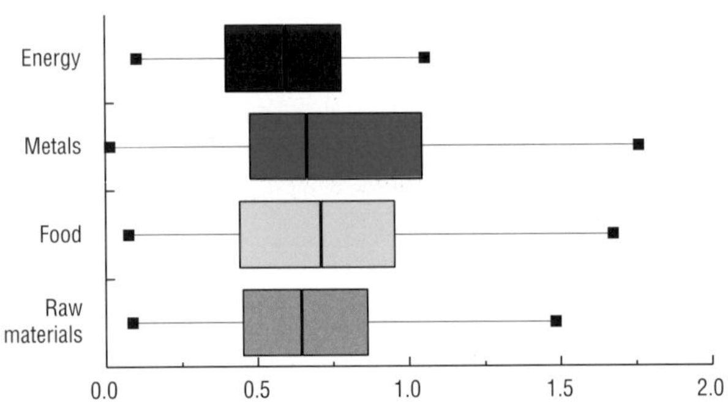

Source: IMF staff calculations.
Note: The vertical line inside each box is the median amplitude within the group; the left and right edges of each box show the top and bottom quartiles. The distance from the black squares (adjacent values) on either side of the box indicates the range of the distribution within that commodity group, excluding outliers. See Appendix 4.2 for a description of the algorithm used to identify peaks and troughs.

of price downswings is slightly greater than that of upswings (Figure 4.13).

The above findings support the related literature (Cashin, McDermott, and Scott, 2002) and earlier literature that found long periods of doldrums punctuated by shorter upward spikes to be characteristic of agricultural commodity prices (Deaton and Laroque, 1992). However, for coffee and cotton, the differences in the length of upswings and downswings are small. This could be related to the fact that both are storable commodities, and therefore inventories may play an important role in smoothing prices in either direction.

Appendix 4.3. Description of the Vector Autoregression Model

In this appendix, we describe the global commodity market model used to determine the sources of commodity price fluctuations described in the section Commodity Market Drivers and Their Macroeconomic Effects.

A Structural Vector Autoregression (VAR) Model for Global Commodity Markets

Drawing on Kilian's (2009) insights into the global oil market, we estimate a structural VAR model of the global commodity market for each of four major commodities: crude oil, copper, coffee, and cotton. Each VAR includes the following set of variables:

$$z'_{i,t} = (\Delta q_{i,t}, \Delta y_t, \Delta k_{i,t}, \Delta s_t, \Delta p_{i,t}), \quad (4.1)$$

where t indexes time, $\Delta q_{i,t}$ is the change in log global production of commodity i, Δy_t is a proxy for the changes in global economic activity, $\Delta k_{i,t}$ is the change in log global inventories of commodity i, Δs_t is the change in the log U.S. real effective exchange rate (REER), and $\Delta p_{i,t}$ is the change in the log real price of commodity i.[48] The structural VAR for each commodity i takes the following form:

[48]For the copper and oil monthly VARs, we take the global industrial production index as a measure of global activity. For agricultural commodities, we use the growth rate of global GDP, since the VARs are estimated at annual frequency. In a robustness check of the results at monthly frequency, we try as an alternative measure of global activity the one proposed by Kilian (2009).

Table 4.8. Statistical Properties of Real Commodity Prices

Commodity	Series Start Date (year: month)	Number of Peak-to-Trough Episodes	Number of Trough-to-Peak Episodes	Peak-to-Trough Average Length	Trough-to-Peak Average Length	Peak-to-Trough Average Amplitude	Trough-to-Peak Average Amplitude	Average Cycle Length	Amplitude between Latest Available Observation and Latest Trough/Peak	Length of the Latest Period
Energy	1973:M2	7	6	31.0	33.0	0.7	0.9	65.3	0.1	17
Coal	1993:M12	4	5	25.0	20.4	0.6	0.7	45.0	–0.1	9
Crude Oil	1973:M2	7	6	31.3	32.7	0.8	0.9	65.3	0.2	15
Natural Gas	1992:M1	6	6	16.7	18.5	0.4	0.5	36.6	0.6	25
Food	1970:M1	7	8	37.9	26.0	0.5	0.4	60.9	–0.2	8
Cocoa	1957:M1	9	10	38.8	28.5	0.9	0.8	63.2	–0.3	22
Coffee	1957:M1	7	8	36.1	40.0	0.9	0.8	77.6	–0.2	6
Tea	1957:M1	10	10	35.7	29.0	0.7	0.6	65.3	0.1	6
Barley	1975:M1	7	8	34.0	24.5	0.7	0.6	57.1	0.0	3
Maize	1957:M1	9	10	39.2	27.9	0.6	0.6	66.6	–0.2	6
Rice	1957:M1	9	8	40.7	33.6	0.8	0.8	76.0	0.2	16
Wheat	1957:M1	10	10	35.6	26.8	0.6	0.5	64.0	0.6	16
Beef	1957:M1	7	7	58.6	31.7	0.5	0.5	81.9	–0.1	6
Lamb	1957:M1	7	8	39.4	39.5	0.5	0.4	72.1	–0.1	11
Poultry	1980:M1	6	6	21.5	40.2	0.2	0.2	67.2	0.0	8
Pork	1980:M1	6	7	37.0	22.1	1.1	0.9	46.3	–0.1	2
Fish	1979:M1	4	5	64.5	25.2	0.9	0.6	82.5	–0.7	6
Shrimp	1957:M1	12	11	24.3	31.2	0.6	0.5	49.5	0.2	18
Coconut Oil	1957:M1	12	13	25.8	25.5	0.9	0.9	51.0	–0.6	8
Olive Oil	1978:M9	4	4	34.5	44.3	0.6	0.5	84.5	–0.8	79
Palm Oil	1957:M1	10	11	27.6	27.7	0.8	0.8	53.7	–0.3	8
Soy Meal	1965:M1	9	10	32.6	25.4	0.7	0.7	55.6	–0.1	4
Soy Oil	1957:M1	9	10	37.3	27.9	0.8	0.7	65.4	–0.1	8
Soybeans	1965:M1	8	8	41.3	25.5	0.7	0.7	70.3	0.2	20
Sunflower Oil	1960:M7	6	7	51.8	39.0	1.0	0.9	89.8	–0.1	4
Bananas	1975:M1	6	6	40.0	31.5	0.8	0.8	69.3	–0.1	8
Fishmeal	1957:M1	9	10	28.4	37.2	0.7	0.7	67.1	–0.4	18
Groundnuts	1980:M1	5	6	37.6	26.5	0.8	0.6	62.0	0.0	3
Oranges	1978:M1	6	5	43.7	23.2	0.9	0.9	69.6	0.3	10
Sugar	1957:M1	7	7	52.9	39.4	1.3	1.2	87.1	–0.1	9
Metals	1970:M1	8	8	33.0	28.5	0.7	0.6	60.1	–0.1	8
Aluminum	1972:M5	6	7	37.5	33.6	0.8	0.7	56.0	–0.2	6
Copper	1957:M1	8	9	42.8	32.8	0.7	0.7	69.0	–0.3	8
Lead	1957:M1	9	10	35.1	26.9	0.9	0.9	59.1	–0.3	6
Nickel	1979:M12	5	6	34.6	27.8	1.1	1.2	57.4	–0.4	8
Steel	1987:M1	4	5	37.3	27.6	0.6	0.7	65.3	–0.1	8
Tin	1957:M1	8	9	44.3	25.0	0.6	0.6	68.0	–0.4	6
Uranium	1980:M1	4	4	39.0	34.0	0.8	1.0	81.0	0.2	19
Zinc	1957:M1	10	11	34.0	26.7	0.7	0.7	58.7	–0.3	8
Gold	1968:M4	6	5	39.0	30.4	0.6	0.7	61.2	1.6	126
Silver	1976:M1	7	7	27.3	32.4	0.8	0.9	57.3	–0.3	6
Raw Materials	1970:M1	5	6	48.6	40.3	0.6	0.5	56.4	–0.3	8
Hardwood Logs	1980:M1	6	6	21.7	32.7	0.6	0.7	59.0	0.5	18
Hardwood, Sawed	1980:M1	5	6	23.2	37.3	0.5	0.6	61.2	0.0	4
Softwood Logs	1975:M1	5	6	45.4	32.3	0.6	0.4	70.4	–0.1	5
Softwood, Sawed	1975:M1	6	6	35.7	34.0	0.5	0.4	72.6	0.1	8
Cotton	1957:M1	12	13	24.9	24.8	0.6	0.5	48.7	–0.7	7
Hides	1957:M1	7	7	58.1	33.9	1.0	1.0	55.7	–0.1	7
Rubber	1957:M1	8	9	41.1	33.9	0.8	0.8	55.3	–0.4	8
Wool	1957:M1	9	9	42.4	29.8	0.7	0.7	69.7	–0.3	4

Source: IMF staff calculations.

Note: All series end in October 2011 (2011:M10) except Crude Oil, which ends in August 2011 (2011:M8). Peaks and troughs are determined according to the Harding and Pagan (2002) algorithm, as described in Appendix 4.2. The length or duration of a phase is quoted in months. The amplitude or height of a phase is expressed in natural log units. See Appendix 4.1 for a full description of the underlying data.

$$z_{i,t} = \alpha_i + \sum_{m=1}^{M_i} A_{m,i}\, z_{i,t-m} + e_{i,t}, \tag{4.2}$$

where $e_{i,t}$ is a mean-zero serially uncorrelated (5×1) vector of innovations, α_i is a (5×1) vector of constants, and $A_{m,i}$ is a (5×5) coefficient matrix for variables at lag m for a total of M_i lags. We assume that the innovations may be expressed as $e_{i,t} = A_{0,i}\,\varepsilon_{i,t}$, where $\varepsilon_{i,t}$ is a vector of mutually and serially uncorrelated structural shocks with variance 1, and $A_{0,i}$ is a coefficient matrix mapping the structural shocks to the contemporaneous reduced-form shocks. To identify production and global demand shocks, we make some assumptions about the structure of the matrix $A_{0,i}$.

Specifically, we assume that the change in a commodity's global production ($\Delta q_{i,t}$) does not respond to other shocks contemporaneously, but only with a lag. This means that the estimated innovation from the production equation represents the structural production shock. In other words, shifts in the demand curve for the commodity due to global activity shocks or other factors do not affect production in the same period, although they may in the next and future periods. This assumption seems justifiable with monthly data, which we have for both crude oil and copper. For coffee and cotton, only annual data on global production are available, but the assumption still seems justifiable, since the production cycles of these commodities are relatively long.[49] Examples of production shocks are unpredictable weather events, such as floods or droughts that adversely impact yields (for agricultural commodities), production disruptions due to unanticipated equipment breakdowns or work stoppages (for oil and metal commodities), or unexpected technological breakthroughs that boost production.

We further assume that global activity (Δy_i) may be contemporaneously affected by the structural production shock, but only with a lag by the other shocks. This means that the estimated innovation from the global activity equation, once the effect of the production shock is accounted for, represents the structural global activity shock. Again, these assumptions seem justifiable at a monthly frequency. Even when the underlying data are annual, it still seems reasonable so long as the commodity in question makes a relatively small contribution to global GDP. Nevertheless, the results for agricultural commodities should be interpreted with caution.[50]

Taken together, these assumptions imply that:

$$e_{i,t} = A_{0,i}\,\varepsilon_{i,t}$$

$$\begin{pmatrix} e^{\Delta q}_{i,t} \\ e^{\Delta y}_{i,t} \\ e^{\Delta k}_{i,t} \\ e^{\Delta s}_{i,t} \\ e^{\Delta p}_{i,t} \end{pmatrix} = \begin{bmatrix} \cdot & 0 & 0 & 0 & 0 \\ \cdot & \cdot & 0 & 0 & 0 \\ \cdot & \cdot & \cdot & \cdot & \cdot \\ \cdot & \cdot & \cdot & \cdot & \cdot \\ \cdot & \cdot & \cdot & \cdot & \cdot \end{bmatrix} \begin{pmatrix} \varepsilon^{\Delta q}_{i,t} \\ \varepsilon^{\Delta y}_{i,t} \\ \varepsilon^{3}_{i,t} \\ \varepsilon^{4}_{i,t} \\ \varepsilon^{5}_{i,t} \end{pmatrix}, \tag{4.3}$$

where 0 indicates that the structural shock does not influence the corresponding reduced-form shock, and a dot indicates that the relationship is unrestricted. Again, under the restrictions shown here, we are able to recover only the structural shocks to production and global activity ($\varepsilon^{\Delta q}_{i,t}$ and $\varepsilon^{\Delta y}_{i,t}$).

Notice that we include changes in a commodity's inventories and in the log U.S. REER in our model, since both variables are known to improve the forecasts of prices and production of oil, metals, and other commodities.[51] Moreover, because they are able to react quickly to new information, these variables likely incorporate forward-looking information about the specific commodity market (in the case of inventories) and global activity (in the case of both inventories and the REER) beyond what is contained in production, activity, and prices themselves. This means that the flow production and global demand shocks identified are more precise in our five-variable VAR than those that are recovered in a three-variable VAR without REER and inventories.

Price fluctuations that are not explained by either demand or production shocks result from a combination of factors we cannot disentangle. Those factors

[49]New coffee trees take about five years to mature (Wellman, 1961). For cotton the assumption might not be as clear cut, since it has a harvest cycle of about a year (Smith and Cothren, 1999).

[50]At annual frequency, a greater concern is that real commodity price changes may correlate with other factors that do drive global GDP but that are not included in the VAR system. This could give rise to an omitted variable bias that would influence the interpretation of the results.

[51]See De Gregorio, González, and Jaque (2005) for the role of the U.S. REER in determining copper prices, and Kilian and Murphy (2010) for the role of crude oil inventories in determining oil prices.

include commodity-specific shocks, but also news about future commodity market developments.[52] This implies that production changes that are either wholly or partly anticipated will show up in the unaccounted-for component of the price, matched to the time the news of the forthcoming change becomes known rather than the time the change actually occurs. An example of such an anticipated production shock might include the recent case of Libya, where political turmoil was expected to disrupt oil production, and thereby the global oil supply, hiking prices in advance.[53] Our results mainly confirm those of Kilian (2009) for the other commodities as well. This means that demand shocks are more important in explaining commodity price fluctuations than unanticipated production shocks.

An alternative exercise we performed also suggests the greater relevance of demand over production shocks, corroborating our VAR results (for the case of oil). We find a positive and significant correlation between revisions in commodity price forecasts and in global real GDP forecasts, suggesting that on balance oil prices are driven by global activity (Figure 4.14). In fact, if forecast revisions in oil prices were more strongly associated with negative commodity production shocks, which adversely affect global GDP, then the commodity price forecast revisions should correlate negatively with global economic activity revisions. We were unable to conduct this analysis for other commodities because of the lack of time series data on Consensus Economics forecasts for other commodity prices.

How much can commodity exporters' GDP be expected to move with changes in the real commodity price driven by global demand or production shocks? To answer this question for copper and oil, we need to make the global demand and production shocks in

Figure 4.14. Correlation of Global Real GDP Growth and Oil Price Forecast Errors

Surprises in global oil price movements correlate positively with surprises in global activity.

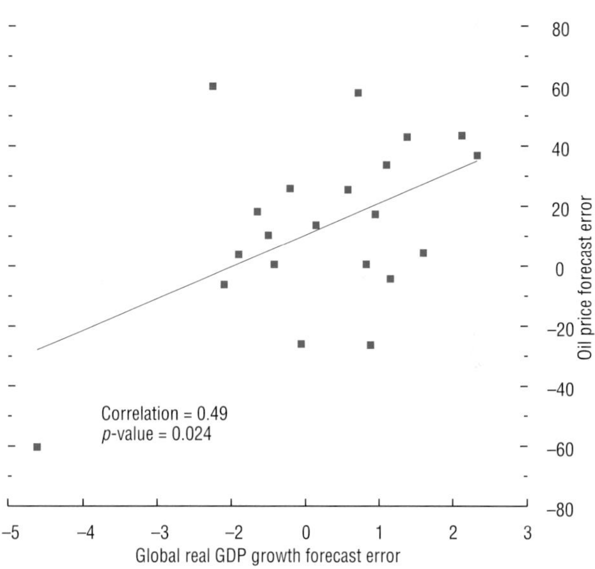

Sources: Consensus Economics and IMF staff calculations.

Note: Forecast errors are calculated as the actual value minus the forecast value. The global real GDP growth forecast error is in percentage points, while the oil price forecast error is in log units times 100. The line shows the least squares line of best fit. See Appendix 4.1 for a full description of the underlying data.

[52]There are various examples of commodity-specific shocks. A preference shift for coffee over tea (as has happened in the past decade) is an example of a shock that is captured by our residual component. Other examples are technological improvements that affect oil intensity, an alternative source of energy, or a global housing boom/bust that affects demand for copper.

[53]The financialization of commodity markets may have exacerbated commodity price sensitivity to news about market prospects (see Chapter 1 in the September 2011 *World Economic Outlook* for a discussion of the role of financialization in influencing commodity prices).

the monthly VAR model comparable with the shocks used in the panel regression, which are at an annual frequency. To do this, we assume that there are a series of shocks for the first 12 months, each equal to the size of the 1 standard deviation shock used in the annual regression. For oil, this results in a 12.2 percent increase in the real price of oil over the year from an annual global demand shock and a 3.8 percent increase from a (negative) global oil production shock. For copper, this is about an 8 percent increase in the real price of copper from a global demand shock and a 3 percent increase from a (negative) global copper production shock. Thus, the elasticity of real GDP for exporters in response to price changes can now be obtained by drawing on the real GDP effects of such commodity price changes over a year (see Table 4.5). For instance for oil, the implied elasticity of real GDP with respect to a global demand-driven oil price change is 0.03 in the impact year and 0.15 three years after the impact year. Although the elasticity with respect to a global production-driven oil price change is comparable in size (0.05 on impact, and –0.14 three years after impact), the effect of the shock on an exporter's GDP is not statistically significant (as seen in Table 4.4).

Robustness

We undertook several robustness checks of our baseline VAR model. These include (1) using the log real commodity price and log U.S. REER in levels instead of differences, since there is no self-evident reason why these variables should be nonstationary; (2) using the real global activity index of Kilian (2009) in the VARs with monthly data instead of the change in log global industrial production; (3) using an alternative deflator for commodity prices based on the SDR basket-weighted wholesale price index instead of the U.S. CPI. Broadly speaking, the results are qualitatively unchanged for all commodities.

Identifying global demand- and production-driven phases

We define a phase as a global demand-driven phase if the contribution to the amplitude of that phase made by the global demand component is at least 25 percent and is bigger than the contribution of the global production component—and vice versa for a production-driven phase. For oil, this results in the identification of four global demand-driven phases, with two downswings (October 1990–December 1993 and October 2000–December 2001) and two upswings (January 1994–October 1996 and January 2002–July 2008). These phases are shown in Figure 4.8. The production-driven phases include one downswing (January 1996–December 1998) and one upswing (January 1999–September 2000).

Appendix 4.4. The Basic Features of the GIMF and Its Application to a Small, Open Oil Exporter

The Global Integrated Monetary and Fiscal model (GIMF) is a microfounded, multicountry, multisector dynamic general equilibrium model that features a wide array of real and nominal types of friction considered relevant in recent macroeconomic literature.[54] For the purposes of this chapter, we use a two-region version of the GIMF comprising a small, open economy oil exporter and the rest of the world, which is a *net* oil importer. The oil sector is modeled along the lines described in Chapter 3 of the April 2011 *World Economic Outlook*. International borrowing by this small, open oil exporter is modeled such that the sovereign risk premium rises with the level of total net debt. In the calibration here—a debt level of 100 percent of GDP—a 20 percentage point decrease (increase) in the debt level would generate a 53 (103) basis point decrease (increase) in the risk premium. In contrast, at a debt level of 30 percent of GDP, a 20 percentage point decrease (increase) in the debt level would generate an 11 (16) basis point decrease (increase) in the risk premium.

Fiscal Policy

The fiscal policy rule is defined by a simple numerical target for the government fiscal-balance-to-GDP ratio that aims to stabilize debt around its long-term target while minimizing output and inflation volatility. It takes the following form:

[54]A full description of the GIMF can be found in Kumhof and others (2010) and Kumhof and Laxton (2009a).

$$gs_t = gs^* + d^{tax}\frac{(\tau_t - \tau_t^{pot})}{GDP_t} + d^{com}\frac{(c_t - c_t^{pot})}{GDP_t}, \quad (4.4)$$

where gs_t is the fiscal-surplus-to-GDP ratio; gs^* is its long-term target; τ_t and c_t are the actual non-oil tax revenues and oil royalties, respectively; and τ_t^{pot} and c_t^{pot} are the *potential* level of tax revenue and oil royalties.[55] Differences between actual and potential values are *gaps*. The coefficients d^{tax} and d^{com} determine the type of rule that is adopted.[56] The choice of d^{tax} and d^{com} provides a continuum of rules, of which three calibrations are discussed in this chapter: (1) a balanced budget rule when d^{tax} and d^{com} are equal to zero, (2) a structural surplus rule when d^{tax} and d^{com} are equal to 1, and (3) a countercyclical rule when d^{tax} and d^{com} are greater than 1.[57]

To implement the surplus-to-GDP ratio prescribed by the rule, the government, in principle, has a menu of fiscal instruments that can be used. However, for simplicity, we assume that the government satisfies the fiscal rule by changing the labor income tax rate. As mentioned, the qualitative results do not change if a different fiscal instrument is used to satisfy the fiscal rule. To determine the optimal rule, alternative calibrations of the fiscal rule parameters are evaluated to find the minimum loss function of the standard deviations of inflation and output. We evaluate the net present value of discounted household utility for the analysis of permanent changes in the price of oil.

[55]More precisely, tax revenues are given by the sum of labor and capital revenues raised in the non-oil sector, plus consumption taxes and transfers. Potential tax revenues are defined as current tax rates times tax bases at the long-term equilibrium. Potential oil revenues are calculated based on long-term values of commodity output and price.

[56]By construction the fiscal surplus and debt-to-GDP ratios are guaranteed to return to their long-term targets because eventually all *gaps* close after the temporary shocks unwind. Kumhof and Laxton (2009b) have shown that this class of rules is particularly well suited to capturing periods of relatively strong (weak) economic conditions and is therefore effective for stabilizing business cycle fluctuations.

[57]For a more detailed discussion of the fiscal rule and the government sector, see Snudden (forthcoming).

Box 4.1. Macroeconomic Effects of Commodity Price Shocks on Low-Income Countries

Commodity price shocks can have large economic, social, and political effects on low-income countries (LICs), whether they are commodity importers or exporters. Most LICs are net importers of food and fuel, and many face substantial import bills for oil products in particular. At the same time, commodities account for more than half of total goods exports for about a third of LICs, implying that swings in commodity prices can lead to large swings in LICs' external balances, creating winners and losers, depending on their trade structure and the specific commodities involved. Global commodity price shocks also tend to create strong inflation and social pressures in LICs because food prices, which account for nearly half of the consumption basket in LICs, are highly correlated with other commodity prices.[1] The resulting squeeze on real household incomes can increase poverty and exert political pressure for mitigating fiscal measures, which in turn could have a negative impact on public finances.

Recent experience highlights the significance of commodity prices for LICs. The spike in food and fuel prices during 2007–08 created significant inflation pressure (Figure 4.1.1) until 2009, when commodity prices slumped during the global financial crisis. In late 2010 and early 2011, LICs faced a renewed surge in global commodity prices. This time, global price increases were more synchronized across commodities than during 2007–08, softening the impact on LICs that export nonfuel commodities. Inflation pressures were also more contained in most LICs, in some cases due to good local harvests. Moreover, about half of LICs took fiscal measures to mitigate the social and inflation impact of the shock, with a median budgetary cost estimated at more than 1 percent of GDP. Measures included food and/or fuel price subsidies (with only a few explicitly targeted to the poor), safety net expenditure measures, and reductions in taxes and import tariffs.

The author of this box is Julia Bersch. It is based on IMF (2011a). The set of low-income countries in this box includes all countries eligible for concessional financing from the IMF under the Poverty Reduction and Growth Trust, except Somalia, which has been excluded due to a lack of data.

[1]This compares with a food share of less than 20 percent in the consumption baskets of Organization for Economic Cooperation and Development countries.

Figure 4.1.1. Headline Inflation in Low-Income Countries and the World Commodity Price Index

Most low-income countries experienced only a modest uptick in headline inflation in 2011.

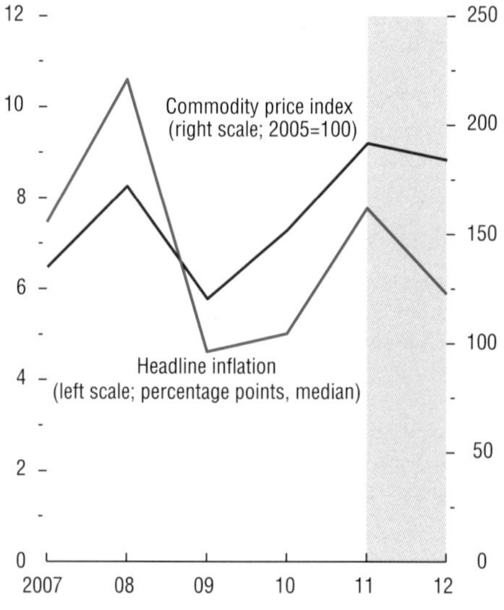

Sources: September 2011 *World Economic Outlook*; and IMF staff estimates.

Simulating the Macroeconomic Effects of Another Spike in Global Commodity Prices

We examine the possible implications of a further global commodity price shock using the IMF's newly developed vulnerability exercise framework for LICs.[2] The scenario is constructed using market expectations embedded in commodity futures options, and the shocks for different commodities are aligned with the prices at the top 7 percent of the expected probability distribution.[3] The impact of the shock is then simulated on a country-by-country basis, taking into account the

[2]Details are in IMF (2011a).

[3]Under this specific scenario, food prices are assumed to increase by 25 percent in 2011 and 31 percent in 2012 relative to the baseline forecast; fuel prices by 21 percent in 2011 and 48 percent in 2012; and metal prices by 21 percent in 2011 and 36 percent in 2012.

Box 4.1. *(continued)*

experience of past shock episodes and countries' different trade structures and consumption baskets.

The scenario analysis illustrates that a further spike in commodity prices could have severe macroeconomic and social consequences. Even though the impact on growth would be modest, the price shock would push 31 million people below the poverty line, mainly because of higher inflation and the absence of efficient social safety nets (Figure 4.1.2). Countervailing fiscal measures, modeled on the basis of past experience, could worsen the median fiscal balance by more than 1 percent of GDP in 2012, with about three-quarters arising from higher oil prices, and the other quarter from higher food prices (Figure 4.1.3).

The external impact of the commodity price scenario would be negative for a large majority of LICs, with a median deterioration in the trade balance of almost 3 percent of GDP (Figure 4.1.4). This deterioration would be driven mainly by higher oil prices, with a smaller impact from higher food prices. Only net oil exporters would benefit from higher prices. Net food exporters would fare only slightly better than net food importers, as both would be negatively affected by higher oil prices. For LICs experiencing a negative terms-of-trade shock, external financing needs could increase by about $9 billion, much of which would be accounted for by a small number of large noncommodity exporters.

Policy Responses to Commodity Price Shocks and Policies to Build Resilience

Many LICs used their macroeconomic policy buffers during the recent crisis, so another global commodity price shock may present difficulties.[4] The standard "first-best" fiscal policy advice of passing on higher prices to consumers may not be feasible in most LICs because they lack comprehensive social safety nets to support the vulnerable. It is also challenging to find pragmatic and cost-effective "second-best" solutions given limited fiscal room. Conducting monetary policy in response to commodity price shocks, in particular food price shocks, also poses significant challenges because policymakers need to choose between accommodating higher inflation and tightening policies that exacerbate real costs. However, even though the direct impact of higher food prices on headline inflation is usually much larger in LICs than in more advanced economies, inflation inertia is relatively low. Hence, an accommodative monetary policy stance is less likely to lead to persistent inflation.[5]

Figure 4.1.2. Inflationary Impact of Higher Commodity Prices in Low-Income Countries in 2011 and 2012
(Percentage points, median)

Under the higher global commodity price scenario, inflation in low-income countries could double relative to the baseline projection, driven mainly by higher food prices.

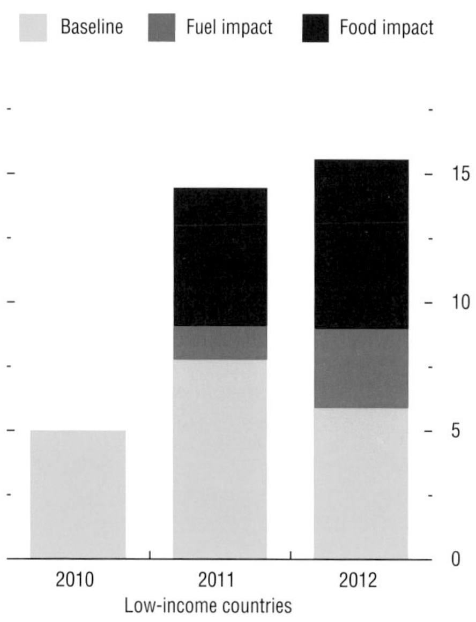

Sources: September 2011 *World Economic Outlook*; and IMF staff estimates.
Note: The scenario gauges the impact of increases in global food and fuel prices compared with the baseline. For food, the price increases used were 25 percent in 2011 and 31 percent in 2012; for fuel, 21 percent and 28 percent, respectively.

[4]For a detailed analysis of how LICs fared during the global crisis, see IMF (2010).

[5]See Chapter 3 of the September 2011 *World Economic Outlook* for an analysis of monetary policy implications of commodity-price-induced inflation in advanced and emerging market economies. This work underscores the importance of "targeting what you can hit" as a way of building monetary policy credibility and delivering better macroeconomic outcomes.

Box 4.1. *(continued)*

Figure 4.1.3. Impact of Higher Commodity Prices on the Fiscal Balance for Low-Income Countries in 2012
(Percent of GDP, median)

The fiscal balance of the median low-income country would deteriorate by more than 1 percent of GDP in 2012, mainly due to higher global fuel prices.

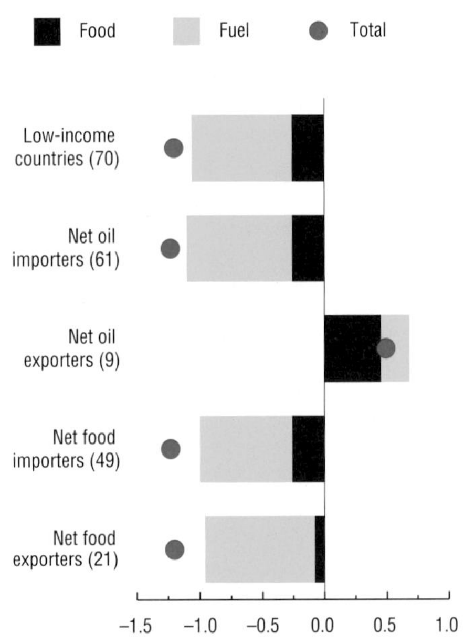

Sources: September 2011 *World Economic Outlook*; and IMF staff calculations.
Note: The estimates of the fiscal impact are calculated using revenue and expenditure elasticities to changes in global food and oil prices. The policy response is assumed to be similar to that in the 2007–08 episode of high global food and oil prices. The calculations are based on the median of differences, so the sum of the components may differ from the total. The numbers in parentheses indicate the sample size (number of economies).

Figure 4.1.4. Impact of Higher Commodity Prices on the Trade Balance for Low-Income Countries in 2012
(Percent of 2010 GDP, median)

Although some countries would gain from higher global commodity prices, for the median low-income country the 2012 trade balance would worsen by almost 3 percent of GDP, with most of the impact coming from oil.

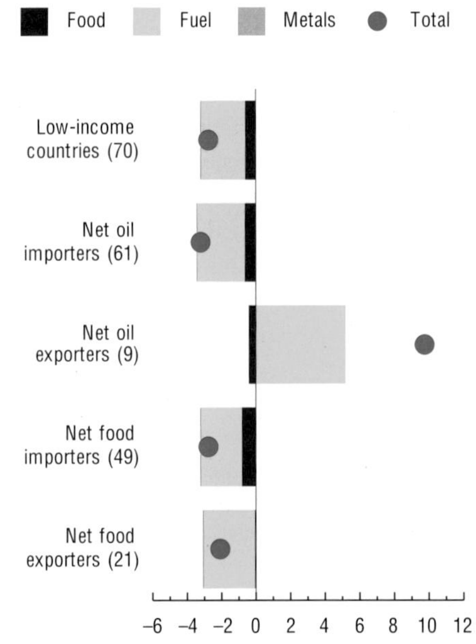

Sources: September 2011 *World Economic Outlook*; and IMF staff calculations.
Note: The scenario simulated the impact of global price increases for food, metal (except gold and uranium), and fuel (31, 36, and 48 percent above the baseline, respectively). The calculations are based on the median of differences, so the sum of the components may differ from the total. The numbers in parentheses indicate the sample size (number of economies).

While coping well with shocks is important, countries can take steps before a crisis occurs to reduce their exposure or create space to prepare for future shocks. Besides building policy buffers during good times, LICs can (1) make their budgets more structurally robust, (2) put in place stronger and more flexible social safety net systems, (3) pursue reforms to encourage domestic saving and deepen their financial sectors, and (4) explore policies to encourage greater diversification in their production and exports.

Box 4.2. Volatile Commodity Prices and the Development Challenge in Low-Income Countries

Recent discoveries of natural resources in many low-income countries (LICs) combine with volatile commodity prices to pose both great opportunities and great challenges for these countries. In many cases, the production horizon is short, meaning that there is only a small window of opportunity to translate resource windfalls into development gains.[1] At the same time, trying to do too much too fast creates its own challenges.

The difficulties are partly analytic. The conventional recommendation, based on the permanent income hypothesis (PIH), is to save most resource income in a sovereign wealth fund, consisting of low-yielding financial assets (for example, Davis and others, 2001; Barnett and Ossowski, 2003; Bems and de Carvalho Filho, 2011). This helps preserve resource wealth, ensure intergenerational equity, and maintain stability.

However, this approach overlooks the longer-term development needs in these capital-scarce, credit-constrained countries. The above analyses generally combine the PIH with an assumption that the capital account is open and that the return to capital—including to public capital—is equal to world interest rates. Substantial empirical evidence, however, indicates that the rate of return to public capital investment in LICs may be well above world interest rates.[2] Limited access to world capital markets and weak domestic tax systems may leave many LICs unable to exploit this opportunity prior to a boom in natural resource exports. Indeed, several studies using models with investment find that front-loading productive public investment can be optimal (Takizawa, Gardner, and Ueda, 2004; van der Ploeg and Venables, 2011; Araujo and others, 2012).

Despite the theoretical appeal of LICs investing their resource income, historical evidence does not generally support the idea that natural resource abundance promotes economic growth—the so-called natural resource curse.[3] For example, the experience of four Latin American countries (Bolivia, Ecuador, Mexico, Venezuela) in the 1970s shows no obvious supply-side effects of growth beyond the resource windfall period (Sachs and Warner, 1999).

All this suggests that LICs should attempt to invest resource income, but with caution. Given the volatile nature of commodity prices, spending resource income as it accrues implies a highly volatile government spending path that aggravates economic instability and makes it harder to execute investment plans efficiently. Moreover, spending a large foreign exchange windfall domestically can lead to real appreciation, which can hurt the traded-goods sector (Dutch disease). Because LICs often suffer from poor governance and production bottlenecks, ramping up public investment is also likely to run into inefficiencies related both to converting resource income to public capital and to absorptive capacity constraints.

To address these potential problems, Berg and others (forthcoming) propose a "sustainable investing" approach, which involves using an investment fund to save some resource income and any increase in nonresource tax receipts.[4] Public investment is scaled up gradually, in line with institutional and absorptive capacity constraints. This approach can minimize the impact of volatile commodity prices in the domestic economy, mitigate Dutch disease effects, and reduce the costs of absorptive capacity constraints. When the magnitude of investment scaling-up is beyond the annuity value of the investment fund, further fiscal adjustments are required.

The author of this box is Susan Yang.

[1]For example, Ghana started to produce oil in 2011, and its reserve from the recent discovery is expected to run out by early 2020 (IMF staff projection).

[2]For example, the median annual rate of return among all the World Bank's projects has risen from about 12 percent during 1987–88 to 24 percent during 2005–07 (World Bank, 2010).

[3]As surveyed by van der Ploeg (2011), although an average negative correlation exists between growth and the export share of natural resources, many countries, such as Botswana and Chile, have escaped the curse.

[4]Collier and others (2010) also propose investing through a sovereign liquidity fund, which mainly aims to smooth the government investment path with resource income. The creation of a separate fund can be thought of as an intellectual construct to help identify the dynamics of an appropriate fiscal policy. In practice, while institutional factors may argue against fragmentation in the form of a separate fund, the insights as far as the trajectory for government saving and spending would remain valid.

Box 4.2. *(continued)*

This approach in effect preserves exhaustible natural resource wealth in the form of public capital that can increase the productivity of private production. Because consumption is also raised permanently, the approach is largely consistent with the PIH principle.

Recent experience among LICs suggests that the vast majority have not followed the PIH-based approach in managing natural resource income (see Appendix II in Baunsgaard and others, forthcoming). For example, during the recent oil price surge, domestically financed capital spending in Chad increased from 2.1 percent of non-oil GDP in 2003 to 12.6 percent during 2008–10 (IMF, 2011b). Timor-Leste, on the other hand, has followed the PIH-based approach for a sustained period. Since oil production began in early 2000, it has built a sizable petroleum fund that reached 886 percent of non-oil GDP in 2011 (IMF, 2012). Capital expenditure remained low before 2011, but the government recently launched a strategic development plan that includes large infrastructure spending to be partially financed by withdrawals from the petroleum fund.

References

Abbas, S. M. Ali, Nazim Belhocine, Asmaa A. ElGanainy, and Mark A. Horton, 2010, "A Historical Public Debt Database," IMF Working Paper 10/245 (Washington: International Monetary Fund).

Adler, Gustavo, and S. Sebastián Sosa, 2011, "Commodity Price Cycles: The Perils of Mismanaging the Boom," IMF Working Paper 11/283 (Washington: International Monetary Fund).

Araujo, Juliana, Bin Grace Li, Marcos Poplawski-Ribeiro, and Luis-Felipe Zanna, 2012, "Current Account Norms in Natural Resource Rich and Capital Scarce Economies" (unpublished; Washington: International Monetary Fund).

Barnett, Steven, and Rolando Ossowski, 2003, "Operational Aspects of Fiscal Policy in Oil-Producing Countries," in *Fiscal Policy Formulation and Implementation in Oil-Producing Countries*, ed. by Jeffrey M. Davis, Rolando Ossowski, and Annalisa Fedelino (Washington: International Monetary Fund).

Barsky, Robert B., and Lutz Kilian, 2002, "Do We Really Know That Oil Caused the Great Stagflation? A Monetary Alternative," *NBER Macroeconomics Annual 2001,* pp. 137–83.

Batini, Nicoletta, and Douglas Laxton, 2005, "Under What Conditions Can Inflation Targeting Be Adopted? The Experience of Emerging Markets," paper presented at "Monetary Policy Under Inflation Targeting," Ninth Annual Conference of the Central Bank of Chile (Santiago), October 20–21.

Baunsgaard, M. Thomas, Mauricio Villafuerte, M. Marcos Poplawski-Ribeiro, and C. Christine Richmond, forthcoming, "Fiscal Frameworks for Natural-Resource-Intensive Developing Countries," IMF Staff Discussion Note (Washington: International Monetary Fund).

Beidas-Strom, Samya, 2011, "Economic Policy Spillovers: Saudi Arabia in the Global Economy," Chapter 6 in *Gulf Cooperation Council Countries: Enhancing Economic Outcomes in an Uncertain Global Economy,* ed. by Samya Beidas-Strom, Tobias N. Rasmussen, and David O. Robinson (Washington: International Monetary Fund), pp. 81–93.

Bems, Rudolfs, and Irineu de Carvalho Filho, 2011, "The Current Account and Precautionary Savings for Exporters of Exhaustible Resources." *Journal of International Economics*, Vol. 84, No. 1, pp. 48–64.

Berg, Andrew, Rafael Portillo, Susan Yang, and Luis-Felipe Zanna, forthcoming, "Public Investment in Resource Abundant, Low-Income Countries," IMF Working Paper (Washington: International Monetary Fund).

Bond, Marion E., 1987, "An Econometric Study of Primary Commodity Exports from Developing Country Regions to the World," *IMF Staff Papers,* Vol. 34, No. 2, pp. 199–227.

Broda, Christian, 2004, "Terms of Trade and Exchange Rate Regimes in Developing Countries," *Journal of International Economics,* Vol. 63, No. 1, pp. 31–58.

Cashin, Paul, C. John McDermott, and Alasdair Scott, 2002, "Booms and Slumps in World Commodity Prices," *Journal of Development Economics*, Vol. 69, No. 1, pp. 277–96.

Céspedes, Luis Felipe, and Andrés Velasco, 2011, "Was This Time Different? Fiscal Policy in Commodity Republics," BIS Working Paper No. 365 (Basel: Bank for International Settlements).

Chen, Yu-Chin, Kenneth S. Rogoff, and Barbara Rossi, 2010, "Can Exchange Rates Forecast Commodity Prices?" *Quarterly Journal of Economics,* Vol. 125, No. 3, pp. 1145–94.

Chinn, Menzie, and Hiro Ito, 2006, "What Matters for Financial Development? Capital Controls, Institutions, and Interactions," *Journal of Development Economics*, Vol. 81, No. 1, pp. 163–92.

———, 2008, "A New Measure of Financial Openness," *Journal of Comparative Policy Analysis*, Vol. 10, No. 3, pp. 307–20.

Collier, Paul, and Benedikt Goderis, 2007, "Commodity Prices, Growth, and the Natural Resource Curse: Reconciling a Conundrum," CSAE Working Paper No. 2007–15 (Oxford: University of Oxford, Center for the Study of African Economies).

Collier, Paul, Frederick van der Ploeg, Michael Spence, and Anthony J. Venables, 2010, "Managing Resource Revenues in Developing Economies," *IMF Staff Papers*, Vol. 57, No. 1, pp. 84–118.

Davis, Jeffrey, Rolando Ossowski, James Daniel, and Steven Barnett, 2001, *Stabilizing and Saving Funds for Non-Renewable Resources: Experience and Fiscal Policy Implications,* IMF Occasional Paper No. 205 (Washington: International Monetary Fund).

Deaton, Angus, 1999, "Commodity Prices and Growth in Africa," *Journal of Economic Perspectives*, Vol. 13, No. 3, pp. 23–40.

———, and Guy Laroque, 1992, "On the Behaviour of Commodity Prices," *Review of Economic Studies,* Vol. 59, No. 1, pp. 1–23.

De Gregorio, José, Hermann González, and Felipe Jaque, 2005, "Fluctuations in the Dollar, Copper Price, and Terms of Trade," Working Paper No. 310 (Santiago: Central Bank of Chile).

De Gregorio, José, and Felipe Labbé, 2011, "Copper, the Real Exchange Rate, and Macroeconomic Fluctuations in Chile," in *Beyond the Curse: Policies to Harness the Power of Natural Resources,* ed. by Rabah Arezki, Amadou N. R. Sy, and Thorvaldur Gylfason (Washington: International Monetary Fund).

Demirel, Ufuk Devrim, 2010, "Macroeconomic Stabilization in Developing Economies: Are Optimal Policies Procyclical?" *European Economic Review,* Vol. 54, No. 3, pp. 409–28.

Eissa, Nada, and Hilary Williamson Hoynes, 2004, "Taxes and the Labor Market Participation of Married Couples: The Earned Income Tax Credit," *Journal of Public Economics,* Vol. 88, Nos. 9–10, pp. 1931–58.

Erten, Bilge, and José Antonio Ocampo, 2012, "Super-Cycles of Commodity Prices Since the Mid-Nineteenth Century," DESA Working Paper No. 110 (New York: United Nations Department of Economic and Social Affairs, February).

Eyzaguirre, Nicolás, Martin Kaufman, Steven Phillips, and Rodrigo Valdés, 2011, "Managing Abundance to Avoid a Bust in Latin America," IMF Staff Discussion Note 11/07 (Washington: International Monetary Fund).

Feenstra, Robert, Robert Lipsey, Haiyan Deng, Alyson Ma, and Hengyong Mo, 2005, "World Trade Flows: 1962–2000," NBER Working Paper No. 11040 (Cambridge, Massachusetts: National Bureau of Economic Research).

Frankel, Jeffrey, 2011, "How Can Commodity Exporters Make Fiscal and Monetary Policy Less Pro-Cyclical?" Harvard Kennedy School Faculty Research Working Paper No. 11-015 (Cambridge, Massachusetts: Harvard Kennedy School).

Hamilton, James D., 2011, "Historical Oil Shocks," in *Handbook of Major Events in Economic History,* ed. by Randall E. Parker and Robert M. Whaples (New York: Routledge).

Harding, Don, and Adrian Pagan, 2002, "Dissecting the Cycle: A Methodological Investigation, *Journal of Monetary Economics,* Vol. 49, No. 2, pp. 365–81.

Heap, Alan, 2005, *China—The Engine of a Commodities Super-Cycle* (New York: Citigroup Smith Barney).

Heenan, Geoffrey, Marcel Peter, and Scott Roger, 2006, "Implementing Inflation Targeting: Institutional Arrangements, Target Design, and Communications," IMF Working Paper 06/278 (Washington: International Monetary Fund).

Husain, Aasim M., Kamilya Tazhibayeva, and Anna Ter-Martirosyan, 2008, "Fiscal Policy and Economic Cycles in Oil-Exporting Countries," IMF Working Paper 08/253 (Washington: International Monetary Fund).

Ilzetzki, Ethan, Carmen M. Reinhart, and Kenneth S. Rogoff, 2008, "The Country Chronologies and Background Material to Exchange Rate Arrangements in the 21st Century: Which Anchor Will Hold?" (unpublished; College Park, Maryland: University of Maryland).

International Monetary Fund (IMF), 2009, "Fiscal Rules—Anchoring Expectations for Sustainable Public Finances," SM/09/274 (Washington). blog-pfm.imf.org/files/paper.pdf

———, 2010, "Emerging from the Global Crisis: Macroeconomic Challenges Facing Low-Income Countries," Policy Paper (Washington).

———, 2011a, *Managing Global Growth Risks and Commodity Price Shocks—Vulnerabilities and Policy Challenges for Low-Income Countries,* Policy Paper (Washington).

———, 2011b, *Chad: Staff Report for the 2011 Article IV Consultation,* IMF Country Report No. 11/302 (Washington).

———, 2012, *Democratic Republic of Timor-Leste: 2011 Article IV Consultation,* IMF Country Report No. 12/24 (Washington).

Kaminsky, Graciela L., 2010, "Terms of Trade Shocks and Fiscal Cycles," NBER Working Paper No. 15780 (Cambridge, Massachusetts: National Bureau of Economic Research).

Keane, Michael P., 2010, "Labor Supply and Taxes: A Survey," Working Paper No. 160 (Sydney: University of Technology, School of Finance and Economics).

Kilian, Lutz, 2009, "Not All Oil Price Shocks Are Alike: Disentangling Demand and Supply Shocks in the Crude Oil Market," *American Economic Review,* Vol. 99, No. 3, pp. 1053–69.

Kilian, Lutz, and Dan Murphy, 2010, "The Role of Inventories and Speculative Trading in the Global Market for Crude Oil," CEPR Discussion Paper No. 7753 (London: Centre for Economic Policy Research).

Kilian, Lutz, Alessandro Rebucci, and Nikola Spatafora, 2009, "Oil Shocks and External Balances," *Journal of International Economics,* Vol. 77, No. 2, pp. 181–94.

Kumhof, Michael, and Douglas Laxton, 2009a, "Fiscal Deficits and Current Account Deficits," IMF Working Paper 09/237 (Washington: International Monetary Fund).

———, 2009b, "Simple, Implementable Fiscal Policy Rules," IMF Working Paper 09/76 (Washington: International Monetary Fund).

———, 2010, "Chile's Structural Fiscal Surplus Rule: A Model-Based Evaluation," *Journal Economía Chilena* (The Chilean Economy), Vol. 13, No. 3, pp. 5–32.

———, Dirk Muir, and Susanna Mursula, 2010, "The Global Integrated Monetary Fiscal Model (GIMF)—Theoretical Structure," IMF Working Paper No. 10/34 (Washington: International Monetary Fund).

Laeven, Luc, and Fabian Valencia, 2008, "Systemic Banking Crises: A New Database," IMF Working Paper No. 08/224 (Washington: International Monetary Fund).

———, 2010, "Resolution of Banking Crises: The Good, the Bad, and the Ugly," IMF Working Paper 10/146 (Washington: International Monetary Fund).

Medas, Paulo, and Daria Zakharova, 2009, "A Primer on Fiscal Analysis in Oil-Producing Countries," IMF Working Paper 09/56 (Washington: International Monetary Fund).

Medina, Leandro, 2010, "The Dynamic Effects of Commodity Prices on Fiscal Performance in Latin America," IMF Working Paper 10/192 (Washington: International Monetary Fund).

Ossowski, Rolando, Mauricio Villafuerte, Paolo A. Medas, and Theo Thomas, 2008, *Managing the Oil Revenue Boom: The Role of Fiscal Institutions,* IMF Occasional Paper No. 260 (Washington: International Monetary Fund).

Radetzki, Marian, 2006, "The Anatomy of Three Commodity Booms," *Resources Policy,* Vol. 31, No. 1, pp. 56–64.

Rafiq, M. Sohrab, 2011, "Sources of Economic Fluctuations in Oil-Exporting Economies: Implications for Choice of Exchange Rate Regimes," *International Journal of Finance and Economics,* Vol. 16, No. 1, pp. 70–91.

Roger, Scott, 2010, "Inflation Targeting Turns 20," *Finance & Development,* Vol. 47, No. 1, pp. 46–49.

Sachs, Jeffrey D., and Andrew M. Warner, 1999, "The Big Push, Natural Resource Booms and Growth," *Journal of Development Economics,* Vol. 59, No. 1, pp. 43–76.

Smith, C. Wayne, and J. Tom Cothren, eds., 1999, *Cotton: Origin, History, Technology, and Production* (New York: Wiley).

Snudden, Stephen, forthcoming, "Designing Fiscal Rules for Oil-Exporting Countries," IMF Working Paper (Washington: International Monetary Fund).

Takizawa, Hajime, Edward Gardner, and Kenichi Ueda, 2004, "Are Developing Countries Better Off Spending Their Oil Wealth Upfront?" IMF Working Paper 04/141 (Washington: International Monetary Fund).

van der Ploeg, Frederick, 2011, "Natural Resources: Curse or Blessing?" *Journal of Economic Literature,* Vol. 49, No. 2, pp. 366–420.

———, and Anthony J. Venables, 2011, "Harnessing Windfall Revenues: Optimal Policies for Resource-Rich Developing Economies," *Economic Journal,* Vol. 121, No. 551, pp. 1–30.

Venables, Anthony J., 2010, "Economic Geography and African Development," *Papers in Regional Science,* Vol. 89, No. 3, pp. 469–83.

Wellman, Frederick L., 1961, *Coffee: Botany, Cultivation, and Utilization* (London: Leonard Hill, and New York: Interscience Publishers).

World Bank, 2010, *Cost-Benefit Analysis in World Bank Projects* (Washington).

IMF EXECUTIVE BOARD DISCUSSION OF THE OUTLOOK, MARCH 2012

The following remarks by the Acting Chair were made at the conclusion of the Executive Board's discussion of the World Economic Outlook *on March 30, 2012*

Executive Directors noted that global prospects are gradually strengthening again, but the recovery remains tenuous and risks are firmly to the downside. Improved activity in the United States and policies in the euro area have reduced the threat of a sharp global slowdown. However, the recent improvements are very fragile, and many sovereigns and banks remain under substantial pressure. The present calm offers a golden opportunity for policymakers to finally get ahead of the crisis. Policymakers must continue implementing the fundamental changes required to achieve lasting stability, which is a prerequisite for healthy growth over the medium term. With output gaps remaining large in advanced economies, policies must also be calibrated with a view to supporting still-weak growth in the near term.

Directors agreed that a weak recovery will likely resume in the major advanced economies, and activity is expected to remain relatively solid in most emerging and developing economies. Nevertheless, growth projections for most regions have been revised down relative to the September 2011 *World Economic Outlook,* mainly on account of the damage done by deteriorating sovereign and banking sector developments in the euro area. The euro area is still projected to go into a mild recession in 2012. Job creation in advanced economies will likely remain sluggish. Growth in emerging and developing economies is also projected to slow in 2012 but is expected to reaccelerate in 2013, helped by easier macroeconomic policies and strengthening foreign demand.

Directors noted that recent policy steps have been crucial in stabilizing euro area financial markets. They cautioned, however, that sovereign risks are still elevated and that pressures on European banks remain, including from sovereign risk, weak euro area growth, high rollover requirements, and the need to strengthen capital cushions. Together, these pressures have induced a broader drive to reduce balance sheet size. While much of the deleveraging to be undertaken by euro area banks will likely be in the form of capital generation or the sale of securities and other noncore assets, some of it will likely lead to a reduced supply of credit to the real economy. Directors agreed that, while further shrinkage of European banks' balance sheets is healthy, the potentially negative consequences of a synchronized large-scale deleveraging remain a concern.

Directors generally agreed that the most immediate concern is that a reintensification of the euro area crisis will trigger a more generalized flight from risk and disorderly deleveraging by European banks. They noted IMF staff stimulations indicating that the recurrence of funding pressures comparable to those seen in fall 2011 could have substantial repercussions for the credit supply in the euro area and beyond.

Directors stressed that other downside risks continue to loom large. Geopolitical uncertainty could trigger a sharp increase in oil prices. Excessively tight macroeconomic policies could also push another major economy into sustained deflation. Additional risks include disruption in global bond and currency markets, with sudden increases in interest rates as a result of high budget deficits and debt, and rapidly slowing activity in some emerging market economies. However, growth could also be better than projected if policies improve further, financial conditions continue to ease, and geopolitical tensions recede.

Directors concurred that policymakers in Europe should build on recent progress and market improvements to push ahead with the implementation of agreed-on reforms and complete the policy agenda. The key priority over the near term is to build a sufficient, robust, and credible firewall in Europe to deter contagion. Further progress on bank restructuring and resolution should complement the increases in bank capital and provisioning already under way. Just as important are far-reaching institutional reforms that remedy design flaws in the economic and monetary union that contributed to the crisis, including policies for further integration that reinforce financial stability. Turning to macroeconomic policies, sufficient fiscal consolidation is taking place, and the pace of near-term fiscal adjustment plans should be calibrated to avoid undue pressure on demand in the near term, without undermining fiscal sustainability. With fiscal multipliers likely on the high side in the weak current environment, a gradual but steady pace of adjustment is preferable to heavy front-loading, as long as financing allows. Given prospects for very low domestic inflation, policy rates should be cut where feasible and unconventional support should be maintained or expanded further when some markets are under acute pressure.

Directors observed that in the United States and Japan there is still an urgent need for strong, sustainable fiscal consolidation paths over the medium term. Also, further monetary easing may be needed in Japan to ensure that it achieves its inflation objective over the medium term. More easing would also be needed in the United States if activity threatens to disappoint. More generally, given the weak growth prospects in the major economies, countries with room for fiscal policy maneuvering can reconsider the pace of consolidation. Others should let automatic stabilizers operate freely for as long as they can readily finance higher deficits. However, putting public finances on a sounder footing over the medium term remains a key requirement for sustainable growth. The environment of high uncertainty also puts a premium on broad and proactive communication strategies to bolster confidence and credibility.

Directors emphasized that beyond the short term, the challenge for advanced economies is to improve the weak medium-term growth outlook. Financial sector reform must address many weaknesses brought to light by the financial crisis, including problems related to institutions considered too big or too complex to fail, the shadow banking system, and cross-border collaboration between bank supervisors. Progress in the design and implementation of credible medium-term adjustment plans is accelerating, but there is still a long way to go, including in the largest economies. The reform of entitlement programs, together with renewed efforts to strengthen fiscal frameworks, is crucial as a way to greatly reduce future spending without significantly harming demand today and can help rebuild market confidence in the sustainability of public finances. Growth-enhancing structural reforms must also be deployed on many fronts.

Directors noted that the key near-term challenge for emerging and developing economies is to appropriately calibrate macroeconomic policies to address the significant downside risks from advanced economies while keeping in check overheating pressures from strong activity, high credit growth, and renewed risks from energy prices. The appropriate response will vary. For economies that have largely normalized macroeconomic policies, the near-term focus should be on responding to adverse spillovers and lower external demand from advanced economies and dealing with volatile capital flows. Other economies should continue to rebuild macroeconomic policy room, which eroded during 2008–09, and strengthen prudential policies and frameworks. The slower pace of fiscal adjustment envisaged in 2012 in emerging market economies is appropriate in the context of weaker growth and given their relatively strong fiscal positions. Monetary policymakers need to be vigilant that oil price hikes do not translate into broader inflation pressures, and fiscal policy must contain damage to public sector balance sheets by targeting subsidies only to the most vulnerable households.

Directors agreed that the latest developments suggest that global current account imbalances are no longer expected to widen, following their sharp reduction during the Great Recession. This is largely because the excessive consumption growth that characterized economies that ran large external deficits prior to the crisis has been wrung out and has not been offset by stronger consumption in surplus economies. Accordingly, the global economy has experienced a loss of demand and growth in all regions relative to the boom years just before the crisis. Rebalancing activity in key surplus economies toward higher consumption, supported by more market-determined exchange rates, would help strengthen their prospects as well as those of the rest of the world.

Directors underscored that austerity alone cannot treat the economic malaise in the major advanced economies. Policies must also ease the adjustments and better target the fundamental problems—weak households in the United States and weak sovereigns in the euro area—by drawing on resources from stronger peers. Policymakers must guard against overplaying the risks related to unconventional monetary support and thereby limiting central banks' room for policy maneuvering. While unconventional policies cannot substitute for fundamental reform, they can limit the risk of another major economy falling into a debt-deflation trap, which could seriously hurt prospects for better policies and higher global growth.

STATISTICAL APPENDIX

The Statistical Appendix presents historical data as well as projections. It comprises five sections: Assumptions, What's New, Data and Conventions, Classification of Countries, and Statistical Tables.

The assumptions underlying the estimates and projections for 2012–13 and the medium-term scenario for 2014–17 are summarized in the first section. The second section presents a brief description of changes to the database and statistical tables. The third section provides a general description of the data and of the conventions used for calculating country group composites. The classification of countries in the various groups presented in the *World Economic Outlook* is summarized in the fourth section.

The last, and main, section comprises the statistical tables. (Statistical Appendix A is included here; Statistical Appendix B is available online.) Data in these tables have been compiled on the basis of information available through early April 2012. The figures for 2012 and beyond are shown with the same degree of precision as the historical figures solely for convenience; because they are projections, the same degree of accuracy is not to be inferred.

Assumptions

Real effective *exchange rates* for the advanced economies are assumed to remain constant at their average levels during the period February 13–March 12, 2012. For 2012 and 2013, these assumptions imply average U.S. dollar/SDR conversion rates of 1.543 and 1.544, U.S. dollar/euro conversion rates of 1.315 and 1.316, and yen/U.S. dollar conversion rates of 79.7 and 79.9, respectively.

It is assumed that the *price of oil* will average $114.71 a barrel in 2012 and $110.00 a barrel in 2013.

Established *policies* of national authorities are assumed to be maintained. The more specific policy assumptions underlying the projections for selected economies are described in Box A1.

With regard to *interest rates,* it is assumed that the London interbank offered rate (LIBOR) on six-month U.S. dollar deposits will average 0.7 percent in 2012 and 0.8 percent in 2013, that three-month euro deposits will average 0.8 percent in 2012 and 2013, and that six-month yen deposits will average 0.6 percent in 2012 and 0.1 percent in 2013.

With respect to *introduction of the euro,* on December 31, 1998, the Council of the European Union decided that, effective January 1, 1999, the irrevocably fixed conversion rates between the euro and currencies of the member countries adopting the euro are as follows:

1 euro	=	13.7603	Austrian schillings
	=	40.3399	Belgian francs
	=	0.585274	Cyprus pound[1]
	=	1.95583	Deutsche mark
	=	15.6466	Estonian krooni[2]
	=	5.94573	Finnish markkaa
	=	6.55957	French francs
	=	340.750	Greek drachma[3]
	=	0.787564	Irish pound
	=	1,936.27	Italian lire
	=	40.3399	Luxembourg francs
	=	0.42930	Maltese lira[1]
	=	2.20371	Netherlands guilders
	=	200.482	Portuguese escudos
	=	30.1260	Slovak koruna[4]
	=	239.640	Slovenian tolars[5]
	=	166.386	Spanish pesetas

[1]Established on January 1, 2008.
[2]Established on January 1, 2011.
[3]Established on January 1, 2001.
[4]Established on January 1, 2009.
[5]Established on January 1, 2007.

See Box 5.4 of the October 1998 *World Economic Outlook* for details on how the conversion rates were established.

What's New

- As in the September 2011 *World Economic Outlook,* fiscal and external debt data for Libya are excluded for 2011 and later due to the uncertain political situation.
- Data for the Syrian Arab Republic are excluded for 2011 onward due to the uncertain political situation.
- As in the September 2011 *World Economic Outlook,* Sudan's data for 2011 exclude South Sudan after July 9. Projections for 2012 and onward pertain to the current Sudan.
- Starting with the April 2012 *World Economic Outlook,* the stock of reserves data previously found in Table A15 of the Statistical Appendix are no longer available. For country-specific historical data on reserves, please refer to the IMF's *International Financial Statistics.*

Data and Conventions

Data and projections for 184 economies form the statistical basis of the *World Economic Outlook* (the WEO database). The data are maintained jointly by the IMF's Research Department and regional departments, with the latter regularly updating country projections based on consistent global assumptions.

Although national statistical agencies are the ultimate providers of historical data and definitions, international organizations are also involved in statistical issues, with the objective of harmonizing methodologies for the compilation of national statistics, including analytical frameworks, concepts, definitions, classifications, and valuation procedures used in the production of economic statistics. The WEO database reflects information from both national source agencies and international organizations.

Most countries' macroeconomic data presented in the *World Economic Outlook* conform broadly to the 1993 version of the *System of National Accounts* (SNA). The IMF's sector statistical standards—the *Balance of Payments Manual, Fifth Edition* (BPM5), the *Monetary and Financial Statistics Manual* (MFSM 2000), and the *Government Finance Statistics Manual 2001* (GFSM 2001)—have all been aligned with the 1993 SNA. These standards reflect the IMF's special interest in countries' external positions, financial sector stability, and public sector fiscal positions. The process of adapting country data to the new standards begins in earnest when the manuals are released. However, full concordance with the manuals is ultimately dependent on the provision by national statistical compilers of revised country data; hence, the *World Economic Outlook* estimates are only partially adapted to these manuals. Nonetheless, for many countries the impact of conversion to the updated standards will be small on major balances and aggregates. Many other countries have partially adopted the latest standards and will continue implementation over a period of years.

Consistent with the recommendations of the 1993 SNA, several countries have phased out their traditional *fixed-base-year* method of calculating real macroeconomic variable levels and growth by switching to a *chain-weighted* method of computing aggregate growth. The chain-weighted method frequently updates the weights of price and volume indicators. It allows countries to measure GDP growth more accurately by reducing or eliminating the downward biases in volume series built on index numbers that average volume components using weights from a year in the moderately distant past.

Composite data for country groups in the *World Economic Outlook* are either sums or weighted averages of data for individual countries. Unless noted otherwise, multiyear averages of growth rates are expressed as compound annual rates of change.[1] Arithmetically weighted averages are used for all data for the emerging and developing economies group except inflation and money growth, for which geometric averages are used. The following conventions apply.

- Country group composites for exchange rates, interest rates, and growth rates of monetary aggregates are weighted by GDP converted to U.S. dollars at market exchange rates (averaged over the preceding three years) as a share of group GDP.
- Composites for other data relating to the domestic economy, whether growth rates or ratios, are weighted by GDP valued at purchasing power parity (PPP) as a share of total world or group GDP.[2]

[1]Averages for real GDP and its components, employment, per capita GDP, inflation, factor productivity, trade, and commodity prices, are calculated based on the compound annual rate of change, except for the unemployment rate, which is based on the simple arithmetic average.

[2]See Box A2 of the April 2004 *World Economic Outlook* for a summary of the revised PPP-based weights and Annex IV of the May 1993 *World Economic Outlook*. See also Anne-Marie Gulde

- Composites for data relating to the domestic economy for the euro area (17 member countries throughout the entire period unless noted otherwise) are aggregates of national source data using GDP weights. Annual data are not adjusted for calendar-day effects. For data prior to 1999, data aggregations apply 1995 European currency unit exchange rates.
- Composites for fiscal data are sums of individual country data after conversion to U.S. dollars at the average market exchange rates in the years indicated.
- Composite unemployment rates and employment growth are weighted by labor force as a share of group labor force.
- Composites relating to external sector statistics are sums of individual country data after conversion to U.S. dollars at the average market exchange rates in the years indicated for balance of payments data and at end-of-year market exchange rates for debt denominated in currencies other than U.S. dollars.
- Composites of changes in foreign trade volumes and prices, however, are arithmetic averages of percent changes for individual countries weighted by the U.S. dollar value of exports or imports as a share of total world or group exports or imports (in the preceding year).
- Unless noted otherwise, group composites are computed if 90 percent or more of the share of group weights is represented.

Classification of Countries

Summary of the Country Classification

The country classification in the *World Economic Outlook* divides the world into two major groups: advanced economies and emerging and developing economies.[3] This classification is not based on strict criteria, economic or otherwise, and it has evolved over time. The objective is to facilitate analysis by providing a reasonably meaningful method of organizing data. Table A provides an overview of the country classification, showing the number of countries in each group by region and summarizing some key indicators of their relative size (GDP valued by PPP, total exports of goods and services, and population).

Some countries remain outside the country classification and therefore are not included in the analysis. Anguilla, Cuba, the Democratic People's Republic of Korea, Montserrat, and South Sudan are examples of countries that are not IMF members, and their economies therefore are not monitored by the IMF. San Marino is omitted from the group of advanced economies for lack of a fully developed database. Likewise, the Marshall Islands, the Federated States of Micronesia, Palau, and Somalia are omitted from the emerging and developing economies group composites because of data limitations.

General Features and Composition of Groups in the *World Economic Outlook* Classification

Advanced Economies

The 34 advanced economies are listed in Table B. The seven largest in terms of GDP—the United States, Japan, Germany, France, Italy, the United Kingdom, and Canada—constitute the subgroup of *major advanced economies,* often referred to as the Group of Seven (G7). The members of the *euro area* and the *newly industrialized Asian economies* are also distinguished as subgroups. Composite data shown in the tables for the euro area cover the current members for all years, even though the membership has increased over time.

Table C lists the member countries of the European Union, not all of which are classified as advanced economies in the *World Economic Outlook*.

Emerging and Developing Economies

The group of emerging and developing economies (150) includes all those that are not classified as advanced economies.

and Marianne Schulze-Ghattas, "Purchasing Power Parity Based Weights for the *World Economic Outlook,*" in *Staff Studies for the World Economic Outlook* (International Monetary Fund, December 1993), pp. 106–23.

[3]As used here, the terms "country" and "economy" do not always refer to a territorial entity that is a state as understood by international law and practice. Some territorial entities included here are not states, although their statistical data are maintained on a separate and independent basis.

The *regional breakdowns* of emerging and developing economies are *central and eastern Europe (CEE), Commonwealth of Independent States (CIS), developing Asia, Latin America and the Caribbean (LAC), Middle East and North Africa (MENA),* and *sub-Saharan Africa (SSA).*

Emerging and developing economies are also classified according to *analytical criteria.* The analytical criteria reflect the composition of export earnings and other income from abroad; a distinction between net creditor and net debtor economies; and, for the net debtors, financial criteria based on external financing sources and experience with external debt servicing. The detailed composition of emerging and developing economies in the regional and analytical groups is shown in Tables D and E.

The analytical criterion by *source of export earnings* distinguishes between categories: *fuel* (Standard International Trade Classification—SITC 3) and *nonfuel* and then focuses on *nonfuel primary products* (SITCs 0, 1, 2, 4, and 68). Economies are categorized into one of these groups when their main source of export earnings exceeds 50 percent of total exports on average between 2006 and 2010.

The financial criteria focus on *net creditor economies, net debtor economies,* and *heavily indebted poor countries* (HIPCs). Economies are categorized as net debtors when their current account balance accumulations from 1972 (or earliest data available) to 2010 are negative. Net debtor economies are further differentiated on the basis of two additional financial criteria: *official external financing* and *experience with debt servicing.*[4] Net debtors are placed in the official external financing category when 66 percent or more of their total debt, on average between 2006 and 2010, is financed by official creditors.

The HIPC group comprises the countries that are or have been considered by the IMF and the World Bank for participation in their debt initiative known as the HIPC Initiative, which aims to reduce the external debt burdens of all the eligible HIPCs to a "sustainable" level in a reasonably short period of time.[5] Many of these countries have already benefited from debt relief and have graduated from the initiative.

[4]During 2006–10, 40 economies incurred external payments arrears or entered into official or commercial bank debt-rescheduling agreements. This group is referred to as *economies with arrears and/or rescheduling during 2006–10.*

[5]See David Andrews, Anthony R. Boote, Syed S. Rizavi, and Sukwinder Singh, *Debt Relief for Low-Income Countries: The Enhanced HIPC Initiative,* IMF Pamphlet Series No. 51 (Washington: International Monetary Fund, November 1999).

Table A. Classification by *World Economic Outlook* Groups and Their Shares in Aggregate GDP, Exports of Goods and Services, and Population, 2011[1]

(Percent of total for group or world)

		GDP		Exports of Goods and Services		Population	
	Number of Economies	Advanced Economies	World	Advanced Economies	World	Advanced Economies	World
Advanced Economies	**34**	**100.0**	**51.1**	**100.0**	**62.4**	**100.0**	**14.9**
United States		37.4	19.1	15.3	9.5	30.4	4.5
Euro Area	17	27.9	14.3	41.5	25.9	32.2	4.8
Germany		7.7	3.9	13.1	8.2	8.0	1.2
France		5.5	2.8	5.6	3.5	6.2	0.9
Italy		4.6	2.3	4.6	2.9	5.9	0.9
Spain		3.5	1.8	3.3	2.0	4.5	0.7
Japan		11.0	5.6	6.8	4.2	12.5	1.9
United Kingdom		5.6	2.9	5.7	3.5	6.1	0.9
Canada		3.5	1.8	3.9	2.4	3.4	0.5
Other Advanced Economies	13	14.5	7.4	26.9	16.8	15.4	2.3
Memorandum							
Major Advanced Economies	7	75.3	38.5	54.9	34.2	72.4	10.8
Newly Industrialized Asian Economies	4	7.7	3.9	15.3	9.5	8.3	1.2
		Emerging and Developing Economies	World	Emerging and Developing Economies	World	Emerging and Developing Economies	World
Emerging and Developing Economies	**150**	**100.0**	**48.9**	**100.0**	**37.6**	**100.0**	**85.1**
Regional Groups							
Central and Eastern Europe	14	7.2	3.5	9.2	3.4	3.0	2.6
Commonwealth of Independent States[2]	13	8.8	4.3	10.7	4.0	4.9	4.2
Russia		6.2	3.0	6.9	2.6	2.4	2.1
Developing Asia	27	51.2	25.1	42.6	16.0	61.5	52.3
China		29.3	14.3	25.1	9.4	23.1	19.6
India		11.6	5.7	5.0	1.9	20.7	17.6
Excluding China and India	25	10.4	5.1	12.6	4.7	17.7	15.1
Latin America and the Caribbean	32	17.8	8.7	14.7	5.5	9.9	8.4
Brazil		5.9	2.9	3.5	1.3	3.3	2.8
Mexico		4.3	2.1	4.4	1.6	1.9	1.7
Middle East and North Africa	20	10.0	4.9	17.3	6.5	6.7	5.7
Sub-Saharan Africa	44	5.0	2.5	5.5	2.1	14.0	11.9
Excluding Nigeria and South Africa	42	2.5	1.2	2.9	1.1	10.4	8.9
Analytical Groups							
By Source of Export Earnings							
Fuel	27	17.8	8.7	28.5	10.7	11.5	9.8
Nonfuel	123	82.2	40.2	71.5	26.9	88.5	75.3
Of Which, Primary Products	22	2.5	1.2	2.7	1.0	5.1	4.4
By External Financing Source							
Net Debtor Economies	121	48.2	23.6	38.9	14.7	60.7	51.6
Of Which, Official Financing	29	2.2	1.1	1.5	0.6	8.8	7.5
Net Debtor Economies by Debt-Servicing Experience							
Economies with Arrears and/or Rescheduling during 2006–10	40	4.8	2.4	4.2	1.6	9.4	8.0
Other Net Debtor Economies	81	43.4	21.2	34.7	13.1	51.3	43.6
Other Groups							
Heavily Indebted Poor Countries	38	2.3	1.1	1.9	0.7	10.7	9.1

[1]The GDP shares are based on the purchasing-power-parity valuation of economies' GDP. The number of economies comprising each group reflects those for which data are included in the group aggregates.

[2]Georgia and Mongolia, which are not members of the Commonwealth of Independent States, are included in this group for reasons of geography and similarities in economic structure.

Table B. Advanced Economies by Subgroup

Major Currency Areas		
United States		
Euro Area		
Japan		
Euro Area		
Austria	Germany	Netherlands
Belgium	Greece	Portugal
Cyprus	Ireland	Slovak Republic
Estonia	Italy	Slovenia
Finland	Luxembourg	Spain
France	Malta	
Newly Industrialized Asian Economies		
Hong Kong SAR[1]	Singapore	
Korea	Taiwan Province of China	
Major Advanced Economies		
Canada	Italy	United States
France	Japan	
Germany	United Kingdom	
Other Advanced Economies		
Australia	Israel	Sweden
Czech Republic	Korea	Switzerland
Denmark	New Zealand	Taiwan Province of China
Hong Kong SAR[1]	Norway	
Iceland	Singapore	

[1]On July 1, 1997, Hong Kong was returned to the People's Republic of China and became a Special Administrative Region of China.

Table C. European Union

Austria	Germany	Netherlands
Belgium	Greece	Poland
Bulgaria	Hungary	Portugal
Cyprus	Ireland	Romania
Czech Republic	Italy	Slovak Republic
Denmark	Latvia	Slovenia
Estonia	Lithuania	Spain
Finland	Luxembourg	Sweden
France	Malta	United Kingdom

Table D. Emerging and Developing Economies by Region and Main Source of Export Earnings

	Fuel	Nonfuel Primary Products
Commonwealth of Independent States[1]		
	Azerbaijan	Mongolia
	Kazakhstan	Uzbekistan
	Russia	
	Turkmenistan	
Developing Asia		
	Brunei Darussalam	Papua New Guinea
	Timor-Leste	Solomon Islands
Latin America and the Caribbean		
	Ecuador	Bolivia
	Trinidad and Tobago	Chile
	Venezuela	Guyana
		Peru
		Suriname
Middle East and North Africa		
	Algeria	Mauritania
	Bahrain	
	Islamic Republic of Iran	
	Iraq	
	Kuwait	
	Libya	
	Oman	
	Qatar	
	Saudi Arabia	
	Sudan	
	United Arab Emirates	
	Republic of Yemen	
Sub-Saharan Africa		
	Angola	Burkina Faso
	Chad	Burundi
	Republic of Congo	Central African Republic
	Equatorial Guinea	Democratic Republic of Congo
	Gabon	Guinea
	Nigeria	Guinea-Bissau
		Malawi
		Mali
		Mozambique
		Sierra Leone
		Zambia
		Zimbabwe

[1]Mongolia, which is not a member of the Commonwealth of Independent States, is included in this group for reasons of geography and similarities in economic structure.

Table E. Emerging and Developing Economies by Region, Net External Position, and Status as Heavily Indebted Poor Countries

	Net External Position		Heavily Indebted Poor Countries[2]
	Net Creditor	Net Debtor[1]	
Central and Eastern Europe			
Albania		*	
Bosnia and Herzegovina		*	
Bulgaria		*	
Croatia		*	
Hungary		*	
Kosovo		*	
Latvia		*	
Lithuania		*	
Former Yugoslav Republic of Macedonia		*	
Montenegro		*	
Poland		*	
Romania		*	
Serbia		*	
Turkey		*	
Commonwealth of Independent States[3]			
Armenia		*	
Azerbaijan	*		
Belarus		*	
Georgia		*	
Kazakhstan		*	
Kyrgyz Republic		•	
Moldova		*	
Mongolia		•	
Russia	*		
Tajikistan		•	
Turkmenistan	*		
Ukraine		*	
Uzbekistan	*		
Developing Asia			
Islamic Republic of Afghanistan		•	•
Bangladesh		•	
Bhutan		*	
Brunei Darussalam	*		
Cambodia		*	
China	*		
Republic of Fiji		*	
India		*	
Indonesia	*		
Kiribati		•	
Lao People's Democratic Republic		*	
Malaysia	*		
Maldives		*	
Myanmar		*	
Nepal		*	
Pakistan		*	
Papua New Guinea	*		
Philippines		*	
Samoa		*	
Solomon Islands		*	
Sri Lanka		*	
Thailand	*		
Timor-Leste	*		
Tonga		*	
Tuvalu		•	
Vanuatu		*	
Vietnam		*	
Latin America and the Caribbean			
Antigua and Barbuda		*	
Argentina		*	
The Bahamas		*	
Barbados		*	
Belize		*	
Bolivia	*		•
Brazil		*	
Chile		*	
Colombia		*	
Costa Rica		*	
Dominica		*	
Dominican Republic		*	
Ecuador		•	
El Salvador		*	
Grenada		*	
Guatemala		*	
Guyana		•	•
Haiti		•	•
Honduras		*	•
Jamaica		•	
Mexico		*	

Table E. *(concluded)*

	Net External Position		Heavily Indebted Poor Countries[2]
	Net Creditor	Net Debtor[1]	
Nicaragua		*	•
Panama		*	
Paraguay		*	
Peru		*	
St. Kitts and Nevis		*	
St. Lucia		*	
St. Vincent and the Grenadines		•	
Suriname		•	
Trinidad and Tobago	*		
Uruguay		*	
Venezuela	*		
Middle East and North Africa			
Algeria	*		
Bahrain	*		
Djibouti		*	
Egypt		*	
Islamic Republic of Iran	*		
Iraq	*		
Jordan		*	
Kuwait	*		
Lebanon		*	
Libya	*		
Mauritania		*	•
Morocco		*	
Oman	*		
Qatar	*		
Saudi Arabia	*		
Sudan		*	*
Syrian Arab Republic		•	
Tunisia		*	
United Arab Emirates	*		
Republic of Yemen		*	
Sub-Saharan Africa			
Angola	*		
Benin		*	•
Botswana	*		
Burkina Faso		•	•
Burundi		•	•
Cameroon		*	•
Cape Verde		*	
Central African Republic		•	•
Chad		*	*
Comoros		•	*
Democratic Republic of Congo		•	•
Republic of Congo		•	•
Côte d'Ivoire		*	*
Equatorial Guinea		*	
Eritrea		•	*
Ethiopia		•	•
Gabon	*		
The Gambia		*	•
Ghana		•	•
Guinea		*	*
Guinea-Bissau		•	•
Kenya		*	
Lesotho		*	
Liberia		*	•
Madagascar		*	•
Malawi		•	•
Mali		•	•
Mauritius		*	
Mozambique		*	•
Namibia	*		
Niger		*	•
Nigeria	*		
Rwanda		•	•
São Tomé and Príncipe		•	•
Senegal		*	•
Seychelles		*	
Sierra Leone		*	•
South Africa		*	
Swaziland		*	
Tanzania		*	•
Togo		•	•
Uganda		*	•
Zambia		*	•
Zimbabwe		*	

[1]Dot instead of star indicates that the net debtor's main external finance source is official financing.

[2]Dot instead of star indicates that the country has reached the completion point.

[3]Georgia and Mongolia, which are not members of the Commonwealth of Independent States, are included in this group for reasons of geography and similarities in economic structure.

Box A1. Economic Policy Assumptions Underlying the Projections for Selected Economies

Fiscal Policy Assumptions

The short-term fiscal policy assumptions used in the *World Economic Outlook* (WEO) are based on officially announced budgets, adjusted for differences between the national authorities and the IMF staff regarding macroeconomic assumptions and projected fiscal outturns. The medium-term fiscal projections incorporate policy measures that are judged likely to be implemented. In cases where the IMF staff has insufficient information to assess the authorities' budget intentions and prospects for policy implementation, an unchanged structural primary balance is assumed unless indicated otherwise. Specific assumptions used in some of the advanced economies follow. (See also Tables B5 to B9 in the online section of the Statistical Appendix for data on fiscal net lending/borrowing and structural balances.[1])

Argentina: The 2012 forecasts are based on the 2011 outturn and IMF staff assumptions. For the outer years, the IMF staff assumes unchanged policies.

Australia: Fiscal projections are based IMF staff projections and the 2011–12 budget, 2011–12 mid-year economic and fiscal outlook, and the Australian Bureau of Statistics.

Austria: Projections take the federal financial framework 2013–16 as well as associated further implementation needs and risks into account.

[1]The output gap is actual minus potential output, as a percent of potential output. Structural balances are expressed as a percent of potential output. The structural balance is the actual net lending/borrowing minus the effects of cyclical output from potential output, corrected for one-time and other factors, such as asset and commodity prices and output composition effects. Changes in the structural balance consequently include effects of temporary fiscal measures, the impact of fluctuations in interest rates and debt-service costs, and other noncyclical fluctuations in net lending/borrowing. The computations of structural balances are based on IMF staff estimates of potential GDP and revenue and expenditure elasticities. (See the October 1993 *World Economic Outlook*, Annex I.) Net debt is defined as gross debt minus financial assets of the general government, which include assets held by the social security insurance system. Estimates of the output gap and of the structural balance are subject to significant margins of uncertainty.

Belgium: IMF staff projections for 2012 and beyond are based on unchanged policies.

Brazil: For 2012 the projection is based on the budget and subsequent updates to plans announced by the authorities. In this and outer years, the IMF staff assumes adherence to the announced primary target and further increases in public investment in line with the authorities' intentions.

Canada: Projections use the baseline forecasts in the Economic Action Plan 2012, Jobs, Growth, and Long-Term Prosperity, March 29, 2012. The IMF staff makes some adjustments to this forecast for differences in macroeconomic projections. The IMF staff forecast also incorporates the most recent data releases from Finance Canada (the January 2012 Fiscal Monitor, updated March 29, 2012) and Statistics Canada, including federal, provincial, and territorial budgetary outturns through the end of the fourth quarter of 2011.

China: For 2011, the government is assumed to continue and complete the stimulus program it announced in late 2008. The withdrawal of the stimulus is assumed to start in 2011, resulting in a negative fiscal impulse of about 1½ percent of GDP. For 2012, the government is assumed to slow the pace of fiscal consolidation; the fiscal impulse is assumed to be neutral.

Denmark: Estimates for 2012–13 are aligned with the latest official budget estimates, adjusted where appropriate for the IMF staff's macroeconomic assumptions. For 2014–17, the projections incorporate key features of the medium-term fiscal plan as embodied in the authorities' 2011 Convergence Program submitted to the European Union.

France: Estimates for 2011 are based on the preliminary data on outturn for the central government only. Projections for 2012 and beyond reflect the authorities' 2011–14 multiyear budget, adjusted for two fiscal packages and differences in assumptions on macroeconomic and financial variables, and revenue projections.

Germany: The estimates for 2011 are preliminary estimates from the Federal Statistical Office of Germany. The IMF staff's projections for 2012 and beyond reflect the authorities' adopted core federal government budget plan adjusted for the differences

Box A1. *(continued)*

in the IMF staff's macroeconomic framework and staff assumptions about fiscal developments in state and local governments, the social insurance system, and special funds. The projections also incorporate the authorities' plans for a 2013–14 tax reduction. The estimate of gross debt includes portfolios of impaired assets and noncore business transferred to institutions that are winding up as well as other financial sector and EU support operations.

Greece: Macroeconomic, monetary, and fiscal projections for 2012 and the medium term are consistent with the policies agreed to between the IMF staff and the authorities in the context of the Extended Fund Facility. The data include fiscal data revisions for 2006–09. These revisions rectify a number of earlier statistical shortfalls. First, government-controlled enterprises whose sales cover less than 50 percent of production costs have been reclassified into the general government sector, in line with Eurostat guidelines. A total of 17 such enterprises were identified and included, including a number of large loss-making entities. The inclusion implies that the debt of these entities (7¼ percent of GDP) is now included in headline general government debt data and that their annual losses increase the annual deficit (to the extent that their called guarantees were not already reflected). Second, the revisions reflect better information on arrears (including tax refund arrears, arrears on lump-sum payments to retiring civil servant pensioners, and arrears to health sector suppliers) and corrections of social security balances as a result of corrected imputed interest payments, double counting of revenues, and other inaccuracies. Finally, new information on swaps also became available and helps further explain the upward revision in debt data.

Hong Kong SAR: Projections are based on the authorities' medium-term fiscal projections.

Hungary: Fiscal projections include IMF staff projections of the macroeconomic framework and of the impact of recent legislative measures as well as fiscal policy plans announced at the end of December 2011.

India: Historical data are based on budgetary execution data. Projections are based on available information on the authorities' fiscal plans, with adjustments for IMF staff assumptions. Subnational data are incorporated with a lag of up to two years; general government data are thus finalized well after central government data. IMF and Indian presentations differ, particularly regarding divestment and license auction proceeds, net versus gross recording of revenues in certain minor categories, and some public sector lending.

Indonesia: The 2011 central government deficit was lower than expected (1.1 percent of GDP), reflecting underspending, particularly on public investment. The 2012 central government deficit is estimated at 1.0 percent of GDP, lower than the revised budget estimate of 1.5 percent of GDP. This reflects current plans to raise domestic fuel prices by 33 percent. However, because the system of fuel subsidies remains unchanged, increasing oil prices will have a negative budgetary impact in the absence of a comprehensive fuel subsidy reform. The low projected budget deficit also reflects ongoing budget execution problems. Fiscal projections for 2013–17 are built around key policy reforms needed to support economic growth—namely, enhancing budget implementation to ensure fiscal policy effectiveness, reducing energy subsidies through gradual administrative price increases, and continuous revenue mobilization efforts to create room for infrastructure development.

Ireland: Fiscal projections are based on the 2012 budget and the Medium-Term Fiscal Statement (published November 2011), which commits to a €12.4 billion consolidation over 2012–15. The fiscal projections are adjusted for differences between the macroeconomic projections of the IMF staff and those of the Irish authorities.

Italy: Fiscal projections incorporate the impact of the government's announced fiscal adjustment package (July 2010 measures covering 2011–13; July–August 2011 measures covering 2011–14: and December 2011 measures covering 2012–14). The estimates for the 2011 outturn are preliminary. The IMF staff projections are based on the authorities' estimates of the policy scenario (as derived, in part, by the IMF staff), including the above-mentioned medium-term fiscal consolidation packages and adjusted mainly for differences in macroeconomic assumptions and for less optimistic assumptions

Box A1. *(continued)*

concerning the impact of revenue administration measures. After 2014, a constant cyclically adjusted primary balance net of one-time items is assumed.

Japan: The projections assume fiscal measures already announced by the government (except for consumption tax increases) and gross earthquake reconstruction spending. The medium-term projections assume that expenditure and revenue of the general government are adjusted in line with current underlying demographic and economic trends (excluding fiscal stimulus and reconstruction spending).

Korea: Fiscal projections assume that fiscal policies will be implemented in 2012 as announced by the government. Projections of expenditure for 2012 are in line with the budget. Revenue projections reflect the IMF staff's macroeconomic assumptions, adjusted for discretionary revenue-raising measures included in the 2009–11 tax revision plans. The medium-term projections assume that the government will continue with its consolidation plans and balance the budget (excluding social security funds) by 2013, consistent with the government's medium-term goal.

Mexico: Fiscal projections for 2012 are broadly in line with the approved budget, while projections for 2013 onward assume compliance with the balanced budget rule.

Netherlands: Fiscal projections for 2011–15 are based on the authorities' Bureau for Economic Policy Analysis budget projections, after adjusting for differences in macroeconomic assumptions. For 2016–17, the projections assume that fiscal consolidation continues at about the same pace as in 2015.

New Zealand: Fiscal projections are based on the authorities' 2011 budget and IMF staff estimates. The New Zealand fiscal accounts switched to New Zealand International Financial Reporting Standards in Budget 2007/08. Backdated data have been released back to 1997.

Portugal: Projections reflect the authorities' commitments under the EU- and IMF-supported program for 2012–13 and IMF staff projections after that.

Russia: Projections for 2012–14 are based on the non-oil deficit as a percent of GDP implied by the 2012–14 medium-term budget and IMF staff revenue projections. The IMF staff assumes an unchanged non-oil federal government balance as a percent of GDP during 2015–17.

Saudi Arabia: The authorities base their budget on a conservative assumption for oil prices with adjustments to expenditure allocations considered in the event that revenues exceed budgeted amounts. IMF staff projections of oil revenues are based on WEO baseline oil prices discounted by approximately 5 percent, reflecting the higher sulfur content in Saudi crude oil. On the expenditure side, wages are assumed to rise at a natural rate of increase in the medium term with adjustments for recently announced changes in the wage structure. In 2013 and 2016, 13th-month pay is awarded based on the lunar calendar. Transfers increased in 2011, primarily due to a one-time transfer to specialized credit institutions. Interest payments are projected to decline in line with the authorities' policy of reducing the outstanding stock of public debt. Capital spending is in line with the priorities established in the authorities' Ninth Development Plan, and recently announced capital spending on housing is assumed to start in 2012 and continue over the medium term.

Singapore: For fiscal year 2012/13, projections are based on budget numbers. For the remainder of the projection period, the IMF staff assumes unchanged policies.

South Africa: Fiscal projections are based on the authorities' 2012 budget and policy intentions stated in the Budget Review, published February 22, 2012.

Spain: The 2011 numbers are based on the authorities' estimated outturns for the general government for the year. For 2012 and beyond, the projections are based on measures implemented during the course of 2012 and the authorities' deficit target for 2012. The draft budget for 2012 was not available at the time of the IMF staff forecast.

Sweden: Fiscal projections for 2012 are broadly in line with the authorities' projections. The impact of cyclical developments on the fiscal accounts is calculated using the Organization for Economic Cooperation and Development's latest semi-elasticity.

Box A1. *(continued)*

Switzerland: Projections for 2010–17 are based on IMF staff calculations, which incorporate measures to restore balance in the federal accounts and strengthen social security finances.

Turkey: Fiscal projections assume that current expenditures will be in line with the authorities' 2012–14 Medium-Term Program but that capital expenditures will be exceeded given projects initiated in 2011.

United Kingdom: Fiscal projections are based on the authorities' 2012 budget announced in March 2012 and the Economic and Fiscal Outlook by the Office for Budget Responsibility published along with the budget. These projections incorporate the announced medium-term consolidation plans from 2012 onward. The projections are adjusted for differences in forecasts of macroeconomic and financial variables and exclude the temporary effects of financial sector interventions and the effect on public sector net investment in 2012–13 of transferring assets from the Royal Mail Pension Plan to the public sector.

United States: Fiscal projections are based on the January 2012 Congressional Budget Office baseline, adjusted for IMF staff policy and macroeconomic assumptions. The key near-term policy assumptions include a continuation of the payroll tax cut during 2012, an extension of emergency unemployment benefits into 2013 (one year beyond the current law), and automatic sequestration of spending beginning in 2013—triggered by the November failure of the Joint Select Committee on Deficit Reduction. In the medium term, the IMF staff assumes that Congress will continue to make regular adjustments to the alternative minimum tax parameters and to Medicare payments (DocFix) and will extend certain traditional programs (such as the research and development tax credit). Tax cuts for the middle class enacted under President George W. Bush are projected to be extended permanently, but Bush-era tax cuts for higher-income taxpayers are expected to be allowed to expire in 2014 (one year later than under current law). The fiscal projections are adjusted to reflect the IMF staff's forecasts of key macroeconomic and financial variables and different accounting treatment of the financial sector support and are converted to the general government basis.

Monetary Policy Assumptions

Monetary policy assumptions are based on the established policy framework in each country. In most cases, this implies a nonaccommodative stance over the business cycle: official interest rates will increase when economic indicators suggest that inflation will rise above its acceptable rate or range; they will decrease when indicators suggest that prospective inflation will not exceed the acceptable rate or range, that prospective output growth is below its potential rate, and that the margin of slack in the economy is significant. On this basis, the London interbank offered rate (LIBOR) on six-month U.S. dollar deposits is assumed to average 0.7 percent in 2012 and 0.8 percent in 2013 (see Table 1.1). The rate on three-month euro deposits is assumed to average 0.8 percent in 2012 and 2013. The interest rate on six-month Japanese yen deposits is assumed to average 0.6 percent in 2012 and 0.1 percent in 2013.

Australia: Monetary policy assumptions are in line with market expectations.

Brazil: Monetary policy assumptions are based on current policy and are consistent with the gradual convergence of inflation toward the middle of the target range by the end of 2012.

Canada: Monetary policy assumptions are in line with market expectations.

China: Monetary tightening built into the baseline is consistent with authorities' forecast of 14 percent year-over-year growth for M2 in 2012.

Denmark: The monetary policy is to maintain the peg to the euro.

Euro area: Monetary policy assumptions for euro area member countries are in line with market expectations.

Hong Kong SAR: The IMF staff assumes that the Currency Board system remains intact and projects broad money growth based on the past relationship with nominal GDP.

India: The policy (interest) rate assumption is based on the average of market forecasts.

Box A1. *(concluded)*

Indonesia: Bank Indonesia is expected use a combination of macroprudential measures and policy rate increases to limit the second-round impacts of proposed increases in fuel prices.

Japan: The current monetary policy conditions are maintained for the projection period, and no further tightening or loosening is assumed.

Korea: Monetary policy assumptions incorporate a hike of 25 basis points in the second half of 2012 and two hikes of 25 basis points each over the course of 2013.

Mexico: Monetary assumptions are consistent with attaining the inflation target.

Russia: Monetary projections assume unchanged policies, as indicated in recent statements by the Central Bank of Russia. Specifically, policy rates are assumed to remain at the current levels, with limited interventions in the foreign exchange markets.

Saudi Arabia: Monetary policy projections are based on the continuation of the exchange rate peg to the U.S. dollar.

South Africa: Monetary projections are based on the assumption that the authorities follow an estimated policy reaction function.

Sweden: Monetary projections are in line with Riksbank projections.

Switzerland: Monetary policy variables reflect historical data from the national authorities and the market.

Turkey: Broad money and the long-term bond yield are based on IMF staff projections. The short-term deposit rate is projected to evolve with a constant spread against the interest rate of a similar U.S. instrument.

United Kingdom: The projections assume unchanged policy rates through 2013 and a modest amount of additional quantitative easing in 2012—assumptions that are roughly in line with market expectations.

United States: Given the outlook for inflation and sluggish growth, the IMF staff expects the federal funds target to remain near zero until the fourth quarter of 2014. This assumption is consistent with the Federal Open Market Committee's statement following its January 2012 meeting (and reaffirmed at their February meeting) that economic conditions are likely to warrant an exceptionally low federal funds rate at least through late 2014.

List of Tables

Output

Inflation

Financial Policies

Foreign Trade

Current Account Transactions

Balance of Payments and External Financing

Flow of Funds

Medium-Term Baseline Scenario

Table A1. Summary of World Output[1]
(Annual percent change)

	Average									Projections		
	1994–2003	2004	2005	2006	2007	2008	2009	2010	2011	2012	2013	2017
World	**3.4**	**4.9**	**4.5**	**5.2**	**5.4**	**2.8**	**–0.6**	**5.3**	**3.9**	**3.5**	**4.1**	**4.7**
Advanced Economies	**2.8**	**3.1**	**2.6**	**3.0**	**2.8**	**0.0**	**–3.6**	**3.2**	**1.6**	**1.4**	**2.0**	**2.7**
United States	3.3	3.5	3.1	2.7	1.9	–0.3	–3.5	3.0	1.7	2.1	2.4	3.3
Euro Area	2.2	2.2	1.7	3.3	3.0	0.4	–4.3	1.9	1.4	–0.3	0.9	1.7
Japan	0.9	2.4	1.3	1.7	2.2	–1.0	–5.5	4.4	–0.7	2.0	1.7	1.1
Other Advanced Economies[2]	3.8	4.1	3.4	3.9	4.2	0.8	–2.2	4.5	2.5	2.1	3.0	3.3
Emerging and Developing Economies	**4.4**	**7.5**	**7.3**	**8.2**	**8.7**	**6.0**	**2.8**	**7.5**	**6.2**	**5.7**	**6.0**	**6.3**
Regional Groups												
Central and Eastern Europe	3.4	7.3	5.9	6.4	5.4	3.2	–3.6	4.5	5.3	1.9	2.9	4.0
Commonwealth of Independent States[3]	0.6	8.2	6.7	8.8	9.0	5.4	–6.4	4.8	4.9	4.2	4.1	4.2
Developing Asia	7.0	8.5	9.5	10.3	11.4	7.8	7.1	9.7	7.8	7.3	7.9	7.9
Latin America and the Caribbean	2.5	6.0	4.7	5.7	5.8	4.2	–1.6	6.2	4.5	3.7	4.1	4.0
Middle East and North Africa	3.9	6.2	5.6	6.1	5.6	4.7	2.7	4.9	3.5	4.2	3.7	4.4
Sub-Saharan Africa	4.0	7.1	6.2	6.4	7.1	5.6	2.8	5.3	5.1	5.4	5.3	5.5
Memorandum												
European Union	2.6	2.6	2.2	3.6	3.4	0.5	–4.2	2.0	1.6	0.0	1.3	2.1
Analytical Groups												
By Source of Export Earnings												
Fuel	2.4	8.0	6.8	7.6	7.4	5.0	–1.3	4.6	4.5	4.8	4.1	4.1
Nonfuel	4.9	7.4	7.4	8.4	9.1	6.3	3.8	8.1	6.6	5.9	6.5	6.8
Of Which, Primary Products	3.8	5.6	6.3	6.2	6.8	6.3	1.8	7.1	6.6	5.7	5.7	5.7
By External Financing Source												
Net Debtor Economies	3.6	6.5	6.0	6.8	6.9	4.7	0.9	6.9	5.2	4.3	4.9	5.5
Of Which, Official Financing	3.4	6.4	6.4	6.0	5.9	6.3	5.2	5.5	7.1	5.8	5.8	5.9
Net Debtor Economies by Debt-Servicing Experience												
Economies with Arrears and/or Rescheduling during 2006–10	2.6	7.1	7.8	7.7	7.6	5.8	1.9	6.9	6.1	4.1	4.4	5.0
Memorandum												
Median Growth Rate												
Advanced Economies	3.3	4.0	3.1	4.0	3.8	0.8	–3.5	2.3	1.8	0.8	2.0	2.4
Emerging and Developing Economies	4.1	5.3	5.6	5.7	6.3	5.1	1.8	4.5	4.3	4.1	4.1	4.4
Output per Capita												
Advanced Economies	2.1	2.4	1.9	2.3	2.0	–0.7	–4.3	2.6	1.0	0.8	1.5	2.1
Emerging and Developing Economies	3.1	6.4	6.1	7.1	7.5	4.9	1.6	6.3	5.3	4.7	5.1	5.3
World Growth Rate Based on Market Exchange	**2.9**	**3.9**	**3.4**	**4.0**	**4.0**	**1.4**	**–2.2**	**4.2**	**2.8**	**2.7**	**3.3**	**3.9**
Value of World Output (billions of U.S. dollars)												
At Market Exchange Rates	31,416	42,136	45,571	49,342	55,678	61,167	57,761	63,075	69,660	71,897	75,522	94,028
At Purchasing Power Parities	39,234	52,658	56,794	61,638	66,755	70,030	70,139	74,604	78,897	82,647	87,251	111,088

[1]Real GDP.

[2]In this table, Other Advanced Economies means advanced economies excluding the United States, Euro Area countries, and Japan.

[3]Georgia and Mongolia, which are not members of the Commonwealth of Independent States, are included in this group for reasons of geography and similarities in economic structure.

Table A2. Advanced Economies: Real GDP and Total Domestic Demand[1]

(Annual percent change)

	Average									Projections			Fourth Quarter[2]	Projections	
	1994–2003	2004	2005	2006	2007	2008	2009	2010	2011	2012	2013	2017	2011:Q4	2012:Q4	2013:Q4
Real GDP															
Advanced Economies	**2.8**	**3.1**	**2.6**	**3.0**	**2.8**	**0.0**	**–3.6**	**3.2**	**1.6**	**1.4**	**2.0**	**2.7**	**1.2**	**1.6**	**2.2**
United States	3.3	3.5	3.1	2.7	1.9	–0.3	–3.5	3.0	1.7	2.1	2.4	3.3	1.6	2.0	2.6
Euro Area	2.2	2.2	1.7	3.3	3.0	0.4	–4.3	1.9	1.4	–0.3	0.9	1.7	0.7	–0.2	1.4
Germany	1.5	0.7	0.8	3.9	3.4	0.8	–5.1	3.6	3.1	0.6	1.5	1.3	2.0	0.9	1.6
France	2.2	2.3	1.9	2.7	2.2	–0.2	–2.6	1.4	1.7	0.5	1.0	2.0	1.3	0.5	1.4
Italy	1.7	1.7	0.9	2.2	1.7	–1.2	–5.5	1.8	0.4	–1.9	–0.3	1.2	–0.4	–2.0	0.7
Spain	3.6	3.3	3.6	4.1	3.5	0.9	–3.7	–0.1	0.7	–1.8	0.1	1.8	0.3	–2.5	1.3
Netherlands	2.9	2.2	2.0	3.4	3.9	1.8	–3.5	1.6	1.3	–0.5	0.8	1.9	–0.3	0.5	1.0
Belgium	2.5	3.3	1.7	2.7	2.9	1.0	–2.8	2.3	1.9	0.0	0.8	1.7	1.0	0.4	0.6
Austria	2.3	2.6	2.4	3.7	3.7	1.4	–3.8	2.3	3.1	0.9	1.8	1.8	1.4	1.4	1.8
Greece	3.5	4.4	2.3	4.6	3.0	–0.1	–3.3	–3.5	–6.9	–4.7	0.0	2.9	–4.5	–4.5	3.2
Portugal	2.7	1.6	0.8	1.4	2.4	0.0	–2.9	1.4	–1.5	–3.3	0.3	1.5	–2.6	–2.3	1.3
Finland	3.8	4.1	2.9	4.4	5.3	0.3	–8.4	3.7	2.9	0.6	1.8	2.0	1.4	0.3	2.6
Ireland	7.5	4.5	5.3	5.3	5.2	–3.0	–7.0	–0.4	0.7	0.5	2.0	2.9	1.0	1.6	2.2
Slovak Republic	4.4	5.1	6.7	8.3	10.5	5.8	–4.9	4.2	3.3	2.4	3.1	3.6	3.4	2.0	3.7
Slovenia	4.1	4.4	4.0	5.8	6.9	3.6	–8.0	1.4	–0.2	–1.0	1.4	2.0	–3.2	2.3	1.3
Luxembourg	4.4	4.4	5.4	5.0	6.6	0.8	–5.3	2.7	1.0	–0.2	1.9	3.1	–0.4	1.0	2.5
Estonia	5.7	6.3	8.9	10.1	7.5	–3.7	–14.3	2.3	7.6	2.0	3.6	4.0	5.1	2.9	3.2
Cyprus	4.3	4.2	3.9	4.1	5.1	3.6	–1.9	1.1	0.5	–1.2	0.8	3.0	–1.2	0.5	0.8
Malta	. . .	–0.5	3.7	2.9	4.3	4.1	–2.7	2.3	2.1	1.2	2.0	2.3	0.1	3.1	1.2
Japan	0.9	2.4	1.3	1.7	2.2	–1.0	–5.5	4.4	–0.7	2.0	1.7	1.1	–0.6	2.0	1.8
United Kingdom	3.5	3.0	2.1	2.6	3.5	–1.1	–4.4	2.1	0.7	0.8	2.0	2.8	0.5	1.5	2.3
Canada	3.5	3.1	3.0	2.8	2.2	0.7	–2.8	3.2	2.5	2.1	2.2	2.2	2.2	2.0	2.3
Korea	5.7	4.6	4.0	5.2	5.1	2.3	0.3	6.3	3.6	3.5	4.0	4.0	3.4	4.9	2.8
Australia	3.8	4.1	3.1	2.7	4.7	2.5	1.4	2.5	2.0	3.0	3.5	3.5	2.3	3.2	3.4
Taiwan Province of China	4.7	6.2	4.7	5.4	6.0	0.7	–1.8	10.7	4.0	3.6	4.7	5.0	2.5	4.6	3.9
Sweden	3.2	3.7	3.2	4.6	3.4	–0.8	–4.8	5.8	4.0	0.9	2.3	2.4	1.2	3.0	0.4
Hong Kong SAR	2.7	8.5	7.1	7.0	6.4	2.3	–2.6	7.0	5.0	2.6	4.2	4.4	2.9	4.9	2.7
Switzerland	1.3	2.5	2.6	3.6	3.6	2.1	–1.9	2.7	1.9	0.8	1.7	1.9	1.2	0.9	2.1
Singapore	5.4	9.2	7.4	8.8	8.9	1.7	–1.0	14.8	4.9	2.7	3.9	4.0	3.6	5.4	2.7
Czech Republic	. . .	4.7	6.8	7.0	5.7	3.1	–4.7	2.7	1.7	0.1	2.1	3.5	0.6	0.7	2.4
Norway	3.2	4.0	2.6	2.4	2.7	0.0	–1.7	0.7	1.7	1.8	2.0	2.1	1.8	1.3	2.5
Israel	4.3	4.8	4.9	5.6	5.5	4.0	0.8	4.8	4.7	2.7	3.8	3.5	3.7	2.9	3.6
Denmark	2.4	2.3	2.4	3.4	1.6	–0.8	–5.8	1.3	1.0	0.5	1.2	1.8	0.7	0.3	2.3
New Zealand	3.7	4.5	3.3	1.0	2.8	–0.1	–2.1	1.2	1.4	2.3	3.2	2.3	1.8	2.2	4.5
Iceland	3.4	7.8	7.2	4.7	6.0	1.3	–6.8	–4.0	3.1	2.4	2.6	2.9	2.7	1.1	3.3
Memorandum															
Major Advanced Economies	2.6	2.8	2.3	2.6	2.2	–0.4	–4.0	3.0	1.4	1.5	1.9	2.5	1.1	1.5	2.1
Newly Industrialized Asian Economies	5.1	5.9	4.8	5.8	5.9	1.8	–0.7	8.5	4.0	3.4	4.2	4.3	3.1	4.8	3.1
Real Total Domestic Demand															
Advanced Economies	**2.9**	**3.1**	**2.6**	**2.8**	**2.4**	**–0.4**	**–4.0**	**3.1**	**1.2**	**1.1**	**1.8**	**2.6**	**0.7**	**1.5**	**1.9**
United States	3.8	3.9	3.2	2.6	1.2	–1.5	–4.4	3.4	1.6	2.0	2.3	3.5	1.5	1.9	2.6
Euro Area	. . .	1.9	1.8	3.1	2.8	0.3	–3.7	1.1	0.5	–1.1	0.4	1.4	–0.5	–0.6	0.9
Germany	1.1	0.0	–0.2	2.7	1.9	1.3	–2.6	2.4	2.3	0.7	1.0	1.2	1.8	0.7	1.1
France	2.2	2.6	2.6	2.7	3.1	0.1	–2.4	1.3	1.7	–0.2	0.7	1.9	0.5	0.4	0.9
Italy	1.9	1.4	0.9	2.1	1.4	–1.2	–4.4	2.1	–0.9	–3.4	–1.0	1.0	–3.3	–2.6	–0.1
Spain	3.8	4.8	5.0	5.2	4.1	–0.5	–6.2	–1.0	–1.7	–3.7	–0.3	1.4	–2.9	–2.8	1.0
Japan	0.8	1.5	1.0	0.9	1.1	–1.3	–4.0	2.7	0.1	2.4	1.4	1.1	0.5	1.7	1.8
United Kingdom	3.7	3.4	2.1	2.4	3.3	–1.8	–5.4	2.9	–0.8	0.7	1.5	2.9	–0.7	1.4	1.5
Canada	3.1	3.9	4.6	4.2	3.8	2.7	–2.9	5.2	3.2	2.3	2.4	1.8	2.5	2.9	2.3
Other Advanced Economies[3]	3.7	4.7	3.4	4.0	4.9	1.5	–2.8	5.6	2.7	2.3	3.2	3.4	1.6	4.1	2.2
Memorandum															
Major Advanced Economies	2.7	2.9	2.3	2.4	1.7	–0.9	–4.0	3.0	1.2	1.4	1.7	2.6	0.9	1.4	1.9
Newly Industrialized Asian Economies	4.1	4.8	2.9	4.2	4.5	1.4	–3.0	7.4	2.4	2.5	3.4	4.1	0.9	5.0	1.7

[1]In this and other tables, when countries are not listed alphabetically, they are ordered on the basis of economic size.
[2]From the fourth quarter of the preceding year.
[3]In this table, Other Advanced Economies means advanced economies excluding the G7 (Canada, France, Germany, Italy, Japan, United Kingdom, United States) and Euro Area countries.

Table A3. Advanced Economies: Components of Real GDP

(Annual percent change)

	Averages										Projections	
	1994–2003	2004–13	2004	2005	2006	2007	2008	2009	2010	2011	2012	2013
Private Consumer Expenditure												
Advanced Economies	**3.0**	**1.5**	**2.6**	**2.7**	**2.5**	**2.4**	**0.0**	**–1.3**	**2.0**	**1.3**	**1.2**	**1.9**
United States	3.8	1.8	3.3	3.4	2.9	2.3	–0.6	–1.9	2.0	2.2	2.2	2.6
Euro Area	. . .	0.7	1.5	1.8	2.1	1.7	0.4	–1.2	0.9	0.2	–0.6	0.4
Germany	1.2	0.6	0.4	0.2	1.5	–0.2	0.6	–0.1	0.6	1.5	0.5	0.8
France	2.2	1.2	1.5	2.4	2.4	2.3	0.2	0.2	1.3	0.3	0.1	0.7
Italy	1.7	0.0	0.7	1.2	1.4	1.1	–0.8	–1.6	1.2	0.2	–2.1	–1.1
Spain	3.3	1.1	4.2	4.1	4.0	3.5	–0.6	–4.3	0.8	–0.1	–0.9	0.6
Japan	1.1	0.8	1.2	1.5	1.1	0.9	–0.9	–0.7	2.6	0.0	1.1	1.6
United Kingdom	3.9	0.7	3.0	2.1	1.8	2.7	–1.5	–3.5	1.2	–1.2	0.5	1.6
Canada	3.2	2.9	3.3	3.7	4.2	4.6	3.0	0.4	3.3	2.2	2.1	2.1
Other Advanced Economies[1]	4.0	2.9	3.7	3.5	3.7	4.7	1.2	0.2	3.8	2.8	2.4	3.2
Memorandum												
Major Advanced Economies	2.8	1.4	2.4	2.5	2.3	1.9	–0.4	–1.4	1.9	1.3	1.3	1.8
Newly Industrialized Asian Economies	4.8	3.1	3.0	3.9	4.0	4.8	1.0	0.3	4.7	3.4	2.7	3.7
Public Consumption												
Advanced Economies	**2.2**	**1.1**	**1.7**	**1.2**	**1.6**	**1.8**	**2.1**	**2.3**	**1.2**	**0.0**	**–0.3**	**–0.9**
United States	1.9	0.4	1.4	0.6	1.0	1.3	2.2	2.0	0.9	–1.2	–1.6	–2.7
Euro Area	. . .	1.2	1.6	1.6	2.1	2.2	2.3	2.6	0.5	0.1	–0.8	–0.2
Germany	1.4	1.3	–0.6	0.3	0.9	1.4	3.1	3.3	1.7	1.4	0.6	0.7
France	1.1	1.3	2.1	1.3	1.5	1.5	1.2	2.3	1.2	0.9	0.5	0.3
Italy	0.9	0.4	2.5	1.9	0.5	1.0	0.6	0.8	–0.6	–0.9	–0.7	–0.9
Spain	3.3	1.9	6.2	5.5	4.6	5.6	5.9	3.7	0.2	–2.2	–7.6	–2.4
Japan	3.0	1.2	1.5	0.8	0.0	1.1	–0.1	2.3	2.1	2.1	2.3	–0.5
United Kingdom	2.2	1.0	3.4	2.2	1.5	0.6	1.6	–0.1	1.5	0.1	0.0	–1.1
Canada	1.4	2.3	2.0	1.4	3.0	2.7	4.4	3.6	2.4	1.2	1.4	1.3
Other Advanced Economies[1]	2.9	2.4	1.9	2.1	3.0	3.0	2.9	3.3	2.6	1.7	1.8	1.7
Memorandum												
Major Advanced Economies	1.9	0.8	1.6	0.9	1.0	1.3	1.8	2.0	1.2	–0.1	–0.3	–1.4
Newly Industrialized Asian Economies	3.6	3.0	2.4	2.4	3.7	3.9	3.2	4.6	3.1	1.9	2.9	2.2
Gross Fixed Capital Formation												
Advanced Economies	**3.6**	**0.9**	**4.4**	**4.1**	**4.2**	**2.3**	**–2.8**	**–12.3**	**2.3**	**2.4**	**2.6**	**3.6**
United States	5.3	0.7	6.3	5.3	2.5	–1.4	–5.1	–15.2	2.0	3.7	4.8	5.9
Euro Area	. . .	0.2	2.2	3.2	5.7	4.7	–1.0	–12.1	–0.5	1.4	–1.5	0.9
Germany	0.4	1.8	–0.2	0.8	8.2	4.7	1.7	–11.4	5.5	6.4	1.5	1.7
France	2.9	1.2	3.0	4.4	4.2	6.3	0.2	–8.9	–1.3	3.0	0.6	1.0
Italy	3.0	–1.5	2.0	1.3	3.4	1.8	–3.7	–11.7	2.1	–1.9	–5.5	–1.5
Spain	6.0	–2.0	5.1	7.1	7.1	4.5	–4.7	–16.6	–6.3	–5.1	–7.5	–1.0
Japan	–1.0	–0.7	0.4	0.8	1.5	0.3	–4.1	–10.6	–0.2	0.5	4.7	0.9
United Kingdom	4.6	1.2	5.1	2.4	6.4	8.1	–4.8	–13.4	3.1	–1.2	3.3	5.2
Canada	5.0	4.0	7.7	9.3	7.0	3.6	2.0	–13.2	10.0	6.9	4.7	4.1
Other Advanced Economies[1]	4.1	3.4	6.4	4.9	5.6	6.5	–0.1	–6.0	7.8	2.5	3.1	4.2
Memorandum												
Major Advanced Economies	3.4	0.7	4.2	3.8	3.6	1.2	–3.5	–13.2	2.2	2.9	3.4	3.8
Newly Industrialized Asian Economies	3.5	2.5	6.2	2.2	3.8	4.4	–3.1	–4.3	11.3	–0.5	2.2	3.4

Table A3. Advanced Economies: Components of Real GDP *(concluded)*

	Averages										Projections	
	1994–2003	2004–13	2004	2005	2006	2007	2008	2009	2010	2011	2012	2013
Final Domestic Demand												
Advanced Economies	**2.9**	**1.4**	**2.8**	**2.7**	**2.7**	**2.3**	**0.0**	**–2.6**	**1.7**	**1.3**	**1.2**	**1.7**
United States	3.8	1.4	3.5	3.3	2.5	1.4	–1.0	–3.6	1.8	1.8	1.9	2.3
Euro Area	. . .	0.7	1.7	2.0	2.9	2.4	0.5	–2.8	0.5	0.4	–0.8	0.3
Germany	1.1	0.9	0.1	0.3	2.6	1.1	1.3	–1.7	1.7	2.4	0.8	1.0
France	2.0	1.2	2.0	2.5	2.5	2.9	0.4	–1.1	0.8	0.9	0.3	0.7
Italy	1.8	–0.2	1.3	1.3	1.6	1.2	–1.2	–3.2	1.0	–0.4	–2.5	–1.1
Spain	3.9	1.1	4.0	4.8	5.2	5.0	4.1	–0.7	–6.1	–1.0	–3.6	–0.3
Japan	0.9	0.6	1.0	1.2	1.0	0.8	–1.5	–2.3	2.0	0.5	2.0	1.0
United Kingdom	3.6	0.8	3.4	2.2	2.4	3.1	–1.4	–4.4	1.6	–0.9	0.8	1.6
Canada	3.1	3.0	3.9	4.4	4.6	4.0	3.0	–2.1	4.5	3.0	2.5	2.4
Other Advanced Economies[1]	3.7	2.9	3.9	3.5	3.9	4.8	1.2	–0.7	4.4	2.5	2.4	3.2
Memorandum												
Major Advanced Economies	2.7	1.1	2.6	2.5	2.3	1.6	–0.6	–3.0	1.8	1.4	1.4	1.6
Newly Industrialized Asian Economies	4.2	3.0	3.7	3.2	3.9	4.6	0.4	–0.2	5.8	2.2	2.6	3.4
Stock Building[2]												
Advanced Economies	**0.0**	**0.0**	**0.3**	**–0.1**	**0.1**	**0.1**	**–0.2**	**–1.1**	**1.1**	**–0.1**	**0.0**	**0.1**
United States	0.0	0.0	0.4	–0.1	0.1	–0.2	–0.5	–0.8	1.6	–0.2	0.1	0.1
Euro Area	. . .	0.0	0.2	–0.2	0.2	0.4	–0.1	–0.9	0.6	0.1	–0.4	0.0
Germany	0.0	0.0	–0.1	–0.4	0.1	0.8	0.0	–0.8	0.6	–0.1	–0.1	0.0
France	0.1	0.0	0.6	0.1	0.2	0.2	–0.3	–1.3	0.5	0.8	–0.5	0.0
Italy	0.0	–0.1	0.0	–0.4	0.5	0.2	0.0	–1.1	1.1	–0.5	–0.6	0.1
Spain	0.0	0.0	0.1	–0.1	0.3	–0.1	0.2	0.0	0.0	0.1	0.0	0.0
Japan	0.0	0.0	0.5	–0.3	–0.1	0.3	0.2	–1.6	0.8	–0.5	0.3	0.4
United Kingdom	0.1	0.0	0.0	0.0	–0.1	0.3	–0.4	–1.0	1.3	0.0	0.0	0.0
Canada	0.1	0.0	0.1	0.5	–0.2	–0.1	–0.2	–0.8	0.6	0.1	–0.3	0.0
Other Advanced Economies[1]	0.0	0.0	0.6	–0.1	0.1	0.1	0.3	–1.9	1.0	0.2	0.0	0.0
Memorandum												
Major Advanced Economies	0.0	0.0	0.3	–0.2	0.1	0.1	–0.3	–1.0	1.2	–0.2	0.0	0.1
Newly Industrialized Asian Economies	–0.1	0.0	0.8	–0.2	0.3	–0.1	0.8	–2.5	1.4	0.1	–0.1	0.0
Foreign Balance[2]												
Advanced Economies	**–0.1**	**0.3**	**–0.1**	**0.0**	**0.2**	**0.5**	**0.5**	**0.4**	**0.2**	**0.4**	**0.3**	**0.3**
United States	–0.5	0.1	–0.7	–0.3	–0.1	0.6	1.2	1.1	–0.5	0.0	0.0	–0.1
Euro Area	. . .	0.3	0.4	–0.1	0.2	0.2	0.1	–0.6	0.8	1.0	0.8	0.5
Germany	0.3	0.4	1.1	0.8	1.1	1.5	–0.1	–2.8	1.4	0.8	–0.1	0.6
France	0.0	–0.1	–0.2	–0.7	0.0	–0.9	–0.3	–0.2	0.1	0.0	0.7	0.3
Italy	–0.2	0.3	0.3	0.0	0.1	0.3	0.0	–1.2	–0.4	1.4	1.6	0.7
Spain	–0.4	0.4	–1.7	–1.7	–1.4	–0.8	1.5	2.8	0.9	2.5	1.9	0.4
Japan	0.1	0.3	0.8	0.3	0.8	1.1	0.2	–1.5	1.7	–0.8	–0.3	0.3
United Kingdom	–0.3	0.2	–0.6	–0.2	0.1	–0.1	0.8	1.1	–0.5	1.0	0.0	0.5
Canada	0.3	–1.1	–0.8	–1.6	–1.4	–1.5	–2.1	0.2	–2.2	–0.8	–0.3	–0.2
Other Advanced Economies[1]	0.4	0.8	0.5	0.9	1.0	0.7	0.3	1.5	0.7	0.8	0.6	0.6
Memorandum												
Major Advanced Economies	–0.2	0.1	–0.2	–0.1	0.2	0.5	0.6	0.1	0.0	0.1	0.1	0.2
Newly Industrialized Asian Economies	0.6	1.6	1.3	2.1	1.9	2.0	0.7	1.9	1.8	2.1	1.3	1.3

[1]In this table, Other Advanced Economies means advanced economies excluding the G7 (Canada, France, Germany, Italy, Japan, United Kingdom, United States) and Euro Area countries.
[2]Changes expressed as percent of GDP in the preceding period.

Table A4. Emerging and Developing Economies: Real GDP[1]

(Annual percent change)

	Average									Projections		
	1994–2003	2004	2005	2006	2007	2008	2009	2010	2011	2012	2013	2017
Central and Eastern Europe[2]	**3.4**	**7.3**	**5.9**	**6.4**	**5.4**	**3.2**	**–3.6**	**4.5**	**5.3**	**1.9**	**2.9**	**4.0**
Albania	6.3	5.7	5.8	5.4	5.9	7.5	3.3	3.5	2.0	0.5	1.7	2.5
Bosnia and Herzegovina	. . .	6.3	3.9	6.0	6.2	5.7	–2.9	0.7	1.7	0.0	1.0	3.5
Bulgaria	0.6	6.7	6.4	6.5	6.4	6.2	–5.5	0.4	1.7	0.8	1.5	4.5
Croatia	4.3	4.1	4.3	4.9	5.1	2.2	–6.0	–1.2	0.0	–0.5	1.0	2.5
Hungary	3.2	4.8	4.0	3.9	0.1	0.9	–6.8	1.3	1.7	0.0	1.8	2.2
Kosovo	. . .	2.6	3.8	3.4	6.3	6.9	2.9	3.9	5.0	3.8	4.1	4.6
Latvia	4.8	8.7	10.6	10.5	9.6	–3.3	–17.7	–0.3	5.5	2.0	2.5	4.0
Lithuania	. . .	7.4	7.8	7.8	9.8	2.9	–14.8	1.4	5.9	2.0	2.7	3.9
Former Yugoslav Republic of Macedonia	1.1	4.6	4.4	5.0	6.1	5.0	–0.9	1.8	3.0	2.0	3.2	4.0
Montenegro	. . .	4.4	4.2	8.6	10.7	6.9	–5.7	2.5	2.4	0.2	1.5	2.2
Poland	4.5	5.3	3.6	6.2	6.8	5.1	1.6	3.9	4.3	2.6	3.2	3.8
Romania	2.1	8.5	4.2	7.9	6.3	7.3	–6.6	–1.6	2.5	1.5	3.0	4.0
Serbia	. . .	9.3	5.4	3.6	5.4	3.8	–3.5	1.0	1.8	0.5	3.0	3.5
Turkey	2.7	9.4	8.4	6.9	4.7	0.7	–4.8	9.0	8.5	2.3	3.2	4.6
Commonwealth of Independent States[2,3]	**0.6**	**8.2**	**6.7**	**8.8**	**9.0**	**5.4**	**–6.4**	**4.8**	**4.9**	**4.2**	**4.1**	**4.2**
Russia	0.7	7.2	6.4	8.2	8.5	5.2	–7.8	4.3	4.3	4.0	3.9	3.8
Excluding Russia	0.3	10.8	7.6	10.5	10.0	5.6	–3.1	6.0	6.2	4.6	4.6	4.9
Armenia	7.5	10.5	14.1	13.2	13.7	6.9	–14.1	2.1	4.4	3.8	4.0	4.0
Azerbaijan	2.2	10.2	26.4	34.5	25.0	10.8	9.3	5.0	0.1	3.1	1.9	3.1
Belarus	2.3	11.4	9.4	10.0	8.6	10.2	0.2	7.7	5.3	3.0	3.3	5.0
Georgia	. . .	5.9	9.6	9.4	12.3	2.3	–3.8	6.3	7.0	6.0	5.5	5.5
Kazakhstan	2.1	9.6	9.7	10.7	8.9	3.2	1.2	7.3	7.5	5.9	6.0	6.4
Kyrgyz Republic	1.1	7.0	–0.2	3.1	8.5	7.6	2.9	–0.5	5.7	5.0	5.5	5.0
Moldova	–3.1	7.4	7.5	4.8	3.0	7.8	–6.0	7.1	6.4	3.5	4.5	5.5
Mongolia	3.7	10.6	7.3	8.6	10.2	8.9	–1.3	6.4	17.3	17.2	11.8	9.1
Tajikistan	0.5	10.6	6.7	7.0	7.8	7.9	3.9	6.5	7.4	6.0	6.0	6.0
Turkmenistan	4.3	14.7	13.0	11.0	11.1	14.7	6.1	9.2	14.7	7.0	6.7	6.1
Ukraine	–2.3	12.1	2.7	7.3	7.9	2.3	–14.8	4.1	5.2	3.0	3.5	3.5
Uzbekistan	2.5	7.4	7.0	7.5	9.5	9.0	8.1	8.5	8.3	7.0	6.5	5.5

Table A4. Emerging and Developing Economies: Real GDP[1] *(continued)*

	Average 1994–2003	2004	2005	2006	2007	2008	2009	2010	2011	Projections 2012	2013	2017
Developing Asia	**7.0**	**8.5**	**9.5**	**10.3**	**11.4**	**7.8**	**7.1**	**9.7**	**7.8**	**7.3**	**7.9**	**7.9**
Islamic Republic of Afghanistan	. . .	1.1	11.2	5.6	13.7	3.6	21.0	8.4	5.7	7.2	5.8	6.6
Bangladesh	5.1	6.1	6.3	6.5	6.3	6.0	5.9	6.4	6.1	5.9	6.4	7.3
Bhutan	6.8	5.9	7.1	6.8	17.9	4.7	6.7	10.6	5.9	7.0	9.9	4.0
Brunei Darussalam	2.4	0.5	0.4	4.4	0.2	–1.9	–1.8	2.6	1.9	3.2	1.6	3.6
Cambodia	7.4	10.3	13.3	10.8	10.2	6.7	0.1	6.0	6.1	6.2	6.4	7.7
China	9.4	10.1	11.3	12.7	14.2	9.6	9.2	10.4	9.2	8.2	8.8	8.5
Republic of Fiji	2.7	5.5	2.5	1.9	–0.9	1.0	–1.3	–0.2	2.0	1.5	1.7	2.3
India	6.0	7.6	9.0	9.5	10.0	6.2	6.6	10.6	7.2	6.9	7.3	8.1
Indonesia	3.1	5.0	5.7	5.5	6.3	6.0	4.6	6.2	6.5	6.1	6.6	7.0
Kiribati	3.9	0.2	0.3	1.2	0.5	–2.4	–2.3	1.4	1.8	2.5	3.0	2.0
Lao People's Democratic Republic	6.1	7.0	6.8	8.6	7.8	7.8	7.6	7.9	8.3	8.4	7.1	5.7
Malaysia	5.4	6.8	5.3	5.8	6.5	4.8	–1.6	7.2	5.1	4.4	4.7	5.0
Maldives	8.1	10.4	–8.7	19.6	10.6	12.2	–4.7	5.7	7.4	4.4	3.5	3.5
Myanmar	. . .	13.6	13.6	13.1	12.0	3.6	5.1	5.3	5.5	6.0	5.9	6.5
Nepal	4.5	4.7	3.5	3.4	3.4	6.1	4.4	4.6	3.5	4.2	3.8	3.9
Pakistan	3.9	7.5	9.0	5.8	6.8	3.7	1.7	3.8	2.4	3.4	3.5	3.5
Papua New Guinea	1.2	0.6	3.9	2.3	7.2	6.6	6.1	7.6	8.9	7.7	4.0	4.9
Philippines	3.8	6.7	4.8	5.2	6.6	4.2	1.1	7.6	3.7	4.2	4.7	5.0
Samoa	4.4	4.2	7.0	2.1	1.8	4.3	–5.4	0.2	2.1	1.4	1.9	2.7
Solomon Islands	–0.1	8.1	12.9	4.0	6.4	7.1	–4.7	7.0	9.3	6.0	4.0	4.0
Sri Lanka	4.4	5.4	6.2	7.7	6.8	6.0	3.5	8.0	8.2	7.5	7.0	6.5
Thailand	3.4	6.3	4.6	5.1	5.0	2.6	–2.3	7.8	0.1	5.5	7.5	5.0
Timor-Leste	. . .	4.4	6.5	–3.2	11.7	14.6	12.8	9.5	10.6	10.0	10.0	10.0
Tonga	2.1	2.2	0.7	–4.5	–2.4	0.5	0.9	1.6	1.5	1.4	1.5	1.8
Tuvalu	. . .	–1.4	–4.0	2.9	5.5	7.6	–1.7	–0.5	0.4	1.5	1.3	1.2
Vanuatu	2.0	4.5	5.2	7.4	6.5	6.2	3.5	2.2	3.3	4.0	4.0	4.0
Vietnam	7.4	7.8	8.4	8.2	8.5	6.3	5.3	6.8	5.9	5.6	6.3	7.5

Table A4. Emerging and Developing Economies: Real GDP[1] *(continued)*

	Average									Projections		
	1994–2003	2004	2005	2006	2007	2008	2009	2010	2011	2012	2013	2017
Latin America and the Caribbean	**2.5**	**6.0**	**4.7**	**5.7**	**5.8**	**4.2**	**–1.6**	**6.2**	**4.5**	**3.7**	**4.1**	**4.0**
Antigua and Barbuda	2.9	3.2	7.6	12.8	7.2	1.5	–10.3	–8.9	–0.5	1.0	2.5	3.5
Argentina[4]	0.8	8.9	9.2	8.5	8.7	6.8	0.9	9.2	8.9	4.2	4.0	4.5
The Bahamas	4.2	0.9	3.4	2.5	1.4	–1.3	–5.4	1.0	2.0	2.5	2.7	2.5
Barbados	1.9	4.8	3.9	3.6	3.8	–0.2	–4.2	0.2	0.5	0.9	1.5	3.1
Belize	5.0	4.6	3.0	4.7	1.3	3.5	0.0	2.7	2.5	2.8	2.5	2.5
Bolivia	3.4	2.7	6.8	2.8	5.3	6.1	3.4	4.1	5.1	5.0	5.0	5.0
Brazil	2.5	5.7	3.2	4.0	6.1	5.2	–0.3	7.5	2.7	3.0	4.1	4.1
Chile	4.6	6.8	6.3	5.8	5.2	3.0	–0.9	6.1	5.9	4.3	4.5	4.5
Colombia	2.3	5.3	4.7	6.7	6.9	3.5	1.7	4.0	5.9	4.7	4.4	4.5
Costa Rica	4.4	4.3	5.9	8.8	7.9	2.7	–1.0	4.7	4.2	4.0	4.2	4.5
Dominica	1.9	0.8	–1.7	3.6	3.9	7.8	–0.7	0.3	0.5	1.5	1.7	1.9
Dominican Republic	4.9	1.3	9.3	10.7	8.5	5.3	3.5	7.8	4.5	4.5	4.5	5.0
Ecuador	2.4	8.8	5.7	4.8	2.0	7.2	0.4	3.6	7.8	4.5	3.9	3.4
El Salvador	3.4	1.9	3.6	3.9	3.8	1.3	–3.1	1.4	1.4	2.0	2.5	3.5
Grenada	5.2	0.1	12.5	–4.4	6.3	1.7	–5.7	–1.3	1.1	1.5	2.0	2.5
Guatemala	3.4	3.2	3.3	5.4	6.3	3.3	0.5	2.8	3.8	3.1	3.2	3.5
Guyana	3.0	1.6	–1.9	5.1	7.0	2.0	3.3	4.4	4.2	3.9	6.3	3.2
Haiti	0.9	–3.5	1.8	2.2	3.3	0.8	2.9	–5.4	5.6	7.8	6.9	5.0
Honduras	2.9	6.2	6.1	6.6	6.2	4.1	–2.1	2.8	3.6	3.5	3.5	4.0
Jamaica	0.9	1.3	0.9	2.9	1.4	–0.8	–3.1	–1.4	1.5	1.0	1.0	1.5
Mexico	2.6	4.0	3.2	5.1	3.2	1.2	–6.3	5.5	4.0	3.6	3.7	3.3
Nicaragua	4.2	5.3	4.3	4.2	3.6	2.8	–1.5	4.5	4.7	3.7	4.0	4.0
Panama	3.9	7.5	7.2	8.5	12.1	10.1	3.9	7.6	10.6	7.5	6.6	5.1
Paraguay	1.4	4.1	2.9	4.3	6.8	5.8	–3.8	15.0	3.8	–1.5	8.5	4.7
Peru	4.3	5.0	6.8	7.7	8.9	9.8	0.9	8.8	6.9	5.5	6.0	6.0
St. Kitts and Nevis	3.6	3.8	9.2	3.5	5.0	4.0	–5.6	–2.7	–2.0	1.0	1.8	3.5
St. Lucia	1.2	6.0	–2.6	7.4	1.5	5.8	–1.3	3.4	0.2	1.9	2.4	2.6
St. Vincent and the Grenadines	3.5	4.6	3.0	6.0	3.1	–0.6	–2.3	–1.8	–0.4	2.0	2.0	3.5
Suriname	2.5	8.5	4.5	4.7	4.6	4.1	3.5	4.5	4.5	4.9	5.4	5.5
Trinidad and Tobago	7.2	7.9	6.2	13.2	4.8	2.7	–3.3	0.0	–1.3	1.7	2.4	2.6
Uruguay	0.7	4.6	6.8	4.1	6.5	7.2	2.4	8.9	5.7	3.5	4.0	4.0
Venezuela	–0.9	18.3	10.3	9.9	8.8	5.3	–3.2	–1.5	4.2	4.7	3.2	2.9
Middle East and North Africa	**3.9**	**6.2**	**5.6**	**6.1**	**5.6**	**4.7**	**2.7**	**4.9**	**3.5**	**4.2**	**3.7**	**4.4**
Algeria	3.2	5.2	5.1	2.0	3.0	2.4	2.4	3.3	2.5	3.1	3.4	4.3
Bahrain	4.2	5.6	7.9	6.7	8.4	6.3	3.1	4.5	1.8	2.0	2.8	2.9
Djibouti	0.2	3.0	3.2	4.8	5.1	5.8	5.0	3.5	4.5	4.8	5.0	5.8
Egypt	4.8	4.1	4.5	6.8	7.1	7.2	4.7	5.1	1.8	1.5	3.3	6.5
Islamic Republic of Iran	4.2	6.1	4.7	6.2	6.4	0.6	3.9	5.9	2.0	0.4	1.3	2.0
Iraq	. . .	. . .	. . .	6.2	1.5	9.5	4.2	0.8	9.9	11.1	13.5	8.8
Jordan	4.2	8.6	8.1	8.1	8.2	7.2	5.5	2.3	2.5	2.8	3.0	4.4
Kuwait	3.5	11.2	10.4	5.3	4.5	5.0	–5.2	3.4	8.2	6.6	1.8	3.9
Lebanon	3.6	7.5	1.0	0.6	7.5	9.3	8.5	7.0	1.5	3.0	4.0	4.0
Libya	0.0	4.4	10.3	6.7	7.5	5.4	–0.1	2.5	–61.0	76.3	21.0	4.3
Mauritania	2.9	5.2	5.4	11.4	1.0	3.5	–1.2	5.1	3.6	5.3	6.1	5.3
Morocco	3.9	4.8	3.0	7.8	2.7	5.6	4.9	3.7	4.3	3.7	4.3	5.9
Oman	3.2	3.4	4.0	6.9	5.3	12.9	1.1	4.0	5.5	5.0	4.0	3.8
Qatar	8.1	17.7	7.5	26.2	18.0	17.7	12.0	16.6	18.8	6.0	4.6	7.0
Saudi Arabia	2.2	5.3	5.6	3.2	2.0	4.2	0.1	4.6	6.8	6.0	4.1	4.2
Sudan[5]	6.1	3.9	7.5	10.1	11.5	3.2	3.0	4.5	–3.9	–7.3	–1.5	1.7
Syrian Arab Republic[6]	2.5	6.9	6.2	5.0	5.7	4.5	5.9	3.4	. . .	. . .	. . .	. . .
Tunisia	4.5	6.0	4.0	5.7	6.3	4.5	3.1	3.1	–0.8	2.2	3.5	6.7
United Arab Emirates	6.1	10.1	8.6	8.8	6.5	5.3	–3.3	0.9	4.9	2.3	2.8	3.7
Republic of Yemen	5.0	4.0	5.6	3.2	3.3	3.6	3.9	7.7	–10.5	–0.9	2.9	4.5

Table A4. Emerging and Developing Economies: Real GDP[1] *(concluded)*

	Average									Projections		
	1994–2003	2004	2005	2006	2007	2008	2009	2010	2011	2012	2013	2017
Sub-Saharan Africa	**4.0**	**7.1**	**6.2**	**6.4**	**7.1**	**5.6**	**2.8**	**5.3**	**5.1**	**5.4**	**5.3**	**5.5**
Angola	6.7	11.2	20.6	20.7	22.6	13.8	2.4	3.4	3.4	9.7	6.8	6.2
Benin	4.7	3.1	2.9	3.8	4.6	5.0	2.7	2.6	3.1	3.5	4.7	4.9
Botswana	6.6	6.0	1.6	5.1	4.8	3.0	–4.9	7.2	4.6	3.3	4.6	4.3
Burkina Faso	5.9	4.5	8.7	5.5	3.6	5.2	3.2	7.9	5.6	5.0	6.4	7.0
Burundi	–1.1	3.8	4.4	5.4	4.8	5.0	3.5	3.8	4.2	4.8	5.0	6.0
Cameroon[7]	3.7	3.7	2.3	3.2	3.4	2.6	2.0	2.9	4.1	4.1	4.5	5.0
Cape Verde	7.2	4.3	6.5	10.1	8.6	6.2	3.7	5.2	5.0	4.3	4.4	5.0
Central African Republic	0.9	1.0	2.4	3.8	3.7	2.0	1.7	3.3	3.1	4.1	4.2	5.7
Chad	5.2	33.6	7.9	0.2	0.2	1.7	–1.2	13.0	1.6	6.9	0.1	2.6
Comoros	1.5	–0.2	4.2	1.2	0.5	1.0	1.8	2.1	2.2	2.5	4.0	4.0
Democratic Republic of Congo	–1.6	6.6	7.8	5.6	6.3	6.2	2.8	7.0	6.9	6.5	6.7	5.7
Republic of Congo	1.9	3.5	7.8	6.2	–1.6	5.6	7.5	8.8	4.5	3.1	5.4	4.3
Côte d'Ivoire	1.7	1.6	1.9	0.7	1.6	2.3	3.7	2.4	–4.7	8.1	6.2	6.7
Equatorial Guinea	37.0	38.0	9.7	1.3	21.4	10.7	5.7	–0.8	7.1	4.0	6.8	5.2
Eritrea	3.6	1.5	2.6	–1.0	1.4	–9.8	3.9	2.2	8.7	7.5	3.4	–3.2
Ethiopia	4.0	11.7	12.6	11.5	11.8	11.2	10.0	8.0	7.5	5.0	5.5	6.5
Gabon	1.4	1.4	3.0	1.2	5.6	2.3	–1.4	6.6	5.8	5.6	2.3	2.3
The Gambia	3.9	7.0	–0.3	0.8	4.0	6.5	6.7	5.5	3.3	–1.7	9.7	5.6
Ghana	4.6	5.3	6.0	6.1	6.5	8.4	4.0	7.7	13.6	8.8	7.4	5.7
Guinea	4.0	2.3	3.0	2.5	1.8	4.9	–0.3	1.9	3.6	4.7	4.8	14.4
Guinea-Bissau	0.2	2.8	4.3	2.1	3.2	3.2	3.0	3.5	5.3	4.5	4.7	4.5
Kenya	2.5	4.6	6.0	6.3	7.0	1.5	2.6	5.6	5.0	5.2	5.7	6.5
Lesotho	3.6	2.4	3.1	4.4	4.9	4.7	3.6	5.7	4.2	5.2	2.2	3.1
Liberia	. . .	2.6	5.3	7.8	9.4	4.7	2.8	5.0	6.4	8.8	5.1	8.6
Madagascar	2.2	5.3	4.6	5.0	6.2	7.1	–4.1	0.5	0.5	2.9	5.1	5.4
Malawi	2.6	5.5	2.6	2.1	9.5	8.3	9.0	6.5	5.5	4.3	4.1	4.1
Mali	4.9	2.3	6.1	5.3	4.3	5.0	4.5	5.8	2.7	6.0	5.8	5.3
Mauritius	4.2	5.5	1.5	4.5	5.9	5.5	3.0	4.1	4.1	3.6	4.0	4.2
Mozambique	8.3	7.9	8.4	8.7	7.3	6.8	6.3	6.8	7.1	6.7	7.2	7.8
Namibia	3.6	12.3	2.5	7.1	5.4	3.4	–0.4	6.6	3.6	4.0	4.2	4.4
Niger	3.3	–0.8	8.4	5.8	3.1	9.6	–0.9	8.0	2.3	14.0	6.6	5.5
Nigeria	5.5	10.6	5.4	6.2	7.0	6.0	7.0	8.0	7.2	7.1	6.6	6.6
Rwanda	3.5	7.4	9.4	9.2	5.5	11.2	4.1	7.5	8.8	7.6	7.0	6.5
São Tomé and Príncipe	2.4	4.5	1.6	12.6	2.0	9.1	4.0	4.5	4.9	5.5	6.0	3.5
Senegal	3.8	5.9	5.6	2.4	5.0	3.7	2.1	4.1	2.6	3.8	4.5	5.4
Seychelles	2.1	–2.9	6.7	6.3	9.9	–1.0	0.5	6.7	4.9	2.8	3.7	3.9
Sierra Leone	–1.0	7.4	7.2	7.3	6.4	5.5	3.2	5.0	5.3	35.9	9.1	4.3
South Africa	3.0	4.6	5.3	5.6	5.5	3.6	–1.5	2.9	3.1	2.7	3.4	3.7
Swaziland	2.8	2.3	2.2	2.9	2.8	3.1	1.2	2.0	0.3	–2.7	–0.9	0.3
Tanzania	4.5	7.8	7.4	7.0	6.9	7.3	6.7	6.5	6.7	6.4	6.7	7.0
Togo	3.3	2.1	1.2	4.1	2.3	2.4	3.4	4.0	4.1	4.4	4.6	4.1
Uganda	7.0	6.8	6.3	10.8	8.4	8.8	7.2	5.9	6.7	4.2	5.4	7.0
Zambia	1.0	5.4	5.3	6.2	6.2	5.7	6.4	7.6	6.6	7.7	8.3	7.7
Zimbabwe[8]	. . .	–5.7	–5.7	–3.5	–3.6	–17.6	5.8	8.1	9.3	4.7	6.3	3.6

[1]For many countries, figures for recent years are IMF staff estimates. Data for some countries are for fiscal years.

[2]Data for some countries refer to real net material product (NMP) or are estimates based on NMP. For many countries, figures for recent years are IMF staff estimates. The figures should be interpreted only as indicative of broad orders of magnitude because reliable, comparable data are not generally available. In particular, the growth of output of new private enterprises of the informal economy is not fully reflected in the recent figures.

[3]Georgia and Mongolia, which are not members of the Commonwealth of Independent States, are included in this group for reasons of geography and similarities in economic structure.

[4]Figures are based on Argentina's official GDP data. The IMF has called on Argentina to adopt remedial measures to address the quality of these data. The IMF staff is also using alternative measures of GDP growth for macroeconomic surveillance, including data produced by private analysts, which have shown significantly lower real GDP growth than the official data since 2008.

[5]Data for 2011 exclude South Sudan after July 9. Data for 2012 and onward pertain to the current Sudan.

[6]Data for Syrian Arab Republic are excluded for 2011 onward due to the uncertain political situation.

[7]The percent changes in 2002 are calculated over a period of 18 months, reflecting a change in the fiscal year cycle (from July–June to January–December).

[8]The Zimbabwe dollar ceased circulating in early 2009. Data are based on IMF staff estimates of price and exchange rate developments in U.S. dollars. IMF staff estimates of U.S. dollar values may differ from authorities' estimates. Real GDP is in constant 2009 prices.

Table A5. Summary of Inflation

(Percent)

	Average 1994–2003	2004	2005	2006	2007	2008	2009	2010	2011	Projections 2012	2013	2017
GDP Deflators												
Advanced Economies	**1.7**	**2.0**	**2.1**	**2.1**	**2.2**	**2.0**	**0.8**	**1.0**	**1.4**	**1.5**	**1.5**	**1.8**
United States	1.9	2.8	3.3	3.2	2.9	2.2	1.1	1.2	2.1	1.3	1.5	1.9
Euro Area	2.0	1.9	1.9	1.8	2.4	2.0	0.9	0.7	1.4	1.8	1.4	1.6
Japan	–0.8	–1.4	–1.3	–1.1	–0.9	–1.3	–0.5	–2.1	–2.0	–0.2	–0.1	0.8
Other Advanced Economies[1]	2.2	2.4	2.0	2.2	2.5	3.0	0.9	2.5	1.9	2.2	2.2	2.1
Consumer Prices												
Advanced Economies	**2.1**	**2.0**	**2.3**	**2.4**	**2.2**	**3.4**	**0.1**	**1.5**	**2.7**	**1.9**	**1.7**	**1.9**
United States	2.4	2.7	3.4	3.2	2.9	3.8	–0.3	1.6	3.1	2.1	1.9	2.0
Euro Area[2]	2.0	2.2	2.2	2.2	2.1	3.3	0.3	1.6	2.7	2.0	1.6	1.8
Japan	0.0	0.0	–0.3	0.2	0.1	1.4	–1.3	–0.7	–0.3	0.0	0.0	0.9
Other Advanced Economies[1]	2.3	1.8	2.1	2.1	2.1	3.8	1.5	2.4	3.3	2.4	2.3	2.2
Emerging and Developing Economies	**19.8**	**5.9**	**5.7**	**5.6**	**6.5**	**9.2**	**5.2**	**6.1**	**7.1**	**6.2**	**5.6**	**4.5**
Regional Groups												
Central and Eastern Europe	37.7	6.6	5.9	5.9	6.0	8.1	4.7	5.3	5.3	6.2	4.5	3.8
Commonwealth of Independent States[3]	62.9	10.4	12.1	9.4	9.7	15.6	11.2	7.2	10.1	7.1	7.7	6.5
Developing Asia	6.1	4.1	3.7	4.2	5.4	7.4	3.0	5.7	6.5	5.0	4.6	3.6
Latin America and the Caribbean	25.7	6.6	6.3	5.3	5.4	7.9	6.0	6.0	6.6	6.4	5.9	5.6
Middle East and North Africa	8.2	6.6	5.6	7.6	10.1	13.6	6.6	6.9	9.6	9.5	8.7	6.9
Sub-Saharan Africa	20.2	7.6	8.9	6.9	6.9	11.7	10.6	7.4	8.2	9.6	7.5	5.3
Memorandum												
European Union	4.2	2.3	2.3	2.3	2.4	3.7	0.9	2.0	3.1	2.3	1.8	1.9
Analytical Groups												
By Source of Export Earnings												
Fuel	32.9	9.8	9.6	9.1	10.2	15.0	9.4	8.2	10.2	9.0	8.7	7.7
Nonfuel	16.6	5.0	4.8	4.7	5.6	7.9	4.2	5.6	6.5	5.6	4.9	3.9
Of Which, Primary Products	19.3	4.0	5.1	5.2	5.3	9.2	5.1	3.8	5.9	5.5	4.5	4.1
By External Financing Source												
Net Debtor Economies	22.0	5.6	5.9	5.9	6.2	9.0	7.4	7.2	7.4	7.2	6.3	4.7
Of Which, Official Financing	19.7	6.6	7.8	7.6	8.0	13.7	9.1	6.5	9.7	10.9	8.7	5.4
Net Debtor Economies by Debt-Servicing Experience												
Economies with Arrears and/or Rescheduling during 2006–10	19.1	7.9	8.1	8.8	8.3	11.5	6.5	8.0	11.6	12.2	10.1	7.3
Memorandum												
Median Inflation Rate												
Advanced Economies	2.3	2.1	2.1	2.3	2.1	3.9	0.7	2.0	3.1	2.2	1.9	2.0
Emerging and Developing Economies	6.7	4.4	5.5	6.0	6.3	10.3	4.0	4.4	5.8	5.2	5.0	4.0

[1]In this table, Other Advanced Economies means advanced economies excluding the United States, Euro Area countries, and Japan.

[2]Based on Eurostat's harmonized index of consumer prices.

[3]Georgia and Mongolia, which are not members of the Commonwealth of Independent States, are included in this group for reasons of geography and similarities in economic structure.

Table A6. Advanced Economies: Consumer Prices

(Annual percent change)

	Average									Projections			End of Period[1]	Projections	
	1994–2003	2004	2005	2006	2007	2008	2009	2010	2011	2012	2013	2017	2011	2012	2013
Advanced Economies	**2.1**	**2.0**	**2.3**	**2.4**	**2.2**	**3.4**	**0.1**	**1.5**	**2.7**	**1.9**	**1.7**	**1.9**	**2.5**	**1.8**	**1.7**
United States	2.4	2.7	3.4	3.2	2.9	3.8	–0.3	1.6	3.1	2.1	1.9	2.0	3.0	1.9	1.9
Euro Area[2]	2.0	2.2	2.2	2.2	2.1	3.3	0.3	1.6	2.7	2.0	1.6	1.8	2.7	1.9	1.5
Germany	1.4	1.8	1.9	1.8	2.3	2.8	0.2	1.2	2.5	1.9	1.8	2.0	2.3	1.9	1.8
France	1.6	2.3	1.9	1.9	1.6	3.2	0.1	1.7	2.3	2.0	1.6	2.0	2.3	2.0	1.6
Italy	2.9	2.3	2.2	2.2	2.0	3.5	0.8	1.6	2.9	2.5	1.8	1.5	3.7	1.8	0.8
Spain	3.2	3.1	3.4	3.6	2.8	4.1	–0.2	2.0	3.1	1.9	1.6	1.5	2.4	1.7	1.5
Netherlands	2.5	1.4	1.5	1.7	1.6	2.2	1.0	0.9	2.5	1.8	1.8	1.8	2.2	1.8	1.8
Belgium	1.7	1.9	2.5	2.3	1.8	4.5	0.0	2.3	3.5	2.4	1.9	1.9	3.2	2.0	1.8
Austria	1.6	2.0	2.1	1.7	2.2	3.2	0.4	1.7	3.6	2.2	1.9	1.9	3.6	1.9	1.9
Greece	5.3	3.0	3.5	3.3	3.0	4.2	1.3	4.7	3.1	–0.5	–0.3	1.4	2.2	0.8	0.0
Portugal	3.2	2.5	2.1	3.0	2.4	2.7	–0.9	1.4	3.6	3.2	1.4	1.5	3.8	2.6	1.3
Finland	1.6	0.1	0.8	1.3	1.6	3.9	1.6	1.7	3.3	2.9	2.1	2.0	2.6	2.8	2.2
Ireland	3.1	2.3	2.1	2.7	2.8	3.1	–1.7	–1.6	1.1	1.7	1.2	1.8	1.9	1.5	1.3
Slovak Republic	8.3	7.5	2.8	4.3	1.9	3.9	0.9	0.7	4.1	3.8	2.3	2.8	4.7	2.8	2.1
Slovenia	9.6	3.6	2.5	2.5	3.6	5.7	0.9	1.8	1.8	2.2	1.8	2.1	2.1	2.3	1.9
Luxembourg	1.9	2.2	2.5	2.7	2.3	3.4	0.4	2.3	3.4	2.3	1.6	1.5	3.2	1.9	1.4
Estonia	12.9	3.0	4.1	4.4	6.6	10.4	–0.1	2.9	5.1	3.9	2.6	2.8	4.1	3.5	2.6
Cyprus	3.0	1.9	2.0	2.2	2.2	4.4	0.2	2.6	3.5	2.8	2.2	2.0	4.2	2.2	2.2
Malta	3.0	2.7	2.5	2.6	0.7	4.7	1.8	2.0	2.4	2.0	1.9	2.2	1.3	1.8	2.6
Japan	0.0	0.0	–0.3	0.2	0.1	1.4	–1.3	–0.7	–0.3	0.0	0.0	0.9	–0.2	0.2	0.1
United Kingdom[2]	1.7	1.3	2.0	2.3	2.3	3.6	2.1	3.3	4.5	2.4	2.0	2.0	4.7	2.0	2.0
Canada	1.8	1.8	2.2	2.0	2.1	2.4	0.3	1.8	2.9	2.2	2.0	2.0	2.7	2.0	2.0
Korea	4.1	3.6	2.8	2.2	2.5	4.7	2.8	2.9	4.0	3.4	3.2	3.0	4.2	3.2	3.0
Australia	2.6	2.3	2.7	3.5	2.3	4.4	1.8	2.8	3.4	2.7	3.0	2.4	3.1	3.5	2.4
Taiwan Province of China	1.4	1.6	2.3	0.6	1.8	3.5	–0.9	1.0	1.4	1.3	1.8	2.0	–3.5	1.3	1.8
Sweden	1.6	1.0	0.8	1.5	1.7	3.3	2.0	1.9	1.4	2.5	2.0	2.0	0.4	3.1	2.0
Hong Kong SAR	1.7	–0.4	0.9	2.0	2.0	4.3	0.6	2.3	5.3	3.8	3.0	3.0	5.7	3.8	3.0
Switzerland	0.9	0.8	1.2	1.1	0.7	2.4	–0.5	0.7	0.2	–0.5	0.5	1.0	0.2	–0.5	0.5
Singapore	1.0	1.7	0.5	1.0	2.1	6.6	0.6	2.8	5.2	3.5	2.3	2.0	5.5	2.5	2.2
Czech Republic	. . .	2.8	1.8	2.5	2.9	6.3	1.0	1.5	1.9	3.5	1.9	2.0	2.4	3.2	1.8
Norway	2.2	0.5	1.5	2.3	0.7	3.8	2.2	2.4	1.3	1.5	2.0	2.5	0.2	1.7	2.2
Israel	6.1	–0.4	1.3	2.1	0.5	4.6	3.3	2.7	3.4	2.0	2.0	2.0	2.2	2.3	2.0
Denmark	2.1	1.1	1.8	1.9	1.7	3.4	1.3	2.3	2.8	2.6	2.2	1.8	2.5	2.7	2.4
New Zealand	2.0	2.3	3.0	3.4	2.4	4.0	2.1	2.3	4.0	2.1	2.4	2.0	1.8	2.6	2.5
Iceland	3.1	3.2	4.0	6.8	5.0	12.4	12.0	5.4	4.0	4.8	3.5	2.5	5.5	4.1	2.9
Memorandum															
Major Advanced Economies	1.8	2.0	2.3	2.3	2.2	3.2	–0.1	1.4	2.6	1.8	1.6	1.8	2.6	1.6	1.5
Newly Industrialized Asian Economies	2.8	2.4	2.2	1.6	2.2	4.5	1.3	2.3	3.6	2.9	2.7	2.6	2.3	2.7	2.6

[1]December–December changes. Several countries report Q4–Q4 changes.
[2]Based on Eurostat's harmonized index of consumer prices.

Table A7. Emerging and Developing Economies: Consumer Prices[1]
(Annual percent change)

													End of Period[2]		
	Average								Projections				Projections		
	1994–2003	2004	2005	2006	2007	2008	2009	2010	2011	2012	2013	2017	2011	2012	2013
Central and Eastern Europe[3]	**37.7**	**6.6**	**5.9**	**5.9**	**6.0**	**8.1**	**4.7**	**5.3**	**5.3**	**6.2**	**4.5**	**3.8**	**6.4**	**5.3**	**4.1**
Albania	10.3	2.9	2.4	2.4	2.9	3.4	2.2	3.6	3.4	1.9	3.0	3.0	1.7	3.1	3.0
Bosnia and Herzegovina	. . .	0.3	3.6	6.1	1.5	7.4	–0.4	2.1	3.7	2.2	2.1	2.4	2.7	2.2	2.1
Bulgaria	62.5	6.1	6.0	7.4	7.6	12.0	2.5	3.0	3.4	2.1	2.3	3.0	2.0	2.1	2.5
Croatia	10.7	2.0	3.3	3.2	2.9	6.1	2.4	1.0	2.3	2.2	2.4	3.0	2.0	2.5	2.7
Hungary	14.0	6.8	3.6	3.9	7.9	6.1	4.2	4.9	3.9	5.2	3.5	3.0	4.1	5.0	3.2
Kosovo	. . .	–1.1	–1.4	0.6	4.4	9.4	–2.4	3.5	7.3	0.6	1.2	1.3	3.6	1.0	1.9
Latvia	9.8	6.2	6.9	6.6	10.1	15.3	3.3	–1.2	4.2	2.6	2.2	2.1	3.9	2.0	2.4
Lithuania	. . .	1.2	2.7	3.8	5.8	11.1	4.2	1.2	4.1	3.1	2.5	2.2	3.5	3.3	2.3
Former Yugoslav Republic of Macedonia	12.4	–0.4	0.5	3.2	2.3	8.4	–0.8	1.5	3.9	2.0	2.0	2.0	2.8	2.0	2.0
Montenegro	. . .	3.1	3.4	2.1	3.5	9.0	3.6	0.7	3.1	2.0	1.1	1.3	2.8	1.7	1.3
Poland	12.8	3.5	2.1	1.0	2.5	4.2	3.5	2.5	4.3	3.8	2.7	2.5	4.6	3.2	2.5
Romania	53.2	11.9	9.0	6.6	4.8	7.8	5.6	6.1	5.8	2.9	3.1	3.0	3.1	3.6	3.0
Serbia	. . .	10.6	16.2	10.7	6.9	12.4	8.1	6.2	11.2	4.1	4.3	3.8	7.0	4.5	4.0
Turkey	67.3	8.6	8.2	9.6	8.8	10.4	6.3	8.6	6.5	10.6	7.1	5.5	10.4	8.6	6.2
Commonwealth of Independent States[3,4]	**62.9**	**10.4**	**12.1**	**9.4**	**9.7**	**15.6**	**11.2**	**7.2**	**10.1**	**7.1**	**7.7**	**6.5**	**9.2**	**7.7**	**7.4**
Russia	57.5	10.9	12.7	9.7	9.0	14.1	11.7	6.9	8.4	4.8	6.4	6.5	6.1	6.2	6.5
Excluding Russia	79.1	9.0	10.6	8.8	11.5	19.5	10.1	7.9	14.0	12.7	10.7	6.4	17.0	11.3	9.5
Armenia	72.9	7.0	0.6	3.0	4.6	9.0	3.5	7.3	7.7	4.0	4.2	4.0	4.7	4.5	4.0
Azerbaijan	62.4	6.7	9.7	8.4	16.6	20.8	1.6	5.7	7.9	5.6	6.1	6.0	5.6	5.6	6.5
Belarus	175.7	18.1	10.3	7.0	8.4	14.8	13.0	7.7	53.2	66.0	35.8	6.9	108.7	38.4	27.5
Georgia	. . .	5.8	8.2	9.2	9.2	10.0	1.7	7.1	8.5	1.7	5.5	6.0	2.0	5.0	6.0
Kazakhstan	59.9	6.9	7.5	8.6	10.8	17.1	7.3	7.1	8.3	5.5	7.0	6.0	7.4	6.4	6.8
Kyrgyz Republic	29.4	4.1	4.3	5.6	10.2	24.5	6.8	7.8	16.6	4.1	8.1	5.9	5.7	8.0	7.5
Moldova	34.6	12.4	11.9	12.7	12.4	12.7	0.0	7.4	7.6	5.5	5.0	5.0	7.8	5.0	5.0
Mongolia	24.2	7.9	12.5	4.5	8.2	26.8	6.3	10.2	9.5	13.6	12.5	7.0	11.1	14.2	10.8
Tajikistan	105.9	7.2	7.3	10.0	13.2	20.4	6.5	6.5	12.4	7.9	8.4	7.0	9.3	9.0	7.3
Turkmenistan	146.2	5.9	10.7	8.2	6.3	14.5	–2.7	4.4	5.8	6.2	7.0	7.0	5.3	7.0	7.0
Ukraine	70.2	9.0	13.5	9.1	12.8	25.2	15.9	9.4	8.0	4.5	6.7	5.0	4.6	7.9	5.9
Uzbekistan	91.6	6.6	10.0	14.2	12.3	12.7	14.1	9.4	12.8	12.7	10.9	11.0	13.3	11.0	11.0

Table A7. Emerging and Developing Economies: Consumer Prices[1] *(continued)*

	Average									Projections			End of Period[2]	Projections	
	1994–2003	2004	2005	2006	2007	2008	2009	2010	2011	2012	2013	2017	2011	2012	2013
Developing Asia	**6.1**	**4.1**	**3.7**	**4.2**	**5.4**	**7.4**	**3.0**	**5.7**	**6.5**	**5.0**	**4.6**	**3.6**	**5.2**	**5.3**	**3.9**
Islamic Republic of Afghanistan	. . .	13.2	12.3	5.1	13.0	26.8	–12.2	7.7	11.2	4.5	5.0	5.0	7.7	5.0	5.0
Bangladesh	5.2	6.1	7.0	6.8	9.1	8.9	5.4	8.1	10.7	10.4	7.9	4.8	10.6	9.6	6.8
Bhutan	6.1	4.6	5.3	5.0	5.2	8.3	4.4	7.0	8.6	8.4	7.3	5.5	6.8	8.5	6.3
Brunei Darussalam	1.1	0.9	1.1	0.2	1.0	2.1	1.0	0.4	2.0	1.6	1.4	1.3	1.8	1.6	1.4
Cambodia	5.3	3.9	6.3	6.1	7.7	25.0	–0.7	4.0	5.5	4.0	3.6	5.7	4.9	5.5	4.6
China	4.9	3.9	1.8	1.5	4.8	5.9	–0.7	3.3	5.4	3.3	3.0	3.0	4.1	3.5	2.5
Republic of Fiji	2.7	2.8	2.3	2.5	4.8	7.7	3.7	5.5	8.6	4.9	4.5	3.5	7.0	4.8	4.5
India	7.0	3.9	4.0	6.3	6.4	8.3	10.9	12.0	8.6	8.2	7.3	4.0	6.6	8.5	6.3
Indonesia	13.7	6.1	10.5	13.1	6.7	9.8	4.8	5.1	5.4	6.2	6.0	4.0	3.8	7.5	5.2
Kiribati	2.5	–0.9	–0.3	–1.5	4.2	11.0	8.8	–2.8	2.8	2.5	2.0	2.5	2.8	2.5	2.0
Lao People's Democratic Republic	29.7	10.5	7.2	6.8	4.5	7.6	0.0	6.0	8.7	6.7	5.3	3.5	9.7	6.0	4.8
Malaysia	2.7	1.4	3.0	3.6	2.0	5.4	0.6	1.7	3.2	2.7	2.5	2.5	3.2	2.7	2.5
Maldives	2.1	6.3	2.5	3.5	7.4	12.3	4.0	4.7	12.1	11.5	8.3	3.0	15.0	8.0	8.0
Myanmar	. . .	3.8	10.7	26.3	32.9	22.5	8.2	8.2	4.2	5.8	6.3	5.3	5.0	5.4	5.3
Nepal	6.5	4.0	4.5	8.0	6.2	6.7	12.6	9.5	9.6	7.8	7.4	5.5	9.7	7.2	6.9
Pakistan	7.3	4.0	9.3	8.0	7.8	10.8	17.6	10.1	13.7	12.0	12.5	14.0	13.3	11.0	11.5
Papua New Guinea	11.5	2.1	1.8	2.4	0.9	10.8	6.9	6.0	8.4	6.8	6.7	6.5	6.9	6.8	6.7
Philippines	6.3	5.6	7.8	5.6	3.0	8.2	4.2	3.8	4.8	3.4	4.1	4.0	4.2	4.2	4.0
Samoa	4.0	7.8	7.8	3.5	4.7	6.3	14.6	–0.2	2.9	7.5	4.0	4.0	2.9	5.5	4.0
Solomon Islands	9.6	6.9	7.0	11.1	7.7	17.4	7.1	1.0	6.7	5.3	4.2	4.6	7.1	5.2	4.6
Sri Lanka	9.4	9.0	11.0	10.0	15.8	22.4	3.5	6.2	6.7	7.5	8.0	6.0	4.9	9.1	7.0
Thailand	3.6	2.8	4.5	4.6	2.2	5.5	–0.8	3.3	3.8	3.9	3.3	3.0	3.5	5.5	1.6
Timor-Leste	. . .	3.2	1.1	3.9	10.3	9.0	0.7	6.8	13.5	13.0	8.0	8.0	17.4	9.5	8.0
Tonga	5.1	10.8	8.5	6.1	7.4	7.4	3.5	3.9	5.3	4.5	5.3	6.0	5.4	4.5	6.0
Tuvalu	. . .	2.4	3.2	4.2	2.3	10.4	–0.3	–1.9	0.5	2.6	2.7	2.7	. . .	. . .	. . .
Vanuatu	2.5	1.4	1.2	2.0	3.9	4.8	4.3	2.8	1.2	2.6	3.0	3.0	1.8	3.0	3.0
Vietnam	5.1	7.9	8.4	7.5	8.3	23.1	6.7	9.2	18.7	12.6	6.8	5.0	18.1	9.5	5.9

Table A7. Emerging and Developing Economies: Consumer Prices[1] *(continued)*

	Average									Projections			End of Period[2]	Projections	
	1994–2003	2004	2005	2006	2007	2008	2009	2010	2011	2012	2013	2017	2011	2012	2013
Latin America and the Caribbean	**25.7**	**6.6**	**6.3**	**5.3**	**5.4**	**7.9**	**6.0**	**6.0**	**6.6**	**6.4**	**5.9**	**5.6**	**6.7**	**6.3**	**5.9**
Antigua and Barbuda	2.2	2.0	2.1	1.8	1.4	5.3	–0.6	3.4	3.3	4.5	2.8	2.4	3.9	3.4	3.0
Argentina[5]	4.2	4.4	9.6	10.9	8.8	8.6	6.3	10.5	9.8	9.9	9.9	11.0	9.8	10.3	10.3
The Bahamas	1.7	1.2	2.0	1.8	2.5	4.4	2.1	1.0	2.5	2.0	2.0	2.0	4.0	1.5	2.0
Barbados	1.8	1.4	6.1	7.3	4.0	8.1	3.7	5.8	9.4	6.4	5.6	4.4	9.5	6.0	5.3
Belize	1.7	3.1	3.7	4.2	2.3	6.4	2.0	–0.2	1.9	3.2	2.5	2.5	3.8	2.5	2.5
Bolivia	5.5	8.1	5.2	4.1	8.7	10.3	6.5	2.5	9.9	4.9	4.5	4.0	6.9	5.0	4.4
Brazil	52.7	6.6	6.9	4.2	3.6	5.7	4.9	5.0	6.6	5.2	5.0	4.5	6.5	5.0	5.0
Chile	5.4	1.1	3.1	3.4	4.4	8.7	1.5	1.4	3.3	3.8	3.0	3.0	4.4	3.2	3.0
Colombia	14.2	5.9	5.0	4.3	5.5	7.0	4.2	2.3	3.4	3.5	3.1	3.0	3.7	3.1	3.1
Costa Rica	12.9	12.3	13.8	11.5	9.4	13.4	7.8	5.7	4.9	5.4	6.0	4.0	4.7	6.5	5.5
Dominica	1.2	2.4	1.6	2.6	3.2	6.4	0.0	3.2	2.3	2.5	2.5	1.5	4.0	2.0	2.3
Dominican Republic	9.3	51.5	4.2	7.6	6.1	10.6	1.4	6.3	8.5	5.5	5.5	4.0	7.8	6.0	5.0
Ecuador	33.0	2.7	2.1	3.3	2.3	8.4	5.2	3.6	4.5	5.7	4.8	3.0	5.4	5.7	4.5
El Salvador	4.4	4.5	4.7	4.0	4.6	7.3	0.4	1.2	3.6	4.5	3.4	2.8	5.1	4.0	2.8
Grenada	1.6	2.3	3.5	4.3	3.9	8.0	–0.3	3.4	3.0	3.2	2.2	2.0	3.5	2.4	2.2
Guatemala	8.0	7.6	9.1	6.6	6.8	11.4	1.9	3.9	6.2	4.6	4.6	4.0	6.2	5.0	4.5
Guyana	6.7	4.7	6.9	6.7	12.2	8.1	3.0	3.7	5.7	5.5	5.6	5.6	6.2	4.9	6.2
Haiti	19.0	28.3	16.8	14.2	9.0	14.4	3.4	4.1	7.4	7.7	7.0	3.4	10.4	8.0	4.9
Honduras	15.1	8.0	8.8	5.6	6.9	11.5	8.7	4.7	6.8	5.2	6.4	6.0	5.6	6.3	6.2
Jamaica	13.4	13.5	15.1	8.5	9.3	22.0	9.6	12.6	7.5	6.9	6.8	6.6	6.0	6.9	6.5
Mexico	15.0	4.7	4.0	3.6	4.0	5.1	5.3	4.2	3.4	3.9	3.0	3.0	3.8	3.6	3.1
Nicaragua	8.2	8.5	9.6	9.1	11.1	19.8	3.7	5.5	8.1	9.0	6.8	6.9	8.0	7.5	7.3
Panama	1.0	0.5	2.9	2.5	4.2	8.8	2.4	3.5	5.9	6.0	5.5	4.0	6.3	6.2	5.5
Paraguay	10.9	4.3	6.8	9.6	8.1	10.2	2.6	4.7	6.6	5.0	5.0	4.1	4.9	5.0	5.0
Peru	7.2	3.7	1.6	2.0	1.8	5.8	2.9	1.5	3.4	3.3	2.6	2.0	4.7	2.6	2.3
St. Kitts and Nevis	3.1	2.2	3.4	8.5	4.5	5.3	2.1	1.0	5.4	2.8	1.8	2.5	1.2	2.1	2.5
St. Lucia	2.6	1.5	3.9	3.6	2.8	5.5	–0.2	3.3	2.8	3.2	2.3	2.5	4.8	2.0	2.6
St. Vincent and the Grenadines	1.3	2.9	3.4	3.0	7.0	10.1	0.4	0.8	3.2	2.7	1.6	2.5	4.7	0.7	2.6
Suriname	62.0	9.1	9.9	11.3	6.4	14.6	–0.1	6.9	17.7	6.3	5.5	4.0	15.3	7.5	4.0
Trinidad and Tobago	4.2	3.7	6.9	8.3	7.9	12.0	7.0	10.5	5.1	5.4	4.0	4.0	5.3	4.0	4.0
Uruguay	18.6	9.2	4.7	6.4	8.1	7.9	7.1	6.7	8.1	7.4	6.6	6.0	8.6	7.0	6.0
Venezuela	39.1	21.7	16.0	13.7	18.7	30.4	27.1	28.2	26.1	31.6	28.8	27.3	25.2	33.4	28.7
Middle East and North Africa	**8.2**	**6.6**	**5.6**	**7.6**	**10.1**	**13.6**	**6.6**	**6.9**	**9.6**	**9.5**	**8.7**	**6.9**	**9.4**	**9.0**	**8.7**
Algeria	9.4	3.6	1.6	2.3	3.6	4.9	5.7	3.9	4.5	5.5	4.5	4.3	4.5	6.5	4.5
Bahrain	0.9	2.2	2.6	2.0	3.3	3.5	2.8	2.0	1.0	1.0	1.5	2.0	1.0	2.0	2.0
Djibouti	2.5	3.1	3.1	3.5	5.0	12.0	1.7	4.0	5.1	4.3	2.5	2.5	7.6	2.0	1.3
Egypt	5.1	8.1	8.8	4.2	11.0	11.7	16.2	11.7	11.1	9.5	12.1	7.0	11.8	10.8	12.7
Islamic Republic of Iran	21.4	15.3	10.4	11.9	18.4	25.4	10.8	12.4	21.3	21.8	18.2	15.5	19.6	18.0	18.2
Iraq	. . .	. . .	. . .	53.2	30.8	2.7	–2.2	2.4	6.0	7.0	6.0	4.0	6.0	7.0	6.0
Jordan	2.5	3.4	3.5	6.3	4.7	13.9	–0.7	5.0	4.4	4.9	5.6	4.4	3.3	4.9	5.4
Kuwait	1.7	1.3	4.1	3.1	5.5	10.6	4.0	4.0	4.7	3.5	4.0	4.1	4.7	3.5	4.0
Lebanon	4.1	1.7	–0.7	5.6	4.1	10.8	1.2	4.5	5.0	4.0	3.3	2.0	3.1	4.5	2.0
Libya	0.7	1.0	2.9	1.4	6.2	10.4	2.4	2.5	14.1	1.9	–2.3	5.0	14.1	1.9	–2.3
Mauritania	4.9	10.4	12.1	6.2	7.3	7.3	2.2	6.3	5.7	5.3	6.1	5.1	5.5	6.0	6.3
Morocco	2.5	1.5	1.0	3.3	2.0	3.9	1.0	1.0	0.9	2.0	2.5	2.6	0.9	2.0	2.5
Oman	–0.3	0.7	1.9	3.4	5.9	12.6	3.5	3.3	4.0	3.2	3.0	2.7	3.3	3.1	3.0
Qatar	2.5	6.8	8.8	11.8	13.8	15.0	–4.9	–2.4	2.0	4.0	4.0	5.0	2.0	4.0	4.0
Saudi Arabia	0.4	0.4	0.6	2.3	4.1	9.9	5.1	5.4	5.0	4.8	4.4	4.0	5.3	4.7	4.2
Sudan[6]	36.4	8.4	8.5	7.2	8.0	14.3	11.3	13.0	18.1	23.2	26.0	12.3	18.9	28.2	25.9
Syrian Arab Republic[7]	3.2	4.4	7.2	10.4	4.7	15.2	2.8	4.4	. . .	. . .	. . .	. . .	. . .	. . .	. . .
Tunisia	3.5	3.6	2.0	4.1	3.4	4.9	3.5	4.4	3.5	5.0	4.0	3.5	3.5	5.0	4.0
United Arab Emirates	3.0	5.0	6.2	9.3	11.1	12.3	1.6	0.9	0.9	1.5	1.7	2.1	1.2	1.6	1.8
Republic of Yemen	22.6	12.5	9.9	10.8	7.9	19.0	3.7	11.2	17.6	17.1	14.1	8.0	22.7	16.1	12.0

Table A7. Emerging and Developing Economies: Consumer Prices[1] *(concluded)*

	Average									Projections			End of Period[2]	Projections	
	1994–2003	2004	2005	2006	2007	2008	2009	2010	2011	2012	2013	2017	2011	2012	2013
Sub-Saharan Africa	**20.2**	**7.6**	**8.9**	**6.9**	**6.9**	**11.7**	**10.6**	**7.4**	**8.2**	**9.6**	**7.5**	**5.3**	**9.7**	**8.6**	**7.0**
Angola	413.6	43.6	23.0	13.3	12.2	12.5	13.7	14.5	13.5	11.1	8.3	4.5	11.4	10.0	7.0
Benin	7.5	0.9	5.4	3.8	1.3	8.0	2.2	2.1	2.7	7.0	3.5	2.8	1.8	7.2	3.5
Botswana	8.7	7.0	8.6	11.6	7.1	12.6	8.1	6.9	8.5	7.8	6.7	6.0	9.2	6.7	6.6
Burkina Faso	5.2	–0.4	6.4	2.4	–0.2	10.7	2.6	–0.6	2.7	2.5	2.0	2.0	5.1	2.5	2.0
Burundi	14.6	11.8	1.2	9.1	14.4	26.0	4.6	4.1	14.9	10.3	8.4	5.5	14.9	10.3	8.4
Cameroon[8]	6.1	0.3	2.0	4.9	1.1	5.3	3.0	1.3	2.9	3.0	3.0	2.5	2.7	3.0	3.0
Cape Verde	3.9	–1.9	0.4	4.8	4.4	6.8	1.0	2.1	4.5	2.1	2.0	2.0	3.6	2.3	2.3
Central African Republic	5.6	–2.2	2.9	6.7	0.9	9.3	3.5	1.5	0.7	2.5	1.9	1.8	1.3	1.8	2.0
Chad	7.3	–4.8	3.7	7.7	–7.4	8.3	10.1	–2.1	1.9	5.5	3.0	3.0	10.8	5.5	3.0
Comoros	5.0	4.5	3.0	3.4	4.5	4.8	4.8	3.9	6.8	5.6	3.1	3.4	7.0	4.3	2.0
Democratic Republic of Congo	382.7	4.0	21.4	13.2	16.7	18.0	46.2	23.5	15.5	12.7	9.4	7.3	15.4	9.9	9.0
Republic of Congo	7.7	3.7	2.5	4.7	2.6	6.0	4.3	5.0	1.9	2.7	2.9	2.6	3.0	3.0	2.5
Côte d'Ivoire	6.3	1.5	3.9	2.5	1.9	6.3	1.0	1.4	4.9	2.0	2.5	2.5	1.9	1.5	2.5
Equatorial Guinea	9.3	4.2	5.7	4.5	2.8	4.3	7.2	7.5	7.3	7.0	7.0	6.9	7.3	7.0	7.0
Eritrea	13.0	25.1	12.5	15.1	9.3	19.9	33.0	12.7	13.3	12.3	12.3	12.3	12.3	12.3	12.3
Ethiopia	2.4	8.6	6.8	12.3	15.8	25.3	36.4	2.8	18.1	33.9	23.1	9.0	38.1	25.4	15.5
Gabon	5.0	0.4	1.2	–1.4	5.0	5.3	1.9	1.4	1.3	2.3	2.6	3.0	2.3	2.3	2.6
The Gambia	4.7	14.3	5.0	2.1	5.4	4.5	4.6	5.0	4.8	4.7	5.5	5.0	4.4	5.0	6.0
Ghana	27.8	12.6	15.1	10.2	10.7	16.5	19.3	10.7	8.7	9.6	8.9	7.0	8.6	9.8	9.0
Guinea	5.0	17.5	31.4	34.7	22.9	18.4	4.7	15.5	21.5	15.0	11.2	5.9	20.5	12.0	8.7
Guinea-Bissau	13.6	0.8	3.2	0.7	4.6	10.4	–1.6	1.1	5.0	3.5	2.5	2.0	3.3	2.1	1.7
Kenya	8.9	11.8	9.9	6.0	4.3	15.1	10.6	4.1	14.0	10.6	5.2	5.0	18.6	7.0	7.0
Lesotho	8.4	4.6	3.6	6.3	9.2	10.7	5.9	3.4	5.6	5.2	4.6	4.7	6.4	2.9	4.1
Liberia	. . .	3.6	6.9	7.2	13.7	17.5	7.4	7.3	8.5	5.2	4.2	5.0	11.4	3.3	3.4
Madagascar	15.0	14.0	18.4	10.8	10.4	9.2	9.0	9.2	10.6	8.9	8.5	5.0	10.5	9.0	8.5
Malawi	30.9	11.4	15.5	13.9	8.0	8.7	8.4	7.4	7.6	11.1	11.9	11.3	9.7	12.1	12.0
Mali	5.0	–3.1	6.4	1.5	1.5	9.1	2.2	1.3	3.1	6.1	2.2	2.7	5.3	6.0	3.4
Mauritius	6.0	4.7	4.9	8.7	8.6	9.7	2.5	2.9	6.5	4.8	5.6	4.4	4.9	5.2	5.6
Mozambique	20.6	12.6	6.4	13.2	8.2	10.3	3.3	12.7	10.4	7.2	5.6	5.6	5.5	5.6	5.6
Namibia	8.9	4.1	2.3	5.1	6.7	10.4	8.8	4.5	5.8	6.7	5.9	4.5	7.2	6.2	5.7
Niger	6.0	0.4	7.8	0.1	0.1	10.5	1.1	0.9	2.9	4.5	2.0	2.0	1.4	4.5	2.0
Nigeria	22.0	15.0	17.9	8.2	5.4	11.6	12.5	13.7	10.8	11.2	9.7	7.0	10.3	11.0	9.5
Rwanda	13.0	12.0	9.1	8.8	9.1	15.4	10.3	2.3	5.7	7.9	6.8	5.0	8.4	7.5	6.0
São Tomé and Príncipe	27.7	13.3	17.2	23.1	18.6	32.0	17.0	13.3	14.3	8.3	4.9	3.0	11.9	6.0	4.0
Senegal	4.9	0.5	1.7	2.1	5.9	5.8	–1.7	1.2	3.4	3.0	2.2	2.1	2.7	2.8	2.1
Seychelles	2.5	3.9	0.6	–1.9	5.3	37.0	31.7	–2.4	2.6	6.3	3.6	3.1	5.5	5.0	3.1
Sierra Leone	15.5	14.2	12.0	9.5	11.6	14.8	9.2	17.8	18.5	11.5	9.1	5.4	16.9	11.0	7.5
South Africa	7.2	1.4	3.4	4.7	7.1	11.5	7.1	4.3	5.0	5.7	5.3	4.7	6.1	5.5	5.3
Swaziland	8.6	3.4	4.9	5.2	8.1	12.7	7.4	4.5	6.1	7.2	6.7	5.2	7.8	5.1	9.0
Tanzania	13.4	4.1	4.4	5.6	6.3	8.4	11.8	10.5	7.0	17.4	9.5	5.4	10.9	15.6	7.9
Togo	6.5	0.4	6.8	2.2	0.9	8.7	1.9	3.2	3.6	1.5	3.0	2.3	1.5	1.0	6.1
Uganda	4.7	5.0	8.0	6.6	6.8	7.3	14.2	9.4	6.5	23.4	7.6	0.0	15.7	15.0	5.3
Zambia	29.5	18.0	18.3	9.0	10.7	12.4	13.4	8.5	8.7	5.6	5.2	5.0	7.2	6.0	5.0
Zimbabwe[9]	. . .	. . .	. . .	. . .	. . .	. . .	6.2	3.0	3.5	6.2	5.1	5.0	4.9	6.5	5.0

[1]In accordance with standard practice in the *World Economic Outlook*, movements in consumer prices are indicated as annual averages rather than as December–December changes during the year, as is the practice in some countries. For many countries, figures for recent years are IMF staff estimates. Data for some countries are for fiscal years.

[2]December–December changes. Several countries report Q4–Q4 changes.

[3]For many countries, inflation for the earlier years is measured on the basis of a retail price index. Consumer price index (CPI) inflation data with broader and more up-to-date coverage are typically used for more recent years.

[4]Georgia and Mongolia, which are not members of the Commonwealth of Independent States, are included in this group for reasons of geography and similarities in economic structure.

[5]Figures are based on Argentina's official consumer price index (CPI-GBA) data. The IMF has called on Argentina to adopt remedial measures to address the quality of these data. The IMF staff is also using alternative measures of inflation for macroeconomic surveillance, including data produced by provincial statistical offices and private analysts, which have shown considerably higher inflation figures than the official data since 2007.

[6]Data for 2011 exclude South Sudan after July 9. Data for 2012 and onward pertain to the current Sudan.

[7]Data for Syrian Arab Republic are excluded for 2011 onward due to the uncertain political situation.

[8]The percent changes in 2002 are calculated over a period of 18 months, reflecting a change in the fiscal year cycle (from July–June to January–December).

[9]The Zimbabwe dollar ceased circulating in early 2009. Data are based on IMF staff estimates of price and exchange rate developments in U.S. dollars. IMF staff estimates of U.S. dollar values may differ from authorities' estimates.

Table A8. Major Advanced Economies: General Government Fiscal Balances and Debt[1]

(Percent of GDP unless noted otherwise)

	Average							Projections		
	1996–2005	2006	2007	2008	2009	2010	2011	2012	2013	2017
Major Advanced Economies										
Net Lending/Borrowing	. . .	–2.2	–2.0	–4.5	–10.0	–8.7	–7.7	–6.8	–5.5	–3.6
Output Gap[2]	0.4	0.8	0.8	–1.0	–5.9	–4.0	–3.8	–3.7	–3.2	–0.1
Structural Balance[2]	. . .	–2.6	–2.5	–3.9	–6.2	–6.5	–5.9	–5.0	–4.0	–3.4
United States										
Net Lending/Borrowing	. . .	–2.0	–2.7	–6.7	–13.0	–10.5	–9.6	–8.1	–6.3	–4.4
Output Gap[2]	1.0	0.9	0.1	–2.2	–7.0	–5.1	–5.1	–4.9	–4.4	0.0
Structural Balance[2]	. . .	–2.4	–2.8	–5.0	–7.5	–7.8	–7.2	–5.9	–4.4	–4.3
Net Debt	43.4	48.5	48.2	53.7	65.9	73.1	80.3	83.7	86.7	88.4
Gross Debt	62.7	66.6	67.2	76.1	89.9	98.5	102.9	106.6	110.2	113.0
Euro Area										
Net Lending/Borrowing	–2.4	–1.3	–0.7	–2.1	–6.4	–6.2	–4.1	–3.2	–2.7	–1.1
Output Gap[2]	0.0	1.4	2.7	1.6	–3.5	–2.4	–1.4	–2.3	–2.2	–0.3
Structural Balance[2]	–2.5	–2.4	–2.3	–2.9	–4.4	–4.2	–3.2	–1.8	–1.3	–0.9
Net Debt	55.3	54.3	52.0	54.0	62.2	65.8	68.4	70.3	71.5	69.5
Gross Debt	70.6	68.6	66.4	70.2	79.9	85.7	88.1	90.0	91.0	86.9
Germany[3]										
Net Lending/Borrowing	–2.6	–1.6	0.2	–0.1	–3.2	–4.3	–1.0	–0.8	–0.6	–0.2
Output Gap[2]	–0.6	1.0	2.7	2.3	–3.7	–1.5	0.2	–0.4	–0.2	0.0
Structural Balance[2,4]	–2.5	–2.3	–1.1	–0.9	–1.2	–2.2	–1.0	–0.6	–0.5	–0.1
Net Debt	45.2	53.0	50.4	50.0	56.6	56.8	56.1	54.1	53.4	52.4
Gross Debt	61.9	67.9	65.2	66.7	74.4	83.2	81.5	78.9	77.4	71.1
France										
Net Lending/Borrowing	–2.9	–2.4	–2.7	–3.3	–7.6	–7.1	–5.3	–4.6	–3.9	–0.5
Output Gap[2]	0.0	0.1	0.7	–0.7	–4.2	–3.6	–2.6	–2.7	–2.5	0.0
Structural Balance[2,4]	–2.8	–2.3	–3.0	–2.9	–4.8	–4.6	–3.4	–2.5	–1.9	–0.2
Net Debt	53.9	59.6	59.5	62.3	72.0	76.6	80.4	83.2	84.9	78.8
Gross Debt	60.4	63.9	64.2	68.3	79.0	82.4	86.3	89.0	90.8	84.6
Italy										
Net Lending/Borrowing	–3.3	–3.3	–1.5	–2.7	–5.4	–4.5	–3.9	–2.4	–1.5	–1.1
Output Gap[2]	0.6	2.0	2.8	1.0	–4.5	–2.9	–2.3	–3.8	–4.1	–1.1
Structural Balance[2,5]	–4.4	–4.0	–3.2	–3.5	–3.6	–3.3	–2.9	–0.4	0.6	–0.5
Net Debt	94.8	89.3	86.9	88.8	97.1	99.0	99.6	102.3	102.6	98.8
Gross Debt	109.9	106.1	103.1	105.8	116.1	118.7	120.1	123.4	123.8	118.9
Japan										
Net Lending/Borrowing	–6.0	–3.7	–2.1	–4.1	–10.4	–9.4	–10.1	–10.0	–8.7	–7.5
Output Gap[2]	–0.8	–0.4	0.3	–1.6	–7.3	–3.6	–4.6	–3.0	–1.8	0.1
Structural Balance[2]	–5.7	–3.5	–2.2	–3.6	–7.4	–7.9	–8.1	–8.7	–7.9	–7.5
Net Debt	60.3	81.0	80.5	95.3	106.2	112.8	126.6	135.2	142.7	165.5
Gross Debt[6]	144.9	186.0	183.0	191.8	210.2	215.3	229.8	235.8	241.1	256.6
United Kingdom										
Net Lending/Borrowing	–1.5	–2.6	–2.7	–4.9	–10.4	–9.9	–8.7	–8.0	–6.6	–1.0
Output Gap[2]	0.5	1.1	2.2	1.3	–3.3	–2.7	–3.2	–4.0	–3.7	0.0
Structural Balance[2]	–1.8	–3.5	–4.0	–6.5	–9.0	–7.8	–6.3	–5.1	–3.8	–0.7
Net Debt	37.3	38.0	38.1	46.0	60.9	71.1	78.3	84.2	87.2	82.6
Gross Debt	42.4	43.1	43.9	52.5	68.4	75.1	82.5	88.4	91.4	86.8
Canada										
Net Lending/Borrowing	0.5	1.6	1.6	0.1	–4.9	–5.6	–4.5	–3.7	–2.9	–0.5
Output Gap[2]	0.6	1.7	1.7	0.2	–4.0	–2.4	–1.7	–1.5	–1.3	0.1
Structural Balance[2]	0.2	0.8	0.5	–0.6	–2.5	–4.1	–3.6	–2.8	–2.2	–0.6
Net Debt	48.9	26.3	22.9	22.6	28.3	30.4	33.3	35.4	36.9	35.6
Gross Debt	85.1	70.3	66.5	71.1	83.6	85.1	85.0	84.7	82.0	73.6

Note: The methodology and specific assumptions for each country are discussed in Box A1 in the Statistical Appendix. The country group composites for fiscal data are calculated as the sum of the U.S. dollar values for the relevant individual countries.

[1]Debt data refer to the end of the year. Debt data are not always comparable across countries.

[2]Percent of potential GDP.

[3]Beginning in 1995, the debt and debt-services obligations of the Treuhandanstalt (and of various other agencies) were taken over by the general government. This debt is equivalent to 8 percent of GDP, and the associated debt service to 1/2 to 1 percent of GDP.

[4]Excludes sizable one-time receipts from the sale of assets, including licenses.

[5]Excludes one-time measures based on the authorities' data and, in the absence of the latter, receipts from the sale of assets.

[6]Includes equity shares.

Table A9. Summary of World Trade Volumes and Prices

(Annual percent change)

	Averages										Projections	
	1994–2003	2004–13	2004	2005	2006	2007	2008	2009	2010	2011	2012	2013
Trade in Goods and Services												
World Trade[1]												
Volume	6.9	5.4	10.6	7.8	9.3	7.9	2.9	–10.5	12.9	5.8	4.0	5.6
Price Deflator												
In U.S. Dollars	0.2	4.2	9.4	5.2	5.2	7.5	11.3	–10.6	5.5	10.9	–0.2	–0.2
In SDRs	0.2	3.2	3.5	5.5	5.6	3.3	7.7	–8.4	6.7	7.1	2.1	–0.2
Volume of Trade												
Exports												
Advanced Economies	6.2	4.4	9.3	6.2	8.9	6.8	1.9	–11.5	12.2	5.3	2.3	4.7
Emerging and Developing Economies	8.7	7.7	13.3	11.9	11.5	10.5	4.7	–7.7	14.7	6.7	6.6	7.2
Imports												
Advanced Economies	6.9	3.7	9.3	6.3	7.8	5.2	0.5	–12.2	11.5	4.3	1.8	4.1
Emerging and Developing Economies	7.0	9.4	15.8	12.1	11.9	14.9	9.0	–8.1	15.3	8.8	8.4	8.1
Terms of Trade												
Advanced Economies	0.2	–0.6	–0.4	–1.5	–1.1	0.3	–2.0	2.3	–1.0	–1.7	–0.9	0.1
Emerging and Developing Economies	0.3	1.5	3.3	4.9	2.8	1.1	2.9	–4.3	2.0	3.2	0.6	–1.1
Trade in Goods												
World Trade[1]												
Volume	7.1	5.3	10.6	7.8	9.2	7.2	2.4	–11.7	14.3	6.3	3.7	5.6
Price Deflator												
In U.S. Dollars	0.3	4.5	9.2	5.7	5.8	7.6	12.1	–11.8	6.6	12.1	0.1	–0.2
In SDRs	0.2	3.5	3.3	6.0	6.2	3.5	8.5	–9.6	7.7	8.3	2.4	–0.2
World Trade Prices in U.S. Dollars[2]												
Manufactures	0.2	2.6	5.1	2.7	2.5	6.0	6.7	–6.6	2.4	7.2	0.2	0.2
Oil	5.6	14.3	30.7	41.3	20.5	10.7	36.4	–36.3	27.9	31.6	10.3	–4.1
Nonfuel Primary Commodities	–0.3	7.4	15.2	6.1	23.2	14.1	7.5	–15.7	26.3	17.8	–10.3	–2.1
Food	–0.8	6.1	14.0	–0.9	10.5	15.2	23.4	–14.7	11.5	19.7	–7.5	–3.1
Beverages	1.2	6.6	–0.9	18.1	8.4	13.8	23.3	1.6	14.1	16.6	–22.2	1.6
Agricultural Raw Materials	–1.0	3.0	4.1	0.5	8.8	5.0	–0.8	–17.0	33.2	22.7	–13.2	–3.4
Metal	1.4	12.9	34.6	22.4	56.2	17.4	–7.8	–19.2	48.2	13.5	–10.5	–0.7
World Trade Prices in SDRs[2]												
Manufactures	0.2	1.6	–0.6	3.0	3.0	1.9	3.3	–4.3	3.5	3.6	2.5	0.2
Oil	5.5	13.2	23.6	41.6	21.0	6.4	32.1	–34.8	29.3	27.2	12.8	–4.1
Nonfuel Primary Commodities	–0.4	6.3	9.0	6.3	23.8	9.6	4.1	–13.6	27.7	13.8	–8.2	–2.1
Food	–0.9	5.1	7.8	–0.7	11.0	10.7	19.5	–12.6	12.7	15.7	–5.4	–3.2
Beverages	1.2	5.6	–6.3	18.3	8.8	9.4	19.4	4.1	15.4	12.7	–20.4	1.6
Agricultural Raw Materials	–1.1	2.0	–1.6	0.8	9.3	0.9	–3.9	–14.9	34.7	18.6	–11.2	–3.4
Metal	1.4	11.8	27.3	22.7	56.9	12.8	–10.7	–17.2	49.8	9.7	–8.4	–0.7
World Trade Prices in Euros[2]												
Manufactures	0.6	1.0	–4.4	2.5	1.7	–2.9	–0.7	–1.4	7.5	2.2	6.0	0.1
Oil	6.0	12.6	18.9	41.0	19.5	1.4	27.1	–32.7	34.3	25.5	16.7	–4.2
Nonfuel Primary Commodities	0.0	5.7	4.8	5.9	22.3	4.5	0.1	–10.9	32.6	12.3	–5.1	–2.2
Food	–0.5	4.5	3.7	–1.1	9.6	5.6	14.9	–9.8	17.0	14.1	–2.1	–3.2
Beverages	1.6	5.0	–9.9	17.8	7.5	4.2	14.8	7.3	19.8	11.2	–17.7	1.5
Agricultural Raw Materials	–0.7	1.5	–5.3	0.3	8.0	–3.8	–7.6	–12.3	39.9	17.0	–8.2	–3.5
Metal	1.8	11.2	22.4	22.2	55.0	7.5	–14.1	–14.6	55.5	8.3	–5.3	–0.7

Table A9. Summary of World Trade Volumes and Prices *(concluded)*

	Averages										Projections	
	1994–2003	2004–13	2004	2005	2006	2007	2008	2009	2010	2011	2012	2013
Trade in Goods												
Volume of Trade												
Exports												
Advanced Economies	6.4	4.2	9.0	5.8	8.8	5.8	1.5	–13.3	14.0	5.7	2.3	4.8
Emerging and Developing Economies	8.6	7.2	12.4	11.9	10.8	9.5	4.3	–8.4	15.0	6.4	5.9	6.5
Fuel Exporters	4.4	4.4	11.4	9.0	5.3	5.3	3.9	–8.1	7.0	4.4	4.8	2.5
Nonfuel Exporters	10.1	8.4	12.7	12.9	13.1	11.4	4.6	–8.5	18.2	7.2	6.4	8.3
Imports												
Advanced Economies	7.2	3.7	9.7	6.6	8.1	4.7	–0.1	–13.1	13.3	5.1	1.3	4.2
Emerging and Developing Economies	7.1	9.2	16.1	11.9	11.2	14.3	8.3	–9.3	16.0	9.4	8.1	7.9
Fuel Exporters	3.8	9.7	15.2	15.4	13.1	23.0	14.0	–12.4	8.3	9.0	9.3	5.8
Nonfuel Exporters	8.0	9.1	16.3	11.2	10.8	12.4	7.0	–8.5	17.9	9.6	7.8	8.3
Price Deflators in SDRs												
Exports												
Advanced Economies	–0.1	2.3	1.7	3.5	4.1	3.3	5.2	–6.8	4.9	6.5	1.1	–0.2
Emerging and Developing Economies	2.0	6.3	8.7	13.1	11.1	4.8	13.9	–13.7	12.7	12.3	4.0	–0.8
Fuel Exporters	4.4	10.2	15.0	28.9	17.6	7.0	24.9	–25.4	20.8	20.9	7.9	–3.1
Nonfuel Exporters	1.2	4.6	6.5	7.1	8.3	3.9	9.2	–8.0	9.5	8.9	2.3	0.2
Imports												
Advanced Economies	–0.2	2.8	2.4	5.2	5.4	2.8	8.0	–10.1	6.1	8.1	2.0	–0.2
Emerging and Developing Economies	1.4	4.6	4.7	6.9	7.9	3.7	10.8	–9.3	10.7	7.6	3.6	0.5
Fuel Exporters	1.5	4.6	4.2	8.3	7.8	4.4	9.2	–4.9	8.1	5.1	3.9	1.1
Nonfuel Exporters	1.4	4.5	4.7	6.7	7.9	3.6	11.1	–10.4	11.4	8.2	3.5	0.4
Terms of Trade												
Advanced Economies	0.1	–0.6	–0.7	–1.6	–1.3	0.4	–2.5	3.6	–1.1	–1.5	–1.0	–0.1
Emerging and Developing Economies	0.6	1.6	3.9	5.7	2.9	1.1	2.8	–4.8	1.8	4.3	0.4	–1.4
Regional Groups												
Central and Eastern Europe	0.2	–0.1	0.8	0.6	–4.0	1.4	–2.8	3.1	–1.7	0.7	1.2	0.0
Commonwealth of Independent States[3]	2.7	5.5	11.8	14.5	8.7	2.3	14.4	–19.0	12.7	11.3	4.9	–1.4
Developing Asia	–0.8	–0.7	1.1	–0.9	–0.8	0.0	–3.2	5.5	–6.3	–1.1	–1.1	–0.2
Latin America and the Caribbean	1.1	2.7	5.9	4.8	6.6	1.6	3.0	–7.8	10.5	8.0	–3.0	–1.0
Middle East and North Africa	2.0	4.0	6.4	17.8	6.8	1.2	11.1	–17.2	7.9	12.6	3.1	–5.3
Sub-Saharan Africa	. . .	3.9	5.0	10.6	7.7	4.1	10.6	–13.9	11.0	7.9	1.5	–2.4
Analytical Groups												
By Source of Export Earnings												
Fuel Exporters	2.9	5.4	10.3	19.0	9.1	2.5	14.3	–21.5	11.8	15.1	3.9	–4.1
Nonfuel Exporters	–0.2	0.1	1.7	0.4	0.3	0.3	–1.8	2.7	–1.7	0.6	–1.2	–0.2
Memorandum												
World Exports in Billions of U.S. Dollars												
Goods and Services	7,210	17,921	11,316	12,867	14,835	17,248	19,707	15,755	18,758	21,982	22,763	23,980
Goods	5,817	14,487	9,070	10,366	11,995	13,868	15,902	12,383	15,084	17,958	18,642	19,600
Average Oil Price[4]	5.6	14.3	30.7	41.3	20.5	10.7	36.4	–36.3	27.9	31.6	10.3	–4.1
In U.S. Dollars a Barrel	21.03	79.31	37.76	53.35	64.27	71.13	97.04	61.78	79.03	104.01	114.71	110.00
Export Unit Value of Manufactures[5]	0.2	2.6	5.1	2.7	2.5	6.0	6.7	–6.6	2.4	7.2	0.2	0.2

[1] Average of annual percent change for world exports and imports.

[2] As represented, respectively, by the export unit value index for manufactures of the advanced economies and accounting for 83 percent of the advanced economies' trade (export of goods) weights; the average of U.K. Brent, Dubai, and West Texas Intermediate crude oil prices; and the average of world market prices for nonfuel primary commodities weighted by their 2002–04 shares in world commodity exports.

[3] Georgia and Mongolia, which are not members of the Commonwealth of Independent States, are included in this group for reasons of geography and similarities in economic structure.

[4] Percent change of average of U.K. Brent, Dubai, and West Texas Intermediate crude oil prices.

[5] Percent change for manufactures exported by the advanced economies.

Table A10. Summary of Balances on Current Account

	2004	2005	2006	2007	2008	2009	2010	2011	Projections 2012	2013	2017
					Billions of U.S. Dollars						
Advanced Economies	**–207.8**	**–396.6**	**–433.5**	**–324.0**	**–496.4**	**–86.8**	**–85.4**	**–102.8**	**–157.6**	**–80.3**	**–255.8**
United States	–628.5	–745.8	–800.6	–710.3	–677.1	–376.6	–470.9	–473.4	–509.9	–499.0	–695.6
Euro Area[1,2]	121.6	51.9	53.7	45.6	–100.8	6.2	37.5	41.0	93.6	124.7	160.2
Japan	172.1	165.7	170.4	211.0	157.1	141.8	195.9	120.2	130.0	166.2	129.0
Other Advanced Economies[3]	127.0	131.7	143.0	129.8	124.5	141.8	152.2	209.5	128.7	127.7	150.6
Memorandum											
Newly Industrialized Asian Economies	87.1	83.2	99.0	128.3	86.5	123.8	137.2	134.8	127.8	132.8	161.5
Emerging and Developing Economies	**215.8**	**412.6**	**644.1**	**633.0**	**676.3**	**294.7**	**400.6**	**476.3**	**450.3**	**373.3**	**271.3**
Regional Groups											
Central and Eastern Europe	–55.1	–61.1	–89.0	–136.2	–159.9	–49.5	–81.8	–114.1	–108.7	–113.2	–160.1
Commonwealth of Independent States[4]	63.5	87.6	96.3	71.7	108.0	41.8	72.4	112.5	106.2	52.8	–62.4
Developing Asia	90.2	137.2	268.6	399.7	405.9	300.6	303.6	201.3	145.9	189.9	483.9
Latin America and the Caribbean	22.0	35.8	50.1	13.9	–32.1	–22.4	–55.2	–68.2	–107.2	–119.0	–181.2
Middle East and North Africa	103.1	213.9	287.5	271.4	353.3	52.0	186.2	366.0	439.7	399.0	272.5
Sub-Saharan Africa	–7.9	–0.7	30.6	12.5	1.2	–27.8	–24.6	–21.1	–25.6	–36.3	–81.5
Memorandum											
European Union	68.6	–4.3	–34.4	–66.9	–183.8	–15.9	–24.6	17.1	51.1	90.6	154.6
Analytical Groups											
By Source of Export Earnings											
Fuel	185.8	352.5	481.6	435.2	596.6	142.1	322.8	586.6	663.4	552.0	263.4
Nonfuel	30.1	60.1	162.5	197.7	79.7	152.7	77.8	–110.3	–213.1	–178.7	7.9
Of Which, Primary Products	–0.1	–0.9	10.0	7.8	–15.7	–2.1	–4.2	–18.2	–26.7	–23.9	–15.1
By External Financing Source											
Net Debtor Economies	–60.6	–90.3	–116.9	–227.3	–374.5	–190.0	–278.0	–343.1	–415.5	–427.7	–554.3
Of Which, Official Financing	–5.2	–6.0	–3.5	–5.4	–12.2	–9.4	–11.4	–13.4	–18.5	–16.1	–18.3
Net Debtor Economies by Debt-Servicing Experience											
Economies with Arrears and/or Rescheduling during 2006–10	–3.4	–6.7	–3.7	–13.8	–30.1	–24.7	–31.5	–38.9	–48.8	–48.1	–55.2
World[1]	**8.0**	**16.1**	**210.6**	**309.0**	**179.9**	**207.9**	**315.3**	**373.5**	**292.8**	**292.9**	**15.4**

Table A10. Summary of Balances on Current Account *(concluded)*

									Projections		
	2004	2005	2006	2007	2008	2009	2010	2011	2012	2013	2017
					Percent of GDP						
Advanced Economies	**–0.6**	**–1.1**	**–1.2**	**–0.8**	**–1.2**	**–0.2**	**–0.2**	**–0.2**	**–0.4**	**–0.2**	**–0.5**
United States	–5.3	–5.9	–6.0	–5.1	–4.7	–2.7	–3.2	–3.1	–3.3	–3.1	–3.5
Euro Area[1,2]	1.2	0.5	0.5	0.4	–0.7	0.0	0.3	0.3	0.7	1.0	1.1
Japan	3.7	3.6	3.9	4.8	3.2	2.8	3.6	2.0	2.2	2.7	1.9
Other Advanced Economies[3]	1.9	1.8	1.8	1.4	1.3	1.7	1.6	2.0	1.2	1.1	1.1
Memorandum											
Newly Industrialized Asian Economies	6.5	5.5	5.9	7.0	5.0	7.7	7.2	6.5	5.9	5.7	5.3
Emerging and Developing Economies	**2.4**	**3.8**	**5.0**	**4.0**	**3.5**	**1.6**	**1.9**	**1.9**	**1.7**	**1.3**	**0.7**
Regional Groups											
Central and Eastern Europe	–5.6	–5.2	–6.8	–8.3	–8.3	–3.1	–4.7	–6.0	–5.6	–5.5	–5.8
Commonwealth of Independent States[4]	8.2	8.7	7.4	4.2	5.0	2.5	3.7	4.6	4.0	1.7	–1.5
Developing Asia	2.6	3.4	5.6	6.6	5.5	3.8	3.2	1.8	1.2	1.4	2.5
Latin America and the Caribbean	1.0	1.3	1.6	0.4	–0.7	–0.6	–1.1	–1.2	–1.8	–2.0	–2.4
Middle East and North Africa	9.6	16.0	18.1	14.6	15.2	2.5	7.8	13.2	14.5	12.7	7.1
Sub-Saharan Africa	–1.5	–0.1	4.3	1.5	0.1	–3.1	–2.4	–1.8	–2.0	–2.6	–4.5
Memorandum											
European Union	0.5	0.0	–0.2	–0.4	–1.0	–0.1	–0.2	0.1	0.3	0.5	0.8
Analytical Groups											
By Source of Export Earnings											
Fuel	10.3	15.2	16.6	12.2	13.1	3.8	7.4	11.2	11.4	8.8	3.3
Nonfuel	0.4	0.7	1.6	1.6	0.5	1.1	0.4	–0.6	–1.0	–0.8	0.0
Of Which, Primary Products	0.0	–0.3	2.9	2.0	–3.5	–0.5	–0.8	–2.9	–3.9	–3.2	–1.5
By External Financing Source											
Net Debtor Economies	–1.2	–1.6	–1.8	–2.8	–4.0	–2.2	–2.7	–3.0	–3.5	–3.4	–3.3
Of Which, Official Financing	–2.6	–2.7	–1.4	–1.8	–3.4	–2.5	–2.8	–3.4	–4.3	–3.5	–2.9
Net Debtor Economies by Debt-Servicing Experience											
Net Debtor Economies with Arrears and/or Rescheduling during 2006–10	–0.8	–1.4	–0.6	–2.0	–3.5	–3.0	–3.3	–3.6	–4.3	–4.0	–3.5
World[1]	**0.0**	**0.0**	**0.4**	**0.6**	**0.3**	**0.4**	**0.5**	**0.5**	**0.4**	**0.4**	**0.0**
Memorandum											
In Percent of Total World Current Account Transactions	0.0	0.1	0.7	0.9	0.5	0.7	0.8	0.9	0.6	0.6	0.0
In Percent of World GDP	0.0	0.0	0.4	0.6	0.3	0.4	0.5	0.5	0.4	0.4	0.0

[1]Reflects errors, omissions, and asymmetries in balance of payments statistics on current account, as well as the exclusion of data for international organizations and a limited number of countries. See "Classification of Countries" in the introduction to this Statistical Appendix.

[2]Calculated as the sum of the balances of individual Euro Area countries.

[3]In this table, Other Advanced Economies means advanced economies excluding the United States, Euro Area countries, and Japan.

[4]Georgia and Mongolia, which are not members of the Commonwealth of Independent States, are included in this group for reasons of geography and similarities in economic structure.

Table A11. Advanced Economies: Balance on Current Account

(Percent of GDP)

	2004	2005	2006	2007	2008	2009	2010	2011	Projections 2012	2013	2017
Advanced Economies	**–0.6**	**–1.1**	**–1.2**	**–0.8**	**–1.2**	**–0.2**	**–0.2**	**–0.2**	**–0.4**	**–0.2**	**–0.5**
United States	–5.3	–5.9	–6.0	–5.1	–4.7	–2.7	–3.2	–3.1	–3.3	–3.1	–3.5
Euro Area[1]	1.2	0.5	0.5	0.4	–0.7	0.0	0.3	0.3	0.7	1.0	1.1
Germany	4.7	5.1	6.3	7.4	6.2	5.9	6.1	5.7	5.2	4.9	3.6
France	0.5	–0.5	–0.6	–1.0	–1.7	–1.5	–1.7	–2.2	–1.9	–1.5	–0.4
Italy	–0.3	–0.8	–1.5	–1.2	–2.9	–2.1	–3.5	–3.2	–2.2	–1.5	–1.6
Spain	–5.2	–7.4	–9.0	–10.0	–9.6	–5.2	–4.6	–3.7	–2.1	–1.7	0.0
Netherlands	7.6	7.4	9.3	6.7	4.3	4.2	6.6	7.5	8.2	7.8	5.8
Belgium	3.2	2.0	1.9	1.6	–1.6	–1.7	1.5	–0.1	–0.3	0.4	1.4
Austria	2.2	2.2	2.8	3.5	4.9	2.7	3.0	1.2	1.4	1.4	1.6
Greece	–5.9	–7.4	–11.2	–14.4	–14.7	–11.0	–10.0	–9.7	–7.4	–6.6	–1.1
Portugal	–8.3	–10.3	–10.7	–10.1	–12.6	–10.9	–10.0	–6.4	–4.2	–3.5	–2.8
Finland	6.2	3.4	4.2	4.3	2.6	1.8	1.4	–0.7	–1.0	–0.3	0.3
Ireland	–0.6	–3.5	–3.5	–5.3	–5.6	–2.9	0.5	0.1	1.0	1.7	4.0
Slovak Republic	–7.8	–8.5	–7.8	–5.3	–6.6	–3.2	–3.5	0.1	–0.4	–0.4	–0.7
Slovenia	–2.6	–1.7	–2.5	–4.8	–6.9	–1.3	–0.8	–1.1	0.0	–0.3	–1.4
Luxembourg	11.9	11.5	10.4	10.1	5.1	6.5	7.7	6.9	5.7	5.6	6.0
Estonia	–11.3	–10.0	–15.3	–15.9	–9.7	3.7	3.6	3.2	0.9	–0.3	–3.4
Cyprus	–5.0	–5.9	–7.0	–11.8	–15.6	–10.7	–9.9	–8.5	–6.2	–6.3	–6.5
Malta	–5.9	–8.7	–10.0	–5.3	–5.3	–8.3	–6.4	–3.2	–3.0	–2.9	–2.7
Japan	3.7	3.6	3.9	4.8	3.2	2.8	3.6	2.0	2.2	2.7	1.9
United Kingdom	–2.1	–2.6	–3.2	–2.5	–1.4	–1.5	–3.3	–1.9	–1.7	–1.1	–0.5
Canada	2.3	1.9	1.4	0.8	0.3	–3.0	–3.1	–2.8	–2.7	–2.7	–2.0
Korea	4.5	2.2	1.5	2.1	0.3	3.9	2.9	2.4	1.9	1.5	0.7
Australia	–6.1	–5.7	–5.3	–6.2	–4.3	–4.2	–2.8	–2.2	–4.6	–5.1	–6.1
Taiwan Province of China	5.8	4.8	7.0	8.9	6.9	11.4	9.3	8.8	8.0	8.4	8.9
Sweden	6.6	6.8	8.4	9.2	8.7	7.0	6.3	6.7	3.0	2.9	7.1
Hong Kong SAR	9.5	11.4	12.1	12.3	13.7	8.6	5.5	4.1	3.2	3.5	6.4
Switzerland	13.4	14.1	14.9	8.9	2.2	11.0	15.6	14.0	12.1	11.6	9.8
Singapore	17.1	21.4	24.5	25.8	13.9	16.2	24.4	21.9	21.8	21.3	18.6
Czech Republic	–5.0	–0.9	–2.1	–4.4	–2.1	–2.5	–3.0	–2.9	–2.1	–1.9	–1.8
Norway	12.6	16.1	16.4	12.5	15.9	10.8	12.4	14.6	14.8	13.7	9.5
Israel	1.7	3.1	4.8	2.7	0.9	3.6	2.9	0.1	–0.9	0.0	1.0
Denmark	3.3	4.1	3.1	1.4	2.6	3.5	5.5	6.2	4.8	4.5	4.7
New Zealand	–5.7	–7.9	–8.3	–8.2	–8.8	–2.6	–3.4	–4.1	–5.4	–6.3	–7.1
Iceland	–9.8	–16.2	–25.7	–15.7	–28.3	–11.8	–8.4	–6.5	–2.8	–1.5	–2.8
Memorandum											
Major Advanced Economies	–1.3	–1.8	–1.9	–1.2	–1.4	–0.6	–1.0	–1.1	–1.1	–0.9	–1.3
Euro Area[2]	0.8	0.1	–0.1	0.1	–1.6	–0.3	–0.5	–0.3	0.7	1.0	1.1
Newly Industrialized Asian Economies	6.5	5.5	5.9	7.0	5.0	7.7	7.2	6.5	5.9	5.7	5.3

[1]Calculated as the sum of the balances of individual Euro Area countries.
[2]Corrected for reporting discrepancies in intra-area transactions.

Table A12. Emerging and Developing Economies: Balance on Current Account

(Percent of GDP)

									Projections		
	2004	2005	2006	2007	2008	2009	2010	2011	2012	2013	2017
Central and Eastern Europe	**–5.6**	**–5.2**	**–6.8**	**–8.3**	**–8.3**	**–3.1**	**–4.7**	**–6.0**	**–5.6**	**–5.5**	**–5.8**
Albania	–4.0	–6.1	–5.6	–10.4	–15.1	–13.5	–11.6	–13.2	–13.2	–12.5	–8.0
Bosnia and Herzegovina	–16.2	–17.1	–8.0	–10.7	–14.1	–6.3	–6.1	–8.3	–7.8	–7.1	–4.7
Bulgaria	–6.4	–11.7	–17.6	–25.2	–23.2	–8.9	–1.3	1.9	2.1	1.6	–1.3
Croatia	–4.1	–5.3	–6.7	–7.3	–8.9	–5.0	–1.0	0.9	0.4	–0.2	–2.6
Hungary	–8.4	–7.5	–7.4	–7.3	–7.4	–0.2	1.1	1.6	3.3	1.2	–3.3
Kosovo	–8.4	–7.4	–6.7	–8.3	–15.3	–15.4	–17.4	–20.3	–18.3	–18.3	–13.9
Latvia	–12.9	–12.5	–22.6	–22.4	–13.2	8.7	3.0	–1.2	–1.9	–2.5	–3.3
Lithuania	–7.6	–7.0	–10.6	–14.5	–13.3	4.7	1.5	–1.7	–2.0	–2.3	–3.3
Former Yugoslav Republic of Macedonia	–8.1	–2.5	–0.4	–7.1	–12.8	–6.8	–2.2	–2.8	–5.0	–6.2	–5.0
Montenegro	–7.2	–8.5	–31.3	–39.5	–50.6	–29.6	–24.6	–19.4	–19.7	–20.0	–18.9
Poland	–5.2	–2.4	–3.8	–6.2	–6.6	–4.0	–4.7	–4.3	–4.5	–4.3	–3.9
Romania	–8.4	–8.6	–10.4	–13.4	–11.6	–4.2	–4.5	–4.2	–4.2	–4.7	–4.9
Serbia	–12.1	–8.7	–10.2	–16.1	–21.6	–7.1	–7.2	–9.1	–8.6	–7.9	–5.6
Turkey	–3.7	–4.6	–6.1	–5.9	–5.7	–2.2	–6.3	–9.9	–8.8	–8.2	–7.9
Commonwealth of Independent States[1]	**8.2**	**8.7**	**7.4**	**4.2**	**5.0**	**2.5**	**3.7**	**4.6**	**4.0**	**1.7**	**–1.5**
Russia	10.1	11.1	9.5	5.9	6.2	4.0	4.7	5.5	4.8	1.9	–1.9
Excluding Russia	2.2	1.3	0.6	–1.3	0.8	–1.9	0.5	1.9	1.5	1.3	–0.3
Armenia	–0.5	–1.0	–1.8	–6.4	–11.8	–15.8	–14.7	–12.3	–11.0	–9.5	–6.9
Azerbaijan	–29.8	1.3	17.6	27.3	35.5	23.6	29.1	26.3	21.8	16.4	5.0
Belarus	–5.3	1.4	–3.9	–6.7	–8.2	–12.6	–15.0	–10.4	–6.2	–6.5	–5.9
Georgia	–6.9	–11.1	–15.1	–19.7	–22.6	–11.3	–11.5	–12.7	–10.3	–9.3	–6.8
Kazakhstan	0.8	–1.8	–2.5	–8.1	4.7	–3.5	2.0	7.6	6.6	5.6	2.9
Kyrgyz Republic	4.9	2.8	–3.1	–0.2	–8.1	0.7	–6.9	–3.1	–4.8	–4.2	–2.9
Moldova	–1.8	–7.6	–11.3	–15.2	–16.2	–8.6	–8.3	–10.6	–9.7	–9.9	–7.8
Mongolia	1.2	1.2	6.5	6.3	–12.9	–9.0	–14.9	–30.4	–24.4	–1.8	8.8
Tajikistan	–3.9	–1.7	–2.8	–8.6	–7.6	–5.9	2.1	–2.3	–3.6	–5.0	–4.4
Turkmenistan	0.6	5.1	15.7	15.5	16.5	–16.0	–11.7	1.8	2.1	1.3	0.2
Ukraine	10.6	2.9	–1.5	–3.7	–7.1	–1.5	–2.2	–5.6	–5.9	–5.2	–5.3
Uzbekistan	7.2	7.7	9.1	7.3	8.7	2.2	6.2	5.8	2.8	3.0	1.2

Table A12. Emerging and Developing Economies: Balance on Current Account *(continued)*

	2004	2005	2006	2007	2008	2009	2010	2011	Projections 2012	2013	2017
Developing Asia	**2.6**	**3.4**	**5.6**	**6.6**	**5.5**	**3.8**	**3.2**	**1.8**	**1.2**	**1.4**	**2.5**
Islamic Republic of Afghanistan	–4.7	–2.7	–5.6	1.3	0.9	–2.8	1.7	–0.1	–1.1	–2.6	–4.6
Bangladesh	–0.3	0.0	1.2	0.8	1.4	2.8	1.7	–0.4	–1.0	–0.6	0.0
Bhutan	–32.6	–4.8	14.8	–2.4	–10.5	–5.5	–11.6	–18.3	–33.2	–36.5	–17.2
Brunei Darussalam	42.2	47.3	50.1	47.8	48.9	40.2	45.5	54.2	52.6	53.4	65.3
Cambodia	–2.2	–3.8	–0.6	–0.9	–4.5	–3.5	–4.0	–9.6	–10.6	–9.7	–5.2
China	3.6	5.9	8.6	10.1	9.1	5.2	5.1	2.8	2.3	2.6	4.3
Republic of Fiji	–12.6	–9.3	–18.1	–14.2	–18.1	–7.6	–11.3	–11.9	–9.8	–18.6	–7.6
India	0.1	–1.3	–1.0	–0.7	–2.5	–2.1	–3.3	–2.8	–3.2	–2.9	–2.4
Indonesia	–0.2	–1.0	3.0	2.4	0.0	2.5	0.8	0.2	–0.4	–0.9	–1.2
Kiribati	–25.2	–34.4	–17.6	–19.3	–16.8	–26.6	–15.4	–22.4	–27.2	–24.0	–27.8
Lao People's Democratic Republic	–17.9	–18.1	–9.9	–15.7	–18.5	–21.0	–18.2	–19.4	–19.6	–22.0	–14.3
Malaysia	12.1	15.0	16.7	15.9	17.7	16.5	11.5	11.5	10.8	10.4	8.6
Maldives	–11.4	–27.5	–23.2	–28.4	–34.3	–21.0	–17.4	–13.2	–21.6	–17.2	–19.0
Myanmar	2.4	3.7	7.1	0.6	–2.7	–2.8	–0.9	–2.6	–4.3	–3.4	–5.1
Nepal	2.7	2.0	2.1	–0.1	2.7	4.2	–2.4	–0.9	2.5	0.0	–0.1
Pakistan	1.8	–1.4	–3.9	–4.8	–8.5	–5.7	–2.2	0.2	–1.9	–2.1	–3.7
Papua New Guinea	2.3	6.1	7.6	3.1	12.0	–7.3	–8.4	–34.3	–30.5	–21.8	6.2
Philippines	1.8	1.9	4.4	4.8	2.1	5.6	4.5	2.7	0.9	1.0	1.9
Samoa	–8.4	–9.6	–10.2	–16.0	–6.5	–3.1	–8.1	–15.1	–14.2	–13.9	–8.4
Solomon Islands	16.8	–6.7	–9.1	–15.7	–20.5	–21.4	–30.3	–11.6	–12.7	–15.6	–11.8
Sri Lanka	–3.1	–2.5	–5.3	–4.3	–9.5	–0.5	–2.2	–7.5	–7.3	–7.5	–5.8
Thailand	1.7	–4.3	1.1	6.3	0.8	8.3	4.1	3.4	1.0	1.4	1.0
Timor-Leste	11.4	32.2	50.0	65.1	66.7	51.7	48.1	55.0	43.5	36.2	20.2
Tonga	0.4	–5.0	–5.5	–5.5	–8.1	–7.8	–3.9	–4.0	–3.8	–2.6	–3.3
Tuvalu	–2.5	14.9	14.3	0.4	–31.4	14.9	–15.5	–9.6	–10.7	–10.0	–11.4
Vanuatu	–4.5	–8.8	–6.0	–8.0	–11.4	–7.1	–6.0	–6.3	–7.2	–7.0	–6.7
Vietnam	–3.5	–1.1	–0.3	–9.8	–11.9	–6.6	–4.1	–0.5	–1.6	–1.4	–1.2

Table A12. Emerging and Developing Economies: Balance on Current Account *(continued)*

	2004	2005	2006	2007	2008	2009	2010	2011	Projections 2012	2013	2017
Latin America and the Caribbean	**1.0**	**1.3**	**1.6**	**0.4**	**–0.7**	**–0.6**	**–1.1**	**–1.2**	**–1.8**	**–2.0**	**–2.4**
Antigua and Barbuda	–13.1	–18.8	–27.8	–30.6	–27.3	–19.2	–12.9	–10.8	–13.7	–15.5	–15.6
Argentina[2]	1.7	2.6	3.2	2.4	1.6	2.1	0.6	–0.5	–0.7	–1.1	–1.9
The Bahamas	–2.4	–8.4	–17.7	–16.4	–14.9	–11.4	–11.7	–17.0	–18.4	–19.4	–12.2
Barbados	–8.3	–8.0	–4.8	–2.7	–9.6	–5.6	–8.2	–8.4	–8.3	–7.1	–3.6
Belize	–14.7	–13.6	–2.1	–4.1	–10.6	–5.9	–3.1	–1.6	–3.0	–3.9	–6.6
Bolivia	3.5	5.5	10.6	11.0	12.0	4.0	4.9	2.2	1.6	1.1	0.1
Brazil	1.8	1.6	1.3	0.1	–1.7	–1.5	–2.2	–2.1	–3.2	–3.2	–3.4
Chile	2.6	1.5	4.6	4.1	–3.2	2.0	1.5	–1.3	–2.4	–2.4	–2.1
Colombia	–0.8	–1.3	–1.9	–2.8	–2.9	–2.1	–3.1	–2.8	–2.7	–2.4	–2.0
Costa Rica	–4.3	–4.9	–4.5	–6.3	–9.3	–2.0	–3.5	–5.2	–5.5	–5.5	–5.1
Dominica	–16.0	–21.0	–12.9	–20.8	–26.9	–21.3	–21.1	–23.9	–25.6	–19.8	–15.0
Dominican Republic	4.8	–1.4	–3.6	–5.3	–9.9	–5.0	–8.6	–7.9	–6.9	–6.7	–5.7
Ecuador	–1.6	1.0	4.4	3.6	2.5	–0.3	–3.3	–0.3	0.5	0.6	–2.4
El Salvador	–4.1	–3.6	–4.1	–6.1	–7.1	–1.5	–2.3	–5.9	–4.8	–4.1	–3.0
Grenada	–1.6	–21.2	–25.2	–26.6	–24.5	–24.1	–25.5	–22.9	–24.0	–26.2	–20.3
Guatemala	–4.9	–4.6	–5.0	–5.2	–4.3	0.0	–1.5	–2.8	–3.2	–3.4	–3.6
Guyana	–6.7	–10.1	–13.1	–11.1	–13.2	–9.1	–9.5	–13.7	–12.3	–20.6	–10.1
Haiti	–1.6	0.7	–1.5	–1.5	–4.4	–3.5	–2.6	–3.5	–4.5	–5.5	–3.7
Honduras	–7.7	–3.0	–3.7	–9.0	–15.4	–3.7	–6.2	–8.6	–7.8	–6.3	–5.3
Jamaica	–6.3	–9.3	–10.2	–16.9	–18.1	–10.9	–8.1	–9.9	–12.5	–12.4	–7.7
Mexico	–0.7	–0.7	–0.5	–0.9	–1.4	–0.6	–0.3	–0.8	–0.8	–0.9	–1.3
Nicaragua	–14.5	–14.3	–13.4	–17.8	–23.8	–12.2	–14.4	–17.8	–19.8	–18.7	–13.3
Panama	–7.5	–4.9	–3.1	–7.9	–10.9	–0.7	–10.8	–12.7	–12.5	–12.4	–7.7
Paraguay	2.1	0.2	1.4	1.5	–1.9	0.5	–3.4	–1.2	–3.5	–1.4	–1.3
Peru	0.0	1.4	3.1	1.4	–4.2	0.2	–1.7	–1.3	–2.0	–1.9	–1.5
St. Kitts and Nevis	–16.2	–14.9	–15.8	–18.1	–25.6	–25.7	–20.6	–14.0	–18.7	–17.9	–16.0
St. Lucia	–10.5	–17.0	–28.6	–32.4	–28.4	–12.6	–15.2	–17.1	–16.9	–16.0	–14.5
St. Vincent and the Grenadines	–19.6	–18.0	–19.3	–28.0	–32.9	–29.4	–31.6	–28.8	–25.1	–22.9	–14.0
Suriname	–10.3	–13.0	7.7	10.5	9.6	–1.0	2.0	1.1	–13.0	–15.2	0.8
Trinidad and Tobago	12.4	22.5	39.6	24.8	30.6	8.2	19.9	20.7	20.0	18.2	10.1
Uruguay	0.0	0.2	–2.0	–0.9	–5.7	–0.4	–1.2	–2.2	–3.6	–3.2	–1.7
Venezuela	13.8	17.7	14.8	8.7	11.9	2.6	4.9	8.6	7.4	5.6	2.0
Middle East and North Africa	**9.6**	**16.0**	**18.1**	**14.6**	**15.2**	**2.5**	**7.8**	**13.2**	**14.5**	**12.7**	**7.1**
Algeria	13.0	20.5	24.7	22.8	20.1	0.3	7.5	10.3	10.0	7.9	4.6
Bahrain	4.2	11.0	13.8	15.7	10.2	2.9	3.4	4.2	7.1	9.5	6.7
Djibouti	–1.3	–3.2	–11.5	–21.4	–24.3	–9.1	–5.8	–12.6	–12.1	–11.9	–9.5
Egypt	4.3	3.2	1.6	1.7	0.5	–2.3	–2.0	–2.0	–2.6	–2.1	–1.3
Islamic Republic of Iran	0.5	7.6	8.5	10.6	6.5	2.6	6.0	10.7	6.6	5.1	2.1
Iraq	. . .	6.2	19.0	12.5	19.2	–13.8	–1.8	7.9	9.1	10.8	11.3
Jordan	0.1	–18.0	–11.5	–17.2	–9.3	–4.9	–5.6	–9.5	–8.3	–6.8	–4.1
Kuwait	26.2	37.2	44.6	36.8	40.9	24.4	29.6	41.8	46.2	41.9	34.5
Lebanon	–15.3	–13.4	–5.3	–6.8	–9.2	–9.8	–10.8	–14.4	–14.2	–13.4	–11.0
Libya	21.1	38.3	51.0	43.5	38.0	14.9	20.9	4.4	15.4	23.6	11.5
Mauritania	–34.6	–47.2	–1.3	–17.2	–14.8	–10.7	–8.8	–6.5	–18.3	–13.7	–3.9
Morocco	1.7	1.8	2.2	–0.1	–5.2	–5.4	–4.2	–7.4	–5.9	–6.0	–5.0
Oman	4.5	16.8	15.4	5.9	8.3	–1.3	8.8	13.2	12.9	8.3	–9.3
Qatar	22.4	29.9	25.1	25.4	28.7	10.2	26.3	28.4	31.5	29.0	8.3
Saudi Arabia	20.8	28.5	27.8	24.3	27.8	5.6	14.8	24.4	27.9	22.7	14.0
Sudan[3]	–2.2	–7.9	–7.0	–4.4	–4.7	–7.9	0.7	2.1	–4.6	–4.0	–1.4
Syrian Arab Republic[4]	–3.1	–2.2	1.4	–0.2	–1.3	–3.6	–3.3	. . .	. . .	. . .	. . .
Tunisia	–2.4	–0.9	–1.8	–2.4	–3.8	–2.8	–4.8	–7.4	–7.1	–7.1	–5.8
United Arab Emirates	6.1	12.4	16.3	6.9	7.9	3.4	3.1	9.2	10.3	10.4	9.1
Republic of Yemen	1.6	3.8	1.1	–7.0	–4.6	–10.2	–3.7	–3.5	–1.0	–3.9	–5.2

Table A12. Emerging and Developing Economies: Balance on Current Account *(concluded)*

	2004	2005	2006	2007	2008	2009	2010	2011	Projections 2012	2013	2017
Sub-Saharan Africa	**–1.5**	**–0.1**	**4.3**	**1.5**	**0.1**	**–3.1**	**–2.4**	**–1.8**	**–2.0**	**–2.6**	**–4.5**
Angola	3.8	18.7	29.6	21.7	12.7	–8.9	10.4	8.1	9.7	6.2	–5.0
Benin	–7.0	–6.3	–5.3	–10.2	–8.1	–8.9	–7.2	–7.9	–7.6	–7.4	–5.1
Botswana	3.5	15.2	17.2	15.0	6.9	–5.8	–5.2	–6.8	–4.1	–1.4	0.7
Burkina Faso	–11.0	–11.6	–9.1	–8.2	–11.2	–4.4	–3.6	–4.4	–8.0	–6.9	–6.1
Burundi	–5.4	–5.4	–22.9	–5.9	–1.8	–11.5	–9.9	–12.9	–12.3	–8.7	–7.8
Cameroon	–3.4	–3.4	1.6	1.4	–1.2	–3.7	–2.8	–3.5	–4.8	–3.3	–3.1
Cape Verde	–14.3	–3.5	–5.4	–14.7	–15.7	–15.6	–12.5	–12.5	–12.1	–10.5	–8.4
Central African Republic	–1.8	–6.5	–3.0	–6.2	–9.9	–8.1	–9.9	–6.9	–7.6	–6.8	–4.2
Chad	–17.1	1.2	5.9	11.6	9.0	–4.0	–3.5	–17.7	–10.0	3.3	–2.4
Comoros	–4.6	–7.4	–6.0	–5.7	–10.9	–7.7	–6.9	–9.9	–11.1	–9.6	–7.8
Democratic Republic of Congo	–3.0	–13.3	–2.7	–1.1	–17.5	–10.5	–6.9	–8.7	–7.8	–6.5	–5.7
Republic of Congo	–5.7	3.7	3.6	–6.5	2.3	–7.4	5.1	6.2	4.3	3.8	–1.1
Côte d'Ivoire	1.6	0.2	2.8	–0.7	1.9	7.0	1.1	6.7	–2.8	–3.0	–4.8
Equatorial Guinea	–21.6	–6.2	7.7	5.0	9.1	–17.1	–24.1	–9.7	–9.0	–6.6	–7.5
Eritrea	–0.7	0.3	–3.6	–6.1	–5.5	–7.6	–5.6	0.6	2.8	2.6	–2.5
Ethiopia	–1.4	–6.3	–9.1	–4.5	–5.6	–5.0	–4.4	–0.2	–8.4	–7.6	–5.2
Gabon	11.2	22.9	15.6	17.0	24.2	6.3	9.1	12.0	11.7	7.5	3.7
The Gambia	–4.5	–10.3	–6.9	–8.3	–12.1	–12.3	–15.7	–14.1	–17.9	–14.9	–12.2
Ghana	–2.2	–4.4	–7.1	–8.0	–10.8	–3.2	–7.3	–10.0	–6.9	–6.0	–8.1
Guinea	–2.5	–1.0	–4.6	–11.7	–10.3	–9.9	–12.4	–6.4	–36.1	–39.7	3.5
Guinea-Bissau	1.4	–2.1	–5.6	–3.5	–4.9	–6.4	–8.3	–6.2	–7.2	–6.9	–4.3
Kenya	0.1	–1.4	–2.2	–3.7	–7.4	–5.7	–6.5	–11.8	–9.6	–8.4	–5.5
Lesotho	9.8	–1.0	14.6	6.2	10.3	–3.4	–15.1	–16.6	–11.2	–15.4	–0.2
Liberia	–20.2	–37.4	–13.8	–28.7	–57.3	–38.2	–43.4	–43.2	–60.5	–58.7	–10.2
Madagascar	–10.6	–11.6	–9.9	–12.7	–20.6	–21.1	–9.7	–7.4	–6.3	–5.5	–0.6
Malawi	–11.2	–11.9	–11.3	1.0	–9.7	–5.5	–1.2	–3.4	–2.1	–1.8	–1.6
Mali	–7.9	–8.5	–4.1	–6.9	–12.2	–7.3	–12.6	–10.2	–10.3	–9.0	–8.3
Mauritius	–1.8	–5.0	–9.1	–5.4	–10.1	–7.4	–8.2	–10.3	–11.1	–10.1	–5.7
Mozambique	–10.7	–11.6	–10.7	–9.7	–11.9	–12.2	–11.7	–13.0	–12.7	–12.4	–10.8
Namibia	7.0	4.7	13.9	9.1	2.8	1.8	–1.8	–6.2	–4.4	–4.0	–2.2
Niger	–7.3	–8.9	–8.6	–8.2	–13.0	–25.0	–21.1	–28.5	–26.6	–20.7	–11.3
Nigeria	5.6	8.7	25.3	16.8	13.6	7.9	1.3	6.2	7.3	5.3	–0.4
Rwanda	1.8	1.0	–4.3	–2.2	–4.9	–7.3	–6.0	–10.4	–12.5	–8.6	–2.0
São Tomé and Príncipe	–16.0	–11.0	–25.8	–29.8	–22.0	–25.5	–34.1	–33.1	–35.2	–33.6	–9.2
Senegal	–6.9	–8.9	–9.2	–11.6	–14.1	–6.7	–6.1	–8.3	–10.0	–10.7	–7.6
Seychelles	–9.1	–22.2	–15.8	–15.3	–20.2	–9.8	–20.1	–21.6	–22.5	–18.3	–1.7
Sierra Leone	–5.8	–7.1	–5.6	–5.5	–11.5	–8.4	–28.8	–56.4	–10.0	–9.4	–9.5
South Africa	–3.0	–3.5	–5.3	–7.0	–7.2	–4.0	–2.8	–3.3	–4.8	–5.5	–6.0
Swaziland	3.1	–4.1	–7.4	–2.2	–8.2	–13.8	–16.5	–11.1	0.4	–5.7	–6.5
Tanzania	–2.5	–5.1	–8.2	–10.4	–11.9	–10.7	–9.3	–9.7	–12.3	–11.2	–12.0
Togo	–10.0	–9.9	–8.4	–8.7	–6.8	–6.6	–7.1	–7.5	–9.3	–9.3	–7.1
Uganda	0.1	–1.4	–3.4	–3.1	–3.1	–8.7	–9.6	–11.1	–12.5	–10.7	–8.7
Zambia	–10.4	–8.5	–0.4	–6.5	–7.2	4.2	7.1	1.2	1.3	2.6	3.6
Zimbabwe[5]	–8.4	–10.8	–8.5	–7.1	–22.9	–24.2	–23.1	–17.5	–15.7	–14.9	–12.0

[1]Georgia and Mongolia, which are not members of the Commonwealth of Independent States, are included in this group for reasons of geography and similarities in economic structure.
[2]Calculations are based on Argentina's official GDP data. See footnote to Table A4.
[3]Data for 2011 exclude South Sudan after July 9. Data for 2012 and onward pertain to the current Sudan
[4]Data for Syrian Arab Republic are excluded for 2011 onward due to the uncertain political situation.
[5]The Zimbabwe dollar ceased circulating in early 2009. Data are based on IMF staff estimates of price and exchange rate developments in U.S. dollars. IMF staff estimates of U.S. dollar values may differ from authorities' estimates.

Table A13. Emerging and Developing Economies: Net Financial Flows[1]

(Billions of U.S. dollars)

	Average									Projections	
	2001–03	2004	2005	2006	2007	2008	2009	2010	2011	2012	2013
Emerging and Developing Economies											
Private Financial Flows, Net	110.1	242.4	320.7	299.4	700.1	259.5	285.2	527.0	521.0	394.7	460.0
Private Direct Investment, Net	155.6	187.5	293.2	303.6	440.2	479.6	313.9	332.0	418.3	403.8	421.2
Private Portfolio Flows, Net	–32.1	16.9	41.1	–39.5	105.9	–72.9	86.0	232.9	101.1	79.3	99.3
Other Private Financial Flows, Net	–13.4	38.1	–13.7	35.3	154.1	–147.1	–114.7	–37.9	1.6	–88.4	–60.5
Official Financial Flows, Net[2]	–10.1	–68.4	–95.0	–163.9	–92.6	–97.8	135.0	74.7	–109.8	–109.7	–112.9
Change in Reserves[3]	–189.1	–414.6	–590.6	–755.4	–1,210.0	–724.9	–520.3	–873.8	–831.6	–733.3	–724.6
Memorandum											
Current Account[4]	93.6	215.8	412.6	644.1	633.0	676.3	294.7	400.6	476.3	450.3	373.3
Central and Eastern Europe											
Private Financial Flows, Net	23.6	49.7	102.1	117.6	182.4	153.5	25.9	79.7	88.9	95.3	112.1
Private Direct Investment, Net	14.4	30.6	37.8	64.1	74.7	67.5	30.4	21.7	33.7	35.1	39.0
Private Portfolio Flows, Net	2.4	15.7	20.8	0.9	–4.2	–10.4	9.0	27.1	28.8	23.8	28.4
Other Private Financial Flows, Net	6.9	3.4	43.5	52.5	111.8	96.4	–13.5	30.9	26.5	36.4	44.6
Official Flows, Net[2]	5.4	9.6	3.3	5.0	–6.1	20.5	48.4	35.1	21.8	11.3	3.0
Change in Reserves[3]	–6.9	–12.8	–43.6	–32.3	–36.4	–4.0	–29.0	–36.8	–14.4	–2.0	–6.6
Commonwealth of Independent States[5]											
Private Financial Flows, Net	6.9	5.6	29.1	51.6	129.2	–97.9	–63.1	–22.6	–60.7	–55.2	–17.4
Private Direct Investment, Net	5.1	13.2	11.7	21.4	28.3	50.6	16.2	10.3	22.0	16.8	23.5
Private Portfolio Flows, Net	1.6	4.7	3.9	4.9	19.5	–31.5	–9.5	10.1	–5.2	–1.8	2.2
Other Private Financial Flows, Net	0.1	–12.3	13.5	25.4	81.4	–117.0	–69.7	–43.0	–77.5	–70.3	–43.0
Official Flows, Net[2]	–1.4	–10.1	–18.3	–25.4	–6.0	–19.0	42.4	0.2	–8.6	–8.3	–12.1
Change in Reserves[3]	–20.7	–54.9	–77.1	–127.9	–168.0	27.0	–7.9	–52.7	–44.0	–36.5	–19.0
Developing Asia											
Private Financial Flows, Net	54.7	162.4	126.8	97.6	206.5	83.0	188.7	331.8	303.2	264.9	241.1
Private Direct Investment, Net	55.0	68.3	131.9	131.6	175.4	169.6	104.1	160.1	168.1	163.2	149.9
Private Portfolio Flows, Net	–2.9	39.6	15.5	–46.3	64.0	9.1	56.8	101.3	64.7	69.8	75.3
Other Private Financial Flows, Net	2.6	54.4	–20.7	12.4	–32.9	–95.7	27.8	70.3	70.4	31.9	15.9
Official Flows, Net[2]	–9.6	–19.9	–3.2	2.7	1.3	–6.6	20.2	21.4	9.7	15.0	13.8
Change in Reserves[3]	–120.5	–245.5	–281.0	–361.5	–612.2	–491.5	–467.3	–584.5	–468.5	–441.0	–461.3
Latin America and the Caribbean											
Private Financial Flows, Net	28.0	17.3	45.4	29.9	94.6	74.1	64.8	127.7	198.9	155.3	151.3
Private Direct Investment, Net	53.6	50.5	57.3	32.8	90.7	98.3	70.2	77.1	133.4	128.7	130.4
Private Portfolio Flows, Net	–14.1	–21.5	2.9	15.9	39.5	–11.8	34.2	72.7	44.2	29.7	28.2
Other Private Financial Flows, Net	–11.4	–11.8	–14.9	–18.8	–35.7	–12.4	–39.6	–22.1	21.3	–3.1	–7.3
Official Flows, Net[2]	15.1	–10.6	–38.7	–56.0	–4.7	4.2	43.4	46.7	17.1	34.4	31.1
Change in Reserves[3]	–9.7	–24.3	–36.3	–52.5	–133.6	–50.6	–49.7	–104.6	–119.4	–60.9	–43.2
Middle East and North Africa											
Private Financial Flows, Net	–5.0	–3.3	–3.7	–1.7	68.8	37.7	54.7	20.1	–18.5	–86.7	–62.4
Prlvate Direct Investment, Net	13.9	13.1	35.9	45.0	48.9	58.2	62.0	40.5	28.7	26.1	33.3
Private Portfolio Flows, Net	–15.1	–23.6	–1.1	–20.3	–11.4	3.2	0.6	26.1	–16.9	–41.0	–34.6
Other Private Financial Flows, Net	–3.8	7.2	–38.5	–26.4	31.2	–23.7	–7.9	–46.6	–30.2	–71.7	–61.0
Official Flows, Net[2]	–19.9	–37.2	–30.2	–60.8	–76.2	–106.1	–35.7	–59.5	–176.8	–187.9	–170.7
Change in Reserves[3]	–30.7	–58.3	–129.5	–151.6	–231.2	–186.6	23.1	–91.7	–164.4	–166.2	–169.0
Sub-Saharan Africa											
Private Financial Flows, Net	1.8	10.8	21.0	4.3	18.7	9.1	14.1	–9.7	9.2	21.1	35.2
Private Direct Investment, Net	13.6	11.7	18.5	8.7	22.1	35.4	31.0	22.2	32.6	33.8	45.1
Private Portfolio Flows, Net	–4.0	2.0	–0.9	5.5	–1.6	–31.5	–5.2	–4.4	–14.5	–1.2	–0.2
Other Private Financial Flows, Net	–7.8	–2.9	3.3	–9.9	–1.8	5.3	–11.7	–27.4	–8.9	–11.6	–9.7
Official Flows, Net[2]	0.3	–0.3	–7.8	–29.5	–0.9	9.2	16.3	30.7	27.1	25.9	21.9
Change in Reserves[3]	–0.5	–18.7	–23.2	–29.6	–28.4	–19.1	10.5	–3.5	–20.9	–26.8	–25.5
Memorandum											
Fuel Exporting Countries											
Private Financial Flows, Net	–8.6	–8.2	0.9	8.8	125.4	–144.5	–67.7	–78.1	–150.3	–214.9	–155.8
Other Countries											
Private Financial Flows, Net	118.6	250.6	319.8	290.6	574.7	404.0	352.9	605.0	671.3	609.6	615.8

[1]Net financial flows comprise net direct investment, net portfolio investment, other net official and private financial flows, and changes in reserves.

[2]Excludes grants and includes transactions in external assets and liabilities of official agencies.

[3]A minus sign indicates an increase.

[4]The sum of the current account balance, net private financial flows, net official flows, and the change in reserves equals, with the opposite sign, the sum of the capital account and errors and omissions.

[5]Georgia and Mongolia, which are not members of the Commonwealth of Independent States, are included in this group for reasons of geography and similarities in economic structure.

Table A14. Emerging and Developing Economies: Private Financial Flows[1]

(Billions of U.S. dollars)

	Average 2001–03	2004	2005	2006	2007	2008	2009	2010	2011	Projections 2012	2013
Emerging and Developing Economies											
Private Financial Flows, Net	110.1	242.4	320.7	299.4	700.1	259.5	285.2	527.0	521.0	394.7	460.0
Assets	–97.8	–265.8	–335.8	–620.2	–815.6	–584.4	–297.3	–580.8	–553.6	–614.9	–626.8
Liabilities	207.0	508.3	655.0	919.6	1,514.8	841.5	582.6	1,106.0	1,074.0	1,006.5	1,084.2
Central and Eastern Europe											
Private Financial Flows, Net	23.6	49.7	102.1	117.6	182.4	153.5	25.9	79.7	88.9	95.3	112.1
Assets	–6.9	–30.0	–17.8	–56.4	–44.5	–29.3	–10.0	–6.9	10.8	2.0	3.4
Liabilities	30.6	79.7	119.8	173.7	226.0	182.0	36.6	86.8	78.4	93.7	108.9
Commonwealth of Independent States[2]											
Private Financial Flows, Net	6.9	5.6	29.1	51.6	129.2	–97.9	–63.1	–22.6	–60.7	–55.2	–17.4
Assets	–20.6	–53.0	–80.3	–100.1	–160.6	–264.8	–74.0	–103.5	–128.9	–122.1	–110.5
Liabilities	27.5	58.6	109.4	152.0	289.8	167.4	11.1	80.4	68.0	65.2	93.2
Developing Asia											
Private Financial Flows, Net	54.7	162.4	126.8	97.6	206.5	83.0	188.7	331.8	303.2	264.9	241.1
Assets	–19.5	–54.1	–115.7	–221.6	–248.2	–171.1	–92.8	–234.2	–210.6	–273.4	–290.0
Liabilities	73.9	216.3	242.2	319.2	454.1	253.1	281.1	565.8	513.9	538.3	529.9
Latin America and the Caribbean											
Private Financial Flows, Net	28.0	17.3	45.4	29.9	94.6	74.1	64.8	127.7	198.9	155.3	151.3
Assets	–31.9	–45.7	–50.3	–91.9	–114.9	–74.9	–96.6	–160.9	–113.2	–78.1	–79.8
Liabilities	59.0	62.8	94.6	121.8	209.6	148.1	161.1	287.5	312.1	232.4	230.3
Middle East and North Africa											
Private Financial Flows, Net	–5.0	–3.3	–3.7	–1.7	68.8	37.7	54.7	20.1	–18.5	–86.7	–62.4
Assets	–10.1	–71.5	–55.8	–120.3	–213.4	–25.4	–8.3	–46.4	–90.5	–119.1	–118.6
Liabilities	5.1	68.3	52.1	118.6	282.2	63.1	63.0	66.5	72.0	32.4	56.2
Sub-Saharan Africa											
Private Financial Flows, Net	1.8	10.8	21.0	4.3	18.7	9.1	14.1	–9.7	9.2	21.1	35.2
Assets	–8.7	–11.5	–15.8	–29.9	–34.0	–18.8	–15.6	–29.0	–21.2	–24.3	–31.3
Liabilities	10.8	22.7	37.0	34.3	53.1	28.0	29.7	19.0	29.6	44.6	65.7

[1]Private financial flows comprise direct investment, portfolio investment, and other long- and short-term investment flows.
[2]Georgia and Mongolia, which are not members of the Commonwealth of Independent States, are included in this group for reasons of geography and similarities in economic structure.

Table A15. Summary of Sources and Uses of World Savings

(Percent of GDP)

	Averages								Projections		
	1990–97	1998–2005	2006	2007	2008	2009	2010	2011	2012	2013	2014–17
World											
Savings	22.1	21.7	24.0	24.2	24.1	21.9	23.3	24.0	24.4	24.8	25.5
Investment	23.0	21.9	23.2	23.7	23.8	21.7	22.8	23.5	24.0	24.5	25.5
Advanced Economies											
Savings	21.7	20.5	20.9	20.7	19.8	17.2	18.2	18.5	18.6	19.1	19.8
Investment	22.3	21.1	21.5	21.6	21.0	17.7	18.6	18.8	19.2	19.4	20.3
Net Lending	–0.5	–0.5	–0.7	–0.9	–1.2	–0.6	–0.4	–0.3	–0.5	–0.3	–0.5
Current Transfers	–0.4	–0.6	–0.7	–0.8	–0.8	–0.8	–0.9	–0.8	–0.8	–0.7	–0.7
Factor Income	–0.5	0.4	1.1	0.5	0.6	0.3	0.7	0.9	0.7	0.7	0.6
Resource Balance	0.5	–0.3	–1.0	–0.6	–0.8	0.1	0.0	–0.3	–0.3	–0.1	–0.2
United States											
Savings	16.0	16.3	16.4	14.6	13.4	11.5	12.5	12.9	13.1	13.7	15.2
Investment	18.3	19.8	20.6	19.6	18.1	14.7	15.8	15.9	16.3	16.8	18.4
Net Lending	–2.3	–3.5	–4.2	–5.0	–4.7	–3.3	–3.3	–3.0	–3.3	–3.1	–3.3
Current Transfers	–0.5	–0.6	–0.7	–0.8	–0.9	–0.9	–0.9	–0.9	–0.8	–0.8	–0.7
Factor Income	–0.7	1.0	2.2	0.8	1.0	0.4	1.1	1.6	1.5	1.6	1.5
Resource Balance	–1.1	–3.9	–5.6	–5.0	–4.9	–2.7	–3.4	–3.7	–4.0	–3.9	–4.0
Euro Area											
Savings	. . .	21.5	22.3	22.9	21.4	19.0	19.8	20.0	20.3	20.5	20.9
Investment	. . .	21.0	21.9	22.6	22.2	19.0	19.3	19.6	19.5	19.5	19.7
Net Lending	. . .	0.5	0.4	0.3	–0.8	0.0	0.5	0.4	0.8	1.0	1.1
Current Transfers[1]	–0.6	–0.8	–1.0	–1.1	–1.1	–1.1	–1.2	–1.1	–1.0	–1.0	–1.0
Factor Income[1]	–0.6	–0.4	0.3	–0.2	–0.6	–0.2	0.3	0.1	–0.2	–0.4	–0.5
Resource Balance[1]	1.1	1.7	1.2	1.6	0.9	1.4	1.4	1.5	2.0	2.4	2.6
Germany											
Savings	21.9	20.9	24.4	26.7	25.6	22.5	23.4	23.7	23.7	23.3	22.6
Investment	22.8	19.6	18.1	19.3	19.4	16.5	17.3	18.0	18.5	18.5	18.6
Net Lending	–0.9	1.2	6.3	7.4	6.2	5.9	6.1	5.7	5.2	4.9	4.1
Current Transfers	–1.6	–1.3	–1.2	–1.3	–1.3	–1.5	–1.5	–1.3	–1.3	–1.3	–1.3
Factor Income	0.0	–0.2	1.9	1.8	1.3	2.4	2.0	1.9	1.5	1.0	0.7
Resource Balance	0.6	2.7	5.6	7.0	6.2	5.0	5.6	5.1	4.9	5.1	4.6
France											
Savings	19.9	20.4	20.3	20.9	20.1	17.5	18.6	18.8	19.4	19.7	20.7
Investment	19.1	19.1	20.8	21.9	21.8	19.0	19.2	20.1	21.3	21.2	21.4
Net Lending	0.8	1.3	–0.6	–1.0	–1.7	–1.5	–0.6	–1.4	–1.9	–1.5	–0.7
Current Transfers	–0.7	–1.0	–1.2	–1.2	–1.3	–1.4	–1.4	–1.4	–1.3	–1.3	–1.3
Factor Income	–0.1	1.1	1.6	1.7	1.7	1.7	3.0	2.8	1.6	1.6	1.6
Resource Balance	1.6	1.3	–1.0	–1.4	–2.2	–1.7	–2.3	–2.8	–2.2	–1.8	–1.0
Italy											
Savings	20.8	20.8	20.3	20.9	18.7	16.8	16.7	16.4	16.6	17.2	17.7
Investment	20.6	20.7	21.8	22.1	21.6	18.9	20.2	19.6	18.8	18.7	19.2
Net Lending	0.2	0.1	–1.5	–1.2	–2.9	–2.1	–3.5	–3.2	–2.2	–1.5	–1.6
Current Transfers	–0.5	–0.5	–0.9	–0.9	–1.0	–0.9	–1.1	–0.9	–0.9	–0.8	–0.8
Factor Income	–1.8	–0.6	0.2	–0.1	–1.2	–0.7	–0.6	–0.7	–0.8	–0.8	–0.8
Resource Balance	2.5	1.2	–0.8	–0.3	–0.7	–0.5	–1.9	–1.5	–0.5	0.1	0.0
Japan											
Savings	31.7	26.7	26.6	27.7	26.1	22.4	23.3	21.9	23.0	23.7	23.4
Investment	29.7	23.8	22.7	22.9	23.0	19.7	19.8	19.9	20.7	20.9	21.1
Net Lending	2.0	3.0	3.9	4.8	3.2	2.7	3.5	2.0	2.2	2.7	2.3
Current Transfers	–0.2	–0.2	–0.2	–0.3	–0.3	–0.2	–0.2	–0.2	–0.2	–0.1	–0.1
Factor Income	0.8	1.6	2.7	3.1	3.1	2.5	2.4	3.0	2.7	2.7	2.8
Resource Balance	1.4	1.5	1.4	1.9	0.4	0.5	1.4	–0.7	–0.4	0.2	–0.4
United Kingdom											
Savings	15.6	15.5	14.2	15.8	15.6	12.7	12.1	12.9	13.1	14.2	16.6
Investment	17.2	17.4	17.5	18.2	17.0	14.2	15.4	14.8	14.8	15.3	17.1
Net Lending	–1.6	–1.9	–3.2	–2.5	–1.4	–1.5	–3.3	–1.9	–1.7	–1.1	–0.6
Current Transfers	–0.7	–0.9	–0.9	–1.0	–1.0	–1.1	–1.4	–1.4	–1.1	–1.1	–1.1
Factor Income	–0.3	1.1	0.7	1.5	2.3	1.5	0.6	1.4	0.7	0.7	0.7
Resource Balance	–0.6	–2.2	–3.1	–3.0	–2.7	–1.8	–2.5	–1.8	–1.4	–0.8	–0.2

Table A15. Summary of Sources and Uses of World Savings *(continued)*

	Averages								Projections		
	1990–97	1998–2005	2006	2007	2008	2009	2010	2011	2012	2013	2014–17
Canada											
Savings	16.4	21.8	24.4	24.1	23.6	17.9	19.1	20.0	20.6	21.0	21.7
Investment	19.0	20.3	23.0	23.2	23.2	20.9	22.2	22.8	23.2	23.6	24.0
Net Lending	–2.5	1.6	1.4	0.8	0.3	–3.0	–3.1	–2.8	–2.7	–2.7	–2.3
Current Transfers	–0.1	0.0	–0.1	–0.1	–0.1	–0.2	–0.2	–0.2	–0.3	–0.3	–0.3
Factor Income	–3.6	–2.6	–0.9	–0.9	–1.1	–1.0	–1.0	–1.2	–1.3	–1.2	–1.6
Resource Balance	1.1	4.1	2.4	1.9	1.5	–1.8	–2.0	–1.3	–1.1	–1.2	–0.4
Newly Industrialized Asian Economies											
Savings	34.6	32.2	32.5	33.4	32.6	31.2	33.7	32.4	31.7	31.5	31.0
Investment	32.7	26.5	26.4	26.2	27.6	23.5	26.4	26.0	25.9	25.8	25.7
Net Lending	1.9	5.7	6.1	7.2	4.9	7.7	7.3	6.5	5.9	5.7	5.3
Current Transfers	–0.1	–0.5	–0.7	–0.7	–0.6	–0.6	–0.8	–0.8	–0.8	–0.8	–0.7
Factor Income	0.8	0.4	0.6	0.7	0.9	0.7	0.8	0.7	0.7	0.6	0.7
Resource Balance	1.2	5.9	6.2	7.2	4.7	7.7	7.2	6.5	6.0	5.8	5.3
Emerging and Developing Economies											
Savings	23.7	26.3	32.8	33.1	33.6	32.1	32.9	33.6	33.7	33.9	33.8
Investment	26.2	25.1	27.8	29.2	30.1	30.5	31.0	31.8	32.1	32.7	33.0
Net Lending	–1.9	1.2	5.0	4.0	3.4	1.7	1.9	1.8	1.6	1.2	0.7
Current Transfers	0.7	1.3	1.8	1.6	1.5	1.4	1.3	1.1	1.0	1.0	1.1
Factor Income	–1.6	–1.9	–1.8	–1.6	–1.6	–1.5	–1.5	–1.8	–1.7	–1.4	–1.1
Resource Balance	–0.9	1.8	5.1	4.0	3.6	1.7	2.1	2.6	2.2	1.7	0.8
Memorandum											
Acquisition of Foreign Assets	1.9	4.7	10.6	12.6	6.9	4.9	6.8	5.7	4.9	4.4	3.7
Change in Reserves	1.1	2.5	5.9	7.7	3.8	2.9	4.0	3.3	2.7	2.5	2.3
Regional Groups											
Central and Eastern Europe											
Savings	20.1	17.3	16.6	16.3	16.7	16.0	16.2	16.8	16.7	16.9	17.3
Investment	22.0	21.0	23.4	24.7	25.0	19.1	20.8	22.7	22.2	22.4	22.9
Net Lending	–1.8	–3.8	–6.8	–8.4	–8.3	–3.0	–4.6	–6.0	–5.6	–5.5	–5.6
Current Transfers	1.8	2.0	1.8	1.6	1.5	1.7	1.5	1.6	1.5	1.4	1.3
Factor Income	–1.3	–1.4	–2.3	–2.9	–2.4	–2.3	–2.2	–2.5	–2.3	–2.3	–2.1
Resource Balance	–2.3	–4.5	–6.3	–7.1	–7.5	–2.6	–4.0	–5.2	–4.9	–4.7	–4.8
Memorandum											
Acquisition of Foreign Assets	0.9	2.7	6.1	4.8	1.7	1.7	2.7	–0.1	0.4	0.5	0.2
Change in Reserves	0.4	1.4	2.5	2.2	0.2	1.8	2.1	0.8	0.1	0.3	0.1
Commonwealth of Independent States[2]											
Savings	. . .	27.1	30.2	30.7	30.1	21.9	26.2	29.1	28.8	28.7	26.6
Investment	. . .	20.2	23.0	26.7	25.2	19.1	22.4	24.4	24.9	27.0	27.3
Net Lending	. . .	6.9	7.3	4.0	4.8	2.8	3.8	4.7	3.9	1.6	–0.7
Current Transfers	. . .	0.6	0.4	0.3	0.4	0.4	0.3	0.3	0.3	0.3	0.3
Factor Income	. . .	–3.0	–3.3	–2.9	–3.4	–3.6	–3.7	–3.8	–3.4	–3.0	–2.3
Resource Balance	. . .	9.2	10.3	6.8	8.0	5.8	7.1	8.2	7.1	4.4	1.4
Memorandum											
Acquisition of Foreign Assets	. . .	9.3	14.9	17.5	10.0	1.5	6.1	5.4	4.5	2.9	1.7
Change in Reserves	. . .	4.0	9.8	9.8	–1.2	0.5	2.7	1.8	1.4	0.6	0.3
Developing Asia											
Savings	31.7	34.3	42.6	43.5	43.8	45.3	44.4	43.5	43.3	43.5	43.6
Investment	33.6	31.9	37.0	36.9	38.3	41.4	41.2	41.7	42.1	42.1	41.6
Net Lending	–1.9	2.3	5.5	6.6	5.4	3.8	3.2	1.8	1.1	1.4	2.0
Current Transfers	1.0	1.8	2.2	2.2	2.1	1.9	1.7	1.4	1.4	1.4	1.7
Factor Income	–1.7	–1.5	–0.9	–0.5	–0.3	–0.5	–0.4	–0.7	–0.6	–0.3	–0.2
Resource Balance	–1.3	2.1	4.3	5.0	3.7	2.4	1.8	1.0	0.3	0.3	0.6
Memorandum											
Acquisition of Foreign Assets	3.2	5.4	11.2	13.4	7.6	6.8	8.4	5.5	4.8	4.5	4.5
Change in Reserves	1.9	3.8	7.5	10.1	6.6	5.9	6.1	4.1	3.6	3.4	3.5

Table A15. Summary of Sources and Uses of World Savings *(continued)*

	Averages								Projections		
	1990–97	1998–2005	2006	2007	2008	2009	2010	2011	2012	2013	2014–17
Latin America and the Caribbean											
Savings	19.0	19.1	23.3	23.0	22.8	20.0	20.5	21.2	20.9	21.1	21.3
Investment	21.0	20.5	21.7	22.6	23.8	20.6	21.8	22.7	23.0	23.3	23.7
Net Lending	–2.1	–1.4	1.6	0.4	–0.9	–0.6	–1.3	–1.5	–2.1	–2.1	–2.4
Current Transfers	0.9	1.5	2.1	1.8	1.6	1.4	1.3	1.1	1.1	1.1	1.1
Factor Income	–2.4	–3.0	–3.0	–2.7	–2.7	–2.5	–2.5	–2.8	–2.7	–2.5	–2.4
Resource Balance	–0.5	0.1	2.6	1.3	0.2	0.5	0.0	0.2	–0.5	–0.7	–1.0
Memorandum											
Acquisition of Foreign Assets	1.2	2.3	2.9	5.8	2.4	4.4	5.2	4.8	2.4	1.9	1.2
Change in Reserves	0.9	0.5	1.7	3.6	1.2	1.2	2.1	2.1	1.1	0.7	0.5
Middle East and North Africa											
Savings	22.4	30.0	41.1	40.6	42.5	31.5	35.6	39.6	40.9	39.4	36.2
Investment	24.4	23.4	22.9	26.3	27.1	29.0	27.8	26.6	26.3	26.8	27.6
Net Lending	–2.0	6.6	18.3	14.6	15.0	3.0	8.1	13.4	14.7	12.8	8.4
Current Transfers	–2.2	–1.0	–0.4	–0.8	–0.8	–1.4	–1.2	–1.5	–1.5	–1.8	–1.9
Factor Income	1.5	0.6	0.9	1.1	0.6	0.2	–0.3	–0.8	–0.5	–0.2	0.9
Resource Balance	–1.3	7.0	18.0	14.5	15.5	3.8	9.4	15.5	16.5	14.7	9.6
Memorandum											
Acquisition of Foreign Assets	1.7	8.4	24.8	28.0	15.7	4.5	9.2	14.1	13.9	12.9	9.2
Change in Reserves	0.8	3.4	9.5	12.4	8.0	–1.1	3.8	5.9	5.5	5.4	3.8
Sub-Saharan Africa											
Savings	15.6	16.7	25.2	23.7	22.4	19.6	19.8	19.7	19.5	19.4	19.5
Investment	16.7	18.8	20.6	21.9	21.9	22.3	21.8	21.2	21.1	21.8	22.7
Net Lending	–1.2	–2.1	4.6	1.8	0.4	–2.8	–2.0	–1.5	–1.7	–2.4	–3.2
Current Transfers	2.0	2.3	4.6	4.6	4.5	4.7	4.2	3.8	3.4	3.3	3.1
Factor Income	–3.0	–4.8	–3.9	–5.3	–6.0	–4.3	–4.8	–5.2	–5.4	–5.4	–4.3
Resource Balance	0.0	0.3	3.8	2.5	1.7	–3.4	–1.6	–0.2	0.1	–0.4	–2.1
Memorandum											
Acquisition of Foreign Assets	1.2	2.4	8.4	7.9	3.8	2.4	2.4	2.5	3.7	4.2	3.0
Change in Reserves	0.9	1.2	4.1	3.4	2.0	–1.2	0.3	1.7	2.0	1.8	1.3
Analytical Groups											
By Source of Export Earnings											
Fuel Exporters											
Savings	22.7	30.3	39.3	38.2	38.4	28.5	32.3	36.0	36.4	34.9	31.4
Investment	26.0	22.7	22.7	26.3	25.3	24.6	24.8	25.0	24.9	26.2	26.7
Net Lending	–1.3	7.6	16.6	12.0	12.8	4.1	7.6	11.1	11.4	8.6	4.5
Current Transfers	–3.2	–1.6	–0.3	–0.6	–0.6	–1.0	–0.9	–1.0	–1.0	–1.1	–1.1
Factor Income	0.1	–1.6	–1.6	–1.6	–2.3	–2.2	–2.6	–3.0	–2.8	–2.4	–1.4
Resource Balance	1.9	10.8	18.7	14.5	16.0	6.9	10.9	15.1	15.1	12.2	7.2
Memorandum											
Acquisition of Foreign Assets	1.7	9.3	21.3	23.3	14.0	3.5	7.8	11.0	10.6	8.8	5.6
Change in Reserves	0.2	3.5	10.0	10.8	3.6	–1.5	3.0	4.5	4.2	3.4	2.0
Nonfuel Exporters											
Savings	23.9	25.4	31.0	31.7	32.1	33.0	33.0	32.9	33.0	33.6	34.4
Investment	26.0	25.7	29.3	30.0	31.5	31.9	32.6	33.5	34.1	34.4	34.6
Net Lending	–2.0	–0.3	1.7	1.7	0.6	1.1	0.5	–0.6	–1.0	–0.8	–0.2
Current Transfers	1.4	1.9	2.4	2.3	2.2	2.0	1.8	1.6	1.6	1.5	1.7
Factor Income	–1.9	–2.0	–1.8	–1.6	–1.4	–1.3	–1.3	–1.5	–1.4	–1.2	–1.0
Resource Balance	–1.5	–0.2	1.1	1.0	–0.2	0.4	–0.1	–0.7	–1.3	–1.2	–0.9
Memorandum											
Acquisition of Foreign Assets	1.9	3.7	7.4	9.4	4.7	5.2	6.6	4.4	3.4	3.2	3.2
Change in Reserves	1.3	2.2	4.7	6.8	3.8	4.0	4.3	3.0	2.3	2.2	2.3

Table A15. Summary of Sources and Uses of World Savings *(concluded)*

	Averages								Projections		
	1990–97	1998–2005	2006	2007	2008	2009	2010	2011	2012	2013	2014–17
By External Financing Source											
Net Debtor Economies											
Savings	19.3	19.4	22.5	22.7	21.7	21.0	21.5	21.5	21.2	21.6	22.4
Investment	21.5	21.4	24.1	25.5	25.8	23.1	24.2	24.5	24.8	25.1	25.7
Net Lending	–2.3	–2.0	–1.7	–2.7	–4.0	–2.1	–2.7	–3.0	–3.5	–3.4	–3.3
Current Transfers	1.8	2.6	3.0	2.9	2.9	2.9	2.6	2.5	2.5	2.5	2.4
Factor Income	–1.9	–2.3	–2.5	–2.5	–2.5	–2.2	–2.3	–2.5	–2.5	–2.5	–2.3
Resource Balance	–2.1	–2.3	–2.3	–3.2	–4.4	–2.9	–3.1	–3.1	–3.6	–3.5	–3.4
Memorandum											
Acquisition of Foreign Assets	1.1	2.3	4.1	5.9	1.6	2.7	3.7	2.8	1.4	1.4	1.1
Change in Reserves	0.9	1.1	2.5	3.9	0.7	1.5	2.0	1.5	0.6	0.7	0.7
Official Financing											
Savings	17.4	19.0	22.8	23.4	21.6	21.7	22.4	23.3	22.5	22.9	23.1
Investment	19.7	21.3	23.4	23.5	23.9	23.3	24.2	25.8	26.2	26.0	25.8
Net Lending	–2.3	–2.4	–0.6	–0.1	–2.3	–1.6	–1.8	–2.5	–3.7	–3.1	–2.8
Current Transfers	4.8	7.6	10.7	11.4	11.0	10.8	10.8	11.4	11.0	10.6	10.0
Factor Income	–2.6	–3.1	–2.5	–1.2	–1.6	–1.6	–1.5	–2.0	–2.3	–2.4	–2.8
Resource Balance	–4.6	–7.0	–8.8	–10.3	–11.7	–10.8	–11.0	–12.0	–12.4	–11.3	–10.0
Memorandum											
Acquisition of Foreign Assets	1.5	1.7	0.2	3.3	0.9	2.8	2.4	1.8	1.5	1.7	1.6
Change in Reserves	1.5	1.2	1.2	2.3	1.3	1.3	2.0	1.1	1.3	1.6	1.8
Net Debtor Economies by Debt-Servicing Experience											
Economies with Arrears and/or Rescheduling during 2006–10											
Savings	14.9	17.0	22.8	22.2	20.8	18.9	19.7	20.2	20.0	20.4	20.7
Investment	18.8	19.0	23.2	24.1	24.8	21.7	23.8	24.8	25.2	25.3	24.9
Net Lending	–3.9	–2.0	–0.3	–1.9	–4.0	–2.8	–4.0	–4.6	–5.3	–4.8	–4.2
Current Transfers	1.7	3.9	5.6	5.0	4.5	4.5	4.2	3.6	3.5	3.3	3.2
Factor Income	–3.6	–4.0	–2.9	–2.8	–3.7	–3.1	–3.8	–3.9	–3.8	–3.6	–3.2
Resource Balance	–2.1	–1.9	–3.1	–4.0	–4.9	–4.4	–4.7	–4.4	–5.1	–4.6	–4.2
Memorandum											
Acquisition of Foreign Assets	2.9	2.6	3.3	5.7	1.3	1.2	2.3	2.9	1.1	1.1	0.8
Change in Reserves	0.8	0.6	2.0	3.8	0.6	1.7	1.4	0.2	0.6	0.7	0.6

Note: The estimates in this table are based on individual countries' national accounts and balance of payments statistics. Country group composites are calculated as the sum of the U.S. dollar values for the relevant individual countries. This differs from the calculations in the April 2005 and earlier issues of the *World Economic Outlook*, where the composites were weighted by GDP valued at purchasing power parities as a share of total world GDP. For many countries, the estimates of national savings are built up from national accounts data on gross domestic investment and from balance-of-payments-based data on net foreign investment. The latter, which is equivalent to the current account balance, comprises three components: current transfers, net factor income, and the resource balance. The mixing of data sources, which is dictated by availability, implies that the estimates for national savings that are derived incorporate the statistical discrepancies. Furthermore, errors, omissions, and asymmetries in balance of payments statistics affect the estimates for net lending; at the global level, net lending, which in theory would be zero, equals the world current account discrepancy. Despite these statistical shortcomings, flow of funds estimates, such as those presented in these tables, provide a useful framework for analyzing developments in savings and investment, both over time and across regions and countries.

[1]Calculated from the data of individual Euro Area countries.

[2]Georgia and Mongolia, which are not members of the Commonwealth of Independent States, are included in this group for reasons of geography and similarities in economic structure.

Table A16. Summary of World Medium-Term Baseline Scenario

	Averages				Projections			
	1994–2001	2002–09	2010	2011	2012	2013	2010–13	2014–17
				Annual Percent Change				
World Real GDP	**3.5**	**3.6**	**5.3**	**3.9**	**3.5**	**4.1**	**4.2**	**4.5**
Advanced Economies	3.1	1.4	3.2	1.6	1.4	2.0	2.1	2.6
Emerging and Developing Economies	4.2	6.4	7.5	6.2	5.7	6.0	6.4	6.3
Memorandum								
Potential Output								
Major Advanced Economies	2.5	1.9	0.9	1.2	1.3	1.4	1.2	1.6
World Trade, Volume[1]	**7.4**	**4.4**	**12.9**	**5.8**	**4.0**	**5.6**	**7.0**	**6.3**
Imports								
Advanced Economies	7.8	2.8	11.5	4.3	1.8	4.1	5.4	5.4
Emerging and Developing Economies	6.7	8.8	15.3	8.8	8.4	8.1	10.1	7.8
Exports								
Advanced Economies	7.0	3.3	12.2	5.3	2.3	4.7	6.0	5.4
Emerging and Developing Economies	8.6	7.5	14.7	6.7	6.6	7.2	8.7	7.7
Terms of Trade								
Advanced Economies	0.0	–0.1	–1.0	–1.7	–0.9	0.1	–0.9	–0.2
Emerging and Developing Economies	0.2	1.5	2.0	3.2	0.6	–1.1	1.2	–1.0
World Prices in U.S. Dollars								
Manufactures	–0.8	3.1	2.4	7.2	0.2	0.2	2.5	0.2
Oil	4.7	12.4	27.9	31.6	10.3	–4.1	15.5	–4.6
Nonfuel Primary Commodities	–1.4	6.7	26.3	17.8	–10.3	–2.1	6.9	–2.4
Consumer Prices								
Advanced Economies	2.1	2.0	1.5	2.7	1.9	1.7	2.0	1.8
Emerging and Developing Economies	23.3	6.4	6.1	7.1	6.2	5.6	6.2	4.7
				Percent				
Interest Rates								
Real Six-Month LIBOR[2]	3.7	0.5	–0.6	–1.6	–0.1	0.1	–0.6	0.6
World Real Long-Term Interest Rate[3]	3.4	1.9	1.6	0.2	0.7	1.3	1.0	2.4
				Percent of GDP				
Balances on Current Account								
Advanced Economies	–0.2	–0.8	–0.2	–0.2	–0.4	–0.2	–0.2	–0.3
Emerging and Developing Economies	–0.6	2.9	1.9	1.9	1.7	1.3	1.7	0.8
Total External Debt								
Emerging and Developing Economies	36.9	29.8	25.2	23.8	23.7	23.6	24.0	22.7
Debt Service								
Emerging and Developing Economies	8.8	9.9	8.2	8.4	8.9	9.1	8.7	9.2

[1]Data refer to trade in goods and services.
[2]London interbank offered rate on U.S. dollar deposits minus percent change in U.S. GDP deflator.
[3]GDP-weighted average of 10-year (or nearest maturity) government bond rates for Canada, France, Germany, Italy, Japan, United Kingdom, and United States.

WORLD ECONOMIC OUTLOOK
SELECTED TOPICS

World Economic Outlook Archives

World Economic Outlook: Recessions and Recoveries	April 2002
World Economic Outlook: Trade and Finance	September 2002
World Economic Outlook: Growth and Institutions	April 2003
World Economic Outlook: Public Debt in Emerging Markets	September 2003
World Economic Outlook: Advancing Structural Reforms	April 2004
World Economic Outlook: The Global Demographic Transition	September 2004
World Economic Outlook: Globalization and External Balances	April 2005
World Economic Outlook: Building Institutions	September 2005
World Economic Outlook: Globalization and Inflation	April 2006
World Economic Outlook: Financial Systems and Economic Cycles	September 2006
World Economic Outlook: Spillovers and Cycles in the Global Economy	April 2007
World Economic Outlook: Globalization and Inequality	October 2007
World Economic Outlook: Housing and the Business Cycle	April 2008
World Economic Outlook: Financial Stress, Downturns, and Recoveries	October 2008
World Economic Outlook: Crisis and Recovery	April 2009
World Economic Outlook: Sustaining the Recovery	October 2009
World Economic Outlook: Rebalancing Growth	April 2010
World Economic Outlook: Recovery, Risk, and Rebalancing	October 2010
World Economic Outlook: Tensions from the Two-Speed Recovery—Unemployment, Commodities, and Capital Flows	April 2011
World Economic Outlook: Slowing Growth, Rising Risks	September 2011
World Economic Outlook: Growth Resuming, Dangers Remain	April 2012

I. Methodology—Aggregation, Modeling, and Forecasting

The Global Economy Model	April 2003, Box 4.3
How Should We Measure Global Growth?	September 2003, Box 1.2
Measuring Foreign Reserves	September 2003, Box 2.2
The Effects of Tax Cuts in a Global Fiscal Model	April 2004, Box 2.2
How Accurate Are the Forecasts in the *World Economic Outlook*?	April 2006, Box 1.3
Drawing the Line Between Personal and Corporate Savings	April 2006, Box 4.1
Measuring Inequality: Conceptual, Methodological, and Measurement Issues	October 2007, Box 4.1
New Business Cycle Indices for Latin America: A Historical Reconstruction	October 2007, Box 5.3
Implications of New PPP Estimates for Measuring Global Growth	April 2008, Appendix 1.1
Measuring Output Gaps	October 2008, Box 1.3
Assessing and Communicating Risks to the Global Outlook	October 2008, Appendix 1.1
Fan Chart for Global Growth	April 2009, Appendix 1.2

II. Historical Surveys

III. Economic Growth—Sources and Patterns

IV. Inflation and Deflation, and Commodity Markets

V. Fiscal Policy

The Case for Growth-Indexed Bonds	September 2003, Box 3.4
Public Debt in Emerging Markets: Is It Too High?	September 2003, Chapter 3
Has Fiscal Behavior Changed under the European Economic and Monetary Union?	September 2004, Chapter 2
Bringing Small Entrepreneurs into the Formal Economy	September 2004, Box 1.5
HIV/AIDS: Demographic, Economic, and Fiscal Consequences	September 2004, Box 3.3
Implications of Demographic Change for Health Care Systems	September 2004, Box 3.4
Impact of Aging on Public Pension Plans	September 2004, Box 3.5
How Should Middle Eastern and Central Asian Oil Exporters Use Their Oil Revenues?	April 2005, Box 1.6
Financial Globalization and the Conduct of Macroeconomic Policies	April 2005, Box 3.3
Is Public Debt in Emerging Markets Still Too High?	September 2005, Box 1.1
Improved Emerging Market Fiscal Performance: Cyclical or Structural?	September 2006, Box 2.1
When Does Fiscal Stimulus Work?	April 2008, Box 2.1
Fiscal Policy as a Countercyclical Tool	October 2008, Chapter 5
Differences in the Extent of Automatic Stabilizers and Their Relationship with Discretionary Fiscal Policy	October 2008, Box 5.1
Why Is It So Hard to Determine the Effects of Fiscal Stimulus?	October 2008, Box 5.2
Have the U.S. Tax Cuts Been "TTT" [Timely, Temporary, and Targeted]?	October 2008, Box 5.3
Will It Hurt? Macroeconomic Effects of Fiscal Consolidation	October 2010, Chapter 3
Separated at Birth? The Twin Budget and Trade Balances	September 2011, Chapter 4

VI. Monetary Policy, Financial Markets, and Flow of Funds

When Bubbles Burst	April 2003, Chapter 2
How Do Balance Sheet Vulnerabilities Affect Investment?	April 2003, Box 2.3
Identifying Asset Price Booms and Busts	April 2003, Appendix 2.1
Are Foreign Exchange Reserves in Asia Too High?	September 2003, Chapter 2
Reserves and Short-Term Debt	September 2003, Box 2.3
Are Credit Booms in Emerging Markets a Concern?	April 2004, Chapter 4
How Do U.S. Interest and Exchange Rates Affect Emerging Markets' Balance Sheets?	April 2004, Box 2.1
Does Financial Sector Development Help Economic Growth and Welfare?	April 2004, Box 4.1
Adjustable- or Fixed-Rate Mortgages: What Influences a Country's Choices?	September 2004, Box 2.2
What Are the Risks from Low U.S. Long-Term Interest Rates?	April 2005, Box 1.2
Regulating Remittances	April 2005, Box 2.2
Financial Globalization and the Conduct of Macroeconomic Policies	April 2005, Box 3.3
Monetary Policy in a Globalized World	April 2005, Box 3.4
Does Inflation Targeting Work in Emerging Markets?	September 2005, Chapter 4
A Closer Look at Inflation Targeting Alternatives: Money and Exchange Rate Targets	September 2005, Box 4.1
How Has Globalization Affected Inflation?	April 2006, Chapter 3
The Impact of Petrodollars on U.S. and Emerging Market Bond Yields	April 2006, Box 2.3
Globalization and Inflation in Emerging Markets	April 2006, Box 3.1

Globalization and Low Inflation in a Historical Perspective	April 2006, Box 3.2
Exchange Rate Pass-Through to Import Prices	April 2006, Box 3.3
Trends in the Financial Sector's Profits and Savings	April 2006, Box 4.2
How Do Financial Systems Affect Economic Cycles?	September 2006, Chapter 4
Financial Leverage and Debt Deflation	September 2006, Box 4.1
Financial Linkages and Spillovers	April 2007, Box 4.1
Macroeconomic Conditions in Industrial Countries and Financial Flows to Emerging Markets	April 2007, Box 4.2
Macroeconomic Implications of Recent Market Turmoil: Patterns from Previous Episodes	October 2007, Box 1.2
What Is Global Liquidity?	October 2007, Box 1.4
The Changing Housing Cycle and the Implications for Monetary Policy	April 2008, Chapter 3
Is There a Credit Crunch?	April 2008, Box 1.1
Assessing Vulnerabilities to Housing Market Corrections	April 2008, Box 3.1
Financial Stress and Economic Downturns	October 2008, Chapter 4
Policies to Resolve Financial System Stress and Restore Sound Financial Intermediation	October 2008, Box 4.1
The Latest Bout of Financial Distress: How Does It Change the Global Outlook?	October 2008, Box 1.1
How Vulnerable Are Nonfinancial Firms?	April 2009, Box 1.2
The Case of Vanishing Household Wealth	April 2009, Box 2.1
Impact of Foreign Bank Ownership during Home-Grown Crises	April 2009, Box 4.1
A Financial Stress Index for Emerging Economies	April 2009, Appendix 4.1
Financial Stress in Emerging Economies: Econometric Analysis	April 2009, Appendix 4.2
How Linkages Fuel the Fire	April 2009, Chapter 4
Lessons for Monetary Policy from Asset Price Fluctuations	October 2009, Chapter 3
Were Financial Markets in Emerging Economies More Resilient than in Past Crises?	October 2009, Box 1.2
Risks from Real Estate Markets	October 2009, Box 1.4
Financial Conditions Indices	April 2011, Appendix 1.1
House Price Busts in Advanced Economies: Repercussions for Global Financial Markets	April 2011, Box 1.1
International Spillovers and Macroeconomic Policymaking	April 2011, Box 1.3
Credit Boom-Bust Cycles: Their Triggers and Policy Implications	September 2011, Box 1.2
Are Equity Price Drops Harbingers of Recession?	September 2011, Box 1.3
Cross-Border Spillovers from Euro Area Bank Deleveraging	April 2012, Spillover Feature

VII. Labor Markets, Poverty, and Inequality

Unemployment and Labor Market Institutions: Why Reforms Pay Off	April 2003, Chapter 4
Regional Disparities in Unemployment	April 2003, Box 4.1
Labor Market Reforms in the European Union	April 2003, Box 4.2
The Globalization of Labor	April 2007, Chapter 5
Emigration and Trade: How Do They Affect Developing Countries?	April 2007, Box 5.1
Labor Market Reforms in the Euro Area and the Wage-Unemployment Trade-Off	October 2007, Box 2.2
Globalization and Inequality	October 2007, Chapter 4

VIII. Exchange Rate Issues

IX. External Payments, Trade, Capital Movements, and Foreign Debt

X. Regional Issues

XI. Country-Specific Analyses

XII. Special Topics

UNION COUNTY COLLEGE
3 9354 00202148 9